MARKET IN STATE

Focusing on the evolving relations between the state and market in the post-Mao reform era, Yongnian Zheng and Yanjie Huang present a theory of Chinese capitalism by identifying and analyzing three layers of the market system in the contemporary Chinese economy: a free market economy at the bottom, state capitalism at the top, and a middle ground in between. By examining Chinese economic practices against the dominant schools of Western political economy and classical Chinese economic thought, the authors set out the analytical framework of "market in state" to conceptualize the market not as an autonomous, self-regulating order but as part and parcel of a state-centered order. Zheng and Huang show how state (political) principles are dominant over market (economic) principles in China's economy. As the Chinese economy continues to grow and globalize, its internal balance will likely have a large impact upon economies across the world.

YONGNIAN ZHENG is Professor and Director of the East Asian Institute at the National University of Singapore. He is the author of *The Chinese Communist Party as Organizational Emperor* (2010), *Technological Empowerment* (2007), *Globalization and State Transformation in China* (Cambridge, 2004), and *Discovering Chinese Nationalism in China* (Cambridge, 1999).

YANJIE HUANG is conducting doctoral research on modern Chinese history at Columbia University, New York. He has published papers and book chapters on China's state sector, food security, and monetary history.

Market in State

The Political Economy of Domination in China

YONGNIAN ZHENG

National University of Singapore

YANJIE HUANG

Columbia University, New York

CAMBRIDGE
UNIVERSITY PRESS

CAMBRIDGE
UNIVERSITY PRESS

University Printing House, Cambridge CB2 8BS, United Kingdom

One Liberty Plaza, 20th Floor, New York, NY 10006, USA

477 Williamstown Road, Port Melbourne, VIC 3207, Australia

314–321, 3rd Floor, Plot 3, Splendor Forum, Jasola District Centre, New Delhi – 110025, India

79 Anson Road, #06–04/06, Singapore 079906

Cambridge University Press is part of the University of Cambridge.

It furthers the University's mission by disseminating knowledge in the pursuit of education, learning, and research at the highest international levels of excellence.

www.cambridge.org
Information on this title: www.cambridge.org/9781108473446
DOI: 10.1017/9781108562119

© Yongnian Zheng and Yanjie Huang 2018

First published 2018

Printed and bound in Great Britain by Clays Ltd, Elcograf S.p.A.

A catalogue record for this publication is available from the British Library.

Library of Congress Cataloging-in-Publication Data
Names: Zheng, Yongnian, author. | Huang, Yanjie, author.
Title: Market in state : the political economy of domination in China / Yongnian Zheng, National University of Singapore, Yanjie Huang, Columbia University, New York.
Description: Cambridge, United Kingdom ; New York, NY : Cambridge University Press, 2018. | Includes bibliographical references and index.
Identifiers: LCCN 2018012811 | ISBN 9781108473446 (hardback : alk. paper) | ISBN 9781108461573 (pbk. : alk. paper)
Subjects: LCSH: China–Economic policy. | China–Economic conditions. | Economic development–China. | Government business enterprises–China.
Classification: LCC HC427 .Z457 2018 | DDC 330.951–dc23
LC record available at https://lccn.loc.gov/2018012811

ISBN 978-1-108-47344-6 Hardback
ISBN 978-1-108-46157-3 Paperback

Contents

List of Figures	*page* vii
List of Tables	ix
Preface	xi
Introduction	1
PART I THEORY	27
1 Market, State, and Capitalism: Theories of Political Economy and China	29
2 Market in State: A Theory of Chinese Political Economy	78
PART II HISTORY	129
3 The State and Market in Imperial China	131
4 Origins of the Modern Chinese Political Economy: Geopolitics, Mobilization, and State-Building	190
PART III CONTEMPORARY INSTITUTIONS	247
5 Grassroots Capitalism and Marketization: Dynamics of Market Reform in the Contemporary Era	249
6 The Middle Ground: The Nexus between the State and Private Enterprises	298
7 The Money Regimes: Fiscal and Monetary Reforms and Their Limits	339

8   State Capitalism: The Centrally Managed State-Owned
    Enterprises and Economic Domination   378

Conclusion   425

Bibliography   447
Index   469

Figures

3.1 Concentric circles of organizational dependency in the
    traditional imperial system   *page* 140
4.1 Share of defense in PRC budget and GDP, 1950–1993   240
6.1 The political opportunity structure for private entrepreneurs 329
7.1 Share of central and local revenues, 1991–2016   349
7.2 Land transfer and local revenue, 1999–2016   354
8.1 Capitalization of state-owned and state-holding
    manufacturing enterprises, 1998–2015   391
8.2 Share of the state sector in overall economy   392
8.3 Profits of centrally managed and locally managed SOEs,
    2002–2016   393
8.4 Total assets and profits of centrally managed SOEs   394
8.5 SOEs' contribution to fiscal revenue   399
8.6 Return on capital for state and nonstate enterprises   407
8.7 Intersectoral wage differentials in Zhejiang, 2008   409

Tables

8.1 List of main sectors in the strategic market   *page* 390
8.2 Political Bureau members with business administration
    background (2012)   405

Preface

This book is both the fruit of our long-term intellectual speculation and the product of our troubled times. The book was conceived more than a decade ago when Yongnian completed his research project on *Globalization and State Transformation in China* (Cambridge University Press, 2004). He certainly did not foresee this research project kickstarting a series of related projects on China's party-state system of the time. In 2005, after spending several resourceful research years with the East Asian Institute (EAI), National University of Singapore, Yongnian moved to the University of Nottingham to head the China Policy Institute and subsequently to embark on a research project on the Chinese Communist Party (CCP). In 2010, the findings of that project were laid out in a book entitled *The Chinese Communist Party as an Organizational Emperor*, which discusses the historical roots and contemporary transformation of the most powerful, yet understudied, political party of our time – the CCP – and analyzes how the party has dominated the state both within the party-state system and outside society. For Yongnian, the project raised more questions than it solved. For one, to fully examine the transformation of the Chinese state, it is necessary to account for the tremendous economic power of the party-state and the huge state sector under its aegis. For another, a theoretically grounded and historically informed research program on contemporary institutions seems to hold promise for other major institutions in a society like China. In this sense, the book raised interesting questions for related research.

We embarked on the market-in-state project after we met at the EAI in late 2008, when Yongnian returned to direct the institute and Yanjie joined the institute as a junior researcher. The idea of a book project on the Chinese political economy system gradually took shape during frequent discussions among ourselves or with colleagues and visitors at the EAI over dinner or afternoon tea. Our main concerns were the well-exposed down-sides of China's epic growth story: the increasingly imbalanced economic structure, the eroding basis of social trust, the widening gap of income inequality, and other social costs of high growth. We could not accept mainstream diagnoses of these problems, which put all the blame squarely on either immoral and destructive market forces or a corrupt and ineffi-cient Chinese state. A shared concern for these contemporary issues and debates led us to conclude that a timely theoretical intervention was needed in the very concept of the market in the Chinese context.

When the global financial crisis sent seismic waves across the Asia-Pacific region in 2008, we watched developments in China anxiously as a stimulus package of 4 trillion yuan impinged on an already overheated economy and an anomic society. We had mixed feelings about the crisis in China: It was indeed the worst external shock that had hit the Chinese economy since reform, but it also presented opportunities for again reforming the Chinese economy and rebuilding society. We anticipated a quick and decisive response, but the sheer amount of credit that the Chinese government pumped into the economy through the state sector still caught us off guard. Within a couple of years, the assets and invest-ment portfolios of centrally managed state-owned enterprises (SOEs) and their subsidiaries ballooned. Although China has successfully prevented a nightmarish economic outcome and engaged in meaningful social reforms, plans for comprehensive social reforms and economic rebalancing have been shelved. Meanwhile, credit expansion for physical infrastructure and real estate has led to rising inflation, increasing inequality, and a disturbing housing bubble. Our disappointment with these developments and our intellectual curiosity about the logic behind all these led us to explore ways to try to make sense of market–state relations in China from both historical and contemporary angles.

The writing of this book took about six years. The first few chapters to be generated from our initial probing were the historical chapters and the one on centrally managed SOEs. We were very fortunate to have the oppor-tunity to present an earlier draft of the chapter on SOEs at a conference on public sector reforms in China and India held at the Copenhagen Business School in late September 2011, where we received positive feedback from our host, Kjeld Erik Brødsgaard, and several other scholars. However, the drafting of other chapters and the conceptualization of the market in state proved more difficult than expected. We had to sift through a wealth of empirical materials and gradually expand the scope of investigation to the fiscal systems, market reforms, and the relationship between the state and private entrepreneurs. Meanwhile, we firmed up the theoretical chapters that spelt out clearly the ideas of the market in state. The first draft was ready by July 2015. By the time we came to the final draft in December 2017, we had already gone through three rounds of revision, partly to refine our arguments and partly to respond to rapidly evolving external events.

Despite all our endeavors, we were unable to account for the full complexity of the Chinese economy as it enters another unpredictable "new normal" phase of slower growth, mounting social challenges, and hard structural reforms. Without restructuring the economy and protecting society, China will risk not only the "middle income trap" but also major social upheaval. The stakes are high but the outcome remains uncertain. Notably, any institutional outcome from these troubled post-crisis times, if durable, must combine with the mixed economy, characterized by a balance between the state and market and a truly comprehensive program of social protection.

In the long process of researching and writing this book, we have benefited from fruitful discussion with and constructive feedback from our colleagues at the EAI, other research institutes, and teaching departments of the National University of Singapore. Wang Gungwu, a renowned historian of China and the institute's chairman, has provided us with unfailing intellectual and moral support. With insightful comments and observations, he has always encouraged us to transcend prevailing concerns and analyze China's history from the angle of an ancient civilization and its changing position in the world. John Wong, an economist on modern China in the Southeast Asian region, has also unreservedly shared with us many of his views on the modern Chinese political economy. We would also like to thank, among many of our EAI colleagues, Chen Chien-Hsun, Chen Gang, Chen Kang, Lance Gore, Kong Tuan Yuen, Lye Laing Fook, Qi Dongtao, Qian Jiwei, Shan Wei, Yu Hong, Sarah Tong Yueting, and Zhao Litao, whose ideas and comments have inspired us at different stages.

We would also like to thank our friends and colleagues who have shared with us their interests and research findings on similar topics during friendly exchanges in Singapore and elsewhere. These intellectual exchanges were especially stimulating. We would particularly like to thank Daniel A. Bell, Kjeld Erik Brødsgaard, Peter Nolan, Lawrence J. Lau, Barry Naughton, Christine Wong, Dwight Perkins, Justine Lin Yifu, Lin Shuanglin, Yu Yongding, Ge Yanfeng, Gong Sen, Hou Yunchun, David Li Daokui, Li Jiange, Li Shi, Liu Shijin, Wu Guoguang, Andrew Warder, Jean Oi, Lynn White, Joseph Fewsmith, and Jae Ho Chung.

On the business side, we benefited greatly from many intensive discussions and interviews with Chinese entrepreneurs in both the state and private sectors, particularly many members of the China Entrepreneur Club. They not only provided us with their personal experiences of doing business in China, but also offered rich insights into how the Chinese political economy works. Our special thanks go to Mo Daoming, a successful entrepreneur based in Guangzhou and Hong Kong, for his great assistance rendered during the many years of our research. Mo is an exceptional entrepreneur in today's China. Besides sharing his rich business experience with us, he linked us to many other entrepreneurs for us to expand on our research bases. Many of his insights were reflected in our research in one way or another. Equally important were our frequent discussions with Chinese government officials at both the central and local levels. Without their insights, it would have been more difficult for us to conceptualize market–state relations in China today.

For years, Yongnian has attended the annual China Development Forum organized by the China Development Research Foundation. Regular attendees include Fortune 500 companies, international organizations, and academic institutions. Since its inception, it has been one of the most important occasions for anyone seeking an understanding of China's economic reforms. Yongnian has taken the opportunity to exchange views with CEOs of multinational companies, research experts from international organizations, and university scholars. He would particularly like to thank, among others, Masahiko Aoki (who passed away in 2015), Michael J. Boskin, Martin Feldstein, Ricardo Melendez-Ortiz, Stephen S. Roach, Mouriel Roubini, Michael Spence, Nicholas Stern, Joseph Stiglitz, Ronnie C. Chan, Fan Gang, Lu Mai, Lu Zhongyuan, Vincent H. S. Lo, and Wu Jinglian.

Both authors also want to acknowledge the excellent editorial support and guidance provided by Stephen Acerra, Karen Maloney, Grace Morris, Anwarali Shaheer, Kristy Barker, and Kristina Deusch. Karen deserves special mention as she worked on our manuscript from its initial review right through to the end of its publication. We would also like to express our heartfelt thanks to the three anonymous reviewers who offered invaluable suggestions during the review process.

Last but not least, we want to thank our family members, particularly Lijun and Jielu, for their contribution to the projects. Their selfless moral and intellectual support has been vital in our scholarly pursuit.

Introduction

This research is an attempt to reconsider the basic theoretical premises of China's political economy. We believe that China's political economy has been seriously misunderstood in the West, and this misunderstanding has created various forms of confusion and conflict among scholars and policy makers in China and the West. Some radical reconceptualizations will help clarify perceptions and misperceptions about China, and thus contribute to our China knowledge and policy making.

In this research, we conceptualize the Chinese political economy system by investigating the interconnectedness between the polity and the economy. While we often refer to China's historical experience, the main focus is on contemporary China. Methodologically, our research questions are positive ones, namely, what the Chinese political economy system is, how it is formed, how it has evolved, and how it functions now.

China's political economy is becoming increasingly important in the field of China studies. In Europe and North America, concepts and theories of political economy have been developed to explain the long process of economic development and growth of the West. Ever since the advent of the modern age, when China began to encounter dominant Western powers, Chinese scholars have gradually accepted "standard" Western political-economic concepts and theories, such as the free market and capitalism, and applied them in interpreting China's economic development and growth.[1] Their explanations, however, remain problematic

---

[1] Chinese acceptance of Western economics was not a simple process of linear development, of course. Rather, it was mediated and influenced by various political forces and institutional settings. But the overall trend in the late nineteenth and early twentieth centuries was toward full embrace and indigenization of economic research. See Paul B. Trescott, *Jingjixue: The History of Introduction of Economic Ideas to Modern China* (Hong Kong: Chinese University Press, 2007).

and misleading. We believe that in seeking to explain China, a scientific
concept and theory must be based on China's own experiences, just as
scholars in the West have developed concepts and theories based on
Western experiences.

Despite China's long history, Chinese scholars had not developed a
systemic theory of political economy as their Western counterparts did.[2]
Nevertheless, the country had a rich history of practicing different forms of
political economy systems in different periods. Conceptualizing Chinese
experiences of political economy is an important intellectual enterprise
for political and economic theorists and policy analysts. Given the fact that
contemporary China has been in transition for more than three decades
and is the largest living laboratory for all fields of social science, such
an endeavor will shed new light on various important research areas in
political economy in general and the Chinese state and economy in
particular, and thus improve and deepen our understanding of China. This
is particularly true in policy circles, since there is increasing uncertainty
about the rise of China.

In this day and age, all theoretical questions related to the rise of China
are the subject of heated debate. As the second largest economy in the
world, China is exercising increasingly greater influence worldwide. Yet, its
political economy system remains a mystery. Is China a market economy?
What does capitalism mean in the Chinese context? Is China an example of
so-called state capitalism? Perhaps most important of all, what is the
relationship between state and market in China, and how has it come into
being? Why is this perennially inefficient model, in the eyes of neoliberal
economists, so efficient in managing economic crises? Needless to say, such
questions have immense implications for theoretical development and
policy analysis. Questions such as these have often puzzled China scholars,
as they find it difficult to apply dominant theories in economics and
political science to China. As a result, many countries are not certain
what kind of China policy they should have. Without a sufficient level
of knowledge as to what China is, it is not easy to have an effective
China policy.

Our motivation to write this book was twofold: first, intellectual curiosity; second, policy considerations. Over the years, we have been puzzled by

---

[2] As it is used in China today, the term "political economy" (*zhengzhi jingjixue*) refers
mostly to an adapted Marxist theory of political economy. But imperial China did have a
tradition of policy-oriented political economy studies under the umbrella term *jingji*,
literally (Confucian) management of the world.

the long-lasting debate over two related aspects of China's development, namely, market economy and capitalism. We believe that the key to understanding China's recent economic miracle and its likely future lies in a theoretically informed analysis of its ideas and structures in the past and the present. Driven by the urgency of this task, our work here represents an attempt to present a theoretically informed analysis of China's political economy based on its historical experiences and contemporary transformations.

CHINA AND THE MARKET ECONOMY

The first debate between China and the West is about China's market economy status. Since the reform and the beginning of the open door policy, the Chinese economy has undergone an impressive transition to an increasingly market-oriented system. The country has been the beneficiary of global trade and financial investment, and has emerged as an economic power with seemingly unlimited growth potential. Its economic integration into the world system, however, has also generated conflicts between China and the West. Among others, China's market economy status is one of the main issues.

When China joined the World Trade Organization (WTO) in 2001, it agreed to be treated as a nonmarket economy (NME) for up to fifteen years, with the goal of developing into a market economy by the end of the transitional period. By doing so, the Chinese leadership wanted to demonstrate its determination to move the country toward a market economy. A country that is subject to antidumping investigations is classified as either a "market economy" (ME) or a "non-market economy" (NME). While Russia was recognized by the United States as a ME in 2002, China remained in the NME league, together with Albania, Cambodia, Kazakhstan, and Vietnam. The consequence of being classified as a NME is that in antidumping investigations, China's input factory prices cannot be used in the calculation of fair market value of end export products. Price data from a "surrogate" country such as India are typically used instead. The use of surrogate country data often leads to unfavorable rulings for Chinese exporters, and higher dumping duties. In many cases, the choice of surrogate country is a significant source of bias, often serving as a convenient tool to accommodate political pressure from domestic competitors.

From a Chinese perspective, since joining the WTO and reforming its legal system, the country has liberalized its economic system, resulting in unprecedented growth in economic activity and free trade. For China, market economy status is important, as it relates to the antidumping cases in international trade disputes. Understandably, for many years after joining the WTO, when China's leaders met their counterparts from the United States and Europe, they would urge them to recognize China's status as a market economy.

However, from a Western perspective, China is not ready to be granted market economy status, as it is still far from being a market economy in a Western sense.[3] The Chinese state continues to be the ultimate economic decision-making authority. There are still so many areas where the market does not function to regulate the economy, such as poorly defined or protected property rights, an outdated labor system, a continued stranglehold on the financial system, currency fluctuations, and other aspects of macroeconomic policy. All these forms of control and regulation on the part of the Chinese state thwart entrepreneurial activity and reduce economic growth.

Among all these problematic areas, China's state-owned enterprises (SOEs) have generated lasting debate among external observers and become the hallmark of the country's political economy system. Certainly, the sheer size and scope of China's SOE sector has made that country unique among the world's major economies. Due to this gigantic sector, more than anything else, China's system has been coined "state capitalism," an economic system in which commercial economic activity is undertaken by the state, with management and organization of the means of production carried out in a capitalist manner. The system of state capitalism has often drawn scrutiny from abroad and criticism at home. Writing in 2008, Jonathan Woetzel, then McKinsey's Shanghai Office Director, said in a McKinsey report:

For many years, the West has viewed China's state-owned enterprises in black or white. In one portrayal, they are infiltrators to be viewed with suspicion. An example: Aluminum Corporation of China's (Chinalco) recent multibillion-dollar purchase of a stake in Rio Tinto has raised fears about China's agenda for the acquisition of Australia's resources. The other version sees state-owned companies as muscle-bound goons: without the smarts of a private company but with plenty of brawn. In this characterization, they are relics of a failed economic experiment that still dominate the national economy, controlling natural resources, utilities, and many other vital sectors. Their power and

---

[3] The most recent iteration of this position came from the Trump administration, which, ironically, had rejected the idea of free trade on many occasions. See "US Seeks to Deny China's Market Economy Status in the WTO," *Financial Times*, November 30, 2017.

influence – particularly their links to the ruling Communist Party and government – have given partners and competitors pause.[4]

While many both inside and outside China have actively urged China to carry out large-scale systematic privatization and to substantially shrink the state sector, China's SOE sector was strengthened rather than weakened by such reforms in the late 1990s. Many in China have perceived the SOE sector as an advantage for the country, not a disadvantage. The SOE sector has been performing many key functions which the private sector cannot bear. For example, SOEs are employed by the state to build large-scale infrastructure, to promote economic growth, to balance a private sector that is perceived as greedy, and, more importantly, to cope with serious economic crises such as the 1997–1998 Asian Financial Crisis and the 2008 Global Financial Crisis. Meanwhile, SOEs can be faulted for their relative economic inefficiency, overexpansion, and self-serving political autonomy while performing these functions.

Due to these problems, there is no consensus in the West as to whether China should be granted market economy status. The issue has been debated in the United States and Europe for years. From a strategic point of view, some have argued that while China is not a "free market" yet, by granting it market economy status, the West would be able to offer a welcoming step in the right direction for a freer, more prosperous China. The country needs to be pushed to liberalize its economy and increase global competition.

Both within and outside China, for those who believe that China should be granted market economy status, there are reasonable arguments. A few arguments include: First, barring a few strategic economic sectors with significant government ownership (such as in banking, telecommunications, transport, and energy, none of which are abnormal in many other market economies), most other sectors in China are competitive, with hundreds of companies as players and razor-thin profit margins. Second, China's privatization is incremental. A sweeping privatization policy cannot occur overnight. The West should recognize China's developments in market liberalization. Third, failure to acknowledge China's market economy status could hamper trade relations between the West and China. The West is much wealthier because of China, and China's export industry flourishes because of free trade. In other words, free trade makes society

---

[4] Jonathan R. Woetzel, "Reassessing China's State-Owned Enterprises," *The McKinsey Quarterly*, July 2008, p. 1.

better off while protectionism makes it worse off. Fourth, the refusal to grant China market economy status is largely political. It is nonsensical and, in a sense, discriminatory. Treating China as a nonmarket economy is at odds with willingly recognizing Russia as having market economy status.

It is not so difficult to discover a similar logic behind the arguments of those both for and against granting China market economy status – namely, that China will become "more like us," in James Fallows' term.[5] Those who are pro-China believe that a more liberal China policy will make that country more liberal; those who are against it believe that a harder China policy will force the country to be more liberal. Indeed, China has been regarded as a postsocialist transitional economy, or a semimarket economy in transition.

Nearly two decades after China joined the WTO, the country is now the largest trading nation in the world. The country has moved from capital shortage to capital surplus, and its capital has gone up globally. While market economy status is no longer important for China, the West, particularly the United States, continues to raise questions about the nature of state capital. For instance, under the Obama administration, the United States tried to convince eleven Pacific nations to join a "next generation" trade agreement called the Trans-Pacific Partnership (TPP). Had it succeeded, it would have been the most important trade initiative since the 2001 launch of the WTO's Doha round collapsed, since it would bind two of the largest economies – namely, the United States and Japan – into a bloc covering 40 percent of global output. The TPP excluded China, but included Vietnam. This was a deliberate move. The TPP was the United States' "trade pivot" to Asia, and it was expected that Beijing might be pushed into reforming its economy so it could join at a later stage.[6] Again, the purpose was to promote economic liberalization in China. One can predict that as long as China's economic system does not run along the same lines as those in the West, such battles will continue in the future.

Therefore, for the scholarly community, the question of whether China will become a free market economy remains important. Among scholars and policy makers in both China and the West, the common position is to view China's economic transition as a process from planned economy to

---

[5] James Fallows, *More Like Us: Making America Great Again* (New York, NY: Houghton Mifflin, 1989).

[6] David Pilling, "Round Two in America's Battle for Asian Influence," *The Financial Times*, April 1, 2015.

market economy. The question is how complete this transition is. There is no doubt that since reform, China's economy is becoming increasingly market-oriented and less planned. But two conceptual questions can be raised. First, do scholars and policy makers in and outside China understand the market economy in the same way? Second, is the market in China becoming similar to those we can observe in the West? If we add these two questions to the "great divergence" debate, we can raise the question: Will China and the West converge in terms of development of the market economy?

Empirically speaking, the answer to this question is rather certain: China is not going to become a market economy such as we have seen in the West. For example, while China is moving toward a market economy, the state has consistently emphasized that the SOE sector should occupy a central position in the country's economic structure. This was confirmed once again in the most important document on economic reform in the post-Deng Xiaoping era, passed at the Third Plenum of the Eighteenth Chinese Communist Party in November 2013. The leadership overwhelmingly emphasized marketization as the direction of China's economic reform, but it also reiterated that state ownership is a "pillar" and "foundation" of China's distinctive economic system and its "socialist market economy." Therefore, one must go back to the basic question: What is China's political economy system? Without an answer to this question, we will continue to misperceive China.

CHINA AND CAPITALISM

The second, and related, debate between China and the West is about the relationship between the market economy and capitalism. Here our intellectual curiosities lay in both economic growth and capitalist development.

The thrust of the debate was also nicely captured in the concept of the Great Divergence, which, as historian Kenneth Pomeranz frames it, centers on the following question: "Why did sustained industrial growth begin in Northwest Europe, despite surprising similarities between advanced areas of Europe and East Asia in the eighteenth and nineteenth century?"[7] Phrased another way: "Why was China not able to develop a system of

---

[7] Kenneth Pomeranz, *The Great Divergence: China, Europe, and the Making of the Modern World Economy* (Princeton, NJ: Princeton University Press, 2000), p. 1.

modern capitalism even though there was the period of the 'sprouts of capitalism'"?[8] Over the years, scholars both within and outside China have struggled to identify perceived important factors which led to different paths of economic development in China and the West, but have met with limited success.

There have been two different answers to this question: "long-term lock-in theories" and "short-term accident theories," following the terms of historian Ian Morris.[9] The "long-term lock-in theories" came first. From Montesquieu onward, and during the nineteenth century, the predominant scholarly view of China in the West was of an "oriental despotism" without the self-propelling political and economic dynamism. This view of China as a country "without a history" reached its apogee in Karl Marx's writings. In Marx's view, Asiatic despotism was characterized by an absence of private property in land; large-scale, state-run irrigation systems in agriculture; autarchic village communities combining craft with tillage and communal ownership of the soil; bureaucratic cities; and a despotic state machine which appropriated the bulk of the economic surplus. Unlike European political economy, which Marx viewed as progressing from slavery to serfdom, feudalism, capitalism, and ultimately communism, the Asiatic mode merely had cycles of dynastic rise and fall, not an evolutionary history. This led Marx to view the violent intrusion of Western colonialism in a positive light, liberating Asian peoples from "Oriental despotism."

Based on the Marxist concept of the Asiatic mode of production, Karl Wittfogel, in his monumental work *Oriental Despotism: A Comparative Study of Total Power*, came up with an analysis of the nature of China's political economy system.[10] According to Wittfogel, over the course of the imperial period, China had developed not only private property but also considerable commercialization, monetization, and handicraft industries; however, due to the specific feature of Chinese ecology, the state had a special function to play in organizing large-scale hydraulic works, which necessitated the development of a full-time professional bureaucracy and allowed a despotic monarchy to retain its political dominance despite the rise of commerce. This complex hydraulic system

---

[8] For example, David Faure, *China and Capitalism: A History of Business Enterprise in Modern China* (Hong Kong: Hong Kong University Press, 2006), pp. 11–12.

[9] Ian Morris, *Why the West Rules – For Now: The Patterns of History and What They Reveal About the Future* (London: Profile Books, 2011), pp. 11–13.

[10] Karl August Wittfogel, *Oriental Despotism: A Comparative Study of Total Power* (New Haven, CT: Yale University Press, 1957).

of political economy was highly stable, with merely cyclical change as the fortunes of dynasties waxed and waned.

Such a critical view of China's political economy was also present and dominant among Western Sinologists of older generations. For example, historian John Fairbank and his coauthors distinguished two basic models of industrialization: the British model and the Chinese model. In the British model, modernization was endogenous. According to Fairbank and his colleagues,

the traditional pre-industrial order itself provided a framework for gestation. The commercial revolution of the mercantile period and the agricultural revolution following it were the necessary precursors of the industrial revolution in England. Endogenous, i.e., internally generated, forces played a dominant role in the rise of disequilibriating forces in the form of new inventions, advances in technology and innovations.[11]

By contrast, China was seen to fit into the second basic model of industrialization, in which traditional equilibrium needed to be disturbed exogenously before modernization could take place:

China of the early nineteenth century had a circular flow economy in which production was absorbed in consumption, with very little if any net saving, so that the economy merely reproduced itself without advancing. While there was some commercialization of the economy, it was not a major disequilibriating change.[12]

Joseph Needham, who produced the multivolume magnum opus *Science and Civilization in China*, also tended to take this view.[13] Needham recognized that China occupied a fairly dominant position in global technical progress up to around 1500. For Needham, the puzzle was: Given that the effects of all Chinese inventions and engineering solutions on the technology of post-Renaissance Europe were self-evident, why did they not lead to a similar upsurge of industrialism in China? Needham suggested that social analysis provides the answer to this question, arguing that Chinese "bureaucratic feudalism" was able to digest a wide array of discoveries and inventions which acted like time bombs in the social structure in the West.

---

[11] J. K. Fairbank, A. Eckstein, and L. S. Yang, "Economic Change in Early Modern China: An Analytic Framework," *Economic Development and Cultural Change* 9 (1960), p. 2.

[12] *Ibid.*, pp. 4–5.

[13] Joseph Needham, *Science and Civilization in China* (Cambridge: Cambridge University Press, 1954–2008). To date, twenty-seven volumes have been published.

The "short-term accident theories" came into existence in response to the "long-term lock-in theories" and were put forward by the California School of global history, including historians such as Bin Wong and Kenneth Pomeranz. According to these scholars, whatever we look at – ecology or family structures, technology and industry or finance and institutions, standards of living or consumer tastes – the similarities between China and the West, and in particular between China's Yangtze River Delta and Britain, vastly outweighed their differences as late as the nineteenth century. In that case, why did industrialization and capitalist development occur in the West and not in China? Pomeranz essentially argued that Western Europe, and above all Britain, just got lucky. The West's first stroke of luck was the accidental discovery of the Americas, creating a market for cheap produce and a West-dominated trading system that provided incentives to industrialize production. A second and important lucky break was that Britain alone in the world had conveniently located coalfields, as well as rapidly mechanizing industries.[14]

Inside China, particularly since the establishment of the People's Republic in 1949, economic development and capitalism in the premodern era has been a major research topic, if not a political one, and a huge amount of scholarly research has been devoted to the economic history of the Ming and Qing dynasties in search for the "sprouts of capitalism."[15] Outside the Marxist school, liberally minded Chinese scholars have produced general works on the imperial Chinese state and economy, which mirrored the bias of oriental despotism. For example, Wang Yi refines the oriental despotism thesis in his magisterial survey of the fiscal system of the late Ming dynasty by arguing that the system was characterized by irregular taxes and surcharges, predatory officials and fiscal agents, and ruthless exploitation

---

[14] Kenneth Pomeranz, *The Great Divergence* (Princeton, NJ: Princeton University Press, 2000). See the Introduction for the historical context and conceptualization of the Great Divergence, and the Conclusion for the role of historical contingencies.

[15] The most representative of this body of scholarship is the voluminous *Zhongguo zibenzhuyi fazhanshi* (in three volumes) produced by the Chinese Academy of Social Sciences under the editorship of Xu Dixin and Wu Chengming. The first volume deals with the question of underdevelopment of Chinese capitalism in Ming Qing China following a Marxist framework. For the English version of the first volume, see Xu Dixin and Wu Chengming, eds., *Chinese Capitalism, 1522–1840*, English translation by Li Zhengde, Liang Miaoru, and Li Siping, edited and annotated by C. A. Curwen (London: Macmillan Press Ltd, 2000).

of the peasants by the rich and powerful, all underwritten by the autocratic nature of the imperial power.[16]

While the despotic image of imperial Chinese polity continues to prevail in more ideologically inclined works, it is in many ways not supported by empirical data on imperial Chinese state and economy. For one thing, apart from a short interregnum of aggressive state-building in the early Ming (1368–1449), the imperial Chinese state was a very small one with only limited direct control over its vast society, in comparison with both the modern Chinese state and its contemporary Western state in the absolutist cast.[17] It is hard to conceive such a minimalist state with despotic powers to make wishful economic policies without negotiating with a myriad of economic forces outside its direct control. In fact, as we shall discuss in this book, it is the weakness rather than the despotic power of the imperial Chinese state that led to the lack of development of a capitalist system in late imperial China.

The Chinese Marxists have also come under heavy fire. For example, economists Chris Bramall and Peter Nolan have observed that, greatly influenced by the standard Marxist view of capitalism and China, scholars in China confine themselves to three sets of Marxist objectives when they examine China's economic history[18]: first, to evaluate the degree to which early modern China used a "capitalist" mode of production; second, to examine the nature of the "force of production"; and third, to analyze the interrelationship of the economic "base" of the "forces" and "relations" of production with the "superstructure of politics, law and ideology." Not surprisingly, their conclusions were often Marxist. For example, according to Wu Chengming, who coauthored a multivolume economic history of China from the year 1500, while premodern China developed capitalist elements, this embryonic capitalism developed extremely slowly and, even in the 1840s, amounted to only a tiny fraction of the national economy.[19] Although scholars in China have gathered a large amount of historical material and data, the traditional view of Marxism has constrained their

---

[16] Wang Yi, *Zhongguo huangquan zhidu yanjiu* (A Study of the Institutions of Emperorship in China) (Beijing: Beijing University Press, 2007), pp. 986–990.

[17] For a fuller discussion, see H. Lynman Miller, "The Imperial Chinese State," in David Shambaugh, ed., *The Modern Chinese State* (New York, NY: Cambridge University Press, 2001), pp. 16–40.

[18] Chris Bramall and Peter Nolan, "Introduction: Embryonic Capitalism in East Asia," in Xu and Wu, eds., *Chinese Capitalism*, pp. xiii–xl.

[19] Xu and Wu, eds., *Chinese Capitalism*, p.18

interpretations of China's economic history, and thus have rendered their interpretations not beyond those of scholars in the West.

In addition to various methodological issues, scholars are frequently influenced by the ideologies and politics of a given time when interpreting China's political economy system. As Bramall and Nolan observed:

A wide range of views has been advanced about the nature of the Chinese early modern economy. In the outside world, the selection and interpretation of evidence about the traditional Chinese economy were heavily influenced in the nineteenth century by Europe's own dynamic progress. In the twentieth century, the analysis of the traditional Chinese economy has been heavily affected by the struggle against communism, by ignorance of the Chinese language, by China's political turmoil pre-1949 and by China's long cultural isolation after the 1949 revolution. Within China, views have been affected by nationalist sentiments, by intense political struggle pre-1949, by the restrictions placed on freedom of scholarship for much of the post-1949 period and by the limited interaction between Mainland Chinese and foreign scholars until the 1980s.[20]

More often than not, in their endeavors to compare China and the West, scholars pointed either to factors which had existed in China but not in the West, or factors which had existed in the West but not in China.[21] While such comparative studies are useful in demonstrating the differences or similarities between China and the West, sometimes such endeavors did not improve our knowledge of the Chinese political economy system. In some cases, they led to distortion. Also, since scholars' focus was not on conceptualizing the Chinese political economy system, their efforts produce little generalized knowledge of China.

Of course, we do not intend to answer all these grand questions in this research. However, we do attempt to shed light on these questions by setting out a political economy approach. By doing so, we intend not only to satisfy our own intellectual curiosity, but also to stimulate others' interest in the nature of Chinese political economy.

CHINA AND ITS CONTEMPORARY ECONOMIC MIRACLE

To address these old, grand questions about the Chinese political economy, we analyze the structure and mechanisms of contemporary Chinese political economy that lie behind China's economic miracle and its

---

[20] Bramall and Nolan, "Introduction: Embryonic Capitalism in East Asia," p. xviii.

[21] For example, Eric Jones, *The European Miracle: Environments, Economies and Geopolitics in the History of Europe and Asia*, 3rd ed. (Cambridge: Cambridge University Press, 2003).

political development. These two interrelated domains provide the central questions for our research.

First, China's economic miracle has posed enormous new intellectual challenges for the scholarly community. We need to explore the formation of new types of state–market relations, capital–society relations, and state–society relations after China's reform and the introduction of the open door policy. Even though China has opened its door wide to the West, its political economy system remains unknown to us since we cannot find another system that closely resembles it in other places of this world.

Scholars have attempted to use various concepts and theories put forward in the context of development experiences in the West to explain China's economic miracle.[22] However, they have found it difficult to use any established concepts and theories of Western economics to satisfactorily explain it. Among others, Justin Lin Yifu, a Chicago-trained Chinese economist at Beijing University and then Chief Economist and Senior Vice President of the World Bank, has set out why and how the existing concepts and theories could not give a convincing explanation for China's economic miracle. For many years, he has called for Chinese economists to be innovative and creative in searching for new explanations.[23] Indeed, Lin and his colleagues have searched for new concepts and theories that they believe would be more capable of explaining China's development experiences. For instance, they have attempted to place China in the context of the East Asian miracle.[24] Despite their great efforts, such explanations do not go beyond the existing Western analytical frameworks. Concepts and theories which have developed in social sciences in the West have been extensively and intensively applied to the case of contemporary China since China's economic reform. While scholars are aware of the political–institutional context of China's economic reform during the early years of China's ascendance, they tend to believe that China is making a transition

---

[22] There is a growing body of literature in this area. For a survey of the field, see Barry Naughton, *The Chinese Economy: Transition and Growth* (Cambridge, MA: MIT Press, 2007) and Loren Brandt and Thomas G. Rawski, eds., *China's Great Economic Transformation* (New York, NY: Cambridge University Press, 2008).

[23] Justin Lin Yifu, "Chuangxin jingjixue lilun wei hexie shehui zuo gongxian" (To Innovate Theories of Economics and To Contribute to Harmonious Society), speech at the 2006 Beijing Forum, available at http://theory.people.com.cn/GB/40557/72701/72717/4971204.html [Accessed on May 3, 2009].

[24] For example, Justin Yifu Lin, Fang Cai, and Zhou Li, *The China Miracle: Development Strategy and Economic Reform*, A Friedman Lecture Fund Monograph, published for the Hong Kong Centre for Economic Research and the International Centre for Economic Growth by The Chinese University Press, 1996.

from a planned economy to the market economy seen in the West.[25] Indeed, a growing body of literature on China's political economy regards China as "transitional," explicitly implying that China is inevitably developing into a Western type of market economy.

In recent years, there has been another group of scholars in China – traditionally dominant Marxist economists who have found that their explanations have been greatly threatened by those produced by new generations and Western-trained economists, and who have tried to revive Marxist economics in China.[26] But Marxist economics does not explain China's development either, and its revival is mainly targeted at explaining the negative social consequences caused by rapid economic development. The debate between Marxist economists and other schools continues to be staged more on ideological than on academic grounds. Marxist economics has been used as a tool by Chinese Marxist economists either to provide an ideological justification for the existing regime or to rebut other schools of economics in the West, particularly the neoliberal one. Of course, this does not mean that Marxist economics is irrelevant to contemporary China. From the perspective of Marxist political economy, many negative social consequences are part and parcel of China's economic miracle. Marx's main point was that capitalistic development would have destructive impacts on society. China's development has exactly confirmed that Marx was right. Certainly, viable concepts and theories must be able to explain not only how China's economic miracle has been achieved, but also how various forms of social consequence are associated with the process of rapid development. Marxist economics remains relevant since it attempts to explain both the process of economic development and its social consequences. Nevertheless, Marxist economics does not provide an economic solution to the social consequences, and its solution (that is, revolution) is overwhelmingly political and ideological. Indeed, the revolutionary nature of the Marxist doctrine has posed serious intellectual as well as political challenges to the scholarly community in China.

Most Marxists, and the neoliberal economists, have focused largely on China's domestic economic development, with little consideration of

---

[25] For example, in the mid-1990s, Barry Naughton saw the path to market economy as the inevitable end of China's post-Tiananmen economic development. See Barry Naughton, *Growing Out of the Plan: Chinese Economic Reform, 1978–1993* (New York, NY: Cambridge University Press, 1995), pp. 278–288.

[26] For example, Liu Guoguang, "Tan jingji jiaoxue he yanjiu zhongde yixie wenti" (On Some Issues in Teaching and Research in Economics), available at http://www.mjjx.cn/Article/ArticleShow.asp?ArticleID=677 [Accessed on May 3, 2009].

global and comparative perspectives. Having realized the limitations of existing literature, scholars have searched for new explanations for China's development by placing the country in the international context. The study of China's market economy and capitalism is an example of this genre of research with a stress on the global and comparative perspectives. Since reform and the introduction of the open door policy, China has embraced the market economy and capitalism. However, scholars have found that the market economy in China or Chinese capitalism is not of any Western type, but remains uniquely Chinese. They thus call it "capitalism with Chinese characteristics." This form of capitalism has generated enormous economic and social consequences considered undesirable. For example, Huang Yasheng presents a story of two Chinas – an entrepreneurial rural one and a state-controlled urban one. In the 1980s, rural China gained the upper hand, and the result was rapid and broad-based growth. In the 1990s, the state-centered model of urban China triumphed. In this decade the Chinese state reversed many of its productive rural experiments, inflicting long-lasting damage on the economy and society. A weak financial sector, income disparity, rising illiteracy, productivity slowdowns, and reduced personal income growth are the product of the "capitalism with Chinese characteristics" of the 1990s and beyond. While gross domestic product (GDP) grew quickly in both decades, the welfare implications of growth differed substantially. For Huang, to rectify these problems, China has to transform its capitalism into a full-fledged form like that of the West. Huang particularly emphasizes the role of democracy – for instance, in the Indian case – and privatization during this process of transition from "capitalism with Chinese characteristics" to a Western form of capitalism.[27] It is not difficult to see that, as with many other scholars, Huang's explanation is deeply rooted in development experiences in the West, where capitalism implies private ownership and private entrepreneurship. According to this explanation, China seems to have developed in the wrong way. While the government allowed and encouraged development of the private sector, large-scale privatization of the state sector did not take place; instead, China has developed an increasingly large state sector and state capitalism has become dominant in the market.

No concept or theory that ignores this growing state sector will be able to explain the growth of China's economy and its associated problems. However, the concept of "capitalism with Chinese characteristics" does not

---

[27] Huang Yasheng, *Capitalism with Chinese Characteristics: Entrepreneurship and the State* (Cambridge and New York, NY: Cambridge University Press, 2008), pp. 233–240, 256–260.

explain China's market system and all its sociopolitical consequences. For one thing, state capitalism does not capture the extent of the market system in China. State capitalism is only one of the various forms of capitalism that exist in China today. The dominant position occupied by state capitalism does not mean that other types of capitalism have not played a role in promoting China's rapid economic growth, and producing social consequences. In fact, while Huang laments the rise of state capitalism at the cost of private entrepreneurship, he does not highlight the fact that the share of urban employment in the private sector increased from 3 percent to 21 percent from 1995 to 2014, while the share of employment in nonstate sectors in urban China increased from 15 percent to 60 percent.[28] Moreover, state capitalism does not mean that the state can always dominate capital in the form of the assets and economic might of the SOEs, which theoretically belong to the state. There are deep structural contradictions or conflicting interests between the state and its capitalistic agents. While the state attempts to exercise control over its capital, the latter wants to avoid such control by appealing to the market. In terms of research methodology, "capitalism with Chinese characteristics" was largely formulated at the policy level, especially in terms of the policy of the central government. Its focus is on how government policy and development strategy affects the economic behavior of various players. The concept of Chinese capitalism does not point to the structural aspects of China's political economy system, which sometimes are determinant of rather than determined by central government policy. In the literature, more often than not, scholars tend to tell us how government policies have made a Chinese economy that does not converge with the market economy model of the West. But focusing solely on policy-level factors will not lead us to explore how China's political economy system has been configured and how it has actually functioned to make the China that we see now.

OUR RESEARCH AGENDA AND MAIN ARGUMENTS

While all the scholarly efforts just discussed show us how China's development has taken a different path from other countries, they are limited in the sense that they tell us what China is not, but not what China is. More importantly, by comparing China to other countries, especially the developed West, most scholars come to regard China as abnormal and

---

[28] National Bureau of Statistics Database, www.stats.gov.cn/tjsj/ndsj/ [Accessed on April 15, 2015].

the West as normal. For many scholars, to make China normal is to transform it into a Western type of political economy. In their writings, China is assessed, valued, and judged by what has existed and developed in the West. This is apparently implicitly embedded in the literature of postsocialist transition, which views China as a transitional political economy – this transition being one from Chinese characteristics to Western characteristics. These culturally or implicitly ideologically biased approaches tend to undermine our understanding of China, and often unintentionally present a "distorted" image of China.

From the perspective of scientific research, we believe that more often than not, the intellectual puzzles described are more the result of the mechanical application to China of concepts and theories based on experiences of the West than the result of Chinese practice. The purpose of this research is to conceptualize and theorize China's political economy system based on China's own experiences, historical and contemporary. While this research has implications for all the grand questions previously raised, we limit our endeavor to China's political economy system.[29]

All political economy concepts and theories, such as the classical, Marxian, neoclassical, Keynesian, and neoliberal ones, were based on Western experiences in different historical periods, and they have been used to explain China's political economy system. Assumptions are made regarding the universality of these economic concepts and theories, since economics deals with general economic phenomena such as supply and demand, price, and rationality. However, one has to be reflective, at least, when applying them to a different institutional setting in a different historical period. Even within the West, not all concepts and theories are universally applicable to different historical periods, since each concept and theory was a reflection of the economic situation during that period. In fact, we can go one step further to question the universal applicability of all these concepts and theories. When one perceives China from a conceptual and theoretical perspective based on non-China experiences, one will surely regard China as abnormal. But if one can conceptualize or theorize

---

[29] This study is the second in our "trilogy" on China, focusing on China and its modern transformation. In the first, we explored the modern transformation of the Chinese regime. See Zheng Yongnian, *The Chinese Communist Party as Organizational Emperor: Culture, Reproduction and Transformation* (London and New York, NY: Routledge, 2010). The current study focuses on China's political economy system and its modern transformation. In the third, we will focus on state–society relations and its modern transformation.

China's own experiences, the situation might become different, and then "abnormal" might turn out to be "normal."

Therefore, the most important motivation of this research is to conceptualize the Chinese experience of political economy. This book radically departs from the existing theories inside and outside China in its effort to provide a Chinese perspective of political economy on China's development and its consequences. We believe that while scholars can continue to apply Western economic concepts and theories to China, they will have to do so reflectively, since China's political economy system has operated in a typically Chinese way. As the Chinese government has rightly claimed, it is a system with "Chinese characteristics." But the official concept of "socialism with Chinese characteristics" remains an ideological dogma and explains nothing scientifically. A truly universal concept or theory of political economy would have greater explanatory power were it to take the Chinese factors into consideration. The field of Chinese political economy studies is full of imported concepts and theories which are incapable of explaining the actual functioning of the Chinese political economy. Conceptualizing Chinese operation of the political economy system is the target of this research.

We argue that to conceptualize China's political economy system, one has to meet two conditions in terms of research methodology. First, we have to go beyond various policy-level factors to look at structural factors. This is simply because structural factors are more consistent than policy ones. Second, and relatedly, we also have to go beyond a given historical period. It is easy to observe how government policies affect China's economic performance in a given historical period. For instance, Huang Yasheng's study has shown how different sets of government policy in the 1980s and 1990s have produced differentiated economic performance and distributional consequences in these two decades. However, by solely looking at government policies, it is difficult to conceptualize China's political economy system. State policies do affect the performance of the political economy system, but do not necessarily change the nature of the system. Rather, the *longue durée* structural forces of the system determine the kind of policy options available and favorable to the government. Therefore, to conceptualize China's political economy system, we have to examine its consistent features and functioning over longer, and in different, historical periods.

While our focus is the contemporary era in this study, we also consider China's past experiences of economic management. We contend that through early dynasties and up to the contemporary era, China's political economy system can be simply defined by the two concepts of the market: one with or without state intervention. The formation of these two concepts can be traced back to the Confucian and Legalist Schools in the early days of Chinese emperorship. Among other schools of thought, they represented China's mainstream philosophies of state, economy, and society, and relations among them. While the formation of these philosophies was affected by China's physical and geographical environments at that time, the existence of these ideational factors affected the architecture of China's political economy system.

Over China's long history, these two concepts represented two extremes of its political economy system, or two ideal-types. There were periods in which the extreme forms of the Legalist or Confucian School became prevalent, but for the most of time the two concepts were integrated and well balanced, and the two set of actors – market and state – were held roughly in equilibrium. Either the market alone or the state alone was regarded as abnormal. The normality is the coexistence of the market and the state. However, equilibrium does not mean that the power of the state and that of the market are symmetrical. Instead, the relationship between the two is asymmetrical, and state domination of the market is the rule. In this sense, we conceptualize the central idea and practice of China's political economy system as "economic statism." Economic statism played a crucial role in governing a vast country, mobilizing resources for national defense, engaging in huge public projects, and coping with major crises. But the expansion of economic statism often led to disequilibrium between the state and the market. This often led to the state's withdrawal from economic life and its weakening vis-à-vis the market and local elites; the decline of its many public functions; its collapse in the face of external and internal threats; and the destruction of the economy. In either case, disequilibrium was the inevitable outcome and constant adjustment was required to maintain equilibrium. In this sense, we call this "asymmetrical equilibrium." While China's political economy system has been in a process of constant transformation over different historical periods, equilibrium has been reproduced over different times and spaces. The purpose of this study is to highlight and format this asymmetrical equilibrium, an architectonic structure of the political economy that we call "market in state" (MIS).

Despite changes over China's long history, the structure of MIS has remained intact. One might argue that this is simply because China remained an agrarian society for thousands of years before the modern age. But the important question here is why this structure has remained unchanged throughout China's modern age, particularly since Deng Xiaoping's reform and open door policy, when China experienced rapid industrialization, a growing market economy, capitalist development, urbanization, and all the other aspects that were also observed during the transition periods of the West.

There is consensus that since reform and the introduction of the open door policy, China has transformed itself from a planned economy to a more market-based one. In economic terms, a market economy is an economy based on the division of labor in which the prices of goods and services are determined in a free price system set by supply and demand. At the other end, a planned economy system is one in which a central government determines the price of goods and services using a fixed price system. Of course, despite the post-Mao transition, China's political economy system still differs drastically in many aspects from those seen in the West. But this does not matter, and one can still regard China as a sui generis market economy.

Under Mao Zedong, following first the Soviet model and then his ad hoc mobilization models, the revolutionary state attempted to build a socialist economy structure which aimed at providing greater equality and giving the "proletariat" or working class greater ownership of the means of production. In terms of its conceptual ideals, it was a centrally planned economy. The system functioned through the imposition of production quotas and goods were cleared through a central planning authority. Even prices for allocation of goods and services were predetermined by the state. But in terms of historical context, the system was an extension of the modern mobilization state developed in response to war and social disruption since the nineteenth century.

In the initial period, this system saw some great economic achievements. The state was able to mobilize all available sources for fast economic growth. However, a successful Communist system was deemed to be unattainable. Since the state controlled every productive element, there was no incentive for individuals, and this eventually led to a situation of "socialism with poverty." Also, under this system, government mandarins appropriated too much power, and corruption became excessive. Mao tried to solve this problem by radically decentralizing power from the central state to local states, but decentralization from the state to enterprises never really took place.

Since reform and the introduction of the open door policy, China's official definition of its political economy system is "socialist market economy." With the decline of the state mobilization model, market mechanisms have been introduced and widely utilized across the economy. As Deng emphasized, since the market is only a tool or means to liberalize a country's productive forces, both capitalism and socialism can make use of market mechanisms. In this sense, China's socialist market economy is a radical departure from the old planned economy. This system is now characterized by some key features. First, the state continues to own key industries such as heavy industry, energy, and infrastructure. However, state ownership does not mean state control. More often than not, the state retains controlling ownership of many enterprises on the "commanding heights," but the central government has little effective direct control over SOEs' operations. Second, private ownership is allowed in many competitive sectors of the economy. Indeed, privately owned enterprises have become the backbone of the economic system. Most of the economic growth is attributed to the private sector. Third, the market is given a free hand to allocate and distribute the country's resources based on the forces of supply and demand. It demonstrates the essential features of efficiency, growth, and production of surplus value generally associated with capitalist economies. It is worth noting that while the free market has largely supplemented central economic planning in the economy, the government still guides overall national economic development through "indicative planning." Fourth, the role of the market in social sectors is more pervasive than is the case in many Western countries, especially the welfare states of continental Europe. The state has attempted to privatize various social sectors previously run by the state, such as health care, education, and public housing, which are still run by the state in many Western countries. The introduction of market-oriented reform in the social sectors has also contributed to China's economic growth.

In some aspects, China's "socialist market economy" is even more capitalistic than many market economies in the West. It is understandable that this system has come under criticism. Orthodox Marxists criticize it on the grounds that the socialist market economy restores capitalist commodity relations and production while further disempowering the working class, leading to a sharp increase in social inequality and the formation of a growing capitalist class. Others believe that the Chinese system has embraced too many elements of market capitalism, resulting in a "state capitalist" type of economic system.

However, we believe that the development of these characteristics does not mean that China and the West converge in terms of fundamental principles of market–state relations. In the real world, market economies do not exist in a pure form, as societies and governments regulate them to varying degrees rather than allowing self-regulation by market forces. While no country has ever had within its borders an economy in which all markets were free, almost all economies in the world today are mixed ones with varying degrees of free market and planned economy traits. As a matter of fact, the terms "free economy" and "market economy" are sometimes used synonymously. However, as the German ideas and practice of social market economy have demonstrated, a free economy can operate and even prosper with heavy government intervention that upholds social justice and checks overconcentration of market power.[30] In most economies, the price system is not entirely free but under some measure of government control or heavily regulated, sometimes combined with state-led economic planning that is not extensive enough to constitute a planned economy. Different perspectives exist as to how strong a role the government should have in both guiding the market economy and addressing market failures inequality is not a market failure.

This is also true from the perspective of the evolution of capitalism in world history. Capitalism in the West generally refers to an economic system in which the means of production are all or mostly privately owned and operated for profit, and in which investments, distribution, income, and production and pricing of goods and services are determined through the operation of a market economy. It is usually considered to involve the right of individuals and groups of individuals acting as "legal persons" or corporations to trade capital goods, labor, land, and money. While capitalism has been dominant in the Western world since the end of feudalism, after waves of transformation, today the most common form of capitalism behaves like a mixed economy, containing both privately owned and state-owned enterprises, combining elements of capitalism and socialism, or mixing the characteristics of market economies and planned ones. In different historical periods, some Western economies experimenting with socialism had adopted measures such as nationalization, redistribution of wealth among the rich and poor, minimum wage measures, and policies of demand management along Keynesian lines.

However, in most forms of contemporary capitalism, there is no central planning authority and the prices are decided by the economic forces of supply and demand. Even the functioning of the government will have to follow market principles, since a government's operation depends on direct

---

[30] Christian L. Glossner and David Gregosz, *The Formation and Implementation of the Social Market Economy: Incipiency and Actuality* (Berlin: Konrad Adenauer Stiftung, 2011), pp. 32–33.

taxes to survive and policy is made through a bargaining process between powerful economic and social interests. The Chinese will never understand why in the West, a government, even a central (federal) government, could be shut down due to fighting between opposing political parties. In general, we can conceptualize various forms of capitalism in the West as "state in market." This is a system in which market (economic) principles are dominant over state (political) principles. By contrast, we characterize China's political economy system as "market in state." Through this concept, we argue that despite the existence of different forms of capitalism and the functioning of market principles, China's political economy system is one in which state (political) principles are dominant over market (economic) principles. With the rise of this form of Chinese capitalism, the family of capitalism now has a new, but powerful, member.

Our aim at the intellectual level is to describe and explain this new family member in the typology of world political economies. More specifically, the purpose of this research is multifold: to conceptualize China's political economy system as "market in state," to describe how this system is developed and has evolved, to explain how it functions, and to explore the social and political consequences of this system.

This research also has some important policy implications. At the policy level, our purposes look to the future. We want to make some contributions to an important policy area for the contemporary world, namely, the future of capitalism. Contemporary capitalism is in crisis, as demonstrated during and in the aftermath of the 2007–2008 global financial crisis. The financial crisis has exposed fundamental weaknesses in the West's political-economic systems. Today, many in the West are disillusioned with the workings of their economic and political systems – particularly as they have watched governments bail out bankers with taxpayers' money and then stand by impotently as financiers continue to pay themselves huge bonuses. Scholars such as Thomas Piketty have begun to consider capitalism in the twenty-first century.[31]

Chinese capitalism has not only produced an unprecedented economic miracle in the past three decades, but has also succeeded in coping with various economic crises such as the 1997–1998 Asian financial crisis and the 2007–2008 global financial crisis. So far, it has sustained its growth momentum, albeit at a lower rate. While the scholarly community has been very critical of the Chinese variety of capitalism, the functioning of this

---

[31] For example, Thomas Piketty, *Capitalism in the Twenty-First Century*, translated by Arthur Goldhammer (Cambridge, MA: Harvard University Press, 2014).

system is unfairly understudied. We believe that varieties of capitalism can draw lessons and experiences from one another. There is no reason to ignore this Chinese variety of capitalism.

THE ORGANIZATION OF THE BOOK

The book is divided into three parts. The first two chapters of the first part attempt to answer the question of what China's political economy system is and is not. One of our arguments is that while China's economy is increasingly market-oriented, it is not developing, or will not develop, into a Western-type political economy system.

Chapter 1 answers the question of what China is not. We discuss basic characteristics of the political economy system in the West, and show how they have developed and been institutionalized historically. We show that the market system is a unique product of Western history, and no other place can easily repeat such a history; neither can such a system be produced elsewhere. This chapter also examines the political economy system which has developed in other East Asian economies, since scholars tend to place China into this group of economies. We argue that while China's political economy system has similar characteristics with these East Asian economies, there are also major differences between the two. By comparing China's political economy system with other systems, we hope to emphasize the dominant feature of China's political economy system, namely, "market in state."

Chapter 2 answers the question of what China is. We examine the two concepts of the market in Chinese history and identify key issues that these Chinese concepts sought to address. Our aim is to develop a theory of political economy in China. China's political economy system is defined as power relations of state domination of the market. These relations are in asymmetrical equilibrium. The domination of state power, however, does not mean that the market is a helpless actor; instead, it has capacity to exercise its influence over the state. The interaction between the state and the market is mutually transforming. We identify three levels of market in China – grassroots, middle ground, and national – and discuss how the state related itself to market players at different levels and the rationales behind these relationships. We want to identify the Chinese logic underneath the practice of its political economy system. We believe that the Chinese political economy approach, once conceptualized and theorized, is better capable of explaining contemporary China than any political economy approach originating elsewhere.

The two chapters in the second part tackle the historical evolution of China's political system. Chapter 3 furnishes an analysis of how the political economy system of imperial China functioned and demonstrates how the MIS approach operated. Our discussion focuses on the fiscal capacity of the imperial state and demonstrates how imperial China established a unique type of order that gradually evolved to integrate an omnipotent emperorship, a complex hierarchy of imperial agents, and the world of common people in a political economy system which operated on power and authority provided by the emperorship and its agents.

Chapter 4 examines the transformation of the MIS system in modern times, as China began to interact with Western powers. We focus on the geopolitical factors and believe that these, particularly the interactions between the imperial state and minorities, impacted on the formation of the MIS system in imperial China. In the modern era, China's entire system, political and economic systems included, was reshaped by a new set of geopolitical factors faced by the country. Facing a new geopolitical environment, China's traditional MIS system was transformed to meet the challenges of modern state-building. The system not only survived the process of modern state-building; it was reinforced and radicalized by the nascent party state. We show that the interactions between geopolitics, state-building, and political economy run through China's entire modern period, from the late Qing, through the Republic era, to the late 1970s before the post-Mao reform.

The third part of the book turns to contemporary China and constitutes the main body of the book. These chapters examine in detail how the MIS system of China's political economy has developed and functioned in the contemporary era. We consider again the three levels of the market system – grassroots, middle ground, and national level – and how the state realized dominance over the market while continuing to accommodate it.

Chapter 5 covers what we call grassroots capitalism. This is a large area of small-scale economic activity, including millions of peddlers and household retailers. We examine how the grassroots market grew out of the Maoist planning system. To explain the process, we follow some pioneering market actors in the smooth marketization of the 1980s and trace their fate as they move into the 1990s, when market development follows the political logic of the state.

Chapter 6 turns to what we call middle-ground capitalism, and examines the nexus between the private sector and the state. While the state has never ceased to reposition itself vis-à-vis private capital, it has been always centrally concerned with overriding political objectives of economic or production growth and employment. For that purpose, it has been willing to make concessions and maintain limits that were hardly conceivable in a typical free market economy. This chapter explains the various institutional arrangements between the state and private enterprises, demonstrating both the flexibility and the rigidity of the MIS system in different local conditions.

Chapter 7 examines how a new fiscal and monetary arrangement constantly evolves away from a planned system and into an array of complex market and state organizations. We focus on the interactions among the central state, local governments, and various private interests in the process of monetization. The chapter shows that the process of monetization and financialization is not simply a story of reform and development as directed by the central party state. Instead, through a series of fiscal and financial innovations, local and private interests have become a shaping force in the process of China's monetization just as much as the central state. We are interested in the process by which various political-economic hybrids are created in the middle ground between the state and market.

Chapter 8 focuses on state capitalism. It answers the question of why China's centrally managed SOEs are organized as they are. We explain how the state sector – and particularly centrally managed SOEs – has differentiated itself from the state sectors of both the imperial era and the Maoist era, and how the state has established various mechanisms through which it continues to exercise its domination over the state sector. By doing so, we demonstrate that while the purpose of the market-oriented reform in the contemporary era was to fundamentally change the Maoist planned economy, it does not mean that China's SOEs operate in the same way as private firms in the market system in the West.

In the Conclusion, we summarize the major findings of this research. We also highlight some of the main social and political consequences of the MIS system of China's political economy, although this subject deserves a separate study. We point to some inherent contradictions within this system, and the challenges this system faces today.

PART I

THEORY

1

Market, State, and Capitalism

Theories of Political Economy and China

A political economy system is a set of institutional arrangements with regard to the relationship between the state and market. China's political economy system consists of a particular set of institutions that mediate the state and market. Compared to other political economy systems worldwide, it has its own unique and distinguished structural features. Before we describe these features, it is necessary to consider other political economy systems, since such a comparison will enable us to see how unique China's political economy system is. Nevertheless, in a book about China, it is impossible for us to discuss other political economy systems in detail; nor can we make a comprehensive comparison between China and these other systems. In this chapter, we shall discuss China in the context of two of the main political economy systems in modern times, namely, market capitalism in the West – typically in the contemporary United States – and strategic capitalism in East Asia's newly industrial economies, especially in Japan and South Korea. Market capitalism originated in Western Europe and then spread to other parts of the world. During the process, capitalism transformed according to local conditions, as reflected in the writings of economic historians and in the more recent literature on "varieties of capitalism." In the East Asian sphere where China is located, the variety of capitalism that has developed is strategic capitalism, and thus China is conventionally regarded as ascribing to this variety of the strategic capitalism. However, here, by placing China in the realms of both Western market capitalism and East Asian NIEs, we will be able to categorize China's as a new variety of capitalism by highlighting similarities and differences between it and other forms of capitalism.

It is certainly not an easy task to define China's political economy system. Scholars inside and outside China frequently find that they do not have proper terms, concepts, and theories to describe China's unique political economy system. They have to borrow existing ones, which have been developed in the West and used to explain various Western political economy systems, to interpret and understand China's. Terms and concepts such as capitalism, liberalism, Marxism, Keynesianism, fascism, and state corporatism are often on the list, among many others. However, doing this does not help much. The application of these terms and concepts has led to our current situation: We do not understand China's political economy system today.

China's post-Mao economic reform is market-oriented, and its target is to transform a planned economy into a market economy with "Chinese characteristics." After more than three decades of reform, China is increasingly integrated into the world economic system, but the country has not developed into a Western-type political economy system. While the market now plays an important role in the economy, and even an excessive role in some social sectors such as health, education, and housing, China's political economy system has grown, and has its own characteristics. Scholars and policy analysts have thus begun to search for other terms to describe China. The latest conceptual invention to have gained popularity in describing China is "state capitalism."[1] While this new term captures one of the main features of China's political economy system, namely, the dominant role of state-owned enterprises (SOEs) in the economy, it does not explain many other increasingly important market realms, such as the growing private sector; nor does it answer many important questions such as how the system actually functions, how the state dominates the market, and how the state and the market coexist.

Our argument is that while China's economy has been increasingly market-oriented since the late 1970s, it is not developing – nor will it develop – into an American-type political economy system. Therefore, it will be useful to highlight some basic characteristics of the political economy system in the West, and discuss how they have developed and institutionalized historically. We contend that the market system is a unique product of Western history, and no other place can easily repeat such a history; neither can such a system be produced elsewhere. A comparison between the political economy systems in the West and in

---

[1] See, for example, "The Rise of State Capitalism: The Emerging World's New Model," *The Economist*, January 21–27, 2012.

China will serve as a background for us to understand China's political economy system in later chapters.

Another political economy system that is often used in comparison with China's is the one underlying the so-called East Asian Miracle, namely, the political economy system which has developed in other East Asian NIEs, first in Japan and later in the "four little dragons" (South Korea, Singapore, Taiwan, and Hong Kong). It is understandable that scholars tend to rank China among these East Asian NIEs, since geographically and culturally much of China is a part of East Asia, and in some respects China's recent economic development pattern resembles these East Asian NIEs. Moreover, a negative side of the East Asian miracle, namely, crony capitalism – a capitalism where business success depends on a close relationship with government officials – also applies to China. In recent years, scholars within China have increasingly applied this term to characterize their country's political economy system. While it is certainly correct that China's political economy system has similar characteristics to these East Asian NIEs, to say that China ascribes to the East Asian model does not help us understand the relationship between the state and the economy in China. Therefore, it will also be useful to highlight some main characteristics of the East Asian model in terms of the relationship between the state and market before we turn to discuss China's political economy system.

Through such a comparison, this chapter aims to answer the question of what China is *not*, and to provide a background for Chapter 2, where we will answer the question of what China *is*. In this way we hope to highlight one dominant feature of China's political economy system, that is, "market in state" (MIS). Through this term we attempt to conceptualize state domination of the market in China's political economy system. Several features of this system will be discussed in detail in later chapters, but they can be summarized here. First, the MIS approach recognizes that there is a system of markets and the market as a social field, and this recognition is critical for the legitimate existence of a market at an institutional level. The state allows the market to exist and to function. Second, the state and the market coexist in the same mixed-economy system. Third, the market always operates within the rules and boundaries set by the state, but the state may often disobey the rules and boundaries set by the market. In both the Western and East Asian political economy systems, there is a boundary between the state and the market, and the market field is autonomous. The difference between these two systems is the degree to which the state can penetrate the market: In the West, the boundary of the market field is protected by laws and political cultures, while in East Asian economies, both laws and political cultures allow the state to penetrate the market field deeply. In both systems, although the state has developed different means to intervene in and regulate economic activities, it has to follow market principles. In this sense, the state has to live within the boundaries set by the market. By contrast, in China, while in principle there is a boundary between the state and the market, the market is not autonomous and its function is sometimes not guaranteed by laws and political cultures; it must live within the boundaries set by the state in order to survive. In terms of Max Weber's "ideal type," one can say that the Chinese system is characterized by "market in state," while the political economy system in the West is characterized by "state in market," and the East Asian NIEs by interpenetration of market and state.

In comparing China with these political economy systems, we focus on both conceptual and empirical levels, for two reasons. First, by considering both, we will see how economists construct their concepts and theories. We believe that while economists often construct their concepts and theories at an abstract level, their thinking and reasoning is inevitably affected by the empirical world in which they live. We thus refer to two bodies of economic literature: that by economists and that by economic historians. Second, we want to provide a historical background for the later chapters, in which we will discuss China's political economy system in the traditional and the contemporary eras. While traditional China did not develop a modern discipline of economics or political economy, this does not mean that China did not have its unique thoughts and ideas on the economy. On the contrary, one can argue that China had its own "discipline of economics" which dealt with issues related to the economy. But China's discipline of economics tends to be less understood, even unduly misunderstood, by the modern concept of the economy. The fact that Chinese economic thinkers did not present a systematic body of thought meant their discipline of economics was drastically different from that of their Western counterparts. For many in the West, Chinese thinkers had, at most, provided some random thoughts on the economy. In this book, we attempt to put together a collection of these seemingly random thoughts to make China's discipline of economics a more systematic body of economic knowledge. Furthermore, when conceptualizing contemporary China's political economy system as "market in state," we also attempt to reflect its actual functioning and capture the essence of this unique system.

THE STATE VERSUS THE MARKET IN THE WEST

Political Economy Approaches in the West

In the classical West, as in ancient China, the state and the economy were initially considered as inseparable and vertically ordered. In Ancient Greece, the equivalent of economy (*oikonomia*) referred to the management of household (*oikos*), whereas the earliest conception of the state was the Platonic *politeia*, the form or the constitution of the polis. During the late Republic and the Empire, while practicing a kind of cosmopolitan statecraft similar to the Qin–Han empires in China, the Romans largely accepted this vertical division between *oikos* and *polis* in its Aristotelian and post-Aristotelian casts. Like the ancient Chinese Confucian philosophers, who held the family to be a basic unit and the foundation of the state, classical thinkers also generally regarded the *oikos* or household as a fundamental building block of the polity, upon which basic social, economic, and educational functions of the polity rested.[2]

The classical idea of *oikonomia* held sway during the classical and early medieval periods. With the rise of medieval scholasticism, however, another idea arose: that of the economy as the proper management of human affairs, oriented to a divinely inspired Common Good, and ensuring the economy is autonomous from worldly powers. The medieval scholastic thinkers thus developed a system of the economy as an analytical system expressed in an abstract and universalistic language of theology.[3] In comparison, this kind of abstract economy, autonomous from statecraft and everyday livelihoods, was never well developed in premodern and even modern Chinese thought. This is an important divergence between Chinese and Western economic thought that persists to this day. But the medieval schoolmen were not prepared to regard the economy as a self-regulating system centered on market exchange. When the Church dominated all aspects of Western spiritual life, the economy likewise was a function of divine providence rather than secular economic activities.

It was not until the Reformation and the Enlightenment, from the sixteenth to the eighteenth centuries, that the concept of the economy grew away from normative divine laws and became associated with its own

---

[2] D. Brendan Nagle, *The Household as the Foundation of Aristotle's Polis* (New York, NY: Cambridge University Press, 2006), pp. 300–301.

[3] For a detailed discussion of scholastic economics, see Joseph Schumpeter, *History of Economic Analysis* (London: George Allen & Unwin Ltd., 1954), pp. 82–107.

positive rules. A byproduct of the great social, cultural, and intellectual transformation of the seventeenth and the eighteenth centuries was the rise of both the fiscal state and market exchange at the heart of a new mercantilist economy in Western Europe and especially in France. The significance of the former was represented by an even earlier group of economic and fiscal practitioners who regarded gold and silver in the state coffers, derived from a favorable trade balance and highly regulated markets, as the ultimate form of wealth. The centrality of the latter was championed by the physiocrats, a group of *philosophes* who held that all wealth came from agriculture – a combination of land and labor – and should be allowed to circulate in an impeded circular flow. For the physiocrats, the principle of laissez-faire, rather than the economic controls of the mercantilists, represented the application of the natural law in economic domain.[4] In historical terms, both schools have deep roots in the history of the most important Europe absolutist state: Bourbon France, in the late eighteenth century. Whereas the mercantilists embodied the interventionist fiscal and trade policy of increased state-building, the physiocrats advocated trade liberalization and deregulation when the rising bourgeois class began to challenge state controls. But despite their differences, neither the physiocrats nor the mercantilists treated the economy as separate from the process of nature or state-building. This was still an age before the Great Transformation and the myth of the self-regulating market.

In the early nineteenth century, the discipline of political economy, focusing on the construction of the free market as a distinctive field of inquiry, finally took shape. This new discipline inherited from its predecessors the methodological division into two approaches: a market-centered approach that treated the economy as a market-based process, and a more state-centered approach that focuses on the power dynamics or political aspects of the market process. As we will see later, there are also similarities and differences between these two schools and the two traditional Chinese schools of thought, namely, the Confucian School (Confucianists) and the School of Law (Legalists). In general, the political economy system in the West primarily places emphasis on the market, while state power is central to the Chinese political economy system.

In very broad terms, the market-centered approach is represented by thinkers ranging from political economists from the classical school, such

---

[4] For a discussion of the representative thinkers from the two camps and their historical backgrounds, see Henry William Spiegel, ed., *The Growth of Economic Thoughts* (Durham, NC: Duke University Press, 1991), pp. 171–198.

as Adam Smith and David Ricardo; through the neoclassical school; to contemporary neoliberal economists. There have been strong arguments for markets' capability to regulate themselves and for the policy of laissez-faire to be taken up by states in a given society. As mentioned earlier, in the history of economic ideas, the classical political economists of the nine-teenth century were the first to treat the economy as a system separable in principle from religion, politics, and other social realms such as family life. Their argument for the market as a self-regulatory field assumed that the market system operates at a higher and more universalistic order than the state. The separation of the economy from the state and other social organizations means that there is a clear boundary between the economy and the rest of society, even as the market constantly interacts with society. This view differentiates the modern Western political economy system from that of China. As we will see in later chapters, in the writings of premodern China's rough equivalents of these classical economists, the economy was regarded as an integral part of the state, and the market as a tool of government. The economy itself was never a separable reality from the state and other social organizations, but rather a means for the state to create and increase its wealth and maintain an orderly society.

The neoclassical theory developed since the end of the nineteenth century, founded by Alfred Marshall, continued this tradition, treating the economy as a separable system of social order that operates at a higher level than the state. Unlike the earlier classical thinkers, neoclassical economists steered away from natural law thinking and developed the concept of the market to a further level of abstraction by associating its fundamentals with the positivist laws of human action and mathematical theory of demand and supply. Followers of this line of thought further defined the relation of politics to economics in terms of market failure and public goods, which allowed limited realms of state action to provide for smooth functioning of the market. For the neoclassical thinkers, economics refers principally to private acts of transaction in pursuit of individual goals of utility and profit maximization, with the state a secondary actor responsible for ensuring the orderly functioning of the market in line with social interests.[5] Again, their efforts to base economics on an abstract *homo*

---

[5] For example, Alfred Marshall was among the most enthusiastic supporters of state intervention, but state intervention only served to ensure that the market contributed to common goods. See Simon J. Cook, *Foundations of Alfred Marshall's Science of Economics: A Rounded Globe of Knowledge* (New York, NY: Cambridge University Press, 2009), pp. 129–133.

economicus have few parallels in Chinese economic thought, since the latter has always conceptualized human actions in relational terms and as moral actions. Like the beliefs of Adam Smith, Alfred Marshall's theory has few contemporary repercussions in early twentieth-century China.

But it would be incorrect to say that modern economists only pay attention to the economic realm. From classical economists to contemporary neoliberal economists, views on market self-regulation are closely related to views on how human society ought to be organized. In other words, they are all interested not only in a positive question – how social order is organized – but also in a normative one – how social order should be organized. In their writings, society is regarded as organizing itself and developing according to its own laws, processes, and imperatives. These thinkers believe that the vitally important social institutions do not develop according to plans articulated and instituted by political decisions, but according to underlying and unintended imperatives of group life.

Economists thus tend to conceptualize and theorize how a society *should* function based on their observations and understanding of how a society *does* function. While there is a huge gap between how a society functions and how a society should function, it seems that economists did not have difficulty in accepting such a great leap. As Karl Polanyi correctly pointed out in his *Great Transformation*, such acceptance was a result of two changes that took place toward the end of the eighteenth century and in the first half of the nineteenth. The first change happened in the economic realm. The rapidly expanding factory system altered the relationship between commerce and industry. Production involved large-scale investment of funds with fixed obligations to pay for those provided funds. Producers were less willing to have either the supply of inputs or the vents for output controlled by governments. The second, and closely related, change was the development of economic liberalism as a body of ideas that provided justification for a new set of public policies that facilitated transformation of land, labor, and capital into the "fictitious commodities" of a self-regulated market system. Land (nature), labor (people), and capital (power of the purse) were not in fact produced for sale; nor did the available quantity of land, labor, and capital disappear inconsequentially when relationships of supply and demand produced low input prices. This issue was particularly acute in the case of labor and led to the dismal conclusions of classical economics. According to Polanyi, the philosophy called laissez-faire was "born as a mere penchant for non-bureaucratic methods ... [and] evolved into a veritable faith in man's secular salvation through a self-regulating market."[6] Polanyi described this evolution of British thought from the humanistic approach of Adam Smith, who wrote in a time of "peaceful progress," through Malthus' acceptance of poverty as part of the natural order, and on to the triumphant liberalism of the more prosperous early nineteenth century.

Within this background, it is not difficult to understand why classical economists focused on market society while their contemporary political philosophers placed an emphasis on civil society. The term "civil society" refers to "social organizations occupying the space between the household and the state that enable people to co-ordinate their management of resources and activities."[7] Like market society, the concept of civil society was a product of the Enlightenment. It was first formulated by John Locke and Adam Ferguson.[8] The concept was coined during the period in which Western European society was undergoing a great transformation from feudalism to mercantile capitalism. "Because the concept was invented at the time when the divine right of kings was challenged, and the new bourgeoisie pressed for the abolition of feudal social order, it was assumed that civil society itself was born at that time."[9] Implicit in the concept of civil society was the notion that only a market economy could ensure that contractual associations were sufficiently flexible and adaptive to create civil society. At the normative level, both classical economists and political philosophers preferred a spontaneous social order to the one planned or imposed by the state.

This line of thinking was already apparent in the writings of Adam Smith, who saw the rise of civilized modern society as the result of profit-seeking behavior rather than of any plan known to and instituted by a political process or public authority. For Smith, the transition from the "savage state of man" to civilized society was the historical work of capitalism. Yet, it was also the unintended consequence of a multitude of actions taken for purely private purposes. Later, Karl Marx took this idea even much further and described the process by which epochal changes were brought about in methods of production, social relations, and ways of

---

[6] Karl Polanyi, *The Great Transformation: The Political and Economic Origins of Our Time* (Boston, MA: Beacon Press, 1944), p. 135.

[7] Robert Layton, *Order and Anarchy: Civil Society, Social Disorder and War* (Cambridge: Cambridge University Press, 2006), p. 3.

[8] John Locke, *Two Treaties of Government* (Cambridge: Cambridge University Press, 1960) (first published 1689); and Adam Ferguson, *An Essay on the History of Civil Society* (Cambridge: Cambridge University Press, 1995) (first published 1767).

[9] Layton, *Order and Anarchy*, p. 9.

life, all as unintended consequences of the pursuit of private gain. Marx's materialist concept of history expresses with particular force the subordination of politics and of the decisions of a public authority to the immanent and inexorable forces set loose and operating within society.

In classical economics, there is a division and thus a boundary between the economy and polity, and the market and the state. Of course, there is also a division and boundary between the state and society in terms of politics. Each actor behaves in its own domain and realm. Then what should be the duties of each realm? Adam Smith tended to put more emphasis on market society than on the state, calling the former "a Society of Perfect Liberty." He first emphasized an independent and autonomous realm of the economy in which everyone was free to exchange and trade in the market:

> Every man, as long as he does not violate the laws of justice, is left perfectly free to pursue his own interest his own way, and to bring about his industry and his capital into competition with those of any other man, or order of men. The sovereign is completely discharged from a duty, in the attempting to perform which he must always be exposed to innumerable delusions, and for the proper performance of which no human wisdom or knowledge could ever be sufficient – the duty of superintending the industry of private people and of directing it toward the employments most suitable to the interest of society.[10]

Then what remains for the state? Smith goes on to describe three duties of great importance that the state must perform. In this context, he gives us a classical definition of the role of the state:

> According to the system of natural liberty, the sovereign has only three duties to attend to; three duties of great importance, indeed, but plain and intelligible to common understanding: first, the duty of protecting the society from the violence and invasion of other independent societies; secondly, the duty of protecting, as far as possible, every member of the society from the injustice or oppression of every other member of it, or the duty of establishing an exact administration of justice; and thirdly, the duty of erecting and maintaining certain public works and certain public institutions, which it can never be for the interest of any individual, or small number of individuals, to erect and maintain; because the profit could never repay the expense to any individual or small number of individuals, though it may frequently do much more than repay it to a great society.[11]

By "public works" and "public institutions," Smith had in mind primarily those aimed at facilitating commerce (roads, bridges, canals) and

---

[10] Adam Smith, *The Wealth of Nations* [1776] (New York, NY: Modern Library, 1937), p. 651.
[11] *Ibid.*, p. 651.

"promoting instruction of the people,"[12] or in today's words, public infra-structure. Smith rails against the impertinences of meddlesome officials who seek to substitute their own wishes for those of the market. While celebrating the role of private industry and the market, he also recognizes that government has an indispensable role to play.

Classical economics emphasizes that a market economy operates according to laws rooted in the ongoing reproduction and expansion of a system of material interdependence between persons – a social division of labor. This process follows laws that are independent of the wills and desires of persons and human organizations. To be sure, individuals within a market economy act independently and according to their desires. The matrix of individual wants directly determines what happens in the market. Behind these private wants stands an objective structure of repro-duction whose requirements dominate the individual in the formation of his private interests. This domination justifies the theory in focusing on the objective process of reproduction rather than on the subjective process of ranking opportunities or making choices. Classical economics thus sees the market as an institution allowing maximum scope for free exchange and hence efficiency. The market allows one to reshuffle resources and commodities to achieve their most desirable use.

Separateness of the economy does not mean its independence from the other aspects of social life. Nor does it imply that the economy can stand alone. Even those economists who are most committed to the idea of market self-regulation maintain that the market depends on the state for a set, albeit a limited set, of requirements for its own survival. As already mentioned, Smith insisted that the state not only maintain internal order and security against foreign invasion, but also engage in substantial public works where the private sector lacked the means needed given the scale of the project. Separateness does not mean either complete autonomy or the absence of significant state involvement in economic life. However, it is clear that whatever role classical and neoclassical economists assign to the state, it is the market, not the state, that dominates and should dominate social order.

A second school – Marxism – can be regarded as responding to the classical approach to the economy and the market. While, like the classical scholars, Karl Marx himself put an overwhelming emphasis on economic forces in bringing about historical changes, he nevertheless advanced a

---

[12] *Ibid.*, p. 681.

critique of the classical claims for market self-regulation by highlighting the real relationship between the state and the market field. Marx did not intend to justify state-regulated capitalism, but rather attempted to demonstrate that capitalism was not viable in the long run. Marx did not assign a great role to the state since he believed it was only an agent of the capitalist class; instead, he placed much emphasis on classes, which he regarded as a natural product of capitalism.

Scholars after Marx, or new Marxist scholars, have developed a state-centered approach, attempting to overthrow the classical idea of the economy as a reality *sui generis*. This approach identifies politics with the use of power and, by finding power in the economy, claims to have established that the economy is political. The term "political economy" strikes a radically new chord. It advances claims about the political nature of the economy, insisting on this political nature whether the market is subject to government regulation or not.

Although classical economics also gives the state a role in the economy by referring to market failure, for the Marxian theorists, a state-centered approach need not begin with market failure in identifying the role of politics vis-à-vis the economy. Such theory assumes that the state has its own ends, and that pursuit of those ends has implications for economic affairs and institutions. Therefore, the state may seek to control the economy not to correct market failure, but to impose purposes of its own. Political economy begins with the imperatives of political rather than economic affairs. It refers to the imposition of political agenda on the economy.

For Marxism, the market economy is not so much a mechanism for maximizing the private welfare of individuals generally as it is a means of facilitating the capitalist's appropriation of surplus value and accumulation of capital. The market makes sense as a social institution because it makes possible self-aggrandizement and private accumulations of wealth in the form of capital. If economists from the classical to the contemporary neoliberal schools have attempted to consider the production side, the Marxian school has challenged the mainstream with another set of important questions: Is the system fair? Who benefits from the process of capitalistic production? Who loses from the process of unequal exchange?

From the *oikos* and *politeia*, for the economists from classical to contemporary neoliberalism, the market is neutral and apolitical; for Marxist economists, it is political. The Marxist question of who engages economic activities and operates the market is important. It introduces a political dimension into the market process. Indeed, as will be discussed in

Chapter 2, it an important question in the Chinese tradition of political economy is always: Who operates the market – the state or private individuals? This remains important in contemporary China, since the political struggles between the state sector, in which state agencies are the actors, and the private sector, in which private individuals are the actors, have dominated the economic realm.

THE MARKET SYSTEM AND CAPITALISM

From classical theories to contemporary neoliberalism, economists often treat the economy as analytically separable from politics. But in our actual world, both the economy and politics coexist, and they are integral parts of a given society. Capitalism is not only an economic order, but also a social order and a political order. When economists construct their theories on the market, it is unavoidable to treat the market field as separable from politics and society; nevertheless, this does not mean the two are separable in reality. Therefore, in discussing the market system and capitalism, we have to be aware of whether they are understood in abstract or actual terms.

As a matter of fact, in constructing their theories, economists often treat the market and capitalism at an abstract level. In the literature of economics, a market is usually defined as any one of a variety of different systems, institutions, procedures, social relations, and infrastructures whereby personal trade and goods and services are exchanged, forming part of the economy. Put simply, it is an arrangement that allows buyers and sellers to exchange things.[13] There are two roles in the market: buyer and seller. Conceptually, the market is a structure that allows buyers and sellers to exchange any type of goods, services, and information. The exchange of goods or services for money is defined as a transaction. Market participants consist of all the buyers and sellers of a good who influence its price. Along this basic line of thinking, various theories and models concerning the basic market forces of supply and demand have been developed. The market facilitates trade and enables the distribution and allocation of resources in a society. It allows any tradable item to be evaluated and priced. A market emerges spontaneously or is constructed deliberately by human interaction to enable the exchange of rights of services and goods. At this abstract level, the term "market" is generally

[13] Arthur O'Sullivan and Steven M. Sheffrin, *Economics: Principles in Action* (Upper Saddle River, NJ: Pearson Prentice Hall, 2003), p. 28.

used in two ways. The first is to denote the abstract mechanisms whereby supply and demand meet each other and deals are made. Here, reference to markets reflects ordinary experience and the places, processes, and institutions in which exchanges take place.[14] Second, the market is often used to signify an integrated, all-encompassing, and cohesive capitalist economy.

The market is not the only structuring force in a society. A market that runs under laissez-faire policies is called a free market. It is "free" in the sense that the government makes no attempt to intervene through taxes, subsidies, minimum wages, price ceilings, and so forth. Market prices may be distorted by a seller or sellers with monopoly power, or a buyer with monopoly power. Such price distortions can have an adverse effect on market participants' welfare and reduce the efficiency of market outcomes. Furthermore, the level of buyers' organization or negotiation power affects the functioning of the market. Markets in which price negotiations meet equilibrium still do not arrive at desired outcomes, though, since both sides are believed to experience market failure.

When economists think about the market, they often link it to capitalism. Their interest is in how the functioning of capital in the market leads to capitalism, and they have formulated different forms of the relationship between the market and capital. But when considering the term "capitalism," often its meaning becomes ambiguous. Indeed, many economic historians have avoided using the term "capitalism." If the market is abstract, capitalism may be even more so. Economists often have to use different terms to describe different forms of capitalism, such as mercantilism, free-market capitalism, social-market economy, state capitalism, corporate capitalism, and so on. This is also the case with regard to China. While the scholarly community has employed the term "capitalism" to describe post-Mao China, within China the term "socialist market economy," not "capitalism," has been used to refer to the political economy system developed in the post-Mao reforms.

The fact that the market exists under different forms of capitalism means that the market and capital are related, but the two are not identical. According to Robert Heilbroner:

[14] M. Callon, "Introduction: The Embeddedness of Economic Markets in Economics," in Michel Callon, ed., *The Laws of the Markets* (Oxford and Malden, MA, Basic Blackwell, 1998), p. 2.

Capitalism is a much larger and more complex entity than the market system we use as its equivalent, and a market system is larger and more complex than the innumerable individual encounters between buyers and sellers that constitute its atomic structure. The market system is the principal means of binding and coordinating the whole, but markets are not the source of capitalism's energies nor of its distinctive bifurcation of authority. Markets are the conduits through which the energies of the system flow and the mechanism by which the private realm can organize its tasks without the direct intervention of the public realm.[15]

The market is a part of capitalism, but not the whole. The discrepancy between the two is great. The market is fundamentally a means of organizing production and distribution, while capitalism is the larger social order in which the market plays a crucial role.[16] In other words, the market is "the organizing principle of capitalism."[17] In this sense, capitalism can be defined as an economic system in which capital can accumulate and expand itself endlessly through the market.

In talking about capital, one also needs to make sense of the difference between capital and wealth. At the conceptual level, there is often confusion regarding the relationship between the two. While wealth can *become* capital, capital and wealth are not the same things. The value of wealth often inheres in its physical characteristics, and that of capital in its use to create a larger amount of capital. Typically, this use takes place as money is converted into commodities such as raw materials, the raw materials are converted into finished goods and services, and the finished goods are sold on the market – not to make a profit for retirement but to buy more raw materials to start the process over again. Because of this endless turnover, the physical characteristics of commodities have nothing to do with their function to generate wealth.[18] Marx thus defined capitalism as a process in which capital realizes the self-expansion in the market.

Adam Smith made this expansion of production a central feature of what he called "a Society of Perfect Liberty." Expansion begins because the most readily available means for a capitalist to better his condition is to save a portion of his profits and invest it in additional equipment, thereby adding to the potential output of his enterprise, and thus to his future income. The accumulation process exerts its immediate impact on the social environment by multiplying the productivity of labor. Smith expected that process of growth to come to a halt as soon as society

---

[15] Robert L. Heilbroner, *21st Century Capitalism* (New York, NY: W. W. Norton & Company, 1993), p. 96.
[16] *Ibid.*, p. 30.   [17] *Ibid.*, p. 34.   [18] *Ibid.*, p. 46.

had built all the capital it needed.[19] By contrast, early twentieth-century economist Joseph Schumpeter believed that the most formidable means of capital accumulation was the displacement of one process or product by another at the hands of giant enterprises. What Schumpeter called the process of "creative destruction" is still believed to remain the central agency of change in all capitalist economies.[20]

The market system and capitalism have also been examined in actual or substantive terms – that is, how the two have functioned and evolved – by scholars other than mainstream economists. Today, scholars in economic history and sociology are skeptical of the idea that it is possible to develop a theory of the market to capture the essence or unifying principles of the markets.[21] For economic geographers, reference to regional, local, or commodity-specific markets can serve to undermine assumptions of global integration, and highlight geographic variations in the structures, institutions, histories, path dependencies, forms of interaction, and modes of self-understanding of agents in different spheres of market exchange.[22] Reference to actual markets can show capitalism not as a totalizing force or completely encompassing mode of economic activity, but rather as "a set of economic practices scattered over a landscape, rather than a systemic concentration of power."[23]

The market is not abstract, and it exists in different sizes and at different levels within and across national territories. Both sizes and levels matter since, historically speaking, the market correlates to the physical marketplaces which would often develop into small communities, towns, and cities. In other words, the market is not merely a part of the economy, but also a social institution. The idea of the economy as a socially and historically specific institution is an important one. In speaking of the economy, one already assumes the existence of a separable entity: a place, a sphere, a moment of the whole, a distinct set of relations between persons not in essence political or familial. This usage parallels the historical

---

[19] Adam Smith and Edwin Cannan, eds., *An Inquiry into the Nature and Causes of the Wealth of Nations* (Chicago, IL: Chicago University Press, 2009), pp. 195–196.

[20] John E. Elliot, "Introduction," in Joseph A. Schumpeter, *The Theory of Economic Development* (New Brunswick, NJ and London: Transaction Books, 1983), pp. xxvii–xxviii.

[21] Richard Swedberg, "Markets as Social Structures," in Neil Smelser and Richard Swedberg, eds., *The Handbook of Economic Sociology* (Princeton, NJ: Princeton University Press, 1994), p. 258.

[22] J. Peck, "Economic Geographies in Space," *Economic Geography* 81:2 (2005), pp. 129–175.

[23] J. K. Gibson-Graham, *Postcapitalist Politics* (Minneapolis, MN: University of Minnesota Press, 2006), p. 2.

emergence of the economy as a separate institution. The mid-twentieth-century economist and economic historian Karl Polanyi in particular drew our attention to this aspect of modern social organization: "A self-regulating market demands nothing less than the institutional separation of society into an economic and political sphere."[24]

HISTORICITY OF THE MARKET SYSTEM AND CAPITALISM

When we go beyond theories at the abstract level and consider the market and capitalism at an actual level, it is not difficult to discover the historicity of the capitalist market economy. The historicity of market–state relations is key to grasping the essence of the modern economy and the market, and understanding the market's impact on the transformation of society. It is particularly important if one wants to see why a given form of capitalism has its own historical roots, and various forms of capitalism in the West cannot be automatically repeated in other parts of the world.

In this regard we can refer to the writings of many economic historians, such as Karl Polanyi, Fernand Braudel, and Robert Heilbroner.[25] As already mentioned, when economists construct their theories, they tend not only to regard the economy as separable from the polity and society, but also to treat economic variables such as labor, land, and capital at an abstract level. At an abstract level, everything tends to be universal, without geographical, national, or cultural boundaries. In doing so, more often than not, economists unconsciously "bridge" the gap between what something is and what it should be. But for economic historians, there is no such thing as a market system that exists without geographical, national, and cultural boundaries. The market can exist within different geographical, national, and cultural backgrounds and function in different ways. Every market system is a unique product of a given geographical, national, and cultural entity. Both the market system and capitalism in the West are unique products of the West and its geographical, national, and cultural developments. Of course, even within the West, there have been different forms of the market and capitalism in different times and spaces.

---

[24] Polanyi, *The Great Transformation*, p. 71.

[25] Polanyi, *The Great Transformation*; Fernand Braudel, *Civilization and Capitalism, 15th–18th Century*, vol. 1: The Structures of Everyday Life, vol. 2: The Wheels of Commerce, and vol. 3: The Perspective of the World, translated from the French by Siân Reynolds (New York, NY: HarperCollins, 1981, 1982, 1985); Robert L. Heilbroner, *The Nature and Logic of Capitalism* (New York, NY: W. W. Norton & Company, 1985).

In his *The Great Transformation*, Karl Polanyi demonstrated why the market economy is a relatively modern development. Polanyi looked at the economies of various great empires through time and explained how these economies changed. According to him, every human society has had an economy of some kind, but not until recently has any economy been controlled by the markets. In the premarket-economy eras, instead of the economy being ruled by social relations, social relations ruled the economy.

In ancient economies, the role of markets in a national economy was limited because markets were too far from one another. Unlike in modern economies, which are self-regulating and dominated by markets and market prices, in earlier economies gain and profit did not play an important part. Early economies were driven by social relationships rather than self-interest. In early economies, humans sought out material goods that would enhance their social standing, social assets, and social claims rather than personal gains. Thus, in these economies, what we perceive as economic exchange was in fact embedded in larger, complex networks of social exchanges based on the principle of equal values. For instance, when one tribal member gives to another tribal member, they can expect something of equal worth in return from that tribal member or another member of the tribe. So, if a tribe member gives some food to another tribe member, that tribe member will give back something of the same worth. If it is not in material form, the tribe member will give his or her time by helping in some type of physical labor, such as planting crops or taking part in a hunt. The giver might not get something back right away but the receiver must give back something of equal worth within a certain amount of time or they will lose status in the tribe. Rituals and ceremonies were developed to ensure that reciprocity went smoothly. Since everything is shared collectively in tribal societies, maintaining social ties is incredibly important to the individual. All social obligations are reciprocal and best fulfill the tribe's interest. If an individual acted in his or her own self-interest rather than in the interest of the tribe, it could be fatal to that individual. If individuals were unable to behave reciprocally, they would lose status; if the individual lost enough of their status they could be cut off from the tribe and would become an outcast. An outcast from the tribe had little hope of surviving.

How members of a tribe receive what they need is determined by two factors: reciprocity and redistribution. Symmetry and centricity help economic systems that are based on reciprocity and redistribution to work without written records or any kind of public administration. Reciprocity means what one gives to another today will be matched tomorrow by one's taking. Redistribution in tribal societies most often comes about through the tribal chieftain or headman. It is the tribal chieftain who gains goods from tribal members and redistributes the wealth to the members. The bigger the territory, the greater amount of goods the land produces, and the greater the need for redistribution and for the division of labor for everyone to receive the goods that their survival is dependent on.

According to Polanyi, in the ancient economy, local trade was limited to goods that were too heavy or perishable to travel over long distances, and were found in the region in which they were being traded. External trade is the trade of goods that are absent from the regions in which they are being exchanged. Neither local or external trade were very competitive; internal trade was. Goods were exchanged more and there was greater bartering in internal trade than in local or external trade. Polanyi did not believe that bartering led to the development of market economies; rather, it was just an aspect of the systems of reciprocity and redistribution. Bartering was a type of social relationship that implied trust and confidence.

While Polanyi informed us of the purpose and function of the market in early civilizations and the ancient world, the French economic historian Braudel demonstrated how the market has developed and evolved since early modern Europe. In his three-volume *Civilization and Capitalism*, Braudel described how the market, and capitalism, grew from the fifteenth to the eighteenth centuries, and explored the deepest structures of the market and capitalism by compiling descriptive detail rather than building theoretical constructs, as mainstream economists usually do. Braudel did not believe that the market exists at an abstract level and he avoided using all economic theory in his discussion.

According to Braudel, modern capitalism was deeply rooted in the preindustrial modern world. He claimed that there are long-term cycles in the capitalist economy which developed in Europe in the twelfth century. City-states, and later nation-states, followed each other sequentially as centers of these cycles: Venice and Genoa in the thirteenth through fifteenth centuries (1250–1510), Antwerp in the sixteenth century (1500–1569), Amsterdam in the sixteenth through eighteenth centuries (1570–1733), and London (and England) in the eighteenth and nineteenth centuries (1733–1896). He used the concept of "structures" to denote a variety of organized behaviors, attitudes, and conventions, as well as literal structures and infrastructures. He argued that structures that were built up in Europe during the Middle Ages contributed to the successes of present-day European-based capitalist cultures. He attributed much of this to the long-standing independence of city-states, which, though later subjugated by larger geographic states, were not always completely suppressed.[26]

Braudel thus argued that capitalists have typically been monopolists and not, as is usually assumed, free entrepreneurs operating in competitive markets. Capitalists did not specialize and did not use free markets. He thus diverged from both liberal (Adam Smith) and Marxian interpretations of capitalism. In Braudel's view, under capitalism the state has served as a guarantor of monopolists rather than as the protector of competition it is usually portrayed as. He asserted that capitalists have had power and cunning on their side as they have arrayed themselves against most of the local population.[27]

In the same vein, the economic historian Heilbroner tended to believe that the birth of the market system and capitalism is a unique historical product of the West. He traced the market system and capitalism to the fall of the Roman Empire. According to him, the fall of the Roman Empire was crucial for the market system since it not only indicated that the social hierarchy of the empire was incompatible with a capitalist order at every level, but also created a historical condition for the rise of the market order: The shattered ruins of the empire provided an extraordinary setting in which such an order would emerge during the thousand-year period of feudalism. The disappearance of the empire left Europe without a unifying law, currency, and government, and broken into a large amount of isolated and self-dependent towns, manorial estates, and petty fiefdoms. It was the very fragmentation of feudal life that paved the way for the transformation that followed. By the ninth century, merchant adventurers insinuated themselves into the affairs of the manor and especially the town, and by the fourteenth century their descendants became the political authorities of expanding "burgh" or urban life. They played a role that was both indispensable for the evolving feudal order and ultimately subversive of it: essential because the feudal rulers were continually forced to turn for loans to their resident burghers, some of whom were by now very rich; subversive because the commercial way of life for which the lenders stood was ultimately incompatible with feudal dominance. By the end of the seventeenth century, a bourgeois (burgher) class had already become politically powerful in England; by the end of the eighteenth century it was the real master of France; by the end of the nineteenth century, it was the dominant political force in the world.

---

[26] Cf Braudel, *Civilization and Capitalism*, vol. 1.
[27] Cf Braudel, *Civilization and Capitalism*, vol. 2.

With the coming to power of the bourgeoisie in the West, there arose the lineaments of a new social order as well; new money-minded values were its most noticeable aspect, but the spread of a new form of economic life was by far the most important. In the country, the institution of serfdom, in which the serf paid a portion of his crop to his lord and kept the rest for himself, gave way to a quite different institution in which a capitalist farmer paid his hands a wage but owned the entirety of the product they brought forth. In the town, the relationship of master and apprentice, under the strict supervision of guild rules, became that of employer and worker, under no regulation save that of the marketplace for labor. In the big cities, money making moved from the suspect periphery of life to its esteemed center.

In other words, the fall of the Roman Empire generated conditions for the separation of the economy and polity. A rising merchant class was capable of challenging, and in the end taking precedence over, the aristocratic world around it. A true realm of power and authority came into existence in a network of farms, household industries, and trading links that for the first time considered itself out from under the thumb of the state and capable of managing its own affairs with a minimum of political guidance or restraint – a kind of state within a state.

Thus, as the institutions of feudalism were gradually phased out, in their place appeared those of an order of economic freedom that Adam Smith called the "Society of Perfect Liberty." In such a society, workers could move freely from one location or occupation to another, which as serfs and apprentices they could not; and capitalists could raise or lower their prices as they saw fit, which as guild members they could not. Thus the capitalistic institutions took shape. "Capitalism" entered the English language sometime in the middle of the nineteenth century.[28]

MODERN INDUSTRIAL CAPITALISM

While capitalism had already come a long way, industrialization drastically transformed it by assigning an unprecedented role to the market. The market system had developed and evolved since the fall of the Roman Empire. But once it began to dominate the economy, the nature of the economic system changed. According to Polanyi, economies that were driven by markets changed societies and greatly influenced how they were run.

---

[28] Heilbroner, *21st Century Capitalism*, pp. 50–52.

Markets can control the prices of goods only when there are many markets in close proximity to one another and many traders bartering and haggling over the price of goods. When markets play a greater role in controlling the economy, they also play a greater role in controlling society. When economies are no longer shaped by social relationships but rather by markets, societies change their social relationships. Societies and social relationships are reshaped to accommodate the market economy. Thus it was industrialization that gave rise to the self-regulating market (SRM).

Polanyi regarded the rise of the SRM as "the fount and matrix of the system" and the "innovation which gave rise to a specific civilization."[29] What he called "the Great Transformation" is the history of the SRM: of its emergence from the Industrial Revolution of the late eighteenth and early nineteenth centuries, taking place within a thoroughly commercial though not yet thoroughly market-organized economy; its nurturing through the efforts of the liberal economists and statesmen of England in the first decades of the nineteenth century; and finally its demise, as a consequence of the "protective reaction" counteracting the consequences of the SRM. Polanyi differentiated between economic systems in which there were markets and the "starkly utopian" SRM of the nineteenth century. Markets are human interactions organized by price, quality, and quantity of traded goods and services. The SRM was a society-wide system of markets in which all inputs into the substantive processes of production and distribution were for sale and in which output was distributed solely in exchange for earnings from sales of inputs. Polanyi believed that the SRM could not survive – not because of the distributional consequences that played the major role in Marx's explanation of the inevitable collapse of capitalism, but because the "starkly utopian" nature of the SRM gave rise to a spontaneous countermovement, even among those enjoying increased material prosperity. Society is vital to humans, as social animals, and the SRM was inconsistent with a sustainable society.

According to Polanyi, the Industrial Revolution was "an almost miraculous improvement in the tools of production," but was also an equally powerful revolution in economic organization that was in part a consequence of the introduction of the new machines into an already commercially organized economy, and in part a social experiment.[30] Up to the time of the Industrial Revolution, the economies of much of Western Europe had been quite thoroughly commercialized: Cottage industries,

---

[29] Polanyi, *The Great Transformation*, p. 3.   [30] *Ibid.*, p. 33.

paid agricultural labor, and thriving trade in towns meant that most people earned money and used that money to buy the material stuff of life. However, control and regulation of markets by governments and other organizations were also widespread and common. Markets were controlled and heavily regulated by governments and society; they did not control the basic functioning of society until the beginning of the nineteenth century, when "market society" was born in England.[31]

Polanyi thus demonstrated that economies could be and had been organized in ways other than through an SRM. The organization of production and distribution in many societies had been accomplished through social relationships of kin or community obligations and counterobligations (reciprocity), and other societies employed redistributive systems. In much of Western Europe, a combination of redistributive and reciprocal systems dominated through the end of the feudal and manorial era and came to be increasingly supplemented and then replaced by market trading, the control and encouragement of which was a major focus of medieval municipal and mercantilist national governments.[32]

The rise of the market system and capitalism led to accumulation and material progress. But from the very beginning, the elevation of material well-being was accompanied by a new form of social misery. This made its initial appearance in Elizabethan England in the form of the "enclosures" of land. Enclosures meant that land traditionally available as a "commons," where poor peasants could build their huts, graze their beasts, and grow a few vegetables, was now taken over by its legal owners, mainly landed gentry, for the exclusive use of sheep grazing. This double-edged process took a different guise a century later. By that time, the active centers of accumulation had moved to the manufactories about which Smith wrote. The outputs of these burgeoning industries undoubtedly benefited the middle-class consumers who bought them, and the profits they earned benefited their owners. What is not so certain is whether benefits also accrued to the workmen. Their wages were low and their working conditions were miserable. By the early nineteenth century, the still small-scale manufactories were eclipsed by the "dark Satanic mills" where women and children labored under brutal conditions for less than subsistence pay. This underside of Dickensian England is well known.

Polanyi called the continuing tension and conflict between the efforts to establish, maintain, and spread the SRM and the efforts to protect people

---

[31] *Ibid.*, pp. 45–46; 133. [32] *Ibid.*, pp. 66–67.

and society from the consequences of its workings "the double movement."
On one side was a concerted philosophical and legislative program to
establish the SRM, from the enclosures of the 1790s, through the Poor
Law Reform of 1834, to the Ricardian Bank Charter Act of 1844 and the
repeal of the Corn Laws in 1846. On the other side was a widely varying,
unorganized set of movements, legislative reforms, and administrative
actions to limit the effects of self-regulation, from the Chartists, through
early legislation to limit the hours and places of work of women and
children, through the growth of labor unions and the emergence of the
Bank of England as lender of last resort, to the reimpositioning of tariffs
on foodstuffs and the first legislation presaging the welfare state. As the
SRM was impaired in operation, justifications for international economic
cooperation and the liberal state weakened.

Polanyi's explanation of the tensions in and collapse of the self-
regulating economies that developed in the first half of the nineteenth
century differs sharply from that of Marx and Marxian economists.
Though Polanyi argued that perception and response to the damages of
the SRM varied by class, and therefore "the outcome was decisively influenced by the character of the class interests involved," it was not unfair
distribution of total output via exploitation that caused the tensions in and
ultimate collapse of the SRM system.[33] Polanyi argued that the working
class did not rise up to overthrow the system; rather, land owners and
bankers as well as merchants, whose interests were often threatened by
fluctuations in trade, joined workers in seeking protection. As they got this
protection, the SRM was "impaired," eventually reaching the point of
collapse. Increased protection so impaired the SRM that it could no longer
coordinate the world's economy when World War I destroyed Europe's
balance of power. The struggle to restore the nineteenth-century system by
reestablishing the gold standard destroyed the international financial
system. Meanwhile, dictatorships in some places, and more benign management elsewhere, emerged in nationally varying responses to the collapse
of the SRM system.[34]

While few mainstream economists nowadays cite *The Great Transformation*, Polanyi's double-movement thesis continues to dominate debates
in public policy today. As neoliberalism founded on faith in secular salvation through the natural emergence of a self-regulating market system
has spread in Central and Eastern Europe and in Asia, Africa, and Latin

---

[33] *Ibid.*, p. 161.   [34] *Ibid.*, pp. 211–215.

America, so too have calls for protection of man, nature, and national interests. The framework that Polanyi provided for understanding the collapse of nineteenth-century civilization and the rise of the troubled twentieth remains powerful. As French sociologist Pierre Bourdieu suggests, the market model is becoming self-realizing, in virtue of its wide acceptance in national and international institutions through the 1990s.[35] So is the countermoment to the market. As will be discussed in later chapters, this is, of course, exactly what is taking place in contemporary China.

KEYNESIANISM

Classical and neoclassical economists divided a social order into two independent and legally divorced realms. This separation, as a social construct, is more abstract than actual. It is a useful theoretical tool for economists to construct their concepts and theories, but the market system is an integral part of society and capitalism is not only a purely economic order – more importantly, it is also a political order. A boundary between the economy and the state exists, but at the same time the two realms are mutually dependent and married for life. The state has its own domains, with its institutions of law and order, its apparatus of force, and its ceremonial functions; the economy has its own, with its factories and stores, banks and markets, want ads and unemployment offices. It is the business of the state to govern and that of the economy to produce and distribute. But to govern the society, the state will have to lay down rules and regulations for the economy, and it must intervene in economic affairs. At the same time, the economy will inescapably intrude on the governing function, sometimes in ways that are antithetical to public interest, such as in the realms of foreign policy and national defense, and sometimes in ways that are inseparable from it, such as in the formulation of economic policy.

The economy and the state are so interdependent that each realm will not function without the other. For instance, the realm of capital cannot perform its accumulative task without the complementary support of the state. On the other hand, a government is dependent on the healthy condition of the economy for the revenues it needs for its own goals. Marx was among a few early political economists who saw the economy and the

---

[35] Pierre Bourdieu, *Acts of Resistance: Against the Tyranny of the Market* (New York, NY and London: The New Press, 1999), p. 95.

state as inseparable. He observed that the economics of capitalism was dominated by the "contradictions" generated by its drive for production, and its politics by the "class struggles" stemming from its mode of distribution. As discussed previously, Smith, while celebrating a spontaneous economic order directed by an invisible hand, also emphasized that the state must play a role for such an economic order to function.

In this sense, capitalism is truly a political order. The central political issue in capitalism is the relationship between business and government, or between the economy and the state.[36] So the question is not whether the economy and the state are separable, but how the two live together. From the perspective of political economy, the role of the state, not that of the economy, is the key for any social order. The state must balance its interest in the economy, and in the social order.

Historically speaking, as Heilbroner pointed out, the realm of capital has had the upper hand. The state could wield its stronger weapon, namely, the power to tax, but the ability to tax would be an empty privilege if the economy were not operating satisfactorily. In ordinary times, the first concern of the state is to assist and support the accumulation of capital. Far from "crowding out" the private sector, the government makes way for it to move in. It is not out of weakness but as a result of considerations of its own interest that the business of government is business. In modern times, with the development of an international market, the role of the state in promoting business has greatly expanded. By the mid-nineteenth century, the state had everywhere been openly associated with the promotion of bourgeois interest at home and abroad. In the contemporary era of globalization, the state has taken on functions needed to protect the economy from the increasingly threatening consequences to which an unregulated market could lead.

At the same time, the state must maintain the domestic order by protecting society, which, more often than not, is undermined by endless expansion of capital. For instance, the beginning of the accumulation process brought disquiet to Elizabethan England through the enclosure of the commons. Throughout the nineteenth century and most of the twentieth century, such disquiet persisted, often with growing intensity. To maintain the social order, the state in Europe began to introduce measures to protect society. This is exemplified by the introduction of the first social security legislation, by German Chancellor Otto Bismarck.

---

[36] Heilbroner, *21st Century Capitalism*, p. 68.

Such minimum measures of social protection were undertaken more for the interests of capital than for the interests of the working class. The functioning of capital needs a minimum social order. At this time, legislative and regulatory measures introduced by the state were very repressive. The introduction of social protection measures was due to a deep fear of class hostility on the part of the state. Both the state and business were convinced that "there was little that government could do to solve the problem of economic instability, except to allow the system to recover its 'natural' vitality. Political intervention was not only contrary to the nature of things but useless to boot."[37]

The turning point was the Great Depression in the 1930s, which radically changed intellectual perceptions of the economy and society and introduced great changes in mainstream economics. Capitalism unquestionably stood nearer to overthrow or collapse at this point than at any time in Marx's life. In Germany, Italy, and Spain, this gave rise to fascism, which introduced a change in the relation of the realms: the subordination of the economy to the state. While such subordination did not take place in the democratic nations, the government had to expand its role in the economy far beyond Adam Smith's original list of activities. The new role involved striving for what was called "full employment." It is worth noting that this was still very different from subordinating the private sector to the ambitions of the public sector, because the expanded role of the state stopped far short of permitting it to guide, much less take over, the activities of the private sector. Full employment meant only that economic growth would be pushed to its feasible limits.[38]

This new role of the state was addressed by John Maynard Keynes. In his book *General Theory of Employment, Interest, and Money*, published in 1936, Keynes proposed a "somewhat comprehensive socialization" of investment as necessary to rescue capitalism from the danger of chronic unemployment. According to Heilbroner, "what Keynesian economics provided was a rationale for using the public realm in a previously undreamt of way: as a fiscal agency of the capitalist order, charged, as a minimal responsibility, with the prevention of massive unemployment and, as a maximal one, with the attainment of full employment."[39]

Keynesianism was not only a reaction to the Great Depression, but also wanted to introduce new elements to mainstream economics by adding new roles to the state. Prior to Keynes' *General Theory*, the mainstream

[37] *Ibid.*, p. 84.   [38] *Ibid.*, p. 85.   [39] *Ibid.*, p. 86.

"classical" and "neoclassical" economic belief was that the economy existed in a state of general equilibrium, meaning that the economy naturally consumes whatever it produces because the needs of consumers are always greater than the economy's capacity to satisfy those needs. This perception is reflected in Say's Law and in the writings of David Ricardo, which state that that individuals produce so that they can either consume what they have manufactured or sell their output in order to buy someone else's output. This perception assumes that if a surplus of goods or services exists, they would naturally drop in price to the point at which they would be consumed.

Keynesian economists believe that, in the short run, productive activity is influenced by aggregate demand (total spending in the economy), and that aggregate demand does not necessarily equal aggregate supply (the total productive capacity of the economy). Instead, it is influenced by a host of factors and sometimes behaves erratically, affecting production, employment, and inflation. Keynesian economists argue that private sector decisions sometimes lead to inefficient macroeconomic outcomes which require active policy responses by the public sector, particularly monetary policy actions by the central bank and fiscal policy actions by the government to stabilize output over the business cycle. Keynesian economics thus advocates a mixed economy – predominantly private sector, but with a role for government intervention during recessions.

Keynes overturned the mainstream thought of the time and brought about greater awareness that problems such as unemployment are not a product of laziness, but the result of a structural inadequacy in the economic system. He argued that because there was no guarantee that the goods produced by individuals would be met by demand, unemployment was a natural consequence. He viewed the economy as unable to maintain itself at full employment and believed it was necessary for the government to step in and put underutilized savings to work through government spending.

Before Keynes, a situation in which aggregate demand for goods and services did not meet supply was referred to by classical economists as a general glut, although there was disagreement among them as to whether such a thing was possible. Keynes argued that when a glut occurred, it was the overreaction of producers and the laying off of workers that led to a fall in demand and perpetuated the problem. Keynesian economists therefore advocate an active stabilization policy to reduce the amplitude of the business cycle, which they rank among the most serious of economic problems. According to this theory, government spending can be used to increase aggregate demand, thus increasing economic activity and reducing unemployment and deflation.

Keynes argued that the solution to the Great Depression was to stimulate the economy through some combination of two approaches: a reduction in interest rates (monetary policy), and government investment in infrastructure (fiscal policy). By reducing the interest rate at which the central bank lends money to commercial banks, the government sends a signal to commercial banks that they should do the same for their customers. Government investment in infrastructure injects income into the economy by creating business opportunities, employment, and demand and reversing the effects of the imbalance.

During the latter part of the Great Depression, World War II, and the postwar economic expansion (1945–1973), Keynes' ideas became widely accepted in the developed nations, serving as the standard economic model for Roosevelt's New Deals and then postwar reconstructions in Western Europe. But it lost some influence to the neoclassical synthesis following the stagflation of the 1970s. The advent of the global financial crisis in 2008 caused a resurgence in Keynesian thought in developed as well as developing countries.

Keynesianism assigned a greater role to the state than to the market and has been criticized by liberal economists, particularly neoclassical economists. For instance, Austrian economist Friedrich Hayek criticized Keynesian economic policies for what he called their fundamentally "collectivist" approach, arguing that such theories encourage centralized planning, which leads to malinvestment of capital, which is the cause of business cycles. Hayek also argued that Keynes' study of the aggregate relations in an economy is fallacious, as recessions are caused by microeconomic factors. Hayek claimed that what start as temporary governmental fixes usually become permanent and expanding government programs, which stifle the private sector and civil society.[40]

In contemporary China, the influence of Keynesianism was mixed. On the one hand, liberal economists have propagated neoliberal economics, and the economic writings of Hayek, Friedman, and others have been their bible. The government's economic reform policy was characterized by radical decentralization and the development of the private sector in the 1980s and by privatization in the 1990s. To liberal economists, the fact that all these liberal policies have promoted China's economic growth seems to

---

[40] Friedrich Hayek, *The Collected Works of F. A. Hayek* (Chicago, IL: University of Chicago Press, 1989), p. 202.

indicate that China has followed and should follow neoliberalism in its economic reform. On the other hand, whenever the economy lacks growth dynamics and particularly when there is an economic crisis, the government frequently appeals to Keynesianism.[41] Indeed, large-scale government investment has been a major source of China's economic growth during crises. In this sense, China's economy is close to what was proposed by Keynesianism: a mixed economy.

We do not want to go into the detail of this policy debate on the source of China's economic growth, since this book seeks to explain how China's political economy system functions, not how China has achieved its economic growth. But at this stage, we do need to point out the difference between China's political economy system and Keynesianism. Despite the deceptive similarities between Keynesianism and Chinese policies, there are important structural differences between the two. In Keynesianism, the state expands its role in the economy, but does not replace the market. Although Keynesianism assigns the state a major role in coping with economic problems, the market system is still the main actor in the economy. In this sense, Keynesianism is supplementary to mainstream economics in the West. On the contrary, in China's MIS political economy system, while the market exists, it must be subordinate to the state and operate within the boundaries set by the latter. We will see in later chapters that it is quite misleading to call this system Keynesian. Government investment is undertaken not only to promote growth or cope with economic crisis but also, and more importantly, to enhance the government's capability to regulate and constrain the market.

NEW INSTITUTIONAL ECONOMICS

In contemporary China, scholarly and policy communities often turn to new institutional economics (NIE) as a framework of analysis. NIE is

---

[41] For example, in a World Bank study of the recent Chinese stimulus package, World Bank economists continued to employ the Keynesian framework of analysis, identifying its sources of successful implementation and potential room for improvement. See Shahrokh Fardoust, Justin Yifu Lin, Xubei Luo, "Demystifying China's Stimulus Package," *Policy Research Working Paper No. 6221* (Washington, DC: World Bank, October 2012), pp. 1–25. In another discussion paper, Malcolm Warner chronicles the sustained intellectual interests and policy influence of Keynesianism and post-Keynesianism in China's reform era, but he appears to perceive a gap between Western theory and China's murky policy practices. See Malcolm Warner, "On Keynes and China: Keynesianism 'with Chinese Characteristics'," *Cambridge Judge Business School Working Paper No. 2/2014* (Cambridge: University of Cambridge, 2014).

an economic perspective that attempts to extend economics by focusing on the social and legal norms and rules that underlie economic activity, with analysis beyond earlier institutional economics and neoclassical economics.

Intellectually, NIE has its roots in two articles by Ronald Coase, "The Nature of the Firm" (1937) and "The Problem of Social Cost" (1960).[42] In the latter, Coase argued that if we lived in a world without transaction costs, people would bargain with one another to produce the most efficient distribution of resources, regardless of the initial allocation. This is superior to allocation through litigation. However, many welfare-maximizing reallocations are often forgone because of the transaction costs involved in bargaining. With potentially high transaction costs, the law ought to produce an outcome like the one that would result if transaction costs were eliminated. Central to Coase's theory is the argument that without transaction costs, alternative property right assignments can equivalently internalize conflicts and externalities. Therefore, comparative institutional analysis arising from such assignments is required in order to make recommendations about efficient internalization of externalities and institutional design, including law and economics.

NIE is built on a complex set of methodological principles and criteria. NIE economists work within a modified neoclassical framework in considering both efficiency and distribution issues. NIE analyses cover a wide range of subjects, including organizational arrangements, property rights, transaction costs, credible commitments, modes of governance, persuasive abilities, social norms, ideological values, decisive perceptions, gained control, enforcement mechanism, asset specificity, human assets, social capital, asymmetric information, strategic behavior, bounded rationality, opportunism, adverse selection, moral hazard, contractual safeguards, surrounding uncertainty, monitoring costs, incentives to collude, hierarchical structures, bargaining strength, and so on.[43]

Although no single, universally accepted set of definitions has been developed, most scholars conducting research under the NIE methodological principles and criteria follow Douglass North's demarcation

---

[42] Ronald Coase, "The Nature of the Firm," *Economica* 4:16 (1937), pp. 386–405; and "The Problem of Social Cost," *Journal of Law and Economics* 3 (1960), pp. 1–44.

[43] Since the NIE literature continues to grow at speed, further aspects can be added to this list. A large amount of work on NIE has been published in the Political Economy of Institutions and Decisions series published by Cambridge University Press. James E. Alt and Douglass C. North are its founding editors; its current editors are Randall Calvert and Thrainn Eggertsson.

between institutions and organizations. Institutions are the "rules of the game," consisting of both the formal legal rules and the informal social norms that govern individual behavior and structure social interactions (institutional frameworks). Organizations, by contrast, are groups of people and the governance arrangements they create to coordinate their team action against other teams that also perform as organizations. Firms, universities, clubs, medical associations, unions, and others are some examples. However, since some institutional frameworks are in reality always "nested" inside other broader institutional frameworks, this demarcation is always blurred in actual situations.

NIE has gained great influence in contemporary China. There are several reasons behind its growing influence. First, compared to other mainstream economic theories, NIE is much closer to the reality of Chinese economy. While mainstream economic theories are popular in classrooms, Chinese economists find they are often less relevant to China's economic reality, and cannot support an understanding of what is happening to China's economy. Second, its influence is also related to the concept of "institutions." The post-Mao economic reform is identified as institutional reform. Contemporary Chinese economists appeal to NIE not only for its methodological capability to explain the country's economic phenomena, but also, more importantly, for clues as to what kinds of institutions China should develop in reforming its old economic institutions and making new ones. Third, understandably, and just as in the West, NIE is most popular among liberal economists. Among the many aspects that NIE has explored, the most popular in China are organizational arrangements, property rights, transaction costs, and credible commitments. The concept of private property rights has gained particular significance. Fourth, there is a consensus among these scholars that market-oriented institutional reforms should not follow NIE prescriptions blindly, but instead need to innovate and adapt to China's initial conditions. To the NIEs, it was the adaptive indigenization of important legal and institutional reforms, such as legally enforceable contracts and protection of private property, that contributed to China's phenomenal economic growth and structural transformations.[44]

Like other economic schools, NIE's explanation for China's economic growth is still a set of post hoc explanations based on "universal" Western concepts of the market. While it is true that China's economic

---

[44] For a summary of this argument, see Qian Yingyi, "How Reform Worked in China," *William David Working Paper No. 473*, June 2002, pp. 1–50.

transformations have brought about many of the market-oriented institutional changes predicted by NIE, they were perhaps not a good predictor
of China's modern economic transformation. From the use of enforceable
contracts to well-defined property rights and limited liability, at various
times and places the premodern Chinese economy exemplified many of the
institutional features of a modern market economy, but it never yielded
sustained industrial development, much less a modern capitalist system. In
many cases of failed industrial projects, the underdevelopment of a functioning state usually played a key role.[45] Likewise, scholars who have
considered the role of laws and contracts in contemporary economic
transformations have demonstrated that China's economic transformation
in recent decades was not primarily the product of legal reforms; rather,
economic changes produced legal changes.[46] This is not a rejection but a
reminder of one shortcoming of the NIE: It has taken an overly simplistic
view of the role of state in economic life in China. As we shall discuss,
China's historical experience of state-building and market–state relations
in the late imperial and Maoist eras has had a shaping influence on China's
contemporary political economy.

In this book, we are not overly interested in whether NIE can explain
economic reform and development in the contemporary era. As a political
economy approach, NIE can explain some parts of the Chinese economy,
but not others. Like other schools of Western economic thought, NIE is
also based on economic experiences in the West. All the aspects of the
theory that NIE has developed are the product of economic development
in the West. In this sense, NIE is not so different from other schools of
economics, from classical to contemporary neoliberalism. When NIE
economists extend the theory to explain economies in the non-Western
world, its explanatory power often tends to be limited and weakened. Our
argument is that, as with the other economic theories, NIE does not tell us
how China's political economy system functions.

[45] The economic and legal historian Madeine Zelin shows that a contract-based corporate
system could still function with minimum state intervention: see Madeleine Zelin, "A
Critique of Property Rights in Prewar China," in Madeline Zelin, Jonanthan K. Okco, and
Robert Gardella, eds., *Rights of Property in Early Modern China* (Stanford, CA: Stanford
University Press, 2004), pp. 30–33. But this is not to say that the state was only a marginal
actor. For a typical study of quick local industrialization with significant institutional
innovations, see Madeleine Zelin, *The Merchant of Zigong: Industrial Entrepreneurship in
Early Modern China* (New York, NY: Columbia University Press, 2006).
[46] Donald Clark, Peter Durrell, and Susan Whiting, "The Role of Law in China's Economic
Development," in Loren Brandt and Thomas Rawski, eds., *China's Great Economic
Transformation* (New York, NY: Cambridge University Press, 2008), pp. 420–422.

THE DEVELOPMENTAL STATE THEORY AND THE
EAST ASIAN NIES

We have so far discussed economics from classical, to neoclassical, to contemporary neoliberalism, and from Keynesianism to NIE. All these theories have developed from economic experiences in the West. While they have been used to explain economies in the non-Western world, they are not political economy theories of non-Western economies. This is why we need to develop a Chinese political economy theory to explain China's political economy system. This rationale, however, can be questioned, since there is a political economy theory of developmental states in East Asian NIEs and for many, China, as a part of East Asia, belongs to this political economy system. To justify our rationale, we highlight some main features of the political economy system of developmental states in East Asia and demonstrate why China does not belong to this system.

In the post-World War II era, East Asia has emerged as the most dynamic region of the world economy, in a situation comparable to the eighteenth-century rise of the West. Within a few decades of the war's end, the region dramatically raised its average income in relation to the West's, while those in all other "developing" regions – Latin America, Africa, West Asia, and South Asia – either fell or remained constant. For this simple reason, the term "East Asian miracle" came into existence. Two questions follow: What political economy theory can explain the East Asian miracle? How did the political economy system of East Asia function to produce such a miracle?

As in any political economy system, relations between the state and the market are central to the East Asian miracle. For contemporary neoclassical economists, the East Asian political economy is not a unique system and its miracle can be explained by neoclassical economics. As discussed earlier, in neoclassical economics, the essential economic functions of a government include:

(1) Maintaining macroeconomic stability;
(2) Providing physical infrastructure, especially that which has high fixed costs in relation to variable costs, such as harbors, railways, irrigation canals, and sewers;
(3) Supplying "public goods," including defense and national security, education, basic research, market information, the legal system, and environmental protection;

(4) Contributing to the development of institutions to improve markets for labor, finance, technology, etc.;
(5) Offsetting or eliminating price distortions which arise in cases of demonstrable market failure;
(6) Redistributing income to the poorest in sufficient measure for them to meet basic needs.

As discussed earlier, the state's role in the economy has been controversial and economists' perceptions of it have changed over time in the West. In the industrialized world, due to the Great Depression and the difficulties of wartime, the state was assigned a substantial role in repairing market failures in the post-World War II era, particularly the 1950s and 1960s. With the rise of development economics, this state-centered approach was also taken up by economists dealing with under-developed countries and made the basis of the newly emerging discipline of development economics. Many of the special circumstances experienced by underdeveloped countries, such as low private saving, dependence on primary product exports, declining prices of exports in relation to imports, small internal markets, limited stock of human capital, the presence of few entrepreneurs adept at large-scale organization, and pervasive underemployment all meant an even more important role was required for the state than was the case in the more developed countries.

Nevertheless, in the late 1960s and early 1970s, the role of the state was downgraded in both developed and less developed economies. In the less developed countries, the state was perceived to have played a negative role in the economy. For example, the use of the state to promote import-substituting industrialization during the 1950s and 1960s had resulted in inefficient industries requiring permanent subsidization, with little prospect of achieving international competitiveness. Also, extensive government intervention tended to generate "rent-seeking" on a significant scale, diverting economic agents' energies away from production and into lobbying for increased government subsidies and protection. In contrary, some of the most successful of the less developed economies – mainly the so-called four little dragons, including Taiwan, South Korea, Hong Kong and Singapore – had achieved extraordinary industrial growth by using an outward-oriented model driven by market incentives and a strong private sector. For neoclassical economists, these experiences show that whether or not the neoclassical prescription is followed decides the failures or successes of less developed economies.

For scholars in the neoclassical school, there is no need for a new political economy theory to explain the East Asian miracle; neoclassical economics can perform this task. In the neoclassical view, the engine of development in East Asia is not so much capital formation as efficient allocation of resources. Once institutional arrangements are in place to generate efficient allocation of resources, investment can be left to take care of itself. The necessary institutional arrangements for generating efficient resources use are competitive markets, particularly domestic markets integrated with international markets. Therefore, government should leave it to private producers operating through market mechanisms to supply all but certain "public goods."

There is a body of literature presenting neoclassical explanations for the East Asian miracle. Hugh Patrick interprets Japanese economic performance as due primarily to the actions and efforts of private individuals and enterprises responding to the opportunities provided in markets for commodities and labor with a greater degree of freedom. According to Patrick, while the government has been supportive and indeed has done much to create an environment of growth, its role has often been exaggerated.[47] Edward Chen asserts that in East Asian economies, "state intervention is largely absent. What the state provided is simply a suitable environment for the entrepreneurs to perform their functions." Such practices as "directing resources to the desired channels by state intervention" are part of central planning and have no part in the development of the East Asian economies.[48] The hypergrowth of the East Asian economies demonstrates that "the free market environment provides the necessary mechanism to gear the economies towards their optimal points on the production possibilities frontier."[49] Milton Friedman and Rose Friedman also argued: "Malaysia, Singapore, Korea, Taiwan, Hong Kong and Japan – relying extensively on private markets – are thriving ... By contrast, India, Indonesia, and Communist China, all relying heavily on central planning, have experienced economic stagnation."[50]

Simply put, from the neoclassical perspective, East Asian economies do better than other newly industrializing ones because the East Asian state

---

[47] Hugh Patrick, "The Future of the Japanese Economy: Output and Labor Productivity," *Journal of Japanese Studies* 3:2 (Summer 1977), p. 239.

[48] Edward Chen, *Hyper-Growth in Asian Economies: A Comparative Study of Hong Kong, Japan, Korea, Singapore and Taiwan* (London: Macmillan, 1979), p. 41.

[49] Chen, *ibid.*, p. 185.

[50] Milton Friedman and Rose Friedman, *Free to Choose: A Personal Statement* (New York, NY: Harcourt Brace Jovanovich, 1980), p. 57.

barely interferes in the working of the market. While neoclassical econo-mists do not necessarily deny the role of the state, the state in neoclassical economics is only marginal and supplementary. The East Asian NIEs thus present no fundamental challenge to the neoclassical model of market-oriented development.

Dissatisfied with the neoclassical explanation, scholars in other social sciences, such as political science, sociology, and business management, have attempted to develop other explanations for the East Asian miracle. Some emphasize Confucian values and frugal consumption preferences, combined with a get-up-and-go entrepreneurialism. Others emphasize external demand generated by the rhythm of Western capital accumulation linked to Western defense against communism. Still others emphasize techniques of business management.

Among all these non-neoclassical explanations, the most popular of the unorthodoxies stresses the importance of the role of the government in the economy. This body of literature has had various terms ascribed to it, such as "the developmental state," "alliance capitalism," and "strategic capitalism." After the 1997 Asian financial crisis, it was often called "crony capitalism."

In this literature, most scholars place the role of the state at the center of the East Asian miracle. They believe that government intervention was the principal factor behind East Asian success. Robert Wade has given a succinct summary of this explanation:

A more tenable formulation is a synergistic connection between a policy system and a mostly private market system, the outputs of each becoming inputs for the other, with the government setting rules and influencing decision-making in the private sector in link with its view of an appropriate industrial and trade profile for the economy. Through this mechanism, the advantages of markets (decentral-ization, rivalry, diversity, and multiple experiments) have been combined with the advantages of partially insulating producers from the instabilities of free markets and of stimulating investment in certain industries selected by government as important for the economy's future growth. This combination has improved upon the results of free markets.[51]

Chalmers Johnson developed a theory of the capitalist developmental state, initially based on his case study on the role of Japan's Ministry of

---

[51] Robert Wade, *Governing the Market: Economic Theory and the Role of Government in East Asian Industrialization*, 2nd edn. (Princeton, NJ: Princeton University Press, 2004). p. 5.

International Trade and Industry (MITI) in promoting economic development.[52] According to Johnson, the institutional arrangements of all high-performance East Asian economies have some common features:

(1) The top priority of state action, consistently maintained, is economic development, defined for policy purposes in terms of growth, productivity, and competitiveness rather than in terms of welfare. The substance of growth/competitiveness goals is derived from comparisons with external reference economies which provide state managers with models for emulation;

(2) The state is committed to private property and the market and limits its interventions to conform with this commitment;

(3) The state guides the market with instruments formulated by an elite economic bureaucracy, led by a pilot agency or "economic general staff";

(4) The state is engaged in numerous institutions for consultation and coordination with the private sector, and these consultations are an essential part of the process of policy formulation and implementation;

(5) While state bureaucrats "rule," politicians "reign." Their function is not to make policy but to create space for the bureaucracy to maneuver, while also acting as a "safety valve" by forcing the bureaucrats to respond to the needs of groups upon which the stability of the system rests: that is, to maintain the relative autonomy of the state while preserving political stability. This separation of "ruling" and "reigning" goes along with a "soft authoritarianism" when it comes to a virtual monopoly of political power in a single political party or institution over a long period of time.

---

[52] Chalmers Johnson wrote extensively on the developmental state. His writings on this subject include: "MITI and Japanese International Economic Policy," in Robert A. Scalapino, ed., *The Foreign Policy of Modern Japan* (Berkeley, CA: University of California Press, 1977), pp. 227–279; *MITI and the Japanese Miracle: The Growth of Industrial Policy, 1925–1975* (Stanford, CA: Stanford University Press, 1982), pp. 305–307; "Political Institutions and Economic Performance: A Comparative Analysis of the Government-Business Relationship in Japan, South Korea, and Taiwan," in F. Deyo, ed., *The Political Economy of the New Asian Industrialism* (Ithaca, NY: Cornell University Press, 1987), pp. 227–279; and "The Developmental State: Odyssey of a Concept," in Meredith Woo-Cumings, ed., *The Developmental State* (Ithaca, NY: Cornell University Press, 1999), pp. 32–60.

After Johnson, other scholars also found similar evidences in other East Asian economies, particularly the "four little dragons."[53] In his study on South Korea, Parvez Hasan draws attention to the role of the state. According to his observation:

The Korean economy depends in large measure on private enterprise operating under highly centralized government guidance. In South Korea, the government's role is considerably more direct than that of merely setting the broad rules of the game and in influencing the economy indirectly through market forces. In fact, the government seems to be a participant and often the determining influence in nearly all business decisions.[54]

Edward Mason and his coauthors come to a similar conclusion in their study of government–business relations:

The rapid economic growth that began in South Korea in the early 1960s and has accelerated since then has been a government-directed development in which the principal engine has been private enterprise. The relationship between a government committed to a central direction of economic development and a highly dynamic private sector that confronts the planning machinery with a continually changing structure of economic activities presents a set of interconnections difficult to penetrate and describe. Planning in South Korea, if it is interpreted to include not only policy formulation but also the techniques of policy implementation, is substantially more than "indicative." The hand of government reaches down rather far into the activities of individual firms with its manipulation of incentives and disincentives. At the same time, the situation can in no sense be described in terms of a command economy.[55]

Drawing on the evidence from East Asian economies, particularly Taiwan, Robert Wade has developed what he called a "governed market theory." He observed that all three economies (Japan, South Korea, and Taiwan)

have in common an intense and almost unequivocal commitment on the part of government to build up the international competitiveness of domestic industry – and thereby eventually to raise living standards. This commitment led all three governments to create rather similar policies and organizations for governing the market. Their outstanding economic success makes it plausible to suggest

---

[53] For a brief introduction of these "four little dragons," see Ezra F. Vogel, *The Four Little Dragons: The Spread of Industrialization in East Asia* (Cambridge, MA: Harvard University Press, 1991).

[54] Parvez Hasan, *Korea, Problems and Issues in a Rapidly Growing Economy* (Baltimore, MD: Johns Hopkins University Press, 1976), p. 29.

[55] Edward S. Mason, Mahn Je Kim, Dwight H. Perkins, Kwang Suk Kim, and David Cole, *The Economic and Social Modernization of the Republic of Korea* (Cambridge, MA: Harvard University Press, 1980), p. 24.

that they have created a more competitive form of capitalism, from which other countries would be wise to learn.[56]

According to Wade, the superiority of East Asian economic performance is due in large measure to a combination of the following factors: (1) very high levels of productive investment, making for fast transfer of newer techniques into actual production; (2) more investment in certain key industries than would have occurred in the absence of government intervention; and (3) many industries' exposure to international competition, in foreign markets if not at home.[57]

It is not so difficult to see that the difference between the neoclassical theory and the developmental state theory mainly lies in their different emphases on the roles of the market and of the state. Neoclassical theory emphasizes efficient resource allocation as the principal general force for growth, and therefore interprets superior East Asian performance as the result of more efficient resource allocation than is the case in other late developing economies. This more efficient resource allocation comes from more freely functioning markets, including closer integration of domestic product markets into international markets. Hence these countries show the virtues of "getting the prices right," where "right" means domestic prices in line with international prices. For example, in its report *The East Asian Miracle*, published in 1993, the World Bank argued: "in large measure, the HPAES [High Performing Asian Economies, eight across East and Southeast Asia] achieved high growth by getting the basics right."[58] For neoliberal economists, East Asian experience supports the proposition that liberalized markets are the best way to organize economies. The state should protect property rights and ensure the supply of public goods, but not impart directional thrust. More specifically, the state should create and sustain efficient, rent-free markets; an efficient, corruption-free public sector able to supervise the delivery of a narrow set of inherent public services; and decentralized arrangements of participatory democracy. The more these conditions are in place, the more development and prosperity will follow.

By contrast, the developmental state theory emphasizes capital accumulation as the principal general force for growth, and interprets superior East Asian performance as the result of a level and composition of

---

[56] Wade, *Governing the Market*, p. 7.   [57] *Ibid.*, p. 26.

[58] The World Bank, *The East Asian Miracle: Economic Growth and Public Policy* (New York, NY: Oxford University Press, 1993), p. 5.

investment different from what would have been produced by both the neoclassical theories and the "interventionist" economic policies pursued by many other least developed countries (LDCs). Government policies deliberately got some prices "wrong," to change the signals to which decentralized market agents responded, and used nonprice means to alter the behavior of market agents. The resulting high level of investment generated fast turnover of machinery, and hence fast transfer of newer technology into actual production.[59]

However, the difference between neoclassical theory and the developmental state theory is not as big as it first appeared. The latest research has offered a somewhat more balanced analysis. For instance, Dwight Perkins, who has been involved in economic decision making in many Asian economies, argued that while the overall economic policy has been positive, no single economic policy has been effective regionwide. He found that interventionist policies that worked well in some economies failed elsewhere. In his research, he employed a more dynamic approach to consider the changing role of the state in different historical periods. State policies that worked well in one historical period might fail in another. Income distribution is a good example: Initially egalitarian East Asian societies have now ended up in very different places, with Japan maintaining a modest gap between rich and poor while other states, such as Hong Kong and Singapore, have witnessed widening income disparities in the age of globalization. Despite its rapid economic growth since the reform and the beginning of the open door policy, China has become one of Asia's most unequal economies.[60]

Another grand synthesis of developmental state and neoclassical theory comes from Justin Lin's New Structural Economics (NSE). Drawing on his vast experience in the Chinese economy and other developing economies, Lin argues that in developing economies such as China, the state could make a significant contribution to sustained economic growth by adapting to the country's changing comparative advantages. Rather than championing aggressive state intervention to create factor prices favorable for industrialization, as earlier development economists Gerschkron and Kutznets suggested, NSE advocated that the state should limit its role to the

---

[59] Wade, *Governing the Market*, p. 29.

[60] Dwight H. Perkins, *East Asian Development: Foundations and Strategies* (Cambridge, MA: Harvard University Press, 2013). Also, see Vu Minh Khuong, *The Dynamics of Economic Growth: Policy Insights from Comparative Analyses in Asia* (Cheltenham: Edward Elgar, 2013). Vu provided a more comprehensive analysis by focusing on economic governance on the part of the state.

provision of information, incubation of new industries, and encouragement of foreign investment, while relying on the market to play a central
role in industrial upgrading and diversification.[61] In a way, Lin's suggestion
reflected some regional experiences of China's reform-era industrialization
and economic globalization, such as those in Zhejiang and Guangdong,
which we shall discuss in Chapter 6. While the theory is intended as a
lesson for China and other developing countries, it seems to explain only
parts of China's diverse and complex experience.

   Both the developmental state theory, neoclassical theory, and their
various syntheses have tried to explain China. On one hand, scholars have
applied the developmental state theory to analyze economic development
in China.[62] Wade and his coauthors argued that capitalist developmental
states (CDS) and socialist developmental states (SDS), though their ideologies and economic systems are very different, share the greatest similarity –
that is, "they are successful examples of ... development as a national
endeavor guided by a strong and pervasive state."[63] On the other hand, for
neoclassical scholars, China, just as other economies in the East Asian
region such as Taiwan and South Korea, has been reforming itself in line
with the Anglo-American economic model, discarding the remnants of
developmental statism.

   Apparently, what theory fits China depends on the aspect of China's
development on which one wants to focus. If one focuses on the development of grassroots private sector and the market system, then reform-era
China fits the neoclassical theory. On the other hand, if one focuses on the
role of the state in the development of the private sector and the market
system, then China fits the developmental state theory. Also, it is not
difficult for one to collect ample evidence to support either neoclassical
theory or the developmental state theory. We will not discuss this issue
further, since our goal is not to argue which theory explains the case of
China better, but to explore China's unique pattern of the political economy system. Our discussion of how scholars have viewed the East Asian
economies is put forward to serve our argument that China is not a part of
the East Asian model, just as it is not a part of the Western market system

---

[61] Justin Lin Yifu, *New Structural Economics: A Framework for Rethinking Development Policy*, (Washington, DC: The World Bank), pp. 28–29.

[62] Gordon White, ed., *Developmental States in East Asia* (London: The Macmillan Press, 1988); and Gordon White, "Developmental States and Socialist Industrialization in the Third World," *Journal of Development Studies*, 21:1 (1984), pp. 97–120.

[63] Gordon White and Robert Wade, "Developmental States and Markets in East Asia," in Gordon White, ed., *Developmental States in East Asia*, p. 26.

or the Keynesian model. This is simply due to the following two factors. First, in the East Asian model, there is still a boundary between the state and the market, despite synergetic industrial policy and institutional intermediaries such as *Keiretsu*. The key question for the East Asian model is not whether the state or the market should exist, but what role each should play in the economy. By contrast, the unique aspect of China's political economy system is the state's domination of the market.

Second, central to the East Asian model is the relationship between the state and the private sector. China, of course, also has this dimension. However, in addition to this, China has a few structural conditions that are absent from other East Asian economies, such as the continued domination of the centrally managed SOEs, the corporate local developmental states, and the still powerful state planning agencies such as the National Commission for Development and Reform (NCDR). As we will show in later chapters, this single factor can change the relationships between the state and the market, and between the state and the private sector.

CONCLUSION

In this chapter, we have discussed several key political economy theories in the West and East Asia. Our purpose is not to answer the questions whether these theories can explain China, which theory can better explain China, and how a given theory can be improved. Instead, by highlighting some key aspects of these theories, we want to answer the question of what China is *not*. We believe that all these theories were developed based on their theorists' observations of the key features and functioning of different political economy systems. China's political economy system might be explained partially by each political economy theory discussed here, and some theories might better explain China than others. The purpose of this research is far beyond a simple examination of all these theories; instead, it is twofold: first, we want to consider how China's political economy system functions; second, based on our observations, we want to conceptualize this political economy system. Based on our review of these key political economy theories, the following points are particularly relevant for our discussion of China in later chapters.

First, the conceptual separation of the polity and the economy reflects a unique historical experience of the West and cannot precisely characterize experiences of development in other societies. As discussed in this chapter, even in the West, the state and the market were not always separate or to be perceived to be separable in historical terms. Historically speaking, in different times and spaces there were seemingly capitalist-like societies, such as Ancient Greece, with its flourishing international trade, or Rome, which sported a kind of stock market in the forum, or sixteenth-century Florence, with its moneyed life. In all these cases, the governing authority of the state was legally unbounded. However, as Heilbroner emphasized, the idea that the material activities of farmers, artisans, and merchants were not under the authority of the state would never have occurred to Aristotle, Cicero, or Machiavelli. If the state did not much meddle in these activities it was because it had more important things to do, such as the conduct of war and the celebration of its own majesty, and because these economic tasks were sufficiently routinized, or marginal, to be left to themselves.[64] In the contemporary era, such a separation did not appear in noncapitalist societies, particularly in centrally planned socialist states, including Maoist China.

Economists espousing theories from classical to neoliberal political economy tend to regard the separation of the polity and the economy as normal, and nonseparation as abnormal. By so doing, they have transformed the perspective they take in their observations of the West's unique experience from positive to normative. With this transformation, an ideological inclination becomes inevitable when their political economy theories are applied to explain China. Certainly, their explanations of China are often value-loaded. While this cannot completely be avoided, since nothing is absolutely value-free in social sciences, it affects the effectiveness of an explanation. A more effective way to avoid this is to avoid simply applying existing political economic theories to China and instead construct a new theory based on our observations of the functioning of China's political economy system. This, of course, is the purpose of our research.

Second, and relatedly, we must keep in mind that economic theories based on development experiences in the West are unique but not universal. As C. B. Macpherson pointed out, there is a model of the market underlying Anglo-American liberal-democratic political economy and philosophy since the seventeenth and eighteenth centuries which assumes that persons are cast as self-interested individuals who enter into contractual relations with other such individuals, concerning the exchange of goods or personal capacities cast as commodities, with the motive of maximizing pecuniary interest. The state and its governance systems are cast as

---

[64] Heilbroner, *21st Century Capitalism*, p. 69.

outsiders in this framework.[65] This model came to dominate economic thinking in the later nineteenth century, as economists such as Ricardo, Smith, Mill, and Jevons, and later neoclassical economists, shifted from references to geographically located marketplaces in the West and toward an abstract "market."[66] This tradition is continued in contemporary neo-liberalism, including NIE, where the market is held up as optimal for wealth creation and human freedom and the state's role is imagined as minimal, reduced to that of upholding and keeping stable property rights, contract, and money supply. This allowed for boilerplate economic and institutional restructuring under circumstances of structural adjustment and post-Communist reconstruction, including China.[67] Moreover, it is also worth noting that even in the Anglo-American liberal market economies, a variety of hybrid institutional orderings and new markets have emerged, such as those for carbon trading or rights to pollute. In some cases, such as emerging markets for water, different forms of privatization of various aspects of previously state-run infrastructure have created hybrid private–public formations and graded degrees of commodification, commercialization, and privatization.[68]

One needs to be particularly cautious when these political economy approaches are employed to examine economic development in non-Western societies. In *The Communist Manifesto*, written in 1848, Karl Marx predicted that European capitalism would expand into different parts of the world and have a huge impact.[69] In his "world system theory," Immanuel Wallerstein extensively discussed capitalism's spread from Europe to the rest of the world.[70] Today, the concept of "global capitalism" has become key in many social science disciplines.[71] However,

---

[65] C. B. MacPherson, *The Political Theory of Possessive Individualism: From Hobbes to Locke* (Oxford: Clarendon Press, 1962), p.3.

[66] Swedberg, "Markets as Social Structures," p. 258.

[67] David Harvey, *A Short History of Neoliberalism* (Oxford: Oxford University Press, 2005).

[68] Karen Bakker, "Neoliberalizing Nature? Market Environmentalism in Water Supply in England and Wales," *Annals of the Association of American Geographers* 95:3(2005), pp. 542–565.

[69] Karl Marx, "The Communist Manifesto," in Robert C. Tucker, ed., *The Marx–Engels Reader* (New York, NY: W. W. Norton, 1972).

[70] Immanuel Wallerstein, *The Modern World-System I: Capitalist Agriculture and the Origins of the European World-Economy in the Sixteenth Century* (New York, NY: Academic Press, 1974); *The Modern World System II: Mercantilism and the Consolidation of the European World-Economy, 1600–1750* (New York, NY: Academic Press, 1980); and *The Modern World-System III* (San Diego, CA: Academic Press, 1989).

[71] For a systematic survey of the expansion of global capitalism in the twentieth century, see Jeffry R. Frieden, *Global Capitalism: Its Fall and Rise in the Twentieth Century* (New

this should not lead to confusion with another fact: that the market often grows in non-Western societies not because a state has adopted a neoliberal political economy policy, but because the market helps the state to achieve economic development. The market is not something that spread from the West to other parts of the world; it can grow in any society. Global capitalism and different forms of local market systems coexist in many societies. As both idea and practice, global capitalism often expands into non-Western states, and the market in these states becomes an extension of the market system in the West. The market in these states is integrated into the world system by the needs of global capitalism. But this is not always the case. In some states, global capitalism is "imported" by non-Western states to promote economic development in their own societies. In these cases, the market is integrated into the world system by the needs of the non-Western states. But in all these cases, global capitalism must interact with the market that has grown out from these non-Western societies, and in their interaction, both global capitalism and local market systems are mutually transformed.

Third, our discussion in this chapter indicates that just as the market exists in different forms in different times and spaces, the boundary between the state and the market also changes over time and space. As Polanyi, Braudel, and others have shown, while the market exists in different historical periods, its forms and the ways it functions are different, and its nature changes. Various forms of the market have existed, from the semifeudal and peasant economies widely operative in many developing economies, to the informal markets, barter systems, worker cooperatives, or illegal trades that occur even in most developed countries. Various modes of articulation have arisen between transformed and hybridized local traditions and social practices and the emergence of the world economy. Capitalist markets include and depend on a wide range of geographically situated economic practices that do not follow the market model. Economies are indeed hybrids of market and nonmarket elements.[72]

The relations between the state and the market also change, not only in different stages of a given country's economic history, but also in countries

---

York, NY: W. W. Norton, 2006). Also see Robert Gilpin, *Global Political Economy: Understanding the International Economic Order* (Princeton, NJ: Princeton University Press, 2001).

[72] Timothy Mitchell, *Rule of Experts* (Berkeley, CA: University of California Press, 2002), p. 270.

which are in different stages of economic development. It is not difficult to observe that states in the later developing or less developed world play a more important role than those in the developed world. Almost all now-developed countries went through stages of industrial assistance policy being put in place by the state before their firms' capabilities reached the point at which a policy of free trade was declared to be in the national interest. Britain was protectionist when it was trying to catch up with Holland. Germany was protectionist when trying to catch up with Britain. The United States was protectionist when it was trying to catch up with Britain and Germany, right up to the end of World War II. Japan was protectionist for most of the twentieth century up to the 1970s; Korea and Taiwan to the 1990s. Hong Kong and Singapore were the great exceptions on the trade front, in that they did have free trade and they did catch up. Hong Kong and Singapore are usually regarded as city-states, not as economic countries. But even in these cases, particularly in Singapore, the state played an important role in promoting economic development, a role similar to that played in Japan and other East Asian "little dragons."[73]

Of course, in all such cases, the role of the state is not to adopt measures against the market but to assist the growth of the market. By and large, countries that have caught up with the club of wealthy industrial countries have tended to follow the prescription of Friedrich List, the German catch-up theorist writing in the 1840s: "to allow freedom of trade to operate naturally, the less advanced nation must first be raised by artificial measures to that stage of cultivation to which the English nation has been artificially elevated."[74]

It is also important to note that even within the new clubs of wealthy industrial countries, such as the OECD, there are different forms of relationship between the state and the market. Drawing on concepts of institutional variance and path dependency, "varieties of capitalism" theorists such as Peter Hall and David Soskice have identified two dominant modes of economic ordering in the developed capitalist countries, namely, "coordinated market economies" such as Germany and Japan,

---

[73] For discussions of the role of the Economic Development Board in promoting Singapore's economic development, see Linda Low, Toh Mun Heng, Soon Teck Wong, Tan Kong Yam, and Helen Hughes, *Challenge and Response: Thirty Years of the Economic Development Board* (Singapore: Times Academic Press, 1993).

[74] F. List, *The National System of Political Economy* [1885] (New York, NY: Augustus Kelley, 1966), p. 131.

and Anglo-American "liberal market economies."[75] While in Anglo-American liberal market economies the market continues to dominate, in coordinated market economies such as Japan and Germany the state has implemented varying degrees and types of environmental, economic, and social regulation; taxation and public spending; fiscal policy; and government provisioning of goods, all of which have transformed markets in uneven and geographical varied ways and created a variety of mixed economies.

Fourth and more fundamentally, there is an increasing challenge to the neoliberal assumption of self-interest maximization. There are now a few streams of economic sociological analysis of markets focusing on the role of the social in transactions, and the ways transactions involve social networks and relations of trust, cooperation, and other bonds. Economic geographers draw attention to the ways in which exchange transactions occur against the backdrop of institutional, social, and geographic processes, including class relations, uneven development, and historically contingent path dependencies. As Michel Callon summarizes, each economic act or transaction occurs against, incorporates, and reperforms a geographically and cultural specific complex of social histories, institutional arrangements, rules, and connections. These network relations are simultaneously bracketed, so that persons and transactions may be disentangled from thick social bonds. The character of calculability is imposed upon agents as they come to work in markets and are "formatted" as calculative agencies. Market exchanges contain a history of struggle and contestation that produced actors predisposed to exchange under certain sets of rules. As such, market transactions can never be disembedded from social and geographic relations and there is no sense in talking of degrees of embeddedness and disembeddedness.[76]

One thing was clear when we conducted our research on China: The Chinese market and market system is a unique product of its culture and history, including its more recent interaction with the West. While we do not want to go too deep into the cultural realm, there is an important question to ask: Why have the Chinese organized their market in their own unique way? The market is important, but more important is the way it is organized. The ideas and methods behind the organization of the market matter not only for the market, but also for the relations between the

---

[75] Peter A. Hall and David W. Soskice, *Varieties of Capitalism: The Institutional Foundations of Comparative Advantage* (New York, NY: Oxford University Press, 2001).

[76] Callon, "Introduction."

market and other elements (for example, polity and social forces). On one hand, the market is organized by other social elements, such as the state; on the other, the market also organizes society. Certainly, there is a continuous interaction between "to organize" and "to be organized." Such interactions often reflect deeply rooted ideational factors in a society.

When we come to China's political economy system, all the questions raised by economists from the classical to the contemporary neoliberalist schools can be raised again and reanswered, including, among others: What is the *raison d'être* of the market and the polity? Are the market and the polity separable? Are the market and society separable? And what are the relations among the market, the polity, and society? To answer these questions, we turn first to the Chinese political economy system.

2

Market in State

A Theory of Chinese Political Economy

In Chapter 1, we attempt to answer the question of what China is *not*, by comparing China with other political economy systems. In this chapter, we will answer the question of what China *is*. To do so, we will consider the practice of China's political economy system. Over its long history, China has not been able to provide a set of concepts and theories of its political economy system, even though the various dynastic states which we know today as imperial China had rich experience in practice. When we consider the historical practice of China's political economy system, we will see that some key themes and issues of political economy that often existed in the West could also be found in China. In Chapter 1, we briefly discussed some key concepts in various approaches of political economy in the West and East Asian newly industrialized economies (NIEs). The discussion in this chapter will illustrate that while China has also encountered similar issues in dealing with relations between the state and the market, it has addressed these key issues differently. We believe that there has been a Chinese logic underlying the practice of its political economy system throughout its long history. China's political economy is typically Chinese, a product of Chinese history, philosophy, and culture in the *longue durée*. We are also confident that the Chinese political economy approach, once conceptualized and theorized, is better able to explain contemporary China than any political economy approach originated elsewhere. It will be used to illustrate how China has created an economic miracle, and the social consequences of this miracle that have been seen in the post-Mao era. The purpose of this chapter is to conceptualize the Chinese political economy system, or to construct a Chinese theory of political economy.

This chapter is divided into three sections. The first section discusses the relationship between the state and the economy at the level of classical

Chinese political philosophy. In Chapter 1, we demonstrate that in economic theory, from the classical to contemporary neoliberalism, certain philosophical assumptions underlie relations between the state and the economy in the West. This set of philosophical ideas was based on the unique historical practices during the formation of the market system in the West, and has served as the intellectual foundation of capitalism ever since. The same is true in the case of China: Early Chinese ideas on the relationship between the state and the economy were formed in a particular historical period, but continued to affect the thought of economic thinkers and policy makers in later times. Even though there have been changes over time, with new elements added to that thinking in different times and spaces, the *core* of this economic philosophy does not change.

The second section focuses on the economic policy debates on relations between the state and the economy which took place during the formative years of imperial China – the Qin and early Han periods. As discussed in Chapter 1, in the West, political economists have developed various political economy theories across two millennia. This is not the case in China. Over its several thousand years of history, China was never able to develop any systematic school of political-economic theory such as those seen in the West. Nevertheless, this does not mean that Chinese economic thinkers and policy makers did not engage in economic thinking and debate. In China, political economy was taken more as a practical subject, less as a theoretical one. Historically speaking, the Chinese state was among the earliest to introduce economic policy. How imperial China's economic thinkers and policy makers thought about relations between the state and the economy was reflected in the policy debates in different dynasties. Our mission here is not to examine different policy debates in detail – this is too much for one chapter. Rather, in this chapter we shall focus on some key recurrent themes of state–economy relations in imperial Chinese political economy, especially the themes articulated and emphasized by the early policy debates of the Qin and Han periods. We believe that early formulations of policy discourse affected the development of China's political economy thinking in later dynasties. It provided an ideational frame and set up an economic philosophical foundation for Chinese economic thinkers and policy makers.

The third section of the chapter discusses how different forms and layers of the market coexist in the same political economy system. As we will see, there was no consensus among different schools of thought on the state and the economy in China. Indeed, the geographical size of China, from the first unified Qin Empire (221 BC) to the present day, has determined that there were diverse needs in the economy. It is understandable that the various economic thinkers and policy makers developed diverse policy discourses. For example, from a governmental perspective, a centralized political economy system was usually preferred. The government is not just an economic actor; more importantly, it is a political actor whose fundamental role is to provide and maintain a social order. The economy is only one aspect of its governance responsibilities. From a societal perspective, however, a decentralized political-economic system can be desirable, since such a system often enables a society to develop an autonomous system of self-government. To govern such a vast country, China's political economy system would have to be sufficiently pragmatic to reflect and accommodate various perceptions of the state and the economy. A practical solution is to allow the coexistence of different forms of economic organizations that function in different realms of the economy. We will identify the three layers of the market: the grass roots, where rural marketplaces flourish; the national market, where state monopolies and strategic concerns reign; and the middle market in between, where state agents and private actors interact.

Such a market system is very close to the "mixed economy" of our modern parlance. To a great degree, the coexistence of these markets means their mixture and interpenetration. The concept of the mixed economy has now gained immense popularity since the Chinese Communist Party (CCP) formally endorsed the term at its Third Plenum of the Eighteenth Congress in 2013. A mixed economy has become the goal of China's economic institutional reform.[1] However, the term mixed economy does not capture the essence of China's political economy system, namely, "market in state". China's political economy system is characterized by the existence of a market hierarchy and state domination of the market. An examination of the coexistence of the market's three levels will show how the state dominates, and sustains its domination of, the market system while accommodating the market, and how the market operates within the boundaries set up by the state. We will also demonstrate that the game between the state and the market is not always a zero-sum one, but is frequently win–win. In their interaction, the state and the market can mutually empower each other.

---

[1] The CCP Central Committee's Decision on Major Issues Concerning Comprehensively Deepening Reforms, available at http://news.xinhuanet.com/politics/2013–11/15/c_ 118164235.htm [Accessed on 13 April 2017].

THE CHINESE STATE AND THE ECONOMY

While the political economy was dominated by a powerful centralized state in the heyday of Chinese empire, the political economy system in the early modern West was characterized by decentralization. In medieval and early modern Europe, states, the Church, market towns, and other substate polities all had overlapping jurisdictions and their own principles with which to regulate their economic activities; they also interacted with and influenced each other. This allowed Enlightenment statecraft thinkers and political economists to counter the mercantilist state regulations of the day and envision the economy as an independent and distinctive natural order. As discussed in Chapter 1, there was a conceptual separation of state and economy. The economy was regarded as separable from the state, and as an autonomous realm. Over time, the role of the state has evolved and its scope expanded, but there remains a definite boundary between the state and the economy. This is also true in the case of East Asian NIEs.

However, when we consider China, we find that the defining feature of its political economy system is centralization. From very early times, the state has both encompassed and penetrated society to a remarkable degree. Although the level of this penetration ebbed and flowed in line with the rise and fall of dynastical states, the conceptual framework of the state as both dominating and caring for society members has remained unchanged. As such, in Chinese political philosophy, the imperial state – headed by the cosmological ruler, or the Son of Heaven – was defined as the source of moral values and the power which fashions society and the economy. French historian Jacques Gernet pointed to this aspect of the Chinese system:

One could say that in China, the state is all. History explains this. The state was not an organism which developed little by little and was obliged to make a place for itself among other powers, as was the case in the West, where the state had to impose itself on the independent powers of the Church, of feudalism and of the nobility, come to terms with the merchants, and seek the support of the financiers. In China, the state was an established reality from the beginning, or in any case from the time when the formula was worked out in the state of Qin, before it was extended to the whole of the Chinese realm. It was the great organizer of society and of territory.[2]

---

[2] Jacques Gernet, "Introduction," in Stuart R. Schram, ed., *The Scope of State Power in China* (Hong Kong: The Chinese University of Hong Kong Press, 1985), p. xxxli.

The state is manmade everywhere, and takes many forms, related to the historical conditions prevalent when it is made. Historians have found that while the modern state, distinguished by a centralized bureaucratic system, developed in Western Europe in the period between the fifteenth and nineteenth centuries, all the essential traits that European historians attribute to the concept of the modern state developed much earlier in China. Administrative division into districts answerable to the central authorities occurred in China in the third century BC, whereas in Europe nothing similar was seen prior to the French Revolution, which established departments and prefectures.[3]

As such, two important questions are in order. First, what justifies the centralized Chinese state? Second, what is the relationship between the state and the economy? In preindustrial Europe, the decentralized structure of the state and the separation of the state and the economy, the Church, and the burghers (a prototype of civil society) were conditioned by the historical circumstances at the time the modern European state was formed. As mentioned in Chapter 1, the classical economics developed in the late eighteenth and nineteenth centuries was not only a reflection of the relationship between the state and the economy at that time, but also a normative justification of this relationship. This is certainly also true in China. While the centralized structure of the state was conditioned by historical circumstances, a political philosophy centered on Confucianism was also developed to justify this structure. In China, the government's responsibilities are central to this justification. It is within the frame of government responsibilities that the relationship between the state and the economy was justified. The economy was regarded only as part of the state, and an aspect of government responsibilities over society.

The centralized dominant state structure was justified by the state's responsibilities, which in turn arose from the idea of *tianming*, the Mandate of Heaven given to those who ruled the world, or All Under Heaven (*tianxia*). This idea first emerged when the founder of the Shang Dynasty (1600–1100 BC) overthrew the Xia Dynasty (2100–1600 BC), claiming that the Xia emperor had lost his Mandate of Heaven. But throughout the Shang, the dynastic god of *Di*, rather than *tian*, reigned supreme. When the much smaller state of Zhou defeated the Shang Dynasty and founded the West Zhou (1100–771 BC), many people asked why Heaven had previously given power to Shang, but had now changed its mind and

---

[3] *Ibid.*

endorsed Zhou. The Zhou rulers explained that Shang had lost its Mandate of Heaven, using the concept of *geming*, or revolution, to describe a successful change of dynastic house (*geming* literally means "removing the Mandate").[4] If a ruler was considered to have lost the mandate to rule, a revolutionary (*geming*) moment would naturally follow. John Fairbank characterized Chinese history as a series of dynastic cycles, with new dynasties replacing the old ones every several hundred years. Each time, the doomed emperors were accused of being ruthless, fatuous, rotten, and ultimately lacking in virtue. The concept of the "Mandate of Heaven" was employed to justify not only the "right to rule" but also the "right to rebel." The changing dynasties illustrate how the illegitimate regimes were removed and replaced.

Once an existing ruler began to lose its Mandate of Heaven, the Mandate became open to whoever won out among the competing forces. The Chinese have never believed that the royal family has an eternal hereditary bloodline, and they do not necessarily respect the royal bloodline of the ruling dynasty. On the contrary, they believe that everyone has an equal chance to become emperor. In other words, the Chinese hold a typically Machiavellian idea of power, and they do not care where their rulers come from or how they came to power as long as they hold the Mandate of Heaven. Whether they were in power because of peaceful power transfer, court conspiracy, or dynastic wars, it was the capability or fortune of the founders in the name of Heaven that determined the right to rule. However, the Chinese do care what their rulers do. Once an emperor is in position, he must bear responsibility and rule by virtue. Legitimacy does not come from the way a leader obtains power, but lies instead in the way he exercises it.

For a Chinese emperor, the most vital matter was to avoid being overthrown. According to Jacques Gernet,

The only problem for the Chinese state, in the course of its long history, was to prevent the development of powers other than its own, such as that of the merchants, the armies, the religious communities, and to prevent dangerous splits at the top. It is this which explains the constant effort to devise mechanisms and arrangements capable of preventing the development of parallel powers, not only outside the central state power, but also within it.[5]

---

[4] Wang Gungwu, "A Revolution is a New Mandate," in Wang Gungwu, *Renewal* (Hong Kong: The Chinese University of Hong Kong Press, 2013), pp. 85–106.

[5] Gernet, "Introduction," p. xxxli.

The question, then, is what the ruler can and should do to avoid such a misfortune. The fundamental condition for avoiding such a loss of the Mandate is an adequate material or economic basis for All Under Heaven to survive and thrive. In China's political economy tradition, the Confucian school has emphasized the state's role in providing society with equitable and adequate material well-being so it can better maintain the moral values of the subjects and the harmony of the realm, while the Legalists have focused on its role in producing material goods to ensure sufficient resources and fiscal capacity for defense and other public purposes. In both cases, material wealth is indispensable for the state. The ruler and his state need material wealth for to ensure the presence of both moral values and material goods in governing society.

Central to Confucianism is a moral philosophy. It is worth noting that the rulers of China had emphasized the role of morality long before Confucius. When the rulers of Zhou were asked what the Mandate of Heaven meant, the reply was: "Heaven does not favor anybody; only morality makes Heaven trust you."[6] The Mandate of Heaven was closely related to morality. Later, Confucius developed systematic teaching on morality as the basis for the "Mandate of Heaven." He elaborated that the concept of a good government was fundamentally a matter of morality. He did not question the emperors' hereditary right to rule, but he insisted that their first duty was to set a proper example in terms of sound moral conduct. In the Confucian scheme, the ruler was to be a role model for moral behavior, displaying benevolence, filial piety, faithfulness, courtesy, integrity, and frugality. If an emperor does not behave correctly, he cannot expect his people to do so. If the ruler behaves in a moral fashion, protecting the people, the people will voluntarily obey him and Heaven will forever entrust to him the power to govern. In fact, for Confucianists, the Mandate of Heaven and morality are sometimes interchangeable terms. John Fairbank and Edwin Reischauer have commented that it is remarkable that Confucius argued that the ruler's virtue and the contentment of the people, rather than power, should be the true measures of political success.[7]

---

[6] Cited in Yanqi Tong and Shaohua Lei, *Social Protest in Contemporary China, 2003-2010: Transitional Pains and Regime Legitimacy* (Routledge: London and New York, NY, 2014), p. 28.

[7] John Fairbank and Edwin Reischauer, eds., *China: Tradition and Transformation* (George Allen & Unwin, Sydney, 1979), p. 44.

Furthermore, to be moral, or to be seen as moral, the ruler has to protect his people and rule by benevolence. According to Confucius, the central theme of benevolence is showing compassionate care for the people. Officials should behave like parents, accepting a duty to plan for and worry ahead of the people, and enjoy the fruits of action after the people. Specifically, benevolent governance includes the socializing of moral values, encouraging agricultural production, recruiting the best and most capable to the government, exercising fairness in legal enforcement, and allocating duties to the subjects of the realm equally.

The Legalists, meanwhile, emphasized the role of the state in producing material goods for collective use, especially in security, and sometimes in territorial expansion. In this context, the Chinese philosophy of the relationship between the state and the economy is drastically different from that in the West. As discussed in Chapter 1, the concept of economics in the West comes from the Ancient Greek *oikonomia*, or "management of a household/administration." *Oikonomia* is from *oikos* (house) and *nomos* ("custom" or "law"). *Oikonomia* thus meant "rules of the household," namely, the domestic arts taught to young women, or at the very most the art of managing one's patrimony. Only in the nineteenth century did economics became the social science that analyzes the production, distribution, and consumption of goods and services. As discussed in Chapter 1, it was not the actions of the centralized state, which had only just begun to find a foothold in Europe and barely existed in North America, that brought economic preoccupations forth in the West; rather, it was the activities of merchants, colonial settlers, and other actors with varying degrees of state backing. It is understandable that terms such as profit, interest, and efficiency have dominated the field of economic discourse since the eighteenth century – a field dominated by the merchants autonomously. It makes sense that the Western notion of the economy is linked to the development of commercial capitalism and the modern state.

By contrast, in China, the economy was regarded as an integral aspect of the emperor's benevolent governance, and thus not separable from the state. The Chinese state did not have a notion of the economy as an autonomous realm. The economy was managed – far more an instrument in the service of the state than an autonomous force to which the state was exposed. China does not have a term equivalent to the Western "economy." The modern Western term was translated into the Chinese *jingji*, which has been used since ancient times as an abbreviation of *jingshi jimin*, literally "to order the world and succor the people." The term evokes the social responsibilities of the state, its consistent interventions to maintain the equilibrium between factors such as money and food supply or surplus and penury, and its role in shaping the environment through such things as canals, roads, and fortifications.[8] In other words, the purpose of the "economy" (*jingji*) is not about itself, but about All Under Heaven, or society in a very large sense, which the economy is only one part of. Even today, when the Chinese use the term *jingji* to refer to the modern economy, the term still carries these ancient meanings, at least on the part of the state.

It is not difficult to see the difference in the historical itineraries followed at the two extremities of the Eurasian continent. "Economic" thought appeared in China with the first manifestations of centralization in the realm of the state, and remains rudimentary today. As Gernet pointed out, it was in fact the very intervention of the state which served to disguise and conceal the mechanisms of the economy.[9] These very different paths of historical development gave rise to different conceptions of the state and the economy throughout their long histories and to this day.

In China, the *jingji* philosophy treats the economy as inseparable from the state and justifies state domination of the economy. This philosophy has shaped all aspects of the historical Chinese economy. For instance, it influenced the development of financial institutions in China. In Europe, one can argue that the development of modern financial institutions such as national debt and shareholding companies produced capitalism. As Marianne Bastid, a French historian focusing on China, has emphasized, "in various European countries, the growth of the modern state corresponds to the development of the financial state, imposing itself on the judicial state and gradually crushing it with its weight."[10] Capitalism remains a system in which the debt-financing of the state is the overriding and dominant concern. Clearly, in the modern systems of the West, the Exchequer or Ministry of Finance (or its equivalent) is all-powerful in mediating the economy and the state. But this has not at all been the case in China. As Bastid correctly points out, "in contrast to such historical development on the European continent, the financial administration in China had from ancient times always been an essential aspect of the machinery and of the functions of the central power, linked to the economic responsibilities of the emperor."[11] As a matter of fact, in China there

---

[8] Gernet, "Introduction," p. xxxi.   [9] *Ibid.*

[10] Marianne Bastid, "The Structure of the Financial Institutions of the State in the Late Qing," in Schram, ed., *The Scope of State Power in China*, p. 51.

[11] *Ibid.*

was no such thing as a strict financial system or domain, nor was there even an economic function as we understand it in the West, although a Board of Revenue had existed since the seventh century. At the close of the nineteenth century there was no separate, specialized administration responsible for the overall management of public finance, from the central to the local levels. In traditional China, the Board of Revenue, equivalent to the Ministry of Finance in the West, had functions that were not directly related to financial management: According to Bastid, "the role of the Board of Revenue in matters for trade regulation, forestry protection and sericulture, or even in organizing the agricultural ceremonies performed by the emperor at the beginning of each year, is more that of a Ministry of Trade or Agriculture than that of Ministry of Finance."[12] As we will see in later chapters, despite drastic changes in modern times, the Ministry of Finance in contemporary China is far less important than its counterparts in the West; it remains purely a tool of the party-state and is subject to its overriding political agenda.

The *jingji* philosophy also affected the nature of China's legal system. Since the state is dominant over its subjects, it never plays the role of arbiter between the different parties. Its laws do not have as their aim the distribution of rights or powers (legislative, executive, and judicial); nor do they seek to provide a framework for the settlement of litigation. These are precisely the functions of law in the West. China's criminal law and administrative regulations are dominant, but because of the operation of other mechanisms already described, even these types of legislation play only a subordinate role – far less important, in the final analysis, than penal or civil law in the West. One can understand why the limitation of the sovereign's rights – so fundamental an aspect of the system of constitutional monarchies in the Western perspective –was not understood in China at the time of the reform attempts toward the end of the Qing Empire in 1905–1908. In the modern age, China sought to learn from the West. However, the imitation of Western institutions was inspired by the desire to copy aspects leading to the success of the West. China was concerned with the means for "enriching the state and strengthening the army" (*fuguo qiangbing*) or procedures to more effectively discover the state of mind of the population. In this context, at the end of the nineteenth and the beginning of the twentieth centuries, Japan was regarded by the Chinese as the most exemplary model. If Japan had become a powerful

---

[12] *Ibid.*, p. 52.

state, this was because it had copied Western institutions, not as an end in itself but as the secret of success. As we will discuss in later chapters, this mindset has not drastically changed in contemporary China.

DISCOURSES ON THE STATE AND THE ECONOMY IN IMPERIAL CHINA

China did not develop a discipline of economics and economic theories like that in the West. There was no theoretical framework available to explain the economic role of the state and the market. This does not mean, however, that China did not have its own economics. In fact, up to the Qin and Han dynasties, China had developed sophisticated methods of economic thinking based on rich experience in all aspects of political-economic life. Since this study is not a history of Chinese political economy thought, we will not provide a systematic survey of China's political thinking; nor will we discuss the economic thought of any individual writer. Instead, we choose to focus on Chinese discourses on the role of the state and the market in economic affairs. But even having narrowed our focus to this subject, it remains unlikely that we can cover such a huge amount of literature. The main document we will discuss in this chapter is *Discourses on Salt and Iron (Yantie lun)*, a document which recorded a large-scale debate on state control of commerce and industry in the Han dynasty.[13] We will also include other relevant writings of that period.

We select this literature for several reasons. First, *Discourses on Salt and Iron* represents the basic political economy arguments during the period in which China's political economy system was formed. In the several thousand years that followed, dynastic changes took place, but there was no significant change in the main themes of China's political economy system as discussed in the text. Second, this document sets out most of the basic arguments and policy proposals regarding the market, the state, and relations between the two from both the Confucian and the Legalist schools. Since the document summarizes the debate, it can be seen to reflect the views held by that generation of key government officials and scholars, and their views on the economic and policy practices of the Qin and the early Han (221–87 BC). Third, most of the key concepts raised and discussed by Confucians and Legalists in this debate also appeared in

---

[13] All citations are from *Discourses on Salt and Iron: A Debate on State Control of Commerce and Industry in Ancient China*, translated from the Chinese of Huan Kuan with Introduction and Notes by Esson M. Gale (Taipei: Ch'eng-Wen Publishing Company, 1967).

the field of modern economics in the West. This enables us to see the differences between Chinese economic thinkers and policy makers and their counterparts in the West. The main problem is that neither Confucians nor Legalists were the kind of professional economists we have seen in the West, and neither formulated any economic theories. However, they often cited cases – that is, their empirical evidence – to support their arguments. This is not dissimilar from what many professional economists in the West did. While it is difficult to identify the author of a specific argument here, this does not matter, since we are only interested in their thinking in terms of economic affairs. Fourth, the issues raised and discussed in the debate reflect real economic life. The focus on real economic life made this debate the most valuable. Participants were not reasoning at an abstract level, but attempting to find the roots of the economic problems that they observed, and their solutions. Indeed, all the key issues discussed in the document have remained consistent from the early dynasties to this day. We believe that it remains the best work on the political economy of China and represents the strongest indigenous Chinese economic thinking.

Compiled by Huan Kuan, a Confucian participant in the Iron and Salt Conference, the *Discourse* reflects vividly the economic, political, and geopolitical choices of the former Han Empire at the crossroads of history. The Conference was held in the fifth year (82 BC–81 BC) after the death of the legendary Emperor Wu of Han (r. 141 BC–87 BC), whose mixed legacy included an expanded imperial state and a society exhausted by decades of war. There were two important historical contexts to the book, one immediate and one *longue durée*.

In the preceding four decades, the Han Imperial Army, under Emperor Wu's capable generals, had expanded the imperial territory in all directions, especially in the North and Northwest, through several punitive campaigns against the powerful Xiongnu Empire, a nomadic state controlling the steppes in Central and North Asia. Although not all campaigns were military successes, the incessant expeditions reversed a century-long trend of nomadic invasions, stalled the Xiongnu expansions into China proper, devastated that empire's state and economy, and secured Han dominance in North and Northwest China. Decades of campaigns required the imperial state to broaden its fiscal base, an objective that Emperor Wu accomplished through such radical means as confiscatory wealth taxes on the rich and a state monopoly on salt and iron. The Legalists were both the planners of these policies and their loyal executive agents.

In the preceding three to four hundred years, North and Central China experienced a period of interstate war known as the Warring States (479–221 BC), during which a succession of total wars between seven states ended with the rise of China's – and arguably the world's – first, albeit shortlived, centralizing state in present-day China proper, the Qin (221–207 BC).[14] During its short reign, the Qin employed the mobilization model developed during the Warring States period in its wars of imperial expansion and its great engineering projects such as the Great Wall and the Mausoleum of the First Emperor. Ironically, this weakened its popular mandate and led to rebellions. The collapse of Qin was both precipitated and followed by a short but intensive period of civil war, culminating in the Han victory in 202 BC. The first Han emperors (r. 202–141 BC), learning from the Qin failure and facing a war-torn economy and society, opted for a *laissez-faire* approach to the economy domestically and a pacifist and defensive stance against the Xiongnu, until Emperor Wu reversed both strategies.

On the eve of the debate on iron and salt held in 81 BC, China had gone through two cycles of state-building: a long cycle during the Warring States and a short cycle during the reign of Emperor Wu. This is the period in which the Confucian–Legalist state took shape, when Confucian scholars began to take a leading position in the state bureaucracy, which in turn was built following the Legalist thinking of the total war.[15] The debate reflected a political situation in which a second mobilization was no longer sustainable and the centralizing state built by the deceased emperor and still guarded by his Legalist lieutenants faced severe challenges from strong local and private interests and their Confucian spokesmen.[16]

---

[14] For a short political analysis of this state-building process as the first in world history, see Francis Fukuyama, *The Origin of Political Order: From Prehuman Times to the French Revolution* (New York, NY: Farrar, Straus and Giroux, 2012), pp. 111–124.

[15] Zhao Dingxin, *Confucian-Legalist State: A New Theory of Chinese History* (New York, NY: Oxford University Press, 2015), p. 239.

[16] For the political background and the issues at stake at the Iron and Salt Conference, see Michael Loewe, "The Former Han Dynasty," in John K. Fairbank and Denis Twitchett, eds., *The Cambridge History of China* vol. 1: The Chin and Han Empires, 221 BC–AD 220 (Cambridge and New York, NY: Cambridge University Press, 1986), pp. 179–190. Examining the conference against its political contexts, Loewe rightly points out its historical significance: It demonstrates that totalitarianism based on the so-called Legalists, which we define as a statist approach, could never be sufficient to govern a large state such as the Han Empire. In a few decades' time the balance would tilt towards Confucianism; it became common to blend Legalist statecrafts with Confucian approaches, as demonstrated by the policy of the succeeding Emperor Xuan of Han

Given the historical context, the terms of the debate between these two schools were more practical than ideological. In other words, both sides attempted to present their arguments not in normative but in positive terms, and drew on their technical knowledge and empirical evidence from economic practice from the Warring States period to the Han dynasty. It is also worth noting that compared to Confucian scholars, who tended to focus on principles, the Legalists focused more on the operational side. This is understandable given that the former came largely from the scholarly community and the latter from the government. The Legalists accused the Confucian scholars of having an unfeasible argument, as reflected in the following paragraph:

We have now "Confucianists by profession" who ... concentrate on learning to discourse on matters unproven and unprovable, wasting day after day consuming valuable time, without contributing in the least to actual working problems.[17]

It is unfair to say that the Confucian scholars conducted their reasoning purely on principle and in a normative sense, since they also frequently presented their arguments based on their observations of the real economic world and attempted to influence the functioning of the real political-economic world. The key difference between the Legalists and Confucian scholars is that the former perceived the issue from the perspective of the ruler and the latter from the perspective of social elites. In the following discussion, we frequently cite the *Yantie lun* at length, for two reasons. First, China's classical economic thinking is often unduly ignored in the context of modern political economy analysis, and a detailed discussion will benefit contemporary readers. Second, by comparing different views on key economic subjects between the Legalist and the Confucian schools, we will provide a contextual background for our generalization of classical Chinese economic thinking – namely, two concepts of the market – which we discuss in the following section.

The debate was organized in line with two key pairs of concepts, namely, production and distribution, state and market. In general terms, the Legalist school emphasized the problem of production and the role of the state in production, while the Confucian school stressed the problem of distribution and the role of the market in distribution.

(r. 74–49 BC). This continued not just in the Han dynasty but also in future empires centered on China proper.

[17] *Ibid.*, pp. 74–75.

Production vs. Distribution

The first pair of concepts in classical Chinese economic thinking is production and distribution. During the Warring States period, different states
developed very different models of economic development in their
attempts to achieve great power status. Policy makers and scholars were
able to observe the differences between these models and their practical
efficacy. During this period, the two main schools – namely, the school of
law, or Legalists, and the Confucian school – were formed. The former was
dominant in the courts of many dominant powers, especially the Qin
state; the latter, articulated by Confucians, remained outside the court.[18]
Within the Legalist school, there were two branches of thought. The
agrarian branch, represented by the *Shang-jun-shu*, stressed the importance of agriculture. The commercial branch, represented by some parts of
the *Guanzi*, laid more emphasis on commerce, particularly the currency
and trade of grain. For the Legalists, the consumption of goods was to be
encouraged as a means of distribution of wealth and to keep the economy
active. Chinese historian Yang Lien-sheng found evidence in the *Guanzi*,
Yantie lun, and *Xunzi* for this active view of the state and showed how
this economic principle was put forward. According to this principle, the
consumption of luxury articles, the brisk circulation of goods, and the
custom of extravagant funerals would all lead to fuller employment, and
the luxurious fashions of the rich would provide work and a livelihood
for the poor. This principle also served as an economic justification for
spending.[19]

Another school, represented by Mo Di, also emphasized production. But
here the concept of production was connected with consumption. For this

---

[18] This by no means suggests that there were only these two schools. Both the Moist School
and the proto-Daoist Huang-Lao School were important at this time, but in the long run
they became less determinant of the Chinese tradition of economic thinking, as the
essential elements of the pre-Qin Moist and Huang-Lao schools were absorbed into
Confucian and Legalist schools. Also, there was no such categorical distinction between
Legalistic and Confucian schools at this formative stage, as is clear from the Salt and Iron
Conference. In fact, Xunzi, a leading Confucian in the fourth century BC, developed a
syncretic theory of statecraft based on rituals and law and made a significant contribution
to legalistic thinking through his disciple, the legalist theorist Han Fei, and the statesman
Li Si. See Zhao Jing, "Fu Guo Xue and the 'Economics' of Ancient China" in Cheng Li,
Terry Peach, and Wang Fang, eds., *The History of Ancient Chinese Economic Thought*
(London and New York, NY: Routledge, 2014), pp. 73–74.

[19] Yang Lien-sheng, "Economic Justification for Spending – An Uncommon Idea in Traditional China," *Harvard Journal of Asiatic Studies* 20 (1957), pp. 36–52.

school, regulated consumption meant equal production. Scholars thus attacked unregulated consumption such as the observance of funeral rites, the performance of music, and aggressive warfare. For this school, indulgence in extravagant luxury was a mark of poor government and social imbalance. It maintained the theory that by manufacturing necessities, to the exclusion of luxuries, the productivity of a nation would increase. This school was not overly historically significant, partly due to the religiosity of its thinking and partly due to the unfeasibility, in reality, of making people consume less.

By contrast, the Confucian economists emphasized distribution. The key word for this school is "equality," or *jun*. Confucius said, "The ruler of a kingdom or the chief of a house is not concerned about his people being few, but about lack of equitable treatment."[20] The idea is to stress the problem of distribution. The Confucian school also considered the problems of production and consumption. The *Da Xue* (Great Learning), a classic text of the Confucian school, says: "Let the producers be many and the consumers few. Let there be activity in the production, and economy in the expenditure. Then the wealth will always be sufficient."[21]

State vs. Market

For the Legalist school, the question is how production can be maximized; for the Confucian scholars, it is how harmony can be achieved through distributive arrangements. To achieve their goals, the former emphasized the role of the state and the latter that of the market. According to the Legalist school, to maximize production is to achieve its economic policy goal, as expressed in the text: "I can expand the territory and enrich the treasury for the Prince."[22] As a matter of fact, this is also the goal pursued by modern Chinese nationalists such as Yan Fu and Liang Qichao – "rich nation and strong army" (*fuguo qiangbing*).[23] For the Legalists, all economic policies should be able to contribute to the wealth of the nation. The question then is not whether the economy is for the state, but how the state can make use of its economy as a tool to achieve its own goal.

---

[20] Cited in "Introduction," *Discourses on Salt and Iron*, p. XXIII.   [21] *Ibid.*   [22] *Ibid.*
[23] John Fitzgerald, *Awakening China: Politics, Culture, and Class in the Nationalist Revolution* (Stanford, CA: Stanford University Press, 1996); and Yongnian Zheng, *Discovering Chinese Nationalism in China: Modernization, Identity, and International Relations* (Cambridge and New York, NY: Cambridge University Press, 1999).

How could the economy serve as a tool for the state? Both the Confucians and the Legalists divided the economy into primary and secondary sectors. The primary sector included agriculture and sericulture; the secondary sector mining, manufacture, and commerce. While both agreed to place an emphasis on the primary sector, they also realized that the two sectors were interdependent and there was a division of labor between the two. The Confucians, particularly Mencius, knew that the various occupations of mankind cannot be undertaken in isolation. For instance, efficient agriculture depended on the provision of iron-made tools, and this derived from the product of the mines and was distributed by merchants. Similarly, conscript or hired workers in the mines required and deserved the products of the farm, and merchants had to be able to concentrate their energies on the distribution of goods without needing to expend effort on fieldwork. In China's traditional vision of social order, the whole society was divided into four classes: scholar, farmer, artisan, and merchant. There was a clear division of labor among these four classes, although they were interdependent in the production of wealth and social order.[24] Therefore, the question for both the Confucians and Legalists was the proportionate effort suitable for these different occupations. Since those who were engaged in industry or commerce handled money and had greater opportunities to benefit, many chose to flee the countryside for the towns, in the hope of acquiring wealth more quickly than would be the case with the drudgery of the fields. As a result, while private fortunes might accumulate, the real wealth of the nation would dwindle.

What then was the solution? According to the Legalist school, the state, not the private sector, must play a dominant role in controlling and regulating economic activities. The Legalists did not believe that the private sector could play a positive role in maximizing production; by contrast, they held that the evils resulting from powerful combinations of interests were due to private manipulation of money and grain prices. For the Legalists, public wealth was of much greater importance than private wealth. To prevent private competition and the resultant inequality of wealth among the people, the Legalists proposed what may be termed "nationalization of capital," and the undertaking of production and trade by the state. They believed that certain occupations in industry and commerce, which were categorized as "inessential" or secondary, would simply lead to private gain, at the expense of the people and to the

---

[24] Michael Loewe, "Attempts at Economic Co-ordination during the Western Han Dynasty," in Schram, ed., *The Scope of State Power in China*, pp. 244–245.

detriment of the commonwealth. The Legalist school thus advocated nationalization of key industries such as the salt and iron industries as a source of public revenues.

Regarding land ownership, the Legalists tended to view land primarily as a source of revenues. So long as more land was potentially available than there was labor to work on it, those who wished to increase the wealth and strength of the empire could see no reason why a limit should be imposed on the extent of an individual's holdings, for the wider the extent of the land possessed and worked by individual owners, the greater the revenue that would accrue to the imperial treasury.

For the Legalist school, national security (defense) and market regulations were the two fundamental reasons for the introduction of state administration of essential commodities and state monopolies in key industries. According to them, the wealth of salt and iron available from remote mountains and lonely marshes could be exploited only by rich and aggressive individuals. Possession of the mountains' resources meant the rapid accumulation of wealth, first by coinage of money, and second by the manufacture of arms. In preindustrial China, the salt and iron industry were highly profitable and required considerable capital outlays and mobilization of labor. Furthermore, private enterprises could mobilize the market potential of these sectors, and engaged in potentially seditious activities. For this reason, state monopolies had to be introduced and established. These measures aimed to centralize financial power in the imperial government as against overpowerful nobles, on the one hand, while on the other preventing the exploitation of the poor by the rich.[25]

It is important to note that while the Legalist school stressed the role of the state, it did not deny the ground for the existence of the market. For Legalists, the purpose of the market is to maximize production for the state. In their view, the market must be regulated by the state, and cannot and should not be operated based on free exchange among market participants. The Legalists were indeed very innovative in discovering (and practicing) mechanisms or technologies via which the state could exercise its power over and govern the market. For instance, they designed a system to "equalize distribution" (*junshu*), or offer equable marketing; its functionaries were to regulate commercial transactions throughout the empire. Their duty appears to have been to purchase staple commodities when cheap and sell them when dear, thus preventing

[25] *Discourses on Salt and Iron*, pp. 30–33.

prices from becoming too low or excessively high. The Legalists argued
that a bureau of "equalization and standardization" (*pingzhun*) to regulate the system of equable marketing should be set up to achieve this goal.
According to the Legalist school:

The true King should restrict and regulate tax-barriers and markets; in his hand
lies the power of adjusting the balance of trade and in his keeping, is the right
utilization of the seasons; for through his control of the ratio of production he can
curb the people. In years of abundance with harvest tall, he stores and bins to
provide for times of scarcity and want; in evil years of dearth he circulates moneys
and goods and tempers the flow of surplus to meet the deficiency . . . It was entirely
due to the stores accumulated through the system of equable marketing and the
hoard in public granaries that the troops were provided for and the distressed
people succored. Thus, the goods of equable marketing and the capital of the
Treasury are not for the purpose of exploiting the people or solely for military uses,
but also for the relief of the needy and as recourse against flood and drought.[26]

By contrast, the Confucian school appreciated the role played by the
market. The Confucian scholars purported to concern themselves primarily with the "people's economy" or the people's livelihood. They believed
that if the problem of the people's economy were solved, the political
or fiscal regimen would take care of itself. According to Confucius: "if
the people enjoy plenty, with whom will the Prince share want? But if
the people are in want, with whom will the Prince share plenty?"[27] The
Confucians thus strongly condemned the Legalist school and its policy of
"enriching the state." They believed that concentration of wealth in the
hands of the state would discourage individual economic initiative. The
Confucians regarded the Legalist financiers as "money grabbers," or "small
men."[28] While the Legalist school did not distinctly differentiate the state
from individual rulers, the Confucians tended to view the state as separable
from the rulers. While the Confucians did not oppose a strong state, they
were concerned that self-interested rulers would grab money from the
people in the name of the state. Thus they placed overwhelming emphasis
on the role of individual initiative, and argued that the state should not
adopt a policy of interference in individual economic activities. For the
Confucian school, the function of the government was to remove all
obstacles to the productivity of labor, or to equality in the distribution of
wealth. The rest would be left to the people. While practical statesmen
responsible for financing an extravagant government sought to control the

[26] *Ibid.*, p. 12.   [27] Cited in "Introduction," *Discourses on Salt and Iron*, p. XXIII.
[28] *Ibid.*

profits of industry and commerce for the benefit of the public exchequer, Confucianism, as represented in the writings of Mencius, called for a *laissez-faire* policy, government by remote influence, and the impressive but inactive "virtue" of the ruler.

Within this conceptual framework, the Confucians opposed the state monopoly in the production of iron and salt, the imposition of the wine tax, and the system of equable marketing, or equalized or balanced transportation. They believed that monopolies would prevent individuals from engaging in private enterprise. All these economic activities on the part of the state meant the state was in competition with people in commerce, and thus created an atmosphere of greed and extravagance among the people, leading them away from essential (agriculture) pursuits to nonessential (commercial) enterprises.[29] Moreover, the Confucians were in favor of state control of land distribution. They believed that the duty of the emperor lay principally in alleviating popular hardship while securing stable fiscal income from land tax. They observed the growing disparities between the rich landowners, with their large properties, and the living conditions of the very poor peasantry. The Confucian school was also suspicious about the argument of national defense presented by the Legalists. It refuted the effectiveness of the grandiose military display and advocated pacifying other races or peoples through the all-rewarding influence of a benevolent rule. According to Confucian scholars, "if one desired to find the way to pacify the people and enrich the country, one would find it in a return to the fundamental; for when the fundamental is established, the way comes of itself."[30]

Technologies (Mechanisms) to Maximize Production

The Legalist school, while stressing the role of the state, also regarded the market as an integral aspect of the process of production. The Legalists discovered the virtue of the market in maximizing production, and provided strong justification as to why the state must play a crucial role in facilitating the market, on one hand, and regulating it, on the other. The maximization of wealth was not only a good in itself; more importantly, it was the necessary condition for the building of state power, especially military might.

---

[29] *Ibid.*, pp. 13–17.   [30] *Discourses on Salt and Iron*, p. 77.

Division of Labor and the Market

First of all, to maximize production, the government has to be open to "both fundamental and branch industries," and to facilitate equitable distribution of goods. A system of division of labor is the key to maximize production. Without state intervention, the market alone will not be able to establish a system of division of labor and will not function to meet the demands of the state and the people. Evidences are ample: "a country may possess a wealth of fertile land and yet its people may be underfed – the reason lying in lack of an adequate supply of agricultural implements. It may possess rich natural resources in its mountains and seas and yet the people may be deficient in wealth – the reason being in the insufficient number of artisans and merchants."[31]

The state therefore must be proactive in establishing the market to facilitate exchange among different products from different fields of production. According to the Legalists,

Markets and courts were provided to harmonize various demands; there people of all classes gathered together and all goods collected, so that farmer, merchant, and worker could each obtain what he desired; the exchange competed, everyone went back to his occupation. Facilitate exchange so that the people will be unflagging in industry ... Thus without artisans, the farmers will be deprived of the use of implements; without merchants, all prized commodities will be cut off. The former would lead to stoppage of grain production, the latter to exhaustion of wealth. It is clear that the salt and iron monopoly and equable marketing are really intended for the circulation of amassed wealth and the regulation of the consumption according to the urgency of the need.[32]

Transportation and Circulation of Goods

Both the Legalists and the Confucians regarded commerce as one of the secondary occupations, but their attitudes toward commerce were radically different. The Confucians believed that the growth of mercantile fortunes detracted from the wealth of the empire, while the Legalists contended that trade had a specific part to play in the economy if the organ of government took the profits. Different views on commerce led to their different attitudes toward transportation.

Among the Legalists, Sang Hongyang argued that trade and the circulation of goods formed an integral part of the universal order, and for this reason, it was a recognizable duty of a sovereign to promote the

---

[31] *Ibid.*, pp. 5–6.   [32] *Ibid.*, p. 6.

distribution of goods across the empire.[33] The Legalist school believed that the state must provide a sound transportation infrastructure for the flow of products and goods. While people depend on merchants for their distribution and on artisans to give them their finished form, the state must facilitate this process. The Legalist school argued that

this is why the Sages availed them of boats and bridges to negotiate rivers and gullies, and domesticated cattle and horses for travel over mountains and plateaus. Thus by penetrating to distant lands and exploring remote places, they were able to exchange all goods to the benefit of the people. The salt and iron monopoly and the equable marketing supported by the myriad people and looked to as the source of supply, cannot conveniently be abolished.[34]

Importantly, a sound transportation infrastructure will empower both the state and the people. According to the Legalists,

Formerly the Princes in the provinces and the demesnes sent in their respective products as tribute. The transportation was vexatious and disorganized; the goods were usually of distressingly bad quality, often failing to repay their transport costs. Therefore, Transportation Officers have been provided in every province to assist in the delivery and transportation and for the speeding of the tribute from distant parts. So the system came to be known as equable marketing. A Receiving Bureau has been established at the capital to monopolize all the commodities, buying when prices are low, and selling when prices are high, with the result that the government suffers no loss and the merchants cannot speculate for profit. This is therefore known as the balancing standard. With the balancing standard people are safeguarded from unemployment; with the equable marketing people have evenly distributed labor. Both measures are intended to equilibrate all goods and convenience the people, and not to open the way to profit and provide a ladder to popular misdemeanor.[35]

In contrast to the state-centered view, the Confucian school believed that a country possesses a wealth of fertile land and yet its people are underfed because merchants and workers prosper unduly while the fundamental occupations are neglected. That a country possesses rich natural resources in its mountains and seas and yet its people lack capital is because the people's necessities have not been attended to, while luxuries and fancy articles have multiplied. The Confucian scholars thus saw the negative impacts of the system of division of labor and overconsumption on the part of the rich. More importantly, they pointed out, just as Marxist

---

[33] J. L. Kroll, "Toward a Study of the Economic Views of Sang Hung-Yang," *Early China* 4 (1978–1979), pp. 11–18.

[34] *Discourses on Salt and Iron*, p. 6.   [35] *Ibid.*, pp. 9–10.

economists would argue, that the self-interested ruling class makes economic policies for their own benefit:

What if the ruling classes should pursue profit themselves? ... when the princes take delight in profit, the ministers become mean; when the ministers become means, the minor officers become greedy, the people become thieves. Thus, to open the way for profit is to provide a ladder to popular misdemeanor.[36]

For the Confucians, the consequences of state intervention may be the exact opposite to what was expected by the Legalist school. When the government leaves alone what the people have most of and exacts from them what they have least of, the people are forced to sell their products at a cheap price to satisfy these demands from above.

In addition to the system of division of labor, the Legalists also tended to emphasize market exchange. They observed: "Where products abound, the people multiply; when the house is near the market, the family will get rich. Getting rich depends on 'methods' and 'statistical calculation,' not on hard manual labor; profits depend on 'circumstances,' not on strenuous farming."[37]

The Confucian school also emphasized the role of the market. However, it is not a market manipulated by the state, but a naturally developed or, in today's terms, *laissez-faire* market that will bring about prosperity and stability. For Confucians, a state-manipulated market could undermine the natural process of production by providing people with the "wrong" incentives. Mencius had envisioned such a market:

Mencius says that if the seasons of husbandry are not distributed there will be more grain than can be eaten. If silks worms and hemp are raised according to the seasons, cloth and silk will be more than what is required for wear. If the axes and bills enter the forest according to season, the timber supply will be more than the demand. Hunting and fishing according to season, fish and game will be more than can be eaten. If you do not do all these things according to the seasons, and on the other hand, you decorate the palaces and dwelling houses, and raise terraces and arbors higher and higher, and if carpenters and mechanics carve the large into the small, the round into the square, so as to represent clouds and mists above and mountains and forests below, then there will not be enough timber for use. If the men folk abandon the fundamental in favor of the nonessential, carving and engraving in imitation of the forms of animals, exhausting the possibilities of manipulation of materials, then there will not be enough grain for consumption.[38]

---

[36] *Ibid.*, p. 8.   [37] *Ibid.*, p. 18.   [38] *Ibid.*, pp. 23–24.

Territorial Expansion and Undeveloped Wealth

Legalist and Confucian scholars also disagreed with each other on how to increase wealth by territorial expansion. The Legalist school pointed to the importance of increasing national wealth by expanding territories. According to the Legalists,

the provinces of the interior, with a great population, where the water supply is not adjusted to fodder-growing requirements, with climate warm and damp, are not suited to raising horses and cattle. When farming, people trudge wearily behind the plough; and when walking, they carry their loads on their backs or on poles. They wear out their strength and still obtain little results. Thus the common people have suffered great hardships, insufficiently provided even with clothing and food. Old men and children have been forced to carry burdens and pull carts on the highways, and even ministers and high officials often rode in ox-carts.[39]

For the Legalists, in order to solve problems such as these, the state has to play an important role in developing unexplored territories.

By contrast, the Confucians are not so interested in exploring undeveloped territories, especially in peripheral areas. They are more cautious about the use of state power to expand taxable land. According to this point of view,

the principle of administration lies in proceeding from the center to the periphery, beginning from the near. Only after those near at hand have attached themselves submissively to the government, steps may then be taken to rally the distant. After the people within are contented, then care will be taken of those afar.[40]

Technologies (Mechanisms) to Dominate the Market

For the Legalist school, to regulate the market is to maximize production and state power. It is also to establish mechanisms which enable the state to dominate the market. The main mechanisms they proposed and, indeed, practiced included money and currency, land, and production ratios.

Money and Credit

The Legalists and Confucians disagreed with each other on both the role of money and credit in the economy, and who should control money and currency. In general, the Confucian school argued that coinage did not necessarily make for a just and happy society, and they were against a

[39] *Ibid.*, p. 92.   [40] *Ibid.*, p. 100.

monetary economy. This is because they believed that a centrally minted coinage, as with the state monopoly in the salt and iron industries, would involve the use of excessive conscript manpower, and thus lead to a failure to work productively in the fields and the risk of starvation. On the other hand, the Legalists regarded centralized control and a monopoly over minting as a means of balancing prices and equalizing distribution. The Legalists wanted the government to use money as a means of circulating goods and relieving distress.

For the Legalists, money and currency were effective mechanisms for the government to maintain its domination of the market and to govern the people. According to their observations:

That the exchange of money and the circulation of commodities do not advantage the people is because goods have been monopolized (by private hands). Even when taking thought for the fundamental and weighing the non-essential, that the people still starve, is because grain is hoarded. The clever are able to utilize the labor of a hundred men, the simple cannot even repay themselves for their own labor. Should the rulers not adjust wealth evenly, there will be among the people property interests mutually detrimental. Thus it is that some accumulate a sufficiency for a hundred years while others are obliged to rest content with husks and chaff. When people are too wealthy they cannot be controlled through salaries; authority will be insufficient to impose penalties upon them. These inequalities cannot be removed except by relieving congestion and evening profit. Therefore the ruler must first accumulate the people's good, conserve their consumption, regulate their surplus, ease their lack, prohibit undue gains and check the source of profit making. Only then will the common people be able to provide for their homes and the needs of every individual be supplied.[41]

On the other hand, the Confucians were skeptical about the role played by money and currency in economic activities. This is largely because they strongly opposed the state monopoly over goods and preferred a natural market, namely, a market not promoted by the state. According to them,

since the gentlemen in office turn their back on honor and scramble for wealth, the big and little devour and overthrow one another by turns. This is the reason that some have a sufficiency for a hundred years and others nothing to fill their emptiness or cover their forms. These who held office in ancient times did not farm; those who tilled did not fish; the gatemen and the watchmen had each their permanent stations and did not attempt to double their income or corner good. In this manner the simple and the clever labored without undermining each other. That is to say, there was no monopoly of goods.[42]

---

[41] *Ibid.*, pp. 25–26.   [42] *Ibid.*, p. 26.

For the Confucians, a natural market was ideal, since at this level of market exchange there is limited use of money and credit, which they believed to be a necessary evil, but one to be checked at all costs.[43] According to them,

the Ancients had markets but no coinage; each exchanged that which he had for that which he lacked, packed his cloth and peddled his silk. Later generations have used tortoise shells and metal currencies, knife coins and cloth as a medium of exchange. But as currency has frequently changed, the people have become increasingly dishonest. Now to correct dishonesty one must resort to simplicity and to prevent mistakes one must fall back upon propriety.[44]

While the Legalists did not deny these negative consequences, they emphasized that new institutions had to be invented to control them. They argued:

When social habits decay they must be met by new laws, nor is this an intentional departure from the Ancients, but in order to correct mistakes and arrest decline. Administration must adjust itself to society, and currency changes with the generation. If there be no interdiction on coinage, the counterfeit will circulate with the genuine. If the officials and the rich vie with one another in extravagance, the lower classes will devote themselves to gain, and thus the two will undermine one another.[45]

Surplus Products
The Legalists also emphasized the role of government control over surplus products and believed that there would be a high political cost if they were in the hands of the private sector. They observed:

The King of Wu (a rebel prince who nearly brought down the Han dynasty) took sole control of the surplus products of the mountains and marshes, taxed his people lightly and gave doles to the poor and humble. Thus he established his personal prestige; when his personal prestige was increased, his heart was moved to rebellion. Thus you see if you do not stop the source early and only worry about

---

[43] This Confucian vs. Legalist debate on the founding of the Chinese empire was much like the Anti-Federalist (later Republicans) vs. Federalist debate about important policy issues like state bank and national debt on the founding of the United States. It is also possible to make a case regarding similar parallels, with Confucian and Legalist concepts of the national polity as less (anti-Federalist) or more centralized (federalist). For the early American case, see George William Van Cleve, "The Anti-Federalist's Toughest Challenge: Paper Money, National Debt, and the Ratification of the Constitution," *Journal of the Early Republic* 34:4 (2014), pp. 529–560.

[44] *Discourses on Salt and Iron*, pp. 27–28.   [45] *Ibid.*, p. 27.

the outcome, the damage will be very great. One family would harm a hundred families, a hundred families would harm the nobles, and the nobles would harm the rule of the Empire. This is why the prohibitory laws are made to prevent it. Now give the people free rein to strive after power and profit and to end the salt and iron monopoly would be to give the advantage to the overbearing and aggressive in the pursuit of their covetous practices. All the evil-minded would come together, cliques would become parties – for the aggressive if not constantly curbed are ungovernable – and combines of disorderly persons would take form.[46]

The Legalists thus placed overwhelming emphasis on the role of law in deterring people's criminal behavior:

Formerly when the Lord of Shang was Chancellor of Ch'in he pursued in internal affairs the policy putting the laws and regulations on a firm basis, of making punishments and penalties harsh and severe, and of ordering government and education. In this no mercy was shown to the criminals and the cheats. In his external policy he managed to obtain profits of a hundred fold and collected taxes on mountains and marshes. The state became rich, the people, strong; weapons and implements were kept ready, complete in every detail, and grain-stores had a surplus. As a result of these measures he was able to wage war on enemy countries, to conquer foreign states, to annex new lands, and to extend wide his territories, without overtaxing the people for the support for the army. The profits derived from the salt and iron monopolies serve sufficient funds for the upkeep of military forces. These measures emphasize conservation and storing up in order to provide for times of scarcity and want. The beneficiaries are many; the state profits thereby and no harm is caused to the masses.[47]

The Legalist school argued that iron implements and soldiers' weapons were important in the service of the empire and should not be made the gainful business of everybody. While the Legalist school saw evil in the private control of production surpluses, the Confucianists saw the same consequence regarding state control. They pointed out that the Legalist school failed to see who benefits from state control and who is disadvantaged by it. According to the Confucians:

Profit does not fall from Heaven, nor does it spring from the Earth; it is derived entirely from the people ... Shang Yang made heavy punishments and harsh laws the foundation of the Ch'in state, and within two generations Ch'in lost the Empire. Not satisfied with the already severe and inhuman laws, he created also the system of mutual responsibility, devised an organization of spying and accusation and increased bodily punishments. The people were terrorized, not knowing even where to place their hands and feet. Not satisfied with the already exacting and numerous taxes and levies, he established abroad prohibitions on the resources of the mountains and seas and set up a hundredfold profit in the interior, while the

[46] *Ibid.*, pp. 30–31.   [47] *Ibid.*, pp. 40–41.

people had no means to express their opinion. The worship of profit and neglect of rectitude, the high regard for might and emphasis on merit, resulted indeed in extension of territory and acquisition of land, but it was just like the case of a man suffering from dropsy and being given water which only increases his illness.[48]

The Ratio of Production

For the Legalists, controlling the ratio of production is another mechanism with which to regulate and control the market. Needless to say, the Legalists placed this in the context of the government's relationship with the people. According to the Legalists:

[The government] has put salt and iron under unified control, developed the profits from mountains and seas, so that the production of goods is on the increase. Thus the government has ample and rich revenues, and people suffer no distress or need. Both the fundamental and the secondary industries are benefited, and all classes are well provided for. All this has been achieved by budgeting and accounting, not by concentrating on the rural occupations, the cultivation of mulberries and grain fields, alone. With powerful recalcitrants among the nation, the common people's livelihood declines. The principle of governing a country consists in removing the noxious and hoeing out the unruly. Only then will the people enjoy equal treatment, and find satisfaction under their own roofs ... [Therefore] the strong could not take advantage of the weak, and the many could not ill-treat the few. The resources of salt and iron are monopolized in order to put down the rich traders and big merchants. Offices are offered for sale and criminals may buy themselves off, thus taking from those who have, to aid the needy, in the interest of equality among the people. Consequently, in spite of the fact that our armies made expeditions east and west, expenditures were well provided for without increasing the levies and taxes.[49]

For the Confucians, however, the key question is who benefits from such practices. For them, the ruler cannot rely on state monopoly over the economy to govern society. The government should leave the market to perform an important role in economic activities; when the government becomes involved in economic activities, the natural social order will be undermined. According to the Confucianists,

the rulers of ceremonial and the social duties are the foundation of a nation, but the lust for power and profit are the bane of administration ... Now the government desires to subtract from the superabundant to add to the needy. And yet the rich grow richer, and the poor grow poorer. Severe laws and penalties are intended to curb the tyrannical and suppress malefactors. Yet the wicked still persist.[50]

---

[48] *Ibid.*, pp. 41–44.   [49] *Ibid.*, pp. 85–88.   [50] *Ibid.*, pp. 86–88.

Control of the Commons

Another most important mechanism for the government to control the market and society is the control of commons, such as parks and ponds. The Legalists provided a strong justification for such government control:

It is clear that under the small manorial roof the expenses are trifling, in comparison with the great expenditure necessitated by the immense undertaking of ruling the Empire. Herein lies the reason for the government's opening up of parks and ponds, and its concentrating under one hand the mountains and the seas, to secure profits that could be used to supplement tribute and levies. We improve canals and sluices, promotes various kinds of agriculture, extend farm and pasture lands, and develop national reservations. Now you [the Confucianists] desire to abolish all these measures, to stop the fountain of income and the source of revenue, with the result that the people, both high and low, will be in dire need, devoid of means of subsistence. Even though we would like to save effort and cut down expenditure, how can we do it?[51]

The Confucians, however, were strongly against government control of commons. They felt such control was not only unproductive but, more importantly, would disturb the natural order of society: Once a government controls commons, it will seek to satisfy its own greed, and will become predatory. According to the Confucian:

The ancients managed to control land so that it would suffice to nourish the people, and the people would have ample means to satisfy demands from above. With offices superfluous, activities irrelevant, ever-changing fashions for prodigalities and vagaries, those unwarrantedly feeding and clothing at the expense of the government are so numerous that it is no wonder we have deficiency above and poverty and distress blow. Yet the present policy is to strive to make ends meet without making an attempt at rigid economy at the source. All kinds of devices are put up to obtain capital: farming, and rearing of animals are taken up; the government competes with the people in fodder production, and with the merchants in the matter of market profits. Such a policy will never help you to make illustrious the ruler's virtue, or become real gerents of the commonwealth. Now that men should till and women should weave, this is the Great Vocation in the Empire. So the ancients subdivided the land to settle the people, and made farming profitable to give them an occupation; as a result, for every occupation there was a plot of land assigned to the individual, and there were no unemployed in the country. At present we see on the other hand the government opening up national reservations, public ponds, and marshes; but the result is that while the commonwealth enjoys in name the rentals from the dykes, all the profit derived from them reverts to the plutocrats. The Metropolitan District, hemmed in by

---

[51] *Ibid.*, pp. 81–82.

rivers and mountains, is greatly overpopulated. With the people flocking to it from all quarters of the Empire, the supply of grain and fuel falls short; but with the public fields rented out, the mulberries and elms, vegetables and fruits fall in production, and the land is not tilled to full capacity. It is our humble opinion that this was not the purpose of the later Emperor in opening up parks and reservations, ponds and weirs. They could be turned over to the people in return for certain levies; the government should get nothing but rents and taxes. Though lease and tax are different terms, they are identical in substance. With such an arrangement, the male population would exert themselves in working in the southern fields, while the women would spend all their effort in the production of woven goods. With fields and fallows worked to capacity, and the production of linen going at full speed, both rulers and subjects would have plenty, and what deficiency and distress would there be?[52]

TWO CONCEPTS OF THE MARKET

So far we have discussed China's classic economic thinkers' different opinions on several key concepts or key aspects of real economic life. The debate recorded in *Yantie lun* was about the Han dynasty's previous policy of state control of commerce and industry, and by that time, economic thinkers and policy makers had been able to observe the performance of previous state economic policies. The practice of state monopoly had mixed consequences. On the one hand, state monopoly enabled the state to effectively accumulate wealth. Treasury deficits disappeared, adequate stores of grain accumulated in the public granaries, and armies on the frontiers once again received adequate supplies. The country at large, however, seethed with discontent. As the Confucian scholars argued, while the ruler benefited from state monopoly, society became its victim. State control of salt led to high prices, and due to its high cost, people were often forced to eat without the use of salt. The iron implements employed on the farms, as supplied by the government monopoly, were also criticized as inferior and unsuitable. The debate reflected policy conflict between the statesmen and government economists who defended the government's policies, and the Confucian scholars who represented the people and argued for the abolition of state control over essential commodities and a return to the *laissez-faire* system of earlier times.

[52] *Ibid.*, pp. 82–84.

Central to this debate is the relationship between the state and the market. Along these lines, and from the above discussion, we can generalize the practice of Chinese political economy and formulate two different lines of thinking regarding the relationship between the state and the market, that is, two concepts of the market: state domination and market domination. While both Legalists and Confucians recognized the coexistence of the state and the market in the economy, their views differed greatly on the roles of the state and the market: The Legalist school focused on the political economy of state domination, while the Confucian school focused on the political economy of market domination. The political economy of state domination, or economic statism, is characterized by the following features:

(1) The state and the market coexist, with the former dominating the latter.

(2) The rationale for the market's existence is for the state to maximize production.

(3) The state should provide the infrastructure for the market to operate. The state should play an important role in promoting the development of the market, and the private sector is not able to and should not try to perform the task of infrastructural development.

(4) The state should promote a system of division of labor and commercial development, as well as playing a role in facilitating the expansion of the market.

(5) All these efforts, however, are to increase the wealth and power of the state, not that of the people.

(6) Therefore, the state should develop and design different mechanisms to control and dominate the market.

(7) The state should control and monopolize key industries and commerce.

(8) The state should regulate the functioning of the market through various methods.

(9) While the state itself is an operator of the market, it should be able to exercise control over other operators of the market.

(10) The goal of the state is to create and maintain a social order from above. The economy is the tool for the state to serve this ultimate goal.

By contrast, the political economy based on naturally formed market and minimum state intervention has these features:

(1)   The state and the market coexist, with the market dominating society.

(2)   The purpose of the market's existence is to increase the wealth of the people, not the state.

(3)   The market is and should be naturally formed and operated;

(4)   State intervention in the market is evil.

(5)   The state is not an abstract concept, but a self-interested organization; therefore, the purpose of the state is to maximize its interest, not that of the people.

(6)   A *laissez-faire* policy will lead to the greatest productivity; the market, as naturally formed and operated, will play an important role in supporting fair distribution of wealth among the people.

(7)   State measures to promote the development of the market are not necessary, since they are measures through which the state seeks to increase its own interest.

(8)   Therefore, the state (emperor) should rule society symbolically, without substantial penetration of power into society.

(9)   State ideology rather than material interest is important in establishing such a symbolic rule of the state over society.

(10) The state should rule over society without disturbing the naturally formed and spontaneous societal order.

Behind these theoretical formulations, private political and economic interests were also at play at the Confucian–Legalist debate. The Legalists were essentially officials and experts in statecraft who had climbed the ladder of bureaucracy and owed their positions to the centralizing state and a strong emperor. Thus, when they defended the fiscal and strategic interests of the state, this was also in the service of their own interests as agents of the imperial state. In contrast, the Confucians were often from the so-called *jushi* (big clans) or were members of local economic and social elites, since only these elites could afford expensive Confucian education and reproduce their wealth and power through acquisition of the cultural capital involved in studying the Confucian classics and gaining qualifications in the topic. When defending common interests or the people, the Confucians set out their clear preference for a decentralized political and economic order in which the local elites had some leeway over the imperial state and its agents, even at the cost of higher economic inequality. In late imperial China (960–1912), there would be a synthesis of the two elite groups through the Civil Service Examination system, which became the main avenue to bureaucratic service, and a synthesis of the two positions in orthodox neo-Confucian political economy, making radical Legalism and Confucianism extreme positions. While there were certainly a number of radical Confucians who supported state interventions in favor of more egalitarian principles throughout Chinese history, historically they remained a minority rather than a majority voice until well into the modern era, as education expanded to new levels of society. As we shall discuss further in the next chapter, the Confucian view came to predominate, and to define the normality of the premodern Chinese political economy.

Beyond the domain of the state and private interests, there remained the realm of geopolitics. Although geopolitics would only become a key determinant as China entered the modern era, its importance was already evident in the debate between the Confucians and the Legalists. The Confucians were generally supporters of the *Tianxia* vision of imperial polity, which favored means such as culture, trade, or what we now call "soft power" to uphold the hegemonic position of the empire. Under their vision, geopolitics was secondary to domestic order, including economic order. But for the Legalists, geopolitical dominance was essential to the survival of the emperor and economic production was the function of military power necessary for geopolitical dominance. Thus Legalists often appeared to support the aggressive policies of imperial expansion throughout the history of imperial China. But again, the Confucian position was dominant throughout the history of imperial China, especially in the late imperial era, when the imperial state was consolidated and streamlined. This was due to the basic fact that the geopolitical situation for the dominant empires in China proper has largely been stable, except in periods of division such as the Song Empire. The only credible threats to China's geopolitical security, which came from the Central Asia Steppes, posed no fundamental challenge to the Confucian geopolitical vision. This situation remained unchanged until the 1840s, when preindustrial China was challenged by industrial powers that were both militarily and economically superior, the consequences of which we shall discuss in Chapter 4. But until then, geopolitics would remain a second-order issue and the Confucian vision would hold sway.

Formulated during the Qin–Han period, these two concepts of the market (and the state) had long, and lasting, impacts on the imperial governments of different dynasties when they built their fiscal systems and formulated their economic policies. One can argue that the two concepts of the market represented a highly institutionalized economic philosophy and culture, providing an ideological frame for economic thinkers and policy makers from ancient times to the contemporary era. Both state domination and market domination are ideal-types of political economy. Normality is the coexistence of the state and market, with the former dominating the latter. In China's long history, there were few periods in which the power of the state was overwhelmingly dominant; rather, it existed and functioned at different levels over time. While the ideal of China's political economy has always been equilibrium between the state and the market, in which the state allows the market to exist and function while private actors accept its domination, equilibrium can be undermined by either the power of the state or its weakness. We thus call this relationship between the state and the market "asymmetrical equilibrium." The predominance of state power over the market often led to the rise of "economic statism," where the state intervened heavily in the market, or even replaced it. But such state monopoly inevitably undermined the very economic foundation of state power by creating inefficiency, disruption, and at times even chaos in the economic life of empire. To restore equilibrium, the state often retreated to allow the market a more salient role. But this cycle of state expansion and retreat has been a recurring feature of Chinese political economy, from China's earliest centralized empires to the party-state of modern times. Our task is to conceptualize this process of state–market interaction.

Furthermore, as debated by the Legalist and Confucian scholars, political economy is not only about the relationship between the state and the market; more importantly, it is about the people and society. Society is an integral part of the relationship between the state and the market. As discussed earlier in this chapter, in the political economy of China, the state and the economy are never considered as two separate domains: Both are part of the imperial realm, or All Under Heaven (*Tianxia*). The economy (and the market) is evaluated in the context of the relationship between the state and society, with the Legalist school focusing on the state and the Confucian scholars on society. This differentiates the political economy of China from that of the West. As discussed in Chapter 1, although the economy and the state are often perceived in the Western social sciences literature as two separate fields of a given society, such a distinction has never been made in China even at a discursive level.[53]

---

[53] Intellectually, such a separation was an important factor leading to the development of different disciplines in the West. It created a division of labor among different disciplines such as economics, politics, and sociology, and thus facilitated their development.

MARKETS AND THE MARKET SYSTEM IN CHINA

Although the Legalists and Confucianists disagreed with each other in most realms of statecraft, the system of governance in traditional China combined the two schools of thought. This was also reflected in the realm of political economy. The Chinese political economy system allows the coexistence of different types of markets, just as proposed by the Legalists and Confucians. The market system in China, from the first imperial state to date, consists of three conceptual layers.[54] These three layers form a market hierarchy, with national markets at the top, market–state inter-actions at an intermediate level, and regional and local grassroots markets at the bottom. Historically, in general, local grassroots markets formed and developed naturally. A typical local grassroots market was a marketplace that required no organization on the part of the state or other major market players. At this level, market participants were individuals who were also, at the same time, market organizers. Such markets could range from a village fair to a temporary market town barely under the govern-ment radar. At the intermediate level, market actors interacted with the economic agents of state and were often controlled by these agents. Typically, second-level markets were the market towns that grew into the political units or even regional centers of power. At the level of the national market, the markets were organized and managed primarily by the state agents and organized economic interests. These institutions include the factory systems controlled by the imperial household agencies, the tribu-tary system controlled by the Board of Rite, or the national salt market controlled by specialized salt agencies. At regional and national levels of marketplaces, individuals could only participate as agents, on behalf of either the state or powerful private interests, since the thresholds for entry to these marketplaces – such as power and capital – dictated that only well-connected and well-placed individuals were allowed. Therefore, two main historical actors in these two levels were the fiscal agents of the state, and state–private partners. In later chapters we will discuss how this

Over China's long history, the lack of such a tradition was a barrier to the development of modern social sciences.

[54] Here we acknowledge our debt to William Skinner's formulation of naturally formed market hierarchies in Sichuan, which we shall discuss later in this chapter and in the next. But our formulation is fundamentally different from Skinner's since it deals with the conceptual dimension of the economic system. The Skinnerian scheme can be regarded as the lower reach, or the first level, of the three-layer market we discuss here.

hierarchical market system functions; the remaining part of this chapter delineates the structure of this multilayered market system.

The Commanding Height: The State Sector and the Market

In various political economy systems in the West, the state is regarded as separable from the economy. The question in such systems is how the state can relate itself to the economy. Various institutions and mechanisms have been developed to enable it to do so. While in theory the state and the economy are two separate and autonomous realms, state intervention has always been present, but to differing degrees in different countries. With the rise of modern regulatory states, the scope of state intervention in the economy has expanded. Nevertheless, the boundary between the state and the economy is apparent and regulated by laws and other institutions, and in line with this boundary, the state itself must follow market principles.

By contrast, in China the state and the economy are regarded as inseparable, and the state is an important – even the most important – economic actor in the national economy. Providing society with material goods is an aspect of state responsibility. To fulfill this economic responsibility the state must organize not only its own economic activities, but also the market system, to maximize its economic output. The role of the state is not much different from that of the merchants who must organize their economic activities and the market. It is also not much different from that of today's global capitalists, who have organized their economic activities and the market on the global stage.

Historically, one of the premodern Chinese state's primary responsibilities was to organize and order economic activities through the market. In addition to its role in military affairs, the state's role in the economy has been clear since ancient times. It is understandable that the state would be interested in mining and metalwork, and in the salt monopoly. For the state, control of the production of these important goods was about not only imperial expansion and national defense, but also meeting the needs of the local population, offering them, as a lesser evil, an alternative to hunger, emigration, or revolt. One aspect of state monopoly in China tends to be ignored: The state only selected a few important industries in which to exercise a monopoly. Across China's long history, these industries included salt, iron, and textiles. As later chapters will show, the state's role in the economy became extremely pervasive, leading to what we have called "economic statism" in a few historical periods, including Wang Mang's reform in the middle of the two Han dynasties; Wang Anshi's reform in the Song dynasty; large-scale social and economic reforms under the first emperor of the Ming dynasty, Zhu Yuanzhang; and Mao Zedong's totalistic economic transformation during the first three decades of the People's Republic. For most of the time, the state's hold over the economy was limited and only in certain industries, although ideologically it always had a mandate to steer and transform the economy.

Furthermore, the state's role in the economy was not only in the field of production, but also in the provision of large-scale infrastructure. This point was emphasized by early liberal economists, including Adam Smith. However, this role was often misunderstood and exaggerated. In his *Oriental Despotism*, German–American historian Karl Wittfogel discussed the formation and development of China's traditional "hydraulic-bureaucratic official-state," following the concept of the Asiatic Mode of Production raised earlier by Karl Marx and Max Weber.[55] Wittfogel came up with an analysis of oriental despotism which emphasized the role of irrigation works, the bureaucratic structures needed to maintain them, and the impact that these had on society, coining the term "hydraulic empire" to describe the system. In his view, many societies – mainly those in Asia, such as China and India – relied heavily on the building of large-scale irrigation works. For this work, the state had to organize forced labor from the population at large. This required a large and complex bureaucracy staffed by competent and literate officials. This structure was uniquely placed to also crush civil society and any other forces capable of mobilizing against the state. Such a state would inevitably be despotic, powerful, stable, and wealthy.

While Wittfogel made a worthy attempt to demonstrate the state's role in the economy, particularly in infrastructural building, his analysis was excessively loaded with ideology, partly due to the political circumstances of the time (his research was conducted during the Cold War). There are several main problems in his analysis. First, he failed to answer the question why the state was responsible for irrigation works. As discussed in Chapter 1, in the West, the economy was regarded as separate from the state. Even though infrastructure work was regarded as part of a government's responsibility by economists such as Adam Smith, no state engaged in large-scale irrigation works of the sort discussed. By contrast, in China, the economy was regarded as being among the government's responsibilities and not separable from the state, and so the government had to bear

---

[55] Karl Wittfogel, *Oriental Despotism: A Comparative Study of Total Power* (New Haven, CT: Yale University Press, 1957).

responsibility for any large-scale infrastructure building, such as irrigation work. Second, Wittfogel misperceived state–society relations as a zero-sum game, largely because of his anticommunist ideological inclination and the common understanding of the communist state as predatory. As we will discuss in later chapters, communism was an extreme form of the statist economy, but China's traditional forms of economy are drastically different from communism. The state and nonstate sectors coexist. State-organized marketplaces can coexist with other forms of marketplace. Third, as Pierre-Etienne Will correctly points out, it is by no means certain that such a generalization of the hydraulic state is tenable in the case of a geographic entity as vast, diverse, and compartmentalized as China. The centralized Chinese state can be defined by many functions and plans other than administration of the various irrigation and hydraulic protection works, even if these are essential in most areas. And even if this sole function is considered, the state and its bureaucracy are not the only factors in question, the only decision makers, and the only executants. While the state was responsible for infrastructure building, it was not the only actor involved. Any large-scale matter, be it a state-owned enterprise or a public project, involves multiple levels, which are not necessarily integrated and which represent options and interests often contradictory to each other.[56] It is in this sense that Will comments: "hydraulic society was stronger than the hydraulic state."[57]

Indeed, China's official ideology – namely, Confucianism – also constrained the state from taking up such large public projects. One main factor in this was that such large projects involved a large number of conscript laborers. From the very beginning, when the state as an organization came into being, conscript labor was needed to transport staple goods, or to build roads, cut canals, and erect lines of fortification. Later, with the growth of the larger political units of the Warring States period, such labor was directed toward the construction of palaces, or to supply other forms of royal requirement. By the time of the Qin and Han empires, emperors were entitled to require the services of able-bodied men for certain tasks in the government. Men were liable to be called up both to serve in the armed forces, in the interest of security, and as laborers to work on public projects. It was always part of the responsibility of provincial and local

---

[56] Pierre-Etienne Will, "State Intervention in the Administration of a Hydraulic Infrastructure: The Example of Hubei Province in Late Imperial Times," in Schram, ed., *The Scope of State Power in China*, p. 295.

[57] *Ibid.*, p. 346.

officials to call up and organize this labor. Mencius thus warned sovereigns that the excessive use of conscript labor would be self-defeating in view of the harm wrought to agriculture, for not only does a lengthy period of call-up remove men from the productive work of the fields at just the time it is required most, but it also imposes on those who are left behind the burden of providing the necessities of life for those serving in the forces or the labor gangs.[58]

More importantly, as discussed in the *Discourses on Salt and Iron*, the state sector and large infrastructure projects were established not only for the purpose of state domination but also to support social equilibrium. They could contribute to the goal of maintaining social order, while avoiding inequalities and speculation which would have negative consequences for social cohesion. Therefore, the state had to reach out to society via the state sector and infrastructure projects. In other words, these were also the economic means through which the state connected itself to society. In this context, in the state sector or in any large state-initiated public project, the state was not the only actor, and many social actors were also involved. What the state pursued was domination over society, but state domination was a process of interaction between the state and social forces. During this process, the market became important, since it was the most effective tool for the state to reach out to society. Without the private sector, it would be difficult to understand how the state organized its economic activities; without the market, it would be difficult to understand how the state sector functioned. In fact, when one looks into the actual functioning of the state sector and public projects, the boundary between the state and the private becomes blurred. Indeed, more often than not, the state had to heavily rely on the private sector to organize its economic activities and the market. That led to the formation of the second layer of the market, namely, the state–private partnership, or the middle ground.

The Intermediary: State–Private Partnership

A state–private partnership can form in two ways. First, the state initiates economic projects and the private sector fulfills the tasks; second, the private sector initiates projects and the state takes them over, making them national institutions. In the former, the state allows and encourages the private sector to take part in state-initiated economic activities; in the

---

[58] Loewe, "Attempts at Economic Co-ordination during the Western Han Dynasty," in Schram, ed., *The Scope of State Power in China*, p. 246.

latter, the state tries to penetrate private economic activities. But one needs to keep in mind that in both cases, this is by no means to suggest that the relationship between the state and the private sector is a more equal one. As emphasized previously, the Chinese imperial state usually retained structural domination of the market and the private sector, but remained open to strategies of cooperation and cooptation. It did not matter whether the state was an initiator or a follower in the actual implementation of a policy. The priority was to make the partnership work as an efficient mechanism.

State initiatives and private participation can be exemplified by the salt monopoly and imperial textile factories. For reasons of political and economic rationality, the state took initiatives to form partnerships with the private salt merchants. In terms of political rationality, the state's organizational capability in governing a vast and diverse territory was limited and constrained by major geographical, environmental, and cultural factors. A partnership with the private merchants could enhance state capacity. In terms of economic rationality, the state could reduce its costs drastically by forming a private sector partnership. The state could frame the boundary in which the private sector engaged in state activities to serve the latter's purposes.

This pattern of partnership is apparent in the salt monopoly, as Thomas Metzger examined in the case of the Liang-huai salt operations.[59] The Liang-huai salt operations were a typically state-owned enterprise, but that state ownership did not mean that all activities were engaged in by the state. Instead, it was a model of state ownership and private operation. During the Qing dynasty, the Liang-huai salt operations involved about 400,000 people. The Qing state did not directly incorporate them into its former bureaucracy. Instead, it allowed nearly all of them to retain private or semiprivate status, and relied on a complex web of cooperation with powerful merchants whose interests sometimes conflicted with its own. The state often sought to advance legal sales and tax collection by promoting a balanced pattern of economic incentives favoring those low-status groups directly engaged in the production, distribution, and consumption of salt, while powerful, high-status merchants often acted to upset such a pattern of incentives by seeking to increase their own immediate profits at

---

[59] Thomas A Metzger, "The Organizational Capabilities of the Ch'ing State in the Field of Commerce: The Liang-huai Salt Monopoly, 1740–1840," in W. E. Willmott, ed., *Economic Organization in Chinese Society* (Stanford, CA: Stanford University Press, 1972), pp. 9–46.

the expense of these lower-status groups, whether by cheating salt makers when measuring salt, fleecing the poorer traders who were financially dependent on them, or raising the prices paid by consumers.[60]

Why did the legally all-powerful state have to coopt such powerful merchants and tolerate divergent interests and often corrupt business behavior? Metzger explains:

> If the merchants had been replaced by officials, the salaries of the latter would have absorbed many of the profits of the monopoly, while the officials themselves would have had similar corrupt behavior. Moreover, officials tended to be unskillful in commercial affairs. The increasing size of the monopoly must have called for increasing inputs of managerial skill which the officials would have been hard-pressed to supply . . . But in having to rely on merchants, the state still had a choice between dealing with a few powerful, large-scale merchants and with many low-status, small-scale merchants. Generally speaking, the officials' attitude toward rich merchants fluctuated between two poles: they could be regarded either as trustworthy, respectable, and able persons with the capital necessary to move goods as the state wished, or as corrupt schemers using financial manipulations to divert profits from both the state and the poorer, honest traders. Conversely, small-scale traders could be regarded as either the foundation of honest, efficient commerce or untrustworthy riffraff and former smugglers who put immediate profits above long-range considerations of cooperation with the state.[61]

Despite the conflicting interests involved, the state was able to manage its domination over its private partners, be they powerful merchants or small-scale traders. Metzger informs us that even in times of crisis, the Qing state was able, through its various agencies, to ensure the steady flow of vast quantities of salt from the coastal pans throughout the Yangtze Valley, constantly adjusting its relationship with private enterprise as the exigencies of the situation demanded.

The imperial factories in Suzhou present another good example.[62] The factories of Suzhou are part of the system of offices assigned to the supply of goods necessary for the life of the imperial court, and in particular the section that supplies textiles and ceremonial dresses. The system goes back to the Qin and continued under various names across the entire imperial period. It was also a typical case of state ownership and private operation. As Santangelo points out, "apart from being linked to the imperial

---

[60] *Ibid.*, p. 19.   [61] *Ibid.*, p. 20.

[62] Paolo Santangelo, "The Imperial Factories of Suzhou: Limits and Characteristics of State Intervention during the Ming and Qing Dynasties," in Schram, ed., *The Scope of State Power in China*, pp. 269–294. Also see E-Tu Zen Sun, "Sericulture and Silk Textile Production in Ch'ing China," in Willmott, ed., *Economic Organization in Chinese Society* (Stanford, CA: Stanford University Press, 1972), pp. 79–108.

household, the textile factories were also deeply rooted in society and in the local economy."[63] Indeed, since enormous families were involved in textile production, it is quite difficult to define these families as "private," "public," or "state." If set against the imperial factories, they can be considered shops or premodern private businesses. However, the factories often vested them with duties and powers that resembled more public functions. Therefore, these factories can actually be seen as mere private businesses of the crown. Moreover, the concentration of the labor force in the factory workshops and the artisans' direct responsibility to the officials prevailed during only part of the textile production required. The rest involved the families and contractors as intermediaries. These factories received payments and raw materials from the officials in charge of the factories for delivering the required products, or even for supplying the artisans who should have worked in the factories.[64]

Of course, state–private partnership was not limited to these cases; it took place in almost all state sectors and in almost all state-initiated public projects. These cases require us to reexamine the nature of the state sector in China from ancient times to the contemporary era. We need to consider the uniqueness of China's state sector. As Willmott points out, we need to search for the "Chinese-ness" of state enterprises. These existed in a complex web between the state and the private sector, and both sides took measures of mutual adaptation. Such a situation "is not found either in the state domination of the economic system of Meiji Japan or in the struggle between city and state in eighteenth-century Western Europe."[65]

Moreover, China's state sector had multiple purposes. It was an instrument of state control over the various sectors of the economy. In this sense, there was no means for the state to develop it into a purely economic sector. Therefore, productivity and competitiveness, which were the most important aspects of the economy in the West, were disregarded in China's state sector. Since economic utility came second to political objectives in the state sector, state-owned enterprises were looked upon not so much as economic enterprises, but rather as political and organizational centers.

Also, the existence of the state sector was a matter of social equilibrium. Aspects of the state sector were usually not taken out of private hands. As already discussed, the state only controlled part of the textile sector. State control was always selective rather than total. Whether the

---

[63] *Ibid.*, p. 270.   [64] *Ibid.*, p. 280.
[65] W. E. Willmott, "Introduction," in Willmott, ed., *Economic Organization in Chinese Society*, p. 3.

state chose to exert control or not depended on various factors, such as those economic activities considered dangerous to social order, certain products of importance, the possibility of obtaining considerable fiscal income, and the importance of certain interventions in terms of public affairs.[66] In this sense, state domination and economic statism are radically different. State domination refers to a situation in which the relationship between the state and the private sector serves the state while at the same time permitting private gain, and involves a compromise between public and private interests at every point.[67] By contrast, economic statism is an extreme case of state domination in which the state excises its total control over the economy by undermining and even eliminating the private sector – a situation seen during the eras of Wang Mang, Wang Anshi, Zhu Yuanzhang, and Mao Zedong.

Private initiatives and state participation can be exemplified by the regional merchant groups that built strategical alliances with the imperial state, such as the Anhui business groups (*Huishang*), the Guangdong Conhang merchants, and the Shanxi banks (*Piaohao*). In these cases, the merchant groups first achieved business success in certain sectors, before cultivating a symbiotic relationship with the fiscal system as economic agents such as procurement agents, sponsors, and financiers for imperial projects. There was both a political and an economic rationale for this type of economic operation. In terms of economic rationality, the state wanted to employ these private enterprises as tools to maintain a normal economic life and to gain fiscal benefits as well. In terms of political rationality, the state was fearful of a growing private sector which could threaten its rule if left undominated by the state. China's traditional official ideology – Confucianism – placed the merchant class at the bottom of the four major classes, namely, scholar, peasant, artisan, and merchant. From the ancient times to this day, the state has encouraged the development of the private sector, but it cannot tolerate large private enterprises or private businesses that are able to threaten the state. When the state's domination over the economy is weakened by private businesses, it will attempt to penetrate these enterprises. But in doing so, the state must balance its two ends: to gain fiscally and to control politically. Compared to a situation in which the state initiates and the private sector follows, here the state had to make greater compromises with the private sector.

---

[66] *Ibid.*, p. 287.
[67] Willmott, "Introduction," in Willmott, ed., *Economic Organization in Chinese Society*, p. 4.

Take the *Piaohao* banks of Shanxi as an example. These were an early Chinese banking institution, also known as Shanxi banks because they were owned primarily by natives of Shanxi. The first *Piaohao* originated from the Xiyuecheng Dye Company of *Pingyao*. To deal with the transfer of large amounts of cash from one branch to another, the company introduced drafts, cashable in the company's many branches around China. Although this new method was originally designed for business transactions within the Xiyuecheng Company, it became so popular that in 1823 the owner gave up the dye business altogether and reorganized the company as a special remittance firm, Rishengchang Piaohao. In the next thirty years, eleven *Piaohao* were established in Shanxi province. By the end of the nineteenth century, thirty-two *Piaohao* with 475 branches were in business, covering most of China.

All *Piaohao* were organized as single proprietaries or partnerships, where the owners carried unlimited liability. They concentrated on interprovincial remittances, and later conducted government services. From the time of the Taiping Rebellion, when transportation routes between the capital and the provinces were cut off, *Piaohao* became involved with the delivery of government tax revenue. The *Piaohao* grew by taking on a role in advancing funds and arranging foreign loans for provincial governments, issuing notes, and running regional treasuries.

The *Piaohao* dealt in interregional remittance transactions and functioned as a quasigovernmental institution. The government regarded the services provided by the *Piaohao* as beneficial. It supported and then used the evolving network of interregional remittances. In the early eighteenth century, the government began to coopt the *Piaohao* network, but it is important to note that the *Piaohao* also benefited from a partnership with the government. Economic historian Susan Jones points out:

Co-optation did not necessarily imply exploitation, for the Shanxi banks flourished under relatively light central government control. They accepted government funds for deposit at no interest and lent the money at usurious rates to other banks. Other loans went to bright young candidates in the civil service examinations at the capital. Later the earnings of these same men were collected in the form of deposits and investments as they moved from post to lucrative post throughout the empire. In its zeal to insure the solvency of this repository of official funds, the government bolstered the established hegemony of the three Shanxi banking cliques by requiring that individuals or companies desiring to found similar institutions be endorsed by members of the established group.[68]

---

[68] Susan Mann Jones, "Finance in Ningbo: The 'Ch'ien Chuang,' 1750–1880," in Willmott, ed., *Economic Organization in Chinese Society*, p. 50.

With government funds to finance an interregional banking system, and with an expanding intermediary role in financial transactions between imperial and provincial treasures, the Shanxi banks were assured of success, and the 1870s and 1880s saw the zenith of their development. Of course, a partnership with the state also involved a high cost. The trade network's geographic proximity to the capital allowed the government to oversee the financial operations that evolved from it, and to coopt them to serve its own fiscal needs. The network's eventual decline was closely related to a decline in government support, due to various factors.[69] This is evident when one compares the *Piaohao* institution with the Anhui business groups (*Huishang*). The story of the *Huishang* is similar to that of the *Piaohao*: The private sector initiates and the state follows. A sustaining network involving the government and high-ranking government officials made the development of the *Huishang* more sustainable than the *Piaohao*.[70]

The Grassroots: Local Market Networks

The market system could be created by the state or by a state–private partnership. This happened in larger geographic areas when the state wanted to create a nationwide or crossregional market for whatever purposes. But beyond this, at the regional and local level, the market existed without much state intervention and without much state–private partnership. It was in this market that Smithian dynamics of growth formed and growth was achieved through free trade and a system of division of labor.[71]

---

[69] This is not the place for a detailed examination of the *Piaohao* institution. For comprehensive surveys and analyses, see Huang Jianhui, *Shanxi piaohao shi* (A History of the Shanxi Banks) (Taiyuan: Shanxi jingji chubanshe, 1992), and Zhang Zhengming, Sun Liping and Bai Lei, eds., *Zhongguo jinshang yanjiu* (A Study of Shanxi Merchants in China) (Beijing: Renmin chubanshe, 2006). For a collection of original materials on the *Piaohao*, see Shanxi Provincial Academy of Social Sciences, ed., *Shanxi piaohao shiliao* (Historical Materials on the Shanxi Banks) (Taiyuan: Shanxi jingji chubanshe, 1992).

[70] For a comprehensive survey and analysis of the *huishang*, see Zhang Haipeng and Wang Tingyuan, *Huishang yanjiu* (A Study of the Anhui Merchant Groups) (Hefei: Anhui renmin chubanshe, 1995).

[71] R. Bin Wong, *China Transformed: Historical Change and the Limits of European Experience* (Ithaca, NY: Cornell University Press, 1997); Kenneth Pomeranz, *The Great Divergence: China, Europe, and the Making of the Modern World Economy* (Princeton, NJ: Princeton University Press, 2000).

The marketplace at this level was well researched by American anthologist William Skinner. Skinner offered an analysis of the economic geography of late imperial China in terms of a set of eight (or nine) macroregions: physiographically bounded regions consisting of core and periphery, regarding which the bulk of trade occurs internally rather than externally. He argued that it is analytically faulty to treat China as a single national market system; rather, economic activity was largely confined within the separate macroregions. He used empirical measures to establish the distinctions between core and periphery, as well as to draw boundaries between adjacent macroregions. As he points out, the economic geography of traditional Chinese economy was largely governed by transport cost, and this meant that China's river systems largely defined the shape and scope of intra- and interregional markets. He demonstrated how human activity was structured by the patterns of social interaction defined by these macroregions.

Skinner made a detailed analysis of the marketing systems of Sichuan, providing an important empirical instance of the abstract geometry of central place theory – the nested hexagons that represent the optimal spatial distribution of towns, villages, and cities. The analysis also creates an important shift of focus from the village to the larger social systems of interchange within which villages are located – the patterns of social interactions that are associated with periodic markets, the flow of ideas associated with the circuits of martial arts specialists, and the likelihood of intersections between economic, cultural, and political processes rooted in the geometry of social exchange.[72]

Markets were formed and operated more naturally and spontaneously at this level than were those created by the state or by a state–private partnership. Of course, this does not mean that no matters of power were involved in these local markets. Local bureaucratic power was often involved in terms of management. However, it was the key player only in the formation of these local marketplaces. This is different from the case of the markets which were created by the state or a state–private partnership. To make this distinction, one can borrow from Skinner's research on the great importance of the city to China in the late imperial period. He developed an idea of a hierarchy of urban systems, and argued that there was an orderly hierarchy of places, ranging from higher-level cities through lower-level cities, market towns, and villages. He distinguished between

---

[72] William G. Skinner, "Marketing and Social Structure in Rural China," *Journal of Asian Studies* 24:1–3 (1964), p. 65.

two types of hierarchy: the administrative–bureaucratic hierarchy of places and the economic–commercial hierarchy of places. These two systems create different characteristics and functions for the cities that fall within them.[73] This distinction can also apply to our concept of the market hierarchy, namely, the market created by the state, the market created by the state–private partnership, and the market formed spontaneously from the bottom up.

Of course, one can go one step further to examine the role of the market in an industry within a large geographic area. This can be exemplified by the Ningbo *Qianzhuang* (banking institutions). Earlier, we discussed the *Piaohao* institutions. The Ningbo *Qianzhuang* and the *Piaohao* institutions existed in almost the same historical period, and they often cooperated and competed in China's financial market. The difference is that the *Piaohao* institutions formed a partnership with the government, while the *Qianzhuang* largely operated without government intervention. In other words, the *Qianzhuang* market was created by social forces alone.

The *Qianzhuang* institutions consist of many small native banks serving local markets and specializing in money conversions. The development of the *Qianzhuang* institutions proceeded with the growth of commerce in the South, which was oriented to coastal and foreign ports, and the corresponding increase in the size and complexity of existing monetary institutions. Commerce in the South was distinguished from that in the North by a greater volume of foreign and coastal trade, by the widespread use of foreign silver coins as the medium of exchange in major commercial centers, and by a high degree of local variation in currency and units of account. A sophisticated local banking system well suited to this area grew up in and around Ningbo, first tied to Shanghai, then expanding from there throughout South and Central China.

Various factors contributed to the survival and development of the *Qianzhuang* institutions. First, its geographical location mattered. Ningbo was miles away from the capital, and this separation protected the *Qianzhuang* institutions from direct government control. As Jones pointed out, the *Qianzhuang* in traditional China were remarkably free of the governmental controls that served to protect and sustain comparably sophisticated banking systems in other cultures. They can thus be viewed as examples of the self-regulating, autonomous, segmentary organizations – based on ties of locality, occupation, and surname – typical of the city in

---

[73] William G. Skinner, ed., *The City in Late Imperial China: Studies in Chinese Society* (Stanford, CA: Stanford University Press, 1977).

late traditional China. Second, in their use of a foreign currency, they won a further measure of autonomy.

Third, and more important, were their independent operation mechanisms. The *Qianzhuang* institutions were independent, small-scale institutions, specific to various local systems. In contrast to the *Piaohao* institutions, most *Qianzhuang* institutions were local and functioned as commercial banks by conducting local money exchange, issuing cash notes, exchanging bills and notes, and discounting for the local business community. The *Qianzhuang* institutions maintained close relationships with Chinese merchants, and grew with the expansion of China's foreign trade. With a few exceptions, interregional ties were limited to the Yangtze delta trade network. Such ties were informal and free from central governmental control, and no government support was received. Also important were their self-governance mechanisms. In the absence of regulation by the central government, and of municipal institutions that might have provided a legal framework for banking operations, the Ningbo banking system created its own regulatory agencies—the guild and the clearinghouse.[74] In 1776, several of these *Qianzhuang* institutions in Shanghai also organized themselves into a guild.[75]

The considerable autonomy of the *Qianzhuang* institutions had its advantages, but also pitfalls. For one thing, they proved to be incapable of adjusting themselves to a changing external environment when macroeconomic stability was in jeopardy, in the absence of a regulatory state. According to Jones, the *Qianzhuang* system was ultimately vulnerable to forces outside the control of its guilds, such as shortages in the native currency supply, an increasing dependence on foreign capital, and the growth of speculative investment in the foreign stock market by bankers and depositors. The central government did not control domestic currency supplies or banking policies through a central agency, nor did it act to check the growing influence of foreign banks in China's increasingly open financial market.[76] While foreign banks' penetration of China eventually led to the decline of the *Qianzhuang* institutions, the demise of *Qianzhuang* could also be interpreted as the result of a weak state unable to protect its indigenous economic institutions.

---

[74] Jones, "Finance in Ningbo," p. 77.

[75] On the development of the *Qianzhuang* in Shanghai, see The Institute of Financial Studies of the People's Bank of China, Shanghai Branch, ed., *Shanghai qianzhuang shi liao* ("Historical Materials of Shanghai *qianzhuang*"), Shanghai, 1961; reprint, Shanghai, 1978.

[76] *Ibid.*

CONCLUSION

In this chapter, we have discussed several key concepts of the political economy and delineated general operational features of the political economy system in China. Political economy is about power relations between the state and the economy. Power is one actor's dominance over another. We use "market in state" (MIS) to refer to a system of political economy whereby a substantial part of the market and market mechanisms is firmly embedded and confined within institutional mechanisms of the state. Such a system of political economy has several distinctive features at both micro and macro levels that set it apart from the models offered by mainstream economic and political economy theories. Under such a system, the political power of the state and its agencies plays a decisive role in the allocation of resources, the process of socioeconomic stratifications, and national economic development, whereas the institutions of modern (or premodern) capitalism are created, dominated, and transformed by the state into a subsidiary order.

China is the best example of such a system. As we discussed in this chapter, one defining feature of the Chinese political economy system is that the coercive power of the state has always allowed it to exercise direct and indirect dominance over the entire national economy through a complex system of political economy institutions, hence ruling out the possibility of an independent economic sphere through a bottom-up process of market development and integration. In premodern history, the imperial state and its institutional or personal agencies far surpassed Western counterparts both in scale and in sophistication during a long imperial era spanning several thousand years. However, while it is worth discussing the historicity of state domination of the economy, the majority of this book seeks to explore how state domination has been reproduced in contemporary China. As will be demonstrated in later chapters, we believe that in the past two hundred years, despite the metamorphosis of China's political economy – which has evolved from an essentially agrarian-based economy in an imperial system, through a Maoist variant of socialism, to its present form of a party-state-dominated system with a mixture of market and statist elements – the structural dynamics and the underlying institution of the Chinese political economy have remained, unmistakably, within the MIS framework.

We conceptualize China's political economy system as "market in state" to answer the key question of what it is. Various concepts and theories formed in the context of non-China empirics have been applied to explain

China's political economy system. Misunderstandings and even distortions can follow. We attempt to conceptualize China's political economy system based on China's empirics, believing that this conceptualization will be able to provide a new angle on the issues surrounding China's political economy system. Our approach offers new answers to some of the old questions. For instance, we show how what we characterize "market in state" has effectively prevented China from developing an independent entrepreneurial class which played a crucial role in the development of both economic and political systems in the West. We also show how "market in state" has also inevitably led to disequilibrium between the state and economy, and thus led to new changes in the relations between the state and the economy.

The research also attempts to look at how state domination is reproducing itself in the contemporary era. We argue that while history will never repeat itself, the state can transform itself in order to reproduce its dominance. Power is about domination, but this cannot remain the same across different times and spaces, since dynamism exists in any power relationship. In "market in state," domination is inevitable, but it is not necessarily absolute. Each economic actor, in order to dominate or to be dominated, has its own particular type of capital. In our case, while "market in state" refers to the domination of the state's power over the economy (the market), the state–market equilibrium means that the state's power over the market cannot be absolute. Disequilibrium appears when the state's power over the market becomes overwhelmingly pervasive. But the power of the state itself will be undermined by the development of such disequilibrium. To support its own interests, the state will have to make efforts to restore such equilibrium; the market will also resist disequilibrium. This book seeks to understand how such equilibrium is achieved, how disequilibrium develops, and how equilibrium is restored. While the norm is state domination of the market, the market is not a helpless actor, and it also actively engages in resisting disequilibrium and restoring equilibrium.

More concretely, this book attempts to explore two issues: first, how the state has realized its dominance of the market in the contemporary era, and second, how the transformation of state dominance of the market has taken place. We assume that society is an area in which interactions between the state and the economy (the market) take place. The state is a part of society, not independent from the latter. The interaction between the state and the economy is mutually transformative. The state reproduces itself and maintains its dominant position through interacting with the economy. Nevertheless, the economy, and economic actors, are not completely helpless, even though they are subordinate to the state; instead, different economic actors process their own power in their fields. Through their continuous struggles with the state, they facilitate its transformation, all while continuously subordinate to it. We hope that this study will be able to answer three related questions regarding China's political economy system today: What is China's political economy system? How does it function? How does it change over time?

PART II

HISTORY

3

The State and Market in Imperial China

From this chapter onwards, we develop the "market in state" (MIS) approach by exploring Chinese political economy in its historical and contemporary forms. In this chapter, our analysis focuses on China's imperial past, before its full confrontation with modern imperial powers in the nineteenth century. In our analysis, we are aware that very Western concepts such as the free market, the modern state, and capitalism are not easily applicable to the Chinese experience. The typical perspective taken in a liberal framework regards the market mechanism as central in creating wealth and allocating resources efficiently, while the state merely evolves functions to safeguard its smooth operation. This process of market-determined development has only limited application to imperial China. From China's first imperial days to the dawn of industrialization, nation-wide industrial and commercial activities were undertaken by agents of the state more often than by private business groups, and were driven by political rather than economic motivations. Meanwhile, early modern Europe's vision of the absolutist state with powerful autonomous institutions to exercise social control and economic regulation also has limited application to the Chinese experience. The late imperial Chinese state, despite its ideological claims regarding the Mandate of Heaven and a complex bureaucracy, was a relatively small and weak early modern state with limited capacities and fragmented authority.[1] Likewise, it is perhaps futile to ask why modern capitalism did not develop in imperial China,

---

[1] Stuart R. R. Schram, ed., *The Scope of State Power in China* (Hong Kong: Chinese University Press, 1985), and *Foundations and Limits of State Power in China* (Hong Kong: Chinese University Press, 1987); H. Lyman Miller, "The Late Imperial State," in David Shambaugh, ed., *The Modern Chinese State* (New York, NY: Cambridge University Press, 1999), pp. 15–40.

before China's deep integration into the historical logics of global capitalism, since the question does not consider the central issues of the premodern Chinese economy and offers little to support an understanding of China on its own terms. The key questions regarding the historical evolution of Chinese political economy therefore center on the basic structures of the system, such as patterns of resource allocation, institutional development, incentive mechanisms, strategies of integration, and the vision and reality of the political economy's order, especially the role played by the traditional imperial state or modern party state.

This chapter is not a history of the Chinese political economy; rather, it is an exercise in historical sociology that tries to synthesize historical literature on premodern Chinese political economy under the MIS framework. In Chapter 2, we discussed some key guiding principles of the Chinese political economy system, as reflected in the policy discourses and the organization of the market system in imperial China. In this chapter, we furnish an analysis of the functioning of this political economy system, mostly based on the experience of the late imperial state, but also with some reference to its earlier historical forms. It is impossible to do full justice to the complexity of historical Chinese political economy in such a limited space. As such, following the spirit of Schumpeterian economic analysis, we shall focus on patterns of the imperial Chinese fiscal system – both its visions and its actual operations.

Our invocation of Joseph Schumpeter is not accidental. In fact, it was he who first argued that the fiscal system is the center of an economic order. While Schumpeter referred to capitalist systems, we believe that this statement is also true for noncapitalist systems such as imperial China. Schumpeter observed that fiscal history has an enormous influence on the history of nations, and fiscal measures – the "economic bleeding" necessitated by the requirements of the state – have created and destroyed industries and economic forms. According to Schumpeter,

in some periods, they explain practically all major events, and in most periods, they explain a great deal ... But even greater than the causal is the symptomatic significance of fiscal history. The spirit of a people, its cultural level, its social structure, the deeds its policy may prepare ... all this and more is written in fiscal history. He who knows how to listen to its message here discerns the thunder of world history more clearly than anywhere else.[2]

---

[2] Joseph A. Schumpeter, "The Crisis of the Tax State," reproduced in Joseph A. Schumpeter, *The Economics and Sociology of Capitalism*, ed. R. Swedberg (Princeton, NJ: Princeton University Press, 1991), p. 101.

By highlighting the fiscal system, we shall demonstrate how the imperial Chinese states established a unique type of order that integrated three principal actors – an omnipotent emperorship, a complex hierarchy of imperial agents, and the world of common people (scholars, peasants, artisans, and merchants) – into a system of political economy. We shall discuss how economic forces of the imperial domain were mobilized and controlled by higher political principles of the emperorship and harnessed and regulated by the political–economic interests of fiscal agents. The imperial state typically followed regular dynastic cycles of growth, stagnation, and decay, while its political economy moved periodically from laissez-faire, to statism, to disorder and decline.

THE IMPERIAL STATE, HOUSEHOLDS, AND THE MARKET

Over China's long history, the relation between imperial state and economic forces have led to the evolution of complex models defying simple characterization. From the second century BC, the central aspect of the political economy was the domination of the core institution of the emperor and ruling family households over millions of ordinary family households – mostly peasant households only indirectly linked to the imperial state. Over the past two thousand years, the imperial state developed various sophisticated approaches of resource extraction and economic management to ensure its effective control over its basis in the agrarian economy.

Despite the well-heeded peril of generalization, a general inquiry into the history of Chinese political economy cannot avoid some general recapitulations. In earlier literature taking a systematic and theoretical approach to Chinese history, scholars of China's imperial past characterized the two millennia of dynastic cycles as a super-stable social system.[3] But recent studies have revealed the system's remarkable variability and significant institutional evolution over time. Take the overall fiscal designs of imperial China as an example. Organizational experiments over two millennia include a number of diverse models, from the highly centralized multilayered fiscal state of the first Qin state and its later, short-lived namesake dynasty; the laissez-faire regime of the early Han;

---

[3] For example, see Jin Guantao and Liu Qingfeng, *Shengshi yu weiji: lun zhongguo fengjian shehui de chaowending jiegou* (Prosperity and Crisis: On the Ultra-Stable Structure of Chinese Society) (Hong Kong: The Chinese University of Hong Kong Press, 1992), pp. 19–62.

military–economic statism under Han Wudi (as discussed in Chapter 2), the utopian statism at the end of Han; the feudalist models from the late Han to the North dynasty; the household-based market model from the North dynasty to the mid-Tang; the highly commercialized model from the reform-era Song to Yuan dynasties; the revived household-based system of a proto-planned economy in the early Ming; and the final late imperial standard of coexistence of a small state and a vibrant market, controlled by that state. The contemporary Chinese planned and market economy can easily find predecessors, especially in the late imperial iteration. Before dipping into its changing forms, we shall make some observations regarding the enduring features of the imperial political economy in terms of state–market relations.

As an agrarian empire, imperial China's political economy consistently featured the uneasy coexistence of subsistent farming households, naturally formed grassroots and local markets, and the fiscal institutions of the coercive state built around the imperial household and a complex bureaucracy.[4] Such coexistence was secured on the premise that the imperial state could hold its disruptive social and economic dynamics within limits while at the same time sustaining a stable tax base. Such a pattern could be

---

[4] There is a large growing body of literature on the economic history of imperial China. The long-run political economy of late imperial China was clouded by methodological and ideological debates: see Albert Feuerwerker, *Chinese Social and Economic History: From the Song to 1900: Report of the American Delegation to a Sino-American Symposium on Chinese Social and Economic History* (Ann Arbor, MI: The Center for Chinese Studies, University of Michigan, 1982). In the 1980s, the Chinese Academy of Social Sciences published the history of capitalistic development in late imperial China: see Xu Dixin and Wu Chengming, translated by Li Zhengde, Liang Miaoru, and Li Siping, edited and annotated by C. A. Curwen, *Chinese Capitalism, 1522–1840* (New York, NY: Saint Martin's Press, 2000). The most comprehensive compilation by Chinese scholars in recent years is the nineteen-volume series *Zhongguo Jingji Tongshi* (A General Economic History of China) (Beijing: The Economic Daily Press, 2005). A general empirical economic history for various dynasties of imperial China was available in the various volumes of the *Cambridge History of China*. Discussions on economic statism and other specific issues of political economy were available in English, Japanese, and Chinese. The most influential synthetic works in recent decades are from the California School, especially Kenneth Pomeranz, *The Great Divergence: China, Europe and the Making of the Modern World Economy* (Princeton, NJ: Princeton University Press, 2000) and Wong Bin, *China Transformed: Historical Change and Limit of European Experience* (Ithaca, NY: Cornell University Press, 1997). The conceptual focus of all these works is the historical process of economic growth and structural change rather than the conceptual and historical relationships between the state and market. In this study, our focus is more on conceptualizing the political economy of imperial China than on historic issues such as economic conditions and the reasons for growth and stagnation, and we do not intend to discuss this body of literature comprehensively, even though we often refer to it.

regarded as an institutional norm in the economic history of imperial China. Of course, as mentioned in Chapter 2, there were periods in which the imperial state attempted total domination or, at the other extreme, completely lost control of agrarian households after a total collapse of the imperial order. Nevertheless, such periods were exceptions rather than the rule. Short-lived statism and near total laissez-faire were only punctuation in an overall period of stable state–market architecture and limited state intervention. In other words, the abnormality of the system emerged periodically as either total state control/transformative reforms or a total relaxation of state control/laissez-faire.

It was never easy for the imperial Chinese state to manage and sustain a balanced economy, since its basic parameters, demography, and ecology, as well as the external threats to it, were constantly changing. From a dynamic point of view, the shifting balance of power between the institutional actors and social forces, and their muddled and entangled relations, always tended to disturb the balance between the state and market, and thus undermined the existing socioeconomic order. The difficulty was partly a result of the technical and organizational limitations of managing a vast premodern state with only limited resources in these areas.[5] More importantly, the political economy of imperial China also suffered from its inherent structural paradoxes, largely arising from the fundamental contradiction between the monolithic power of the emperor in conceptual and structural terms, and the multiplicity of local and social interests under its rule. It is this basic contradiction that lay behind the cycles of imperial rise and decline. Typically, after a period of growth and stagnation, the organizational capacity of the imperial state, or its ability to "order the world," inevitably declined, not least in fiscal capacity. Eventually, as we shall see, this cyclical model would come to an end in the nineteenth century, as the mutually restrictive model of small state and noncapitalist markets eventually failed to stand up to the challenge of modern colonial empires.

In terms of market–state dynamics, the contradiction is underlined by the interplay between state domination and the autonomy of household and local markets, and the cyclical changes involving alterations of normality and abnormality. Our discussion in this chapter elucidates that the

---

[5] For a discussion of the organizational capacity of empires in economic life in general, as well as in the Chinese Empire, see S. N. Eisenstadt, *The Political Systems of Empire: The Rise and Fall of the Historical Bureaucratic Societies* (New York, NY: The Free Press of Glencoe, 1963), pp. 33–51. For a study of the reach of the imperial state at the grassroots level, see Kung-Chuan Hsiao, *Rural China: Imperial Control in the Nineteenth Century* (Seattle, WA: University of Washington Press, 1960).

evolution of the Chinese imperial political economy was a long process, toward a nexus of institutional arrangements that better accommodated and eventually resolved many of its inherent contradictions.

Basic Problems of Economic Management in Imperial China

Across most of the written history, all or parts of China proper were ruled by consecutive imperial dynasties from both Chinese and nomadic origins. The emperor ruled by the perceived virtue of his semidivine persona, in the capacity of the Son of Heaven (*Tianzi*), following a direct line of descent as the most legitimate male heir of the ruling family. The institution of emperorship was indisputably the most important and powerful public institution in traditional China. In legal terms, the emperor has complete ownership of and disposal over his family property, which includes the lives and properties of all his subjects, while also inheriting the hefty responsibility of ensuring the welfare, peace, and prosperity of All Under Heaven (*Tianxia*).

The legal foundation for "economy" (*jingji*), or the management of the realm, came from the imperial idea of the sovereign's lordship over all lives and ownership of all properties of *Tianxia*, or the realm. This idea has a long pedigree that extends at least to the universal kingship of the West Zhou dynasty (ca. 1000 BC). One of the best expressions of such can be found in the Minors Odes in the *Book of Songs*, which reads:

> Under the wide heaven,
> All is the king's land.
> Within the sea-boundaries of the land,
> All are the king's servants.[6]

The idea of the sovereign as ultimate lord over land and people was later restated and refined throughout the history of imperial China. It is ultimately derived from the fact that imperial power, which originated from violence, treated conquered land and people as subjects of its rule and disposition.[7] It can manifest in myriad ways, from direct confiscation, forced migration, and redistribution of land to the execution of any subject, depending on the power and strategy of individual rulers. In reality, for most times and in most places, the imperial power remained notional and

---

[6] http://ctext.org/book-of-poetry/decade-of-bei-shan [Accessed on April 30, 2017].
[7] Liu Zehua, Wang Maohe, Wang Lanzhou, *Zhuanzhi quanli yu zhongguo shehui* (Absolutist Power and Chinese Society) (Changchun: Jining Wenshi Chubanshe, 1988), pp. 28–30.

dormant, exercised through his agents and sometimes usurped by local elites. There were also times when opportunity and personality allowed the imperial power to assume full lordship and ownership. As we shall discuss later in this chapter, the emperors who exercised such powers most freely and profusely included Han Wudi (141–87 BC), Wang Mang (9–23 AD), and the founding emperor of the Ming dynasty, Zhu Yuanzhang (1368–1398). But even in times of relative peace and stability, imperial lordship and ownership underlies the day-to-day of the empire in terms of *jingji*, or "management" through the complex institutional arrangements of its various and multilayered agents.

In socioeconomic terms, the management of the entire empire's economic life resembled what we term "macroeconomic management" today, but in a more static agrarian environment. The principal task of the fiscal system consisted of collecting surplus from tens of millions of mainly agrarian households and other resources through thousands of locally based fiscal units and redistributing the surplus to thousands of budgetary units (mainly military units) and hundreds of thousands of stipend households. And above all, the imperial households were required to retain and redistribute surplus within their own extended families, keep a certain portion of the surplus for their own consumption, and redistribute another part to local agents who helped to collect tax and manage order. The imperial state's capacity to cope with millions of households and tens of thousands of bureaucratic units was founded on a system of power infrastructure that could rival any traditional state in terms of complexity and extensiveness. At the bottom of the system, land, male labor, the household, and persons under households were registered and redefined as fiscal units (*Mu*, *Ding*, *Hu*, and *Kou*), each carrying a specific fiscal obligation to the emperor by its very existence under the imperial domain.[8] Due to limited and uneven penetration of the imperial bureaucracy, households were usually not directly managed by the state fiscal bureaucracy. In late imperial China, tax collection was carried out at times by grassroots fiscal agents – which sometimes included rich and influential households in the local rural community – under the principle of collective

---

[8] *Mu* is the basic unit for area; *Ting* is the fiscal unit for male laborers between maturity and retirement age; *Hu* is the household; *Kou* is the head unit for poll tax. The precise area for *Mu* and age range for *Ting* changed over time. In all cases, these were fiscal units and by no means refered to actual culviated area, labor force, or population under the control of the imperial state. See Hou Jiaju, *Zhongguo Caijin Zhidu Yanjiu* (Study on the Fiscal History of China) (Taipei: Lianjing Publishing House, 1989), pp. 55–56.

responsibility, and at other times by county government runners and tax officers.[9] Grassroots tax agents in turn passed the revenues to county, prefecture, provincial, and finally central government coffers. In principle, central government presided over the entire process. Fiscal revenues that were initially taken in kind or in money were eventually streamlined and monetized into a silver-dominated land tax. Labor services and the poll tax were abolished. For the majority of this time, key military functions such as national defense were largely provided by stipend military households, in Ming, and Manchu banners, in Qing. In the Qing case, the banner households were supplied with farmland, farms, and stipends, depending on their stations and functions.[10]

The late imperial government had other important economic institutions besides the basic fiscal systems of land tax and drafted labor. The nontax channels of imperial finance – or in modern terms, "the state sector" – were historically managed by direct dependents of the emperor, such as eunuch commissioners in Ming and bond servants in Qing, rather than the literati-bureaucrats. They made revenue directly or conducted economic activities for strategic purposes, such as state-controlled trade monopolies, special tax contributions, and state-controlled handicraft industries.[11] The most enduring institutions in this regard include the state salt monopoly, the largely locally run granary system, the monopoly trading system, centralized control of minting, and the operation of imperial factories, mostly in the service of the imperial household.[12]

While the emperor was the head of the family state and had nominal control over all the empire's economic activities, it was impossible for the emperor and his household to take charge of economic management. To make possible what was impossible, the emperor and the imperial government effectively employed multiple layers of agents throughout the domain. Since the imperial power over the economy was complete and inalienable, fiscal agents also inherited despotic powers and economic–fiscal prerogatives in their own specific domain. These agents, including most local bureaucrats, grassroots tax agents, and other imperial delegates,

---

[9] *Ibid.*, pp. 67–78.
[10] Mark C. Elliot, *The Eight Banners and Ethnic Identity in Late Imperial China* (Stanford, CA: Stanford University Press, 2001), pp. 193–195.
[11] Preston Tobert, *The Ching's Imperial Household Department: A Study of its Organization and Principal Functions, 1662–1792* (Cambridge, MA: Harvard University Press, 1977), pp. 75–76.
[12] Zhou Boli, *Zhongguo caizheng shi* (Fiscal History of China) (Shanghai: Shanghai Renmin Publishing House, 1981), pp. 157–159.

collectively formed intermediaries between the imperial state and its tax base, which had specific interests of its own. Given the extent of the empire and the complexity of fiscal organizations, controlling and disciplining these agents became an infinitely difficult task.

When it came to fiscal management, the emperor could choose between the state and local societal agents for economic management, especially at the grassroots level, in dealing with household units. Although institutionally costly and inefficient, the deployment of state agents and the extension of imperial bureaucracy meant a high level of state penetration and control over society and a heightened state capacity. Alternatively, the state might entrust fiscal services to local families and coopt local economic elites, in an implicit system of tax farming, but that would mean a loss of control and effective sharing of fiscal powers with local elites.

The interactions between the emperor, the fiscal agents, and the vast tax base constitute the central dynamics of fiscal life in the imperial state. In principle, the imperial state has to forge a system of multilayered organizational dependency via its fiscal agents so that private households become dependent on the emperor for public goods, and in return accept his dominance. For the sake of analysis, we assume that the fiscal system of imperial China was indeed structured in terms of three-layered concentric circles, with the imperial household at the center, the various tax agents in the middle layer, and tens of millions of registered households at the periphery of organizational dependency (Figure 3.1). In addition, there were always areas of economic life operating outside effective state controls, as powerful economic and social elites legally or illegally dominated the local economy and captured surplus. Most typically, peasant households often sold their land and rented from landlords who had tax exemptions or means of evasion, resulting in a major loss of revenues for the imperial state. Moreover, due to the size of the imperial domain, there was always a central–local dimension to the political economy, as the superior units always had the means of coercion over the inferior ones and the inferior units always had the means of information advantage over the superior ones. This continues in China today.

Once established, there was immense inertia in the imperial system. With few exceptions, the emperor could not restructure the registered household sector. Nevertheless, he could influence the structure of households by changing the tax system and the organization of fiscal agents, inducing certain behaviors to accompany either market or household models. Since these measures amounted to redistribution of surplus, typically from fiscal agents to the grassroots and the emperor, they faced stiff

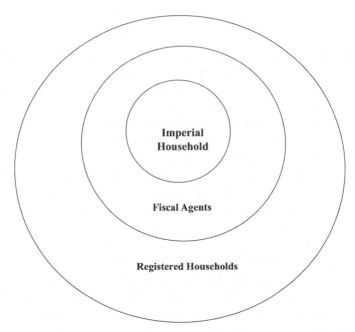

Figure 3.1 Concentric circles of organizational dependency in the traditional imperial system

resistance. There were indeed many experiments with the system of fiscal agents, mostly aimed at creating effective direct control of the imperial household over the household sector, including some reform programs that looked strikingly similar to a modern command economy.[13]

Approaches to Fiscal Management

Like the main types of public goods provision, the mainstay of the fiscal revenue system was remarkably constant throughout the entire imperial China. The three principal taxes of the imperial state were land produce tax, in terms of land produce or money, and proportional to land owned; labor service, in terms of obligatory public work or a monetized service tax;

[13] As later discussions will further illuminate, the Wang Mang and Wang Anshi reforms pursued institutional inventions that extended the effective control of the state to various fields of economic life, such as state banks, state trade agencies, and a profitable manufacturing monopoly. For a comparison between the Wang Anshi reform of the eleventh century and state socialism in the West, see Huang Renyu, *Zibenzhuyi yu ershiyi shiji* (Capitalism and the 21st Century) (Beijing: Sanlian Books, 2001), pp. 459–463.

and per capita money tax, collected either directly or indirectly through the sale of monopolized products such as salt.[14] In addition, there were commercial taxes such as custom and transit taxes, although these were not as important until the mid-nineteenth century. In terms of actual collection, there were also numerous surcharges and ad hoc surtaxes on the principal tax, justified by purposes such as collection fees, conversion, and logistics, but mostly collected upon coercion by the local tax agents. Beside tax revenues, imperial states also derived income from coinage and minting, sale of offices and tax-exemption permits such as monk certificates, and contribution from imperially commissioned merchants.

Despite all the vicissitudes of the tax system, there was remarkable historical continuity in the structure of expenditure. For most dynasties, the bulk of the imperial state's budget went toward maintaining a large standing army to guard the borders and keep internal peace. The other major fixed item in the expenditure was catering for the imperial household and the hereditary elites, as well as payment of the salary and stipends of the civil servants, mostly literati-bureaucrats. Other portions of the revenue had to be used to build and maintain physical and institutional infrastructures, such as the granary system, Imperial Post Services, river control facilities, Grand Canal System, and imperial building projects. During times of natural disaster and foreign invasions, regular fiscal revenues had to be expanded and supplemented with emergency funds to provide disaster relief and military expenditure.[15]

The fiscal problem facing the imperial government was considerably more complex than merely balancing fiscal revenues against expenditures. Other matters to be considered were agency costs to the fiscal agents and efficiency costs because of the constraints of fiscal arrangements such as state monopoly and control of trade. This invisible portion could comprise the larger share of the actual resource extraction and running costs of the empire. It was essentially determined by the structure and strategy of the fiscal system. For example, a strictly hierarchical arrangement with a highly

---

[14] These indirect forms of tax proved to be more stable and enduring: see Hou Jiaju, *Zhongguo caijin zhidu shilun* (Discourse on the History of China Fiscal System) (Taipei: Lianjing Publisher, 1988), pp. 55–56.

[15] The items varied widely across dynasties. At the most mature point of the Qing Empire, about half of the revenues went to support the military, 20 percent to the imperial bureaucracy, and 10–15 percent to the imperial households. The rest was stored for disaster relief. See chapter 2 of Zhou Yumin, *Wanqing caizheng yu shehui bianqian* (Late Qing Government Finance and Social Changes) (Shanghai: Shanghai Renmin Publishing House, 1997) on the early Qing imperial state's incomes.

disciplined system of agents could lead to lower revenues and higher social controls. On the contrary, a revenue-maximizing, market-oriented system might have to share much of the revenues with its self-aggrandizing fiscal agents and run the risk of losing control. A well-balanced approach would have to make compromises between control of the market and state agents.

The design of a fiscal system is important to the fortunes of each dynasty. At the beginning of a dynasty, the imperial state could at times muster sufficient power to reshape social structure through reorganization of the society, forced mass migration, and reallocation of land. This was the case for the founding of the Ming dynasty (1368–1398).[16] Even politically and militarily weaker states would have the autonomy to decide upon a general strategy of economic management vis-à-vis their agrarian economic base, as was the case with the smaller states that implemented a market-oriented open economy during the period of the Five Dynasties (907–979).[17] These fundamental considerations, embodied in fiscal systems instituted at the beginning of each dynasty, largely shaped the fiscal trajectory of each dynasty and the fate of their fiscal regime.

Broadly speaking, there were two general approaches to economic management in late imperial China: the conservative approach and the radical one. The basic distinctions boiled down to two visions of the emperor's economic order and fiscal base. The mainstream or conservative vision, championed by most Confucian scholar-officials, viewed economic management as analogous to household management, in line with the Confucian economic philosophy which we discussed in Chapter 2.[18] In household management, they upheld the golden law of fiscal discipline and self-restraint on behalf of the imperial state. From a typical conservative perspective, economic welfare and social order took precedence over fiscal revenues. Fiscal institutions of the state reflected the economic and social functions of agrarian households, which formed the fiscal basis of the emperorship. This type of economic thinking naturally led to a

---

[16] William Guanglin Liu, *The Chinese Market Economy, 1000–1500* (New York, NY: SUNY Press, 2015), pp. 5–6.

[17] Huge R. Clark, "The Southern Kingdoms between Tang and Song," in Denis Twitchett and Paul Jakov Smith, eds., *Cambridge History of China*, vol. 5 (Cambridge and New York, NY: Cambridge University Press, 2009), pp. 181–182.

[18] It is sufficient to characterize this approach as *liang ru wei chu*, that is, spend only as much as you collect. By implication, the imperial state cannot spend more than the resources from all fiscal units stated in its account books, which were akin to the famous Domesday Book. However, except for population accounting, the dynastic fiscal registers seldom changed much even as the economy expanded, due to the large information costs involved.

noninterventionist principle in fiscal affairs, since wealth in a preindustrial society came mostly in the forms of agricultural produce and its basic means of production – namely, land and labor – which was provided at a fixed level and determined by factors outside state control. The fiscal process was thus a zero-sum game played between the state and agrarian households. Any increase in fiscal revenues could only come at the producers' collective cost. Fiscal expansion through the markets was also viewed unfavorably by most Confucian elites, since excessive state involvement in commerce meant competition with the small private businesses that had the potential to harm their very livelihood.[19] The conventional conservative approach also took a dim view of state control and manipulation of money and credit, especially excessively active interventionist policies to increase the accounting value of the fiscal revenues. At various times, low-level tax in kind, such as through grain and other produce, was the preferred type of taxation.

The radical or reformist approach, usually upheld by the Legalists or radical Confucian reformers, had its roots in a very different vision of economic order. In the typical version of this active view, fiscal considerations took precedence over economic welfare, and state domination was preferred to non-intervention. The imperial state was viewed as an economic actor with limitless capacity to transform the economy. This transformative approach can work at both a market-oriented and a market-suppression level. As a market-oriented monopoly, the state might maximize revenues through a monopoly over natural resources and international trade and controls on money supply.[20] As a market-suppressing state, the state might radically reshape the economic landscape by imposing controls on mobility and curtailing markets at all levels. In contrast to the static view of mainstream Confucians, the reformists found value in state manipulation of market mechanisms, in many ways similar to state socialism or state capitalism of the contemporary world. Moreover, the reformist approach valued motivated fiscal agents who could share the state's agenda of fiscal expansion or radical economic reform. In both cases, the state usually had a radical vision, either to expand its fiscal revenue beyond the norm or to construct a more equitable social

---

[19] One of the most systematic institutional frameworks of this household model was proposed by Huang Zongxi in *Waiting for the Dawn, a Plan for the Prince: Huang Tsung-his's Ming-i-tai-fang-lu*, translated with an introduction by Wm Theodore De Barry (New York, NY: Columbia University Press, 1993), pp. 151–160.

[20] See Alley Rickett, *Guanzi: Political, Economic and Philosophical Essays from Early China* (Princeton, NJ: Princeton University Press, 1985), vol. 1, pp. 1–9.

distribution of income. Following such a transformative vision, the state and its fiscal agents actively dominated and shaped the economy to achieve a utopian vision. Compared with the conservatives' strong preference for substantive tax, reformers tended to favor a more uniform and streamlined tax structure.

The two approaches contain different sets of contradictions. At the heart of the issue was the structure of *organizational dependency*, as the foundation of imperial domination over the economy and society. Under organizational dependency, all subjects of the realm were ultimately dependent on the emperor and the imperial state for their life and welfare, since the emperor and the imperial state were entrusted with ordering the world, or All Under Heaven, by the Mandate of Heaven. Such dependency was guaranteed by proper organization of the family, the bureaucracy, and the imperial household. In installing and upholding the system, the imperial state had to manage a system fraught with dilemma from its very inception. As the chain of dependency extended downward to penetrate society, the emperor often found it increasingly difficult to motivate or control local and social fiscal agents in his interest. For the conservative order, agents' interests could become entwined with those of powerful households, weakening the effective control of the imperial state. For the radical order, agents' interests could lead to a predatory state, destroying the local society and economy in the name of the state. The two approaches both supported self-styled systems of organizational dependency, but neither could sustain them indefinitely.

The household model envisaged the emperor as the head of the family state and a system of organizational dependency that nominally reached all households on the household registry that the emperor, as chief officiate, sacrificially displayed at the Altar to Heaven. In the Confucian ideal, the emperor's rights to tax labor and produce was legitimized by his conferring the usage rights of land to individual farming households.[21] The fiscal systems were further premised on two grounds. First, the state has both the moral obligation and the legitimate fiscal concern to prevent excessive formation of subsystems of organizational dependency, such as annexation and concentration of landed wealth and the excesses of the tax agents. Second, the system had to maintain a measure of social and economic controls, otherwise increasing mobility of labor and capital might weaken households (including kinship and lineage organizations) – the foundations

---

[21] For a typical Confucian view on this issue, see Huang Zongxi, *Waiting for the Dawn*, pp. 95–97.

of the emperor's fiscal power. Both conditions required the emperor to exercise a certain degree of infrastructural power and organizational control. At times, adjustments to the level of power and control required or induced shifts toward the radical model. Similarly, the radical model of economic management has to meet two conditions for it to be sustainable. First, although the emperor could indeed capture larger revenues, fiscal agents' share might also increase further, since it would be more difficult for the central state to control local and societal fiscal agents. Second, it would be able to deal with the consequences of either an overexpansive market or market contractions due to macroeconomic mismanagement, often caused by war and fiscal mobilization.

Organizational Dependency and Its Challengers

The emperorship was characterized by dominance and dependency. Ideally, the emperor could maintain a monopoly over the extraction of surplus products and the mobilization of labor while keeping the level of extraction and mobilization minimal. But this was only an ideal. In fact, the agents (*guan*) and powerful households (*dahu*) were always formidable challengers of the state. Implicitly or explicitly, the emperor had to pre-empt rival households or agents from forging private dependences and stealing his fiscal base. If the presence of the challengers became sufficiently significant, the emperor would have to take action; if such action failed, the imperial system could decline and ultimately collapse. Much of the institutional design and dynamics of the imperial fiscal system were based on this very important concern for balance.

The first category of challengers vying with the emperor was that of large hereditary households with substantial local powers. They came from both inside the imperial household and from its ruling coalition, although this class of competitors generally declined in late imperial China. Apart from income from inheritable lands, they also stood to derive considerable wealth from political power and fiscal privileges, through common practices such as land annexation and market monopolies. By making households and market actors their dependents, they could effectively steal much of the imperial revenues and fiscal base.

The second category of challengers was that of powerful local family clans which constituted another main challenger to the imperial economic order from outside the imperial household. Like the internal challengers, many local family clans possessed both the economic and the coercive resources to provide alternative local orders and make smaller households their economic and political dependents. Sometimes, they even captured local states and gained influence in the central bureaucracy by leveraging large social networks and strategic positions. This class of competitors suffered crushing devastation in the mid-Tang period and never recovered its political clout.[22]

The third category of challengers was that of large merchants and their commercial organizations, built around single household clans and their local networks. While typical merchant families came from trade and commerce, they were usually also landed local elites. Powerful private commercial interests could also capture a significant share of wealth and power through predatory market behavior, especially in grain and credit, thus reducing small household producers to dependency on them. In late imperial China, the standard practice was to co-opt rather than suppress them.

The fourth and most important category was that of state agents and associated interest groups, including the families of central and local agents. On the surface this seems contradictory, since imperial agents derived their power and privileges from the emperor and thus definitely held a stake in the imperial household. However, in reality, the private interests of imperial agents were usually not the same as the emperor's. In practice, almost all state fiscal agents in late imperial China controlled channels and had the leverage to benefit their own interests through organized dependency, especially where the state had chosen to adapt a radical market-oriented or reformist approach to economic management. Their self-profiteering practices ranged from direct land annexation to manipulation of household data, the tax registry, and even official measurements of weight and volume.

The category of state fiscal agents represented a very special interest group. They owed their existence to the emperor, but the organizational dependence between the two was based on a complex, multilayered principal–agent arrangement. This basic arrangement entailed the classic organizational problems of adverse selection, moral hazard, and extremely high costs of information and top-down supervision. Historically, various imperial states evolved elaborate systems of control to deal with this most difficult but indispensable class of actors in the system. Most threatening was their potential to develop hereditary interests. In late imperial China,

---

[22] Nicolas Tackett, *The Destruction of Medieval Chinese Aristocracy* (Cambridge, MA: Harvard University Asian Center, 2016 reprint), pp. 235–238.

the emperor actively coopted this large class of elites and controlled its reproduction via the Civil Service Examination system.

Last, there were marginal social groups outside the imperial household registry, such as religious groups, secret societies, and the growing floating population, or vagrants, in late imperial China. Since the fourteenth century, these marginal elements in the formal imperial system had often developed their own internal ideologies and organizations outside the mainstream social order.[23] These social groups could only pose a threat when the economy suffered a major disturbance, either from natural factors such as changes in the climate or persistent degradation due to social factors such as demographic explosion. As their ranks exploded into the registered households when the social and economic order disintegrated, these marginal groups could become a hotbed for social revolution. In this way, they could become a deadly threat to imperial rule.

We might add a final group of challengers, in the form of foreign powers. Until the eighteenth century, these competing states were nomadic states from North and Northeast China. The threat they presented was not primarily economic but military. As such, we shall not categorize them as a major threat to organized dependency, though they did have an acknowledged role in state-building in China, especially in the founding days of the Manchu Qing dynasty. The real external gamechangers – namely, China's geopolitical challengers, which would eventually reshape Chinese political economy – will be discussed in Chapter 4.

Economic management in a broader sense was the management of organizational dependency. To secure the desired order, the emperor had to keep in check all potential challengers to the order. If successful, the emperor consolidated his rule. Otherwise, the fiscal institution could lose its autonomy and capacity, and decline. Such a fiscal crisis could happen even before the dynasty had formally ended.

The tension between the emperor and the various challengers to the imperial order had profound consequences for the political economy of imperial China. In historical terms, the imperial system evolved toward a more sustainable and all-encompassing order, as the imperial state

---

[23] For a Chinese account on the new social formations collectively known as *youmin* or wondrous people, see Wang Guotai, *Youmin wenhua yu Zhongguo shehui* (Marginal Culture and Chinese Society) (Beijing: Tongxin Publisher, 2007). In economic terms, the basic character of *youmin* is a money-based economy detached from economic production. Thus, *youmin* was the first social category in late imperial China to convert to a "modern" social identity detached from the traditional ritual anchors of ancestral land and clan.

gradually coopted and internalized its organizational rivals. At the basic institution level, the emperor gradually eliminated hereditary fiscal and political privileges for aristocrats. In late imperial China, the remaining hereditary households were reduced to dependent budgetary units under strict imperial administration. The Qing Empire further weakened the hereditary class, reducing their aristocratic prerogatives and making them strictly budgetary units under full imperial control.

Since the early Han, the emperor had strictly enforced the laws of equal partial inheritance for ordinary households while reserving the right of primogeniture to the office of the imperial household. In the period of economic and social transformation between the Tang and Song dynasties, local hereditary households were substantially weakened and replaced by more decentralized, new local elites with fewer hereditary rights. Meanwhile, the imperial state gradually assimilated local elites into the Civil Service Examination and enlisted their service in the provision of local order and public goods. In late imperial China, the system of assimilation and cooptation was so successful that the symbolic capital of a degree became the precondition to elites' social and political status.[24]

Historically, the tensions between the emperor and the commercial elites centered on state monopoly in trade and commerce. But after the states tested and learned the limits of monopoly, an alternative policy of cooptation, in which commercial elites became the dependent agents of the state, became the prevailing institutional arrangement in late imperial China. Relations between the emperor and commercial elites evolved gradually from zero-sum confrontation to informal domination-autonomy. Rather unlike the bourgeois class in the early modern West, commercial and industrial elites in late imperial China were effectively absorbed into a symbiotic existence with the imperial state in the joint production of social order. As the Civil Service Examination set the norm for elite formation, commercial elites were often transformed into degree-holding landed elites within a few generations.[25]

The emperor sought to maximize his control over the fiscal system while conceding the private privileges of agents. But the imperial agents often

---

[24] For an account of the social process of the civil examination system, see Benjamin Elman, *A Cultural History of China's Civil Examinations in Late Imperial China* (Berkeley, CA: University of California Press, 2000), pp. 15–17.

[25] Roy Bin Wong, *China Transformed: Historical Changes and the Limit of European Experience* (Ithaca, NY: Cornell University Press, 1997), pp. 120–121.

proved to be a very potent force, capable of maneuvering within the system and taking collective action against the public interest through a wide range of tactics. Even as the emperor centralized powers and adopted a tighter system of checks and balances, fiscal powers simply sank to the bottom of the grassroots fiscal agents' list of benefits. In general, the imperial state increased its control over its larger and more powerful local agents, including the imperial and provincial bureaucracy. In late imperial China, the grassroots agents were the most formidable ones. Although corruption was increasingly routine in later empires, imperial political control over imperial agents tightened. In the final analysis, the imperial agents, who depended on the emperor for most of their personal fortune, formed no separate organizations of dependency, and thus constituted no challenge to the emperor.[26]

The only exception to this was marginal rival organizations, which grew significantly and became an increasingly destabilizing force in late imperial China. They proved to be the major threat to the late imperial social order. The typical strategy was to provide public goods such as the ever-normal granary to support poor peasant households and implement harsh social controls to keep them from becoming part of the floating population. However, this strategy was ultimately ineffective, as demographic trends outgrew state capacity. From the fourteenth century onwards, armed rebellions organized by popular religious groups, most significantly the White Lotus millenarians, largely replaced domestic political elites and nomadic forces as the principal source of social instability, economic disorder, and political revolution. As such, the late imperial state became increasingly stringent in its control and suppression of popular religions such as these.[27]

We have so far outlined the infrastructure of the imperial political economy. Now we turn to consider the imperial political economy from historical and institutional perspectives. We will examine both the cyclical pattern of normality and abnormality and the historical evolution of the

---

[26] It is necessary to qualify here that it became normal for literati-bureaucrats to socialize and form their own autonomous organizations based on shared origins and ideologies. But these had little to do with their economic resources. In a strictly agrarian economy and under the dominant conservative ideology, the literati-bureaucrats had no sphere of economic dominance except as landlords.

[27] The late imperial response to the White Lotus was a response to the Song-Yuan White Lotus Movements. Indeed, the Ming founding factions partially emerged from and intermingled with late Yuan White Lotus rebels. See B. J. Ter Haar, *The White Lotus Teaching in Chinese Religious History* (Leiden: Brill, 1991), pp. 125–131.

institutions toward the late imperial order, culminating in the eighteenth century. We will also survey essential aspects of the political economy, especially with reference to High Qing or, roughly, the eighteenth century. Much of what follows will center on the institutional embodiments of organizational dependency in its most mature form.

NORMALITY AND ABNORMALITY IN THE IMPERIAL POLITICAL ECONOMY

Cyclical Patterns of Normality and Abnormality

The history of imperial China is often characterized as the rise and fall of territorially unified dynastic empires, with two major interludes of political disunity (220–581 AD; 907–1279 AD). The evolution of the imperial political economy could also be said to follow a parallel cycle, characterized by alternative periods of balance and imbalance between the imperial state and the nonstate economic institutions, the household, and the market. A dialectical dynamic was at work in the process of institutional change, as changes in the social and economic bases and their responses from the imperial state often gave rise to imbalance and crisis. This structural imbalance and subsequent crisis of interdynastic wars, which fatally damaged the economy, in turn created conditions favorable for the restoration of a *household* order.

Alternatively, we can employ the concepts of normality and abnormality. Normality refers to a state of equilibrium in which the imperial state, household, and market coexist, each with a relatively independent function in the organizational structure. This was usually the case when the mainstream Confucian approach to economic management dominated. In contrast, abnormality refers to a state of disequilibrium in which the balanced structure is disturbed and one or more of the basic institutions cease to function. This was roughly the period in which the radical approaches reigned.

There were two types of abnormality. On one extreme of the spectrum was economic statism, when the imperial state sought complete domination over the economy, to the point of elimination of the autonomous household and market sector. In terms of economic management, these conditions could also be defined as a switch from overall management and limited intervention to total domination and control. The other form of abnormality was the extreme market-oriented approach, in which the imperial state sought to mobilize the market fully as its fiscal tool. In stark opposition to statism, this situation arose when the imperial state and the central government lost effective control of the economy and society.

A dynastic cycle was characterized as a cycle consisting of a long period of normality and some brief abnormalities. At the beginning of a new dynasty, when the nascent imperial state was relatively powerful vis-à-vis a society torn apart by civil wars, nomadic invasions, and various disasters, the state could establish organizational control over the autarchic household sector, strictly localized and reduced to a state of bare subsistence. At this initial stage of funding of the empire, most founders of dynasties initially employed a laissez-faire approach to encourage agricultural production. The economy picked up, social order was restored, and the population began to grow. For a few decades – even as much as a century – as the market and the household economy both prospered, the state of normality prevailed.

But as population growth recovered momentum and the local nexus of power and economy revitalized, the fiscal order of the empire began to erode. A commercialized landed economy meant that wealth naturally gravitated to the rich and the powerful, often corresponding to or allied with the fiscal agents of the empire. The private interests of well-knit networks of interest groups begun to dominate the system, leading to increasing fiscal burdens, widening income disparities, and weakened state control. Organizational dependency fragmented and gave rise to many localized orders of domination. The dynastic state either suffered a major crisis or gave way to another new state.

It was usually at this point that reformers came to the stage with plans to remake the fiscal system.[28] If the state survived, the top issues for reformers were imperial government revenues and seething social inequality. There were two strategies for crisis resolution: first, streamlining the economy, creating a money-based and market-oriented fiscal system; second, complete overhaul of the household-based order. If the state collapsed, the new dynasty could either began another laissez-faire cycle or reform society and the economy, following a grand plan.

In most cases, market-oriented reforms accommodated rather than defied the prevailing socioeconomic trends. In these cases, reform simply

---

[28] Except for the short-lived ones, most dynasties have such radical reformers, such as Wang Mang (Early Han), Yang Yan (Tang), Wang Anshi (Northern Song), Jia Sidao (Southern Song), Toktoghan (Yuan), Zhang Juzheng (Ming), Emperor Yongzheng (early Qing), and the reformers of late Qing. But except in the cases of Wang Mang and Wang Anshi, who attempted to create a new theory of the imperial state, all these reforms were only structural adjustments.

meant recognition of long overdue social and economic changes. The two classic cases are the late Tang reform in the late eighth century and the late Ming reform in the late sixteenth century. In the first case, the Tang state replaced the old kindred taxes with a system of uniform land and household taxes and a salt monopoly, in recognition of the collapse of state-allocated family land and the rise of the commercial economy. In the second, the Ming state incorporated labor into land tax and adopted a *de facto* silver standard, in recognition of a commercial economy long based on silver and copper coins. In both cases the fiscal systems were effectively market-promoting, charting the course for a trend of market development in the next few hundred years.

While all of these reforms had some positive effects on the fiscal health of the imperial state, none could sustain a declining empire for long. Alleviation or delay of the fiscal crisis could not possibly resolve the deeper social and political crisis, as the basic structure remained the same. The rise of markets would open opportunities and benefit the empire fiscally, but would also cause weakened organizational dependency, as the fiscal impact of commercialization in the mid-Ming period demonstrated.[29]

In other, more extraordinary circumstances, reforms were a byword for a period of abnormality: either radical statism or state mercantilism. The reforms could amount to a full-scale overhaul of the economy and a paradigm shift, exemplified by the Wang Anshi Reform in the late eleventh century, or could lead to a utopian restructuring of economy and society – but only for a while – such as the Wang Mang Reform of the first century and the Zhu Yuanzhang reform of the late fourteenth century. Although none of this abnormality persisted, these experiments were perhaps particularly revealing of the nature of the imperial political economy and its more profound institutional dilemmas. Moreover, they served as watershed moments and turning points in the institutional history, and offer useful historical parallels for our later analysis. We shall consider economic statism in this regard in more detail later in the book.

---

[29] A classic case study of organizational dependency is Ray Huang's study on the Ming institution of salt monopoly, which was forced to reform from a household-based model under full government control to a market-based model with less control. See Ray Huang, *Taxation and Government Finance in Sixteenth Century China* (New York, NY: Cambridge University Press, 1974), pp. 195–204.

The First Climax of Economic Statism: The Wang Mang Reform

The process of imperial state-building could be seen to date back to the late Warring States period, when the Lord of Shang attempted to reform the kingdom of Qin from a feudal state to a military absolutist state directly controlled by the ruler. The economic process of state-building involved the expropriation of feudal land ownerships and the establishment of an effective state-allocation system. The new state would be based on military merit achieved in universal military services and massive public infrastructure projects designed to enhance agricultural productivity and interregional communication.[30] Thanks to its effective military-economy institutions, the Qin war machine was powerful enough to crush all its less centralized competitors. After Qin Shihuang's territorial unification of China proper, even larger-scale reform was carried out all over that territory, following much the same logic.

The Han Empire revised Qin institutions to make them softer and less coercive while adopting most of its basic administrative framework. The revisions included, among others, a decades-long laissez-faire policy. But things changed course when Han Wudi and his fiscal administration under Shang Hongyang seized power. Determined to harness the wealth of the empire to fight back the Xiongnu, Wudi and his financiers engineered nothing less than a complete overhaul of the fiscal system. Among the new fiscal sources created were salt, iron, and wine monopolies; a punitive tax on property that almost equaled outright confiscation; the centralization of minting; and a first attempt at security-bearing money.[31] All these measures were carried out forcibly, through massive use of coercive state power against wealthy merchant households and local elites.

While Wudi might have masterfully exemplified the extent of coercive powers exercised by a centralized state over its subjects, the Wang Mang Reform a century later marked the real historical climax of economic statism. Since the death of Wudi, the Han Empire had again experienced the rise of powerful locally based social forces such as large landowners and industrialists. Its initial stage corresponded to the historical backdrop of the *Discourse on Salt and Iron*, discussed in Chapter 2. The rise of these

---

[30] Derk Bodde, "The State and Empire of Qin," in Denis Twichett and Michael Loewe, eds., *The Cambridge History of China*, vol. 1, History of Qin and Han (Cambridge and New York, NY: Cambridge University Press, 1986), pp. 34–39.

[31] Nishijima Sadao, "The Economic and Social History of Former Han," in Twichett and Loewe, eds., *Cambridge History of China*, pp. 601–605.

social forces fundamentally changed the socioeconomic balance and weakened the fiscal basis of the empire by seizing control of land and the market, thus making the majority of households and individuals their private dependents. In the first century BC, several reform efforts, including intervening in landholdings and moral exhortations, failed to curb the trend.[32]

When Wang Mang came to power, the desperate state of affairs had aroused a widely shared sense of crisis among the ruling elite, especially the Confucian scholars. An avowed ideologist and reformer, Wang Mang made an unprecedented attempt to transform the system in line with Confucian ideals. According to modern Confucian scholars, the Wang Mang Reform was essentially a statist social experiment to realize a uniform and equalized fiscal base in accordance with a prefabricated Old-Text School classic, with its ideological blueprints outlined in the Book of Zhou Rituals, *Zhouguan Jing*.[33]

Wang Mang's first major policy measure was to declare public (imperial) ownership of land and bonded laborers, a policy that effectively required the imperial state to exercise direct administrative controls over most surplus land and bonded laborers. Land holdings exceeding the upper limits would be confiscated and converted to public land. Markets for bonded laborers were abolished and bonded laborers exceeding their quota were restored to freedom under the aegis of the imperial government. The second measure amounted to the nationalization of the major goods market, or commercialization of the imperial fiscal system, enabled by a variety of policies to monopolize natural resources and essential goods. For the remaining market sector, at all levels of the economy, the state now imposed a flat 10 percent commercial tax and regulated supplies to ensure price stability for important goods. A parallel policy in the financial sector was state control over the credit system, which for the first time put into practice the innovative ideas of state commercial banks, issuing interest-free loans to noncommercial lenders and charging 10 percent interest to commercial lenders.[34] The third measure was a thorough overhaul of the currency system. Wang Mang instituted a highly complex system of exchangeable currencies to replace the simple system put in place by

---

[32] Michael Loewe, "The Former Han," in Twichett and Loewe, eds., *Cambridge History of China*, pp. 204–205.

[33] See Xu Fuguan, *Zhouguan chengli shijian jiqi sixiang xingge* (Zhouguan Jing: Its Time of Compilation and the Characters of Its Thoughts) (Taipei: Taiwan Xuesheng Shuju, 1980), pp. 265–267.

[34] Sadao, "The Economic and Social History of Former Han," pp. 601–605.

previous governments. As the reform deepened, the system underwent a series of simplifications, leading to hyperinflation and the collapse of the inflation system.[35]

Wang Mang's reform was a complete failure. Land and labor systems were aborted after encountering overwhelmingly stiff social resistance. The strongly enforced monopoly and market regulation led to unprecedented market failure and recession. The currency reforms were the worst disaster, creating massive monetary disorder as result of the collapse of the money system and its replacement by barter. Most problematic of all was Wang Mang's inability to check the behavior of his bureaucratic agents, who quickly became more predatory than local magnates in upsetting normal economic orders.[36]

The Wang Mang Reform was a watershed event in the economic and institutional history of imperial China. From a long-term historical view, the reform was a systemic response of the state to a series of institutional changes in the economy after the collapse of the feudal economic order in the late Warring States period. Since the end of the Warring States period, there had been a long period of growth and structural change in productive technology and economic organizations, only punctuated by two periods of war and mobilization. Economic prosperity also led to the development of trade and commerce and a concentration of private wealth.[37] Meanwhile, the imperial state was increasingly marginalized in economic life, with its ideological and moral foundations in a state of crisis. Wang Mang's efforts could be considered as attempts to bring the state back in on an unprecedented scale.

The reform was also consequential for later developments in the next few centuries. As Wang Ming's failure highlighted the emperor's limited ability to enforce radical Confucian doctrines, emperors of the later Han chose to coopt rather than confront the increasingly potent locally based elite family clans, leaving the grassroots markets and households in the hands of local magnates. As the institution of the emperor declined, the late Han central government was frequently captured by powerful family clans and eunuchs' cliques. This was paralleled by the decline of local fiscal organizations, as the landowning class captured most of the agrarian economy's surplus and reduced most imperial subjects to private dependents.[38]

---

[35] *Ibid.*, pp. 628–230.   [36] *Ibid.*, p. 632.   [37] *Ibid.*, pp. 601–605.

[38] Hsu Choyun, *Han Agriculture: The Formation of China's Agrarian Economy* (Seattle, WA: University of Washington Press, 1980), pp. 152–153.

As the late Han state finally collapsed, China entered a period of disunity, punctuated by only a short period of unification under the Jin Empire (265–317 AD). This long period of territorial fragmentation is often termed the Chinese Medieval Age (200–750 AD).[39] Despite the rise and fall of several dynastic houses, the imperial state was never able to unify and integrate the territory politically, nor to exercise full control over the economy. Constant interstate wars and a lack of central authority continued for about three centuries (320–580 AD). In many parts of Northern China, a state of depopulation and destruction prevailed for centuries. Without a strong central state, public goods including basic security and monetary regimes, became scant and costly. Households and village organizations were the most important economic organizations whereas the market was a state-controlled, morally dubious, and geographically separate domain playing a supplementary role.[40] A household-based economy order would dominate throughout most of the country until favorable trends for recentralization of imperial power came to prevail in the area of political development.

The Second Climax of Economic Statism: The Wang Anshi Reform

The political situation began to stabilize around a new group of conquering elites in the late sixth century. China then entered another major period of imperial state-building and economic reorganization, which lasted for the next century and a half. The tide began to turn when the Northern Wei Empire reaffirmed its adherence to the Confucian ideology and carried out land reforms to ensure more equal distribution of the land and tax burdens. Based on the new land regime, a new household-based kindred tax system in the form of a fixed tax on grain per *ding* (labor), textile products per *hu* (household), and obligatory government service was gradually established. The early Tang state was a typical household-based economic order.

The unification of China proper under the Sui (581 AD) and Tang Empires (618 AD) provided the final institutional superstructure for the household-based economic order. Under the new economic order, the imperial state enjoyed a century and a half of economic prosperity and

---

[39] Naito Torajiro, Zhongguo lishi tonglun (A General Theory of Chinese History) (Beijing: Sheke Wenxian Chubanshe, 2006), pp. 14–15.

[40] Hou Xudong, *Beichao cunmin de shenghuo shijie* (Life World of Villagers in the Northern Dynasties) (Beijing: The Commercial Press, 2010), pp. 188–199.

military dominance over its neighbors. However, economic dislocation soon set in as state control of land aggrandizement was lost and inequality in land ownership became firmly established. The fate of dynastic decline was sealed when the An-Shi Civil War (759–770 AD) destroyed the economy of the North. Under the fiscal duress required for survival, Tang rulers eventually replaced the household-based tax with a new system based on property, chiefly land ownership. Private ownership of land was firmly established as a basic economic institution.

The next two centuries saw the onset of a historic transition, during which the economy, society, and polity underwent a series of fundamental changes. After another major civil war in the late eighth century, the imperial state was never able to fully reclaim the territory in the northeast and northwest, leaving the space to the various nomads until some six to ten centuries later. Political power changed hands from locally based families to military strongmen and, ultimately, the literati-bureaucrat class. The economic center of China gradually shifted from north to south, from west to east, with the southeast rice-cultivating regions increasingly emerging as new economic and cultural centers and the main tax base for the empire.[41]

A parallel shift in the economy was also underway. Both agricultural and nonagricultural sectors likewise underwent another sustained period of growth and technological change, underlined by permanent population growth, urbanization, industrialization, and institutional changes. The Song economy in the tenth century produced as much as half of the world's industrial output.[42] This fundamental historical transition, known as the Tang–Song transition, was largely complete by mid-eleventh century. At this point the Song imperial state (established in 960 AD) already had under its control the most affluent society in the world, and it instituted a most complex system of fiscal management. Yet the imperial state also faced severe fiscal constraints in order to maintain a costly military system of professional soldiers and a cumbersome bureaucratic system, as well as a lack of the necessary resources to reclaim the lost northern territory.

Prior to becoming chief minister, Wang Anshi had spent twenty years serving as the head of county and prefectural governments. In stark contrast to the utopianist Wang Mang, who based all his reform ideas on

---

[41] Dieter Kuhn, *The Age of Confucian Rule: The Song Transformation of China* (Cambridge, MA: Harvard University Press, 2009), pp. 217–219.

[42] Angus Maddison, *The World Economy: A Millennial Perspective*, OECD, 2001, p. 15.

Confucius' classics, Wang Anshi derived a large part of his reform programs from practical experience as a local government official. The latter
Wang's combination of this practical experience with classical learning
made him a classic example of a clearly market-oriented reformer who
blended with this the idealism of a statist. In many ways, his program
amounted to a complete rationalization of state finance along the line of
commercialization and nationalization, a proactive attempt to reorientate
the imperial state toward its changed social bases. The new economic order
presupposed the state's elevation of the market from a supplementary
position to that of a fundamental economic institution.

The Wang Anshi Reform was centrally concerned with the plight of
rural households in an unprotected market economy. The rural reform
programs included equalization of land tax, state-sponsored rural credit,
and the replacement of compulsory service with a service tax. The land tax
rate reform aimed to equalize tax burdens according to the quality and
yields of taxable land. The rural credit reform sought to create state-run
agricultural banks targeting poor households in need of liquidity during
the seasonal production cycle. Another major reform transformed each
household's compulsory services into hired services paid by land tax. The
household was to pay a progressively levied service tax according to
household income and wealth, and the local government was expected to
use the tax proceeds to hire those willing to offer the services.[43]

The commercial part of the reform offered major improvements on
earlier empires' monopolies. In addition to extending monopolies to the
sale of key commodities such as salt, wine, and iron, Wang Anshi's new
trade policy offered support to small traders via government procurement and low-interest loans. From the outset, this naturally led to small
traders' organizational dependency on the state rather than powerful
private predators.

The Wang Anshi Reform soon met harsh criticism from the literati-
bureaucrats. The conservatives enlisted moral as well as political arguments against Wang, not least because the reforms breached traditional
fiscal practice. Most of the high officials were landed elite with strong
connections. A retired chief minister pointed out to the emperor the real
stakes involved: When asked by the emperor for his attitude toward the
reforms, which was clearly in the interest of the people at the cost of the

---

[43] Paul Jakov Smith, "Shen Tsung's Reign and the New Policies of Wang An-Shih," in Denis
Twitchett and Paul Jakov Smith, eds., *Cambridge History of China*, vol. 5 (Cambridge and
New York, NY: Cambridge University Press, 2009), pp. 419–424.

literati-bureaucrats, he was reported to have remarked: "the Emperor should co-rule with the literati-bureaucrats (*shidafu*), rather than the petty people (*xiaomin*)."[44]

Ideological issues aside, the new policies did have some inherent weaknesses. Broadly speaking, the reform was very much in the spirit of earlier statist plans, including Wang Mang's. The aim was to reduce small households' dependency on more powerful social actors while increasing their dependency on the imperial state. But there was also a key difference. While Wang Mang simply sought a reification of the Confucian universal ideals, Wang Anshi at least tried to harness the power of market, credit, and money to streamline state finance. Nevertheless, he could not change the system of organizational dependency and replace it with a state-dominated market economy (aka state capitalism), since markets and households were still subject to the political logics of the fiscal agents. While central government revenues expanded rapidly, the private wealth of the fiscal agents – including the officials entrusted with regulating the market and collecting new tax – increased much faster. The state agents' unchecked power enabled an even more exploitative pattern in both the household and market sectors. As in all state-dominated economies, government failures set in and quickly became a new source of corruption and inefficiency.

Wang Anshi was keenly aware of the problem of economic management. The fiscal system and imperial state could not possibly remain apart from the fundamental changes in the socioeconomic structure.[45]

---

[44] Qi Xia, *Wang Anshi bianfa* (The Wang Anshi Reform) (Shanghai: Shanghai Renmin Publishing House, 1957), p. 196.

[45] The debate on Wang Anshi's historical role, political ideals, and performance as a reformer was inextricably associated with and determined by specific historical perspectives on early Song China. From Song to Qing, generations of historians in late imperial China overwhelmingly condemned Wang as opportunistic and as the progenitor of the crisis. The negative evaluations culminated in Qianlong's official verdict pronouncing Wang one of the worst chief ministers there had been. The common justification for such critiques was that Wang undermined the Order (political order) and violated the Way (ideological doctrines) of the late imperial state. Positive evaluations of Wang only gained power after late Qing, when modern state-building again became an important theme. Liang Qichao praised Wang as the greatest political figure in China's history. This had much to do with his strong grasp on the urgency of China's modernization and state-building in the late Qing period. Later historians, especially during Republican China and the 1980s period of the People's Republic, also gave Wang a very high appraisal, given his attempts to modernize and empower the imperial state. Even today, more objective and balanced historical debates are still shaped by the discourses of statism (New Left) and antistatism (neoliberals). For a detailed account of these different perspectives on Wang Anshi, see Li Huarui, *Wang Anshi bianfa*

The reform was generally a failure, and set off a series of chain reactions in the Song and later empires. The failure of the comprehensive reform and the demise of the empire thirty years later helped to shape a predominantly conservative attitude toward economic management that coevolved with the neo-Confucian ideology of the literati-bureaucrats. This was to become the organizing principle of the late empires, according to the grand design of the first Ming emperor Zhu Yuanzhang, who favored rural households and hated the market. But between the fall of the Northern Song and Zhu Yuanzhang's ascendance, the imperial political economy largely continued to operate in line with a highly commercialized model.

The market-oriented approach to revenue maximization taken by Wang reached an unparalleled level under the *Pax Mongolica* that ruled China from 1276 to 1368. The salt monopoly, now running at an unprecedented geographical level, stood out as a main provider of fiscal revenue. Just before the empire began to falter in 1333, the nationwide salt monopoly had become a principal source of revenue, after land and commercial taxes, supplying about 80 percent of central government expenses.[46] Equally impressive was the paper money system, which served as another lucrative source for revenues. After they conquered China, the Mongols inherited and expanded the paper money system of Song and Jin. For four decades, this operated on a viable footing. Beyond 1311, the paper money system managed to survive even as the state had become effectively insolvent, until the hyperinflation of the 1350s destroyed it completely.[47]

Ming Taizu's Reforms and the Household-Centered Organized Dependency

The late imperial official stance on economic management was conservative and agrocentric, stressing order and uniformity as opposed to economic and fiscal efficiency, and moderate control of inequality over radical equalization. As Ray Huang's classic study of the Ming tax system shows, the fiscal system of the Ming Empire was much less "modernist" in its outlook and institutional design than were the Song and Yuan Empires,

yanjiushi (The History of the Studies on the Wang Anshi Reform) (Beijing: Renmin Chubanshe, 2004).

[46] John Dardess, "Shunti and End of Yuan Rule in China," in *Cambridge History of China*, vol. 6 (Cambridge and New York, NY: Cambridge University Press, 2009), p. 566.

[47] Richard von Glahn, *Fountains of Fortune: Money and Monetary Thoughts in China, 1000–1500* (Berkeley, CA and Los Angeles, CA: University of California Press, 1998), pp. 56–60.

not to mention Wang Anshi's ambitious reform project. The Ming system was designed with a view to consolidate the political power of the central imperial state, in that all alternative institutional sources of organizational dependency were systemically suppressed, both inside and outside the imperial state.[48] The design and spirit of this system was largely inherited by the Mongols, with only some modifications and rationalizations to make it more efficient and controllable.

This is not to say that the late imperial system was a natural order. Quite the opposite is true. In the aftermath of the millenarian rebellion and devastating civil wars of late Yuan (1352–1368), the founding emperor of Ming, Zhu Yuanzhang, emerged from the lowest ranks of society and reached the pinnacle of political power within two decades. With radically transcendent ideas about his Mandate, he tried to remake China in accordance with the ideal vision of a household-centered agrarian society and moral economy. The scale and scope of the changes under his rule could well be seen to rival the Maoist Revolution in the People's Republic after 1949. Drastic policy measures included massive forced migration from regions less affected by war to depopulated regions[49]; the imposition of a highly rigid legal code with a strong cosmological claim[50]; the transformation of a cosmopolitan set of cultural customs into reinvented Chinese traditions, imposed on all ethnic and religious groups in China proper[51]; and the setting up of a military establishment based on multinational migrant military households and their garrisons across the country.[52]

The fiscal aspects of the transformation amounted to a reversal of the previous paradigm of market-oriented finance. According to Liu Guanglin's recent study, the reform was fourfold. First, Taizu (Zhu Yuanzhang) not only inherited the Yuan household classification system that controlled professional and social mobility, but went further by imposing stringent

---

[48] Ray Huang, *China: A Micro-History* (Armonk, NY: M. E. Sharp, 2000), pp. 132–133.

[49] For example, 40–80 percent of the early Ming population in central Chinese provinces equivalent to today's Hubei and Hunan were migrants from Jiangxi and elsewhere. See Cao Shuji, *Zhongguo yiminshi*, vol. 5 (History of Chinese Migrations, Vol. 5, Ming Dynasty) (Fuzhou: Fujian Renmin Chubanshe, 1997), pp. 80–100.

[50] Jiang Yonglin, *The Mandate of Heaven and the Great Ming Code* (Seattle, WA and London: University of Washington Press, 2012), pp. 13–15.

[51] Zhang Jia, *Xintianxiazhihua: Mingchu lisu gaige yanjiu* (Renewing the Transformation of the World: A Study of Reforms of Rituals and Customs in Early Ming) (Shanghai: Fudan University, 2015), pp. 275–278.

[52] Zhao Shiyu, "Weisuo junhu zhidu yu mingdai shehui: shehuixue shijiao" (The Garrison System and Ming Chinese Society: A Social History Perspective), *Journal of Tsinghua University (Philosophy and Social Sciences)*, 30:3 (2015), pp. 114–127.

controls on their geographical mobility. Second, he retained paper notes, but tried to manipulate the price of key commodities by monopolizing the money supply. Third, he imposed a new tax system based on payment in kind and compulsory corvée service. Fourth, he forcefully uprooted rich households from the highly commercialized Jiangnan region and resettled them in devastated regions and the borderlands, in order to reclaim the land. All these could be regarded as measures to establish a command or planned economy in an agrarian setting.[53] The second and third approaches involved an inherent contradiction around the use of paper money. This issue would ultimately be resolved in later decades as the early Ming state moved away from paper currency to an unofficial silver economy.[54]

Compared with earlier ages, the late imperial state relied more heavily on ideology than on hard economic and coercive power as the most important infrastructural power. Technical knowledge and administrative competence, which had been valued in career financiers and local officials from Han to Tang, gave way to ideological and moral authority, such as sound Confucian knowledge and personal loyalty to the emperor. The actual fiscal management of local governments was delegated to low-ranking officers – administrative agents of the fiscal officials as imperial agents, unhindered by their lack of political authority and social prestige.[55] This was in accordance with the idea that the empire was an extended household, where structural aspects such as family morals and personal loyalty took precedence over the substantive aspects of state management.

The mid- and late Ming commercial revolution, like the early Han and Tang–Song market revolution, likewise led to the erosion of direct state control over the society and economy, but not of the fundamental model of the political economy. The most salient consequence of such erosion was arguably the rise of private fiscal agents, most noticeably *Xiejia*, private innkeepers who provided lodgings and food to fiscal agents and peasants who carried tax grain to collection points in the early Ming tax system; they came to be seen as key intermediaries between the state and society who organized tax collection, provided financial mediation, insured fiscal transit, and even mediated local litigation.[56] From mid-Ming to Republican

---

[53] William Guanglin Liu, *The Chinese Market Economy 1000–1500* (New York, NY: SUNY Press, 2015), p. 6.
[54] von Glahn, *Fountains of Fortune*, pp. 71–75.   [55] *Ibid.*
[56] Hu Tieqiu, *Ming–Qing xiejia yanjiu* (A Study of Innkeepers in Ming and Qing Dynasties) (Shanghai: Shanghai Guji Chubanshe, 2015), pp. 599–600.

China, these innkeepers became a pillar of the fiscal system. Meanwhile, the corporate lineage gradually evolved as the pillar of the household economic order that integrated both the subsistence and the commercial economies. The corporate lineage provided the household economy diversification and specialization so that its constituent household could survive and even thrive in the late imperial economic environment in which the subsistence and commercial sectors coexisted.[57] New institutions such as innkeepers and lineage, while taking a significant share of state power, ensured that commercialization was never politically subversive: The innkeepers were merely agents of local officials who mediated local government and society, whereas lineage households were highly identified with the state ideology of Confucianism and were symbiotic with the Civil Service Examination system.

In economic terms, such important institutional innovations did not lead to modern capitalism and industrialization, since they worked on different logics and rationales. Despite some well-documented evidence of capitalist production, the put-out system of proto-industrial production rather than large-scale organized production proliferated in rural southern China. In the Yangtze Delta region, the new economic core of imperial China, most households engaged in market-oriented production, especially handicrafts and family textiles, even if marginal productivity was nonpositive, to meet the increasingly monetized agrarian tax and the costs of daily subsistence. In other words, a market sector tended to evolve as an indispensable but only subsidiary sector in the overall subsistence economy dominated by the household economy on the principle of reciprocity and redistribution. Under such a system, surplus was restricted both by the scale of production and the extent of the market, while the very limited profits went to commercial and landed elites, and ultimately the fiscal interests of the state and its organizational dependents.[58] In some cases, such as that of the lower Yangtze, market expansion was principally driven by the scarcity of land and fiscal pressures, which made market-oriented household handicrafts a complement to agricultural products as a source of revenues. Otherwise, autonomous markets remained largely localized and

---

[57] Zheng Zhenman, Michael Szonyi trans., *Family Lineage Organizations in Ming and Qing Fujian* (Honolulu, HI: University of Hawai'i Press, 2001), p. 235.

[58] Nishijima Sadao, *Chugoku Keizaiji Kankyu* (Study on Economic History of China), 2nd ed. (Tokyo: Tokyo University Press, 1982), pp. 862–864.

mostly unspecialized, serving the subsistence needs of community local households rather than a larger region.[59]

On the other hand, factors indispensable for early modern capitalism, such as long-distance trade, large-scale industrial production and luxury consumption goods, and the creation of money and credit, were always present but were regulated by both the state and its household organizations, such as imperial factories, imperial merchant houses, and, most significantly, the Qing Imperial Household Department. Market activities in late imperial China were comparable with those in its European and Japanese counterparts in terms of density and intensity. Unlike in early modern Europe, where the market performed the intricate role of sustaining and improving the livelihood economy in the private sphere, late imperial China oriented itself away from a reformist approach to the normality of economic management. Taking Western European development as a reference, this system of household-centered organized dependency might seem to be inhibiting the growth of capitalism. But as we shall observe from different aspects of its function, this system was a remarkably successful model of a state's domination of the market without resorting to radical or reformist approaches, though it cannot escape the cyclical process of rise and decline.

AUTONOMY AND DOMINATION

The Agrarian Household

The material foundation of the imperial state was an agrarian economy. For more than 2,000 years, the imperial state received the larger part of its fiscal revenue in the form of grain produce and peasant labor from, eventually, well over ten million farming households. Most official sources show the overall land tax rate was reasonably below 10 percent of the total produce. But the real tax burden was much heavier, since the costs of collection, transit, and the amount paid to the tax agents were at least as high.

The agrarian tax gradually became separated from household and substantive grain produce as tax units. During the Sui and early Tang dynasties, land tax was levied on equitable terms on each household on the assumption of equal land holding. But in the late eighth century, as land

---

[59] William Skinner, *Marketing in Rural China* (Ann Arbor, MI: Association for Asian Studies, 1964), pp. 38–39.

holdings came to be concentrated in the minority of propertied households, actual produce on the *de facto* privately owned and rented land became the true tax base in the Two-Tax System, which was institutionalized in all dynasties after the Song.[60]

Corvée labor was another major fiscal institution. In early Ming, there were two types of such compulsory service. About 1–3 percent of households were officially registered as permanent laborers, working in salt production and other government-controlled industries, who turned in their produce as obligatory service and received a subsistence stipend. For all other households, corvée labor in early Ming consisted of compulsory government service on a regular shift basis. From mid-Ming onward, these corvée services were gradually converted into a progressive service tax on registered households; the state used the proceeds to hire workers for public work and the maintenance of imperial infrastructure.[61]

Historically, the agrarian tax system invariably suffered from a gradual erosion of its tax base and other forms of institutional decline over the course of a given dynastic cycle. While progressive and reasonably low in its definition, the tax system always became increasingly regressive and burdensome. This can be explained by the cyclical rise and decline of the centralizing powers of the imperial state. The state was usually at the height of its power vis-à-vis its various challengers in its founding period. As the agrarian economy recovered from dynastic wars, the demographic effect began to exert a decisive influence on the distribution of land and surplus produce, which had become scarce with respect to both population and household. Land ownership gravitated into the hands of the landlords, who had better means to evade tax or pass the burden to the tenants. Formerly small landowning peasants tended to get a disproportionate share of the burden, and became dependent. The imperial state, increasingly losing track of the actual land distribution, had to commit extra resources to extract the same amount of landed tax. But the increasing tax burden would eventually make things worse, as more and more peasants lost lands and means of livelihood. When natural disaster struck, this large chunk of the grassroots society might become vagabonds, join the marauding rebel bands, and eventually coalesce into formidable peasant armies seeking to capture the Mandate of Heaven.

---

[60] Dieter Kuhn, *The Age of Confucian Rule: The Song Transformation of China* (Cambridge, MA: Harvard University Press, 2009), pp. 244–245.

[61] Brook Timothy, *The Troubled Empire: China in the Yuan and Ming Dynasties* (Cambridge, MA: Harvard University Press, 2008), pp. 153–154.

Equally consequential was the organizational involution in the fiscal system in the long run. As the economy recovered, the society tended to evolve away from tight state control. There was commonly a gradual erosion of grassroots fiscal organizations. In response to a loss of information and organizational control, the imperial state invariably faced the challenge of reform. In the Ming and Qing empires, such fiscal reform usually took the form of monetization and rationalization of land-based direct tax. The reforms of Zhang Juzheng (1576–1582) and Yongzheng Emperor (1724–1735) are cases in point.

As the imperial state lost control, agrarian tax tended to exert an increasingly disproportionate burden on the poor; in the later stages of a dynasty, it usually became a source of social instability. Actual revenue from the tax amounted to only a fraction of the land wealth and produce. In most cases, the fiscal agents in between the imperial state and the household producing units got the lion's share of the surplus. Despite the supreme ownership enjoyed by the emperor, the imperial state was crippled by its lack of capacity to control tax and derive full rents from the land. Even at the height of Qianlong's rule in the mid-eighteenth century, total agricultural tax – the mainstay of the late imperial tax system – amounted to less than 10 percent of the total grain output.

Local Government Finance

Ever since China's territorial unification by Qin Shihuang, central–local relations between the imperial state and its local government agents had played an indispensable role in the fiscal and economic management of the empire. The structure of central–local power distribution and the capacity of local states largely defined the limit of the state's reach and the distortions in its policy outcomes.

In general, the balance between central and local states has moved in favor of higher centralization of powers in the emperor and his central bureaucracy at the cost of autonomy for local governments. By the late imperial China period, the emperor had accumulated many organizational strategies to restrain local powers, such as divide and rule, selective centralization, personalized communication channels, and elaborate supervision of the administrative hierarchy over a very long time span.[62] At the same time, local governments lost all their autonomous military and fiscal

---

[62] For a long-term evolution of the control regime, see Jae Ho Chung, "The Evolving Hierarchy of China's Local Administration: Tradition and Change," in Jae Ho Chung

powers and from the Ming dynasty onwards, even legal and fiscal affairs were administered separately by different, parallel, units at the provincial administrative level. From Qing onwards, even county magistrates, not to mention officials at the provincial and circuit levels, were sometimes personally supervised by the emperor at annual reviews, as his own private representatives.[63]

In terms of fiscal resources, local governments had also lost much of their autonomous sources of revenue. In the Ming tax administration, the county/city (*Zhou/Xian*) was essentially the tax collection center, the circuits the account unit, the province a unit of transfer and redistribution, and the central bureaucracy the only control center for all fiscal resources. Much of the revenues were transferred vertically in this way; little was retained in the grassroots collecting units. The ratio between forwarded and retained revenues was around 3:1 or 4:1 for any typical county/city.[64] Despite meager incomes and little maneuverability, the grassroots local governments were to provide most public goods and support all personal and administrative costs.

This tendency toward centralization produced a seemingly contradictory institutional outcome in late imperial China: a rationalized but diminished state. On one hand, there was a higher degree of central government control and considerable rationalization in central–local fiscal relations, in terms of more efficient administration of taxation and basic public goods, from defense to disaster relief. Even information costs were largely reduced by innovations like the Secret Palace Memorial System, which opened channels of personal communication between the emperor and officials at levels above the provincial. Tightened controls directly handled by the emperor in high-stakes fiscal affairs reduced the otherwise unmanageable corruption and misappropriations to a set of more regularized informal rules and, in the mid-Qing case, a formally institutionalized additional anticorruption bonus (*yanglian* salary) to prevent corruption.[65]

However, at the grassroots level, local governments – significantly weakened both fiscally and administratively compared to earlier periods –

and Tao-chiu Lam, eds., *China's Local Administration: Tradition and Change* (London and New York, NY: Routledge, 2010), pp. 1–13.

[63] Shen Daming, *Daqing luli he qingdaide shehuikongzhi* (The Qing Legal Cases and Social Control in Qing Empire) (Shanghai: Shanghai Renmin chubanshe), pp. 109.

[64] Ray Huang, *Taxation and Government Finance in 16th Century Ming China*, pp. 178–179.

[65] Madeleine Zelin, *The Magistrate's Tael: Rationalizing Fiscal Reform in Qing China* (Berkeley, CA: University of California Press, 1992), pp. 117–118.

lost their autonomy to a deeply entrenched local network of powers. In late imperial China, local governments typically depended on the locally based literati gentry and family clans to provide a wide range of public goods, including local education, public health, water works, disaster relief, and law and order.[66] Public goods would otherwise become too costly for the local magistrates, who were constrained both in fiscal resources and manpower under the late imperial state model established by Ming Taizu. But the reliance on the gentry meant a considerable loss of local state autonomy. In late imperial China, the gentry class would loom large not only as intermediaries, but also as self-interested power players between the state and the local society.[67]

The other manifestation of local embeddedness was the actual domination of administrative agents in public and especially fiscal affairs. Since the administrative officers were also household units, the actual everyday administrative power was highly decentralized and locally inherited. The tendency was structurally rooted, but the late imperial state's centralization and subsequent weakening of local governments led to a predominance of low-ranking local officers with both technical and human skills and with local knowledge and connections, resulting in a distortion of the rent-seeking local intermediaries between the state and society. Collectively, this class of unclassified imperial agents would appropriate private wealth at least on a par with total government revenues.[68]

Although there was some rationalization in central–local relations, local governments generally declined and contracted in late imperial China. There was a loss of autonomy vis-à-vis the emperor and the local society. This had a significant impact on the provision of public goods and local economic order. Left without the resources to promote meaningful economic development, local governments were equally incapable of controlling the local elite's encroachment on and even usurpation of state powers. This left them with little room to improve and direct society, except when its activity corresponded to the prevailing ideology and interests of the gentry class. This situation was drastically different from the Tokugawa local states or the *Han* in Japan, which were able to engage in more fiscal

---

[66] Chu Tung-Tzu, *Local Government in China under Qing* (Cambridge, MA: Harvard University Press, 1962), pp. 182–183.

[67] Yuri Pines, *Everlasting Empire: The Political Culture of Ancient China and Its Imperial Legacy* (Princeton, NJ and Oxford: Princeton University Press, 2012), pp. 123–133.

[68] This tendency was called *Guan wu Fengjian, Li you fengjian*, which means there is no (political) feudalism for the *guan* (literati-bureaucrats), but there is (administrative) feudalism for the *li* (hired low-ranking administrative agents of the literati officials).

and other policy innovations according to their local and perceived national interests.[69] As it turned out, local elites would eventually supplement or even replace the state as providers of order and public goods when foreign powers entered the picture. This will be a theme in Chapter 4.

The National Market

As discussed in Chapter 2, Chinese political thinkers have long recognized the state monopoly of the market and money as a potential source of fiscal revenue. The first systemic state theory of market and money was found in *Guan Zi*, a compilation of political theses from no later than the early Han period.[70] About one third of the chapters dealt with fiscal management. According to the theory of *Qing-Zhong* (State Price Theory), the prince could make huge profits through the market by manipulating money, controlling grain supply, and monopolizing essential products such as salt. Besides the ordinary commercial operations of buying low and selling high, the authors of *Guan Zi* argued for the commercialization of the fiscal system as a more effective substitute to agrarian tax. Like the Keynesians in modern times, this school of management argued for reformist state intervention through excessive consumption and employment of labor for public work.

In 80 BC, Han Wudi set up the first empirewide monopoly of salt, iron, and wine to finance his expensive expedition against China's major nomadic rival, the Xiongnu. But the monopoly system caused so much controversy after the death of Wudi that it was gradually dismantled and replaced by market and state taxation, though there were a few failed attempts at remonopolization. The salt monopoly was once more institutionalized as a source of fiscal revenue in the eighth century in the Tang dynasty. It was perfected in successive dynasties, and remained a fiscal

---

[69] For a survey of the local autonomy in the Japanese case, see Harold Botho, "The Han," in John Whitney Hall, ed., *Cambridge History of Japan*, vol. 4 (Cambridge and New York, NY: Cambridge University Press, 1991), pp. 205–225.

[70] *Guan Zi* was probably a collection of policy plans and philosophical papers produced by Jixia Xuegong (the Academy of Jixia, possibly the first policy think-tank in the world) of the Kingdom of Qi during the late Warring States period (fourth to third century BC). The views thus reflected various state-building plans undertaken in the climate of political urgency of the successful Shang Yang centralization reform in the Kingdom of Qin. For a full English translation with an introduction, see Allyn Pickett, *Guanzi: Political, Economic, and Philosophical Essays from Early China, a Study and Translation* (Princeton, NJ: Princeton University Press, 1985).

institution well into the People's Republic.[71] The practice of state monopoly also extended to other key everyday products. For example, there was a system of state monopoly over the distribution and sale of tea which ran intermittently from the eighth century to the end of the imperial era.[72]

Among the key issues facing state monopoly were inefficiency, corruption, and smuggling. Burdened by the institutional costs and loss of income caused by these difficulties, the imperial state usually turned to merchants as fiscal agents while focusing state monopoly on only key processes in the whole value chain. Thus, the evolution of state monopoly was not unlike that of the agrarian tax system. While the imperial state readily adopted full state control over the production, distribution, and sale process in the hope of full monopoly profits, the resultant costs of market failure, rampant corruption, and lower fiscal revenues compelled it to move gradually toward more perfect indirect control.

The most enduring institutional innovation of organizational dependency in state monopoly was the *guanshang* (bureaucrat-merchant comprador) in late imperial China. Alternatively known as "red-hat merchants," the *guanshang* were usually merchant households with special licenses to act as supply agents for the imperial state. Most *guanshang* families had long-standing, stable relations with imperial governments. They operated in every profitable area of business, acting as informal agents of the imperial state or commercial agents of the emperor (in this case, they were called *huangshang*) through organizations like the Imperial Household Department. In return for their loyal service to the empire as intermediaries between market and state, the *guanshang* received low-interest loan advances and derived stable streams of profits from their monopoly.

Although *guanshang* were widespread in the imperial economy, the only *guanshang* groups performing a direct fiscal function were the officially designated salt merchants of late imperial China. Usually a hereditary family business, a designated salt merchant typically operated as both monopoly trader and fiscal agent. A classic example is the Anhuai and Shanxi merchant family clans of late Ming and early Qing, whose principal

---

[71] This institution was rumored to have ended only in 2014. See www.bloomberg.com/news/articles/2014-11-20/china-to-end-salt-monopoly-dating-back-to-ancient-times [Accessed on May 12, 2017].

[72] John Evans, *Tea in China: The History of China's National Drink* (Westport, CT: Greenwood Press, 1992), pp. 58–59.

source of wealth was the state-run salt monopoly. Without political sanction, any large-scale capital accumulation would be difficult.

Behind the proliferation of the *guanshang* and their family wealth was a national market of salt and other commodities that was only partially integrated and subject to political control, despite its vast size and complex structure. Unlike premodern Japan, late imperial China never witnessed any market actors operating on a national scale as retailers or financiers. Even when there were some elements of large-scale enterprises, such as the *piaohao*, they still operated in semiclosed markets and networks (most among themselves), self-governed in the style of traditional households, and kept thinly veiled dependent relations with the imperial state.[73] Measurements and currencies were likewise unified only in the central fiscal administration of the state, where a large variety of standards prevailed for different regions and localities.

The International Market

International trade has long been regarded as an important alternative source of fiscal revenue and a strategic weapon against a foreign country. The theorists in *Guan Zi* talked about outpricing rival states in grain in the interstate markets in order to weaken the rival economically. But it was not until Tang that private wealth from international trade became a worthy tax base.

The late imperial state initially took a positive view of both sea and border trade. From the Tang through Yuan dynasties (seventh to fourteenth century AD) onward, the imperial state operated special trade administrations at each trading port to encourage trade and collect custom duty. There had also been an unsuccessful systemic attempt to establish a state-sponsored trading monopoly in early Yuan.[74] But since the mid-Ming dynasty (fifteenth to nineteenth century AD) through to the entire late imperial era, as strategic concerns weighed in, both trades came to be closely monitored and fell under tight political control. Thus, the official tribune system symbolized by Zheng He voyages in the early fifteenth century largely foreshadowed private trade. Meanwhile, both sea and

---

[73] Huang Jianhui, *Shanxi piaohao shi* (History of Shanxi Banks) (Taiyuan: Shanxi Economic Press, 1996), pp. 159–160.

[74] William Atweh, "Ming and the Emerging World Economy," in Denis Twitchett and Frederick W. Mote, eds., *Cambridge History of China*, vol. 8 (Cambridge and New York, NY: Cambridge University Press, 1988), pp. 377–378.

border trade were made illegal during periods of insecurity in the early sixteenth century, and again in the late seventeenth century. The final settlement was still a rather limited trading monopoly run by officially designated merchants under the direct administration of a custom superintendent, bounded by the framework of the tribune system and existing alongside militarized and highly professionalized smugglers and pirates active along China's east coast.[75]

From the sixteenth century onward, even though China had effectively become a key player in the expanding global trade networks and received a constant influx of silver due to trade surplus, the Ming and Qing courts never regarded custom duty as an important source of state revenue. Rather, strategic and security considerations took precedence over fiscal concerns. The late imperial state imposed a ban on overseas trade several times when security concerns were raised. Their concerns were partially justified by the role of customs in China's fiscal system. Even at the very height of the late Ming market-oriented reform, revenue from customs amounted to less than 5 percent of fiscal revenue.[76]

While scrapping a measure of fiscal benefits as involuntary net exporters in the international system, the Ming and early Qing imperial state kept a watchful eye on foreign ships, goods, and traders. Except for the Portuguese at Macao, no European trading powers obtained any permanent foothold in China in the first three hundred years after they initially entered the China market. This situation would not change until the mid-nineteenth century, when the Qing Empire lost control over its customs and maritime borders.

As in other aspects of the fiscal system, in the eighteenth century, the imperial state used a system of merchant-run monopoly trading companies called the *Conghang* as an intermediary between foreign traders and the imperial government. Unlike modern Western mercantilist organizations such as the English and Dutch East India Companies, the *Conghang* trade organizations were strictly dependent upon the emperor in their capacity as both trade and fiscal agents of the imperial state. As well as the due custom duty, the *Conghang* merchants had to make various contributions

---

[75] Takeshi Hamashita, *Intra-East Asian Trade in Ming Times* (Ithaca, NY: Cornell University Press, 1997), pp. 269–270.

[76] Xu Dixin and Wu Chengming, translated into English by Li Zhengde, Liang Miaoru, and Li Siping, edited and annotated by C. A. Curwen, *Chinese Capitalism, 1522–1840* (New York, NY: Saint Martin's Press, 2000), p. 375.

to the imperial court and local governments in exchange for political protection when the occasion demanded.[77]

Imperial Household Administration

Provision for the imperial household was a key issue in the imperial state's fiscal system. The demand was twofold: namely, imperial income in monetary terms, and material provision in the form of finished products. As discussed previously, due to the conflation of the emperor as both ruling monarch and a head of the imperial household, it was extremely difficult to distinguish between the emperor's household management and the imperial government's public finances, even if they were managed by separate institutions. The material needs of the imperial household could be met directly through the markets or autarchic bureaucratic organizations.

Imperial household management was initially the central issue of state finance. In the Qin and Han dynasties, the imperial household and the imperial state had their own fiscal bases, managed by the *Shaofu* agency, which had the same ranking as chief government financiers. Whereas the state derived its income from agrarian tax, natural resources and imperial lands provided the source of private income for the emperor. This source of revenue was estimated to be very substantial and on a par with government revenues. When Wudi launched his expensive expeditions, he made extensive use of his massive private income.

In the management of the private (imperial household) and public (government) revenues of the imperial state, the *Sansi* (three commissions in charge of taxation, state monopoly, and household registry) system of an integrated administration was an important institutional innovation in the Song dynasty. The Wang Anshi Reform further integrated the three commissions into the Board of Revenue and completed the fiscal centralization. But as imperial power increased, the significance of the imperial household in the fiscal system was not curtailed. The emperor could institutionalize a separate system of fiscal arrangement, controlled and run by his personal agents, such as eunuchs and bonded servicemen, to hold the bureaucratic fiscal system in check.[78]

---

[77] Huang Qichen and Peng Xinping, *Mingqing Guangdong shangren* (Merchants in Ming and Qing Canton) (Guangzhou: Guangdong People's Publishing House, 2003), pp. 307–308.

[78] Du Wanyan and Fang Zhiyuan, "*Mingchao zhengzhi zhidushi*" (Political Institutions of Ming Dynasty), in Bai Gang, ed., *Zhongguo zhengzhi zhidu tongshi* (General History of China's Political Institutions) (Beijing: Renmin Publishing House, 1996), pp. 388–289.

In late imperial China, the imperial household was managed by a separate system of fiscal provision directly under the emperor. In the Ming dynasty, this was the larger part of twenty-four eunuch-run professional bureaucracies specializing in the production, procurement, and provision of goods and services for the emperor, the imperial household, and the Palace. In late Ming, as the fiscal system was fully monetized, eunuch agents were employed to seek out alternative sources of revenues in mining. By this time, the past predatory traditions were being experienced once more, with the eunuch agents exploiting their powers and stirring up local uprisings.[79]

In the Qing dynasty, the emperor sidelined eunuchs and substituted close dependents or the Manchu *Booi* (bond servant) to staff a more integrated bureaucratic system called the Imperial Household Department. Noted especially for its huge size and extensive jurisdiction, the Internal Household Department had under its control the Palace, the imperial estates near Beijing, and locally based imperial factories specializing in luxury goods. As the most mature institutional organization in the imperial household administration, the Imperial Household Department was a giant bureaucratic organization that controlled the cream of the Qing Empire's economic resources, such as public lands, imperial customs, and imperial factories with responsibility for the provision of the emperor's material requirements. As one Qing scholar remarked, the most significant aspect of the *Nei-wu-fu* system was institutionalization of master–servant dependency at the commanding height of the economy. But – this being a major institutional drawback of multiple principal–agency structures – the whole organization functioned through various activities of self-profiteering, embezzlement, exaction, and squeezing.[80]

Autonomous Local Markets

Throughout the imperial era, when the realm was at peace, autonomous local markets thrived. However, local markets were generally not an essential part of the imperial political economy. Neither the conservative-household nor reformist-corporate approaches to economic management

---

[79] Wang Yi, *Zhongguo huangquan zhidu yanjiu* (An Institutional Study of Chinese Emperor) (Beijing: Beijing University Press, 2007), pp. 656–660.

[80] Preston M. Torbert, *The Ch'ing Imperial Household Department: A Study of Its Organization and Principal Functions, 1662–1796* (Cambridge, MA: Harvard University, 1977), pp. 177–178.

regarded autonomous markets as the basis of sound economic order. The Confucian conservatives deemed limited rural markets a necessary complement to household production, but many commercial activities were clearly subject to tight social control. The Legalist reformists did seek to promote exchange and uses of money, but their vision of the market was merely as a fiscal instrument dominated by imperial fiscal agents.

Nevertheless, autonomous markets prospered and played an important role in the daily lives of ordinary people. In his *The Wealth of Nations*, Adam Smith identified imperial China as a curious example of a "sluggish" market economy. The salient features of the market economy have been documented by successive generations of economic historians in China. For example, economic historian Chao Kang argues that China had all the following important features of a market economy as early as the late Warring States period:

a) There was free movement of people between different states in the Warring States;
b) Most land became privately owned; property rights were allowed for free transaction;
c) Complicated social division of labor was already an extensive and firmly established institution; numerous family clans that specialized in certain handicrafts were closely supervised by the government;
d) Exchange of products (market system) had developed very early and was integrated into each city;
e) Virtually everything had a price tag; governance on socio-economic affairs based on quantitative terms had become a standard practice of the early Empires.[81]

Many other features might be added to the list, such as rural market systems, complex market regulations, and extensive trade routes and nationwide merchant networks. Indeed, as discussed in Chapter 2, based on extensive anthropological studies on market structures in early modern China, Skinner identified market-centered clusters of villages as a "standard market community," which functions not just as a domain of economic exchange but also in terms of social and cultural activities above the unit of the natural village.[82]

Markets in late imperial China, embedded in local society, followed various local norms and catered to distinctive regional demands. For

---

[81] Kang Chao, *Man and Land in Chinese History: An Economic Analysis* (Stanford, CA: Stanford University Press, 1986), pp. 2–3.
[82] William Skinner, *Marketing and Social Structure in Rural China* (Ann Arbor, MI: Association for Asian Studies, 2001), pp. 36–37.

instance, throughout late imperial China, markets were less developed and less concentrated in the northern plain compared to the relatively commercialized south. Even within the same macroregion, measurement was not standardized and followed particularities in local markets.[83] This offered a sharp contrast with the state-run measurement system in taxation, where a national measurement standard had been in operation for each dynasty since the first empire.

Late imperial markets also operated on several layers. Unlike late medieval and early modern European towns, late imperial Chinese cities were primarily centers of political power. Throughout the history of imperial China, cities as major commercial centers usually corresponded with imperial capital and the seat of provincial capitals, or political and military power centers. In late imperial times, the process of urbanization and rustication was in constant flux, and the population boom from the early Ming to the late Qing occurred without any significant emergence of an urban civilization such as in the Song dynasty. Indeed, the urbanization level as measured per share of urban population declined significantly from 22 percent at the southern Song peak to 6 percent in the mid-nineteenth century in late Qing.[84] This could perhaps be explained by the decline of the relative size of the state from the Song to the Qing dynasties.

Beyond and above the level of the natural village, intervillage market networks constituted an important economic institution in rural China. According to Skinner's classic study on the rural market in late imperial China, rural market organizations followed a regular pattern, in close accordance with the cyclical and seasonal nature of an agrarian economy. Most of them were limited to serving a few villages or an economic region. Since there were generally no monopolistic powers in control of the demand and supply of goods, the exchanges at the regularly held intervillage fairs were voluntary and on a more or less equal basis. Take Skinner's Sichuan, in late imperial China, for example; there were about 400 such markets, with considerable concentration in the more densely populated areas.

During most periods in late imperial China, when local grassroots markets were flourishing on their own, state regulation of these markets

---

[83] *Ibid.*, pp. 46–47.
[84] Chao Kang, "Cong Hongguan jiaodu kan zhongguo chengshi" (Chinese Urban History from a Macro-Perspective), in *Zhongguo chengshi fazhanshi lunji* (Collected Discussions on the History of Development of Chinese Cities), (Beijing: New Star Publisher, 2006), p. 29.

was only weakly integrated and loosely structured. There were certainly a few military and civil officials at every strategic marketplace responsible for maintaining order and collecting tax, but these posts were symbolic rather than substantive. Before the emergence of more sophisticated tax systems toward the late Qing, the commercial tax service was satisfied with achieving a rather lax annual target. Closer examinations of the geographical distribution of such small market towns would suggest that the service was heavily biased toward markets located in cities or in densely populated areas, reflecting a primarily strategic and political concern.

In comparison with this minimal state intervention, guild organizations such as *Yahang* played a more extensive role in the regulation and management of local markets than grassroots fiscal bureaucracy. Individual merchant households were too weak vis-à-vis the state; *Yahang* as a collective body offered the merchants some measure of protection and resistance against state tax agents. Local government also benefited, as guilds reduced the costs of collecting business tax and maintaining market order. In other words, guilds provided public and collective goods at a lower cost. The advantage and the weakness of this arrangement was evident in a study on *Yahang* brokerages in the Middle Yangtze Region: while facilitating market mechanisms, they frequently turned into a source of exploitation. Meanwhile, the late imperial government only exercised regulatory oversight, rather than directly involving itself in the regulation of the market.[85]

In short, the imperial state's approach to local indigenous markets was different from that in the case of land, key goods markets, and international trade. It was neither a political strategic institution nor a profitable source of revenues, in a system dominated by millions of households and family clans and segregated into a dozen macro- and hundreds of microregions. However, the state could certainly act aggressively: The reformist approach, as a state monopoly devised to increase fiscal revenues, dominated market orders from urban centers, leaving soaring transaction costs and destroying the local autonomous market. Equally formidable was the danger of natural disaster, which usually led to a radical reduction in rural surplus and the closing of rural markets. But this was the exception rather than the rule, and seldom inflicted on a national scale.

---

[85] See Ren Fang, *Mingqing changjiang zhongyou shizhengjingji yanjiu* (Study of Market Towns in Ming and Qing Dynasties) (Wuhan: Wuhan University Press, 2003), pp. 277–290.

The Monetary System

The imperial state practiced, on and off, a monopoly on minting for two thousand years from the period of rule of Wudi, of the Han dynasty. But monetary regimes also varied widely between dynasties. There were long periods of monetary stability, as in the early Han and Tang, as well as short periods of great disturbance, such as during the Wang Mang Reform. Since the period of the Tang dynasty, imperial states have generally upheld a system of stable metallic money under centralized control. The Ming–Qing silver–copper bimetallic system, though largely a creation of economic customs, only became a stable standard under central government tax reforms.

There were, though, long periods of interruption and abnormality. The height of development came in the mid-eleventh-century Northern Song, when China adopted the first paper money system. During the three centuries of Song rule, successive imperial administrations in Song, Jin, Yuan, and early Ming developed the institutions and expertise to keep paper money in circulation, but each prolonged effort always ended in hyperinflation due to a lack of fiscal discipline. The system finally proved to be incompatible with the late imperial fiscal system and faded into history in the early fifteenth century.

Later Ming rulers proved to be inefficient minters and lost their control over the monetary regime soon after the collapse of the paper currency in the mid-fifteenth century. Over the course of the century that followed, a silver-based economy developed in the subnational markets and the more prosperous commercial regions. The imperial state followed these prevailing trends to make silver *de facto* legal currency during the One Whip Law Reform.[86]

It was not until the early Qing that the state began active minting again. But like the Ming rulers, the Qing imperial government adopted a more market-oriented strategy of minimal state intervention. Unlike Ming Taizu, early Qing rulers tended to rely on the market and entrust public funds to private merchants to generate a capital return.[87] Aggressive monetary policy had become such a distant memory by the mid-nineteenth century that some senior officials imagined paper money to be

---

[86] Liang Fangzhong, *The Single Whip Law of Taxation in China*, translated by Wang Yu-chuan (Cambridge, MA: Harvard University Press, 1956), pp. 36–37.

[87] Yang Lien-shen, *Money and Credit in Ancient China* (Cambridge, MA: Harvard University Press, 1962), pp. 98–99.

a fiscal panacea that could be printed at will to generate revenue and pay off foreign debts.[88] Burdened with debt and lacking a sound fiscal basis, the late Qing government was never successful in reestablishing a credit-carrying paper currency or a market for national debts. China had to continue with the silver system until currency reform in 1933 under the Nationalist government.

The development of the credit system in imperial China has also been a slow, tortuous process. For one thing, the state-centered credit system developed in imperial China seemed overwhelmingly to have been a substantive form of consumption credit. The most common type of consumption credit originated from the seasonal nature of agricultural production and consumption for agrarian households. After the national agricultural bank projects under Wang Anshi failed in the Song dynasty, late imperial China turned to the classical approach to counter economic uncertainty in an agrarian economy, with a national granary system run by the state and local elites. By selling and buying grain at controlled prices from government stocks, the state-centered grain system functioned as a financial system that ensured consumption and reproduction of the agrarian economy.[89]

It is likely that the private credit system in late imperial China was underdeveloped in comparison with that of the early modern West. This had much to do with the basic structure of organizational dependency in supranational trade and commerce. Trade was still largely financed through households and local social networks, as in the case of the strategic salt merchants in Yangzhou and foreign trade merchants at Canton. This has a well-known institutional background. As discussed earlier, the late imperial state chose to manage domestic (principally salt) and international trade through its loyal merchant agents. In both cases, organized political protection replaced the credit system and family lineage substituted for incorporation in risk and business management. A full-fledged national credit system had no place under the imperial model of household production and reproduction, since accumulation of land and cultural and sociopolitical capital alone ensured stable reproduction of wealth and power.

[88] William T. Rowe, *China's Last Empire: The Great Qing* (Cambridge, MA: Harvard University Press, 2007), pp. 164–165.
[89] Pierre Etienne-Will and Roy Bin Wang, *Nourish the People: The State Civilian Granary System in China, 1650–1850* (Ann Arbor, MI: University of Michigan Press, 1991), pp. 13–14.

180 *Market in State*

Late imperial China did develop its distinctive indigenous proto-modern banks (*Qianzhuang*) specialized in exchange and small-sum retail banking and large wholesale banks (*Piaohao*) engaging in large-sum banking, especially distant-trade finance. These indigenous credit institutions, naturally family businesses themselves, did not develop from their original shadowy complementary role into well-established autonomous financial institutions until the nineteenth century. Indigenous credit institutions initially prospered despite dynastic declines and the invasion of Western banking institutions, but their decline came equally abruptly, when the crisis in the Qing state deepened and these institutions got deeply involved with politics and state finance.

As was the case throughout the nonhousehold sector of imperial China's economy, the internal organization of traditional banks strictly followed a household-based order. Organizational dependency was forged upon close paternalistic patron–client relations, a strict hierarchy based on seniority, tight personal control of agents, a culture of secrecy and exclusion, and the use of moral persuasion.[90] These key features limited their potential for expansion and adaption to become a national market force and constituted the internal reasons for their decline, as was the case with other traditional indigenous household–corporate bodies. Even at the height of its development, *Piaohao* remained a uniquely Shanxi merchant enterprise and the prosperity of *Qianzhuang* was largely restricted to the Yangtze Delta region.[91] This development was particularly unfortunate since, unlike many other profitable sectors, the late imperial state left the credit market to private players and, in its later days, actively supported indigenous financial enterprises.

Social Control

The free flow of labor, goods, and commercial capital was inherently destabilizing for the household-centered economic order. The household registration system had long been in existence as a fundamental mechanism of social control. Due to logistical difficulties, the systems seldom performed consistently as effective tools of social control. In the Han and Tang dynasties, for example, the registry was not regularly updated, and it lost its relevance to the socioeconomic reality on the ground in the course

---

[90] Huang Jianhui, *Shanxi piaohao shi* (History of Shanxi Banks), (Taiyuan: Shanxi Economic Press, 1995), pp. 51–52.
[91] *Ibid.*, pp. 175–176.

of only a few generations. Until the advent of more rigid social controls, the imperial governments barely had the capacity to police and enforce stronger implementation.[92]

Serious experiments with large-scale social control of the grassroots came much later. To exercise effective controls and minimize factor flow throughout the empire, Ming Taizu carefully devised a system of household registration and a system of grassroots social control. Under the Ming household registry system, households were organized into small sociopolitical units of *Baojia* and held collective accountability for any offenses and transgressions. In the original early Ming design, the new grassroots organizations were to serve social, economic, fiscal, and ideological functions all at once. Despite its atrophy in the mid-Ming, the *Baojia* system remained an important institution until the People's Republic.

The most critical aspects of the grassroots system of powers were the institutions of social controls that limited the mobility of household-bound labor. From the Yuan dynasty onwards, late imperial states had exercised increasing control over the professional mobility of most households. The motivation for the classifications imposed was the emperor's intention to reproduce a fixed ideal distribution of fiscal burdens among registered households.[93] At the first level of division, the late imperial state in the Yuan dynasty (1271–1368) classified all households into military and civilian systems. In the Ming dynasty (1368–1644), within the civilian systems, specialized laborers, especially in the strategically important sector of salt production, were designated as special households with an obligation to contribute unpaid labor to the emperor in the form of tax.

Geographical mobility of individuals and families was another key aspect of social control. Except in the case of state-sponsored migration, the imperial state strictly preferred stable agricultural settlements to internal migration. From the early empires onward, a system of internal passes was in place to prevent the free movement of labor and population. From the early Ming onward, regulations were refined to realize harsher controls and restrictions on travel and migration, based on a system of travel permits and a strict household registry. These measures were further aided by the prevailing cultural and social institutions in rural society, where loyalty and compliance to lineage clans and the rural community reduced the risk of downward mobility.

---

[92] Hsiao, *Rural China*; Wang Fei-ling, *Organizing through Division and Exclusion: China's Hukou System* (Stanford, CA: Stanford University Press, 2005), pp. 36–37.
[93] Huang, *Taxation and Government Finance in 16th Century Ming China*, pp. 21–23.

Although tight social controls were always implemented at the beginning of a dynasty, they seldom lasted long. For one thing, the late imperial state lacked any mechanisms to enforce a rigid social system against the grain of basic trends in economic development and social change. Control institutions declined as people found every loophole to evade control. Ming military service and salt production were good examples of such decline.[94] The collapse of rigid social control left the imperial state ill prepared for an upsurge in the mobile population as a result of natural disasters in the late Ming, which contributed directly to the collapse of the imperial order.[95]

The Qing Empire social control strategy was a revised model of the Ming strict household registry. It was generally more flexible, especially vis-à-vis the migrant and marginal populations. Migration was conditionally legalized, giving rise to a more efficient distribution of resources and the economic prosperity of the eighteenth century. Since there were no other substantive breaks with the late imperial paradigm, the imperial state still lacked any effective source of information and organizational penetration into society. Massive coercive measures were still the only tool of control, even in the event of small perceived challenges.[96]

REPRODUCTION OF THE IMPERIAL ECONOMIC ORDER

We have discussed the basic structure of the political economy system of late imperial China by focusing on various aspects of its fiscal regime. But an important missing link between the imperial state and its economy remained relevant. While both the imperial household and agrarian households were reproduced on the basis of the natural life cycle of the family, the political economy of each empire required an institutionalized process to reproduce itself. In late imperial China, the process was made possible largely through a complex of institutional arrangements centering on the Civil Examination System.[97] It was the Civil Service Examination that enabled political, cultural, and economic processes to be ordered in accordance with life cycles of the family and individuals.

---

[94] *Ibid.*, pp. 36–37.
[95] Li Guangtao, *Mingji liukou shimo* (A Historical Inquiry into the Rebellions of Late Ming) (Taipei: The Academy Sinica, 1962), pp. 30–31.
[96] Phillip Kuhn's study of the sorcery scare in 1768 offered an excellent case study in this category: see *Soul Stealers: The Chinese Sorcery Scare in 1768* (Cambridge, MA: Harvard University Press, 1990), pp. 223–234.
[97] Benjamin A. Elman, *A Cultural History of Civil Examination in Late Imperial China* (Berkeley, CA: University of California Press, 2000), pp. 15–17.

From the Northern Song onward, the examination system became the principal route to political power, and political power the principal source of extraordinary wealth. These institutional arrangements effectively made cultural capital a prerequisite for power and wealth. Yet preparation for the examination was costly, both in terms of the direct education and examination costs and due to the opportunist costs of foregone male labor. Thus, it became the norm for each aspiring family to accumulate wealth and land first, then acquire cultural capital through classical education and examination, and then strive to gain an official position. This in turn facilitated the accumulation of wealth and cultural capital. Whereas landed wealth could be accumulated and inherited, offices and degrees were generally only attainable through competitive examinations, nominally open to all subjects. This can be attested by numerous studies on the economic conditions of the political elite, including both the literati-bureaucrats and the gentry, principally indicating a strong correlation between an official degree, political office, and landed wealth.[98]

Since the bureaucrat-literati and the degree-holding gentry were produced through a similar process, they invariably acquired a double role: a private one as the representative of local family interests in the power structure of the imperial state, and a public one as the local agent of the imperial power. It was thus possible to speak of "rising a household" (*Qijia*) in late imperial Chinese literature as a multigenerational process of cultivation that included wealth accumulation, examination preparation, office-holding, and strategies to preserve elite status. Even if most households would never cross the Provincial Examination threshold to become office-holding elites, this process legitimized the accumulation of wealth in a highly commercial economy, given that it served a larger purpose beyond self-indulgence. By the late Ming, even mid-level merchants had adapted the Confucian ideology of self-cultivation as an ideological justification and form of moral guidance in everyday practice.[99] The household management strategy included the acquisition of landed wealth, the central role

---

[98] For example, Ho Ping-ti, *The Ladder of Success in Imperial China: Aspects of Social Mobility, 1368–1911* (New York, NY: University of Columbia Press, 1962), pp. 12–16; Chung-li Chang, *The Chinese Gentry: Studies on Their Role in Nineteenth-Century Chinese Society* (Seattle, WA and London: University of Washington Press, 1955).

[99] Richard John Lufrano, *Honorable Merchants: Commerce and Confucian Self-Cultivation in Late Imperial China* (Honolulu, HI: University of Hawai'i Press, 1997), pp. 177–180.

of education, and consolidation of social status through the acquisition of further degrees and offices.[100]

In late imperial China, this examination-centered order had several advantages over hereditary aristocracy or sales of prebends, even though it retained some features of both. At a most fundamental level, it meant cultural, political, and economic capital gravitated in an orderly manner to a stratum of elite family households who were deeply dependent on and coopted by the emperor. This was especially true for economic elites such as private merchant households, since wealth, if not converted into degrees and offices, could only invite the grabbing hands of the state. But it was still rational for ordinary families to engage in profit-yielding commercial activities, since this was always the fastest – if not surest – path to wealth, given that the wealth accumulated should in due course be converted to land, degrees, and eventually offices. The system therefore served to buttress the landed agrarian economy and prevent the rise of independent economic elites.

This examination-centered order also encouraged large extended family, kinship, and lineage organizations. Stable and orderly rural organizations based on strong kinship dominated many key economic regions in Southern China during the late empires, and played a decisive role in rural organization and local governance.[101] This development was clearly welcomed by the imperial state. The proliferation of large agrarian households not only reduced the cost of providing public goods, but also helped to strengthen the organization and ideology favored by the household-modeled imperial political economy.

On the surface, the civil service examinations were no more than an exchange between the emperor and the households. However, the system in fact accomplished much more than that. Among the key sociopolitical functions was more effective political control over the invisible private wealth, largely converted to lands, degrees, and offices and subject to direct control by the imperial system. As for the visible landed wealth, the system also implicitly required an exchange of wealth for cultural and political capital, both evaluated and bestowed in a top-down manner by the imperial state. In the long run, economic elites were transformed into cultural

---

[100] Hilary J. Beattie, *Land and Lineage in China: A Study of T'ung-Ch'eng County, Anhui, in the Ming and Ch'ing Dynasties* (Cambridge and New York, NY: Cambridge University Press, 1977), pp. 127–130.
[101] David Faure, *Capitalism in China: A History of Modern Business Enterprise in China* (Hong Kong: Hong Kong University Press, 2006), p. 181.

and political elites loyal to and dependent on the emperor. This aspect of the examination system was highlighted by Max Weber:

The Chinese mandarin is, or rather originally was, what the humanist of our Renaissance period approximately was: a literatus humanistically trained and tested in the language monuments of the remote past ... This stratum, with its conventions developed and modeled after Chinese Antiquity, has determined the whole destiny of China.[102]

Finally, the Civil Examination System also played a function in the internal elite's circulation across the urban political centers and the rural periphery, supplying much-needed stability and order in rural society. For most rural-born literati degree- and office-holders, rural farmland and family clans were both a starting point and an end. Farmland, family clans, and family-owned lands not only formed the center of the literati gentry and officials' domain, but their social identity as both moral agent of the emperor and head of household organizations was also best anchored in the rural households.

In late imperial China, this balanced distribution of cultural capital in rural and urban areas made up for an unbalanced deployment of coercive force in walled cities and peripheral rural regions, since the literati elites (gentry) would naturally defend ideology and rural organization against any offense against the socioeconomic order. This was borne out by the elite responses to historical disruptions such as the Taiping Rebellion, the last and most violent of all uprisings against the imperial socioeconomic order from the periphery.

The Civil Examination System, like any of the imperial state's principal institutions, entailed implicit social and cultural costs for the empire. For one thing, it had a suppressive effect upon creativity and critical thinking, chiefly through its distorting effects on knowledge production and intellectual innovation, since the only useful knowledge under the examination system was classical knowledge and its subsidiary learning.[103] Given that examination success was measured in terms of strictly styled classical essays, alternative thinking and learning was generally not encouraged, even if not suppressed. Deprived of autonomy and firmly oriented to the political system, the knowledge system lost much of its cognitive and

---

[102] Max Weber, *From Max Weber: Essays in Sociology,* translated, edited, and with an introduction by H. H. Gerth and C. Wright Mills (New York, NY: Oxford University Press, 1958), pp. 92–93.
[103] Hoff Toby, *The Rise of Early Modern Science: Islam, China and the West* (Cambridge and New York, NY: Cambridge University Press, 2003), pp. 157–158.

creative capacity with regard to both the natural and social worlds. This basic feature of the knowledge system had an enduring influence on the pattern of China's later historical development.

EPILOGUE: THE VISIONS AND REALITY OF THE IMPERIAL ECONOMIC ORDER

China's unbroken tradition of imperial rule spanning two thousand years created a unique political economy system of state dominance that set the country apart from the predecessors of today's other major economic powers. Since then, generations of Chinese rulers have struggled with the immense chasm between the emperor's nominal dominance of *Tianxia* (All Under Heaven) and the organizational realities created by limited capacity. The economy was no exception. The goal of the late imperial Chinese state was stable domination of millions of mostly agrarian households, in forging a system of organizational dependency with itself at the center. In late imperial China, fiscal affairs were only consolidated under the direct control of the emperor himself or his personal agents. In retrospect, both the household and the market visions of management lacked substantive infrastructure powers. It is in this respect that the mismatch between vision and reality created the most severe challenges experienced by any imperial state-builder, and their successive generations.

If *Tianxia* was to be organized as a household writ large, the emperor had to exercise direct organizational control over every one of its members and impose complete control over both national and local markets. Indeed, there were ambitious emperors, such as the founding emperors of the Qin and Ming dynasties, who experimented with total control and micromanagement. But these were surely the rare exceptions, given the technology, powers, and socioeconomic foundations of their rule. In fact, even late in the empire, the emperor was still only able to exert direct personal control over a few thousand high officials and personal servants. Except in the matters of war and taxes, the emperor mattered little in daily life, and if he did matter, it was through a multilayered agency. This is exemplified in the Chinese saying "the sky was high and the Emperor was far away." The more important issue for the emperor, as it frequently turned out, was alliance with small households against the rich and powerful in struggles of organizational dependency.

If *Tianxia* was to be organized as a global market with the emperor as the sole monopoly, the emperor must have the necessary tools to control all essential goods and, most importantly, sovereign money and credits.

Attempts were made in this direction, but the traditional emperorship proved incapable of supporting a sovereign monetary space, as the Song and Yuan experiments with paper money demonstrated. More critically, since the agrarian economy was simply producing too little surplus to be marketed nationally in a household-based mode of rural production, the market played only a supplementary role, along with households. There was little room for the market to play a decisive and autonomous role in the national economy. In fact, the only national market that the emperor was able to found and monopolize was that of salt. Today it seems quite improbable that the salt monopoly was able to contribute one-sixth to half of total imperial revenues.

The only solution for the traditional emperorship was to organize a system of sustainable organizational dependency, like a concentric circle. Eschewing the historicist arguments of Chinese uniqueness, we must concede that traditional Chinese emperors had little choice but to follow a structure of personal and organizational agents and coopt local social elites. This is achieved with the centrality of the Civil Examination System, which effectively drew official boundaries between private and public, integrating the political, economic, and social institutions of the empire into a process of reproducible order. Ironically, the system's heyday was the early Qing in the eighteenth century, when the *Ancien Régime* in Europe was on the verge of collapse.

Since the imperial system had failed to modernize China in the late nineteenth century, common wisdom faulted the imperial political economy as inefficient and antimodern. This is not entirely true. Judged against its own household-centered agenda, the late imperial state, especially the High Qing state in the eighteenth century, had been remarkably successful not only in regulating and reproducing the agrarian household economy, but also in the growing productive capacity of its population. In fact, the competition between the imperial order and others, especially between the emperor and the elites such as fiscal agents, largely determined its path of evolution. As our discussion suggests, the system of late imperial China – the product of a long process of evolution and institutional innovation – was effective and coherent with its own agenda. The only challenges that the Qing could not surmount were the military ones from an industrialized West and the industrializing Meiji Japan – challenges that could not be foreseen.

There is a particular reason for the emphasis we place on the abnormal statist or reformist approach in our research agenda. For five hundred years, China steered clear of these two approaches, by following the norm of a minimalist state that checked and contained the market through critical institutional arrangements. Compared with earlier periods of Chinese history, the late imperial order enjoyed remarkable stability, but also created problems that it could not resolve. This was the late Qing conundrum of a weak state and an impoverished economy. Thus, when Yan Fu called for the Chinese state to pursue wealth and power based on the principle of social Darwinism, he appealed to a wide audience among the literati. And the only way to achieve these two missions at once was to remake the imperial state through a process of creative destruction. This option was only available in a world of total war, when the imperial political economy system was destroyed through aggressive and revolutionary state-building in the mid-twentieth century.

However, despite the violent transformations experienced over the past century, the contemporary Chinese economy still retains important structural traits of the imperial political economy. This aspect of the legacy remade through wars and the Communist experiment forms the basic structure of the "market in state." It would not be too far-fetched to compare the underlying visions and approaches of Wang Mang, Zhu Yuanzhang, and Wang Anshi with those of Sun Yat-sen, Mao Zedong, and Zhu Rongji. In this sense, all history is contemporary history, *à la* Benedetto Croce. Our analysis of the imperial system thus provides the sites and analytical basis for us to move on to themes regarding the development and structure of the political economy of modern and contemporary China.

In retrospect, it is safe to conclude that imperial China, unlike early modern Europe and Japan, was not the same type of military–fiscal state as that which gave rise to the paradigmatic European modern state.[104] In the Chinese case, the imperial state had a total vision of order and power, but usually had neither the will nor the capacity to realize such a vision. There were few institutional restrictions on market mechanisms in imperial China precisely because the market was not central to the political system of late imperial China. As long as basic peace and social stability were maintained, the late imperial state remained autonomous and self-sufficient. It was both above and encompassing of the market institutions simply because it did not rely on the market for its political survival, unlike the early modern states in Europe that required capital for internal

---

[104] Charles Tilly offers an authoritative comparison between this type of state and the early modern Chinese state: see *Coercion, Capital and European States, AD 990–1992* (Cambridge, MA: Blackwell, 1990), pp. 127–130.

coercion and external war. Capital and coercion, or economy and politics, were structured vertically in the Chinese case. In other words, the market as a social order was conceptually embedded *inside* the state, rather than parallel to or even above the state. This is perhaps the imperial political economy's most important legacy for contemporary China. Theoretically, this is exactly what we conceptualize as the "market in state": that the state, either the *Tianxia* state of the imperial era or the party state in the contemporary era, assumes the dominant and first order in the political cosmology, whereas the market, as one of its most important applications, always remains secondary to the state, at least conceptually.

4

Origins of the Modern Chinese
Political Economy

Geopolitics, Mobilization, and State-Building

In Chapter 3, we outlined the market-in-state (MIS) system in imperial China. In this chapter, we examine the transformation of this system in modern times, as China began to interact with Western powers. In doing so, we focus on both geopolitical and domestic factors. In Chapter 3 we discussed briefly how geopolitical factors, particularly interactions between the imperial state and minorities such as Xiongnu, affected the formation of the MIS system in imperial China. In modern times, China's entire political economy system was reshaped by a new set of geopolitical factors that emerged with the advent of the Western powers that arrived on the east coast with gunboats and demanded open trade and territorial concessions. After repeated defeats by Western powers and Japan, China began to rebuild its state. During this long process of state-building, which spanned a century, the Chinese not only had to fight foreign imperialism to gain sovereignty on the international stage, but also faced an internal struggle for political domination. As Chinese states – first the Qing, and then local and party states – drew on the economy for their political-military agenda on both regional and global scales, the modern system of the Chinese political economy was transformed, in many fundamental ways, into one that was compatible with an aggressive centralizing state and ambitious plans for industrialization. The transformation, however, does not mean that the traditional MIS system completely broke with its past and was replaced by a fully new system. Rather, it means that the system was revamped to meet challenges arising chiefly from a changing geopolitical environment. At both the ideational and practice levels, the MIS system not only survived the process of modern state-building; more importantly, it was reinforced and radicalized by the Kuomintang (KMT)/Chinese Communist Party state that replaced the imperial state as the dominant political institution in China.

GEOPOLITICS, STATE-BUILDING, AND MODERN CHINESE POLITICAL ECONOMY

Long-term geopolitical and security realignment, though frequently mentioned, is usually not a major factor in mainstream narratives of China's contemporary economic transformation as the dominant historical force.[1] In reality, geopolitics and security are perhaps the most important factors in determining China's modern state-building from late Qing through the contemporary reform era. During this period, China faced a totally different situation from earlier centuries, when China's geopolitics, though an important factor, usually facilitated reproduction of the imperial state rather than its fundamental transformation. As we argued in Chapters 1 and 2, this is a key difference between China and European states, such as the Roman Empire and modern colonial empires. In Europe, shifting geopolitical alignments and interstate competition played a key role in fostering modern state-building and a capitalist economy, as the locations, players, and patterns of geopolitical struggles have continued to change over the past two millennia. In China, since the Tang dynasty fell to the British, and even as dominant players changed regularly, the basic rivalry between the steppe world of inner Asia and the agricultural realm of the great drainage plains of the Yellow, Yangtze, and Pearl Rivers – sometimes expressed in North–South rivalries – had shaped the basic pattern of

---

[1] In predominant theories of economic development and political economy – both Chinese and English- languages – Chinese economic history is mostly concerned with comparative internal dynamics, such as China's early modern market development, global trade, and resource endowments. See, for example, Kenneth Pomeranz, *The Great Divergence: China, Europe and the Global Economy*, 2nd ed. (Princeton, NJ: Princeton University Press, 2001), and Giovanni Arrighi, *Adam Smith in Beijing* (New York, NY: Verso, 2009). When global factors are considered, they usually follow the world system approach, which centers on structural factors such as factor flows rather than on geopolitical shifts. See, for example, Andre Gunter Frank, *Reorient: Global Economy in the Asian Age* (Oakland, CA: University of California Press, 1998). In fact, the resurgence of Chinese power is first and foremost military and strategic. China lost almost all of its major international conflicts between 1840 and 1914, but none since 1914. The strategic windfalls that arose from these conflicts, especially the Cold War, paved the way for China's dramatic economic transformation. Even works on China's political economy and modern state-building tend to focus on domestic politics of modern state-building, rather than the importance of war and geopolitics. See Kent Deng, *China's Economy in Modern Times: Changes and Economic Consequences, 1800–2000* (London: Routledge, 2011); Michel Aglietta and Guo Bai, *China's Development: Capitalism and Empire* (London: Routledge, 2012).

China's geopolitics.[2] This is also why we have not singled out the geopolitical factor in our discussions of the imperial political economy. While domestic crises supply the necessary conditions for the imperial collapse, geopolitical factors, particularly the rise of global capitalism and global empires, set the conditions for the late imperial Chinese economy. However, late imperial China was still able to fend off the forces of global capitalism and restrain its direct sphere of influence to small enclaves like Macao and Canton until the late Qing coastal defense collapsed in the face of the Opium War in 1840.

After China's defeat of 1840, geopolitics gradually came to determine its political economy system through successive processes of modern state-building in China. The rise of radical economic statism in twentieth-century China, first in response to Japanese aggression and then in the face of the Cold War encirclement of China, was first and foremost a geopolitical product, when the Chinese state was insufficiently strong or willing to influence its geopolitical environment. It began with the Soviet party-state in KMT-controlled Guangdong and gradually evolved through various international and civil wars. In order to meet the geopolitical and domestic challenges that arose, successive Chinese states gradually instituted a system of economic control and mobilization unprecedented in traditional China: transit tax, private–public partnerships, public debts, state-owned enterprises, state-owned banks, fiat money, state ownership of national resources, and state control of urban and rural land and the grassroots market.

This interaction between geopolitics, state-building, and political economy runs through China's entire modern experience. From this perspective, we divide the process into six periods. The first period is that between 1840 and 1895, when Qing was formerly incorporated into the world system centered on European powers but kept its traditional imperial institutions. This was a period when geopolitics did not directly influence the economy of the empire, since the Qing state only took moderate and experimental steps to reform its economy, mostly at the local level along the coastal provinces. The second period began in 1895 and ended in the late 1920s, when the Chinese world order formally collapsed in the aftermath of the Sino–Japanese War and Chinese elites finally started to reshape the Chinese polity and economy after the model of the West

---

[2] For a discussion of this basic *longue durée* geopolitical situation as it was formed in the aftermath of the Tang collapse, see Frederic W. Mote, *Imperial China, 900–1800* (Cambridge, MA: Harvard University Press, 1999), pp. 23–29.

and Japan. This was also a period of atrophy of the central state and the rise of the market economy at all levels. The third period began in the late 1920s and ended in the early 1950s, when the new political party-state formations took a dominant position in China and led the country through a period of total war and socialist revolution. The fourth, or Maoist, stage, which started in the early 1950s, ushered in a period of increasing global isolation and radical state-building, as well as radical suppression of the market economy at all levels. The fifth period began in 1971, when China gradually moved in the direction of reform and opening. The period opened with China's realignment with the United States and Japan against the Soviet Union, and ended in 1991 when the Soviet Union collapsed and China moved to full-fledged state-centered market reform. The final period started with the collapse of the Soviet Union and is likely to come to an end soon. In this most recent period, sometimes characterized as an era of hypergrowth and the rise of China, the Chinese state and a large chunk of society benefited from its increasing integration with the global economy and the rise of state capitalism. In this era, China has recovered its dominant position in Asia while maintaining stable relations with the United States. For the first time since 1840, China has regained some control over its immediate geopolitical environment and even beyond.

It is worth noting that we do not follow the standard periodization of China's modern history here, since we want to highlight the impact of changing geopolitical environments on the formation of, and changes in, the country's political economy system. The standard periodization was very much marked by major events such as the end of the Anti-Japanese War, the establishment of the People's Republic of China, and the start of the post-Mao reform. We believe that while such events are important politically, they alone do not change China's political economy system. Political economy systems are formed in response to changing geopolitical environments, but once they come into existence, they can survive different political settings by adapting to them. This approach enables us to observe the continuities and changes in certain ideas and practices of China's political economy system through different historical periods. For instance, there is continuity of state-building between the late Qing and the KMT era/early Chinese Communist Party (CCP) era, and between the late years of the Cultural Revolution and the reforms of 1979–1984. Accordingly, the watershed years of 1895, 1929, 1945, 1972, and 1991 sometimes meant much more for China as key moments in its interaction with the world and the society it governed.

This chapter thus traces the rise of China's modern political economy by sketching out the changing international and domestic dynamics of these six periods, with a focus on the first four periods (1840–1979). We argue that geopolitics, state-building, and the "market in state" structure were intimately linked during this period. Of these three factors, geopolitics provided the foundation for the other two, as it determined China's security setting, trade arrangements, and cultural entities. Indeed, much of modern Chinese state-building and the structure of political economy were determined by its geopolitical situation and strategic choices. Especially critical was China's shifting geopolitical balance vis-à-vis its neighbors, Imperial Russia/the Soviet Union to the North and Japan to the east, as well as its changing relations with the dominant global powers of the British Empire and the United States. These factors had a decisive influence on China's trajectory: Market development and demobilization were premised on a stable and secure geopolitical balance with neighbors as well as good relations with the dominant maritime powers, a set of conditions that only became available to China in the late 1970s. This is the reason why this chapter ends with the late 1970s, at which point China became a major shaper of its surrounding geopolitical environment as it built stable and mutually beneficial relations with the United States. Despite China's most recent ambition to become a global maritime power, *Pax Americana* still broadly defines the external conditions for China's economic transformation.

CRISIS AND LOCAL REFORM IN LATE QING, 1840–1895

If not for its decline and fall, the eighteenth-century Chinese economy could have exemplified an ideal model of an economic society under a primarily agrarian empire. In 1800, this system could support one-third of human beings worldwide, owing to its complex systems of production and exchange and perhaps the most elaborate form of bureaucratic government available. Even if per capita incomes, urbanization, and the technical sophistication of statecraft remained comparable to those of preindustrial Western Europe, the late imperial economic order was nevertheless able to support an unprecedented increase in both population, through expansion of production, and, more importantly, intensive agricultural and market development. This great achievement was realized with a minimalist state: by all measurements, the state was at its smallest at this point.[3]

---

[3] Kent Deng, *China's Economy in Modern Times: Changes and Economic Consequences: 1800–2000* (London: Routledge, 2011), pp. 6–7.

But, like many past empires, the Qing Empire was no exception to the iron rule of imperial decline. After reaching a zenith in the late half of the eighteenth century under Emperor Qianlong, the empire had a long and painful gradual decline over the nineteenth century, culminating in the Taiping Rebellion (1850–1864) and three disastrous military confrontations with the British (1840 and 1860), the Anglo-Franco (1860), and finally the Japanese Empires. While earlier historiography tends to stress these landmark confrontations as the cause for the imperial order's fall in 1890, both Western and Chinese scholarship since the 1970s has gradually come to attribute the demise of the imperial system to the very foundations of its success. In economic domains, the late imperial political economy's lack of ability to meet its basic existential objectives was regarded as a natural consequence rather than a major transformation.

The first crisis was a direct result of the demographic revolution brought about by two centuries of peace under Qing rule. Given a favorable economic policy and various positive social and political factors in the household-centered system, China's population in early Qing soon recovered from the dynastic wars and went from 150 to 300 million during the eighteenth century, then reaching 430 million in 1850.[4] The demographic trend had a host of sociopolitical implications for the economic system. Imperial China's per capita grain supply plummeted to dangerously low levels of 200 kg around the turn of the century. Meanwhile, the price of rice rose by 200 percent in the second half of the eighteenth century.[5] The burden of supplying the growing population had begun to be felt in China's borderland regions such as the southwest frontier, where ecological limitations to the subsistence economy compelled the Hakka communities to cultivate the highland.[6]

The second major crisis arose from the imperial army's declining capacity to manage its increasingly restive border and remote regions. During the first century of Qing rule, China's territory expanded to about three times that of the Ming, as the Qing state brought in Manchuria, East Siberia, Taiwan, Xinjiang, and outer Mongolia and consolidated its control over what are nowadays Xinjiang, Tibet, and the Southwest borderland.

---

[4] Ho Ping-ti, *Studies on the Population of China, 1368–1953* (Cambridge, MA: Harvard University Press, 1959), pp. 278–280.
[5] Peng Xinwei, *Zhongguo huobi shi* (A Monetary History of China), (Shanghai: Shanghai People's Publishing House, 2009), pp. 609–610.
[6] Robert B. Marks, *China: Its Environment and History* (Lanham, MD: Rowman & Littlefield, 2011), pp. 206–207.

On the other hand, the costs of military campaigns against borderland rebels and neighboring countries rose steeply, since the military machines of the empire became less efficient and more expensive, as evidenced by most of Qianlong's so-called Ten Campaigns. The situation became even more critical with the rise of the Taiping and the Lian rebels in South and North China proper, the Islamist separatist movement in the Western provinces, and finally, clashes with the militarily more sophisticated Western powers and Japan.

The third looming source of crisis was external. While the emergence of global capitalism and maritime colonial empires eventually transformed the Qing political economy, it would only launch the imperial state into systemic local and central reform after defeat in the two Opium Wars and the Sino–Japanese War. This period thus marked the beginning of China's move into a globally integrated industrial world, a process that is still ongoing to date. According to Bayly, this relentless shift toward industrialization began to kick in at a global level in the 1840s.[7] This turning point coincided with the dynastic decline of, and the last days of internal peace in, the Qing Empire. After its conquest of the Indian subcontinent and Malaya, the British Empire had intensified its activities in South China Sea trade. Conflicts with China arose over access to China's domestic market and later escalated into full-scale military conflicts, namely, the first Opium War of 1840–1842 and the second Opium War of 1856–1860. Following the Qing Empire's defeat in the Opium Wars, the industrialized British Empire and, later, all other Western powers cleared their external hurdles and expanded into China's domestic market. By the 1890s, Western capitals, especially Anglo-American ones, prospered throughout China's modern industrial and commercial sectors, running factories, opening banks, making investments in and offering loans to the Qing government, and engaging in a variety of commercial activities on favorable tax and interest arrangements.[8]

The patchwork of late Qing reforms in the second half of the nineteenth century was the Qing state's response to these three challenges. In this stage (1840–1870s), the response was a paradoxical admixture of modernizing industries that strengthened the local states, and decentralizing state-building efforts that weakened the Qing courts. This was a

---

[7] C. A. Bayly, *The Birth of the Modern World, 1780–1914* (Oxford: Blackwell Publishing, 2004), p. 7.
[8] Immanuel C. Y. Hsu, *The Rise of Modern China* (New York, NY: Oxford University Press, 1999), pp. 430–439.

product of the situation in the mid-nineteenth century. Social upheavals, especially the Taiping Rebellions, had destroyed much of the empire's military and financial resources. To quell the rebellion and reestablish order, the central state had already sanctioned a decentralized fiscal expansion in the rebel areas in the forms of *lijin*, a transit tax for all commodities, and an opium tax. The creation of an independent local fiscal basis was buttressed by the rise of locally based military and political magnates, such as Zeng Guofan and Li Hongzhang, who were loyal to Beijing but not dependent on it fiscally and militarily. Ironically, it was this cohort of local power holders who first broke the ideological hurdles of neo-Confucian exclusivism to embrace the challenges from the West.

Immediately after the Taiping Rebellion, a civil war that almost destroyed the empire's economic heartland in the Mid- and Lower Yangtze regions, the military superintendents and leaders of antirebellion forces began to adopt Western military technologies and economic organization in military-related sectors. In the 1860s, they began to introduce shipyards and machinery, ordnance, and other modern factories in China's maritime provinces. These efforts kickstarted what later historians termed the "Self-Strengthening Movement." During the first phase of this movement, the reformist local officials established more than twenty factories and bureaus (enterprises) for the manufacturing of arms and warships. The four major enterprises were Machinery Bureaus in Jiangnan (1865) and Tianjin (1867), the Foochow Shipbuilding Enterprise (1866), and China Merchants Steamship Company (1872).[9]

While most of these enterprises were government-run, some were based on a new form of economic cooperation between local state and private businesses, known as *guandu shangban* (literally, merchant management under bureaucratic supervision, or public–private partnership). Li Hongzhang first used *guandu shangban* to refer to the ideal framework of the Merchant Company; the term then came to denote a standard model of modern industrial and commercial enterprises established by local officials on behalf of the imperial government but run by merchants with both

---

[9] Ting-Yee Kuo and Kwang Ching Liu, "Self-Strengthening: The Pursuit of Western Technology," in *Cambridge History of China*, vol. 11 (Cambridge: Cambridge University Press, 1978), pp. 522–523; Xu Dixin and Wu Chengming, *Zhongguo ziben zhuyi fazhanshi* (History of Capitalist Development in China), vol. 2 (Beijing: Social Sciences Academic Press, 2006), pp. 380–381.

political connections and business acumen.[10] The initial institutional setting contained many ambiguities regarding the exact division of powers
and obligations between the merchants and the bureaucrats representing
the state. Since the state had a minimal legal framework for its organization
and governance and state support usually came in the form of protection
from local officials, it was impossible to have a clear boundary between the
different forms of modern enterprises based on involvement of state and
private actors (*guanban*, *guandu shangban*, and *shangban*).

In the second phase of the Self-Strengthening Movement, reformist local
superintendents realized that it was no longer adequate to build the defense
industry, and military modernization would also require a system of
modern manufacturing industry and Western-styled schools. From 1872
to 1894, reformist local officials in charge of China's Yangtze, Pearl River
and Beijing-Tianjin regions established twenty-seven new factories in the
civilian industry, including mining, steel, transportation, communications,
and textiles. The most significant of these achievements in the civilian
industry included Merchant Company (transport, 1872), Kaiping Mine
(mining, 1878), Shanghai Telegram Bureau (communications, 1880) and
Hanyang Steel Mill (steel, 1890).[11]

Government-run enterprises were mostly badly run and poorly governed.
Most of them operated as a kind of government department subsidized by
a yearly budgetary stipend while producing at low efficiency, much in line
with the old model of imperial factories. Indeed, the quality of management was so poor that even the Qing government refrained from procur-
ing from its own state-owned military arsenals due to their high prices
and low quality; if it became necessary, procurement was restricted to
their very simple hand weapons.[12] But the *guangdu shangban* model was
also no guarantee of business success. Indeed, it was sometimes more
risky during times of political upheaval. In the case of Kaiping Coal Mine,
a key government mine in Zhili that operated profitably under its first
merchant manager, Yang Tingshu, was sold by the second manager
Zhang Yi to British investors and registered as a limited liability company
in London.[13]

[10] Samuel Chu and Kwangchi Liu, *Li Hung-Chang and China's Early Modernization*
(Armonk, NY: M. E. Sharp, 2000), pp. 9–12.
[11] Xu and Wu, *Zhongguo ziben zhuyi fazhanshi*, vol. 2, pp. 385–386.
[12] Ma Ming and Zhu Ying, *Zhongguo jingji tongshi* (General Economic History of China),
vol. 9 (Changsha: Hunan Publishing House, 2000), pp. 181–182.
[13] *Ibid.*, p. 185.

In addition to government-run or *guangdu shangban* enterprises, private enterprises owned and run by the gentry also began to emerge in this period. Compared with the factories and bureaus founded by the local viceroys, whose capitalization ranged from 200,000 to 6,000,000 taels of silver, private factories were usually quite small; their initial capital seldom exceeded 200,000 taels of silver by the late twentieth century.[14] Except for some textile factories, most private factories were ill-equipped and under-capitalized, lacking technical expertise and sufficient market. In sectors where the state (*guanban*) and public–private partnerships (*guandu shangban*) already took the leads, private factories were sometimes denied access to the market. Even if such access was open, private entrepreneurs were usually burdened with a heavy extra tax contribution. Under these extremely harsh conditions, some private enterprises bought foreign trademarks or filed foreign fiats to secure favorable tax treatment in domestic market competition.[15]

The Self-Strengthening Movement came to a grinding halt in the aftermath of Qing defeat in the Sino–Japanese War of 1894. While most of the industrial and commercial projects would continue into the twentieth century, the failure of local state initiatives to bring about a rich and powerful state capable of defending itself was already evident in the crushing defeat of Li Hongzhang's Beiyang fleet. The movement was not meant to be a thorough transformation of the Qing political economy and Chinese society; as such, its impact on the society and economy was limited. Nevertheless, it marked the beginning of a tradition of local state-building movement, a trend that would dominate the Chinese political economy until the early 1930s. The movement would have been impossible without strong political support from reform-minded figures in Beijing such as the Prince of Gong (Yixin), Wenxiang, and sometimes even the Empress Dowager Cixi, but it essentially consisted of state-funded modern enterprises in defense and defense-related industries under the auspices of powerful viceroys and their central allies. The overwhelming majority of the Confucian literati remained opposed to even a modicum of Westernization until 1895. As such, the reform networks still operated through patronage networks of a few central and local magnates, rather than the economic bureaucracy of the late imperial state. In this sense, the Self-Strengthening brand of modern enterprises was different from the state-owned and state-related modern enterprises, including the *guandu*

[14] *Ibid.*, p. 189.   [15] *Ibid.*, p. 191.

shangban model and the so-called enterprise of the patriotic businessmen: At the center of their identity were powerful individual agents, still with no conception of the organizational structure of a modern state.

QING *XINZHENG* STATE-BUILDING EXPERIMENT AND ITS SUCCESSORS, 1895–1927

Despite its many structural failings, the Qing Empire could still boast a large standing army, considerable fiscal resources, and a complex system of government in the early 1890s. It survived a succession of major upheavals, including the Taiping, the Nian rebels, and rebellions of Islamist minorities of Hui and Uyghur. But this revival soon came to an end when the imperial Beiyang Fleet and infantry suffered a humiliating defeat at the hands of the nascent Japanese Empire in 1894, and again in a disastrous war with an alliance of Western powers and Japan in 1900. The Qing's inability to protect its territorial sovereign and the lives of its subjects against foreign powers became so blatant that even the country's supreme leader, Empress Dowager Cixi, felt the need to carry out thorough reform of the political system.

Apart from the apparent swings in public opinion and the currents of social thought, major internal forces also steered the country into a radical turn. In the coastal and riverine treaty ports, the front line of encounters with foreign political and economic powers, the Han Chinese viceroys had become the effective power brokers between the Manchu emperor, the social forces of gentry, and the foreign economic and military powers. During the political crisis of 1900, three most powerful Southern governor-generals signed an agreement to stay peace with the foreign powers within their own domains, while the government-general of the capital regions (*Zhili*) also tacitly averted any confrontation with foreign powers. If ruling elites continued to resist reforms, local officials were likely to gain further autonomy by taking the matter into their own hands. As diehard conservatives were purged in the aftermath of the 1900 Boxer Movement and the weakening of central authority was further precipitated, it became impossible for the remaining conservative factions in the court to resist more forceful proposals calling for systemic reforms from governors, backed by local elites.

These critical situations gave rise to a new vision of a centralized modern state and a modern economy. In his influential treatise *Shengshi Weiyan* (literally, *Words of Warning in Times of Prosperity*), Zheng Guanyin, a comparator-thinker, outlined a comprehensive strategy of state-building based on government-sponsored economic development and economically driven political and social changes. In his vision of the modern Chinese political economy, the economy, especially trade and commerce, was the foundation of state power and international order; commercial rivalry (*shangzhan*) is better than military rivalry (*bingzhan*) and trade could be used as a weapon against foreign power. For China to succeed in global competition, systemic reforms had to be made in education and commerce, and above all there had to be an elevation of the merchant's status from a very low level in the Confucian vision to the same level as officials and scholars.[16] Zheng's vision of mercantile nationalism became hugely influential in the late 1890s and early 1900s.

The political situation of 1900, when Beijing was sacked and ransacked by Western powers and Japan, introduced groundbreaking policy shifts that largely favored Zheng's vision. Under all these prevailing political and social forces, and directly influenced by the nightmarish experiences of her flight from Beijing to Xi'an in 1900, Empress Dowager Cixi finally made the fateful decision to launch full-scale economic, political, and social reforms in January 1901. The Empress approved, in principle, the famous three joint memorials by the powerful viceroys of Hubei-Hunan and Jiangsu-Jiangxi, Zhang Zhidong, and Liu Kunyi, and adopted a whole range of modernizing measures, following the example of Japan.[17] As comprehensive discussion of these reforms is beyond the scope of this study, this chapter only examines the major measures and consequences of the economic reform.

The first major *xinzheng* economic reform was a complete overhaul of the imperial bureaucracy. In 1906, the reformers founded several important modern agencies, including the Ministry of Commerce and the later Ministry of Agriculture, Industry and Commerce (MAIC), Ministry of Post and Communications, and Ministry of Finance. Between 1906 and 1912, the economic bureaucracies proceeded to create extensive systems of rules and regulations for the sectors under their jurisdiction.[18] During the final decade of the Qing Empire, the new MAIC played a key role in formulating

---

[16] Yen-Ping Hao and Ern-Min Wang, "Changing Chinese Views of the Western Relations, 1840–95," *Cambridge History of China*, vol. 10 (Cambridge: Cambridge University Press, 1978), pp. 193–194.

[17] Hsu, *The Rise of Modern China*, pp. 86–87.

[18] Zhu Ying, "On Late Qing Economic Laws and Regulations," in Douglas R. Reynolds, ed., *China, 1895–1912 State Sponsored Reforms and China's Late-Qing Revolution: Selected Essays from Zhongguo Jindai Shi* (Modern Chinese History, 1840–1919) (New York, NY: M. E. Sharpe, 1995), pp. 101–106.

and implementing ideas of economic modernization. Moreover, the MAIC experiments left the twentieth-century Chinese state entrusting economic modernization to a system of bureaucratic agents.

The second front of reform focused on tax reform. Under the reform proposal of 1904, the Qing court sought to recentralize control over salt gabelle and *lijin* taxes, which had been under provincial control since the Taiping War. But this soon met with fierce resistance. The 1909 reform to place the personnel and finances of salt administration under central control only led to a document of protest, jointly signed by almost half of the empire's local superintendents and governors.[19] Ironically, when the central governments finally issued a comprehensive action plan for centralized salt control as a national indirect tax, it was only four days before the Wuchang revolution.[20]

Meanwhile, the Qing state also carried out reforms of the public–private partnership in favor of private capital. With a consensus that private ownership was more efficient than state ownership and bureaucratic control, the Qing central and local governments privatized many important modern firms, converting *guanban* (state-owned and state-run) models into *guandu shangban* (state-owned and private-run) and *shangban* (private enterprises). Even in state-owned modern sectors, many modern enterprises experienced managerial changes as businessmen were recruited to take charge of them.[21] The final decade of the Qing Empire was thus the golden decade for Chinese private business. In the fifteen years between 1895 and 1910, in the modern sectors, private enterprises overtook both public (*guanban*) and public–private enterprises (*guandu shangban*) in terms of output and capitalization. Except in the military, communication, and railway industries, private capital broke through into most of the modern sectors, especially those closely linked to people's livelihoods, such as the manufacture of flour, textiles, tobacco, matches, and daily-use chemicals.[22]

The social prestige of businessmen also improved significantly. Among the most exemplary of the officials-turned-entrepreneurs was Zhang Jian,

---

[19] Zhou Zhichu, *Wanqing caizheng jingji yanjiu* (Studies in Late Qing Economy and Government Finance) (Jinan: Qilu Book Publisher, 1999), pp. 99–100.

[20] *Ibid.*, pp. 102–103.

[21] Xu and Wu, *Zhongguo ziben zhuyi fazhanshi*, vol. 2, pp. 380–381.

[22] Wang Kui, *Qingmo shangbu yanjiu* (Study on Late Qing Ministry of Commerce) (Beijing: People's Publishing House, 2008), pp. 107–108; K. K. Chan Wellington, "Government, Merchant and Industry to 1911," in *Cambridge History of China*, vol. 11 (Cambridge: Cambridge University Press, 1978), pp. 441–442.

who ranked first in the Civil Service Examination of 1884. His business had a difficult start in the 1890s but experienced a dramatic upsurge in fortune during the *xinzheng* era. A Confucian scholar at heart, Zhang Jian was equally devoted to transforming Nantong, the seat of his silk-making business, into a model modern city by introducing a host of modern institutions in the provision of public services, such as modern schools, orphanages, museums, and public hospitals, following the model of Japan.[23]

Among the most important of the reforms was the Ministry of Finance's effort to build a number of key modern fiscal and financial institutions, including national banks, a centralized budgetary system, and a unified fiat currency. But the reform was also less successful in this area due to political reasons. Following the example of the West, the Qing court established banks in the hope to mobilize private capital for modernization programs. Based on the lessons of the failed national debt programs, the Qing court decided to enlist wealthy landlords and businessmen as active participants and stakeholders. Rather than being a state-dominated enterprise, the new state bank was set up as a private–public joint stock cooperation, with private individuals and the state each contributing half of all the stocks. Through these newly joint stock banks, the Qing court planned to issue new paper money. But despite the increase in bank savings and capital, the imperial state could not mobilize these savings directly. The creation of sovereign money had not been as successful as the building of modern banks, since China lacked a unified legal currency and an integrated money economy to support its circulation. The path to modern statehood in Qing China, as Wenkai He suggests, differed from the cases of Britain and Japan, in that the Qing never established itself as a major bond-issuing borrower in the country's fledging modern financial institutions, such as the Shanghai stock market.[24] It was thus unable to form a virtuous circle with potential domestic lenders and build the institutional infrastructures necessary for a modern monetary system, such as a modern tax system, public debt, state banks, and, above all, the infrastructural power to control both the real sector economy and money supply. These could not be achieved with a few orders, laws, and regulations. They would require more fundamental changes in the political system. ·

---

[23] See Qin Shao, *Culturing Modernity: The Nantong Model, 1890–1930* (Palo Alto, CA: Stanford University Press, 2003), pp. 21–34.

[24] Wenkai He, *Paths towards the Modern Fiscal State: Britain, Japan, and China* (Cambridge, MA: Harvard University Press, 2013), pp. 186–187.

204   *Market in State*

When the Qing rule collapsed in 1912 – without major social disruption – it bequeathed to the new ruling elites in Beijing, who turned out to be reform factions of the old elites, the legacy of a fledging modern market-oriented state. It had established a new set of economic agencies devoted to economic development, built a few dozen modern enterprises run by professional businessmen, and transformed the fiscal system. In fact, while the economy remained agrarian, the fiscal system had expended significantly. From 1839 to 1910, the Qing budgetary income had increased from 42 to 297 million taels, whereas its expenses had climbed from 32 to 336 million taels. The tax base had broadened to take in customs, transit tax, foreign loans, and various sorts of contributions and local surcharges. The early Qing system of centralized control had given way to central dependence on various local resources.[25] In other words, fiscal control had collapsed as fiscal mobilization accelerated.

While the new policy reform project was still largely unfinished by 1911, much of its experiments would continue under Yuan Shikai and his warlord successors, until the last of the old Qing military elites' successors were overrun by the KMT based in Canton and then Nanjing. Yuan, as an enlightened reformer, generally followed the late-Qing reform policy to promote the development of modern industries and the commercial sector.[26] The modern sector of the economy, which was scattered in the areas around the treaty ports, escaped a potentially destructive dynastic war and entered a golden period of strong growth and prosperity. Even the agrarian economy was not much troubled by the change in the Mandate of Heaven, despite dynastic transitions in Chinese history often affecting it. But the final collapse of the Qing court also meant the loss of a traditional source of legitimacy for the new government in Beijing. Surrounded by powerful and sometimes militarized local power configurations, the central government in Beijing had no choice but to allow the locals to take the lead in economic development.

In the 1910s and 1920s, the Beijing government implemented reform measures with aims to establish a secure tax base, a national currency, and an integrated national market. Perpetually in want of additional revenues, the central government relied principally on revenues from the railway

[25] Zhou Yumin, *Wanqing caizheng yu shehui bianqian* (Late Qing Public Finance and Social Changes) (Shanghai: Shanghai People's Publishing House, 2000), pp. 39, 384.

[26] For a review of the economic dimension of the civil war, see Suzanne Pepper, *Civil War in China: The Political Struggle, 1945–1949* (Berkeley, CA: University of California Press, 1978), pp. 95–132.

mainline to finance large parts of its expenditure and foreign debt to make up the shortfall. By the end of the Beijing government in 1927, these two items amounted to more than 1.7 billion silver yuan.[27] While the reliance on foreign loans was a continuation of late Qing practice, the new Beijing government also succeeded in issuing public debt and in the creation of national banks.

The most notable institutional achievements of economic reform in the Beijing era were public debt and the successful minting of silver yuan based on a real silver standard. As discussed previously, late Qing experiments with public debt were largely unsuccessful, but the Beijing government could issue at least 800 million yuan as debt. In addition, the silver yuan coin issued in 1914–1920 proved to be the most widely circulated and reliable silver coin in Chinese history and supplied the basis for further currency reforms under the Nanjing government. Indeed, the silver yuan would outlive later Republican fiat currencies, before its forcible replacement by the RMB under the new Communist government in 1950.

During the Beijing decade, as the central state's financial power was weak and circumscribed, private modern banks prospered in both the Tianjin–Beijing and Shanghai–Jiangsu–Zhejiang areas. Notable financial forces were the North Bank Group (*Beisihang*) and the Southern Bank Group (*Nansihang*), each of which had four regional banks at its core. When the central governments became extremely weak in the aftermath of the paper currency crisis in 1921, the Southern bankers even forced the Ministry of Finance to sell their shares and achieve the full privatization of two of the largest note-issuing banks in China.[28] For a while, the country's monetary authority, defined as the ability to issue large-sum loans and bank notes, rested in the hands of capable private bankers and capitalists, until the Republican state assumed control through the Banking Coup of 1935.

The modern banks held a large portion of the public bonds as reserves and investment against note issuance. The fact that only 35 percent of the debt was taken by the successor KMT state indicated that this mechanism had worked well at least up to and until the 1920s.[29] But as a result of severe indebtedness due to a period of almost continuous war, the Beijing

[27] Albert Feuerwerker, "Economic Trend, 1912–1949," in John K. Fairbank, ed., *Cambridge History of China*, vol. 13 (Cambridge: Cambridge University Press, 1979), p. 101.
[28] Linsun Cheung, *Banking in Modern China: Entrepreneurs, Professional Managers and the Development of Chinese Banks, 1897–1937* (Cambridge: Cambridge University Press, 2007), pp. 113–114.
[29] *Ibid.*, pp. 102.

government had to use almost half of its annual revenues to service its debt and was basically left with no fiscal resources to finance any large-scale development projects.[30] In spite of its low fiscal capabilities and heavy indebtedness, the Beijing government was able to operate a viable fiscal system working in tandem with a complementary monetary system consisting of private banks. As would eventually be seen, the Yuan Shikai silver yuan was to remain the currency of last resort in China until the Communist takeover.

The evolution of China's political economy in the Beijing decade presented a mixed picture. Compared with earlier and later periods of China's history, this was a period of market ascendance, but to nowhere near the status of a national market. It was an era in which private businesses could grow without formal state restriction, but their economic undertakings were inhibited by the undersupply of basic public goods and an uncertain and unstable political situation.[31] But in comparison with late Qing, this period was still a watershed, as it signaled the first efforts to build a modern state and national market. Although neither the last Qing reformers nor their Beiyang successors could muster the power necessary to build such a centralized state, they nevertheless opened the Pandora's Box of economic statism, which had been locked since the failure of Wang Anshi – a fiscally expanding central state capable of mobilizing finance and fiscal resources. This direction set by late Qing reformers was to continue well into the twentieth century.

THE RISE OF THE PARTY-STATE AND THE NANJING DECADE, 1920–1937

The interim time of the early 1920s, an era of defunct central authority and strong local powers, saw transient periods of domination of various local warlords and, to a lesser degree, autonomous modern economic elites in China's political economy. The three major factions – the Anhuai faction, led by Duan Qirui; the Zhili faction, led by Cao Kun and Wu Peifu; and the Fengtian faction, led by Zhang Zuolin – each controlled a large part of Eastern, Central-Northern, and Northeast (Manchuria) provinces.

[30] Kashiwai Kisao, *Kindai Shina Zaiseishi* (Fiscal History of Modern China) (Tokyo: Tokyo Kyoiku Tosho, 1942), pp. 63–64.
[31] For a regional study of how undersupply of public goods undermined the development of private industrial capitals, see Madeleine Zelin, *The Merchants of Zigong: Industrial Entrepreneurship in Early Modern China* (New York, NY: Columbia University Press, 2005).

They were followed by other powerful but peripheral actors in Shanxi (Yan Xishan), Shaanxi (Feng Yuxiang), Guangxi (Li Zongren), and Guangdong (Chen Jiongming).

Aggressive local financing of wars created waves of short-term disturbance and long-term uncertainty in the economy, even as Chinese businesses benefited handsomely from the Great War in Europe. The warlords had even fewer institutionalized fiscal resources than the unified Qing imperial state and the partially unified Yuan Shikai regime. They were considered legitimate receivers of foreign aid. Only very few, powerful and promising warlords had the opportunity to gain financial support from foreign powers, but even in these limited cases, the leading warlords were often constrained by nationalist feeling. As a result, some of the financially depressed warlords took to the markets to search for new forms of military finance, such as extraordinary and prelevied salt gabelles and commercial and transit taxes. The crisis came to a head in the summer of 1923–1924 as the civil war between Zhili, Anhui, and Fengtian reached its full scale. The economic disturbance was of such a degree that the economies of all major cities in the North and East fell into a sharp depression in 1924 for a period lasting up to half a year.[32]

The most potent force was, quite unexpectedly, a resurgent KMT led by Sun Yat-sen under the banner of "three peoples" – nationalism, democracy, and socialism. Although Yuan Shikai and his Beiyang clique dominated the Republican state initially, his chief political rival, Sun Yat-sen, eventually emerged as the visionary and potent state-builder, with his KMT. In Sun's ideological doctrine of *Sanmin zhuyi*, *Minsheng* (people's livelihood) was the cornerstone and the basis of nationalism and democracy. Sun's belief in the transformative power of the state in the economy was reflected in the three revolutions he proposed. The first was land revolution: the equalization of land rights under state ownership. The second was a state-guided industrial revolution, which would bring about a sweeping modernization of the Chinese system. The third was a monetary revolution that would establish a nonconvertible paper currency backed by materials under the control of the state.[33]

---

[32] Arthur Waldron, *From War to Nationalism: China's Turning Point, 1924–1925*, 2nd ed. (Cambridge: Cambridge University Press, 2002), pp. 119–142.

[33] Sun Yat-sen, "Changqi qianbi geming duikang sha'e qinglue" (A Proposed Monetary Revolution against the Aggression of Czarist Russia), in *Sun Zhongshan quanji* (The Complete Works of Sun Yat-sen), vol. 2 (Beijing: Zhonghua shuju, 1986), pp. 544–546.

However, Sun was only a marginal figure in a country riven with powerful warlords in the 1910s. It was not until the early 1920s that he finally managed to carve out an enclave at Guangdong, with his loyal supporter Chen Jiongmin. His opportunity eventually came when Soviet Russia intervened decisively in China's political development. In 1920, after the failure of Communist insurrections in Germany and Hungary, the newly founded Soviet government in Moscow began to search for a credible political ally in Asia, taking a special interest in politically fragmented China. After several rejections by some of China's more powerful warlords, the Soviet Union missions in China successfully explored and forged friendly relations with Sun and his government in Guangzhou.[34] The model which the Soviet Union offered Sun was a party-state with an explicit revolutionary agenda, as the Nationalist Party, or KMT, became a political vehicle for nation-building.[35]

In terms of its policy toward private businesses, the KMT's harshness was almost the very opposite of the lenient approach taken by the Beijing government and many local warlords, though Sun's successors were to soften that stance in the late 1920s. But with the leftist Liao Zhongkai serving as Minister of Finance, the Guangdong Nationalist Government made the first attempt to control the local economy to finance wars by allying with workers and peasants and attacking business and financial elites. In the urban regions, the KMT government sought to impose a system of fiat currency and taxation, such as universal business and corporate income taxes. As expected, Liao's fiscal programs aroused fierce resistance from commercial interests in Guangdong. Local merchants refused to accept the government's badly backed promissory notes, calling strikes and requesting protection from merchant militia backed by the British colonial authority in Hong Kong.[36] This conflict eventually escalated into the Guangzhou Merchant Rebellion of 1924. Although the KMT eventually quelled the rebellion, with Soviet aid, and disarmed the merchant organizations, the Guangzhou and Nanjing KMT leaders later made

---

[34] Tony Saich, *The Origin of the First United Front in China* (Leiden: Brill Academic Press, 1997), pp. 213–215.
[35] For a more detailed discussion, see Yongnian Zheng, "Nationalism and Statism: Chinese Perceptions of the Crisis of State Power," in *Discovering Chinese Nationalism in China: Modernization, Identity, and International Relations* (Cambridge: Cambridge University Press, 1999), pp. 21–45.
[36] Marie-Claire Bergère, "The Chinese Bourgeoisie, 1911–1937," in John K. Fairbank, ed., *The Cambridge History of China*, vol. 13 (Cambridge: Cambridge University Press, 1979), p. 795.

a conscious effort to adopt a more graduated and conciliatory approach to the economic elites, to avoid similar incidents at least at the individual level in its Northern Expedition to unify the country (1926–1928).[37]

The Northern Expedition established the KMT army as a formidable military bloc in 1927, and the Chinese political economy entered the Nanjing Decade with a national government bent on economic modernization and nation-building. The Nanjing Decade was a turning point in the history of China's political economy. Before the KMT government had time to create its own development policies, China's domestic capitalism had already experienced rapid growth and developed its own domestic extensive marketing systems. At the beginning of this period, the KMT benefited immensely from its alliance with China's capitalists, acting in their interest as defenders against the Communists, who had relied heavily on labor movements and urban rebellions in a borrowed Soviet strategy of proletariat revolution. But as the Communist threat to the urban economy and society waned and the Chinese strategy of peasant revolution took shape in the early 1930s, this ad hoc alliance soon proved unsustainable, since it was now the KMT government, bent on fiscal expansion and state-led economic development, whose interests clashed headlong with those of the capitalists.

Immediately after nominal unification in 1928, the KMT held the National Fiscal Conference to address the issue of economic unification, setting out a blueprint of a state-controlled economic system. But at this stage, the KMT was so internally divided and externally threatened that it could not implement even some elements of such rules. The civilian faction headed by Wang Jingwei and Song Ziwen, the military faction headed by Chiang Kai-shek, and the other important factions such as the CC (Central Club) cliques and Hu Hanmin's Guangzhou clique rivaled each other in the realm of political strategy as well as in their approach to the economy. While all these factions agreed on the importance of state control, the civilian faction preferred more coherent and inclusive economic modernization programs, while the military faction stressed strategic and political supremacy over the market above all. The civilian model dominated first, as Wang and Song used the National Economic Commission to mobilize the support of nationalist private entrepreneurs and attempted

---

[37] Hu Qirui, "Jindai Guangzhou Shangren yu Zhengzhi, 1905–1926" (Merchants and Politics, Modern Canton), MA thesis, Taipei: National Chengchi University, 2003, pp. 176–179.

to enlist them for industrial development projects.[38] Later, it gave way to the statist National Resource Commission, as both internal and external political dynamics favored the rise of Chiang, the military faction inevitably carried the day, and the economy moved in the statist direction.

The Great Depression was another factor contributing to the demise of China's nascent private capitalists. When the crisis at the heart of global capitalism first broke out, China was initially shielded by its silver standard. But when the United States enacted the Silver Act, the situation was immediately reversed and severe deflation set in. The first and most direct impact was on the productive sector, and was followed by an important monetary and financial impact. The prices of agrarian products fell, and the situation of China's agrarian economy and agriculture-process industries immediately worsened to such a degree that most of the silk-reeling and cotton-spinning firms faced imminent collapse.[39] As a de facto silver-standard country with no substantial silver reserves,[40] China suffered a serious blow from the American policy to repurchase silver at an elevated price in 1933, which immediately induced an significant outflow of silver and tightening of money and credit in China.

The economic and fiscal crisis of the early 1930s thus posed a major challenge to the nascent Nationalist government. It was worsened by ongoing civil war with the remaining warlords as well as the Communists, who still controlled sizable territory in China's mountainous south. The demand for fiscal resources and control of the national economy thus precipitated the radical economic centralization of 1935, in which year the KMT government's economic leaders launched a coup against the private bankers. In April 1935, Minister of Finance Kong Xiangxi coerced two major private banks – the Bank of China and Bank of Communications – which had become skeptical of the government's ability to serve its bonds to accept further government bonds as reserves, through a combination of a public relations campaign and political pressure. To secure the compliance of Shanghai capitalists, the KMT government mobilized the support of leaders of secret societies, such as Du Yuesheng and the mass media, against the "big financial capitals," by

---

[38] Zanasi Margherita, *Saving the Nation: Economic Modernity in Republican China* (Chicago, IL: University of Chicago Press, 2010), pp. 81–85.

[39] Tomoko Shiroyama, *China During the Great Depression: Market, State and World Economy* (Cambridge, MA: Harvard University Press, 2008), pp. 114–116.

[40] In the 1930s, the dominant currency in China was still various silver yuan or *dayang* established by the Beijing government in the 1910s. It was fully convertible to silver. All major bank notes were also denominated in yuan.

placing on the great bankers the blame for small and medium enterprises' dire economic and financial situation. Eventually, the Shanghai bankers backed down and agreed to accept state control.[41]

After the government established control over major banks, monetary reform was undertaken in late 1935. The reform instituted the fiat *fabi* to replace an assortment of bank notes and silver yuan as the new national currency of the Republic of China. Thanks to the prior coups, the KMT government achieved fuller control over the financial sector and quickly flooded the coffers of banking assets with public bonds. Between 1934 and 1936, the government's group share in total assets increased from 18.2 percent to 72.6 percent, including controlling shares in all four note-issuing banks.[42] As the first *fiat* currency backed by coercive state power, *fabi* marked a watershed moment in China's monetary history.

Despite the KMT's state-building and market-controlling efforts, the capacity of the central state was weakened by ongoing civil war with the Communists, disobedient warlords turned local leaders, foreign invasions from Japan and the Soviet Union, and political struggles at the center throughout the Nanjing Decade. While Chiang Kai-shek had emerged as the top military leader in the 1930s, his faction was challenged from all sides within the Nationalist Party. As Japanese threats increased, the Chiang Kai-shek faction gradually gained control over the party-state organ. In economic terms, there was a rivalry between a state-guided national economy (*minzu jingji*) centered on Southern economic elites and championed by Wang Jingwei and Song Ziwen, and Chiang's own vision of a state-controlled system of banks and heavy industries with technocrats in command. The National Resource Commission's replacement of the National Economic Commission as the actual economic planning agency in late 1935 signaled Chiang's success. With key economic resources under state control, Chiang was ready to implement a hard-line, military-first strategy toward the external enemies of the KMT state (warlord factions, the CCP Red Army, and the Japanese) and delay any substantive reforms to address the rural questions, which were perceived as the top social issue of the day. But all these came too late to aid in war preparations, since the Sino–Japanese War was already knocking at the door by 1936.

---

[41] Parks M. Coble, Jr., *The Shanghai Capitalists and the Nationalist Government, 1927–1937* (Cambridge, MA: Harvard University Press, 1980), pp. 176–177.

[42] Xu Dixin and Wu Chenming, *Zhongguo Zibenzhuyi fazhanshi*, vol. 3 (Beijing: Social Science Academic Press, 2001), pp. 197–209.

Even as the KMT state tightened control of the market, economic development in the modern sectors continued unabated, as industrial entrepreneurship kept on growing throughout the 1920s and early 1930s. Taking the output of 1933 as 100, gross output of industrial production increased from 11.9 in 1912 to 122 in 1936. But more important changes were in the structure of key industries, clearly demonstrating the rise of domestic-based capitalistic production. The cotton cloth sector, for instance, was almost completely dominated by imports and domestic handicrafts in 1905, which together contributed about 88.5 percent of output, but in 1931 it was domestic manufacturers who were contributing 90.9 percent, and exports had increased from nil to 7.1 percent.[43]

KMT economic statism was a direct response to two parallel external challenges in China's more remote regions. The first and primary source was the Japanese in Manchuria and North China. Japanese encroachment on China's Northeast could be traced back to 1894 but it was limited to small-scale colonialization, control of major railway lines, and intelligence gathering. The process suddenly accelerated in the aftermath of China's nominal unification in 1928 and the Great Depression of 1929. In 1931, the Kanto Army launched a surprise attack against the unprepared Northeast Army and overran its main garrisons. It established the puppet state of Manchukou in the next year. After 1934, the Japanese government began to implement economic control and planning in the puppet state. In 1936, it set up the Manchu Heavy Industrial Company, which controlled all key mines and machinery tool factories in Manchuria. In the first Five Year Plan of 1937–1941, which prioritized defense and heavy industries above all, the entire economy became subject to Japanese military mobilization, as the Japanese government assumed full control over Manchuria's key industries.[44]

Another source of economic statism was the Communists' revolutionary state-building efforts in the Chinese Soviets. While the KMT consolidated its control over China's most economically open and advanced Yangtze River region, various serious social crises in rural China also came to a head. In North China, the rural crisis began with state involution and the collapse of gentry-centered protective brokerage between the rural society and the imperial state during the Qing state's modernizing reforms, but

---

[43] Feuerwerker, "Economic Trend, 1912–1949," pp. 54–55.
[44] Nagakane Katsuji, "Manchukou and Economic Development," in Peter Duus, Ramon H. Meyers, and Mark R. Peattle, eds., *The Japanese Informal Empire in China* (Princeton, NJ: Princeton University Press, 1989), pp. 141–145.

full-scale peasant movements would not develop until the Communist forces arrived during the decades of total war.[45] In the already crisis-ridden agrarian regions in China's south and central hinterland, the arrival of the Communists further escalated the situation into open peasant movements and struggles over land.[46] Contrary to the relatively conciliatory approach of the KMT, the CCP adopted a particularly harsh approach vis-à-vis the economic elites under its control. The first CCP peasant revolutions were led by Peng Pai in the Hai-Lu-Feng area, in which the CCP cadres introduced more efficient organization and class-struggle ideology into the rural areas of eastern Guangdong. Later, when the CCP and KMT alliance collapsed in 1927, the CCP took radical land reform as a chief economic and political strategy in its struggle with the KMT in the base areas.

In occupied territories, the CCP also attempted state control of the market. They implemented an even more aggressive system of paper currency at the base areas, and often forced peasants to follow dogmatic land reform programs that included violent excesses.[47] These aggressive fiscal and economic policies were generally less successful than those of the KMT, leaving the CCP regimes beholden to silver yuan or *fabi*, since their excessively predatory nature merely served to contribute to the downfall of Communist order in the Red Areas as both the economic elites and, later, the ordinary peasants fled to more stable areas.[48] But they were nevertheless the preamble for further CCP economic strategies as the CCP survived the Long March and waited for the situation to ripen.

In the early 1930s, even before China entered a period of total war, the competition between the KMT, the Japanese, and the Communists in building institutional structures and material bases for military and political struggles had already foreshadowed things to come. Indeed, the institutional innovations of this period, from fiat currency, state banks, and monopoly of natural resources to the first Five Year Plans, would have an

---

[45] For a discussion of typical rural decline following the Qing modernizing reforms, see Prasenjit Duara, *Culture, Power, and the State: Rural North China, 1900–1942* (Palo Alto, CA: Stanford University Press, 1988), pp. 217–243.

[46] For a discussion on the CCP-inspired peasant movement and its differences from the earlier autonomous types, see Lucien Bianco, "Peasant Movements," in John K. Fairbank, ed., *Cambridge History of China*, vol. 13 (Cambridge: Cambridge University Press, 1979), pp. 305–329.

[47] Peter Zarrow, *China in War and Revolution: 1895–1949* (London: Routledge, 2006), pp. 281–282.

[48] Kathleen Hartford and Steven M. Goldstein, *Single Sparks: China's Rural Revolutions* (New York, NY: M. E. Sharpe, 1989), pp. 69–71.

enduring impact on the trajectory of China's state-led economic development. This multifaceted development toward a war economy with a heavy
Soviet imprint could be best captured by the emergence of a highly
militarized planned economy in the 1930s. While there had been a plethora
of ministerial-level plans along the lines of Sun's original vision, none had
political and financial support from the Nationalist state. But after the
Manchuria Incident of 1931, the Nationalist government strengthened
its planning agencies and began to gear up industrial development for
the impending war with the industrial and military power of Japan. In
the early 1930s, this effort was first manifested in the powerful National
Resource Commission, headed by technocrats such as Weng Wenhao and
Qian Changzhao, and the first substantial industrial plan, the Ten Year
Plan for Heavy Industry of 1936.[49] But this plan had to be shelved after
the outbreak of the Sino–Japanese War in 1937. In his 1939 review of the
Plan's limited achievements, Qian Changzhao, vice commissioner of the
National Resource Commission, considered four insurmountable hurdles
that were frustrating China's bid for heavy industrialization: capital, technology, information, and human resources. Regarding scarcity of capital,
Qian proposed that China should not follow the Soviet path in squeezing
the peasants to finance industrialization. Instead, he suggested that China
could industrialize via trade and foreign investments, which could in turn
finance the urgently needed basic industries and infrastructure building.
In his view, technology, information, and human resources were likely to
throw up more challenges in the near future. In these aspects, aside from
stepping up the training of technical personnel, international cooperation
was the only way to move forward. In the face of the war with Japan, Qian
maintained that the overall strategy would be a state-oriented effort to
encourage technology and industrial development, with a focus on the
defense industry as the central task of the wartime economy.[50] In essence,
the Chinese economy was already geared toward a partial planned economy premised on foreign technology imports on the eve of the total war
with the Empire of Japan. The conditions for such massive technology
imports would only mature in the Cold War, when China became a pivotal
actor in the superpower rivalry.

---

[49] William Kirby, "Continuity and Change in Modern China: Economic Planning in Taiwan
and China, 1943–1958," *The Australian Journal of Chinese Affairs* 24 (1990),
pp. 125–126.
[50] Qian Changzhao, "Liangnianban chuangban zhonggongye zhi jingguo ji ganxiang"
(Experience and Thoughts of Building Heavy Industry in the Last Two and Half Years),
New Economy Biweekly 2 (1939), pp. 29–31.

THE DECADES OF TOTAL WAR AND THE MOBILIZATION ECONOMY, 1937–1953

After July 1937, China entered a period of war and revolution that would ultimately end with Communist unification, strategic alignment with the Soviet Union, and stalemate with the United States in 1953. In these dramatic and fast-moving years, a dozen political and military forces that had dominated mainland China since the late nineteenth century were reduced to only one: The Communist Party, which assumed unprecedented total control over Chinese society, economy, and politics. This was followed by a series of state-led revolutionary reforms that ultimately destroyed the country's traditional social and economic order. The process of state-building through war in this period had an enduring and far-reaching impact on the political and economic institutions of contemporary China.

From mid-1937 to late 1938, although the national armies of China fought valiantly on many fronts, they lost many major cities, railway lines, the coastline, and the entire Yangtze Delta Region to Japan. As such, the economic effects of the Sino–Japanese War effectively ended the golden period of China's nascent national economy. China was divided into territories that were under Japanese control (Manchuria and then northern China), territories first under KMT control and later lost to the Japanese (Yangtze Delta Regions and central China), and territories continuously under KMT (Southwest China). But in each of these regions, there had been a tendency to replace private market capitalism with a command economy.

The Japanese effort to establish a viable order also generally failed to produce desired outcomes. Like the later KMT in the civil war, the Japanese occupational forces were only able to secure control of China's major railway lines, and their penetration of the command economy hardly went deeper than the occupying army. This strategic limitation created difficulty in the procurement of agricultural household products such as grain and cotton cloth. In the early 1940s, Japanese forces needed to encourage rapid urbanization, by urging peasants to move their tools and even their entire households into county seats in order to establish secure control over resources such as cotton cloths. They had little success,[51] and without control over grain and other supplies such efforts were

---

[51] Peng Zeyi, *Zhongguo jindai shougongye shiliao* (Historical Materials on Handicraft in Modern China) vol. 4 (Beijing: Zhonghua Shuju, 1962), p. 135.

futile. In the end, the Japanese occupational authority was compelled to resort to violent means to mobilize resources, such as sporadic raids into the countryside and enforcing inconvertible fiat coupons in the urban markets. In the case of grain, since the Japanese authority was unable to build a mobilization system from the rural grassroots, it had to build a monopoly trading system with the grain merchants to ensure the army's supply.[52]

Meanwhile, the KMT state in retreat in the Southwest had met with a measure of success in developing mobilization and military systems to reach grassroots society. A similar need to mobilize sufficient grain and manpower necessarily demanded that the KMT government should make its way into the countryside in the area under its control. This was a big challenge to the KMT, which had never built many grassroots organizations to replace the traditional rural power networks. To that end, the KMT experimented with a new level of administration below the county level – the township or district – and instituted a nationwide *bao-jia* system as a new power infrastructure. But hardly any new dynamics of mobilization were available. The KMT then turned to coercive means and came to rely on the traditional elites to carry out grain collection and drafting. After 1941, the KMT war machine was able to mobilize 6,000 tons of grain and 150 million soldiers for the war on a yearly basis.[53]

In their effort to fight the Japanese, the KMT had to develop new industrial bases in China's southwest, based on the human and material resources they rescued from the economic center in the Yangtze Delta Region. As a result, the KMT government's withdrawal to the hinterland spawned rapid industrialization in areas under its effective control. Accounting for merely 6 percent of national industrial output and 4 percent of total investment, the modern sector was minuscule before the war. Between 1938 and 1943, the number of modern factories increased by 250 percent and their output quadrupled in KMT-controlled regions, before these fruits of wartime industrialization were devastated by hyperinflation near the end of the war.[54]

---

[52] Liu Zhiying, *Wangwei zhengfu liangzheng shuping* (Outline and Comments on the Grain Policy of Wang Jingwei Puppet Government), Kangri zhanzheng Yanjiu (Study on Sino-Japanese War) 1 (1999), pp. 135–153.

[53] Sasagawa Yuji and Okumura Satoshi, *Tougo no Chugoku Shakai, Chunichi senso shita no sodoin to nozo* (Chinese Society Led by the Guns: Total Mobilization and Countryside during the Sino-Japanese War) (Tokyo: Iwanami Books, 2007), p. 233.

[54] Arthur Young, *China's Wartime Finance and Inflation, 1937–1945* (Cambridge, MA: Harvard University Press, 1965), pp. 221–222.

Despite the newly gained mobilization power and industrial buildup during the war, the KMT was unable to keep inflation low. This was partly caused by the state procurement system, which had reduced the amount of grain and other strategic goods available on markets. More importantly, however, it was the product of pure military overspending vis-à-vis a limited tax base. To combat inflation, the government first fixed wages and the prices of daily necessities. After 1942, a new system was instituted to actively manage inflation, as the government began to buy and sell necessities and export items in order to maintain price stability. But this system also broke down quickly due to a lack of supply. In retrospect, the Chongqing KMT government simply lacked the required capacity, firm territorial control, efficient bureaucracy, and functioning system of communication and transportation to enforce its policy rules over a wider territory.[55]

The inflationary experiences had an immediate impact on the KMT's approach to economic control. War had made the KMT party-state by far the largest economic force in the country. Although the state's intervention in commerce ended badly, its control over the industrial sector was relatively successful. Before the war, the government only controlled up to 11 percent of the nation's industrial capital, but in 1942, state-owned enterprises (SOEs) commanded 17.5 percent of the factories, 70 percent of capital, 32 percent of the workforce, and 42 percent of power consumption in the modern industrial sector in the unoccupied regions.[56] In particular, the state consolidated its control over heavy industries, which expanded faster during the war than in peacetime. The SOEs' expansion in this period of wartime economic crisis was accompanied by an expanding role for the state in providing basic welfare and social services through these SOEs in an explicit effort to address the social and mental consequences of hyperinflation, remaking the factories into organizations carrying both important social and economic functions.[57]

In general, the Communists fared better than both the KMT and the Japanese in their mobilization and control of economic resources. Like many other aspects of its wartime strategy, the Communist Party's economic policies during the Sino–Japanese war were carefully crafted to

---

[55] *Ibid.*, pp. 146–147.

[56] Chen Zhen, ed., *Zhongguo jindai gongyeshi ziliao* (Materials on the Industry of Modern China), vol. 4 (Shanghai: Shanghai Sanlian Books, 1962), p. 1422.

[57] Morris L. Bian, *The Making of the State Enterprise System in Modern China: The Dynamics of Institutional Change* (Cambridge, MA: Harvard University Press, 2005), pp. 142–149.

secure maximum control over land, population, and strategic commodities. But unlike the KMT and the Japanese, the CCP, largely fighting behind and active among the grassroots, had a clear advantage in not being burdened with the need to supply a massive standing army constantly at war, a large urban population, and capital-intensive heavy industries. For each of the major strategic bases, the task of the CCP local authorities' economic branch was to create a material basis for its survival by developing its own grassroots organizations and extracting more resources for its own expansion.

This unique economic and fiscal strategy did not take shape until 1940, when the conflict between the CCP and KMT resurged, and especially after 1942, when the Japanese joined the blockade after tightening control over China's economic resources for the Pacific War. After this, the economy of the CCP's central Shan-Gan-Ning border base faced even more severe material shortages and inflation than the KMT were suffering.[58] The CCP's central leadership responded with a self-reliance model centering on textile production, imposition of a new agricultural tax, and a system of controlled trade, which eventually stabilized the deteriorating economic situation and established a new equilibrium.[59] In addition, the economy's lack of sophistication helped the CCP, as it suffered a relatively smaller amount of substantive damage from hyperinflation as it switched to a self-reliance model.

Among the CCP's experiences of economic management in the base regions, Xue Muqiao's Shandong experiments proved among the most fruitful. The CCP government in Shandong could keep the value of its own regional currency stable – while the *fabi* (KMT) and *weibi* (Japanese) lost most of their value – by backing it with supplies of basic materials or goods available through state-dominated trade. Before issuing currency, the trade bureaus of the base-area CCP government used grassroots organizations to directly secure grain and other commodities from the peasant households under its control. By means of this material standard, money was subject to the livelihood economy and thus controlled by the

---

[58] Schran Peter, *Guerrilla Economy: The Development of Shanxi-Gansu-Ningxia Region* (New York, NY: SUNY Press, 1976), pp. 184–185.

[59] Lyman Von Slyke, "The Chinese Communist Movement during the Sino-Japanese War 1937–1945," in John K. Fairbank, ed., *The Cambridge History of China*, vol. 12 (Cambridge: Cambridge University Press, 1983), p. 795.

Shandong base-area government.[60] Similarly, the Communist local regimes in other regions could secure access to basic materials and prevent the devastating effects of inflation on the economy despite the fiscal crisis in these regions, such as the Shan-Gan-Ning border region, where the CCP Central Leadership was located.[61]

The eight-year Sino–Japanese war was a nightmare for the overall national economy. North China was more severely affected than Southern and Western China as the war segmented national markets, caused dislocations, and reduced the average level of commercial activity across regions. The nascent modern sectors, despite significant output gains in certain state-owned areas of heavy industry, suffered severe overall contractions in output. Gross industrial output in 1945 was only 62 percent of output in 1933. The disintegration of the national market under the KMT was most evident in the precipitous drop in total freight in government-controlled railways. Taking 1912 as the base year, it plummeted from 228 percent of the 1912 level in 1936–1937 to a mere 9 percent in 1943–1944 and recovered to 154 percent in 1945–1946.[62] Such severe levels of devastation left the KMT state with a pyrrhic victory after Japan's surrender in August 1945. The only victorious power in the war was probably the nascent Communist regime, which managed to balance inflation and resource mobilization through control over local markets. This unexpected turn of history placed the CCP in a favorable position when the Civil War started soon after.

The economic and military struggle between the KMT and CCP during the Chinese Civil War (1946–1949) was one of the most dramatic and decisive episodes in the history of Chinese political economy. In the initial stage, it appeared as if the CCP was no peer of the incumbent KMT, since the government's army enjoyed a decisive edge over the CCP's. With superior weapons and naval support from the United States, the KMT had a clear advantage in seeking to fill the political and military vacuum left by the Japanese and had quickly taken over most of the CCP-controlled

[60] Huang Yanjie, "Constructing A National *Oikonomia*: China's Great Monetary Revolutions, 1942–1952," *EAI Working Paper* No. 161. East Asian Institute, National University of Singapore, January 18, 2013, pp. 3–5.
[61] Tang Taomo, "Kangri zhanzheng shiqi Shang-Gan-Ning bianqu de caizheng" (Finance and Economy at the Shan-Gan-Ning Border Region during the Sino-Japanese War), in Institute of Financial Science in the Ministry of Finance, *Geming genjudi de caizheng jingji* (Finance and Economy in the Revolutionary Base Areas) (Beijing: China Caizheng Jingji Chubanshe, 1985), pp. 96–97.
[62] Feuerwerker, "Economic Trends 1912–1949," p. 97.

base regions in the North and Northeast by 1946. But the initial success was soon marred by several serious policy mistakes, including misman-agement of social movements, economic instability, continued political disunity, serious corruption, and failure to strike decisively against CCP forces.[63] The overall strategic failings of the KMT state soon led to a downturn in military fortune and eventual collapses experienced in decisive encounters with the CCP in 1947 and 1948. All these had their roots in the shortcomings of the fiscal system. The KMT state, being forced to garrison centers of consumption – cities and towns – and lacking effective control over much of the agrarian sector, could not muster sufficient resources to fight the Communists, who enjoyed much better control and greater mobilization capacity over their own economic bases. In the end, it forced the weight of the war on to the already fragile monetary and financial system.

The KMT's inability to finance the Civil War via its relatively modern financial system became evident when the Civil War reached its height in 1947. Between 1946 and the first half of 1948, the share of military expenditure in the Nanjing government budget ranged from 60 to 70 percent, almost equivalent to the share of deficit in the total budget.[64] Almost all these deficits were financed by the issuance of unbacked *fabi*. As public confidence collapsed, inflation rates rose much faster than expend-iture, creating a vicious circle of continuous fiscal and monetary crises. During the year of 1947, Shanghai's wholesale price index increased 1,500 percent; in the first eight months of 1948, it was up 6,500 percent.[65] Finally, on the eve of the decisive Huaihai Campaigns in mid-August 1948, the KMT government had to institute a new currency, the Gold Yuan to replace *fabi*, which had been reduced to merely 0.0001 percent of its 1945 value.[66]

As suggested by its name, the Gold Yuan was a gold-backed fiat currency. To make its value stable, the KMT government forcibly nation-alized all gold in the society and imposed price controls on all key commodities. For such extraordinary measures to succeed, the KMT government needed to secure victory on both the home front, against its self-interested state agents, and on the military front, in the battle against

---

[63] Lloyd Eastman, *Seeds of Destruction: Nationalist China in War and Revolution, 1937–1949* (Stanford, CA: Stanford University Press, 1984), pp. 205–228.
[64] Chang Kia-ngau, *The Inflation Spiral: The Experience in China* (Cambridge, MA: MIT Press, 1958), p. 155.
[65] Eastman, *Seeds of Destruction*, p. 134.   [66] Chang, *The Inflation Spiral*, pp. 87–88.

the CCP. This proved impossible. On the home front there was an internal divide between hardliners, such as Chiang Ching-kuo, who wished to crack down on all insider trading, corrupt officials, and moderates or accomplices in crony capitalism. Chiang made a desperate attempt to crack down on speculators and salvage the situation in Shanghai, but eventually failed to stabilize prices due to uncontrollable inflation and rampant speculation.[67] In early October 1948, as the Gold Yuan collapsed, the KMT's economic fate was sealed even before its final military defeat. The CCP, however, had learned how to manage a vast agrarian hinterland with a small and state-controlled modern sector from its experiences of land reform, particularly in the Shandong area. The key to success lay in the implementation of radical land reforms in the agrarian strongholds, to mobilize both human and material resources. The land reforms entailed a complete reorganization of the rural political and economic structure. The CCP was able to adroitly exploit class tensions in rural society while sustaining its war efforts with resources unleashed by the social revolution. The Huaihai campaign between November 1948 and January 1949 has long been held as a classic example of the CCP's mobilization capacity.[68] In addition to a largely peasant army of about 600,000, CCP grassroots organizations mobilized at least five million nonmilitary servicemen and more than 48,000 tons of grain from central, northern, and Eastern China and, mostly, from the neighboring province of Shandong, a CCP stronghold since 1947.[69] The immense mobilization capacity was directly linked to land reforms: Wherever the reforms were well carried out, there were more volunteer peasant soldiers and more victories.[70]

Meanwhile, the CCP grew accustomed to supplying food and other necessities to a limited number of cities and towns under its control, while cutting the KMT-held cities' vital links to the markets. Nowhere was the success of such an economic strategy more salient than the Northeast Liberation Areas. During the Civil War, the CCP's Manchurian authorities experimented with urban economic management, with

---

[67] Eastman, *Seeds of Destruction*, pp. 186–193.

[68] The story was made known to the world largely through a comment made to the Soviet ambassador to Beijing by Chen Yi, a top CCP general at the Huaihai Campaign and later the first mayor of Shanghai, that "the success of Huaihai Campaign was based on 5 million peasant servicemen and their wheelbarrows."

[69] Li Weiguang, *Zhongguo caizhengshi lungao* (Essays on China's Fiscal History) (Beijing: Zhongguo Caizheng Jingji Chubanshe, 2000), p. 255.

[70] Dong Zhikai, *Jiefang zhanzheng shiqi de tudigaige* (Land Reform in the War of Liberation) (Beijing: Beijing University Press, 1987), pp. 95–96.

the objective of supporting the ongoing war while maintaining relative fiscal and monetary stability. This was largely achieved, as the CCP financial system was centralized internally to enforce fiscal discipline and expanded externally to control internal trade and key industries.[71] Unlike the KMT authorities in the south, the CCP North East Financial Commission was able to exercise comprehensive management over the region's industrial, commercial, fiscal, and financial systems to ensure inflation was under control, thanks to the party's domination of all its functional organizations. Again, unlike the hunger-stricken KMT-controlled urban regions, the CCP economy in northeastern China could easily move millions of tons of grain from the post-land reform countryside.

The CCP's logistical feat is rooted in its ability to control the rural economy. After liquidating the rural elites through land reforms in northern China, it was easily able to master the surplus through its own grassroots organizations in the rural area. This involuntary mobilization was nothing like the voluntary mobilization of the old days. The strength of the CCP's economic mobilization power was demonstrated by the fact that it could mobilize as much as 234 and 502 percent of the average grain mobilized yearly by the KMT after Sichuan's liberation in 1950 and during the Great Leap Forward later in 1959.[72] Whereas the KMT relied heavily on a progressive grain tax on all households and contributions from local landlords to meet grain procurement targets, the CCP simply destroyed the rural power structures and replaced them with its own grassroots organizations with a strong, embedded fiscal capacity.

Eventually, it was the CCP's direct transactions with the post-reform peasant household, rather than a gradual integration of regional markets, that constructed the overarching political economic structure. Rather than simply mobilizing the rural economy for the war, the CCP scheme in the Civil War was essentially a political mobilization. Indeed, in some base areas, the CCP integrated dispersed household economies and rural local markets with a superstructure of bureaucratic controls, as in the case of its commercial and monetary systems. This would have been quite impossible under a natural market system in a period of major war and dislocation. In setting up this system, the CCP asserted the values of a

---

[71] Zhu Jianhua, *Dongbei jiefangqu caizhengjingji shigao* (Fiscal and Economic History of North East Liberated Regions) (Haerbin: Heilongjiang People's Press, 1987), pp. 356–357.

[72] Sasagawa Yuji and Okumura Satoshi, *Tougo no Chugoku Shakai, Chunichi senso shita no sodoin to nozo* (Chinese Society Led by the Guns: Total Mobilization and Countryside during the Sino-Japanese War) (Tokyo: Iwanami Books, 2007), p. 233.

single moral economy, which now coincided with the popular under-standing of socialism, as the new command economy existed first and foremost to provide for all agrarian households' basic subsistence and reproduction needs.

Unlike the KMT system, the CCP system of mobilization in the Civil War had consistent appeal for most of China's destitute peasants. Toward the end of the Civil War, the CCP's army far outstripped that of its competitor in terms of material and personnel supply and could replenish its losses with new drafts from the liberated areas and those deserted and surrounded in the KMT garrisons. Overrunning these garrisons brought not only troops and cadres, but also banks, fiscal and commercial agencies, and, more importantly, basic ideas and conceptions of a modern national economy.

This Civil War model of a mobilization economy met an even harsher challenge in the guise of the Korean War between 1950 and 1953. The CCP's experiences in the Sino–Japanese War and the Civil War provided party-state economic bureaucrats with the expertise to manage a wartime economy. The People's Bank of China was initially set up to take care of the monetary supply during the Civil War in 1948. Meanwhile, an inde-pendent, important agency, the Central Finance Commission (CFC), was established in 1949. In the same year, the renminbi (RMB), the future currency of the People's Republic, was founded on the model of material standards developed in the wartime economies of Shandong and Northeast China.[73] Under this system, the value of the RMB was pegged to a designated basket of essential goods controlled and supplied by the state commercial agencies.

For private entrepreneurs, the mobilization campaign in the first years of Communist rule was a fatal blow to their survival. But this was not the original aim of the CCP government. Rather, it was the direct result of war and hyperinflation, as the Communist financial system had finally reined in inflation by March 1950 but continued to impose rigorous fiscal and financial discipline. As the money illusion of hyperinflation disap-peared, the market panicked about credit and input supply, which by now was strictly controlled by the state. Most enterprises simply could not survive the credit squeeze and supply rationing. Facing an imminent collapse of private industry, the CFC immediately set out to rebalance relations between the private economy and public institutions. Although

---

[73] Huang, "Constructing A National *Oikonomia*," pp. 4–11.

the long-term solution to the depression, as Chen Yun remarked in his year-end economic review, was to boost domestic demand by increasing the purchasing power of peasant households, in the short run the government had to rescue private enterprises which had an immediate need, by contracting with private firms in the midst of market dislocations to fulfill the state plans.[74]

Typical contracts between the enterprises and enterprise bureaus of local finance commissions included raw materials, credit lines with state banks, and an imputed profit margin.[75] In line with the ongoing cash control, the contracts imposed extremely harsh restrictions on private credit and required mandatory monthly production and credit reports to the state bank. China then entered the Korean War in October 1950, forcing the state to secure even more supply and seek to further stabilize prices.[76] Taking the cotton industry in Shanghai as an example, between August 1950 and July 1951, the share of state contracts in the output of colored cloth alone increased from 32 percent to 81 percent.[77] Initially only an issue of expediency, state contracts later became institutionalized, as China's international and domestic political economy evolved in favor of tight state control during the Korean War.

But even the contract system proved to be less than sufficient for the Communist state to meet the demands of the war. After repeated failures to acquire sufficient cotton cloth based on state contracts, in January 1951 the CFC imposed an emergency monopoly over the procurement of cotton yarn (an intermediary product for cloth) and cotton cloth from factories.[78] This was the first of many decisions on monopoly trade that

---

[74] Chen Yun, "Guoqu yinian caizheng jingjide zhuangkuang"(Economic and Fiscal Situations in the Past Year), *Chen Yun Wenji* (Collected Works of Chen Yun), vol. 2 (Beijing: Zhongyang wenxian chubanshe, 2005), p. 177.

[75] Chen Yun, "Muqian jingji xingshi he tiaozheng gongshangye yu shuishou zhengce" (Current Economic Situations and Industrial and Fiscal Policy Adjustment), in *Zhonghua renmin gongheguo jingji dangan ziliao xuanbian, zonghejuan* (PRC Selected Economic Archives, General Volume) (Beijing: Zhongguo Wuzi Chubanshe, 1990), pp. 743–744.

[76] This is because China entered the Korean War in October 1950 and the goods market was again hit by a spurt of speculation and sudden price hikes on all basic daily necessities. In the last months of 1950, it seemed that the state was again losing control over the price of cotton cloth.

[77] Yoko Izutani, *Chūgoku kenkoku shoki no seiji to Keizai: taishu undō to shakai shugi taisei* (Politics and Economy in Early PRC: Mass Movement and the Socialist System) (Tokyo: Ochanomizu Books, 2007), p. 72.

[78] The Central Finance Commission, "Guanyu Mianbu tonggou tongxiao de jueding" (Decisions on State Monopoly Trade of Cotton Cloths), in *Zhonghua renmin gongheguo*

appeared, one after another, between 1951 and 1954.[79] Most emblematic-ally, grain was monopolized by the state commercial agency in 1953. At the height of the Korean War, even as full nationalization was still years away, China's private sector was already more or less beholden to the state. In other words, the Korean War prepared the ground for the final national-ization of the private sector in the mid-1950s.

The early Maoist state succeeded in putting in place an economic function that the preliberalization market system had never accomplished: the unification and organization of economic life across the vast territorial reach of the Communist state. Take the use of the new currency as an example. Under the old systems, China's border regions were effectively operating on a separate monetary system from the central state and imperial bureaucracy. But the triumphant march of the People's Liberation Army into China's four quarters and its logistical system ensured that throughout the local economy, from private businesses to peasant house-holds, the RMB was used as a new unit of account.

Under the new circulation system, the whole country was unified eco-nomically. The state-owned supply and sale societies (*gongxiaoshe*, or SSS), which were first organized to stabilize price levels and uphold the material standard of money, effectively covered all traditional or new market outlets in both rural and urban China. The SSS economy in the Maoist era was essentially the household economy writ large. It was a reversal of the market model: Whereas supply and demand determined price and pro-duction, the SSS economy was based on predetermined price and produc-tion levels stipulated by the planning agency. Under this model, subsistence was valued over profit-making and certainty over uncertainty, as smaller units were linked and made subject to ever larger units, which made provisions for them.

This arrangement allowed the state to determine the scale and level of exchange, neither of which was necessarily lower than those of the natural market in late imperial China. For example, in the chaotic years when RMB was first introduced, the state forced economic exchanges between rural and urban sectors (*chengxiang jiaoliu*) to ensure basic economic equilibrium and the survival of many urban businesses.[80] The first time a

---

jingji dangan ziliao xuanbian, shangyejuan (PRC Selected Economic Archives, Domestic Trade Volume) (Beijing: Zhongguo Wuzi Chubanshe, 2000), pp. 54–55.
[79] *Ibid.*, pp. 146–150.
[80] Yu Xinyan, *Zhongguo shangye shi* (A Commercial History of China) (Beijing: Zhongguo shangye chubanshe, 1987), pp. 331–334.

Chinese peasant in a remote province first bought brand new, Shanghai-made cutlery, it may well have been from a local outlet of the newly established SSS rather than the old rural peddlers.

This new system of rural–urban linkage was critical for both Maoist and contemporary models of the Chinese economy. In pre-Mao China, although market-based linkages existed, they could not serve the purpose of economic modernization if the rural area remained the basis of production and the urban area its economic dependent. The rural economic base was largely self-sufficient and needed few urban goods, whereas the urban areas were mainly centers of consumption. Traditional market-based networks of circulation in the early twentieth century ensured the perpetuation of the model, as the countryside's poverty made it an inadequate market for industrial goods and the lack of demand in turn limited the scale of urban industrialization. The Maoist model began to tackle the fundamental logic of the model in earnest, as its very penetration and control ensured the ability to set the pace of trade and the direction of circulation for primary and industrial goods – especially those necessary for agricultural reproduction, such as fertilizers and agricultural machinery. This condition was critical for China's state-based economic integration.

In short, close to two decades of total war not only led to the suppression and collapse of the national market, either through the monetary chaos wrought by the wars or through the state's coercive efforts to mobilize resources, but also led to its assumption by the apparatus of the military state.[81] This change cannot be understood in terms of political and military destruction of economic exchanges. Instead, it was a reorganization of economic exchanges along political and military lines. In terms of scope and depth, such politically and militarily determined exchanges of materials and peoples, as part of the national mobilizations, grew beyond the scope of the traditional market. When the Communist state imposed controls on grain and nearly all daily necessities in 1954, it had achieved something unprecedented. For the first time in Chinese history, economic life within the geographical boundaries of the People's Republic of China was organized and managed under a single political authority in

---

[81] This can be measured by the rapid increase in the number of military troops mobilized. In 1937, the Chinese army numbered about 2.3 million; in 1945, it stood at 6.3 million; in 1949, it was 5.5 million, and it eventually increased to 6.3 million in 1950. This did not include the mobilization of resources and noncombatants, which had to be much higher in 1950 than in 1945.

a top-down manner. The suppression and assumption of the market by the state only paved the way for a more efficient economic system for noneconomic purposes.

COLD WAR TRANSFORMATION OF THE MOBILIZATION ECONOMY, 1953–1979

The two and half decades between 1953 and 1979 were the height of China's modern state-building period. This was also the era immediately predating marketization, characterized by full nationalization and elimination of the market. But, as we will discuss, it was in fact this elimination of the traditional market and social elites that facilitated the reestablishment of the modern market on a much larger scale, and its integration with global capitalism in the post-Mao era of the reform and open door policy.[82] By abolishing the traditional market system, the Communist state prepared the political economy for marketization based on the power infrastructure that it had been building since the earliest revolutions in the base areas, and especially in the period of full-scale total war between 1946 and 1953. The institutions of the Chinese economy in this period, from state-controlled industry and financial systems to the hierarchical distribution system, were directly based on such power infrastructures built in the decade of total war.

We use the term "mobilization economy" instead of "planned economy" for this period to highlight that the Chinese political economy was characterized by political-military mobilization during this critical period, rather than the orderly and rational planning of bureaucratic agencies.[83] For one thing, national planning was hardly the central nature of the economy during this period, as there were various kinds of military, paramilitary, political, and economic mobilizations. Moreover, the mere existence of central plans meant little for the character of the economy. The term "planned economy," in the sense of following central planning, still applies

---

[82] For a short discussion on Maoism's impact on the formation of the market economy in contemporary China, see Robert K. Schaeffer, *Red Inc.: Dictatorship and the Development of Capitalism in China, 1949–1999* (New York, NY: Routledge, 2011), pp. 1–12.

[83] Indeed, it can be argued that rational economic planning in accordance with the principles of modern economics and management thinking happens on a much larger scale in contemporary China, as Chinese economy becomes subject to planning by local governments and larger industrial enterprises, both domestic and foreign. We shall discuss this in the chapters to come.

to today's Chinese economy, though it is certainly not a typical planned economy.[84] Even within the "planned years" there were significant periods of deviation – such as the Great Leap Forward (GLF) and the Cultural Revolution, which stretched over more than half of the whole period – when planning was weak and nonfunctional. Thus, we refrain from using the term planned economy and characterize the Chinese economy between 1953 to 1978 as a mobilization economy with a central command.

The transition from war economy to mobilization economy was rather natural and smooth. This was largely because, in the mid-1950s, there was no organized resistance to the nationalization of the economy. In China proper, the social category of the old rural elite was almost eliminated by land reform between 1947 and 1953, with more recalcitrant groups exterminated physically during the suppression of counterrevolutionaries. Likewise, private capitalists were almost ruined by the monetary crisis of the Civil War and later integrated by the contract system into the state-directed war economy of the early 1950s. Even the organized unions, most of which were fostered by the CCP, now became part of the party-state organizations under full state control.

In November 1952, a Soviet-style National Planning Commission was created with responsibility for making Soviet-style Five Year Plans. After an intensive debate and drafting process, the first Five Year Plan was unveiled in February 1955. At the core of the plan was the construction of 156 major heavy industrial plants supported by the Soviet Union, including forty-four in defense, twenty in metallurgy, fifty-two in energy, twenty-four in machinery, and ten in the chemical, pharmaceutical, and light industries (only one – a large paper mill in Jiamusi, Heilongjiang – was in the last of these).[85] In 1957, China's industry product rose 128.6 percent from 1952, heavy industry by 220 percent, light industry by 83 percent, agriculture by 25 percent, and per capita consumption by

---

[84] During his trip to South China, Deng Xiaoping argued that both socialist and capitalist systems use a planning system, and therefore both systems can use the "market" as a tool to develop their economies. See Zheng Yongnian, "Ideological Decline, the Rise of an Interest-Based Social Order, and the Demise of Communism in China," in John Wong and Zheng Yongnian, eds., *The Nanxun Legacy and Chian's Development in the Post-Deng Era* (London and Singapore: World Scientific and Singapore University Press, 2001), pp. 173–195.

[85] Lin Yunhui, *Xiang shehui zhuyi guodu: zhongguo shehui he jingji de zhuanxing* (Transition to Socialism: The Transformation of Chinese Society and Economy), History of Contemporary China Series, vol. 2 (Hong Kong: Chinese University of Hong Kong Press, 2009), p. 388.

34.2 percent.[86] Part of the achievement was a natural result of economic recovery, but most important was that this was considered the first fruit of the nascent Communist state's big-push policy. Another important reason for the rapid growth was massive Soviet assistance since 1948. The first 156 industrial projects were almost completely built on Soviet technology and had technical assistance from Soviet experts. By 1958, China had more than 10,000 Soviet experts, comprising 90 percent of all foreign experts working in all sectors of the economy and state apparatus.[87]

Despite what many leftists would claim today, economic and social equality in the Maoist mobilization system was an illusion. Rather, the system was characterized by a rigid system of economic and social hierarchy defined by political background, household registration status, professional qualifications, and administrative rank. The equality illusion was a testimony to its uniformity and compartmentalization, akin to a giant military formation that organized all personnel in accordance with function and rank. Horizontally, institutionalized inequality existed between rural residents, urban residents, and residents of metropolitan areas in terms of the supply of livelihood resources. Within the urban working population, the cadre system ranked all officials and workers into thirty levels, with monthly salaries ranging from 560 to 18 yuan. Within the elite population of high-ranking cadres, all material privileges, such as entitlement to food supply and living quarters, were also distributed according to rank.[88] In addition to this ordinary category, there was the "political pariah" category of counterrevolutionaries, criminals, and old elites, whose livelihoods were at the mercy of changing party political lines. Situated outside the "people" category, they were even less visible and moveable than the peasants.[89]

Vertically speaking, salaries, bonuses, and other material entitlements within the state supply system were distributed according to strict professional qualifications and administrative rank. For instance, high-ranking

---

[86] *Ibid.*, pp. 424–425.   [87] *Ibid.*, pp. 430–431.

[88] Yiqing Wu, *The Cultural Revolution at the Margins: Chinese Socialism in Crisis* (Cambridge, MA: Harvard University Press, 2014), pp. 26–28.

[89] Indeed, "citizenship" was politically defined as "loyalty" to the party, particularly Mao Zedong himself, and people's rights were politically allocated. Fierce competition for "citizenship" among different social groups often led to violence, particularly during the Cultural Revolution. See Yang Lijun, *Social Structure and the Cultural Revolution in China: Citizenship and Collective Violence* (in Japanese) (Tokyo: Ochanomizu Shobo, 2003).

cadres, elite professionals, and their families usually had priority regarding material benefits. Within the factory, workers and cadres were two distinctive categories: The former were paid in accordance with skill qualifications, which were closely linked to years of experience; the latter, paid in accordance to administrative rank, usually enjoyed higher pay and better material benefits. In this sense, this system was also like the Soviet planning system, where administrative ranking was the determining factor in distribution.

One central institution of this mobilization system was the *danwei*, which can be loosely translated as "work unit" but in fact included all economic, social, cultural, and political functional organs under the CCP state. Each *danwei* was a closed entity with its own leadership. For bigger *danwei* geographically concentrated in one locality, such as local party-state organs and larger state-run enterprises, there were also a host of social service providers such as kindergartens, schools, hospitals, and housing compounds. *Danwei* of the same function vertically formed a *xitong*, which reached up to a higher-level administrative unit, and eventually to a ministry in the central bureaucracy in Beijing. A key unit in the Maoist system, the *danwei* hailed from the Yan'an days when the nascent Communist state was championing strict organizational control and economic self-reliance. In Maoist China, most urban workers simply worked in one such unit and had no opportunity to shift to another *danwei*.[90] This vertical hierarchy and inequality must be understood in the context of the *danwei* as a self-enclosed unit in a vertical system: Without a labor market, vertical inequalities in the *danwei* based on identity factors were considered a natural fact of life.

Throughout the period, there were two broadly different strategies of economic management. The first approach, singularly championed by Mao Zedong and some provincial leaders after 1956, favored a highly politicized but decentralized mobilization economy and defied the ritualization of Soviet plans. This was a model that Mao had largely followed in wartime days, when strategic and political concerns trumped economic efficiency. Moreover, when confronted by pragmatists, Mao often took a fundamentalist and utopian view of socialism, treating commodities and wages as

---

[90] For a description of the economic function of *danwei*, see Lu Xiaobo, "Minor Public Economy," in Lu Xiaobo and Elizabeth Perry, eds., *Danwei: The Changing Chinese Workplace in Historical and Comparative Perspective* (New York, NY: M. E. Sharpe, 1999), pp. 11–37.

capitalist institutions to be eradicated.[91] The second approach, supported by Liu Shaoqi, Zhou Enlai, Chen Yun, and most top leaders, encouraged demobilization of the wartime economy and its institutionalization into the Soviet-styled centrally planned economy managed by professional bureaucrats rather than party cadres. Both visions would have eliminated the market in the end, but the Maoist one was much radical in its approach to eradicating the capitalist mode of production. Considering the historical perspectives, the Soviet model would have much in common with the Confucian household-centered economy of the old days, whereas the Maoist mobilization, while blatantly antimarket, had the characteristics of the past reformist approach in its stress on strategic and political concerns and the mobilization of state agents. In general, the Maoist approach was dominant throughout the three decades in terms of the economy's general characteristics, while the planned economy dominated spheres such as distribution. But in the immediate afterwar years between 1953 and 1958, the dominance of the Sino–Soviet alliance and a dire need for reconstruction seemed to make the second approach a more favorable one.

The Chinese mobilization economy could have crystallized into a Soviet-style planned economy like that of the Soviet Union itself, had not a changing geopolitical situation again exerted a derailing influence on high politics in Beijing. After the death of Stalin in 1953, Mao gradually moved away from the Soviet political model and came to challenge the post-Stalinist Soviet Communist Party leaders, especially Nikita Khrushchev, as the indisputable head of international communism. The tension between the two Communist powers and geopolitical allies resulted in a war of words, and eventually direct confrontation. As the Mao–Khrushchev conflict escalated into a political and military stand-off between the two largest Communist powers, Mao realized the importance of a national economic base in his bid for world leadership and opted for a series of policy innovations to break new ground in national development.

Mao's departure from the Soviet model was not first earmarked for economic self-empowerment as a new ideological stand against revisionism. In 1956, Mao launched the Hundred Flowers Campaign partially as a Chinese answer to the contemporary anti-Communist uprising in

---

[91] Shi Yun and Li Danhui, *Nanyi jixu de jixu geming: cong pi Lin dao pi Deng* (The Hard-to-Continue Continued Revolution: From Anti-Lin Biao to Anti-Deng Xiaoping Campaigns), History of Contemporary China Series, vol. 2 (Hong Kong: Chinese University of Hong Kong Press, 2008), pp. 504–505.

Poland and Hungary, but led it into a chaotic antirightist campaign.[92] Undeterred by this failure, he made a few daring speeches during his stay at the Fortieth Anniversary of the October Revolution in Moscow, which included among other things predictions of the Communist camp's success over the capitalists, China's preparation for a full-scale nuclear war with the West, and the country's goal of surpassing Great Britain as an industrial power within fifteen years.[93] These points were not just rhetorical. Shortly after his return to China, Mao accelerated China's economic modernization. Unable to launch a full military and political bid for international leadership, Mao decided to resort to economic mobilization, which seemed to have borne unexpected fruit in the early 1950s.

This radical approach to economic development called for paramilitary mobilization of all economic resources in support of a selection of targets, notably steel production. Known as the GLF, the strategy was conceived literally as a big push to realize a leap in production measured in statistical terms. But in his approach to such a unique centralized vision, Mao adopted the policy of decentralizing decision-making powers to local government cadres to achieve optimal incentives for mass mobilization. The best example for this was the national fever for backyard furnaces. In response to Mao's call for rapid industrial progress toward the ability to keep pace with British steel production, local cadres managed to mobilize a historically high number of workers to work on a single vision. Most of the workers, of course, were illiterate peasants and urban residents who worked with so-called backyard furnaces – mostly locally assembled, makeshift steel production equipment that produced low-quality, unusable pig iron at best. From July 1957 to 1958, the number of laborers participating in steel-making increased from a few hundred thousand to ninety million, or one-sixth of the total population.[94] However, the eventual product was worse than dismal: instead of accruing to national product, it caused a direct net loss equivalent to 3.8 percent of GDP in 1958.[95]

[92] Chen Jian, *Mao's China and the Cold War* (Chapel Hill, NC: University of North Carolina Press, 2001), pp. 156–161.

[93] Joseph C. H. Chai, *An Economic History of Modern China* (London: Edward Elgar, 2011), p. 122.

[94] Lin Yunhui, *Wutuobang yundong: cong dayuejin dao dajihuang* (The Utopian Movement: From the Great Leap Forward to the Great Famine), History of Contemporary China Series, vol. 4 (Hong Kong: Chinese University of Hong Kong Press, 2008), p. 200.

[95] *Ibid.*, p. 205.

If the mass steel campaign was still a policy miscalculation, parallel campaigns in the agricultural sector proved to be a fiasco. On October 27, 1957, the *People's Daily* published *The Plan for National Agricultural Development*, urging on "the spirit of revolutionary optimism in increasing grain yield" by "restructuring, limiting and using nature." Key to this utopian drive were collectivization and mass mobilization at the institutional level, and improvements in irrigation and water management and a super-intensive method of seed plantation in the technological arena. Soon enough, various localities began to competitively release legendary hyperyield fields of more than 75 tons per acre (or 10,000 *jin* per *mu*).[96] These kinds of yields were of course an economic fairytale, but politically they served the purpose of boosting morale and legitimizing Mao's vision. While local officials naturally had an incentive to catch Mao's eye, the explosion in final yields was facilitated by extreme decentralization. Despite the yield errors, they were protected by Maoist politics and, unfortunately, became references for making procurement policies. During the years of the GLF, it was estimated that state grain procurement reached a record high of 30–37 percent of the total grain output for various provinces, far above the usual 20–25 percent pre-1958, as the Communist state struggled fiercely to finance unrealistic industrial projects at the cost of peasant households' daily consumption.[97] The result was the well-known great famine which claimed the lives of tens of millions of Chinese peasants.

While the GLF marked the postwar height of the mobilization economy, it was neither a natural nor an inevitable development of the mobilization model. Instead, it reflected Mao's own political predilection for economic disequilibrium, as well as the fatal weakness of the model.[98] The failure

[96] Judith Shapiro, *Mao's War against Nature: Politics and Environment in Revolutionary China* (Cambridge and New York, NY: Cambridge University Press, 2001), pp. 78–79.
[97] Frank Dikötter, *Mao's Great Famine: The History of China's Most Devastating Catastrophe, 1958–62* (New York, NY: Walker Co, 2010), pp. 156–157. In fact, the pre-1958 CCP procurement level was already at least 200 percent above the KMT level: see Sasagawa Yuji and Okumura Satoshi, *Chogo no Chugoku Shakai, Chunichi Senso shita no Sodoin to nozon* (Chinese Society Behind the Guns: Total Mobilization and the Countryside during the Sino-Japanese War) (Tokyo: Iwanami Books, 2007), p. 233.
[98] This tendency led to regular debates between Mao and most other leaders before the Lushan Conference of 1959. The climax came at the Seventh Plenary Session of the Eighth Party Congress held on May 5, 1959, when Mao criticized all *fanmaojin* (anti-foolhardy) leaders – including in these ranks most senior leadership – and stressed that he himself held the ultimate power and was the main receptacle of truth: see Lin Yunhui, *Wutuobang yundong*, pp. 412–417.

of the GLF underlined a basic tension in Maoist mobilization: While it could be mobilized for a concrete collective task, such as the construction of a city or even the production of steel, it lacked the internal incentive structure to mobilize millions of people for real economic growth, which was not a concrete task but an abstract objective. The mobilization model was an entirely guided top-down political force by nature, not by economic rationale. This pattern made the mobilization economy a victim of politics, but it also made it a force for shaping the economy and society. As later developments demonstrated, the mobilization model, unlike the Stalinist model, never gained any internal equilibrium; it also averted the latter's ossification, precisely because of its tendency to change direction and create displacement.

While the GLF was an irreparable disaster for the Maoist mobilization approach, it left some important institutional legacies. For one thing, it left the countryside, which for thousands of years had comprised loosely organized peasant communities, a part of the state-controlled economic system. Organized into production teams, bridges, and communes, all of the rural economy was for a time under direct state control. Also, the household registration system, first implemented in 1958, became a key institution in the Chinese economic system. By classifying people into rural and urban categories and defining them according to their locality of residence, the system provided direct control first over the movement of the population and then over the social privileges of each resident. When Liu Shaoqi and Deng Xiaoping took over the economic leadership in the early 1960s, they attempted to restore equilibrium by allowing private incentives and room for a grassroots market. In the manufacturing sector, Maoist hyperoptimism gave way to rationalism as the planning commission significantly reconsidered all industrial targets and sought to rebalance the different sectors. In agriculture, private plots and the household responsibility system were temporarily allowed. More significantly, Liu presented an open, sweeping critique of Mao's GLF as a policy disaster at the Seven-Thousand Cadres Conference in January 1962.[99]

While smarting from the irrevocable political wounds inflicted by the failed GLF, Mao secretly planned an ideological comeback. In late 1962, his dissatisfaction with the economic policies of Liu and his adherents grew from policy debate to fundamental ideological struggle. This was heightened by realpolitik concern: Mao grew more impatient with Liu

---

[99] Lowell Dittmer, *Liu Shaoqi and the Chinese Cultural Revolution*, revised edition (New York, NY: M. E. Sharpe, 1998), pp. 32–35.

and his lieutenants, whose plan to remove Mao from the political center backfired. Meanwhile, Mao cemented a political alliance with Lin Biao and the People's Liberation Army (PLA) as his loyal supporters, and encouraged radical leftist ideologues to form ideological battle lines against the moderate tendency associated with Liu Shaoqi and Deng Xiaoping. As political tensions continued to mount, the power struggle within the CCP eventually escalated to become the Cultural Revolution of 1966.[100]

While moderates such as Chen Yun and Bo Yibo took control of the economy, the early 1960s were not the golden years of the planned economy. The plan's restoration was overshadowed by political confrontations with both superpowers and eventually derailed by urging for military preparation in 1964. Therefore, despite the moderating measures and urges for Sovietization emanating from pragmatists such as Liu Shaoqi and Zhou Enlai, the mobilization approach continued to steer economic development until the Cultural Revolution due to overriding security concerns. Indeed, the decade of the 1960s saw a few new national programs of mobilization under Mao's tutelage. This was evident in three contemporaneous national projects of war economy: The Three Frontiers Movement, an attempt by the Maoist state to build a system of defense and heavy industry in China's underdeveloped Western and, especially, Southwest frontiers; an essentially autarchical movement for industrial self-reliance that urged local governments to build a basic system of collectively owned, small-scale local industries for local self-sufficiency; and sending millions of educated youth to the countryside and border regions for the purpose of reeducation and urban population control. All these measures ran counter to the basic rationale of a centrally planned economy that was often coupled with regional specializations and rapid urbanization. In terms of economic geography, the Three Frontiers Movement pushed the Chinese economy further from the east and toward the west and center.

While the direct desire to take such drastic measures arose out of war preparation, the result was a historical redistribution of capital, technology, and industrial capacity. At the national level, it also meant a more complete, evenly balanced, and better integrated modern system of manufacturing than had been seen in China's recent past. The unintended suppression of the better placed coastal regions would turn out to

---

[100] For a detailed account of the struggle in the early 1960s, see Roderick MacFarquar, *The Origins of the Cultural Revolution*, vol. 3 (1961–1966) (New York, NY: Columbia University Press, 1999).

be a huge incentive for them to develop and reestablish their link with the global economy. The strategic move from nationwide specialization to small-scale regional autarchy led to an even spread of local industries across the whole of China. Instead of encouraging the formation of a centrally planned system centered on the capital, as in the Soviet Union, the Maoist system created a less nationally but more locally integrated structure of modern industry. Linkages back and forth between millions of smaller enterprises instilled a certain flexibility in a system that was otherwise rigidly divided. For instance, it allowed for the necessary conditions to develop rural collectively owned commune and brigade enterprises (BCEs) as grassroots suppliers to the larger county economy, which later became the precursors to township and village enterprises (TVEs).

The decade of the Cultural Revolution, which spanned the late 1960s and early 1970s, was a critical period for China's political and economic development. It was the period when the Maoist model of political mobilization began to decline under prevailing international and domestic circumstances. The seeds of this decline were already sown when the two wings of mobilization – the military wing, led by Lin Biao, and the ideological wing, led by Jiang Qing and other radicals – came into sharp conflict in the first half of the Cultural Revolution (1966–1971), not only bringing down Mao's handpicked successor but also causing the decline of revolutionary radicalism.[101] When the death of Lin was announced in early 1972, it became apparent that the Cultural Revolution's initial promise had failed.[102] Politically, the Cultural Revolution had become an unsustainable project.

The Cultural Revolution's failure to create a prosperous proletarian society coincided with a period of economic stagnation, as the state-led mobilization of the economy lost its legitimacy after Mao's fallout with Lin Biao and strategic alliance with the top capitalist power. By the time the moderate cadres had got back into the driving seat, the system had generated a host of

---

[101] Frederic Teiwes, "The Maoist State," in David Shambaugh, ed., *The Modern Chinese State* (Cambridge and New York, NY: Cambridge University Press, 2000), pp. 146–149.

[102] Interestingly, as his own writings suggested, the latter-day Lin Biao was not only a follower of Confucianism but also a supporter of the Soviet planned economy, although he did stress some strategic concerns. But to survive the turbulent waters of Maoist politics, Lin simply followed Mao without objecting to his economic policy during the Great Leap Forward and the Cultural Revolution. This is testimony once again to the overriding political nature of the Maoist mobilization approach. It is simply impossible to analyze Mao's "economic strategy" since it was bound up with political and strategic concerns.

contradictions, including an inefficient structure of national and local autarchy, the displacement of millions of educated workers, and an extreme lack of incentive. Mao's final response to these problems, especially the lack of incentive across urban and rural domains, was the old tactic of continued ideological mobilization and decentralization. Among these mobilization strategies were national campaigns to learn from the Model of Daqing oil field for industrial development and the Dazhai (Xiyang commune) model for rural development, both emblematic of the self-sacrificial and self-reliant ethos for development. But moral miracles were, after all, miracles: Even when they worked, they were exceptions rather than the rule. In the early 1970s, it was no longer enough to set models of self-sacrifice and mobilize the whole nation; people had become disenchanted with such ideals.[103]

But there were also exceptional changes that would eventually open up new possibilities for the Chinese economy. For one thing, massive decentralization – Mao's favorite approach to the lack of local incentive – literally dismantled the ramshackle planned system. From 1969 to 1973, when Deng Xiaoping and the moderate cadres had been restored to their leadership role, they initiated a round of policy shifts which reversed Maoist radicalism but consolidated some of its fruits. These changes in many ways foreshadowed the economic reform of the 1980s.

The first major change was further decentralization of the industrial management structure, a legacy of Maoism that largely survived the partial restoration of centralized control. Mao had been consistently critical of centralization. In a new round of reform in the early 1970s, he ordered the radical devolution of industrial management from central to local levels. Of the 3,082 manufacturing and transportation enterprises under nine ministries, the management of 2,237 or 73 percent of all these enterprises was devolved from central ministries to provincial and even subprovincial units. Meanwhile, since the central bureaucracy now supervised much fewer enterprises, the eighty ministry units in 1960 – mostly responsible for economic supervision – were streamlined to only twenty-seven in 1970.[104] The number of ministries and complex bureaucracies would rise in the 1970s and 1980s, and during the similarly grand reforms of Zhu Rongji in the 1990s. Maoist decentralization and streamlining was clearly the progenitor of Zhu's systematic reforms.

---

[103] Chen Yinghong, *Creating the New Man: From Enlightenment Ideals to Socialist Realities* (Honolulu, HI: Hawaii University Press, 2004), pp. 101–106.
[104] Shi and Li, *Nanyi jixu de jixu geming*, pp. 226–227.

The second major change was further fiscal and material decentralization. A system of fiscal contract was established between the central and
local coffers: The central coffers only collected a stipulated amount or share
from the provinces, whereas the provinces reserved the residue for
reinvestment. The provinces were also given larger authority to mobilize
materials and invest in infrastructure for their own projects.[105] Like the
radical decentralization of industrial management, Mao's fiscal decentralization proved premature, as the late 1970s saw further recentralization
under Deng. But it was again a pretrial for the reforms of the 1980s,
especially the fiscal contract that predated the share tax system.

The third major change was wage policy. During the early 1960s and the
first years of the Cultural Revolution, as economic and social welfare
became an appendix to political struggles, wage rates for all workers were
frozen at the 1966 level. This worked particularly to the disadvantage of the
younger workers, who had to forego wage rises proportional to their base
pay. In 1972, wage rates in all state-run enterprises were adjusted upwards
in three batches according to the workers' years of work. At the same time,
bonus and piece wages were abolished in support of equality. The gross
salary rose by about 28 percent.[106]

These measures to incentivize the local economies needed to be understood on a bigger geopolitical canvas. In the early 1970s, China's geopolitical position shifted from an extremely precarious to a rather stable
one as Mao realigned with the United States against the Soviet Union.
The border skirmish between China and the Soviet Union in 1969 was a
game-changing event. The immediacy of the Soviet threat motivated
China to seek a global balance of power with the United States as a
potential ally. Even before economic pragmatism's victory over ideology
in the early 1990s, strategic pragmatism was triumphant in the early
1970s. The most significant steps in this direction were China's joining
the United Nations in 1971 and hosting Richard Nixon in January 1972.
Between 1971 and 1979, China and the United States undertook a period
of strategic rapprochement, which ultimately resulted in the establishment of formal diplomatic ties in 1979. In February 1979, when Deng
Xiaoping launched the last major action in Vietnam, China had little fear
of Soviet retaliation, since it had already secured the full backing of the
United States and its allies.

---

[105] *Ibid.*, p. 228.   [106] *Ibid.*, pp. 229–230.

The external economic consequences of this rapprochement were immediate. After 1972, China began to rely heavily on Western, instead of Soviet, sources for the modern industrial technology required for industrial development. From 1973 to 1975, China's external trade grew exponentially. Exports in 1974 were already 300 percent of exports in 1970. From 1972 to 1978, China introduced at least twenty-seven industrial systems from seven Western countries, in particular the United States, the Netherlands, and Japan.[107] At the height of the wave of Western technology introduction, Hua Guofang famously endorsed the "foreign leap forward," a massive Mao-style mobilization campaign to update China's industrial base by exchanging oil reserves for imported machinery.[108] Even before China's gradual entry to the world market in the reform years, it had already begun to import world-class technology for its industrial development.

In general, China's changing global alignment ushered in a period of gradual demobilization and demilitarization of the domestic economy, as overriding military priorities and political struggles gave way to modernization of the economy and society. In 1975, the "Four Modernizations" program was formally reenshrined as a leading policy goal, as Zhou Enlai reaffirmed the government's commitment to build a modernized socialist power by the end of the twentieth century.[109] As Figure 4.1 demonstrates, the demilitarization process, as indicated by the share of defense spending in the budget and GDP, proceeded at full pace in the 1970s (with the exception of the 1979 border war with Vietnam), after a period of remobilization under the Maoist model from 1958 to 1969.

Meanwhile, the social dislocation caused by Maoist mobilization paved the way for the final transformation of the system in the 1980s. From 1968 to 1980, seventeen million Chinese youth, mostly high school graduates, were rusticated to receive "proletariat education."[110] When the mobilization period ended, the bulk of educated youth returnees fought for their right to return and eventually went back to their urban hometowns in search of new work and a new life. To accommodate their immediate needs, Deng Xiaoping and other leaders had to make necessary and radical

---

[107] *Ibid.*, pp. 300–302.

[108] Susan Shirk, *The Political Logic of Economic Reform in China* (Berkeley, CA: University of California Press, 1993), p. 55.

[109] Zhou Enlai, "Zhengfu gongzuo baogao" (Report of the Government's Work), *People's Daily*, January 21, 1975.

[110] Michel Bonnin, *The Lost Generation: The Rustication of Chinese Youth (1968–1980)*, translated by Krystynya Horko (New York, NY: Columbia University Press, 2013), p. iv.

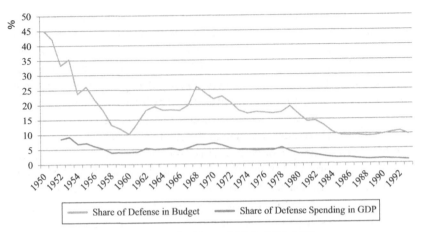

Figure 4.1 Share of defense in PRC budget and GDP, 1950–1993
Source: Compiled by the authors, calculated from National Bureau of Statistics Database

policy changes, including the creation of collectively owned cooperative economies and single-household enterprises, which immediately became a solution for returnee employment and commercial growth.[111] Those who were socially displaced in the Maoist period, such as educated youth, proved to be the vanguard of the Dengist reform, since they could not be otherwise demobilized and absorbed into the regular system. For these social and economic groups, Maoist forced mobilization through state campaigns transmuted into Dengist individual-based self-mobilization through the market.

Taking a broader scope, one of the most prevalent dislocations in the aftermath of the Cultural Revolution was the collapse of labor discipline and initiative across all economic domains. The lack of mechanisms to incentivize and discipline workers was a hallmark of an economy structured on public ownership. But for China, the situation was aggravated by repeated political overmobilization since the mid-1960s, which had eroded even the collective political zeal that used to fuel the mobilization economy. In 1974, this had led to a systemic crisis, including industrial safety problems, malfunctioning of basic infrastructure, and a failure to meet

[111] The China Economic Reform Foundation, *Zhongguo gaige yu fazhan baogao* (A Report on China's Reform and Development) (Beijing: Zhongguo jingji chubanshe, 2002), pp. 89–91.

basic planning goals.[112] Deng Xiaoping's economic rectification (*zheng-dun*) in 1975 was the first solution to this problem. Deng's formal rationale involved three things: Maoist antirevisionist theories, retention of group solidarity, and all-out development of the national economy. But only the latter was effectively reflected in Deng's action plan, since his approach focused on leadership accountability and the centrality of scientific and technical know-how.[113] Both the rationale and the approach proved to be rather effective. Although Deng's larger project failed due to vehement ideological attacks, the economic rectification of 1975 foreshadowed the direction ahead for the mobilization economy: Economic dislocations could only be addressed by a reorientation from politics to the economy. Observers today are often tempted to blame the Maoist system's elimination of the market and lack of economic growth for the low income earned by the average Chinese person. While it is fair to say that the elimination of the market has resulted in stunted income growth, it is too simplistic to dismiss the Maoist decades as a detour. The Maoist state bequeaths us a set of contradictions: A powerful mobilization state that completely dominates and directs the market, and an inefficient economy and a poor population suffering under a lack of market mechanisms. But the contradiction is not insoluble; under a rigidly centrally planned system, mobilization is not incompatible with money and the market, as China's subsequent monetization demonstrates. It is hard to imagine that state-led economic reform can be possible without the capacity to mobilize. Even the extreme mass poverty measured in market prices later proved to be useful for economic reform, facilitating the Communist state's radical turn from the vanguard of revolution to the vanguard of development by once again mustering the popular mandate – narrowly defined by Deng's proverbial call that "to get rich is glorious."

The Chinese economy and society emerged from the decades of mobilization and remobilization with a completely different structure from most of its Third World counterparts. The first characteristic was the prevalence of state control of the modern industries. In 1979, the state sector alone controlled 78.5 percent of China's industrial output and employed 78.4 percent of urban workers, making it by far the dominant force in the urban modern sector.[114] The second characteristic was substantial industrialization without urbanization. The third characteristic was

---

[112] Shi and Li, *Nanyi jixu de jixu geming*, p. 529.   [113] *Ibid.*, pp. 551–553.
[114] Jin Zheng, *State-Led Privatization in China: The Politics of Economic Reform* (London: Routledge, 2013), pp. 29–30.

China's low GDP and income. Measured in US dollars, China's per capita GDP was as low as one-fiftieth of the United States' in 1979.[115] This, however, understates living standards and broader social well-being, in terms of literacy, basic health care, and industrial development, among others. Indeed, in the World Bank's *World Development Report 1979*, China's literacy rate, food consumption, and life expectancy ranked among those of middle-income countries, while its income ranked clearly among low-income countries.[116] This apparent contradiction is a good indicator of the distortionary or suppressive nature of the Maoist economy, a system that is geared toward political and strategic concerns rather than economic growth but nevertheless cares about the general welfare of its people, for strategic ends. Last, but perhaps most importantly, the Maoist decades created a new Chinese state that is *qualitatively* different from the traditional Chinese state, together with a Chinese people that is qualitatively different from the traditional Chinese subjects. The new state and the new people are mirror images of one another: While the state is created to mobilize millions for a collective objective through its complex paramilitary machinery, the new generation of Chinese people is ready to answer such a call and mobilize as a group, following a strong sense of collective identity.

EPILOGUE: ORIGINS OF THE CONTEMPORARY ECONOMIC MIS SYSTEM

Although contemporary economists and historians usually call 1979 the start of China's great economic transformation, this watershed moment was in fact more political than economic. As we have discussed, various structural conditions for such a transformation were created in earlier decades, whereas the real transition from socialism would not begin until the mid-1990s. But the year 1979 and the transitional period between that year and 1991 were still critical for Chinese economic reform from a geopolitical perspective. During this decade, the Soviet Union – once

---

[115] According to the World Bank, China's per capita GDP in 1979 was $260 – on a par with Sierra Leone, Tanzania, Haiti, and Pakistan, and only a small fraction of the United States' $10,630 and the Soviet Union's $4,110. In terms of income, China would rank as a low-income country. See World Bank, *World Development Report 1981* (Oxford: Oxford University Press, 1981), p. 134.

[116] By the late 1970s China's life expectancy at birth was sixty-four, the infant mortality rate was 9.4 per thousand, and the adult literacy rate was 66 percent. These would have ranked China as a middle-income country. *Ibid.*, pp. 134 and 174.

China's most important ally and most formidable foe – declined and disintegrated. This basic geopolitical shift left China in control of its immediate geopolitics by land for the first time in a century. Meanwhile, its temporary alliance with the United States, by far the most potent global sea power, helped China's reintegration with the global economic order. By the early 1990s, despite the bleak events of the Tiananmen Square crackdown, China was in a favorable position to demobilize not only physically but also psychologically and, by force of demobilization, initiate economic reform on a full scale.

War and economic mobilization, followed by demobilization and reconstruction is arguably a set sequence of historical development in modern capitalist society. This was the case with American capitalism, postwar European capitalism, and the Japanese Empire in the late Meiji and Taishō days, as well as China in the last quarter of the twentieth century. From 1895 to 1972, parts or all of China engaged in continuous war and economic preparation for war, either with major foreign powers or among themselves. There have been only three, sporadic reconstructions: the Qing *xinzheng* reform of 1903–1911, the Nanjing Decade of 1927–1937, and the first Five Year Plan of 1952–1957, although all of these periods were also interpreted and eventually ended by military and political mobilization. But even in these three periods of short-lived state-building and state-led industrialization, China witnessed transformative changes in terms of institution-building and industry growth: The *xinzheng* reform first introduced a centralized state in control of the economy; the Nanjing Decade established a national currency, state banks, and SOEs; the first Five Year Plan in the early 1950s laid down a loose structure of planning systems and China's first national system of modern industries. But unlike the Soviet Union under Stalin, in which the political command system managed to institute a centrally planned and nationally integrated economy, the Chinese party-state had only built a command mobilization system, not a planned economy. Most notably, the Chinese command economy never instituted a Soviet-style system of economic accounting, even in the most industrialized city of Shanghai.[117]

After Mao's signature GLF, however, Cold War China moved into a distinctive pattern of development under the personal strategic command of the Chairman. Mao, as an idealist and a strategist, pushed the

---

[117] Lin Chaochao, Sulian jingji hesuanzhi yu zhongguo jihua jingji (Soviet Economic Accounting and Chinese Planned Economy), *Shilin (Historical Review)* 1 (2016), pp. 171–172.

command-and-mobilization character of the system to its logical limits in the late 1960s and then kickstarted a dramatic transformation in the early 1970s. During Mao's rule, the Chinese economy was dominated by intensive political mobilization and strategic reorientations. While these Maoist decades were not exactly decades of war, the country's development continued to be largely shaped by war and preparation for war throughout. Apparently, this was directly reflected in the changing size of the PLA. The PLA expanded throughout much of the Maoist period, playing a shaping role in the political, economic, and technological domains. The PLA formally reached its maximum size and influence not in the Second World War or the Civil War, but during the Cultural Revolution. In 1975, the PLA had 6.6 million personnel, excluding paramilitary and other affiliates, before gradually declining to merely 2.3 million more recently.[118] Since Deng Xiaoping began this mass demobilization, huge amounts of resources have been diverted from the military to the civilian sectors; more importantly, economic control has been removed to make room for market mechanisms and private and foreign capital, though key features of the mobilization system have remained, in their many configurations.

Delayed for at least two decades, China's reconstruction began again in the late 1970s and the early 1980s, a return to normality through demobilization, depoliticization, and marketization of the economy and society. The demobilization of the PLA, which began in the late 1970s, was an important locus of China's marketization, not least in freeing up resources for the civilian sector and economic development. Indeed, military mobilization also had a more direct role: During the 1980s, to create jobs for massive demobilized veterans, the PLA was sanctioned and even encouraged to engage in a variety of business ventures. This naturally went well with the PLA's resources and political clout, resulting in an explosion of market-based entrepreneurship.[119] At a societal level, only the demobilization of millions of educated youth, who came from the countryside to the cities only to find little formal employment, could rival PLA demobilization for the role played in marketization. By the end of demobilization, China was a much less militarized society than major world powers such as the United States, the Soviet Union, and many other powers.[120]

---

[118] Xuezhi Guo, *China's Security State: Politics, Philosophy and Evolutions* (Cambridge: Cambridge University Press, 2012), p. 226.

[119] See James C. Mulvenon, *Soldiers of Fortune: The Rise and Fall of the Chinese Military-Business Complex, 1978–1998* (Armonk, NY: M. E. Sharpe, 2001), pp. 51–77.

[120] From 1953 to 1989, China's military spending was routinely over 5 percent of GDP, and sometimes could run as high as 8 percent. From 1989 to 2014, China's military spending

Besides the direct impact of demobilization, the post-Mao reconstruction of the Chinese economy also meant the institutionalization of certain wartime structures and the transformation of others. For the modern Chinese state and market, demobilization was not a simple restoration of a largely traditional order's premobilization state. Rather, it meant the institutionalization of key wartime structures, such as the national fiat currency, state banks, SOEs, state ownership of land and natural resources, state control of science and technology, the household registration system, and above all, the Five Year Plans and planning agencies, on top of all national economic affairs. Collectively, these apparatuses of centralized state control formed the overarching structure of the state-dominated market economy of the reform years. As Chapter 5 elucidates, despite the rampant marketization of the past few decades, the overarching structures of the Maoist state remain largely unchanged in many key sectors of the economy.

The period between 1840 and 1979, and especially the critical transformations between 1937 and 1952, provided the immediate historical background to China's contemporary economic reform. During this period, global political upheaval meant an ever harsher struggle for the Chinese state's geopolitical survival. To survive in an environment of constant war and geopolitical struggle, the modern Chinese state, born in the late days of the Qing Empire, began to develop extensive capacities of economic mobilization and market control. Such developments came to a head during the era of total war and the Cold War in the guise of the Maoist system, when the state gradually moved to a complete suppression of the market and direct political mobilization of resources. Broadly speaking, China's contemporary MIS system had its origins in the state-building process during this period. More specifically, it had its origins in the Maoist state and its decline in the 1970s, which gave rise to the Dengist reforms in the 1980s and beyond. To understand the contemporary MIS system in China, we need to note that the state is a continuation of that modern state created through war and war preparation over a long period of time, while the market is a recent creation under the aegis of this modern state. As such, the modern Chinese MIS

was less than 2 percent of GDP. This is considered relatively low in comparison with most world powers, such as the United Kingdom, France, Russia, or the United States. National Bureau of Statistics, *China Statistical Year Books* (Beijing: China Statistical Year Book Publisher, various years).

system as we know it today is a distinctive mobilization system, rather than a regulatory state or *Rechtsstaat* (a state with rule of law) such as can be observed in the West. Its regulatory or legal functions are still in the early stages of evolution. This innovative creation of a market, and the continuation of the mobilization state in the reform era since 1979, will be the topic of the chapters to come.

PART III

CONTEMPORARY INSTITUTIONS

5

Grassroots Capitalism and Marketization

Dynamics of Market Reform in the Contemporary Era

In Chapters 3 and 4, we sketched out the basic path of the Chinese political economy's historical evolution during the late imperial and modern periods. In late imperial China, the normality of the Chinese political economy was characterized by multilayered market systems subject to weak or strong penetration of state power during periods of normality or abnormality. From mid-nineteenth to the late twentieth century, the modern Chinese state was transformed in the crucible of geopolitical shifts, military–political mobilizations, and the socioeconomic dislocations that went along with these. When the process of militarized state-building ended in the early 1970s, the modern Chinese state began to transform itself once again along the lines of demobilization and globalization under the *Pax Americana*. This new stage of state transformation constitutes the immediate context of China's political economy in recent decades, and a return to normality in the cyclical movement of the "market in state".

The spectacular growth of markets at almost all levels of the Chinese economy is perhaps the single most important part of the transformation. Within a mere three decades, China has seen the rise of the market as a central organizing institution of economic life in which all economic entities, including not only minuscule household entrepreneurs but also the economic arms of the central and local states, operate as legally defined market actors. These include some of the world's largest companies in terms of assets and revenues, descended or constructed from the key units in the planned system. Even the last bastion of the planned economy – the Chinese Ministry of Railway, which had been organized and operated in a semimilitary way for decades – was incorporated in March 2013.[1]

[1] http://news.xinhuanet.com/2013lh/2013–03/10/c_114968104.htm [Accessed on April 17, 2014].

Meanwhile, Chinese society has also experienced a sweeping marketization that reaches into every fiber of the social fabric. Whereas the Maoist state exercised full control over every single source of material existence for its subjects, from cradle to grave, post-Mao society is so completely market-ized and monetized that it is almost the reverse of the Maoist social order.

From this chapter onward, we shall shift our focus from theory and history to the development of the market-in-state (MIS) system in contemporary China. Our task is twofold. First, we discuss how the triple-layered market system has been developed and how capitalism functions at each level. Second, we explore how the state has attempted to coopt and control market forces while embracing and promoting market-oriented economic development. In this chapter, we discuss how the market has grown out of the Maoist system. We particularly focus on the grassroots market, while discussing how economic reforms at other levels have affected grassroots market development. We will not discuss the party-state's cooptation of and control over different market actors. At this level, party-state control over the private sector is not as important and substan-tial as that over the next two levels. Various control mechanisms form the theme of the coming chapters, in which we shift to the middle ground and the state sector. But first we will focus on the expansion and limita-tions of the market in China, as it operates outside the political logics of the state. We shall examine the opening of boundaries and frontiers, as well as their closures and transformations in the age of reform. In doing so, we shall follow some pioneering market actors as marketization proceeds rapidly in the 1980s, and trace their fate as they move into the 1990s, when market development was subject to the political logic of the recentralizing state. In the first part of the chapter, we shall focus on the growing zone of small-scale market activities, particularly small-scale market actors such as peddlers and household retailers – an area in which grassroots capitalism germinates and flourishes – sketching out the boundaries between grass-roots capitalism and the state as the early sprouts of capitalism negotiated with the state for survival and prosperity. In the second part, we shall turn to the process of state-led market formation and its limitations as eco-nomic reform entered full swing in the late 1990s.

MARKETIZATION IN THE CONTEMPORARY ERA

China's contemporary market economy, officially defined as a "socialist market economy," traveled a long way before its eventual recognition and legitimization by the Chinese state. It is worth noting that under the Maoist order, the market as a system of economic exchange was never fully eliminated. At the national level of foreign trade, China had to deal with its trading partners in the international market in global market terms and standards. At the intermediary level, state commerce agencies effectively acted as market agents in accordance with the so-called Marxist Principle of Values, even in the absence of a national market. And above all, the market survived in government-controlled grassroots markets or in vaguely controlled areas as underground markets even in the early 1970s.[2]

The most important traces of underground market in prereform China were located at the fringes of the state-controlled economic system and in the gray zone between the collective units and the households, such as street peddlers traversing in the urban back alleys, the private plots the peasants kept for their survival, and the Commune and Brigade Enterprises (CBEs) in rural communes. As economic actors, these market entities were dependent on or attached to the prevailing order of things as marginal, but not insignificant or dispensable, parts of the system. There were patches of markets that were deemed as marginal and thus tolerable for the order.[3]

China's various forms of underground market actors began to emerge into the daylight when the Third Plenary Session of the Eleventh Congress of the CCP in 1978, retrospectively defined as the origin of China's economic reform, brought economic development and modernization to the forefront as the overriding task of the party. Meanwhile, these actors had to struggle with pressure from their bureaucratic superiors – local commerce agencies for the peddlers, grassroots commune governments for the household farmers, and township and county governments for the CBEs – for ideological and political control but sometimes also for vital interests. Nevertheless, with support from the reform-oriented central and provincial leaderships, the market adventurers got the upper hand.

Initial marketization in the late 1970s and early 1980s was a classic case of the convergence of politics and economic logic, with underground and bottom-up market forces meeting the high politics of post-Mao China. Just as the protomarket actors fought for recognition and a space of survival, Deng Xiaoping and his reformist lieutenants were engaged in a decisive battle against the Leftists planners and hardliners who had maintained their ideological loyalty to the socialist principles of political economy.

---

[2] Dwight Perkins, *Market Controls and Planning in Communist China* (Cambridge, MA: Harvard University Press, 1966), pp. 75–76.

[3] Andrew H. Wedeman, *From Mao to Market: Rent Seeking, Local Protectionism, and Marketization in China* (New York, NY: Cambridge University Press, 2003), pp. 40–41.

When the grassroots pioneers met trouble, the party's leadership often intervened directly to save the day. China's most famous peddler-turned-entrepreneur of the early 1980s, for instance – Nian Guangjiu – was saved from the verge of demise several times by central leaders such as Deng. The famous Xiaogang Experiment, which literally amounted to a rebellion against the official economic order, likewise only survived thanks to vehement support from Wan Li, the Party Secretary of Anhui. This top-down linkage was to become the *modus operandi* for China's market reform.[4]

The sprouts of the market survived in the ideological battleground as Deng rose to become head of the party leadership. Although the party's formal ideology only adopted the term socialist market economy in 1992, market-oriented reformists had carried the day by 1979, when the pragmatic–reformist tendency triumphed in the aftermath of theoretical and political struggle. The Leftist *raison d'état* could not have been consistently defended, as the socialist planned economy could not possibly be squared with the empirical principle of economic efficacy. As the Dengist principle "practice is the sole criterion for truth" became established as the new ruling mantra in the aftermath of the Truth Debate, the CCP leadership had already subscribed to a utilitarian and thus pragmatic exegesis of its ideological classics in support of political legitimacy and policy formulation. The key message in Deng's ideological attacks on Hua Guofeng's principle of blind obedience to Mao's words in the Truth Debate, for example, was that there existed objective economic laws that transcended and trumped Hua's supposedly irrational mobilization approach.[5] Meanwhile, at the two officially convened Wuxi Conferences in 1979, Chinese planners and economists likewise endorsed the Law of Value (*jiazhi guilü*) and called for integration of plan and market.[6]

The final moment of legitimization for the market-oriented reforms arrived at the Third Plenary Session of the Twelfth Party Congress in 1984, when the Central Committee ruled that the commodity economy was compatible with the planned economy and the Marxist Principles of

---

[4] For an analytical account of the event against its grand historical background, see Kent G. Deng, *China's Political Economy in Modern Times: Changes and Economic Consequences, 1800–2000* (London and New York, NY: Routledge, 2011), pp. 75–77.

[5] Ironically, the champion of this message was Hu Qiaomu, who supported Deng against Hua. He would come to number among the key political conservatives who published the influential editorial "Act in Accordance with Economic Laws, Step up the Four Modernizations" in *People's Daily* in October 1978. See Joseph Fewsmith, *Dilemmas of Reform in China: Political Conflict and Economic Debate* (London: Routledge, 1994), pp. 60–61.

[6] *Ibid.*, pp. 62–65.

Values. Such wording seems to have carefully avoided the politically sensitive issue of the market. In reality, there is little practical difference between a commodity and a market economy. The problem of definition was further entrenched by policy design, since the planned economy was never enshrined by the Constitution as China's legitimate economic order.[7] The policy guideline of 1984 thus gave marketization a new impetus. Although the socialist market economy would only become official eight year later, in the Fifteenth Party Congress in 1992, the main ideological battles had already been concluded in 1984. As the major ideological obstacle to the bottom-up growth of the market had been removed, the market economy entered a golden age of growth in the 1980s.[8]

Since the planned system was still the dominant ideological conceptualization and, functionally, the pillar of the national economy, marketization in the 1980s rested on an institutional innovation, namely, a dual-track system and a continuation of the late Maoist practice of decentralization in the planned system. The dual-track system distinguished between two kinds of prices: market price and planned price. Planned prices were made artificially low on input and high in the product market, whereas market prices were determined by market conditions of demand and supply after economic actors fulfilled the planned quota.

The Maoist logic of decentralization was pushed further and institutionalized within the planned system. Greater managerial powers to make business decisions were passed down from the central government and ministries to enterprises and local governments. This loose hierarchical arrangement was mediated through a contract system: Enterprises or local governments only delivered a contracted sum of profits and taxes to the central coffers. The first system allowed for the creation of a market outside the central planned system, and the second encouraged local governments and enterprises to support marketization both inside and outside the planned system. The effects of such reform have been to carve out a market sector in the overall economy without really dismantling the state sector.

Market development entered a new stage in the mid-1990s, when a new generation of reformers headed by then Premier Zhu Rongji abolished much of the dual-track system and introduced market-oriented reforms in

---

[7] Ou Yangsong, *Gaige kaifang koushushi* (Oral History of the Reform and Opening Up) (Beijing: Renmin University Press, 2014). Online version available at: http://fuwu.12371 .cn/2014/01/14/ARTI1389669347440974_8.shtml [Accessed on June 15, 2014].

[8] For a discussion of the ideological shift, see Yongnian Zheng, *Globalization and State Transformation in China* (Cambridge: Cambridge University Press, 2004), pp. 72–79.

the state sector. Although private enterprises continued to expand throughout the decade and even beyond, most of the leading pioneers of the 1980s faltered. Most star performers in the private sector hit a growth ceiling and town and village enterprises (TVEs) also decreased in importance.

More critically, at the structural level, the state emerged as a major promoter and engine of economic growth. By the early 2000s, domestic private market players had ceased to dominate the stage as unambiguous champions. Instead, a variety of players with ambiguous identities emerged on the central political stage. Their ranks included such a divergent set of actors – including state-backed large private entrepreneurs; large foreign-invested enterprises; denationalized but partially state-owned enterprises (SOEs), companies allied with or even created by the local governments; and large centrally managed SOEs – that observers have found concepts such as market economy or state capitalism wanting in their attempts to characterize the system. Either forming close informal personal networks or institutionalizing relationships with the government via the party-state's alliance system, these heterogeneous players shared with each other only a desire to weave a network of interests between the state and the market.

This process of marketization produced the basic system of contemporary Chinese political economy as we know it today. Scholars have debated about the nature of the economic order that emerged. The most vocal critic of the existing Chinese political economy is Yasheng Huang. In his *Capitalism with Chinese Characteristics*, Huang criticizes the reform of the 1990s as a reversal of the promarket reforms, arguing that it is characterized by state suppression of a genuine market-based economic development model. But since, again, it is endemic to the political model, political reform is inevitable for market growth.[9] Many mainland Chinese scholars hold the opposite position. Hu Angang and Wang Shaoguang, for example, regard the neoliberal free market as a fictional model and call for a stronger central state capable of stabilizing the economy and steering economic transition.[10] While few scholars object to an efficient expanding market mechanism and limitations on state interventions, the point of debate centers on the role of the state: whether and how far its power should expand vis-à-vis a market economy.

---

[9] Yasheng Huang, *Capitalism with Chinese Characteristics: Entrepreneurship and the State* (New York, NY: Cambridge University Press, 2008), pp. 295–298.

[10] Hu Angang and Wang Shaoguang, *The Chinese Economy in Crisis: State Capacity and Tax Reform* (New York, NY: M. E. Sharpe, 2001), pp. 125–128.

The promarket camp is correct in observing that post-reform China differs decisively from the East Asian NIEs. Since the mid-1990s, and especially after the Global Financial Crisis in 2008, China has indeed seen an expansion of large state enterprises and tax revenues at the expense of small and medium enterprises. All these developments make the state agents more resistant to market-oriented reform. However, contrary to Huang's observation and expectation, the Chinese economy fared rather well during the Global Economic Crisis and maintained an abated yet respectable growth rate of 7.5 percent in the aftermath.

The pro-state school also has a point: To date, the Chinese government has been able to push through important reforms up to a certain point and keep the economy stable and growing following the restructuring of the fiscal state. The massive macroeconomic interventions of 1997 and 2009 would be unimaginable if the state had not pushed reforms to counteract market-oriented development. Yet the state capacity championed by scholars such as Hu and Wang has turned out to be a blessing as well as a curse. The Chinese government now annually amasses huge tax revenues, but the benefits of fiscal expansion accrue to well-connected groups and regions, rather than leading to balanced development.[11]

In retrospect, both camps tend to highlight and foreground concepts of market and state and treat them as mutually exclusive forms of organization. Market and state often interpenetrate in post-reform China. The state-led marketization since the mid-1990s is best characterized as a partial marketization of the state apparatus and thus the disappearance of institutional boundaries between the market and state. During this process, the communist state, a behemoth comprising industrial enterprises, commercial agents, service providers, and bureaucratic regulators, was transformed into a number of functionally differentiated groups of institutional actors, including both market and nonmarket actors.[12] Meanwhile, relations between marketized and nonmarketized state agencies were increasingly disciplined by economic rationales and intermediated by a new financial system as the economy became the highest level of politics. For instance, the central government expected not only the recapitalized large SOEs but also local governments to deliver growth and tax revenues as a measure of performance. Overall, this momentous shift from market-based to

---

[11] For an assessment of the problems, see Chen Yun, *Transition and Development in China: Towards a Shared Growth* (London: Ashgate, 2008), pp. 184–191.

[12] Dali Yang, *Remaking the Chinese Leviathan* (Stanford, CA: Stanford University Press, 2004).

state-controlled efficiency causes a vertical interpenetration of the state and the market in the contemporary era, which is different from earlier patterns of penetration. This area of mutual interpenetration, as we discussed in the earlier conceptual chapters, is defined as the middle ground.

However, the marketization of the state is only part of the reform process, which also includes an equally powerful political incorporation of market actors in the middle ground. As we will examine in detail in the following chapters, not only does the CCP retain full control over personnel appointment of its key economic arm, the centrally managed SOEs, but it also routinely enlists private entrepreneurs into its affiliated consultative organizations, such as the National People's Congress (NPC) and the Chinese People's Political Consultative Conference (CPPCC). Private entrepreneurs' participation in these organizations, and thus their interpenetration with the state, is very high considering their relative population.[13] In addition, most lucrative and strategic businesses, such as energy, telecommunication, and national-level banking and financial services are reserved for the national champions, namely, large SOEs and state-owned financial companies, directly run by the CCP and its appointees.

While capitalism and the modern market system conceptually deny natural limits or boundaries, there is clearly an institutional and ideological limit or boundary. In the Chinese case, the limit or boundary is determined by the historically contingent *raison d'état* of the contemporary party-state: a broadly defined version of social stability and regime survival, which includes economic objectives such as growth, fiscal revenues, and macroeconomic stability.

Contemplating China's recent marketization from a historical angle, one needs to keep in mind the long process of China's modern state-building, especially during the Maoist period. As discussed in Chapter 4, China's prereform state-building, which started in late Qing and culminated with the Maoist experiment, provided essential conditions and impetus for rapid market growth, especially the capacity of the central and local states to mobilize and control the marketization process, the physical infrastructure, the financial sources and human capital required for industrialization, and the political and administrative boundaries that kept the national market fragmented and segregated. Incidentally, the last condition proved to be the most powerful: It created the potential for rapid marketization when the boundaries between the

---

[13] Teresa Wright, *Accepting Authoritarianism: State–Society Relations in China's Reform Era* (Stanford, CA: Stanford University Press, 2010), pp. 49–52.

state and market were loosened and eventually removed, but it also kept marketization in check when the boundaries were revamped and institutionalized. Where the boundaries were gradually removed, marketization prospered and the market became the dominant economic order; where the boundaries were revamped and institutionalized, market actors were coopted into the political order of the unitary state.

The logic of marketization is closely related to the unitary state. It is not so much about back-and-forth between plan and market or between market and state. Rather, the growth or nongrowth of the market follows a simple rule of thumb: Scale of market equates to political significance and invites state cooptation. This simple rule poses a perennial dilemma for China's nonstate market actors: When they are small, they are full-fledged market players without access to state-controlled resources and privileges; once they grow bigger, they are beholden to the state and certain central or local leaders, and even in that case, conditions to enter selective markets still apply. The state does not just pick winners from the market; it also manages and structures the market in such a way to keep its loyal agents – and itself – as the winners and stakeholders. In a way, this pattern of MIS harks back to the analytical account of the historical relationship between the imperial state and the market actors, discussed in the chapters on China's historical experiences.

MARKETS GROW FROM THE MARGINS: 1978–1994

Most new actors in the newly liberalized market of the early 1980s shared a common standing at the disreputable margins of Maoist society, such as unemployed youth, returnees from the labor camps, and semilegal peddlers in a desperate bid for survival.[14] In a way, grassroots entrepreneurship in the long 1980s was also the creation of a gradual loosening of state controls and the reconstruction of a market–state relationship at the margins of the socialist society by marginal actors that were latent in the Maoist system. As the reforms led by the central government made real progress in the key urban sectors, these nascent economic forces were more complementary than subversive of the existing order. These people's stories were indeed remarkable: They were quick to act upon any marginal

---

[14] A lot of these "parvenus" had a bad reputation among the urban population even in coastal cities like Ningbo in the mid-1980s. See State Council Research Office, *Geti jingji diaocha yu yanjiu* (Investigations and Studies on the Household Enterpreneurs) (Beijing: Jingji kexue chubanshe, 1986), p. 69.

policy changes, while careful not to challenge the state; once they crossed the political red line, they were doomed. In the discussion that follows we shall consider two celebrated cases, namely, an entrepreneur named Nian Guangjiu and the Daqiu village. In the first case, a marginal entrepreneur grasped business opportunities during the demise of the Maoist order and became a pioneer of marketization in the early 1980s, as the demonstrative power of his case won him timely interventions from the state in favor of the market. In the second case, a charismatic leader led an array of village enterprises through their best years but fell into disgrace as he crossed the line of the market arena into the dangerous area of politics and state laws. Our discussion of these cases will also elucidate that this line was dynamic and highly political, rather than rigidly defined by law. Even the smallest grassroots entrepreneurs could have agency in market reform when the powerful state, led by a dominant political force, was prepared to retreat.

The Melon Seed Boom of the Early 1980s

Nicknamed China's most illuminative grassroots entrepreneur, Nian Guangjiu of Wuhu City, Anhui Province, is a classic example of bottom-up entrepreneurship emerging from the margins of the Maoist order. The son of a street vendor, Nian learned the basics of business when he was a helper for his father. In the 1960s, he practiced various trades at the margin of the socialist system, such as selling fruit and long-distance peddling. But doing private business during the Cultural Revolution was neither glorious nor safe. He was sentenced to a year in jail for speculation and profiteering (*touji dabao*), or challenging the state trade monopoly, during that time.[15] Illiterate and without any institutional affiliation, Nian had few choices but to continue his career as an underground peddler in the early 1970s, after his release. This time he chose to sell roasted melon seeds, a favorite household snack in southern China. His trade's conditions of existence were extremely harsh. He spent the night roasting seeds and the day playing a hide-and-catch game with local cadres.[16]

Nian's effort paid off handsomely in the long run. The harsh years in hiding had improved not only his skill as a melon-seed roaster but also his

---

[15] For a description of Nian's early life, see Wenxian Zhang and Ilan Alon, *Biographical Dictionary of New Chinese Entrepreneurs and Business Leaders* (Cheltenham: Edward Elgar Publishing, 2009), pp. 129–130.

[16] Qiu Jian, "Nian Guangjiu yu shazi guangzi de liangci fuchen" (Two Rises and Falls of Nian Guangjiu and The Fool Melon Seed), *Yanhuang chunqiu* (China through the Ages) 4 (2000), p. 43.

business acumen as a small business owner. His skill and acumen were further enhanced by circumstances within the centrally planned economy: The state had a monopoly over production and distribution of the snack, and since the state-run local factories only produced poor, salty melon seeds, potential customers had been yearning for an affordable and tasty alternative for festival and daily consumption. Therefore, when the reformers loosened strict state controls on peddlers, Nian was in a prime position to expand his business beyond his hometown and quickly made his way into major markets like Shanghai. During the Spring Festival of 1982, Nian's Fool's Seeds sold hundreds of tons in the Shanghai market alone; faced with extraordinarily long queues of customers, shops selling Fool's Seeds had to establish a quota of 500 grams for each buyer.[17]

Nian's phenomenal success soon brought trouble. To meet the unexpected surge in demand from Shanghai and other urban markets, he had to buy other brands of melon seeds and package them as Fool's Seeds for sale. But the shrewd Shanghainese soon spotted the difference and turned against Nian. Following in the footsteps of leading dailies, the local Wuhu Bureau of Commerce quickly intervened, finding evidence of false labeling, tax evasion of RMB43,000, and "illegally" employing more than seven workers – all typical offenses for China's household enterprises.[18] After momentous success, Nian had fallen from grace.

But fortune was again on the side of the peddler. Thanks to national and even international news reports about his story, Nian became a sort of involuntary national champion of the market, and thus a weathervane for China's economic reform. Thus, even before he wrote to Huang Huang, the then Anhui Party Secretary, in March 1984, singing a song of loyalty and pledging allegiance to the party line, Nian was named several times in the speeches of top leaders, each time with mixed messages of approval and criticism: approval of his business success; criticism of his illegal practices, especially overemployment. But this eventually led to China's top leader, Deng Xiaoping, coming to his aid. On October 22, 1984, at a Plenary Session of the Central Advisory Committee, Deng mentioned the Fool's story:

There are things that we can wait to see. The problem of employment raised some time ago indeed causes some commotion. People are extremely worried.

---

[17] *Ibid.*, p. 44.
[18] *Ibid.*, p. 45. At that time, private employers had to justify their employment as noncapitalistic and nonexploitative by citing Marx's classic definition of capitalistic exploitative enterprises as employing more than seven workers.

My opinion is to wait two years and see. Does this thing change our big picture (*daju*)? Once you take the move (to arrest him), people will say that our policy has changed and their mind will grow restless. If you enforce laws upon a mere Fool's Melon Seeds, how many people will be affected? If the people's mind become restless, it is no good. What is there to be afraid of it we allow the Fool to operate for a while? Has it already harmed socialism?[19]

Deng's timely advice to wait and see immediately offered an exception to the law and set Nian free to continue his melon seed business. This time, Nian decided to join two collectively owned enterprises in Wuhu. Again, he took a big business risk with a premier offer on a national scale. He raised the unit price per pack by ten cents, and promised 150,000 prizes across a few million packs. In two weeks, total sales climbed to 2.3 million. But then the storm came. Too many commercial enterprises rushed to offer prizes for sale, and the ensuing disorder in the market alarmed the Ministry of Commerce and caused a sudden ban on all premier offers. Nian's jointly owned firm, with registered capital of less than RMB300,000, suffered a backbreaking loss of RMB630,000.[20]

After this fatal crisis, Nian became embroiled in a conflict with vice-directors appointed by the district government, who subsequently sought legal means at the local level to eliminate his business. In September 1989, three months after the prodemocracy protest, Nian was again investigated and convicted by a local court, this time not for his business misdemeanors – the nature of which had become ambiguous after the reform announcement – but for his ethical errors. Nian was convicted of sexual immorality (*liumangzui*) for having an extramarital affair, remarrying a much younger woman, and having an unregistered, illegitimate child. The local municipal court sentenced him to three years in jail with three years' abeyance.

Unconvinced by the court ruling and fearing further local persecution, Nian again appealed to the heavens. In a tortuous and roundabout way, his letters eventually reached Deng. This decision came at the right time, as Deng had started to reverse the post-Tiananmen austerity. And for all his reputation as China's number one peddler, the top leadership answered him again. In January 1992, during Deng's landmark Southern Tour, the

---

[19] Deng Xiaoping, "Zai zhongyang guwenweiyuanhui disanci huiyi shang de jianghua" (Speech at the Third Plenary Session of the Central Advisory Committee), *Deng Xiaoping wenxuan III* (Collected Works of Deng Xiaoping) (Beijing: Zhongyang Wenxian Chubanshe, 1993), p. 91.

[20] Qiu Jian, "Nian Guangjiu yu shazi guangzi de liangci fuchen," p. 46.

de facto top leader came to the aid of the number one peddler by mention-
ing his name in his famous Southern Tour Speech:

The current Eighth Plenary Session of the Eighth Party Congress is a good session
in that it reaffirms the Household Responsibility System. In an early stage of the
rural reform, in Anhui emerged the issue of Fool's Melon Seeds. At that time,
people felt uncomfortable with him and proposed to remove him, citing that he
has made a million. I said we should not move. Once we move, people will say that
policy has changed. Then our loss will outrun our gain. There are numerous things
like this. If they are dealt inappropriately, these things can easily upset our policy
guideline and affect the overall reform scheme.[21]

Again, unlike the American Supreme Court ruling, the central argument
of China's top leader here is less about legality or morality and more about
the overall political calculus of loss and gain. As an illiterate turned
household entrepreneur, Nian was nothing like the business tycoons and
large landlords with which the party had to deal in earnest and in principle
in the 1950s. Moreover, the patronage offered to Nian came at the critical
moment of reform, when Deng was about to launch his legendary Southern Tour, a political tour de force that ultimately cleared the way for
comprehensive economic reforms. Faced with stiff local resistance, the
state simply needed to maintain reform by stabilizing the expectations of
tens of millions of household entrepreneurs. Deng's comment was thus
not about the business success of such actors but rather the overall
direction of market-oriented reforms, which far transcended the fate of
small market actors.

Later developments have testified to Deng's observation. Under Deng's
personal patronage, Nian was no longer an easy target for local cadres.
But his economic fortunes eventually declined vis-à-vis the growing
market as China moved into a new stage of market expansion in the
1990s. Nian's biggest contribution to marketization was apparently
limited to the first salvo of marketization. Although one of his sons was
a more capable manager and Fool's Seeds remained a noted brand on the
national market, the scale of business remained modest and the production base limited to Wuhu. While the melon seed business ran as usual,
the Fool's enterprise gradually ceased to serve as a national emblem as its
relative weight and significance dwindled. Ironically, this is also the very

---

[21] Deng Xiaoping, "Zai wuchang, Shenzhen, Zhuhai, shanghai dengdi de tanhua yaodian"
(Summary of Conversations at Wuchang, Shenzhen, Zhuhai and Shanghai), *Deng
Xiaoping wenxuan* (Collected Works of Deng Xiaoping) (Beijing: Zhongyang Wenxian
Chubanshe, 1993), p. 371.

reason why Fool's Seeds and Nian secured the party's protection in the first place: The company's small scale ensured that it was representative and controllable.

Deng's patronage was critical for millions similar to Nian Guangjiu. Like Nian, most of these grassroots entrepreneurs typically hailed from relatively uneducated social margins and impoverished parts of the countryside, with little chance of moving to the state sector. For these people, entrepreneurship is a choice but also a necessity for a good life. After the meteoric rise of Nian and the first-generation grassroots entrepreneurs, the number of household and private entrepreneurs rose steeply. In today's China, there are as many as forty-five million self-employed household entrepreneurs and another twelve million small private enterprises.[22] Most of these private businesses are smaller than Nian's melon seed business in its early days.

When household entrepreneurship was the most common avenue to wealth, *wan yuanhu* (literally, a household with net wealth of RMB10,000 in the early 1980s) became the most common and honorable title for the new rich. The household entrepreneurs, early leaders in the race to get rich, are no longer cognate with the new rich. Most of the earlier *wan yuanhu* would have seen their fortunes stagnate or grow at a much slower rate when the state-led marketization proceeded to its next stage in the 1990s and beyond. This process is well understood, since household entrepreneurs usually have only little access to technology and capital, and mostly only aim at the local market. Although there are grassroots entrepreneurs who managed to continue to grow their business growing and remain among the richest today, they are the exception rather than the rule.[23] In retrospect, household entrepreneurship provides the first vivid, and still the most enduring, model for bottom-up marketization in China, but as a rule it has failed to develop into the most powerful model for entrepreneurship and marketization in the 1990s and beyond.

---

[22] The Ministry of Commerce, *2013 nian quanguo shichang zhuti fazhan baogao* (Report of National Survey on Development of Market Entities) (Beijing: Ministry of Commerce, 2014), p. 2.

[23] Most successful entrepreneurs in China today come from the so-called Xiahai group (literally, those who "jumped into 'business' sea"), which emerged later than Nian. But there are also exceptions. The most legendary case is Zong Qinghou, Chairman of the Wahaha. Zong, unlike Nian, began with a sales position in a state-owned enterprise, which means more sophisticated social capital.

The Fortunes of the Daqiu Village

The fortunes of the Daqiu village, another model for China's early market reforms, and its head, Yu Zuomin, bear much resemblance to the stories of grassroots entrepreneurs such as Nian Guangjiu. While Yu's rise to fame was as meteoric as Nian's, his decline happened much faster and in an equally political manner. The Daqiu story is worth quoting not only because it is one of the most successful rural collective enterprises in the reform era, but also because it demonstrates very neatly the political logics of markets at work as their scale and ambitions expand. In this, Yu is different from Nian. Whereas Nian and the Fool's Seeds grew from the absolute margins of Maoist society, Yu and his village came from the very heart of the Maoist rural order; whereas Nian's ambition was purely economic, Yu's crossed the line into the domain of politics.

Located 100 miles from the northern metropolitan city of Tianjin, the Daqiu village seemed naturally well inclined toward economic development. In reality, however, this village had been one of the poorest in the Tianjin area due to its low yield and salted land. In the 1960s–1970s, as Yu Zuomin served his first term as party chief of the Daqiu village, the village was in a state of abject poverty. The place was so poor during the Cultural Revolution that of the population of 2,800, 250 males could not afford a bride.[24] Unlike Nian, who unreflectively struggled with his odds and looked to the state whenever in trouble, Yu had a much clearer understanding of and a critical stance toward Chinese politics from the outset. Years later, Yu would recount grudgingly the memories of the 1960s and 1970s, when political movements and Leftist policies were dominant.[25] When times changed, Yu Zuomin's fortunes would also take a drastic turn.

When the household responsibility system gradually grew up and took over the communes in the late 1970s and the early 1980s, Yu and the village leadership decided to take another track. Instead of dividing the meager land and productive resources into agricultural households, Yu set up four village enterprises from 1978 to 1981. These collectively owned enterprises mostly specialized in processing steel spare parts and then building materials, and each were headed by men of his kin and powerful families.[26]

---

[24] Bruce Gilley, *Model Rebels: The Rise and Fall of China's Richest Village* (Berkeley and Los Angeles, CA: University of California Press, 2001), p. 13.
[25] *Ibid.*, pp. 6–7.   [26] *Ibid.*, pp. 21–23.

Yu had a clear strategy when he redesigned the village economy as a corporate group. The four enterprises were kept small and nimble in order to compete in the product market. The governance system was likewise streamlined, with only thirteen top managers in the mid-1980s, but all were experienced and well remunerated. Since small-scale firms found it difficult to get state finance, all the enterprises obeyed a yearly payback rule in terms of investment. In other words, Yu applied the agricultural household rule to management of the corporatized village. In his enterprise, there was a strict preference for retained corporate savings and minimum reliance on external finance.

Like Nian's family enterprise in the urban context, Yu's village enterprises had to grapple with two very fine and often ambiguous legal lines that defined market activities and economic crimes. The first legal line, *zhanwu*, refers to the procurement of materials. The second, *daomai*, refers to obtaining materials at state price and reselling them at market price, which is the standard strategy of survival for collectively owned village and township enterprises (TVEs) under the dual-track system. In the 1980s, as the villages enjoyed national prestige with close patronage from the then Tianjin leader, Li Ruihuan, who later became a member of the Standing Committee of the Political Bureau, the lines posed little threat. It was only when Yu's personal ambitions pushed him further that the rule of law began to apply.

As the Daqiu village enterprises expanded, so did Yu's political ambition. Thanks to the highly centralized nature of the village political economy, the village corporate obeyed strict rules, with Yu Zuomin, the party chief, in charge. As the villagers' income skyrocketed in the 1980s, Yu's reputation and authority as the absolute leader grew each day. Backed by a sense of total power and control, he even openly challenged the institutional disadvantage of the countryside and the official definition of socialism.[27] At that time, due to his control of village public opinion, such transgressions did not lead to direct conflict with the state.

Nevertheless, problems eventually found Yu as his transgressions increased. In the late 1980s, he had grown exceedingly authoritarian and ruthless as a patriarch, often employing thugs to deliver punishments to the disobedient. In 1990 and 1992, two men suspected of challenging Yu and betraying the village business were killed by mobs and thugs in mysterious circumstances. Although Yu had been only indirectly involved

[27] *Ibid.*, pp. 103–104.

in both cases, his deployment of communal violence alarmed the Tianjin government. Despite his national fame as a flagship peasant entrepreneur, the government eventually arrested him in early 1993. Panic-stricken, Yu committed the most egregious error: He called upon the villagers to defend him against the police, and they managed to hold fast for a few days in a stand-off with the police. When Yu was arrested, he was sentenced to a rather severe term of twenty years in prison, eventually dying in jail at the age of seventy.[28]

Yu's demise did not mark the end of the Daqiu story, but it did change the course of its development. While Yu was dealt a decisive blow, the Daqiu enterprises continued its development path. In the years after Yu's demise, the Daqiu collectives followed the standard restructuring into joint stock and private enterprises.[29] Today, even though the village enterprises still have a place in China's steel production, they have never achieved the success of Yu's days. For one thing, concerted efforts became impossible as political struggle ensued around control of public funds in the aftermath of Yu's fall.[30]

It is evident that the central state had sought to keep market and politics separate in dealing with Yu. When Yu focused on economic development of the village, he was rewarded; when he developed the village community into his own personal kingdom, he was punished. The state's legal action against Yu did not involve any further crackdown on the village enterprises as market actors. As with Nian, the central state's top concern was the stability of its policy guideline of marketization. It was also the visible hand of the state that placed Yu's offense as categorically different from Nian's. Compared with Nian, Yu's political clout had grown too large for the state to allow. Therefore, when Yu broke the law twice, the state could not allow the same leniency that it had afforded Nian.

The Daqiu village is not different from other model villages, the sites of TVEs and harbors of early marketization. In many other such model villages run as corporate entities, the village leader often became authoritarian, unruly, and implicitly if not openly rebellious, and state suppression of the strong leader and, later, the introduction of some sort of pluralism seemed inevitable. But economic performance tends to falter under a more pluralistic village government. This is perhaps why marketization and, thus, urbanization in China's countryside usually takes another, politically

---

[28] *Ibid.*, pp. 136–137; 141–142.
[29] Li Mo, "Jinri Daqiuzhuang" (Today's Daqiu Village), *Xiaokang* 9 (2007), pp. 55–57.
[30] *Ibid.*, pp. 52–53.

safer mode: Villagers simply leave their rural hometowns in search of work in the cities and in the hope of settling there. As a result, when villages fail to corporatize and industrialize, they atrophy into rural agricultural hinterland.

Overall, the TVEs were a major force in China's rural marketization in the 1980s, just like peddlers and household enterprises in the urban areas during the same period. As market actors, the TVEs demonstrated maneuverability beyond SOEs: They typically required little start-up capital, produced using simple technologies, and offered well-marketed standardized products. Moreover, their location in the countryside and the still visible hand of local government ensured that they had easy access to cheap land and affordable capital. Their expansion was further aided by the perpetual labor surplus in the rural agricultural sector.[31] This combination of such ideal conditions gave the TVEs a decisive edge from the 1980s through the late 1990s. During this period, marketization in rural China progressed at full pace, as success stories like Daqiu spread nationwide and eventually became eclipsed by other, bigger stories. Within the single year of 1984, for example, the total number of TVEs more than quadrupled from 1.3 to 6 million.[32] In 1996, when TVEs as an economic organization dominated the national economy, they provided 135 million jobs and contributed one-third of China's gross industrial product.[33]

The TVEs model eventually declined after the mid-1990s. While it is true that some more successful TVEs transmigrated into other categories, notably, large private businesses allied with local states, most of the TVEs had never grown out from the booming years into full bloom modern private enterprises. In 2012, while still employing some 160 million workers, the TVEs produced only slightly more than 10 percent of China's gross industrial value-added.[34] The real cause is the next stage of the marketization no longer centers on the TVEs as the most productive sector

---

[31] William A. Byrd and Lin Qingsong, eds., *China's Rural Industry: Structure, Development, and Reform* (Oxford: Oxford University Press, 1990); John Wong, Rong Ma, and Mu Yang, eds., *China's Rural Entrepreneurs: Ten Case Studies* (Singapore: Times Academic Press, 1995).

[32] Barry Naughton, *Growing Out of the Plan: Chinese Economic Reform 1978–1993* (New York, NY: Cambridge University Press, 1995), p. 140.

[33] Bureau of Township and Village Enterprise, Ministry of Agriculture, *Zhongguo xiangzhan qiye tongji ziliao* (Statistical Materials on China's TVEs) (Beijing: Zhongguo nongye chubanshe, 2003), p. 15.

[34] National Bureau of Statistics, *China Statistical Yearbook 2013* (Beijing: Zhongguo tongji chubanshe, 2013).

and the new growth pole of the economy, though it still occupies an indispensable place on the bottom of the hierarchy.

Marketization under the Dual-Track System and the Contract System

As grassroots market actors grew out of the state system, the reform in SOEs began to create a favorable condition for market development. Throughout the 1980s, as the heart of the state sector, the SOEs continued in line with the plan, acting as production units of the state rather than as market actors. Despite extensive adaptation of market mechanisms in the state sector, such as managerial autonomy of the management system and the marketization of sales and procurement, the SOEs remained part of the planned economy and dutifully performed in line with state plans. This curious coexistence of a planned sector and a market sector was made possible by a formal arrangement known as the dual-track system. Under this system, in the product market, planned and market prices were determined differently: The planned actors enjoyed cheaper input and higher state procurement prices, while market actors had to compete on the both the factor and product markets. As the market proliferated throughout the 1980s, planned prices were gradually adjusted to market levels.[35] The system was designed to achieve two goals at the same time, namely, state-directed development of market mechanisms and protection of state-run enterprises, which could enjoy both subsidized input prices and market output prices.

Another key institutional innovation in the 1980s was the contract system.[36] Like the dual-track system, the contract system can be regarded as an amalgam of state and market mechanisms. Broadly defined, the contract system allows the individual agents to engage with market exchange if they fulfill contractual obligations with the state or state agents. This can apply to a variety of economic actors. Under the household responsibility system, peasant households can sell their produce at regulated prices once they have met the state grain procurement. Under the enterprise contract system, SOEs can sell their products on

---

[35] Lawrence Lau, Qian Yingyi, and Gerard Rolland, "Reform without Losers: An Interpretation of China's Dual Track to Transition," *Journal of Political Economy* 108:1 (2000), pp. 135–136.

[36] For an analysis of contracting as a basic approach to political economy in the early reform period, see Susan Shirk, *The Political Logic of China's Reform* (Berkeley, CA: University of California Press, 1993).

the market after they deliver the goods specified in the economic plans. Under the fiscal contract system, province or subprovincial units could retain the tax they collect after they hand in a stipulated amount to the central state coffers. The contractual arrangements in fact carve out a space for the market alongside the plan. If the economic agents fulfill certain plans, they can keep the proceeds from their additional efforts or enhanced productivity for exchange outside the scope of the plan.

Unlike the hierarchical market, which would only emerge later, the dual-track and contract systems allow market mechanisms to operate alongside the state plan. On the positive side, these two systems effectively provide extra incentives for enterprises and individuals to engage in market-oriented activities. As increased productivities are distributed through market mechanisms, such an arrangement effectively enriches and empowers market actors and local states vis-à-vis the central state. But on the negative side, the combination of these two systems tends to abet disorder, inequality, and even chaos. On a macro level, the inherently radical decentralization creates a wedge between a rapidly changing social and economic system and the centralized political system.

These institutional changes of the late 1980s fostered an entrepreneurship boom in urban China. Many of China's well-known businessmen tested the waters and started their first ventures in the late 1980s. These include, among others, Liu Chuanzhi's computer venture in 1989 (which later gave rise to Lenovo), Wang Shi's Vanke in 1988, Ren Zhengfei's Huawei in 1987, Zong Qinghou's Wahaha Group in 1987, Hou Weigei's ZTE in 1985, and Wang Jianlin's Xigang project in 1989 (which later developed into the Wanda Group). While we will examine some of these cases in Chapter 6, we also want to underline some of their similarities here. In all these cases and in various ways, these future business giants in their respective sectors have benefited from the loopholes of the dual-track system, their former expertise, and ties to SOEs, the military, or the universities.[37] This arrangement also provides immense opportunities for rent-seeking and corruption. Typically, inputs or even products could be obtained at the state planned price and the finished goods or products sold at market price.

Since the dual-track and contract systems operated throughout the state and private sectors, state and market crisscrossed and interlocked on the

---

[37] For a detailed analysis, see Zhang Jun, *Shuangguizhi jingjixue: Zhongguo de jingjigaige, 1978–1992* (The Economics of Dual Track System: China's Economic Reform: 1978–1992) (Shanghai: Sanlian Books, 1997).

same institutional and organizational planes. Gradually, internal markets became pervasive across all government agencies. The most common such internal markets were commercial units attached to government agencies and public units, which sometimes had nothing to do with the main functions of the government bureaucracy.[38] Consequently, there was an explosion of corruption and rent-seeking at all scales, especially in grassroots government. Documented corruption increased by 400 percent in the two decades between 1980 and 2000.[39] Even the military became heavily involved in marketization, as it found new ways to keep its material resources gainfully employed, from thinly veiled real estate business to outright armed smuggling.[40]

Meanwhile, the horizontal interpenetration of market and state made it exceedingly difficult for the central state to order the chaotic process of marketization. Thanks to the fiscal contract system, the share of government in GDP declined from 32 percent to 15 percent between 1978 and 1992. Worse still, the share of the central government in the total government revenues declined from 41 percent in 1985 to a mere 22 percent by 1992.[41] The real situation may have been worse, as official revenue data regularly excluded the lists of nontax and extrabudgetary revenues which also belonged to local authorities. A situation known as "feudalist economy" (*zhuhou jingji*) prevailed, in which local leaders often moved around central economic policies at the end of the 1980s, especially against anti-inflation policies that were directed toward curbing excess investment.[42]

The lopsided marketization of the 1980s also caused social problems that cut deep into the political, vocal elites. For example, one of the most serious socioeconomic consequences of marketization was income misalignment

---

[38] Lin Yi-min, "The Institutional Context of Rent-Seeking in Economic Transition," in Tak-Wing Ngo and Wu Yongping, eds., *Rent Seeking in China* (London: Routledge, 2000), pp. 61–63.

[39] He Zengke, "Zhongguo zhuanxingqi fubai he fanfubai yanjiu," *Jingji Shehui Tizhi Bijiao* (Comparative Studies of Social and Economic Systems) 1 (2003), pp. 23–24.

[40] For a detailed study of the commercialization of the military, see James Mulvenon, *The Soldiers of Fortunes: The Rise and Fall of the Chinese Military Business Complex, 1978–1998* (New York, NY: M. E. Sharpe, 2000), pp. 78–138.

[41] Christine Wong and Richard Bird, "China's Fiscal System: A Work in Progress," in Loren Brandt, Thomas Rawski, and John Sutton, eds., *China's Great Economic Transformation* (New York, NY: Cambridge University Press, 2008), pp. 432–433.

[42] Huang Yasheng, *Inflation and Investment Control in China: The Political Economy of Central-Local Relations in the Reform Era* (New York, NY: Cambridge University Press, 1996), pp. 317–334.

between social classes, especially manifested in the expanding income inequality between market actors and rent-seekers on one side and public sector workers on the other, since state sector workers still earned a state-stipulated low wage even as the market sector took the fruits of economic growth. The protection belt on the state sector thus only served to limit the economic prospects of state sector workers. It was very common in the late 1980s and 1990s for professional scientists in most prodigious universities and research institutes to earn much less than street peddlers.[43] This situation was further exacerbated by hyperinflation and rampant rent-seeking among party cadres and government officials. Economic difficulties led to a sense of social deprivation and eventually fueled political activism. The social crisis eventually culminated in protests held by students, intellectuals, and workers between April and June 1989, especially at Tiananmen Square.[44]

MARKETIZATION IN FULL SWING: STATE-LED MARKET REFORM SINCE 1994

Vertical Marketization and the Middle Ground

With the crushing defeat of the reformers at Tiananmen, the strategy to create a horizontal alignment of market economy and democratic government came to a grinding halt. As in the past, political rather than economic failure determined the fate of the path of reform. Faced with the tumultuous demise of communism in Eastern Europe, and especially the collapse of the Soviet Union in the period 1989–1991, the CCP leadership's initial response was to step back from the market and go back to the more

---

[43] This phenomenon is termed *Naoti daogua* (reversal of wage rates between physical and knowledge workers). There is a popular doggerel that runs: scientists making nuclear bombs earn less than hawkers peddling tea eggs; doctors with a lancet in hand are no match for hairdressers with an eel's knife. Although it sounds like a joke, it was a factual depiction of the bewildering income inequality under the Dual Track system. In the late 1980s, a scientist or doctor's average monthly income was only RMB400–600, much lower than that of a household entrepreneur (RMB1,200) or specialized hairdresser (RMB2,000).

[44] Complex social and political matters were behind the students' protests, which were often oversimplified as part of a single-minded social movement for democratization. In fact, one of the most important causes was university graduates' dire economic prospects as cultural elites, vis-à-vis market actors as cultural inferiors. For a discussion, see Zhao Dingxin's *The Power of Tiananmen* (Chicago, IL: University of Chicago Press, 2001), pp. 82–86.

standard planned model. But it soon became apparent, as was well under-stood by Deng Xiaoping, that the market was a necessity, as its retrench-ment had led to joblessness and economic downturn.[45]

As it turned out, the route forward was further and more radical marketization to divert political tensions and address the social griev-ances of alienated classes. Unlike the marketization of the 1980s, the new marketization in the 1990s was marked by a vertical division of the market to create an institutional hierarchy, rather than a horizontal alignment of the market and the state. The logic of MIS stipulates that the state must maintain a tight grip on the market and make the market its fiscal apparatus.

Deng's dramatic Southern Tour of 1992 eventually led to a complete reconstruction of the state-dominated planned economy, which had been interpenetrated and enfeebled by increasingly penetrative market mechan-isms.[46] In the decade that followed, Jiang Zemin and Zhu Rongji personally engineered a series of important reforms that reached almost all corners of China's state and market. These reforms can be roughly divided into three classes: liberalization of the state sector, consolidation of the state sector at the top, and political cooptation of the new market forces.[47]

The first class of reform programs pointed to further liberalization in the form of privatization. The overall requirement was for the state to with-draw from the consumer goods market. Under the new guidelines for SOE reform, the state privatized most loss-making medium and small enter-prises and only retained control over capital-intensive large enterprises. From 1994 to 2001, the total number of state-owned or -run enterprises of all scales declined from more than ten million to 171,000. In other words, about 98 percent of all SOEs were either privatized or restructured into shareholding companies with both state and private capital.[48] This

---

[45] Ezra Vogel, *Deng Xiaoping and the Transformation of Modern China* (Cambridge, MA: Harvard University Press, 2013), pp. 652–653.

[46] For Vogel's historical recounting of the Southern Tour, see *Deng Xiaoping and the Transformation of Modern China*, pp. 664–690; also see John Wong, *The Political Economy of Deng's Nanxun: Breakthrough in China's Reform and Development* (Singapore and London: World Scientific, 2014); John Wong and Zheng Yongnian, eds., *The Nanxun Legacy and China's Development in the Post-Deng Era* (London and Singapore: World Scientific/Singapore University Press, 2001).

[47] Yongnian Zheng, *Globalization and State Transformation in China* (Cambridge: Cam-bridge University Press, 2004), pp. 76–77.

[48] National Bureau of Statistics, *China Statistical Yearbook 2002* (Beijing: Zhongguo tongji chubanshe, 2002).

privatization and semi-privatization cleared the way for market mechanisms to play a decisive role in areas and sectors abandoned by the state.

The reform lifted barriers that had long prevented the flow of goods, capital, and labor across internal borders. Internal and local tariffs, which had been erected by local authorities in the market wars of the 1980s and early 1990s, were mostly relentlessly swept away in the 1990s. With the revision of household registration regulations in 1992, migrant laborers could now move freely and settle in the cities.[49] Following up on the earlier opening of the market, institutional strictures that hindered international trade and finance were likewise eased with the reform of international trade in 1994.[50] Everywhere across the old state–economy boundary, a remarkable decline in administrative hurdles such as quotas, permits, and coupons has been seen from 1994 onwards.

The second class of reform measures aimed to consolidate the state's dominance over the market. This set of reforms includes a sweeping reform of the government, the larger SOEs, and the fiscal system, with a view to reshaping the state sector into one of dynamic economic actors and regulators.

The government reform of the period was explicitly oriented to serve the market economy. Over the 1990s, the State Council abolished most industrial and commercial ministries as undesirable vestiges of the planned system. Meanwhile, several key ministries and regulatory agencies were established to oversee the emergent sectors of modern finance, banking, insurance, state assets, and natural resources in the new environment of marketization and globalization.[51]

The reform of large SOEs reshaped these giant business groups into national or local business groups with large assets and market clout. Following this strategy of scale-building, selected large enterprises were restructured into shareholding companies and groups and recapitalized into capital-intensive business groups with a monopoly over the most lucrative businesses. Over the years, the old paradigm of SOEs as producers of both goods and welfare services was transformed into one of large

[49] Jason Young, *China's Hukou System: Market, Migrant and Institutional Changes* (London: Palgrave Macmillan, 2013), p. 69.
[50] Lee Branstetter and Nicolas Lardy, "China's Embrace of Globalization," in Loren Brandt, Thomas Rawski, and John Sutton, eds., *China's Great Economic Transformation* (New York, NY: Cambridge University Press, 2008) pp. 634–640.
[51] Zheng, *Globalization and State Transformation in China*, pp. 93–97.

profit-making business groups with distinctive market interests of their own.[52] More importantly, the new round of SOE reform created a few dozen national champions or *yangqi* (centrally managed enterprises) on top of the national market, dominating key sectors such as gas, electricity, telecommunication, transportation, banking, and finance.[53]

An even more consequential market-oriented reform was the tax-sharing reform of 1994, which we shall revisit in later chapters. Essentially, this sweeping restructuring of central–local relations abolished fiscal contracts and introduced separate fiscal bases for central and local governments. Most critically, it gave the central government a majority 75 percent share in the new main tax base, value-added tax, thus reversing the fiscal structures of the 1980s in which local governments were the sole residual claimant of local economic growth. In the new system, the central government had a higher stake and share in economic growth, which now became the overriding rule of further reform and the paramount indicator for development. Meanwhile, local governments also became highly motivated to build the local economy and tax base, as then a stake in economic growth was secured for them. A system of central–local incentives that focused overwhelmingly on increasing local and national GDP became the dominant model of economic development in China.[54]

The final class of reforms was not as pronounced as the first two, but was no less consequential for China's future political economy, as it involved less the economic structure, more the entire political and ideological system. Throughout the 1990s, as the market economy attained political legitimacy under a nominally socialist system, the hurdles previously put in place by the Communist Party and political organs were already gradually removed to allow the participation of private entrepreneurs.[55] In 2002,

---

[52] Huang Yanjie and Zheng Yongnian, "China's Centrally-Managed State-Owned Enterprises," in Eric Kjelk Brødsgaard, ed., *Globalization and Public Sector Reform in China* (London: Routledge, 2014), pp. 125–127.

[53] See Chapter 8 for more discussion on the economic and political attributes of these centrally managed SOEs.

[54] This is what we term "GDPism," an informal policy rule that places GDP growth at the center of economic development and thus government policies. For a book-length critique of China's engagement with GDP, see Liu Wei and Cai Zhizhou, *Zouxiashentan de GDP: cong jingji zengzhang dao kechixu fazhan* (Demystifying GDPism: From Economic Growth to Sustainable Development) (Beijing: China CITIC Press, 2006).

[55] For a detailed study of the political status of private entrepreneurs in China, see Chen Jiaxi, *Gaige shidai de Zhongguo minying qiyejia de zhengzhi yingxiang* (Political Influence of Private Entrepreneurs in the Reform Era) (Chongqing: Chongqing Chubanshe. 2007), pp. 51–73.

Jiang Zemin, the then General Secretary of the CCP, made it clear that the party would follow the new "Three Represents" principle – that is, that the CCP now represents China's advanced productive forces, the orientation of China's advanced culture, and the fundamental interests of the overwhelming majority of the Chinese people.[56] However, a more practical exegesis simply legitimizes the party's embrace and cooptation of economic and cultural elites outside the ranks of the party-state. This holds especially true for the private entrepreneurs, who readily took up the ideological signal of the party's vindication of their roles as new elites.

This flexible approach to party ideology and organization is most evidently reflected in the mass enrollments of private entrepreneurs into the party and its affiliated organizations – the People's Congress, the allied democratic parties, and, more significantly, the CPPCC. The official recognition and informal political affiliation of China's market elites completed the formation of a body of coopted economic forces between the central state and the local market. We shall denote this special group of economic elites as the middle ground, and discuss it in the next chapter. The middle ground embraces all market and state actors that lie between the formal institutions of the state and the market, including the coopted private entrepreneurs, the economic agents of the local governments, and the remaining SOEs. In a way, this body of actors has replaced the old vanguard of entrepreneurs who straddled the state and market.

The middle ground has certain advantages over the crisscrossing of state and market which had dominated China's political economy until the late 1990s. For one thing, the market actors are better organized and more manageable from the top under such a system. By ordering market actors in terms of scale and significance and incorporating them into consultative agencies at various levels, the central state could make sure that it allied with the largest and most strategic sectors and actors of the national economy. For another thing, fiscal arrangements with the middle ground allow the state to reap the fruits of economic growth. In the new economic order dominated by the middle ground, fiscal resources are vertically divided and highly concentrated, with the central state having the most stable and privileged share in economic growth, in the forms of a predominant share in value-added tax and various taxes on the large SOEs.

Alongside the rise of the vertical structure and the middle ground was the development of the factor markets. This is no mere coincidence.

---

[56] For an online English Version of the "Three Represent Theory," see http://english.cpc .people.com.cn/66739/4521344.html

Whereas the development of the goods market in the 1980s could be described as gradual state withdrawal and the making of market space, the development of factor markets was a different matter altogether. In fact, during the reform years, the state has made every effort to create and structure factor markets in light of vertical marketization. Vertical marketization since the mid-1990s was premised on vertical division in the markets of labor, credit, land, and natural resources.

Labor

Of the important factors of production, labor, credit, and land in the Polanyian framework of capitalism, labor is most thoroughly marketized in China. Indeed, the most significant market development in the 1990s was precisely the marketization of labor.

The first category of labor is migrant labor. By far the largest group of laborers, migrant workers started their move into the modern manufacturing and service sectors in the 1980s but only moved en masse in the 1990s. At the beginning of the second phase of marketization in the 1990s and onward, they became the dominant force and the frontier.

Migrant laborers had a long pedigree in history. In late imperial China's market economy, peasants often worked in urban areas as itinerant peddlers, handicraft workers, household servants, or in various other manual and low-skilled jobs to scrape out a living. But the level of urbanization and marketization tended to be limited by the nature of the economy.[57] Not only did the gentry reside in the countryside, but merchants also tended to buy land in the countryside and invest in their sons' education in an effort to move up into a family of landed gentry.[58] As such, cities in late imperial China were political and consumption centers dependent on rural resources and productions.

Maoist industrialization changed the picture forever. The Maoist strategy of industrialization was based on the dualism of urban and rural areas. The urban areas continued to be the political centers; moreover, they also became production bases for the new economy. Rural land, on the other hand, was strictly subject to urban-centered national projects of industrialization. In both rural and urban areas, the centrally planned system

[57] Wang Jiafan, *Zhongguo lishi tonglun* (A General Study of Chinese History) (Taipei: Wunan Book Co. 2002), pp. 254–255.
[58] Tang Lixing, *Shangren yu jinshi Zhongguo shehui* (Merchants and Early Modern Chinese Society) (Taipei: The Commercial Press, 1997), pp. 25–26.

prioritized production over consumption. Following the rationale of max-imal production and minimum consumption, the state favored a policy guideline of industrialization without corresponding urbanization.[59]

In 1958, the NPC passed the first regulation on household registration, classifying all households into agricultural and nonagricultural or urban. This regulation enabled control over grain consumption as well as migration: Nonagricultural households consumed grain from state distributors, whereas agricultural households consumed grain produce after state procurement. As such, nonagricultural household status was effectively state-guaranteed entitlement to basic means of subsistence outside the rural agricultural sector. From 1958 to 1978, when the household registration system was strictly implemented, rural youths had little leeway to obtain nonagricul-tural status unless they enrolled in college or joined the army, the only two pathways to state-sector jobs and cadre status.

Over the years, residents with nonagricultural household registration status gradually acquired a number of fringe welfare entitlements. These fringe welfare benefits took in every area that was conceivable, from heavily subsidized housing, education, and healthcare to pensions, and practically ensured employment in a collective factory.[60] Moreover, these residents' easy access to jobs in the urban modern sector ensured better economic opportunities. Although economic and social inequalities were temporarily reduced by the first phase of the reform, which introduced market mech-anisms to the rural margins, the trend was soon reversed in the 1990s, when marketization started to generate income and wealth increased at a much larger scale in urban areas.

Given the huge income and welfare differentials across the urban–rural divide, it is easy to understand why rural peasants would choose to abandon their hometown and move to an urban area even without the Polanyian coercion when the floodgates were finally loosened in the early 1980s. This is not to say that contemporary Chinese factories were not sweatshops. In fact, in the early reforms, factory workers suffered various forms of maltreatment, from low and untimely pay to irregular working

---

[59] Barry Naughton, "Cities in the Chinese Economic System: Changing Roles and Condi-tions for Autonomy," in Debora Davis et al., eds., *Urban Space in Contemporary China: The Potential for Autonomy and Community* (Washington, DC: Woodrow Wilson Center Press and Cambridge University Press, 1995), pp. 61–89.

[60] Martin King Whyte, "The Paradox of Urban–Rural Inequality in Contemporary China," in Martin King Whyte, ed., *One Country, Two Societies: Rural–Urban Inequality in Contemporary China* (Cambridge, MA: Harvard University Press, 2010), pp. 7–12.

hours and a poor working environment.[61] But work in coastal sweatshops was still vastly preferable to agricultural works, especially in terms of the attractive wage rates and opportunities to settle in the cities. The Maoist household registration system thus produced an unintended institutional windfall for the Chinese economy. It had created such a constant economic and welfare gradient between rural and urban China by the late 1970s that when the system came to an end, it unleashed millions of migrant workers, who readily worked in the sweatshops of the Pearl River and Yangtze River Deltas.

The availability of a massive rural migrant labor force was imperative in the smooth marketization of a large sector of Chinese industrial laborers. For one thing, the influx of a rural labor force drove down costs for the private entrepreneurs, making them competitive domestically and internationally. For example, in the year 1998, a typical Chinese factory worker earned only $1,188, while a US blue-collar worker could earn about $35,639; this is not to mention differences in labor regulations and welfare.[62] This competitive edge in labor costs allowed the small and medium Chinese manufacturers who took contracts from bigger domestic and foreign enterprises to survive and prosper.

By 2010, China boasted 260 million migrant workers. The majority have moved from rural to urban, from inland to coastal regions. They constitute the bulk of the urban labor force in the manufacturing and low-end service sector. In other words, most of China's industrial workers are rural migrants with the imprint of a rural identity in terms of household registration status. Around 145 million of them were born after 1980.[63] Better educated than the first generation and with a decidedly urban outlook, they form the most dynamic part of contemporary China's labor force. They are also the most mobile and marketized labor force under the current labor system. Nevertheless, they also bear the brunt of the household registration system's institutional discrimination in their access to welfare and public services in the cities.

Meanwhile, in the urban sector, the pain of marketization is felt across the board in the old state sectors. The first major group is workers of former SOEs that were later privatized or bankrupted. This is the social

---

[61] Martin Levine, *Worker Rights and Labor Standards in Asia's Four New Tigers: A Comparative Perspective* (New York, NY: Springer, 1997), pp. 95–110.

[62] Wang Yanlin, "Cheap Labor and China's Export Capacity," in Kelvin Zhang Honglin, ed., *China as a World Factory* (London: Routledge, 2006), p. 73.

[63] National Bureau of Statistics, "2013 Monitor on Migrant Labors," www.stats.gov.cn/tjsj/ [Accessed on June 18, 2014].

group that experienced the most turbulent time at the birth of the labor market. In 1992, at their height, the SOEs employed as many as 30 million workers, comprising 20 percent of urban employment. In 2012, the SOEs only employed only 12 million workers, comprising about 10 percent of urban employment.[64]

Most of the elderly laid-off workers must have been hoping for lifelong employment security when they entered the factory back in the socialist days. When they were laid off, they were typically only compensated with severance pay amounting to three years' salary, in addition to welfare housing.[65] A significant percentage of the retrenched workers could be reemployed as they reentered the labor force as skilled workers, service sector workers, or self-employed household entrepreneurs; others simply retired earlier or depended on their family. The exact figure is never known, but the rate of reemployment fell precipitately from the late 1990s to early 2000s as elderly lay-offs left the market.[66] These laid-off workers were the major casualties of the reform of the mid-1990s.

The mass laying-off of workers from SOEs did cause major social protests, especially in China's old heavy industrial centers and the Rust Belt in the Northeast and North, where socialist neotraditionalism traditionally had a strong hold. In several cases, the protests caused major local political crises in a few industrial towns in North China at the turn of the millennium, but the government was able to contain the latent labor movement through a variety of strategies of persuasion and appeasement.[67] Such resistance proved to be less lethal to political stability than had been expected, as the economy saw double-digit growth in the first decade.

The next major category of urban labor is vocational school and college graduates since the mid-1990s. Before this time, when the state sector was still a major employer of educated laborers, China had a work assignment system for graduates from all higher education institutions. The assignment

---

[64] National Bureau of Statistics, *China Statistical Yearbook 2013* (Beijing: Zhongguo tongji chubanshe, 2013).

[65] Makoto Itoh, "Theoretical Possibility of a Socialist Market Economy," in Nobuharu Yokokawa, Jayati Ghosh, and Bob Rowthorn, eds., *Industrialization in China and India: Their Impact on the World Economy* (London: Routledge, 2013), p. 163.

[66] Pei Minxin, *China's Trapped Transition: The Limit of Developmental Autocracy* (Cambridge, MA: Harvard University Press. 2009), p. 200.

[67] For the government strategy towards the workers, see Cai Yongshun, *The State and Laid-Off Workers: The Silence and Collective Action of the Retrenched* (London: Routledge, 2006), pp. 82–100.

system was revamped in 1996 as the state sector underwent fundamental restructuring. Until recently, this group of more educated young laborers seemed to have fared relatively well in the midst of spectacular economic growth and job creation. But as the adverse consequences of an aggressive expansion of higher education sector in the late 1990s through early 2000s became evident, there has been a major problem of underemployment, or structural mismatch between educational qualifications and employment opportunities. As a result, many college graduates opt to take tedious national examinations to gain state-sector jobs, even for lower starting pay and a steeper career path.[68]

The final category of new urban labor includes former professionals and officials who previously worked as state employees. This process of voluntary marketization is commonly called *xiahai* (literally "jumping into the sea of business"), a metaphor for joining the market economy and founding a private business. Unlike grassroots entrepreneurs – barefoot peddlers such as Nian Guangjiu, for example – and grassroots cadres such as Yu Zuomin, who have no choice but to enter the market, these professionals and officials often have years if not decades of experience working in the heart of China's state sector, in places such as research institutes, large SOEs, and government agencies. Most of these *xiahai* cadres make only calculated moves: most of these professionals moved to joint ventures to work as consultants, scientists, experts, managers, but some eventually become business owners and make big money.[69] In addition to professional skills and experiences, *xiahai* elites returned and developed elaborate personal networks with former colleagues and friends in the state sector, including the government. This type of implicit network, which has been analyzed extensively by sociologists and anthropologists interested in China, is not the topic of this study.[70] Suffice it to say that the networks they forged around the state system became part of the highest echelons of China's labor market, where the revolving door between the state and the market leadership keeps the business world close to state powers. We shall

[68] Huang Yanjie, "China's Young Generation and How It Augurs for China's Future," in Zheng Yongnian and Gore Liangping Lance, eds., *China Entering Xi Jinping Era* (London: Routledge, 2014), p. 11.

[69] This category of entrepreneurs is not to be confused with the barefoot entrepreneurs in the early stage of reforms. Their success models have always been closely tied to government policies and state-controlled resources. For detailed analysis, see Chapter 6.

[70] For exemplary ethnographical research on the close-knit networks of entrepreneurs and government officials, see Liu Xin, *The Otherness of Self: A Genealogy of the Self in Contemporary China* (Ann Arbor, MI: University of Michigan Press, 2002), pp. 30–50.

come back to these links in Chapter 6 as we move to discuss the privately owned businesses located in the middle ground.

Marketization of labor in China has gone rather smoothly, largely because of a shift in the state-building and economic paradigm since the Maoist days. During the Maoist era, the state regarded individuals as resources to be exploited and sacrificed. As a result, the state tended to exercise direct personal control over human labor when it came to economic management. Under the post-Maoist economic order, the state no longer controls individual workers through a hierarchy of management agencies. Individual laborers are mobilized to seek their own self-interest and contribute only indirectly to the common interest. In other words, the Chinese state now governs labor and population through the markets, as it did in normal imperial times.

The post-Maoist state thus delegates the control and disciplining of labor from the state to market actors such as private entrepreneurs. Laborers are no longer renumerated in line with their political loyalty, physical strength, and years of service. Instead, their value is weighted by the market price of their labor and human capital. This requires, among other things, an intricate system of surveillance and discipline, as well as professional training and basic provisions. Most small and medium enterprises can only deliver such services up to a point. And only very large enterprises can afford such a complex system. The Foxconn Complex in Shenzhen, for example, houses 230,000 workers, mostly young workers from rural backgrounds. Such facilities are likened to a "state within a state," with various amenities such as internal hospitals and sport fields as well as networks of surveillance system and security forces.[71] While such complexes are often places of alienation and exploitation, the state welcomes them – and not only on account of the favorable economic calculus. As political actors, they provide at least a measure of social order and control in the state's economic mobilization of youth.

Still, China's marketization of labor is only partially complete with regard to the vital interests of state employees, such as local and central government employees, large SOEs, and some public agencies, such as hospitals, schools, and universities. This is where the logic of marketization meets the harsh logics of politics. In the early twenty-first century, state employees on the whole continue to enjoy much better welfare packages than private sector workers, in the forms of better pensions,

---

[71] Ren Xuefei, *Urban China* (London: John Wiley & Sons, 2013), pp. 130–132.

higher allowances, and even highly subsidized public houses and medical packages. The cadres, especially the high-ranking officials and managers of SOEs, have access to exorbitant welfare packages and privileges. The concentration of such privileges within the state sector makes reform toward marketization more difficult and tends to entrench such a dualism in the labor market.

The labor market has arguably been the most important product of the Chinese economic reform. It is also the venue in which marketization has made the greatest imprint on the planned economy and the Chinese society. Over the past thirty-five years, the private sector that has dominated the labor market has created hundreds of millions of jobs – or even more; accommodated massive amounts of rural migrants; lifted hundreds of millions of Chinese out of poverty; and fundamentally reshaped the economy.[72] The innermost part of the state sector, now an island of hierarchy and privilege, still stands amid the sea of the labor market, and its size is relatively small.[73]

This hierarchical arrangement produces a defining feature of the Chinese labor system, leading it to differ from advanced economies in two striking ways. First, in advanced economies in the West and East Asia, the best and brightest often choose to compete at the top of the labor market for the highest pay in private sector jobs in finance, business, and law; in China, top talent often eschews market competition and prefers the state sector in the broader sense, including central and local governments, public agencies, and the monopoly sector. Second, the most poor and least educated in most Western and East Asian industrial economies are often entitled to more state welfare support, but in China the situation is almost the reverse: The most poor and the least educated, often skilled rural migrant workers and peasants, also have the most limited access to state welfare support.[74] This has produced a system of self-reinforcing hierarchies of labor regimes, which allows the state as a top employer to play a

---

[72] Scott A. Hipsher, *The Private Sector's Role in Poverty Reduction in Asia* (Oxford: Chandos Publishing, 2010), pp. 107–111.

[73] Of the 300 million urban employees, only thirty million are state-employed, and perhaps only a small fraction of these state employees really has access to the relatively high level of wages and welfare benefits typical of civil servants in well-off localities and centrally managed SOEs.

[74] This is limited to state-sponsored formal welfare programs. The peasants sometimes benefit from real estate development if they happen to live on the margins of urban centers. Most peasant households typically receive much less, in terms of welfare subsidies in social security, education, and healthcare, than their urban counterparts.

dominant role in the labor market and reserve the best talent for its own bureaucracies and the SOEs. As analysis of market structures in the land and capital system demonstrates, this structure is reinforced by an arrangement in other factor markets that are more explicitly dominated by the state.

Factors of Production

While the labor market was gradually marketized in the 1980s and 1990s, capital, land, natural resources, and infrastructure was also increasingly allocated through the market. But unlike labor, which was in relatively abundant supply, key factors of production such as capital, land, and natural resources were relatively scarce throughout much of the reform decades. The marketization of these factors primarily serves the fiscal and financial interests of the state, as it uses the market as a means for mobilization and control. In these three factor markets, the two logics of marketization in the 1980s – decentralization and dual-track – still dominated the game, even as market reforms moved into deeper waters in the 1990s. Instead of granting market actors full access to the factor market, the state entrusted the capital, land, and natural resources to its own economic agents: large state-owned or shareholding banks, centrally managed SOEs, and local municipal governments.

As discussed in our chapters on the history of imperial political economy, there was some free space for local and grassroots market mechanisms for the allocation of key factors such as capital, land, and natural resources before the rise of the modern Chinese state. Nevertheless, these decentralized local markets were hardly constitutive of a capitalist economy. At a time when the monetary system was underdeveloped and market networks only loosely integrated, these factor markets only operated at grassroots or, at best, local levels. The only significant external factor was the fiscal institutions of the imperial state, which, despite its relatively small size vis-à-vis the economy, had a decisive influence on the long-term distribution of land and credit in the rural economy.

The Communist Revolution shook the foundations of this loosely integrated market system. As discussed in Chapter 4, Maoist economic policies tended to perpetuate a wartime economy that eliminated the factor market and made them part of a national economy plan. At the height of the Maoist system, capital, mostly in the form of fiscal imbursement, only served as accounting units in the national plan, whereas land, natural resources, and infrastructure were simply allocated to various administrative units as basic inputs for production in accordance with the plan.

The 1980s reform had already begun to challenge this system. In the initial stage of marketization, there emerged numerous local private entrepreneurs with many inventive programs. They needed labor, land, and other resources to expand their business. Among these factors, the supply of cheap labor had been the least formidable obstacle, as peasants started to move into the cities in the 1980s. For most entrepreneurs, land and bank credit posed much greater challenges. Throughout the 1980s and the early 1990s, capital, land, and natural resources were still strictly controlled by the state. Unlike the intermediary products, these essential factors of production were insufficient in the dual-track system.

Such an arrangement had a profound structural impact on the behavior of private entrepreneurs. Except for foreign-invested enterprises and joint ventures, there were only two choices for most private entrepreneurs: They either remained small in scale, or cooperated with SOEs and local governments to form various revenue-sharing schemes. Only in rare cases did they successfully secure long-term financing from state-owned banks or the stock exchanges and become more or less autonomous economic actors. That was only possible when a private enterprise secured a dominant position in the national or international market and could negotiate with central governments for preferential treatment, such as in the case of China's emerging Internet giants.

Land

The modern Chinese state's strict control over land could be traced back to its founding days. During the founding period of the People's Republic, the state eliminated the intermediate class of landlords and centralized control over rural and urban land by relentlessly carrying out land reforms and collectivization. During the period of high socialism between 1958 and 1978, the land market became irrelevant, as the state held absolute control over the allocation and use of land.

The land market only began to emerge as an institution after reform began. In the Maoist days, the state had monopolized control over rural and urban land. The Constitution of 1982 was the first to recognize state ownership of urban land.[75] It was not until the reform of the 1990s that

[75] Yang Jufeng, "Woguo chengshi tudi suoyouzhi de yanjin he laiyuan" (Origin and Evolution of China's State-Ownership of Urban Land), *Southern Weekly*, June 13, 2007.

this legal arrangement became immensely consequential. As part of the overall marketization of the period, the housing reform of 1994 heralded an exuberant development of the real estate market. The reform was carried out in stages: In the first stage, urban residents bought their current dwelling at a token price; in the latter stage, except for households eligible for welfare housing, urban residents were required to buy commercial flats from real estate agents. As China moved into a period of rapid urbanization in the late 1990s, housing prices began to skyrocket. For example, the average unit housing price in Shanghai increased by at least 300 percent between 2002 and 2012, far outstripping increases in household income and other prices.[76]

The real estate market had immediate consequences for the land market. Whereas housing was almost completely marketized, local government remained the monopsony in the primary urban land market. Under this system, the local state usually defined the use of land and then auctioned off commercial land for a transfer fee. To maximize their land transfer receipts, local governments became the most ardent supporters of a relentless urbanization drive, and skilled dealers of land. In megacities such as Beijing, Shanghai, Tianjin, and Guangzhou, land transfer receipts regularly accounted for 30–40 percent of the local state coffers.[77] And all together, local governments had collected 2–3 trillion of revenues from land transfers since 2009, but in 2013 total receipts had increased to an unprecedented 4.1 trillion.[78] As municipal governments competed for public funds and urbanization, the urban land market became the most important extra-tax resource for local revenues.

In rural China, the situation was quite different. Although the market for land had not been officially established, market mechanisms had become the dominant economic institutions, held in check by limiting systems such as the household responsibility system and the rural land entitlement system. For instance, in cases where all household laborers had moved to the cities as migrant workers, the household could rent out their allotted plots to hired agricultural laborers. However, rural households

---

[76] Wang Lianli, *Zhongguo fangdichan zhie* (The Adversity of China's Property Business) (Hong Kong: Tianxingjian Publisher, 2011), p. 226.

[77] "Tudi caizheng you duozhongyao" (How Important is Land Transfer to Local Revenues), *China Economic Weekly* 14 (2014). Available online at http://finance.people.com.cn/n/2014/0415/c1004–24896199.html [Accessed on June 12, 2014].

[78] The Ministry of Land and National Resource Report of 2013. Available online at www.mlr.gov.cn/xwdt/jrxw/201307/t20130730_1246849.htm [Accessed on June 12, 2014].

could not use their allotted housing land to build houses for rent, since they did not have full property rights to the allotted land outside its designated use. Such commercial use of rural housing land is still pervasive in suburban areas and often leads to a tug-of-war between the local state and the peasantry.[79]

The current land market in China is thus decidedly two-tiered: Urban land use rights are tradable, with local government as the sole seller; rural land uses rights are only partially tradable and subject to conditions. It is hard to qualify such a system as an efficient market mechanism, but it is nonetheless a far cry from the Maoist arrangement, which regarded land as a nonmarketable condition for agricultural and industrial production. The current system could be regarded as empowering local governments through markets, since it decidedly favors the interests of local governments as the monopsony sellers of urban land, and makes all other private parties clients of local developmental policies.

Natural Resources and Infrastructure

The market for natural resources and infrastructure is a bit different from that for land and credit. In the case of land and, especially, credit, the state has strong institutions that take a keen interest in guarding their own turf. In the case of natural resources and infrastructure, private entrepreneurs often have the upper hand in efficient development and exploitation, especially when local states prove to be weak and corrupt. The battle lines are more radically drawn.

In the late 1990s and early 2000s, when the resource-related SOEs suffered from appalling economic inefficiency, the central state experimented with a more market-oriented approach toward key natural resources such as coal, and even oil fields. In Shanxi, China's principal supplier of coal, the local state retained only the largest coal mines and sold small and medium ones to private investors from the 1990s onward. Though some localities had already commenced renationalization and restructuring of coal mines due to problems associated with private exploitation, privatization reached a climax in the period between 2003 and 2007, when national coal prices surged to unprecedented levels. Meanwhile, the problems of private management, especially safety issues,

---

[79] "Xiaochanquanfang daobi tudi gaige" (Bottom-Up Pressure from the Small Ownership House for Land Reform), *Caijing guojia zhoukan* (Economy & Nation Weekly) 7 (2012), pp. 36–38.

also became more acute. As coal prices and production levels soared, private enterprises resorted to convenient and cheap methods of exploitation regardless of heightened risks to often poorly trained and badly equipped miners. As a result, breaches of safety protocols and deadly accidents became prevalent.[80] In response to the human hazard, the state put a sudden halt to privatization and ordered the closure of all small and medium-sized coal mines.

This back-and-forth movement between the market and the state in the allocation of resources and infrastructure dragged on between the 1990s and 2000s. Marketization promised efficiency at the risk of poor governance, whereas state control delivered better risk control but not necessarily good production levels. In the 2000s, as the balance turned to political concerns, the central government gradually switched from marketization to state control. By the early 2010s, the separation seemed stable: whereas the state operated a system of permits and contracts in the natural resources market for matters such as fisheries and timber, it firmly reserved the monopolies in energy, power, communication, and railways. In these key areas of infrastructure provision, the central government ensured full control of centrally managed SOEs (including the former Ministry of Railway) and allowed little leeway for private capital by funneling central fiscal expenditure and state-owned bank loans into multibillion infrastructural projects. The most notable recent example of this is the national high-speed railway networks. This gigantic network of state-of-the-art railways – debuted only in the mid-2000s, and now the longest and most complex railway network in the world – is mainly financed by the central government and operated by the centrally managed China Railway. The state railway system received a noticeable boost from the four trillion RMB stimulus package, which was devoted to the financing of major infrastructural projects such as high-speed railway networks.[81]

---

[80] "Meigai lunhui: Zhongguo meitan siyouhua zaidao guoyouhua" (The Circle of Coal Reform: Chinese Coal Mines from Privatization to Nationalization), *Southern Weekly*, November 6, 2008. Available at www.infzm.com/content/19532 [Accessed on April 15, 2015].

[81] In retrospect, as much as half of the four trillion might have gone toward the construction of high-speed railways. In 2010 alone, investment in high-speed railway was RMB832 billion (USD145 billion). Due to its sheer scale and its long duration to maturity, such an investment would not have been made by any private investor. See Zhang Zhi, "Gaotie shinian" (Ten Years of High-Speed Railways), *Huaxia Shibao*, July 28, 2017.

Financial Market

The financial market is perhaps the most jealously guarded market in China. In this arena, the state has a direct monopoly and indirect control in all major sectors: banks, insurance, the stock market, the bond market, the foreign exchanges, and even the budding venture capital market. China's financial market is firmly centered on four major state banks: the Bank of China, Agricultural Bank of China, Industrial and Commerce Bank of China, and Construction Bank of China. During the banking reform of the 1990s, the Ministry of Finance stripped the national banks of bad loans and transferred them to four asset management companies. After this restructuring, the four banks remerged as multibillion corporate groups.

Such a highly controlled financial system does have weighty consequences for the market actors. In an economy where profit-driven state banks have a virtual monopoly over deposits and loans, small and medium investors have little choice but to bear the high costs of finance. In addition, the tightly regulated nature of the state banking sector means that costs for financing risky investments are particularly high. Meanwhile, until relatively recently, state regulations strictly restricted the creation of autonomous private banks to compete with the state banks. The result of such a systemic mismatch was the institutional innovation of underground or shadow banking, mostly in China's commercially vibrant coastal cities. The most famous hotbed of underground banking is Wenzhou City, Zhejiang province. There, hundreds of underground bankers accepted private deposits at much higher interest rates than state banks and issued short-term loans at equally high interest rates without a stringent approval procedure. Before their comprehensive collapse in 2004, these shadow bankers in Wenzhou had accumulated net assets of RMB277 billion.[82]

One of the chief concerns that prevents China from liberalizing its banking sector is precisely the fear that such Wenzhou-style banks could cause financial and social instability. As in the case of land and natural resources, the logic of marketization is to create a market that is at once fiscally lucrative and politically stabilizing. In a sector as important and sensitive as the financial market, what is more effective than putting a hierarchical array of semimarket entities under the auspices of the state's

---

[82] Cai Mingyue, "Wenzhou minjian ziben de fazhan yu yingdao yanjiu" (Study on the Development and Guidance of Wenzhou's Private Capitals), *Zhejiang Jinrong* (Zhejiang Finance) 1 (2005), p. 26.

own trusted agents? Indeed, despite repeated calls for financial reform from foreign observers and domestic economists, the paradigm of a state-dominated financial sector is never fundamentally challenged. Rather, the regulatory framework has been strengthened repeatedly in the course of past financial crises, and most recently in the guise of a proposed supraministerial commission.[83]

China's markets for land, credit, and natural resources are sharply divided vertically. Indeed, due to its sharp hierarchical structure, there is no integrated national market to speak of. On the lower end, such as the market for rural land, grassroots credit, and traditional resources, the state operates a system of loose control: It is neither market nor state monopoly, but a combination of market mechanisms and state regulations. Such market mechanisms are still very much localized and limited in their scale of mobilization. At the higher reach, such as urban commercial land, large bank loans, stock markets, and high yield natural resources such as minerals, oil, and gas, the state operates a monopoly via its trusted agents, local governments, state banks, and SOEs. The rationale of such an arrangement is not to suppress local or national markets, but to harness them for economic efficiency, while maintaining order and hierarchy. But the effect is indeed a suppression of bottom-up marketization, as local level markets remain primarily segregated whereas national markets remain underdeveloped.

The boundary between the higher and lower ends of the factor market is heavily policed by the state. This explains frequent state crackdowns on borderline activities such as shadow banking, private extraction of minerals, and commercialization of rural nonagricultural land. Sometimes the state also makes room for entrepreneurs, such as in the reform of the coal mine licensing system in the late 1990s. There is a simple rule of thumb to this policy opportunism: Whenever the state feels a need to stimulate economic efficiency, it shifts the boundary higher to allow more space for market actors, but whenever it feels a need to stress order and tighten control, it shifts the boundary lower to claim more space for its own agents. In any case, the arrangement always allows the state to retain most of the rents and profits of the economy.

---

[83] A newly proposed supraministerial organization, the State Commission for Financial Stability and Development, was founded on July 15, 2017. Headed by the Prime Minister, with the President of the Central Bank as deputy head, this new organization is responsible for ensuring overall financial stability and coordinating the existing financial regulatory agencies, including the People's Bank, the Banking Regulatory Commission, the Security Regulatory Commission, and the Insurance Regulatory Commission.

However, the disjoint between a relatively free labor market and a more tightly controlled factor market also creates an enduring tension in the market: Domestic labor is abundant enough for a large scale of production whereas the size of the domestic market is restricted by the size of the factor market. This is partially alleviated by another feature of the Chinese economy: the large export sector that the presence of a massive overseas market allows.

The Roles of Overseas Markets

China has been a labor-exporting country throughout the entirety of modern times – since long before it became a net exporter of industrial goods three decades ago and found success in outbound investment in recent years. In the second half of the nineteenth century, under the forces of global capitalism, Chinese migrants sailed across the world and populated various colonial farms and construction sites, from the trans-American railways to the rubber plantations in the British East Indies.[84] The century-long labor migration continued unabated until the Chinese Exclusion Act of 1882 in the United States and the outbreak of the Pacific War in the British East Indies. In the 1950s, in his usual hyperbolic fashion, Mao Zedong famously proposed to Stalin that China could send one million Chinese workers to develop Soviet Siberia.[85] By the early 1980s, when China rejoined global market networks, Chinese leaders had already realized the huge potential of China's large pool of labor in global competition. During his term as premier, Zhao Ziyang famously spotted the shifts in the global value chain and championed the policy of labor-intensive process export (*liang tou zai wai*, literally "input and output from outside").[86]

This breathtaking development strategy was reinforced by the hierarchical structure of the emergent labor market, as the underprivileged rural laborers were strongly motivated to move to the export-oriented industries in coastal regions in search for better life opportunities. This structure

[84] For an analytical account of Chinese migration in this period, see Adam Mckeown, *China Migration Networks and Cultural Change* (Chicago, IL: University of Chicago Press, 2001), pp. 1–24.
[85] William Kirby, "China's Early Internationalization in Early People's Republic: The Dream of a Socialist World Economy," in Julia Strauss, ed., *The History of the People's Republic of China, 1949–1976* (Cambridge: Cambridge University Press, 2007), p. 34.
[86] Zhao Ziyang, *Gaige Licheng* (Roads to Reform) (Hong Kong: The New Century Press, 2010), pp. 145–147.

allows the highest degree of marketization in the labor market, while leaving much of the factor market in the hands of the state. The state in turn nurtures its own economic agents to take the lion's share of rents and profits from its commanding heights in the domestic market, without the need to take global competition seriously. The boom of a "Made in China" export-oriented manufacturing sector in the global market is thus no longer another case of the Flying Goose Model typical of the East Asian new industrialized economies (NIEs). In the East Asian cases, particularly Japan and South Korea, the state helps to build national champion industries capable of competing in the international arena, keeping the small and medium enterprises mostly focused on the domestic market. In the Chinese case, the national champions are state-owned domestic monopolies and global competitiveness comes from millions of small and medium enterprises.

Under this development scheme, export-oriented small and medium enterprises (SMEs) in coastal China began to expand trade relations with the outside world and integrate the country with the world market. Even as the domestic market was still in the making in the 1980s, small local producers had already realized the importance of the external market and joined the global production networks. During the first wave of marketization in coastal cities such as Wenzhou and Yiwu in Zhejiang and Dongguan in Guangdong, factories with external links began to target familiar markets in the bigger Chinese world, from Hong Kong to Southeast Asia. This wave of SME-led export-oriented industrialization marked a considerable departure, in terms of mode of industrialization and market integration, from China's previous development model based on small-scale intraregional TVEs. Under the new developmental model, Chinese local markets stepped up their integration with the global and national markets. From the early 1990s to the early 2000s, both the national economy and export-oriented provincial economies were becoming increasingly specialized as they integrated with the world market. The average index of regional industrial specialization increased from 0.43 in 1992 to 0.66 in 2004, after a period of small decline from 1980 to 1992.[87]

China's trade with the external world grew steadily in the 1990s. Despite the political aftermath of the Tiananmen movement, China's access to its diaspora networks remained unhindered. Thanks to the diasporic

---

[87] Jiuli Huang, "Foreign Trade, Interregional Trade, and Regional Specialization," in Ming Lu, Zhao Chen, Zhu Xiwen, and Xu Xianxiang, eds., *China's Regional Development: Review and Prospect* (London and New York, NY: Routledge, 2015), pp. 174–175.

networks that were reconnected in the post-Mao years, which had consistently been the major source of investment to China, foreign direct investment (FDI) grew unabated in the wake of the political turbulence and policy uncertainties between 1989 and 1992.[88] Following Deng Xiaoping's call for further economic opening in 1992, local governments began to court foreign capital, and especially overseas Chinese enterprises from Taiwan, Hong Kong, Singapore, and the larger Chinese world, by building various kinds of development zones, typically local manufacturing centers for export process goods. Under such circumstances, before China's official entry to the World Trade Organization (WTO) in 2001, domestic market actors intensified their international economic ties and prepared themselves for the global market.[89]

China's entry of the WTO marked the starting point of another round of explosive growth in trade and foreign investment. Unlike the previous decade, this time the most significant growth occurred outside China's immediate geoeconomic centers and achieved a truly global reach. From 2001 to 2012, China's trade with the world grew from USD 260 billion to USD 2 trillion, making China the world's largest trading nation. Meanwhile, the pattern of Asia-centered trade continued unabated after China's accession to the WTO.[90] In terms of goods content, labor-intensive goods such as textiles have declined to give way to trade in capital-intensive goods and the process trade, such as electronics, since the late 1990s.[91]

In retrospect, the globalization of China's coastal manufacturing economy provided a more important engine for China's marketization than the initial domestic forces after the decline of the horizontal phase of marketization in the 1980s and until the financial crisis of 2008. This is due to the fact that the global market remains more accessible to the Chinese domestic markets for China's most vibrant SMEs. Indeed, studies suggest that international marketization could substitute for domestic political dynamics of marketization, since provinces that opt for a trade-driven growth model have achieved significantly higher degrees of marketization and

---

[88] Ye Min, *Diasporas and Foreign Direct Investment in China and India* (New York, NY: Cambridge University Press, 2014), p. 66.

[89] Doug Guthrie, *China in the Global Economy* (London: Routledge, 2006), pp. 115–117.

[90] The Chinese Academy of Social Sciences, *China Trade Report 2012*, p. 17. Available at: www.iwep.org.cn/upload/2013/03/d20130307160336894.pdf [Accessed on June 12, 2014].

[91] *Ibid.*, p. 31.

rates of economic growth.[92] This is because China's external trade grew at a much faster rate than internal trade in this period, so that an economic interdependency was forged around rather than within China, while political logics still control domestic marketization. A coastal province such as Guangdong is arguably more closely linked with Hong Kong and Southeast Asia than the inland provinces.

Despite China's rapid external marketization, several remarkable patterns persist. The first is the continuing importance of largely labor-intensive process trade in China's total trade, consistently accounting for 40 percent of China's exports. The second is China's large trade surplus with Europe and the United States and its trade deficit with East Asian industrialized economies, especially Taiwan, Japan, South Korea, and Southeast Asia. The third is China's relatively low position in the global value chain, which is still dominated by the West, and even by Japan and South Korea. In comparison with these, China has produced fewer brand names and leading products of a similar technological caliber.[93] The fourth is the continued importance of the US dollar in China's trading settlement, despite China's increasing effort to make the RMB a more important international currency.

Underlying these continued trends are China's own institutional limitations in a global market system. Simply put, China's economic globalization is not in line with the East Asian industrialization strategy to compete with the advanced economies as an extension of or supplement to its domestic process of marketization. In this sense, China's global marketization is not meant to support global domination so much as global accommodation. It is premised on a maximal use of a favorable global market system, which is still dominated by advanced economies, and especially by the United States. No matter how spectacular the growth in trade and investment, China's external marketization is a process that keeps pace with its imbalanced domestic marketization. Pressed by state policy that both mobilizes and controls private enterprises under the overriding political agendas of growth and employment, until very recently, Chinese firms could only challenge the status quo of the global value chain passively as they adapted to global market conditions and

---

[92] Huang Jiuli and Li Kunwang, "Chukou Kaifang, defang jingjiguimo he jingji zengzhang" ("Export Openness, Regional Market Size and Economic Growth"), *Jingji yanjiu* (Economic Studies) 6 (2006), p. 37.

[93] John Pomfret, "Beijing Tries to Push beyond Made in China to Find Name-Brand Innovation," *Washington Post*, May 25, 2010.

rules. Over the years, China has naturally become the center of an East Asian economic network consisting of China and the East Asian NIEs. Driven by a process known as production sharing between China and its neighbors, the structure of East Asian trade networks evolved spontaneously and without the formation of preferential trade treaties.[94]

The existing market system also allows maximum state control over the overall process of globalization. The rule of the game is that whereas goods exchanges are almost fully liberalized, monetary exchanges are strictly and centrally managed. The function of the state in China's global marketization can be most aptly observed in the mandatory foreign exchange settlement system. This system requires that all foreign exchange for Chinese exports be deposited in stipulated banks and managed by the People's Bank of China. In other words, China's exporting firms literally surrender their foreign currency to the monetary authority, which oversees China's exchange rate policy. Despite China's deep involvement in global trade, this system effectively keeps the Chinese domestic market dominated by a single currency, separate from the global market dominated by foreign currencies. This arrangement ensures that the RMB monetary zone corresponds closely with the domestic market. In addition, it empowers the People's Bank to pursue a controlled floating exchange regime, which has been in place since the last exchange reform in 2005.

It is from this domestic perspective that China's economic globalization since the late 1990s can be best appreciated. As discussed previously, China's state-dominated domestic market system creates various institutional ceilings for private market actors. They can expand in a free market environment but only up to a limit. Once they reach that limit, they face difficulties accessing credit, land, natural resources, and other factors of production. In other words, after a certain point, it would be difficult for them to expand their domestic market unless under a special arrangement with the state.[95] Given China's abundant labor supply, domestic enterprises might be able to expand if given the same access to domestic factors and the product market as the state firms are offered. Since this is not the case, the privately owned SMEs must seek an external market. China's three decades of trade expansion have been based on this model.

---

[94] Mona Haddad, "Trade Integration in East Asia: The Role of China and Production Networks," *World Bank Policy Research Paper*, no. 4160, March 2007.

[95] This exception applies particularly to sectors such as the Internet and real estate, where nascent businesses could seek state support or cooperate with local states. Such cases will be discussed in Chapter 6.

While China's biggest enterprises continue to be large SOEs running on domestic monopolies, its most dynamic exporting enterprises are small and medium-sized enterprises that work on outsource contracts and produce for the world market. Their share of overall employment and output grew rapidly thanks to a robust global market until 2008, generating a trade surplus and accumulating foreign reserves.[96] Since under China's foreign reserve system, all foreign earnings must be converted to RMB and deposited in a designated account, the buildup of trade surplus in turn provides the People's Bank with powerful resources for managing the RMB and making strategic foreign investments. The export-oriented SMEs thus play a further strategic role of supporting the monetary system, in addition to maintaining employment and market efficiency through China's integration with the world market.

MARKETIZATION AND ITS LIMITS IN
CONTEMPORARY CHINA

From 1978 onwards, China witnessed three waves of marketization. The first wave was in the 1980s, when the likes of Nian Guangjiu, Yu Zuomin, and millions of grassroots entrepreneurs made their first buckets of gold, following China's initial marketization from the rural margins. This was followed by the second wave in the 1990s, when the state started to dismantle the SOE system, leaving some without a rice bowl but endowing others with ample space for quick expansion. The third market surge was in the early 2000s, when millions of small and medium-sized Chinese enterprises moved into the global market to populate the lower end of a global value chain.

While three waves of marketization have transformed the Chinese economic landscape beyond recognition, the process has not been unequivocally successful for private businesses. The first wave was indeed spearheaded by bottom-up developments of market mechanisms from the rural margins to urban economies, but the second and third waves were of a fundamentally different nature. The second wave was accompanied by the formation of a large middle ground between the market

---

[96] One study has rigorously demonstrated China's financial suppression of SMEs and the growing foreign reserve, as the overall shrinking of the less productive but better financed SOEs vis-à-vis SMEs causes savings to be invested in foreign assets. See Zheng Song, Kjetil Storesletten, and Fabrizio Zilibotti, "Growing Like China," *American Economic Review* 101:1 (2011), p. 237.

and state, rather than the triumph of market forces. The third wave, essentially driven by globalization, was in fact complementary to the state's tightened grip on the domestic market.

This is not to say that the private sector has become less important over the years. In fact, private enterprises now produce as much as 60 percent of China's GDP.[97] In 2013, the private sector also employed the overwhelming majority of China's urban labor force.[98] Most importantly, private enterprises are China's motor of employment creation. In 2013 alone, household and private enterprise provided 12 million new jobs, about 90 percent of the newly created jobs in the labor market.[99] The private sector has been legally established as the cornerstone of China's labor market and, by extension, its social and political stability. This provides enough justification for the central state to keep the market growing and prospering.

The overwhelming majority of these household and private enterprises remain small and operate in limited local and grassroots markets. In a sense, these firms are not really vibrant modern market actors in a textbook fashion. Instead of relying on modern economic institutions and technology, which are invariably controlled by the state, most of these smaller firms are financially self-reliant, household-centered economic entities. According to a survey by the All-China Federation of Industry and Commerce, 60 percent of these small firms have no standing loans from banks and 40 percent consider loans from the state banks the most expensive mode of finance.[100]

The 57 million-strong army of small and medium household and private enterprises constitute the cornerstone of the contemporary state-dominated economy, but they could not possibly replace the state sector in

---

[97] http://finance.people.com.cn/n/2013/0203/c1004–20414645.html [Accessed on 16 June 2014].

[98] This needs further clarification. According to *China Statistical Yearbook 2013*, private enterprises employ only 70 million out of 371 million urban workers. But this largely excludes migrant workers, who are mostly not urban residents but mostly work in urban private enterprises. According to a CASS researcher, in 2011, private sector employees made up 31 percent of the total urban and rural labor force, vis-à-vis 9 percent employed by the state sector. See Feng Xingyuan, "Zhongguo minying qiye de shengcun huanjing" (The Living Condition of China's Private Enterprises), *Financial Times* (in Chinese), December 11, 2012, www.ftchinese.com/story/001047949?full=y [Accessed on June 16, 2014].

[99] www.saic.gov.cn/zwgk/tjzl/zhtj/xxzx/201407/t20140709_146608.html [Accessed on June 16, 2014].

[100] Ba Shusong, "Report on Small and Micro Business: Chinese Experience and Asia Paths," *Boao Review* (April 25, 2014), p. 13.

terms of its fiscal and political role. Collectively, the SMEs have strength in numbers; individually, they are small in scale and negligible in political significance. In the post-Maoist era, as the state retreats and rebuilds its fault lines, these firms only have minimal interaction with the state. The state only comes to their aid in the event of a severe downturn and unemployment, such as during the initial shocks of the Global Financial Crisis, and even in that case only intervenes indirectly through its own economic agents.[101] Besides these emergency actions, the state has little support to offer, since state banks primarily focus on financing the state sector and the local governments only take interests in larger game-changing private enterprises, often from outside and even abroad. But in reverse, the state is also not dependent on SMEs for tax revenues. In 2013, the SOEs contributed 3.6 trillion to the state coffers, about 60 percent of the three principal taxes (value-added tax, corporate sales tax, and corporate income tax). The 110 centrally managed SOEs alone contribute 2.8 trillion, or 46 percent of the central government revenue.[102] This arrangement is not irrelevant in the light of the lessons in the 1980s and 1990s, when rampant tax evasion and false accounting of the politically insignificant SMEs led to major fiscal loopholes.[103]

As small market actors expand outward and upward in economic scale and power, they inevitably enter negotiations with the local state and sometimes even the central party-state, where they meet local states, state banks, SOEs, and other politically significant actors. At this critical interface between the state and market, market actors could either choose to enter the orbit of the state or become its junior partners. If they pursue their political interests instead of entering the orbit or settling with junior partners, they will be in a disadvantaged position, or even explicitly suppressed by the state. Most of the successful private enterprises have been practical enough to avoid such irrational choices. As it turned out, they either allied with local leaders or readily attached themselves to the various mechanisms of systemic political cooptation. In either case, the

---

[101] Besides the RMB4 trillion stimulus packages, which mostly went to the state sector and local governments, the state intervened to cut corporate tax rates and increase rebates for export firms.

[102] Author's calculation based on the Report on Economic Performance of State and State-Controlled Enterprises by the Ministry of Finance: http://qys.mof.gov.cn/zhengwuxinxi/qiyeyunxingdongtai/201401/t20140121_1037861.html [Accessed on June 16, 2014].

[103] Hao Chunhong, "Zhongguo shuishou liushi guimo guji" (Estimation of the Scale of Tax Loss in China), *Zhongyang caijing daxue xuebao* (Journal of the Central University of Economics and Finance) 14 (2004), pp. 15–16.

limit of marketization is partially transcended through the visible hand of the state. But as Chapter 6 shall discuss, this transcendence of market, while it reduces economic risks, is no guarantee of business success, as it introduces another risk – namely, political risk – into the business in the middle ground.

The limits to marketization are determined by the capacity and the interest calculus of the central state vis-à-vis the market, the SOEs, and the local state. No matter how efficient the market can become in generating economic growth, the state consistently regards it as an instrument, rather than the economic foundation of its rule. To harness the economic gains of marketization, the post-Maoist state has cooperated with its own agents and societal forces in fostering regional, national, and global markets, especially in the areas of consumer goods and employment of labor. But to control the political risks of marketization, the central state has also established a hierarchy of semieconomic institutions that keeps the destabilizing political potential of free markets at bay. As this chapter has demonstrated, such measures work quite well with the middle-ground market actors. But as we shall discuss later in the book, the middle-ground effect is the most damaging when market logics penetrate the state apparatus and create principal–agent problems in relations between the central state and local governments, as well as between the central state and the SOEs.

However, the Chinese market economy needs to be taken as a complete system of economic and political institutions with a logic of its own. Therefore, when understanding the limits of marketization, we cannot simply assume stable domination. The side effects of such marketization need to be taken seriously. Just as free substantive markets are held at the bottom of the economic hierarchy, market mechanisms penetrate deeply into the domains of the state and the middle ground between the state and market. The central state, despite its effective management of the local and grassroots market, finds a much tougher challenge with the market actors in the middle ground, and especially its own agents. Thus, when the state has largely succeeded in its control of the bottom-up marketization, it has faced a much more difficult task taming top-down marketization from within the state. These dilemmas will be discussed in the following chapters.

6

The Middle Ground

The Nexus between the State and Private Enterprises

After nearly four decades of economic reform, the private sector has become the largest and most dynamic part of the mixed economy in contemporary China. However, the mere numerical dominance of the private sector does not bespeak a similar structural dominance in terms of power. Indeed, since the early 1990s, there has been a noticeable reversal of the private sector-led marketization process, a strengthening of state economic power, and the institutionalization of an unequal playing field for the state and private enterprises.[1] While the Chinese state has consistently accommodated and repositioned itself vis-à-vis private capital over the past few decades, something fundamental remains unchanged in the logics of state–capital relations, namely, the political rationale of the market economy. The state has been always centrally concerned with the overriding political objectives of economic growth and employment. For that purpose, it is willing to make concessions and maintain limits that are hardly conceivable in a typical free market economy. Both the flexibility and the rigidity of this system are best illustrated by the changing institutional arrangements between state and private capital.

In this chapter, we shall use the concept of the middle ground defined in previous chapters to analyze the nexus between the state and private actors. The middle ground is a space where the state and nonstate actors interact to fulfill a set of mutually agreed economic and political objectives. The space is thus open to constant negotiation between the state and nonstate actors. The latter include politically significant private entrepreneurs and large private business groups that are typically affiliated with, but not constitutive of, the state power apparatus. Since laws and regulations are

---

[1] Yasheng Huang, *Capitalism with Chinese Characteristics: Entrepreneurship and the State* (New York, NY: Cambridge University Press, 2008), pp. 164–167.

constantly negotiated between the state and these enterprises, the middle ground is not a domain of the rule of law. Since large private enterprises depend on the state for protection and market access, their chances of survival and prosperity depend critically on their negotiations with other powerful state actors at both central and local levels. In this chapter, we shall focus on these politically significant private entrepreneurs as they secure vital resources and face limitations placed upon them by the state.

This chapter's discussion of the middle ground consists of three parts. The first part traces the origins of the middle ground in the enterprise reforms of the 1980s and 1990s. We shall demonstrate that China's large private enterprises are not simply an outgrowth of the grassroots enterprises that we discussed in the previous chapter, though many certainly went through such a stage in the early period of reform. More importantly, those enterprises which reach a politically recognizable scale often grow out of the former state sector in terms of their personnel networks, technology, and capital. Like state-owned enterprises (SOEs), but unlike grassroots actors, they rely on policies of favoritism and are subject to state regulations once they pass a certain threshold. Thus, far from being an autonomous force, large private enterprises have been part of the state's transformation since its very beginning, and their middle-ground characteristics have been their defining feature for just as long.

In the second part of the chapter, we shall focus on two broad categories of the market–state nexus: the partnership model and the state agency model. The partnership model describes a situation in which the state supports or sponsors private enterprises without directly supplying key factors of production and controlling the direction of their development. This broadly defined partnership can be further subdivided into at least three subtypes: the private-dominated relationship, or the Wenzhou model; the local service-providing developmental state, or the Suzhou model; and the state sponsorship or industrial policy model, mostly targeted at certain key technological sectors such as the emergent Internet sector. The state agency model describes a somewhat problematic set of relationships between private enterprises and local governments, where the enterprises become agents or vehicles for the local governments' development objectives. This kind of relationship can be problematic in that local government officials and well-connected private entrepreneurs could collude to exploit locally controlled factors of production and harm public interests. This type of relationship can also be further divided into at least two subtypes: first, an interest-sharing alliance, exemplified by the unholy alliance between local officials and developers as agents of urbanization, which we shall discuss further in Chapter 7 from the perspective of local states; second, an excessive developmental state, typified by those reckless local government officials who make daring but rash investment decisions and employ private entrepreneurs to fulfill local development goals.

Finally, we shall focus on the common mechanism of cooptation and domination in the light of China's recent forging of state–market synergy. Careful examination of the various institutional arrangements between the state and private enterprises shows that, while the reform-period Chinese state has actively promoted the development of the private sector, it has been equally active in bringing this sector under its strategy of domination and protection. A common pattern of state–private relations is that when an enterprise is small and without any political and social significance, the state can leave it alone and even foster its growth, but once it grows to a certain designated size and begins to have fiscal weight and even political significance, the state will come to establish a nexus between itself and the enterprise in order to dominate private capital.

SOURCES OF PRIVATE ENTREPRENEURSHIP IN THE CONTEMPORARY ERA

As discussed in earlier chapters, private merchants have always been a significant class in the history of Chinese market economy, though they occupied only a low ranking in the Confucian ideal social order. While they came close to reaching full recognition as elites in the short-lived, late-Qing *Xinzheng* reforms, private entrepreneurs began to suffer state encroachment amid wars and the rise of the party-state in the mid-twentieth century. The nadir for their social status came during early Communist rule, as the economy was nationalized, demarketized, and demonetized. Nevertheless, even in the Maoist era, private enterprise did not die away. It survived under every possible guise. In the agricultural sector, the household private plot was pervasive but before and after the Great Leap Forward (GLF) as a supplement to collective farm economy. Urban private entrepreneurs disappeared briefly between the 1950s and the late 1970s, but underground markets and private household economies continued to operate during the high tide of the GLF and the Cultural Revolution.[2] Meanwhile, numerous commune and brigade enterprises (CBEs) emerged as semiautonomous economic entities

[2] Kelle Tsai, *Capitalism without Democracy: The Private Sector in Contemporary China* (Ithaca, NY: Cornell University Press, 2007), pp. 46–48.

specializing in agricultural machinery and other intermediate industrial products in response to the strategy of decentralization and self-reliance in the latter half of the Cultural Revolution, prefiguring the marketization of the 1980s.[3]

It was not until the Chinese Communist Party took the initiative to endorse rebellious peasants of the Xiaogang Village in Anhui province, who signed a secret avowal to divide up the public land into private household plots, that the real changes began to take place. Since then the household responsibility system (HRS) has been recognized and even promoted as the norm of rural economic organization. Initially started by farmers merely seeking a subsistence level of living, the HRS spreads into other sectors of the economy. Under this new system, while the rural collectives still owned the land, the households were given freedom to make use of the land and other resources and sell their produce in the market, after having met the state fiscal requirements for grain and taxes.[4] Meanwhile, the commune-and-bridge enterprises, recognized as the most productive of all collective enterprises, were likewise promoted as the most desirable rural productive model nationwide.[5] Since the HRS and the CBEs were tiny actors in the popular perception, they were regarded more as supplements to the dominant state sector, where major reforms were carried out to promote efficiency and profitability.[6] Although the new economic organizations were allowed a place in the economy under reform, they were merely supplementary to the state sector and were not actively supported by government policies. This is especially true for the HRS, which was still being carefully watched and circumscribed within certain boundaries in the early 1980s.

The lack of active government support notwithstanding, China's budding nonstate sector developed rapidly in the early 1980s, though it never reached any political prominence. The HRS expanded rapidly into various

---

[3] Wei Zhou, "The Changing Face of Rural Enterprises," *China Perspectives* 50 (2006), p. 22.
[4] The system has undergone several important modifications in the direction of further market liberalization. Today, though only governments and collectives have the right to requisition and sell agricultural land, agricultural households are free to move to the cities and rent their land to tenant farmers, given that they can make a living in the city. Even the household registration system has largely been dismantled, except in major metropolitan areas.
[5] The State Council, "Guanyu fazhan shedui qiye ruogan wenti de guiding" (Policy Circular on Several Problems Regarding the Development of Commune and Brigade Enterprises), July 3, 1979, available at http://fgk.chinalaw.gov.cn/article/xzfg/197907/19790700268333 .shtml
[6] *Ibid.*

models of household businesses. The earliest form of private business was restricted to very humble peddlers, hawkers, caterers, and petty service providers, existing as a supplement to the dominant public sector. Initially, they enjoyed an existence that was at once prosperous, marginal, and uncertain, frequently falling victim to attacks from the ideologically laden party cadres from central to local levels.[7] Until the late 1980s, most of the private businesses were in fact still living under the shadow of the socialist economic system, with their names and capital registered under collective entities.[8] Nevertheless, taken as a sector, the number of household enterprises increased from just 140,000 in 1978 to twelve million in 1986.[9]

Meanwhile, the CBEs also developed quickly, transforming into what are known as town and village enterprises (TVEs) once the rural communes and brigades were abolished. Unlike the old CBEs, the TVEs functioned more like effectively private market actors, with collective ownership interpreted in a loose sense.[10] Throughout the 1980s, the TVEs began to receive massive support from various layers of local government, especially the county and city-level governments, which derived much of their local revenues from their taxes under the new tax contract system in coastal provinces such as Zhejiang. In the mid-1980s, in more developed regions of Zhejiang, the increasingly complex market networks of the TVEs and private enterprises expanded from local and regional to national and global levels.[11]

These emerging economic organizations were at first only complementary to the state sector, operating at a very small scale and supplying intermediate products to larger state firms. But as the new private businesses and TVEs expanded their operations, they soon came into competition with the SOEs and indeed were the more efficient rivals in

---

[7] Yu Lei, *Zhuixun shangye Zhongguo* (A History of Commerce in Contemporary China) (Beijing: CITIC Press, 2009), pp. 25–27.

[8] *Ibid.*, p. 30.

[9] Chen Baorong, *Zhongguo geti jingji* (China's Private Household Economy) (Shanghai: Shanghai Social Science Academy Press, 1990), pp. 1–2.

[10] In many cases, the TVEs and their urban counterparts, the urban collective enterprises, masqueraded as private enterprises. This is an effective strategy to improve productivity without amending the rules. See Wing Thye Woo, "Improving the Performance of Enterprises in Transition Economies," in Wing Thye Woo, Stephen Parker, and Jeffrey Sachs, eds., *Economies in Transition: Comparing Asia and Eastern Europe* (Cambridge, MA: MIT Press, 1997), pp. 315–316.

[11] Sheng Shihao and Zheng Yanwei, *Zhejiang xianxiang: Chanye jiqun yu quyu jingji fazhan* (The Zhejiang Phenomenon: Industrial Clustering and Regional Economic Development) (Beijing: Tsinghai University Press, 2004), pp. 210–211.

many sectors.[12] To protect the state sector from competition, the Chinese government practiced the dual-track system in which private businesses had to pay higher prices for their materials in the input market but also sell at higher prices in the goods market.

The game-changing moment came during the Fourteenth Party Congress in 1992, as the Communist Party officially endorsed the new direction of reforms revealed in Deng Xiaoping's Southern Tour (*Nanxun*, in Chinese) early that year.[13] This Congress was a landmark moment for the nonstate economy in general and the private economy in particular, as the party formally guaranteed the ideological legitimacy of the private economy and the party's commitment to systemic reform of the economy. This new kind of economic system was called the socialist market economy, meaning that the market was enshrined formally into the new economy under the socialist party-state. The foundation of China's political system began to shift from the ideological legitimacy of Communism to an interests-based social order as the ideological faction lost its hold in the long-drawn-out political struggles that had been occurring since the death of Mao.[14]

An equally important factor was China's changing strategic position in the world in the post-Soviet era, as discussed in Chapter 4. With the collapse of the Soviet Union, for the first time in one hundred years, China no longer faced a direct threat from any major regional power. The military situation had direct political – and, subsequently, indirect socioeconomic – implications for China's reform and liberalization, allowing China's relations with the region to reorient toward economic regionalism. The collapse of the Cold War order and its ramifications in Asia removed the last obstacle between China and the establishment of formal diplomatic relations with key regional players such as South Korea and Singapore, as well as entry to key regional organizations such as APEC, alongside two other Greater China economic entities (Taiwan and Hong Kong). By cooperating with ASEAN to make APEC a purely economic institution,

---

[12] Jean Oi, *Rural China Takes Off* (Berkeley, CA: University of California Press, 1999), pp. 14–15.

[13] For an analysis of the impact of Deng's *Nanxun* on the Chinese economy, see John Wong, *The Political Economy of Deng's Nanxun: Breakthrough in China's Reform and Development* (Singapore and London: World Scientific, 2014).

[14] Zheng Yongnian, "Ideological Decline, the Rise of an Interest-Based Social Order, and the Demise of Communism in China," in John Wong and Zheng Yongnian, eds., *The Nanxun Legacy and China's Development in the Post-Deng Era* (London and Singapore: World Scientific/Singapore University Press, 2001), pp. 173–195.

China would make the APEC a framework for its key interest in trade cooperation but conditioned liberalization.[15]

In the 1992 guideline for economic reforms, the central government continued to regard the invigorated SOEs as the main pillar of the socialist market economy. But in the years that followed, the Chinese government found it increasingly difficult to maintain this vision even with the dual-track system in place. Moreover, the problem-ridden dual-track system had become a major source of inefficiency, corruption, and rent-seeking. In 1995, 44 percent of SOEs were loss-making, while the pretax profit rate had fallen to 16.4 percent from 35.9 percent in 1980.[16] In other words, the SOEs had changed from cash cow to major governmental burden, thanks to new market competition coming mainly from the private sector. In 1997, under the new premier, Zhu Rongji, it was decided that sweeping reforms were to be carried out in the SOE sector over the following three years. Between 1997 and 2000, during the high tide of *zhuada fangxiao* (grasping the large and letting go the small) reform, the total number of SOEs in the manufacturing industry declined from 300,000 to 60,000.[17]

The SOE reform in the 1990s was the defining moment in China's economic reform as well as the turning point for its private sector. The impacts were threefold. First, the privatization of the SOEs directly gave rise to several new kinds of enterprise, which were either fully private firms or shareholding companies under *de facto* private control. Many of the largest private enterprises in this period either directly emerged from this process, or grew from the cheap assets acquired in the process. Second, the SOEs' retreat in most manufacturing and service sectors, including almost the whole spectrum of light industry and a large share of heavy industry, provided a large space for private businesses that was soon filled by various kinds of private capital.[18]

The SOE reform in the 1990s opened the floodgate for the *Xiahai* (literally, jumping into the sea of business) movement, as hundreds of

---

[15] Kai He, *Institutional Balancing in Asia-Pacific: Economic Interdependence and China's Rise* (Abingdon and New York, NY: Routledge, 2009), pp. 32–34.

[16] Lin Yifu, Cai Fang, and Zhou Li, *State-Owned Enterprise Reform in China* (Hong Kong: Chinese University Press, 2001), pp. 65–66.

[17] The National Bureau of Statistics Online Database.

[18] We shall discuss the resultant sectorial distribution of state capital in Chapter 8. For now, it is sufficient to say that the state still retains control over the upper-stream sectors that require key factors of production such as land, natural resources, credit, and nationwide infrastructure.

thousands of former elites – including government officials, researchers in the state system, managers in the SOEs, and some public figures – joined the grassroots *parvenu* to become private entrepreneurs. With the rise of new opportunities, the old state system increasingly looked hopeless to the young and ambitious insiders who were inspired by the first generation of private entrepreneurs. They dared to make their move only because they could mobilize informal resources in the state system, such as political connections, technological know-how, and a variety of exceptional policies that made land and state assets cheap for their use.

Lastly, the reform also induced a gradual but profound change in the relations between government and private businesses. Although this was an indirect effect, it has proved to be the most consequential of all three. The loss of many locally managed SOEs and their substitution by private business meant that local governments needed to form new kinds of partnerships with large private businesses. Moreover, the coupling of fiscal and SOE reforms unleashed a structural transformation in the character of local government, from administrative unit to economic actor. As economic actors, local governments sometimes need to find agents in the market to complete their transactions. Some private enterprises, especially real estate firms and other large enterprises, become the agents of local states. In other words, some parts of the private sector effectively form a part of the *middle ground* with the local corporate state.

The reform of the mid-1990s changed the structure of the SOE sector. From 1994 to 2000, most small and medium SOEs which were incompetent and unprofitable were privatized. Privatization took many forms but generally followed two models: management buyout and shareholding reforms. In the first scenario, the old SOE management acquired a certain share of state assets at a discounted rate before proceeding to downsize the labor force and restructure corporate organization, while the state remained a nominal owner. In the second scenario, private entrepreneurs acquired state assets through mergers and acquisitions and the old SOEs became part of a new and enlarged private enterprise. As in the first model, the private entrepreneurs who buy state assets at a discounted rate take on the responsibility for running the old state firm. In both cases, the state often maintains a less than controlling share in the new shareholding firms. In fact, the shareholding reforms affected the corporate structures of most SOEs. Most remaining SOEs that are still under state control are effectively shareholding firms with the state maintaining the controlling share. Here, we focus on the case of private firms created through this reform, namely, the large private enterprises created through private acquisition of state assets.

The SOE reform had yet another important influence on the Chinese government's attitude toward private enterprises, as the expanded private sector took on a new level of political significance. In the first half of the 1980s, even as reform had moved into the urban areas, the state sector still employed 75–80 percent of urban labor and provided fringe welfare for millions of urban households.[19] In the SOE reform of the 1990s, massive layoffs of SOE workers became the norm, as small and medium SOEs could be privatized and shed of their laborers and larger SOEs were made more and more capital-intensive and concentrated in a few selected sectors. As a result, labor-intensive private enterprises, especially in the service sector, were encouraged by the government as a means for reemployment. From 1998 to 2002, it was estimated that 70 percent of laid-off workers from the SOEs found reemployment in the non-state sector.[20] The thrust to create more employment also came from China's huge internal migration, as rural migrant workers moved to the cities in their millions in search of more lucrative employment. In the reform era, the private enterprises inherited wholesale the socialist state sector's function as primary job provider. As employment was the primary pillar of social stability, which was regarded as a top priority for the Chinese government, it became an inbuilt incentive for local governments at all levels to promote the development of private economy.

Another important unintended consequence of the reform of the mid-1990s was the decline of the TVEs. The TVEs were champions of reform and development in the 1980s and continued to prosper in the early 1990s. In 1995, the TVEs constituted almost 40 percent of China's national industrial output.[21] But as reform deepened through the mid- to late 1990s, the TVE sector began to contract in terms of both economic performance and relative weight in the Chinese economy. As the overall productivity of both SOEs and private enterprises improved dramatically during China's SOE reform, the TVEs' productivity growth appeared to have fallen behind. Part of the disadvantage for the TVEs lay in their blurred ownership structure in the light of the enterprise reforms. When the state sector was dominant, this

---

[19] Zhou Xueguang, *State and Life Chance in China: Redistribution and Stratification, 1949–1994* (Cambridge and New York, NY: Cambridge University Press, 1999), p. 42.

[20] Huang Mengfu, *Zhongguo minying jingji fazhan xingshi baogao 2005* (China Private Economy Development Trend Report 2005) (Beijing: China Social Sciences Press, 2006).

[21] National Bureau of Statistics Online Database.

ambiguity had been an advantage, but once the private economy gained full legality and became the norm in most economic sectors, the opposite became true. As a result, the ownership reforms were similarly carried out in the TVEs sector. As the enterprise reform continued, the private character of the TVEs also became established: most of them, like the SOEs, were privatized to become joint-stock companies.

The process of privatization was not conducted in an environment of probusiness legal and regulatory institutions. Laws and regulations were set out in favor of the waning public sector. As a result, the newly incorporated private enterprises often found themselves deeply embedded in the old legal and regulatory framework of public sector enterprises, not to mention the informal networks between the management and government officials, from the very beginning. For one thing, an institutional connection with the party-state still mattered for a company's success and survival, as the newly defined limited liability company and joint-stock company remained embedded within the party-state structure of control. The law, which was originally designed to restructure the problem-stricken SOEs and TVEs, retained some important dimensions of older versions, such as specific requirements for party cells, a Worker's Union and labor commit-tee, and the company's legal responsibility to abide by the Constitution of the Chinese Communist Party for enterprises above a designated scale.[22]

The new millennium saw a new age of private enterprise development. The key engines of reform were the country's further marketization, as post-WTO China integrated more deeply with the world market, and foreign systems of technology, including both imported and indigenous innovations. Both the postreform SOEs and the private enterprises were the beneficiaries of the new changes. Interestingly, among China's largest private enterprises today, some have an extensive overseas market while others have benefited most from technology borrowing and innovations, but only a very small number of top private firms have been successful in combining these two advantages. On balance, China's private enterprises have grown significantly and captured a large chunk of both the domestic and world markets in the past two decades, but relatively few have suc-ceeded in establishing brand names and setting the standard in the global market.[23]

---

[22] Victor Nee and Sonja Opper, *Capitalism from Below: Markets and Institutional Change in China* (Cambridge, MA: Harvard University Press, 2012), p. 120.

[23] Huang Mengfu, *Zhongguo minying jingji fazhan xingshi baogao 2012* (China Private Economy Development Trend Report 2005) (Beijing: China Social Sciences Press, 2013).

THE PARTNERSHIP MODEL: PRIVATE ENTERPRISES
AS THE FIRST MOVERS

The Wenzhou Model: Private-Dominated Partnerships

The Wenzhou model is perhaps the best exemplified model of private-public partnership in China. Indeed, Wenzhou, a municipality city with a population of three million, had a presence in every Chinese market town. Known for their knack for small business and their nationwide trade networks, Wenzhou people created thousands of markets all over China. The best known commercial facilities in multistory commercial buildings or shopping streets containing hundreds of small shops or stalls were either owned, invested in, or inspired by Wenzhou businessmen.

The Wenzhou model is unique but universal. It is unique because few of China's economically advanced coastal cities are like Wenzhou. Taken as a whole Wenzhou is perhaps among one of the very few Chinese cities with a commercial cultural value that completely permeates its social structures, political culture, and belief systems.[24] In other words, it is unique in having a superb commercial culture. But wherever the Wenzhou businessmen go, they carry with them their business model and adapt to local conditions. Thus, although there is only one city of Wenzhou, Wenzhou-run markets are found all over China as a universalizing market force. And as the Wenzhou markets penetrate deep into China's inland and even border regions, they diffuse their commercial cultures and, to various degrees, also change the mode of government–business interaction. Thus, it is very important to understand the Wenzhou model and its diffusion.[25]

Though there is no lack of private entrepreneurship in Chinese local cultures, the Wenzhou culture is unique in that it combines perfectly with a probusiness local state. This culture is shaped by both geography and history. Geographically, until the postreform era, Wenzhou was separated

---

[24] A large amount of the Wenzhou "bosses" in post-Mao China have adopted the Christian faith. By deploying a version of depoliticized Christianity, the Wenzhou entrepreneurial Christians imbue their faith with modern entrepreneurial logics akin to the Weberian protestant ethic. See Nanlai Cao, *Constructing China's Jerusalem: Christians, Power, and Place in Contemporary Wenzhou* (Palo Alto, CA: Stanford University Press, 2010), pp. 34–40.

[25] For a discussion of the development of the Wenzhou model in the 1980s, see Yongnian Zheng, *De Facto Federalism in China* (Singapore and London: World Scientific, 2007), pp. 204–210.

from other regions by mountains on three sides and the nonexistence of railways and highways. Historically, Wenzhou had been an important port in regional trade networks with Taiwan and Southeast China. Under these prevailing conditions, the local culture among businessmen and officials was different from that of other commercial centers in China. In Wenzhou, and to a lesser degree in some other places in Zhejiang and Fujian, the local government had always been sympathetic toward private business whenever possible. Even in the harsh years of high Maoism, the Wenzhou government did not implement the radical policy of nationalization, allowing the private capitalists substantial space.[26]

Since the early stages of the reform, private enterprises from Wenzhou have proliferated locally and expanded far and wide. Unlike in other areas, the local state was at the forefront of various liberalization reforms. From 1980 to 1986, under the initiative of the local government, Wenzhou's state-owned financial system was partially replaced by semistate credit associations. Wenzhou was also the first to see a variety of financial innovations such as floating interest rates, private securities, private joint-stock companies, and even a few private banks.[27] Among these Wenzhou institutional innovations was the joint-stock company, later to become a national institution. The Wenzhou government devised such a model of partnership in the early 1980s, primarily to circumvent ideological hurdles on private capital, since the joint-stock companies could be regarded as nominally collective.[28] But its development soon exceeded the wildest speculations. In 1991, the percentage of private enterprises in Wenzhou's total production had reached more than 80 percent, whereas the share of SOEs dwindled to a mere 10 percent.[29] In 1993, Wenzhou boasted 37,000 private joint-stock companies, accounting for 60 percent of its regional gross product. The Wenzhou model became synonymous with a regional market economy run by small and medium-sized private enterprises.

The Wenzhou model is primarily based on family enterprises operating in small businesses, especially in commercial activities. Adaptability and maneuverability are the hallmarks of such enterprises. But the negative side of such an economic organization is its relative small size and lack of competitiveness in core products and technology. As the Wenzhou

---

[26] Shi Jingchuan and Jing Xiangrong, *Zhidu bianqian yu jingji fazhan: Wenzhou moshi yanjiu* (Institutional Change and Economic Development: A Study of Wenzhou Model) (Hangzhou: Zhejiang University Press, 2004), p. 27.

[27] *Ibid.*, pp. 154.   [28] *Ibid.*, pp. 157.   [29] *Ibid.*, pp. 158.

markets expand to every corner of China and even overseas, the market potential for small family products has been exhausted. First, although the Wenzhou companies have explored far and wide on a spatial scale, the economy has not experienced a fundamental upgrade of employment in its commercial companies such as in modern services and manufacturing. Second, since nationwide market expansion seems to have reached a bottleneck in the 2000s, the commercial wealth accumulated over the reform years has increasing difficulty finding useful outlets in the real economy. For the time being, it seems that the only channels for Wenzhou "hot money" lie in real estate and underground banking, as they provide Wenzhou companies with attractive short-term rates of return comparable with the period of rapid commercial expansion. In the first decade of the current century, Wenzhou companies played a prominent role in a few sectors, notably the once privatized, small-scale coal mines in Shanxi, the local underground finance market in Zhejiang, and the huge property boom all over China – and perhaps even in cities worldwide with large pools of Chinese residents. In fact, even the popular perception of Wenzhou businessmen as owners of market facilities has increasingly been replaced by the Wenzhou *Chaofangtuan* (literally, a group of real estate speculators). It seems that the Wenzhou model has reached a dead end in its evolution from private commercial capitalism to speculative financial capitalism.[30]

But where is the Wenzhou government, which has been so successful in propelling the growth of the market? Indeed, it seems that as Wenzhou and many Zhejiang businessmen are increasingly engaging with the factor market, the role of government is also changing, since land, natural resources, and credit are still effectively under the control of the state. For one thing, the government has become a more active intervening force in the market. In 2011, the Wenzhou government forcefully intervened in the underground banking system, which was on the verge of collapse. Wenzhou is also witnessing a changing mode of relations between the market and local state.

The Suzhou Model: Local Developmental State

Situated at the strategic midpoint between Nanjing and the Hangzhou–Shanghai region, Suzhou was a key industrial hub in late imperial China.

---

[30] Xi Wang, *Wenzhou moshi de lishimingyun* (The Historical Destiny of Wenzhou Model) (Beijing: Economic Science Press, 2005), pp. 148–150.

Many of China's best handicraft industries, including the famous imperial textile factories under the Qing Household Department, were in Suzhou and Nanjing. The local culture was known to be probusiness and respectful of commerce and entrepreneurship. But in late Qing and Republican China, the economy of Suzhou was devastated by the Taiping Rebellion and the Sino–Japanese war. Meanwhile, most of its pivotal economic roles had been taken over by the strategically better situated new metropolitan center of Shanghai. In the ensuing Maoist period, Suzhou's development stagnated further, similar to many other traditional commercial cities in the Yangtze River Delta, until the decentralized model of reform again invigorated the local economy, particularly through the locally sponsored, booming TVEs and the SME sector.[31]

Suzhou's economy took a major global turn with the launch of a Singapore–China consortium project, Suzhou Industrial Park (SIP), agreed on by top members of leadership in China and Singapore in 1994. Based on the Singapore development model, the park developed into a leading industrial and technological manufacturing center and a flagship national economic zone in China. It was able to attract as many as 15,000 firms from China and around the world, including cutting-edge high-tech enterprises in the fields of nanotechnology and biomedicine. In 2012, SIP achieved a GDP of over 200 billion RMB, with per capita GDP similar to Singapore and Hong Kong levels.[32] Over the past few decades, more and more Chinese cities have based their local development models on the experiences of SIP.

Once SIP had matured, the Suzhou government initiated another project which largely adapted the same model of development, by investing heavily in infrastructure, setting up preferential tax policies, introducing streamlined business services, and establishing special agencies to manage day-to-day operations in the park.[33] In these special zones, the government, now designated as the management committee, functions as an autonomous management unit apart from the state hierarchy, with its political and social duties largely minimized and subsumed under economic management. Under this special institutional arrangement, the old problem of

---

[31] For a longer discussion of the early development of the Suzhou model from the view of central–local relations, see Zheng, *De Facto Federalism in China*, pp. 145–151.

[32] "Suzhou gongyeyuan yuyu jinnian jiben shixian xiandaihua" (Suzhou Industrial Park Aims to Realize Modernization), *China Industrial Daily*, December 1, 2012.

[33] Alexius A. Pereira, *State Collaboration and Development Strategies: The Case of the China Singapore Suzhou Industrial Park (1992–2002)* (London: Routledge, 2003), p. 67.

state intervention and domination is minimized. The SIP management is well aware that its performance and survival in the cadre's evaluation system critically depends on the performance and survival of the enterprises in the market it serves. Most of those involved are private, foreign, or jointly owned firms in the technological manufacturing sector with an orientation to the overseas market. The local government thus becomes a probusiness provider of public services.

The Suzhou model has wide implications for China's special economic zones, becoming a paragon of the local developmental state. Although China used to have hundreds of industrial parks in the early 1990s, most of them were generally hastily assembled and poorly managed; SIP, however, is an exceptional case. It was built in full accordance with Singapore's experiences in the 1970s and 1980s and then replicated the market-oriented model of Singapore within a local Chinese context. This soon spread to other parts of China with similar industrial bases and comparative advantages, as local government officials learned from the experiences of Suzhou. Unlike the Wenzhou model, which universalizes through Wenzhou businessmen and other networks, the Suzhou model spread through official channels of training and promotion. One of these channels is the cadres' promotion and circulation system. From the late 1990s onwards, Suzhou became a breeding ground for high-level officials, as cadres who served in Suzhou were promoted to provincial and ministerial positions nationwide.[34] Meanwhile, Singapore, the origin of the SIP model, has hosted as many as 3,000 Chinese cadres in the last two decades, with 900 cadres receiving training in the mayor's course in the Nanyang Technological University.[35] Today, China has eighty-eight National Economic and Technical Development Zones (NETDZs). Most of these zones have adopted policies such as SIP and other successful examples of similar. After years of growth at exponential rates, these NETDZs together constituted 8.8 percent of China's GDP and 17 percent of national exports in 2011.[36]

---

[34] For example, all seven party secretaries of Suzhou since 1994 have become provincial party bosses or ministers in the State Council. See Wang Jun, "Shenzhang yaolan Suzhou chuguo naxie zhongliangji guanyuan" (Which Heavyweight Officials Came from Suzhou, the Cradle of Governors?), *The Beijing News*, January 14, 2014.

[35] Saw Swee Hock and Ge Yun, "Advancing Education Collaborations between China and Singapore," in Saw Swee Hock and John Wong, eds., *Advancing Sino-Singapore Relations* (Singapore: Institute of Southeast Asian Studies, 2014), p. 274.

[36] "The NETDZ as Engine for Creativity," *People's Daily*, July 5, 2012.

Incubating Technological Enterprises: The State Sponsorship Model

Lenovo and Huawei are perhaps the best known examples in this category. Founded in late 1984, Lenovo was not the first of all of China's technological firms, nor was it the boldest. Its founder, Liu Chuanzhi, a researcher in the Computer Science Institute of the Chinese Academy of Sciences, opted not to sever the company's ties with the mother organization and to operate the business under the aegis of the publicly funded national research institute. Under this arrangement, the newly founded technological enterprise could utilize both the resources of the old SOE system and the policy opportunities offered by central and local governments for new enterprises.[37] Later, Liu would benefit immensely from his experiences at and connections with the Chinese Academy of Sciences.

Huawei's meteoric rise from tiny sales agent for a Hong Kong electrical equipment maker to world-class producer of telecommunication equipment shares a similar storyline. The founder, Ren Zhengfei, was a Communist Party member and ex-People's Liberation Army (PLA) officer working in an engineering department. The chairwoman, Sun Yafang, and many other members of the top management team also have experience of work in government agencies and research institutes. Although there is no clear evidence that Ren utilized his government and army connections at the beginning of his career, it was the case that his contractors in the late 1990s included Hong Kong companies connected with the PLA. Such close alliances with the government, the army, and the Communist Party aroused alarm in the United States, as a Congress special report on national security issues surrounding Huawei's attempted takeover of Three Leaves indicated.[38]

Both Lenovo and Huawei enjoy favorable treatment from local governments and state agencies, and have grown fast since their early years. China Academy of Sciences and the Haidian district government provided the necessary ground for Lenovo's growth: The former provides start-up resources for a host of firms, including Lenovo, whereas the latter ensures Zhongguancun district's institutional environment is favorable

---

[37] Ling Zhijun, *The Lenovo Affair: The Growth of China's Computer Giant and Its Takeover of the IBM-PC*, translated by Martha Avery (Singapore: Wiley, 2005), pp. 32–33.

[38] Mike Rogers and Dutch Ruppersberger, *Investigation Report on National Security Issues Posed by Chinese Telecommunication Companies Huawei and ZTE*, a report by Chairman Mike Rogers and Ranking Member C. A. Dutch Ruppersberger of the Permanent Select Committee on Intelligence, Washington, DC, October 2012.

for technological entrepreneurship. For Huawei, the Shenzhen government and the army proved very helpful both in the start-up years and in the company's mature stage. The Shenzhen Special Region (SSR) in particular has created many policy exceptions designed especially for technological firms. Unlike some other localities, the Shenzhen government sought from the outset to minimize regulatory obstacles so that firms could thrive and offer technological firms the best terms, while making a sustained effort to keep its hands off the market.[39]

Under the state-sponsor model, no matter who the actual sponsor is, the entrepreneur and their management team are the real actors; the state agencies or local governments merely provide the breeding ground for development of the enterprise. Unlike in the developmental state model, the state's role in the sponsorship model is a special relationship not restricted to physical and institutional infrastructure, but also includes active support in terms of personnel, finance, and other resources. In other words, it requires a higher level of state involvement and the cultivation of business–government relationships.

As China has moved into the twenty-first century, competition between different localities – especially the more developed regions – has intensified. As a result, local government has become increasingly willing to offer a helping hand to successful private entrepreneurship that brings economic growth, higher tax income, and brand names to a locality. This state sponsorship is more evident in the case of latecomers to the game of growth. The privately owned car manufacturer BYD ("Build Your Dream") is a case in point.

The rise of independent automobile makers such as BYD and Geely is an interesting new development in the sponsorship model in the new millennium. It involves coproduction of private entrepreneurship and state developmental policy against the backdrop of supply network globalization and China's expanding automobile market. Over the past few decades, the global automobile industry, like many other manufacturing industries, has moved toward a model in which major manufacturers only control key technology and the supply chain while outsourcing the manufacturing of subsystems to global network of suppliers.[40] The shift in the global model of auto production has provided enormous opportunities

---

[39] "Weihe Shenzhen nengchu Huawei tengxun" (Why Shenzhen Can Breed Huawei and Tencent), *Changjiang Daily*, March 25, 2013.

[40] Crystal Chang, "The Emergence of the Independent Chinese Auto Industry," available on Globaltrade.net, pp. 17–18.

for China's private startups, who have a disadvantage in terms of technology and capital but a competitive edge in terms of adaptability and maneuverability.

BYD was founded as a rechargeable battery factory in 1995, and its subsidiary BYD Auto Company came about only in 2002. But by 2010, BYD had emerged as the sixth largest car maker in China measured by units sold. This phenomenal success is due in large measure to its successful meshing with national and local development programs. Its key product series – mass-produced hybrid and electrically powered vehicles – came just in time to hit the national industrial upgrading target for clean energy and automobile industry development. This was a novel stance in a country where even the market for traditionally powered cars is only just beginning to mature, and where it is easy to make fast money from cheaply assembled cars. Unlike many more traditional manufacturing firms, the newly established BYD was unswerving in taking risks to ensure it would lead the new market. In seeking to achieve its goal, the company developed close cooperative connections with the Shenzhen government. In 2010, its flagship product, F3DM, became eligible for national and Shenzhen government purchase subsidies up to 40 percent of the vehicle price. In 2010, the company was enlisted by the Shenzhen government to build the first batch of electrical vehicle charging stations under a joint effort with Southern Grid to promote electrical cars.[41] In 2011, BYD electrical cars served as official taxis and buses for the 2011 Summer Universiade at Shenzhen. At the forefront of electrical car-making, BYD won a large share in a new round of government procurement programs in 2013, which ostensibly favored electrical cars over traditional petrol-powered vehicles.[42] Meanwhile, the company made significant inroads into the European market for environmentally friendly electric buses and set up a major production and development center in Hungary in 2017, with a view to competing with Volkswagen, Renault-Nissan, and General Motors for the European market.[43]

A Shenzhen-based company, BYD has two R&D centers – in Shenzhen and Shanghai, respectively – with two production bases in Xi'an and one

[41] "Biyadi Xiongxin yijiu" (BYD: Ambition Unabated), *New Century Magazine*, November 29, 2010.

[42] "Biyadi: yidiandongche mingyi cong minjian kaixiang zhengfu" (BYD: In the Name of Electrical Cars, the Private Players that Drive into the Government), *Time Weekly*, July 24, 2013.

[43] Cecily Liu, "Electric Bus Pioneer Pulls into Wider European Market," *China Daily (Europe)*, December 14, 2016.

forthcoming in Changsha. During the construction of its plants in Xi'an High-tech Zone, the Xi'an government not only granted cheap land but also helped to build infrastructure such as roads, plants, mixer stations, accommodation, and other facilities. The local county government was in such a rush to expropriate land and build the infrastructure that it broke legal procedures and limits on land use set by the central government, and was later fined by the Ministry of Land and Natural Resources.[44] But such intervention seemed to be minor and temporary with regard to BYD's continued expansion in domestic and global markets.

In a sense, state sponsorship is an upgraded version of the local development model. Under this system, the state, at both the local and central levels, formally or informally establishes a platform to support domestic big business in both the domestic and the overseas market. For Huawei, ZTE, Lenovo, and BYD, this support is in terms of direct financial and policy preferences.

China's Internet Giants and the Chinese State

As a special case of successful large domestic privately owned firms (unlike the centrally managed SOEs), China's Internet industry has become a focus point of discussion worldwide. Ever since its initiation, China's Internet has been as well known for its Great Firewalls and tight government censorship as for its rapid development.[45] These two factors have an interesting unintended consequence, namely, the proliferation of indigenous Internet giants across a broad area of business, from online chatting to *weibo* (microblogs), and from e-commerce to online gaming.

Due to concerns about political security, in the Internet sector, unlike in other nonstate sectors, the government has maintained a policy of creating an independent Chinese market, apart from the world market. America-based global giants such as Facebook, Google, Apple, and Amazon are either blocked from or have restricted access to the mainland Chinese market. The market space was quickly taken over by Chinese substitutes such as Renren and Baidu. In other cases, world leaders such as eBay have

---

[44] "Difang zhengfu touzi xinqie, biyadi xi'an xiangmu weigui zao guotubu duban" (Local Government Haste to Investment Cause Ministry of Land and Natural Resources Penalty), *First Finance News*, July 6, 2010.

[45] Yongnian Zheng, *Technological Empowerment: The Internet, State, and Society in China* (Stanford, CA: Stanford University Press, 2008).

been unable to compete effectively with indigenous giants such as Alibaba, Dangdang, and 360 Buy.

Alibaba is China's dominant e-commerce company. Starting late in 2003, it was far behind the global e-commerce company eBay, which had already started its journey in the China market by this time. But by 2012, Alibaba had beaten all its competitors – including eBay – and become a global giant in e-commerce: Its revenues exceeded that of eBay and Amazon combined. According to a BDA study, Taobao, Alibaba's main e-commerce platform, was able to make full use of the market size in China through a "volume to value" strategy by building up traffic and basing its revenue model on advertising, as compared with eBay's strategy of collecting service fees from sellers.[46] More recently, Alibaba has branched out into China's lucrative and sometimes prohibitive banking and financial sectors and secured state approval for an online bank after a record-setting IPO on the New York Stock Exchange in September 2014.[47]

Compared with Alibaba, the success of Baidu, by far China's largest search engine, has as much to do with market strategy as it does with the state's Internet shield. Both Baidu and Google started in the early 2000s and operated with the same business strategies, though Baidu created an initial advantage by employing unmarked advertisements and enabling MP3 searches.[48] But the real key difference was state security concerns over sensitive content. As a domestic firm, Baidu had little option but to cooperate actively with the government's stringent system of internal self-censorship.[49] Google, meanwhile, is widely believed to have opted out of the market after falling out with the Chinese authorities over Internet censorship.[50] Baidu remains a local but not a global giant; Google continues to lead in the overall global market and is the winning party in this market given its combined advantages of superior technology and a global market strategy.[51]

---

[46] BDA China, "Taobao: China's E-Commerce Revolution: An Overview of China's Dynamic E-Commerce Sector," *BDA China Analyst Note*, January 11, 2010.

[47] www.reuters.com/article/2015/05/27/us-alibaba-bank-idUSKBN0OC0SI20150527 [Accessed on May 29, 2015].

[48] Sherman So and J. Christopher Westland, *Red Wired: China's Internet Revolution* (London and Singapore: Marshall Cavendish, 2010) pp. 46–48.

[49] Xiao Qiang, "Baidu's Internal Monitoring and Censorship Document Leaked," *China Digital Times*, April 30, 2009, available at http://chinadigitaltimes.net/2009/04/baidus-internal-monitoring-and-censorship-document-leaked/ [Accessed on March 15, 2015].

[50] *Apple Daily*, "Saying No to Authoritarians: Google Shifts to Hong Kong," March 24, 2010.

[51] *Bloomberg News*, "A Tale of Two Search Engines: Why Google Is Winning, Baidu Isn't," April 30, 2013.

The Weibo case is even more interesting. Sina Weibo – China's foremost microblogging platform, with some 300 million subscribed users – quickly caught the eye of the central government's Internet management agency. As Weibo became the least controlled and most prevalent source of public information, including political rumors, the government stepped up its already close monitoring of all the leading service providers. To survive the censorship system, Sina Weibo routinely conducted self-censorship while at the same time allowing some leakage of not-so-sensitive information within a given time frame, in order to attract greater attention.[52]

It is fair to say that Alibaba, Sina Weibo, and other Internet giants have not received as much fiscal, financial, and other forms of support from the Chinese government as Huawei, ZTE, and Lenovo have. But they received the most important support of all: They operate in the single largest market, created by Chinese government policy to keep political influences from the outside world off the Internet platform, whereas Huawei, ZTE, Lenovo, and BYD must compete with foreign firms in the products market. In this sense, the Internet firms belong to a special class of state-sponsored enterprises in which concerns for state security and business profits have found convergence in the coopted form of market domination.

This special feature of the Internet sector is partly a result of its departure from the traditional infrastructure. In the traditional sectors of infrastructure, the state could simply dominate by dint of the centrally managed SOEs and state ownership of natural resources and infrastructure. In the Internet industry, since technology and data content rather than infrastructure hold the key to market share, such ownership is inconceivable. In fact, the *People's Daily* and the Xinhua News Agency both experimented with state-owned search engines, but so far have made few inroads into the domestic market. *People's Search*, later renamed *Immediate Search* – a flagship project of the *People's Daily* led by the world tennis champion Deng Yaping – merged with Panguson of the Xinhua News Agency in 2013, after the team failed to achieve its initial objectives.[53] But the newly consolidated state search engine remains less competitive than its private challengers. As of July 2017, private search engines occupied more than 99 percent of the Chinese market.[54] Even with a

[52] Zhang Xiaoling, *Transformation in Political Communication in China* (London: Routledge, 2010), pp. 113–114.
[53] Yan Qiang, "Deng Yaping's Jike Xiaoshi" (Deng Yaping's *Immediate Search* Disappear?), *Financial Times* (Chinese edition), November 17, 2013.
[54] According to the StatCounter, Baidu retains an unshakable lead in the market (77.4 percent), followed by Haoso (8.1 percent), Shenma (7.5 percent), Sogou (3.7 percent), and

market open to both domestic state and private players, the pivotal role of the first-mover private Internet giants such as Baidu has remained unshaken, at least for the time being.

For the Internet giants, the most significant political support provided is the state's national information and security policies, which exclude some foreign competitors and make others operate in a more costly policy environment. Some of these Internet giants are able to trade information control for more policy support. But still, the monopolistic or oligopolistic Internet businesses are much less dependent on the state than SOEs such as Sinopec or State Grid and state-sponsored firms such as Lenovo and ZTE. They enjoy a degree of autonomy, thanks to their large scope of operation and a growing Chinese cyberspace. In some cases, political elites such as the "princelings" or "red capitalists" must depend on them to generate extraordinary wealth, as in the case of Alibaba's IPO.[55] This degree of freedom provided by information technology and China's peculiar institutional arrangement sets the Internet giants apart from most other private big businesses.

THE STATE AGENCY MODEL: THE STATE AS THE DOMINANT ACTOR

The Interest Alliance: The Real Estate Model

The real estate sector's rise to the pinnacle of China's economic development model is an unintended outcome of China's tax-sharing reform in 1994. As we will discuss in more detail in Chapter 7 with regard to central–local fiscal relations and local government as corporate actors, the tax-sharing reform makes all local governments dependent on extrabudgetary and extratax revenues. For those local governments bent on speedy economic development, the best and quickest source of revenue is land transfer receipt. As urban land is state-owned and controlled by the local government, any transfer of land to commercial use requires an open bidding process and an exorbitant usage-right transfer payment to the local government by the successful bidder. Land transfer receipts thus

---

Google (1.7 percent). Available at: http://gs.statcounter.com/search-engine-market-share/all/china [Accessed on August 15, 2017].

[55] According to the *New York Times*, Alibaba's shareholders included investment banks and venture capital companies run by sons and grandsons of China's top leaders. See Michael Forsythe, "Alibaba IPO Could Be Bonanza for the Scions of Chinese Leaders," *New York Times*, July 20, 2014.

became an important source of local development funds as China's urbanization moved into full bloom. In the period 1994–2001, land transfer payments were a negligible part of local revenue. Within a decade, they skyrocketed to a staggering 3.15 trillion RMB, accounting for 50 percent of local government revenue in 2011.[56]

The key vehicle for this land-based local fiscal regime is real estate development sponsored by local governments. Thanks to China's rapid economic development and urbanization in the last two decades, there is huge demand for commercial and family housing and ample room for increased housing prices. After paying the huge land receipts, real estate developers could impute the land costs into housing prices. The real estate boom provides local government revenue. The interest alliance between local government and real estate developers becomes perhaps the most closely knit business–local alliance among all the business sectors in the country.

One of the better known examples of this alliance is that between Shanghai tycoon Zhou Zhengyi and top officials in Shanghai in the early 2000s. Zhou was a real estate tycoon and chairman of Shanghai Real Estate, listed on the Hong Kong Stock Exchange. Through his connections with Shanghai officials, he secured the rights to develop several extremely valuable pieces of land in the Jing'an District of Shanghai as part of the Shanghai urban renewal program in 2001. Zhou, working with the district government, turned an originally not-for-profit urban renewal project into a development of a lucrative commercial district, while keeping the evicted residents in the dark. Realizing their loss, the evicted households protested. Some of the most obstinate residents, led by the committed Shen Ting, turned to the court and even created and signed petitions.[57] Meanwhile, Zhou Zhengyi was eventually investigated and arrested due to increasingly vocal protests from traditional and online media.[58] Zhou's fall initially had little to do with the eviction and land development projects, but was rather related to the changing central–local power dynamics. Hu Jintao and Wen Jiabao came to power in 2002, when Zhou's real estate business was at its height. As the new general sectary consolidated power, he was finally

---

[56] Ministry of Land and Natural Resource, *China National Land and Natural Resource Report 2011* (Beijing: Ministry of Land and Natural Resource, January 2012); National Bureau of Statistics, *China Statistical Yearbook 2012* (Beijing: China Statistical Publishing House, 2012).

[57] Qin Shao, *Shanghai Gone: Domicile and Defiance in a Chinese Megacity*, (Lanham, MD: Rowman & Littlefield, 2013), pp. 151–154.

[58] Zheng, *Technological Empowerment*, pp. 128–130.

prepared to face off with some of the disobedient local leaders. Chief among these was the former Shanghai party boss, Chen Liangyu. Zhou's dubious business conduct and his connections with Chen's team placed him on the roll of suspects in a high-level, high-profile anticorruption campaign in 2006. It was quickly found that Zhou was involved in other aspects of financial misconduct, including forging invoices, bribery, embezzlement of public company funds, and providing false information. He ended up with a sixteen-year sentence.

As well as the changing political environment, Zhou's failure was in part attributed to his highly risky strategies during his meteoric rise, and his unruly style. In this sense, Zhou may rank as an outlier rather than the norm. In fact, China's most powerful contemporary real estate tycoons are typically from well-off or well-connected families. Contrary to Zhou, they climb the ladder of wealth only gradually and cultivate a wide net of politically significant connections. Wang Jianlin, China's richest man according to the Hurun List of May 2015, is an exemplary figure in this category.

The son of a Long March veteran, Wang joined the PLA at an early age and rose to vice-regiment rank officer before starting a real estate business in the late 1980s. Building on his personal networks in the army and riding the wave of China's property boom, Wang quickly established his Wanda Group as one of the leading developers in Liaoning. By 2014, the Wanda Group had become the country's leading real estate and on-site entertainment service provider.

While Wang's relations with Bo Xilai, long-time party boss at Dalian and then governor of Liaoning, have been subject to debate,[59] he surely cultivated a network of close relations with several local and central political leaders. According to a *New York Times* report, his Wanda Group includes investors who are very powerful figures in China's top decision-making organ, the Political Bureau.[60] Although there is uncertainty regarding the degree to which the political elites shared the interests of the Wanda Group, an informal alliance with the political elite has visibly protected the Wanda Group from political risks. Wang was remarkably

---

[59] Due to the contemporaneity between the rise of Wang's business empire and that of Bo's political fortunes in Dalian and Liaoning, it is speculated that the two men have close relations. But Wang has denied any connection with Bo other than purely business dealings. See Mei Jingya, "China's Richest Man Denies Connections with Bo Xilai," *Sina English*, available at http://english.sina.com/china/2013/0911/627766.html

[60] Michael Forsythe, "Wang Jianlin, a Billionaire at the Intersection of Business and Power in China," *New York Times*, April 28, 2015.

frank about engagement with the Communist state in the following straightforward remarks in an interview with foreign journalists:

China is a government-oriented economy. No one can say he can run his business entirely without government connections. Anybody who says that he or she can do things alone with any connection with the government in China is a hypocrite . . . But you cannot hook up with government officials too closely. Don't ally your personal interests with the development of the company.[61]

It is evident that the real estate developers critically depend on local government and officials to support their business interests. The degree of closeness is proportional to the economic return and political risks. This business model can be further demonstrated in the case of Zeng Chengjie, a much less illustrious but equally significant case alliance between a developer and local government. Zeng was the boss of a leading real estate company in a mid-sized city, Jishou, in Hunan Province. In 2003, he was awarded a contract to construct amenities such as sports centers, arts centers, and a library on behalf of the Xiangxi government. As the local government was unable to fund the projects, Zeng was granted the right to explore "private channels of social finance," which literally meant illegal fundraising through the promise of high-interest returns. After some initial success, Zeng expanded the scale of private funding based on a Ponzi scheme, but was unable to keep up with exorbitant interest repayments. The finance scheme eventually collapsed, causing great public outcry and social instability.

Meanwhile, as the term of local leadership ended, the new local leadership took control, immediately retracted its support for so-called private social finance, and named the practice illegal. Zeng was thus arrested, tried, and – based on the huge social impact of the Ponzi scheme – sentenced to the death penalty, with all his personal assets to be confiscated. Most crucially, his total assets, which were supposedly enough to repay the principle and interest of the funds raised, were valued by the court at just one-third of their actual value. The unconventional and hasty execution of Zeng again attracted wide criticism from netizens, especially among business elites and legal practitioners. But local people appeared to be overwhelmingly supportive of the court ruling, due to the overwhelming financial and social impacts of Zeng's Ponzi scheme.[62]

---

[61] Malcolm Moore, "The Rise of Wang Jianlin, China's Richest Man," *Daily Telegraph*, September 21, 2013.

[62] Zhang Ying, "Zeng Chengjie: Shengqian sihou" (Zeng Chengjie: Before and After a Death), *Observer Weekly*, July 22, 2013.

Compared with national-level property tycoons such as Zhou Zhengyi, Zeng Chengjie's case is even more illustrative of the asymmetrical nature of the alliance between local government and real estate developers, since developers always need a measure of exemption from laws and regulations to realize extraordinary profits. Safety in such transgressions is only available with political protection. As Zeng's case shows, developers are invariably at the mercy of opportunistic government policies once the game of allowable exceptions exceeds the level of controllable risk and becomes a major threat to social stability. Zeng's case is extreme in that it involves the collective action of thousands, if not tens of thousands, of residents. But it is indeed only when the hidden actors – the people – appear on the stage that the game reveals its more principled rules. The interest alliance of local government and private businesses is only operational insofar as the transaction costs are mainly economic. Once political causes set in, the game changes its operational rules. Just like political figures, developers with the highest and widest political connections are not only more successful but also much safer. But even in that case, this is a political safety built on personal relationships, rather than legal safety based on the rule of law.[63]

This rule of the game does not apply just to the real estate sector; it is also relevant to all private–public economic cooperative projects with state assets such as land, natural resources, and SOE assets in play. The Tonghua Steel Plant Incident is a case in point. On July 24, 2009, thousands of workers – in open defiance of the local government's decision to privatize their factory, and in fear of losing their jobs during the privatization process – staged fierce protests, ransacked the factory office, and killed a corporate executive. The provincial leadership promptly nullified the privatization deal and ensured the protection of workers' interests.[64] In this case, the state had little choice but to give up its avowed protection of property rights in favor of local stability as the workers threatened more radical political action. This was, arguably, a necessary sacrifice to make the stakeholders – namely, the ordinary workers – more peaceful and content, just as Zeng had to be sacrificed to satisfy the demands of many residents who made unwise investments. In this case as in Zeng's, the political calculus of the state triumphed over law. In a world without the rule of law and political

[63] Even as Wang Jianlin emerged unscathed from the Bo Xilai case, Xu Ming, another Dalian tycoon, joined the ranks of "tycoon-felons" accused of economic crimes. See David Barboza, "China Boss's Fall Puts Focus on a Business Ally," *New York Times*, August 21, 2013.

[64] Yang Ling, "Tonggang shijian beiju beihou" (Behind the Tonghua Steel Plant Incident), *Observer Weekly*, September 10, 2009.

accountability, the local government might easily sacrifice its junior partners once the major stakes of political and social stability are in play.

Local Developmental State Derailed: The Wuxi Suntech Power Experiment

The Suzhou model involves the local developmental state and central planners as the actors. In the Suzhou model, the developmental state is market-oriented, whereas in the Pudong model, a state plan is central. This is because industrial policy is always associated with the central plan and there is no local industrial policy to begin with. But in recent years, there has been a silent devolution of industrial policy from central to local governments, as ambitious local governments take on large-scale industrial initiatives in the name of national industrial development. Among the local developmental states, there is a trend to use flagship enterprises as the platform for local industrial policy. Most of these flagship enterprises are SOEs and even centrally owned enterprises. But in some rare cases, private enterprises can play this role as well. When local private enterprises play the flagship in a local industrial initiative in the name of national industrial policy, a new model emerges.

This new model sets out a new relationship between the government and the private enterprise. Under the new model, the local government devotes its full resources to the support of one private entrepreneurial firm and develops a strongly semiotic relationship with this locally based but globally oriented enterprise. The local government not only provides all necessary start-up resources, including capital and land, but also helps along the way to meet the private enterprises' demands in order to secure a swift expansion. Meanwhile, it also makes demands on the enterprises to make sure they comply with its vital interests. The enterprises also develop a complicated relationship with the government: cooperative and high-profile in securing the necessary public resources, heedful and low-profile in finding out every possible strategy to keep its autonomy. In consequence, this model couples the state's mobilization capacity and developmental ambitions with the enterprise's acquisitiveness and thirst for wealth.

The Wuxi Suntech Power experiment is perhaps the classic example in this newly emerged model of state-driven private expansion.[65] The

---

[65] We only outline the Suntech case for analytical purposes. For a good overview of Wuxi Suntech in English, see Charlie Zhu and Bill Powell, "Special Report: The Rise and Fall of China's Sun King," *Reuters*, May 18, 2013.

relatively young Wuxi Suntech Power Electrics, founded by Shi Zhengde in 2001, emerged as a world-class manufacturer of solar panels in the space of only a few years. Suntech's success story was inseparable from that of the Wuxi government's generous support. When Shi, an Australia-trained young solar energy specialist, returned to his home province of Jiangsu in search of a market, his vision of a cutting-edge clean energy enterprise met with the Wuxi government's equally ambitious plan for industrial development. To support the adventure, the Wuxi SASAC invested USD6 million as starting capital in 2001. In 2004, Suntech Power entered a stage of explosive growth and extraordinary profitability; in 2005, the Wuxi government exited and the company was registered as Suntech Power Group in the British Virgin Islands, in order to be listed as a fully fledged private enterprise in the global capital markets. Soon enough, Suntech Power was successfully listed on the NYSE, the first in a line of large Chinese enterprises. In 2007, at the zenith of its expansion, Suntech Power became the world's leading producers of solar panels; its revenues reached a staggering USD1.4 billion, up from USD200 million in 2005.[66] As it rose to global prominence, Suntech became the calling card of the booming Wuxi industrial economy.

But the global financial crisis cast a dark shadow over Suntech Power and China's solar panel industry. Ironically, the decline and fall of Suntech Power could be directly attributed to its extraordinary success. In the haste to save China's rate of economic growth, the central government gave special warrants to local governments to massively invest in the so-called strategic industries, which naturally included the photovoltaic industry. Indeed, the photovoltaic industry was for some years the focus of local government investment. From 2008 to 2011, the number of China's photovoltaic firms increased from less than 100 to 400.[67] Meanwhile, as the market expanded accordingly, the price of polycrystalline silicon, the key intermediary product for solar panels, plummeted from USD150 per kilo in 2006 to about USD35 per kilo in late 2011.[68] Suntech's overexpansive strategies and lack of financial hindsight also took their toll. In the boom days, Suntech set up the European Global Solar Fund and financed Asia Silicon, an upstream producer. These projects proved to be

[66] Qiao Liu, *Corporate China 2.0: The Great Shake Up* (New York, NY: Palgrave Macmillan, 2016), pp. 93–95.
[67] "Zhongguo zaisheng nengyuan luzaihefang" (Whither China's Renewable Energy Industry), *China Energy Daily*, August 8, 2013.
[68] "Duojingui jiage tiaoshui chongji zhongguo qiye" (The Price Jump in Polycrystalline Silicon Moves Chinese Enterprises to Cease Production), *People's Daily*, July 23, 2012.

unsustainable and unreliable once the global financial crisis struck, and immediately damaged Suntech's credit with banks and in the financial markets.[69] In March 2013, burdened by unsustainable debts and misguided investments, Wuxi Suntech officially declared insolvency, its market value having fallen from USD4.9 billion to 149 million.[70]

Wuxi Suntech Power is one of the most prominent cases among China's hundreds of solar-panel producers. Most other large players in the solar energy sector have developed similar relationships with local governments and likewise have thrived on state policies of cheap capital and land, and other financial and administrative support. In this model, although the private enterprise is the actor on the stage, the main source of growth is local government. The enterprise discussed here not only managed to survive for several years but also once captured 70 percent of the global market share, despite ever decreasing profit margins resulting from internal competition. But once the external market is no longer viable, the demand collapses. The solar energy sector, once acclaimed as the prime example of China's industrial upgrade, has fallen into a deep crisis. Overcapacitated, making huge losses, and verging on bankruptcy, the solar energy industry has proven to be a failure for China's industrial policy.

The conundrum of Wuxi Suntech and its sponsor, the Wuxi government, was a miniature version of the problems facing China's more aggressive local development strategy since the global financial crisis. In 2009, when China's economy was struck by a huge slump in export, the government resolved to pump in trillions of investment in support of ten strategic sectors. At the subnational level, provincial and local governments were encouraged to develop the so-called sunrise high-tech industries. The Jiangsu government hand-picked three such sectors: clean energy, biotechnology, and shipbuilding. In due course, flagship enterprises – including Wuxi Suntec and the Rongsheng Heavy Industry Group, China's largest privately owned shipbuilding company – experienced exponential growth in assets and production scale, with heavy local government support. Unable to bear the financial costs of the huge investment in these projects, local governments resorted to a variety of sources of finance, such as bank

---

[69] Alfred Marcus, *Innovation in Sustainability* (Cambridge: Cambridge University Press, 2015), pp. 96–97.
[70] http://english.caijing.com.cn/2013-03-21/112610390.html [Accessed on August 13, 2017].

loans, land sales, and public trusts. In some severely stricken counties in Wuxi, local governments even retained the salaries and benefits of civil servants.[71] According to a Shenzhen-based trust, Jiangsu governments accounted for 30 percent of all investment trusts sold in China by the end of 2012. The Wuxi government alone raised RMB92 billion in this way.[72] As the debt crisis unfolded, Jiangsu's experiment in the years after the global financial crisis would inevitably pose a serious threat to China's financial stability.

The Wuxi Suntech project showcases a new development in the relationships between local states and private enterprises, in which local politics of developmental and global market forces fueled each other on the road to overexpansion and excess capacity. Rather than being an exception to the rule, the Suntech case perhaps exemplified hundreds of such projects ongoing in post-global financial crisis China. On the surface, this new relation between private enterprises and local governments looks like state sponsorship. But in fact, the local government has far surpassed the role of a genuine local sponsor. In the Suntech case, the Wuxi government not only provides a huge amount of investment and large tracts of land, but it becomes the effective coactor as well, making Suntech the flagship project in its own grand design to become the photovoltaic production center for the world. With the full support of the Wuxi government, the Suntech project acquired the advantages of the state-led growth model at the very beginning and gradually conquered a large share of the world market with state sponsorship. Had it acted more rationally, as in the case of the Shenzhen-based BYD, the model might have turned out to be successful. Unfortunately, when the unbridled ambitions of the private entrepreneur met the unbridled ambitions of local officials, the whole project became a reckless effort, driven forward regardless of economic returns based on rational calculations, much like the GLF project in the era of Mao and the brief "foreign leaps" of 1978–1979 under Hua Guofeng, which likewise ran into difficulty when ambitious mobilization plans met with resource bottlenecks.[73]

---

[71] Wang He, Youzou zai hongxian shang de wuxi chengtou (The Wuxi City Investment Co. on the Verge of Bankruptcy), *China Securities Weekly*, June 16, 2012.

[72] Koh Gui Qing, "Is China's Debt Nightmare a Province called Jiangsu?" *Reuters*, July 24, 2013.

[73] Harry Harding, *China's Second Revolution: Reform after Mao* (Washington, DC: The Brookings Institute, 1987), pp. 56–67.

MECHANISMS OF STATE COOPTATION AND DOMINATION

The rise of private entrepreneurs as a major economic and social force is one of the defining changes in contemporary China. As a champion of the reform, the party-state has long reckoned with this change. Since the mid-1990s, the central state has consistently moved in the direction of cooptation. As with the *zhuada fangxiao* principle in the SOE reform, the key factor in membership in the cooptation system is size of assets and scale of production, not matters of political background such as party membership. All entrepreneurs with asset and production levels above a designated size are automatically invited to the cooptation structure. Business success means political privilege, distributed according to the size of the business as a measure of economic power. There is thus a measure and an interpenetration of the coherence of economic power and the accompanied political resources.

The most fundamental step toward this new model of cooptation and domination is a shift in ideological guidelines.[74] From the late 1980s to the 2000s, there was a gradual shift in the party's constitution in the direction of full recognition of the market economy. But the defining moment came only at the Sixteenth Party Congress in late 2002, when the party officially endorsed private entrepreneurs as the representatives of the most productive force in the new guiding theory of *The Three Represents*. Although local governments have long cooperated with local entrepreneurs, the formal system of incorporation only began to be established systemically from 2002.

Unlike large SOEs, large private enterprises, even when they were important players in the national and even international markets, had only indirect institutional links with the state. To date, none of China's most successful and prominent private entrepreneurs have gained seats in China's central decision-making body, the Central Committee of the Communist Party. It was rumored that Liang Wengen, a staunch party member and the chairman of the famed Sany Heavy Industry, was given the opportunity to enter the CCP's Central Committee (CCPCC) as an alternate member at the Eighteenth Party Congress in late 2012. However, he did not enter the CCPCC, possibly due to resistance from hardliners

---

[74] Zheng Yongnian, "Technocratic Leadership, Private Entrepreneurship and Party Transformation," in Zheng Yongnian, *Will China Become Democratic? Elite, Class and Regime Transition* (Singapore: Eastern Universities Press, 2004), pp. 253–281.

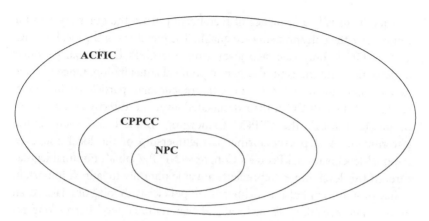

Figure 6.1 The political opportunity structure for private entrepreneurs
Source: Compiled by the authors

and central SOE managers in the party top brass.[75] But still, the mere possibility of a leading private entrepreneur sitting on the party's highest decision-making body is telling evidence of their rising political status at the institutional level.

Based on their absence among the top leadership, it appears that private entrepreneurs are still underrepresented in China's powerful elite circles. This is only half true. While private entrepreneurs never entered the chief party-state organs as their SOE counterparts did, the presence of private entrepreneurs can hardly be underestimated if we take into consideration the wider circles of political consultation, minor parties, and other channels of influence such as the Federation of Industry and Commerce. These organizations constitute a model of cooptation and mutual influence. From the perspective of the central party state, the model could be conceived as four concentric circles (Figure 6.1). In the outermost layer is the All-China Federation of Industry and Commerce (ACFIC), a functional constituency of the Chinese People's Political Consultative Conference (CPPCC). As of late 2016 the ACFIC had 4.7 million members, mostly China's private entrepreneurs with businesses above a designated scale.[76] Once within this range, the private entrepreneurs could communicate with various government departments through a special channel.

---

[75] "First Tycoon in CCP Elite Ranks?" *The Straits Times*, August 8, 2012.
[76] www.acfic.org.cn/zzjg_327/nsjg/hyb/hybsjgk/201704/t20170424_3664.html [Accessed on April 14, 2018].

There is usually a sequence of membership from the outer layer to the center once the entrepreneurs are qualified as members of the local ACFIC. The ACFIC is only one step away from the CPPCC, the party's outer organization and the central organ of political consultation. Once selected as a member of the CPPCC, an entrepreneur may participate in annual sessions of the CPPCC at their designated level and directly launch policy proposals, through the CPPCC framework, to local and even central government. A step even further is membership of the local and even national-level National People's Congress (NPC), China's nominal legislature. At this level, the entrepreneurs are able not only to launch important policy proposals but also to deliberate on policies with local officials. At an even higher level, there is the local and even national-level Party Congress of the CCP, which is the nominal seat of power for the party.

It must be remembered that there is a vertical dimension in this concentric structure – a ladder from the county all the way to the national level. Like the promotion of officials, there is also a merit-based selection procedure for the private entrepreneurs – whom the party purportedly represent as one of the Three Represents – to the center of power. Mostly, the entrepreneurs are weighted primarily by their economic might, social influence, and political loyalties when they are considered for vertical promotion. Only the most fortunate hundred or so elite businessmen, who own politically significant businesses and wield extensive market power, are admitted to the CPPCC, NPC, and Party Congress at the national level. But, considering the size of China, the political opportunities at lower levels are still immense. According to a survey by the ACFIC, about 51 percent of private entrepreneurs had served on the CPPCC and the NPC, mostly at the county and city levels.[77] Perhaps more importantly, the political opportunities for private entrepreneurs have expanded extremely quickly in the past decade. For example, the chances of a private entrepreneur becoming a delegate at county or city level expanded three- and tenfold, respectively, during the past decade.[78]

Within the four-layered structure of cooptation, party membership is key to moving from the outer-layered ACFIC and CPPCC to the inner structure of the NPC and CCPCC. Both the CCP and the rich private entrepreneurs are motivated to move further into this inner layer. For the CCP, this means better control and cooptation of the richest individuals

---

[77] "Zhongguo qiyejia congzheng sanbuqu" (The Trilogy of China's Private Entrepreneurs' March to Politics), available at http://biz.jrj.com.cn/2013/07/31092815609828.shtml
[78] *Ibid.*

and the most active entrepreneurial forces in the society. For the entrepreneurs, this means better protection of their wealth and access to better business opportunities. This holds especially true for those entrepreneurs who come from the grassroots, and can only acquire political resources when they meet the wealth threshold.

Party building in the private sector expanded significantly during the past decade. A survey in 2012 indicated that about one-third of all private entrepreneurs were party members at that time. Of the rest who were not party members, 40 percent showed an interest in party membership. About 60 percent of all private enterprises above a designated size hosted party cells. It has also been found that chances of party membership increase as the overall assets of an enterprise increase. An entrepreneur owning more than RMB100 million in assets has a 53.6 percent likelihood of being a party member. If membership of all eight allied parties is included, nearly all these politically weighty entrepreneurs are coopted into the second layer.[79] Finally, there is the NPC and the CCPCC, convened in Beijing each spring, which offer seats to elites at various levels and sectors of society. In 2015, the NPC and CCPCC plenary sessions included 201 of China's 1,271 richest people. Though they only constituted 4 percent of the Congress, they boasted a combined net worth of USD464 billion and their average worth of USD1.2 billion dwarfed the richest of American legislators.[80]

While the Party has already coopted most of China's private business elites through extensive outlying organizational networks, new strategies are already implemented to cope with the second-generation rich and prepare for their cooptation in advance. In Jiangsu and Zhejiang, where private capital dominates much of the local economy, the provincial party schools have launched programs to train the second-generation rich. Apart from the clear purpose of keeping private capital within the party, the training program also serves to broaden their horizons and strengthen state–business synergy.[81]

At the heart of the new relation between private enterprises and the party-state is the private enterprise's fiscal responsibility as an engine of economic growth and tax contributor, and social responsibility to provide

[79] Chinese Academy of Social Sciences, *China Society Bluebook* (Beijing: Social Sciences Academic Press, 2013), p. 146.
[80] Michael Forsythe, "Billionaire Legislators Ensure the Rich are Represented in China's Legislature," *The New York Times*, March 2, 2015.
[81] "Fuerdai jin dangxiao peixun: wei shulian zhangwo woneiwai zhengshanghuanjing" (Party School Training Second Generation Rich: To Master Business-Government Environment in China and Abroad), *Shidai Zhoubao*, September 19, 2013.

employment and basic welfare. These two basic conditions have long established the implicit terms of exchange between the state and private enterprises. Given that private enterprises deliver the services in the implicit contract, the state must provide political backing and other institutional support for private entrepreneurs. Thus, there is even a measure of tacit protection for those large private entrepreneurs who are outside the grasp of the state's organizational tentacles, provided that they deliver jobs, tax revenue, and economic growth.

Political and economic cooptation of entrepreneurs has also met with institutional limitations. At the macro level, exchange relations between the state and private enterprises have a shaping influence on the behavior of the party-state and especially local governments. As dual actors on economic and political stages, local governments sometimes become more like economic actors entangled with the private interests of the enterprises under their jurisdiction, even as they pursue a probusiness developmental strategy. This leads to an oversupply of fiscal and economic benefits for the big private enterprises and an undersupply of public goods for the wider public, especially ordinary workers and residents. These problems have given rise to sporadic, massive social protests across China, with issues such as labor and land dispute as the leading causes.[82] While the anticorruption campaigns under the current leadership have yielded significant improvements, they cannot resolve the underlying structural issue. The result is sometimes a sacrifce of local intensive and economic growth: As the probusiness developmental state and corruption are sometimes intertwined, anticorruption campaigns have made local officials reluctant to take risks and approve new projects.[83] Eventually, the dilemma boils down to managing the size and the order of the middle ground. As long as the middle ground exists in a world of state-dominated market networks, there must be a balance between size and order.

At the everyday level, market–state exchanges are carried out by agents from the state and business sectors, namely, local officials and private entrepreneurs. And this relationship can only be institutionalized to a certain level, because the officials – as representatives of the interests of the state – always have the incentive to enhance their own interests. Gradually, just as private entrepreneurship becomes the norm for private

---

[82] Yanqi Tong and Shaohua Lei, *Social Protest in Contemporary China, 2003–2010* (New York, NY and London: Routledge, 2014).

[83] Bruce Dickens, *Dictator's Dilemma: The Chinese Communist Party's Strategy for Survival* (New York, NY: Oxford University Press, 2016), pp. 92–93.

business, corruption becomes the norm for officials directly dealing with local government's interest-sharing with private enterprises. However, as private entrepreneurs move up the hierarchy of increasingly state-dominated market networks, they gradually face institutional quandaries in the current configuration of the political economy, since the state still controls the factor markets – including land, natural resources, credit, and most nationwide infrastructural sectors, such as power, transportation, and telecommunications. The basic condition for cooptation is that private enterprises operate in proscribed sectors of the economy and stay clear of the boundaries. Once the private entrepreneurs cross the red line into forbidden areas, even with state support, this becomes dangerous, since the boundaries are fluid and subject to change. This was most vividly demonstrated by the Zhejiang entrepreneurs who invested in Shanxi coal mines. Initially, they were literally invited by the local officials to take over the small collective and state mines on government mining permits. But when the local governments, backed by new central policy directives, forcefully entered the market to renationalize the small and medium-sized mines, those private entrepreneurs were often not paid adequate compensation. For most private entrepreneurs, the change of fortune was immediate once the central government changed gear.[84]

Again, the bigger private entrepreneurs are not entirely powerless vis-à-vis state actors if they grow into *de facto* national and global market actors, especially vis-à-vis local governments, whose power is circumscribed by their jurisdictions. In this case, they often have a socioeconomic constituency to bargain with state agencies. The state, weighing the pros and cons of its interventionist policies, often opts for partial rather than total domination of the market. Thus, a deal becomes possible between the two parties. Taobao or Alibaba's recent tug-of-war with the State Administration of Industry and Commerce (SAIC) was a case in point.

On January 23, 2015, the SAIC released a white paper claiming that 62 percent of the products sold on Taobao, China's largest online commerce platform and a subsidiary of Alibaba Group, are counterfeits, causing Alibaba's NYSE share price to plummet. Instead of capitulating or publicly apologizing, as is more commonly the case, Alibaba's first reaction was to publish through its official Weibo an impassioned, informal open letter, crying foul regarding the SAIC's selective policing. For a week, open exchanges of fire between China's global e-commerce giant and

---

[84] Xu Lingling, "Wenzhou meilaoban de mingyun" (Fate of the Wenzhou Mine Bosses), *The Southern People Weekly*, November 24, 2009.

the state agency led to heated debates in cyberspace, without any further action taken by the SAIC. According to a Sina survey, 48 percent of Chinese netizens supported Taobao while 41 percent backed SAIC's crackdown. Before long, both the white paper and the open letter disappeared from the government's and Taobao's official websites.[85]

Given the opaqueness of the system, what transpired behind the scenes in this week of high tension will always remain a mystery to outsiders. But it is highly possible that Taobao and the SAIC reached a deal which was coordinated by a more powerful arbitrator in a political way. For China's larger private enterprises, this is a clear indication that the state has lost some political ground to some market players in an age of marketization and digitization. The playing field of the market-in-state has become more level for the most powerful enterprises, with high economic and political stakes and even a potential online constituency. In future, the state is likely to be more cautious in wielding its administrative powers vis-à-vis more powerful market players. And even in this case, the SAIC refrained from releasing its report – which had already been circulated internally in early 2014 – ostensibly in anticipation of the Alibaba IPO, which carried as much political as economic significance. This is certainly positive news for the big market players, but is not unambiguously so for the entire system, since such backdoor deals between the powerful state and market players would neither lead to better rule of law nor benefit the shared interests of consumers.

Given all these elaborate arrangements of shared interests and cooptation between the state and private enterprises, do the private entrepreneurs become equal or lesser partners in the management of the economy? The answer is negative. Beside the newly established nexus of cooptation, a larger framework of economic management and control still conditions the nexus of shared interests and sets limits on private enterprise. This part of the system is in fact more fundamental than the cooptation mechanisms. We need to take a historical perspective to get the gist of the system, since much of the dominance we see is a continuation of the earlier mobilization economy.

From 1949 to 1956, the nascent Communist party-state built a structure of cooptation and domination between the party-state and private business. In the process, its dominance was increasingly strengthened and

---

[85] "Taobao dazhan gongshang zongju, ni zhichishei?" (Taobao vs. SAIC: Which Side Do You Support?) *Shanghai Guancha* (Shanghai Observer), available at: http://web.shobserver.com/news/detail?id=3515 [Accessed on May 29, 2014].

cooptation gradually waned as the party-state consolidated its grip on the economy and society. For three decades, domination had been the norm. Since the mid-1990s, there has been a sea change in Chinese government policy toward private enterprises. Today, it is widely felt that there is an effective structure of cooptation between the central state, the local state, and private businesses at all levels. Moreover, direct state suppression of private entrepreneurs has become extremely rare, except for sporadic crackdowns on underground banking and illegal fundraising, and the "red experiments" in Chongqing under Bo Xilai. It seems at first that private entrepreneurs' social and political statuses have recovered to much of their pre-1949 level. But this observation does not stand under careful examination.

First, despite all these changes, the structure of dominance has not declined significantly. On the contrary, it has only become more institutionalized and entrenched in the form of the powerful centrally managed SOEs and the new financial system. The most lucrative sectors, such as energy, power, natural resources, civil aviation, railways, and especially finance and banking, are still under the tight grip of the central state. The SOEs' use of land and credit is still heavily subsidized by the state. An administrative birdcage is still in place for the private enterprises, no matter their size and scale.

Second, the power and prestige of private enterprises and private entrepreneurs are still derived from state support, and sometimes political support from high officials. As the real estate sector demonstrates, the looser the alliance between private enterprises on the one hand and local government and officials on the other, the higher are the political risks for enterprises. The risk is asymmetrically high for entrepreneurs because they will be the first to be punished by the legal system once the political dynamics work in such a way that it is necessary to sacrifice the alliance.

Third, the rise of private enterprises cannot be fully understood independently of the critical changes in the market-in-state system in the reform of the late 1990s. During this fundamental shift, there was a collapse of the absolute political–ideological divide of the private and the public across the government, SOEs, and private enterprises. Replacing the public–private dichotomy is a vertical distinction along the lines of size and scale, in terms of assets, profits, output, and GDP, which set the new standard for the distribution of power and wealth in both the economic and the political domains.

Under the new arrangement, a private entrepreneur with a large enough business can even trump local cadres and leaders in terms of actual political influence. In the new politics of economy measured by the size and scale of resources and output involved, big businesses have managed to find a place just next to large SOEs, whose size and scale are backed by monopoly. Although their institutionalized power may still lag far behind that of top SOE leaders, top private business leaders have the edge in terms of autonomy since they are not as dependent on the party-state for rank and benefits.

Finally, as in other countries, family members of powerful national political elites are often allied with powerful national economic interests in various covert arrangements through ownership of stock or venture capital. In either form, they are typically latecomers who traded power and protection for dry shares when a promising business prepared a stock market listing. The Alibaba and Wanda cases are only the tip of the iceberg. Without necessarily holding controlling shares or sitting on the boards of elite enterprise groups, Chinese political elites are nevertheless able to reap substantial benefits from the cream of burgeoning private capital while offering a degree of protection and assurance to the country's wealthiest business tycoons.

As discussed in the early conceptual chapters, the merging of private and public gives rise to the middle ground, which spans from SOEs and local government to politically significant private businesses. The big business elites, through their formal status in the ACFIC, the CPPCC, the NPC, and even Party Congress and their informal networks with central and local government officials, have become part of the powerful elites as well as middle-ground actors between market and state. This is most clearly demonstrated in the state agent model, especially in the real estate sector, where the invisible hand of the state drives industrial development and entrepreneurial expansions from behind the scenes.

Unlike centrally managed SOEs, big businesses' commercial interests are more closely aligned with the fiscal interests of the local state. Thus, they are naturally less privileged than large centrally managed SOEs even if we discount the political and institutional links between SOEs and the party-state. On the other hand, since private big businesses are subject to less political control from the party-state, they also tend to have more space for adaptation and maneuvering in the market economy. As research on SOEs by the Unirule Institute demonstrated, private enterprises above a designated size perform better than SOEs. In addition, private businesses tend to develop a genuine symbiosis with the local state if they serve the latter's long-run fiscal and economic interests. In the rare case that they are empowered with some degree of freedom in terms of technology and market size, private businesses can even develop some form of symbiosis with the party-state as well.

CONCLUSION

Under China's prevailing political economic order, private entrepreneurs are generally pure economic animals with muffled political ambitions. In this they are almost the mirror image of the country's political elites, who seldom hold substantial wealth. Even though the economic powers of the state and the political values of the market are often shared and negotiated at agencies such as the CCPA and the NPC, political power is not accessible to business elites. For the top class of the business elites who hold political capital, such capital is valuable only insofar as it serves as an instrument for economic benefit and political protection. Indeed, except for village elections, there are few channels for China's private entrepreneurs to access leadership positions at any level of the party-state. But this lack of formal channels of political power has not caused any serious problems so far, as the private entrepreneurs are not typically pro-political reform, especially in the direction of Western-style multiparty democracy.[86]

This unique arrangement certainly enjoys some advantages over earlier models of state–market relations in Republican and Maoist China. Compared with an uncertain future of political mobilization and social disorder, the current system of cooptation does serve the interests of private entrepreneurs, and especially big businesses – so much so that they feel they have a major stake in social and political stability. But no matter what the future course of events, most entrepreneurs have a profound sense of foreboding about future political instability. This is indicated by the high propensity of China's rich entrepreneurs who choose to emigrate or hold foreign passports.[87]

Indeed, as middle-ground actors with the most extensive economic and social capital outside the direct reach of the state, the entrepreneurs might have realized the structural tension in a system which accrues all economic benefits to the middle ground at the expense of the general social interest. Whether this current system of cooptation and domination continues to work is critically dependent on stability at the bottom, where ordinary social members can currently still eke out a living. If social violence and

---

[86] Chen Jie and Bruce J. Dickenson, *Allies of the State: China's Private Entrepreneurs and Democratic Change* (Cambridge, MA: Harvard University Press, 2010), pp. 2–3.
[87] Rachel Wang, "Why China's Rich Want to Leave," *The New Atlantic*, April 11, 2013.

disorder set in, however, the axis of domination–cooptation between the state and private entrepreneurs will no longer be sustained. As the cases of Zhou Zhengyi, Zeng Chengjie, and the Tonghua Steel Plant Incident – as well as many others – have demonstrated, the alliance is still an alliance of convenience rather than one of commitment. When such an alliance ruptures, private enterprises tend to be the sacrifice used by the state to restore a less entrepreneurial but more stable order.

Given all the political risks involved, the highest prize for those economically productive but inherently fragile arrangements between the state and private capital is preferential policies and potential profits without the need to abide by the prevailing laws and regulations.[88] In the MIS system, the interests of powerful private entrepreneurs are often not simply the private interests of the capitalists, but shared special interests of political and economic elites at various levels of the market–state nexus. They are often competitors in the making and unmaking of rules. Thus, the cooptations between state and private entrepreneurs, either in covert or overt forms, present an exception to the rule, or a special arrangement in many cases. Like other actors in the middle ground, private capital has led to rapid growth of market and state power, but less development of rules or institutionalization of the market economy.

---

[88] In fact, in the state-dominated market economy, the concept of "policy" (*zhengce*) is often equivalent to making an exception to the prevailing laws and regulations. The state provision of policy to the private enterprises thus simply means "preferential treatment" or "special license."

7

The Money Regimes

Fiscal and Monetary Reforms and Their Limits

One of the most profound changes in China's economy and society since reform has been the expansion of the money supply and monetization of society. This is most evident in historical comparison with the Maoist era. For three decades under Maoist rule, the role of money in Chinese society was marginalized both at the macro level of national economic management and in micro-level daily economic exchanges. At the height of the Cultural Revolution, demonetization was at such a stage that the People's Bank of China (PBOC), China's nominal monetary authority, was just a small accounting unit under the Ministry of Finance. However, within a mere three decades of reform, the PBOC emerged as one of the most powerful central banks of the world in terms of asset holdings.[1]

This rise of money in contemporary China has been accompanied by a series of sweeping institutional changes and innovations at both central and local levels of the party-state. At the heart of these changes is the transformation of the PBOC from an accounting unit of the Ministry of Finance to a complex central bank entrusted with the important task of macroeconomic management, much in the same light as central banks all over the world. Meanwhile, a number of state-owned and privately owned financial institutions have been created, forming a pyramidal structure from the large state-owned national commercial banks, through privately owned regional banks, to the smallest, local underground bankers.

---

[1] In July 2017, the PBOC's assets amounted to USD5.2 trillion, surpassing the Fed (4.4 trillion), European Central Bank (4.9 trillion), and Bank of Japan (4.5 trillion), based mostly in foreign reserve. See Edward Yardeni and Mali Quantana, "Global Economic Briefing: Central Bank Balance Sheets," *Yardeni Research*, August 21, 2007.

While the financial system is being carved out and differentiated from the fiscal system of the old planned economy, a parallel shift can be observed in the postreform fiscal system itself, describing a tortuous trajectory from centralization to decentralization and then back to drastic recentralization and *de facto* decentralization. This latest move is the local response to fiscal centralization in the form of a myriad of fiscal and financial innovations. Financial interests of the centrally managed state-owned banks, the fiscally thirsty local governments, and various powerful private actors, including millions of small private investors, are constantly negotiating with one another for power and profits.

This chapter examines how a new fiscal and monetary system is constantly evolving away from a planned system and into a complex array of actors straddling financial markets and the fiscal state. We shall focus on the tug-of-war among key players in the financial market, namely, the PBOC, the state-owned banks controlled by agents of the central state, the local governments run by developmentally minded entrepreneurial officials, and larger private market actors in the financial market, acting either on their own or jointly with the local governments. They operate in the murky middle ground, akin to the situation discussed in Chapter 6. The rules are made or unmade not merely through the process of legislation but also through struggles on the ground. As in the enterprise reform, the boundaries between the market and the state are defined by local and private means to mobilize public resources as well as by central capacity in limiting and shaping their actions.

As our analytic narrative and case studies of the reform shall demonstrate, this process of monetization and financialization is not simply a story of central initiative and local response, or vice versa. Rather, through a series of fiscal and financial innovations, local and private interests have become just as much of a shaping force in the fiscal and financial system as the central state. In particular, local governments, which are supposed to be agents of the central authority, have become powerful corporate actors in their own right, in the same way as the centrally managed SOEs that will be discussed in Chapter 8, even as the center consolidated its overall power through selective fiscal and monetary centralization. Although local governments have no legal right to create money and are in control of only limited fiscal resources, they have devised a fiscal–financial regime based on land and nature resources that proves to be more energetic and more reckless than those put in place by the central fiscal and financial agencies. As in previous chapters, here we shall examine the process by which various political–economic hybrids are created in the middle ground between the state and market.

MONETIZATION: REFORMS AND STRUCTURAL CHANGES

The Early Communist System of Money

As discussed in Chapters 3 and 4 on the history of Chinese political economy, the Song and Yuan states operated the world's first state-backed paper money system between the eleventh and fourteenth centuries, before the Ming state abandoned paper money in the early fifteenth century and institutionalized a *de facto* silver standard in the late sixteenth century, establishing a bimetallic standard that continued in operation until the first half of the twentieth century. The new national paper money, *fabi*, established first by the Koumintang (KMT) government in 1935, only had a life span of about thirteen years and was replaced by another, even more short-lived currency, the Gold Yuan, in 1948. Between the late 1940s and early 1950s, silver coin and foreign currencies again served briefly as an effective media of transaction. The third form of national paper money, *Renminbi* (RMB), literally "the people's dollar" – which was established by the Communist regime in late 1948 – proved to be longer-lasting than its predecessors. Under the state-dominated economy, the RMB's value vis-à-vis essential commodities remained relatively intact despite the political and economic upheavals of the mid-century, and remained stable until reform began in 1978.[2]

The remarkable stability of the new currency was testimony to the nature of state control of the economy under the Maoist-era mobilizational system. Unlike all former political regimes, the Communist state was able to secure control of the livelihoods of the entire population through a nationwide system of control over all key factors of production, including land, natural resources, infrastructure, and credit, either as their legal owner or as their only supplier, since the day it took power. In the first three decades of the People's Republic of China, the state also controlled all key commodities, such as food, cloth, steel, and cement, among other essential goods and industrial inputs. The strength of state control is attested by the issue of grain stock during the Great Leap Forward (1958–1962), during which millions perished despite huge stockpiles of grain destined for repayment of Soviet debts. Based on this system of extensive control, the Communist state was able to practice a unique

---

[2] The National Bureau of Statistics, *Xinzhongguo liushinian tongji huibian* (A Collection of Sixty Years' Statistics of People's Republic of China) (Beijing: China Statistical Press, 2010), p. 21.

monetary standard, namely, the commodity standard. As a policy practice, the commodity standard, also known as the material standard, has its origins in wartime mobilizations and monetary stabilizations during the second Sino–Japanese war (1937–1945) and the Chinese Civil War (1945–1949).[3]

As the Communists consolidated and expanded their territorial control, the party-state continued to implement, and even further mobilize, this wartime system during the Cold War. Under the Maoist regime, every *yuan* of RMB in circulation was backed by a basket of goods with equal value, the relative prices of which were of course determined not by market but by planning agencies. To promote industrialization without fomenting social unrest, final industrial outputs were priced at an artificially high level against agricultural products and daily necessities. For the system to work smoothly, consumer goods had to be bought with money as well as equivalent coupons or quotas, which effectively exerted a hard budgetary constraint on households and other organizations. The new fiat money thus became a mere accounting unit for production and consumption. Since household consumption was suppressed to favor industrial investment, money in circulation was only a small and carefully managed sector of the economy. Therefore, it was no wonder that during the Maoist years, the value of the RMB remained remarkably stable.

The legacy of the Communist system of money was multifold. On the positive side, the demonetized economy of planned production and consumption turned out to be a source of huge potential for the post-Mao reform once the institutional and material restraints on household consumption had been loosened. In a matter of a decade, as state control over most commodities loosened and eventually disappeared, domestic commerce revitalized and the coupon system was quickly abolished. For instance, the number of key consumer goods under Ministry of Commerce administration was sixty-five in 1978, twenty-three in 1987, and only fifteen in 1992.[4] Thus the reform began with the gradual dismantling of the old system of control over the production and circulation of commodities. With these changes, the RMB system was no longer dependent on a

---

[3] For example, see Huang Yanjie, "Constructing a National Oikonomia: China's Great Monetary Revolution, 1942–1950," *EAI Working Paper No. 161*, East Asian Institute, National University of Singapore, January 2013.

[4] Wei Liqun, ed., *Shehuizhuyi shichang jingji yu jihua moshi gaige* (The Socialist Market Economy and the Reform of the Planning Economy) (Beijing: Zhongguo jihua chubanshe, 1994), p. 295.

material standard. When the Ministry of Materials, the final remnant of the old system, was abolished in 1993, the transition process was complete.

The negative long-term impact of the system would only become apparent in the later stages of the reform. Among the most important institutional legacies are structural domination of a central party-state and a mobilization approach to money at the local level. As this chapter will demonstrate, the combination of central control and an imperative for economic growth has made local government extremely aggressive in mobilizing local resources for economic growth. Instead of essential goods such as grain and textiles, land and natural resources became the chief sources of locally based economic growth. In the Great Leap Forward, the local party-state demonstrated its capacity to mobilize resources for steel production at the cost of great loss of human lives. The local economic order that emerged since the mid-1990s reform would only enhance this capacity, albeit with much less direct loss of life in the process.

Early Fiscal and Financial Reforms

Until the eve of the economic reform, China's socialist fiscal system remained a highly concentrated system designed to serve the planned economy. Under the old system, there was a common fiscal base for central and local government – namely, the accounting profits of SOEs – which in turn was based on artificially designated high prices for industrial output.[5] A smaller but not insignificant portion of taxes came from artificially low-priced grain and other primary agricultural products from peasants mostly working in collective units. Under the planned system, the Ministry of Finance was responsible for financing economic activities planned by the Central Planning Commission. Since SOEs' profits supplied the main tax base, more industrialized provinces such as Shanghai, Liaoning, and Tianjin had to submit the lion's share of the revenues to the central coffers. For example, Shanghai contributed 14.3 billion of its 16.9 billion to the central coffers, supplying 15 percent of central government revenue.[6] This system allowed the local government little room for maneuver and little incentive for productivity growth.

---

[5] Jinyan Li, *Taxation in the People's Republic of China* (New York, NY: Green Wood, 1991), pp. 13–14.

[6] Zhang Guang, "Zhongguo zhengfujian caizheng guanxi de yanbian," *Journal of Public Administration* (Chinese) 6 (2009), pp. 31–32.

The 1980s saw a major change in the fiscal system. In 1980, the central leadership initiated a fiscal reform characterized by central–local fiscal decentralization. The idea was set out in incentives for the provincial governments to carry out reforms and revitalize the SOEs. A key change in the new system was the creation of separate tax bases for local and central revenues, principally based on the administratively defined centrally (ministerial) and locally managed SOEs. Such measures effectively established the provincial governments as autonomous fiscal actors subject to certain conditions. In addition, a few new locally based tax types were created and designated to the local coffers. However, the new tax base was very insignificant. Within the limited domain of the local tax base, the local governments had some measure of freedom over their own fiscal spending and investment decisions. But overall, the fiscal system was still based on centralized revenue remittance and redistribution.[7]

In 1985, further fiscal reforms were carried out to consolidate initial fiscal decentralizations in the aftermath of the comprehensive reform plan unveiled in 1984. In addition to the central and provincial tax bases that were already clearly demarcated, a shared tax base was carved from business taxes on the nonmonopoly sectors, including foreign-invested or jointly owned enterprises. New measures were taken to ensure that the province as a budgetary unit balanced its budget. Those provinces running a surplus only surrendered a portion of their surplus to the center, whereas those provinces running a deficit can be subsidized from the shared tax base.

In 1987, more drastic reforms were taken to enhance the fiscal incentives for subnational governments to develop their economies. Most provinces established some sort of fiscal contract with the central government. Under the modified system, central and subnational governments established fiscal contracts: Some provinces shared the revenue proportionately with the center, while others split a fixed quota plus a percentage share.[8] In both cases, the subnational units were entitled to a larger share of the yearly increases in fiscal revenues and were responsible for filling more of the gaps. Local governments became the residue claimants and *de facto*

---

[7] Yang Yongzhi and Yang Zhigang, *Zhongguo caizheng zhidu gaige 30 nian* (Thirty Years of China's Fiscal Reform) (Shanghai: Shanghai People's Publishing House, 2007), pp. 78–81.

[8] Lou Jiwei, "The Reform of Intergovernmental Fiscal Relations in China: Lesson Learnt," in The World Bank, *Public Finance in China: Reform and Growth for a Harmonious Society* (Washington, DC: The World Bank, 2009), p. 156.

self-financing fiscal units. After 1988, China entered a five-year period of rapid central fiscal decline, leading to the fiscal reform of 1994.

The central–provincial tax contract also served as a model for subprovincial-level fiscal relations such as province–municipality, munici-pality–county, and county–township fiscal contracts. As contractual rela-tions penetrated the grassroots government, where the market came to assume an increasing role in the 1980s, they became increasingly informal and lax, allowing more impromptu innovations. This created incentives for so-called extrabudgetary revenues. The most significant sources of such extrabudgetary revenues covered nontax levies on and contracted shares in the profits of the TVEs during the booming decade of their development. Given such incentive structures, local corporatism became the norm, as township and village governments invested in promoting and supporting rural industrialization via the TVEs. Meanwhile, the local fiscal arrange-ments also ensured that the local governments could exert full control over the TVEs through institutional channels such as factory management, resource allocation, bureaucratic services, and investment and credit.[9] Many grassroots economies in the 1980s thus conformed to the image of a microscopic market-in-state as local corporatist governments mobilized local economic market forces while controlling their access to key factors of production. This is perhaps the most important upshot of the 1980s reform.

If the fiscal reform was mostly about central–local decentralization, the financial system in the early reform years was characterized as one of a limited financial–fiscal separation and fiscal decentralization. Under a planned system, the financial system was completely absorbed into the fiscal system, with PBOC simply an accounting office in the Ministry of Finance responsible for monetary mobilization and cash flow manage-ment. The financial reform set out to carve an independent state-owned financial system from this fiscal–financial nexus. Things started to change in the late 1970s. In 1979, the PBOC was institutionally separated from the Ministry of Finance to become a nationwide state bank with local branches at all administrative levels, down to the county one. In the next four years, four state-owned commercial banks were established – the Agricultural Bank of China, the Bank of China, the Construction Bank of China, and the Commercial and Industrial Bank of China – to provide loan and credit services in the domains of agriculture, trade, and infrastructure. Until the

---

[9] Jean C. Oi, "Fiscal Reform and the Economic Foundations of Local Corporatism in China," *World Politics* 45:1 (1992), pp. 118–122.

Commercial and Industrial Bank of China was created in 1984, the local branches of the PBOC continued to be the main provider of urban credit and banking services.[10] The PBOC was to remain the major credit provider throughout the early 1990s, until it was designated as the central bank of China and entrusted with macroeconomic policies; major commercial and policy banks then took over all its financial intermediary functions.

Both the fiscal and the financial reforms of the 1980s have served to empower and invigorate local government at the cost of direct central control. As result of fiscal decentralization, local government became very active in expanding its own fiscal base at the cost of the central share, especially since the reform was finalized in 1988. Local governments also became very interventionist and aggressive in its relationships with the local branches of the major state banks and the PBOC. Until the final recentralization in the mid-1990s, the relentless competition for tax bases and profit sources turned local governments against each other through various forms of aggressive local protection.[11] The resultant economic disorder would have an immediate impact on future reforms.

The Fiscal and Financial Reforms of 1994

Compared with the 1980s, China's formal fiscal and financial system today is significantly larger, more centralized, and better equipped, with informal and formal networks on the local and grassroots levels. This contemporary fiscal and financial system can be traced to 1994. It was closely associated with its architect, Zhu Rongji, who was vice executive premier at the time, and a team of technocrats and economists under his aegis. A relentless promoter of economic reform, Zhu Rongji upheld a vision of a strong central state with many macroeconomic capacities as much as he embraced a strong orientation toward market-based economic efficiency.[12] When he first assumed the helm of the reform task force in 1992 as vice executive premier, the Chinese economy was in deep difficulty. Inflation was in double digits, fueled by the investment fever of local governments and worsened by a concurrent weakening of central fiscal capacity. In addition,

---

[10] Nicolas Lardy, *China's Unfinished Economic Revolution* (Washington, DC: The Brookings Institute, 1998), pp. 62–64.

[11] Andrew Wedeman, *From Mao to Market: Rent Seeking, Local Protectionism, and Marketization in China* (New York, NY: Cambridge University Press, 2003), pp. 53–55.

[12] For a narrative of the rise of Zhu Rongji and his reform program, see Zheng Yongnian, *Zhu Rongji xinzheng: Zhongguo gaige de xin moshi* (The New Deal of Zhu Rongji: A New Model of China's Reform) (Singapore: The Global Publishing Co, Inc, 1999).

severe budget and current account deficits threatened the fiscal health of the central state. At the core of the mechanism was malignant competition among local economic actors. Fiscal and financial incentives inherent in decentralized control and the contract system led local governments to war with each other for control of vital marketable resources and levels of productive capacity, but the resultant disorder also facilitated *de facto* marketization and drove national price levels to a new equilibrium.[13]

As discussed in Chapter 5, China's contemporary market system was established in the reform of the mid-1990s. The multifarious reform initiatives that the reformist leadership set up would determine the overall reform agenda for close to twenty years. In January 1994, the central government implemented several reforms aimed at different areas of the economy, all at the same time. The exchange rate reform marked the end of dual-track exchange rates. In its place was a managed float system that allowed the RMB a narrow margin of fluctuation. The *de facto* dollar-pegged exchange rate would remain the standard exchange rate from 1994 until the major exchange rate reform in July 2005. The foreign exchange system also required a great majority of Chinese enterprises to sell their foreign earnings to designated foreign exchange banks; the accounting and management of foreign currency reserves was thus centralized to state banking systems. This system of mandatory settlement was only relaxed in 2003 as the PBOC began to allow enterprises and individuals to buy and sell in the managed exchange market.[14]

As the foreign exchange reform consolidated the central grip on foreign reserves, management of the international trade system was unified nationally and placed under the vertical control of the State Custom Administration. Since the locally fragmented trade system had finally been recentralized, the central government was empowered to start its grand projects of tariff and trade policy readjustment in view of China's full entry into the World Trade Organization (WTO) in December 2001. The foreign trade reform and the institution of a decade-long RMB peg created favorable conditions for the most important tasks of domestic fiscal and financial reform.

The state banking system reform, which began in 1994 and culminated in 1995, marked another decisive step toward a centrally managed financial system. In 1994, three policy banks – the National Development Bank,

---

[13] For a detailed account of the process, see Wedeman, *From Mao to Market*, pp. 241–258.
[14] Xin Li and Dianqing Xu, *From Trade Surplus to Dispute over the Exchange Rates* (Singapore: World Scientific, 2016), p. 149.

China Import-Export Bank, and National Agricultural Development Bank – were set up to take over the policy loan services from the major state commercial banks, separating the banking system into two functionally distinctive subsystems. A parallel project of the financial reform was the central banking reform. Zhu Rongji took it so seriously that he oversaw the entire reform process personally as president of the PBOC (June 1993–June 1995). Toward the end of Zhu's two-year presidency, the PBOC was affirmed as the central bank chiefly responsible for monetary policy authority, or macroeconomic management. By 1995, the central state had assumed control over the financial system.

Most important of all, the tax sharing system was implemented in January 1994 to replace the old system of negotiable contracts between the central and provincial governments. As in the contract system, central and local governments each based their revenue on specific types of taxes, depending on the nature of the economic activities, and drew from a shared portion of national certain taxes. But significant changes were also introduced. Negotiable contracts were abolished to give way to institutionalized tax-sharing. Since 1994, central and local taxes have been administered by the separate and mutually independent bureaucratic agencies of state and local taxation administrations. The new system also made significant changes to the structures and types of tax. A new tax system based on production-based value-added tax (VAT), corporate income tax, and business tax finally replaced the old SOE tax-for-profit system to become the basic taxes, with VAT set as the major tax base. Seeking to enhance central fiscal capacity, 75 percent of VAT went to the central coffers. Under the new system, higher administrative units had the claim to a more institutionalized, stable, and high-quality tax base, leaving the lower levels of local government with a shrinking and less secure tax base.[15] The immediate result of the reform was a reversal of the situation of the 1980s and early 1990s. Central government's share in government revenues leaped from a little more than 20 percent of total revenues in 1994; between 1994 and 2012, at least 50 percent of local tax revenues went to the central coffers (see Figure 7.1).

The reform year of 1994 was indeed a year of momentous change. Over the next few years, for the first time in decades, China would gradually

---

[15] For a detailed account of the well-studied establishment and consequences of the tax-sharing system, see Christine Wong and Richard Bird, "China's Fiscal System: A Work in Progress," in Loren Brandt and Thomas G. Rawski, eds., *China's Great Economic Transformation* (New York, NY: Cambridge University Press, 2008), pp. 429–460.

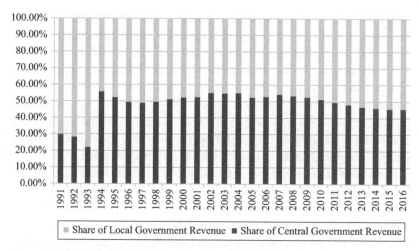

Figure 7.1 Share of central and local revenues, 1991–2016
Source: National Bureau of Statistics. Compiled by the authors

come to have a functioning structure of macroeconomic management, with the central bank, the Ministry of Finance, and a central planning agency responsible for monetary, fiscal, and investment-industrial policies. Most of the post-1994 adjustments under Zhu Rongji were a continuation of the 1994 reform. But later developments, especially the Asian financial crisis of 1997–1998, significantly altered the course of later reform policies under Zhu.

The Making of a New Macroeconomic Architecture

China's financial and fiscal reforms in the late 1990s and early 2000s were built on the achievements of the reform year of 1994. Fiscal reform gradually established a viable central–local fiscal balance in coping with the landscape change in 1994. Through financial reform, the central government gradually constructed a viable system of modern macroeconomic management. The reform of the investment and planning system, culminating in the newly established State Development and Planning Commission (SDPC), marked the end of a central planning system at the institutional level, symbolized by the State Planning Commission (SPC).[16]

---

[16] For a discussion of economic institutional changes under Zhu Rongji, see Yongnian Zheng, *Globalization and State Transformation in China* (Cambridge: Cambridge University Press, 2004), pp. 109–135.

In the fiscal reform arena, the tax-sharing reform of 1994 and follow-up measures brought about two important institutional consequences. The immediate strengthening of central fiscal capacity provided the central government with effective tools of fiscal policy. The newly acquired fiscal capacity soon became useful in terms of fiscal policy and enabled the central government to cope more effectively with various crisis situations. In the event of a severe fall in regional demand, the central government proved quite capable of implementing expansionary fiscal and financial policies without creating too much tension or disequilibrium.

However, the tax-sharing reform also led to a radical weakening of local fiscal capacities and subsequent local government dysfunction, such as inadequate public goods provision and the "grabbing hands" of government institutions, party cadres, and government officials. The often imbalanced local budget also gave rise to extrabudgetary incomes, ranging from revenues from sale or transfer of state-owned assets to miscellaneous fees. The central government responded by institutionalizing central–local transfers and converting some of the miscellaneous fees into the secured tax base.[17] From the late 1990s onward, new sources of revenue related to state-owned land were created and diverted to the local coffers, to soothe local fiscal deficits. However, efforts on these fronts have been less unambiguously successful.

Like the fiscal reform, the financial reform continued largely along the lines of central–local relations. Since the central banking reform of 1994–1995, the major issue for central banking had been to create a viable monetary policy regime. In this regard, the PBOC's local branches had to be restructured to immunize them against the administrative power of local governments. In 1998, this objective was achieved through closing most local branches and creating nine regional ones, each covering several provinces, in the style of regional Federal Reserve Banks. The PBOC has proven to be rather effective in its role as an authority of monetary policy since its creation.

Throughout the 1990s, the key issue for state-owned banks was to address the problem of massive nonperforming loans (NPLs) associated with the restructuring and bankruptcy of inefficient SOEs. These potential lethal heritages prevented the banks from functioning as vital market players. This arduous task took Zhu and his immediate successor, Wen Jiabao, almost a decade to complete, partly via direct fiscal injection of

---

[17] Wong and Bird, "China's Fiscal System," pp. 455–457.

foreign reserves and partly by transferring toxic assets to four state-owned financial asset management corporations. Meanwhile, internal reforms were made in the state banks to diversify their services and modernize their governance in final preparation for the largest among them to be transformed into publicly listed giant financial institutions on both the domestic and international stock markets.[18]

Finally, in 1998, China also moved to reform the last major institutional trappings of the old centrally planned system – the various industrial ministries and two chief planning agencies, the SPC and the State Economic and Trade Commission (SETC). While the industrial ministries were either abolished or corporatized to become centrally managed SOEs, the planning agencies survived the reform to become essential aspects of the new governing superstructure in the new market-in-state system. The old SPC became the National Development Planning Commission (NDPC), assuming control over key commodity prices under a system of "managed float" and long-term investment approval, among others. The SETC's two successors, the State Assets Supervision and Administration Commission and an expanded Ministry of Commerce, continued to play an integrative role in overall macroeconomic management and supervision of the strategic SOE and trade sectors. But for both agencies, the target and the scope of control have become much narrower, limited to a few strategic commodities, long-term investment projects, and key industrial sectors.[19] In other words, these new agencies now sit above a hierarchy of market actors and corporations that make most economic decisions.

In sum, the follow-up reforms of 1994 in financial, fiscal, and planning systems established institutional cornerstones of China's macroeconomic management. In 1998, the recentralized financial and fiscal systems successfully met their first major challenge of macroeconomic management in helping China weather the Asian financial crisis.[20] Through these newly established powerful agents, the central government has been able to create national monetary, fiscal, and investment policies and exercise direct

---

[18] Franklin Allen, Jun Qian, and Meijun Qian, "China's Financial System: Past, Present and Future," in Brandt and Rawski, eds., *China's Great Economic Transformation*, pp. 527–530.

[19] Dali Yang, *Remaking the State Leviathan: Market Transition and the Politics of Governance in China* (Stanford, CA: Stanford University Press, 2004), pp. 39–41.

[20] Wang Mengkui, *China in the Wake of Asia's Financial Crisis* (London and New York, NY: Routledge, 2009), pp. 19–22.

control over the economy, while leaving the work of economic growth and financial innovation to local governments.

Consequences of the New System

The 1994 system is intended to build a centralized, fiscally strong state and an efficient market economy. In the words of two scholars writing at that time, it sought to create "strong state capacity to better serve the economy and shore up the government's authority."[21] Indeed, if strength and efficiency are measured in pure numbers, both objectives have been successfully accomplished. In the first decade after the reform, even as the Chinese economy was achieving double-digit growth, tax revenue growth kept abreast with and in fact surpassed GDP growth, while the central coffers enjoyed a bigger share than all the provinces and local governments combined.[22] As we have just delineated, the structure of the Chinese macroeconomic management seems complete and not dissimilar to the modern Western standard, with a strong central management system.

Another well-expected consequence of the 1994 system is the rise of major state-owned banks in the newly consolidated state-dominated financial sector, similar to the centrally managed SOEs after the reform in that area. China's main state-owned banks and securities, which constitute the bulk of the state-dominated financial sector, behave like the centrally managed SOEs. They are also right in the middle ground, since they are blessed with state-sanctioned monopolies or oligopolistic privileges in certain sectors. Within this regulated monopolistic or oligopolistic structure, Chinese state banks have been able to maintain a large interest rate spread, averaging above 2 percent and sometimes as high as 3 percent. In 2011, this interest spread constituted 75 percent of the net profits for China's five major state-owned commercial banks. Another, less obvious but equally significant, source of new income has been the bank's newfound privilege to straddle two markets: the traditional market of indirect finance and the emergent market of direct finance. Large state banks could enjoy limited access to a large and growing pool of national savings at the same time as relatively open access to the more competitive financial markets. At the height of economic growth, new financial markets serve

---

[21] Wang Shaoguang and Hu Angang, *Zhongguo guojia nengli baogao* (China State Capacity Report) (Shenyang: Liaoning Renmin Chubanshe, 1993).

[22] Jiwei Lou and Wang Shulin, *Public Finance in China: Reform and Growth for a Harmonious Society* (Washington, DC: The World Bank, 2008), pp. 158–159.

to finance ever growing numbers of high-return and high-risk projects, and sometimes also high-risk private projects via underground banking through the private loan markets.

The most important unintended consequence is, arguably, corporatization of local governments. In terms of risk-taking capacities, effective assets and debts, and the scale of their economic undertakings, China's local governments behave like large corporate entities.[23] This development, although noted previously at lower levels of government in the development of rural collective-owned enterprises, only emerged as a dominant trend in the aftermath of the tax-sharing reform. Since the tax reform assigned the lion's share of major taxes to the central government and the centralized system required high performance (i.e., economic development), local leaders were perpetually seeking an alternative off-budget source of finance to fuel local economic development. The transfer of land via a land auction system instituted in 1998, as well as more than a dozen locally based taxes on real estate, provided an ideal platform for local government to engage in exchanges with developers, bankers, and other entrepreneurs. Urban land use rights were transferred to the real estate developers based on the land's economic value. The real estate developers in turn imputed the value of this transfer into the final prices of properties. From 2000 to 2012, this source of local revenue rose steadily to become the top source of local finance, at up to 50 percent of regular tax revenue, before recently starting to fall to more reasonable levels (Figure 7.2). Under the fiscal drives of local government, with the acquiescence of the central government, and fueled by an influx of foreign capital, the value of both land and real estate has soared ahead of GDP growth since 1998.[24]

In addition to land transfer as a direct source of fiscal revenue, since financial centralization freed state banks from local political influence, local governments began to use state-owned urban land as a sort of mortgage to secure bank loans, via a specialized platform known as local government financing vehicles (LGFVs). Unlike direct land sales through the land use rights bidding system, these financing platforms turned the

---

[23] The scale of local government economic operations could be deduced from the scale of local government debt. In 2004, total local government debt was only about RMB1 trillion, but official estimates expected it to rise to RMB11.5 trillion by the end of 2017. See http://yss.mof.gov.cn/2017zyys/201703/t20170324_2565725.html [Accessed August 15, 2017].

[24] Lijian Sun and Shengxing Zhang, "An Externally Dependent Economy and Real Estate Bubbles," in Ross Garnaut and Ligang Song, eds., *China: Linking Markets for Growth* (Canberra: Asia Pacific Press, 2007), pp. 360–361.

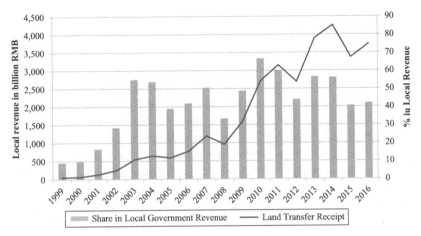

Figure 7.2 Land transfer and local revenue, 1999–2016
Source: China Land and Natural Resources Yearbook (1999–2013), Ministry of Finance and National Bureau of Statistics Official Database. Compiled by the authors

land reserves of local governments into cash flow via bank loans from state-owned banks. By the end of 2010, the number of LGFVs had grown from virtual nonexistence to about 10,000 strong.[25] The funds mobilized through these financing vehicles, together with the land transfer receipts, were then reinvested to develop various infrastructures, which in turn served to raise the future price of land. Thus, the entire cycle of land-based development could continue until the completion of the whole industrialization and urbanization process.

The terminal symptoms of the local addition to economic growth could be summarized as GDPism or GDP syndrome. What China calls "GDPism" is in another term blind worship of GDP growth. From the early days of the reform, growth data and local GDP growth have been the key evaluation criteria for local government cadres, among other socio-economic indicators.[26] Under the supreme command of GDP growth, local cadres could often court investment, offering a variety of favorable conditions such as local tax exemption, zero land costs, lenient environment

[25] People's Bank of China, 2011, *Zhongguo quyu jingrong yinxing baogao* (China Regional Economy Operation Report 2011), available at POBC website: www.pobc.gov.cn.
[26] Hongbin Li and Li-an Zhou, "Political Turnover and Economic Performance: The Incentive Role of Personnel Control in China," *Journal of Public Economics*, 86:9–10 (September 2005), p. 1761.

regulations, and even recruitment of cheap workers. The point of such measures was to create favorable terms of trade for large state and private businesses seeking larger profits, since the additional costs, from land leases to environmental damage, could be absorbed by the local state.

Meanwhile, most entrepreneurial local governments, abetted by soaring land and property prizes, have made unwise investments and thus accumulated huge debts in the process. According to a report from the National General Audit Office, by the end of June 2013, total local government debts had reached RMB17.9 trillion, or about 33 percent of China's GDP in 2012. Of these 17.9 trillion, 10.9 trillion are direct bank loans, while the rest are debts either guaranteed or backed by local governments.[27]

Another unintended consequence, related to the first, is the rapid development of a land-based economy under full local government control, and a real estate sector. During the past two decades, land changes have been closely associated with value creation under a resource-intensive development model. This is evidenced in the relationship between land use rights change and GDP growth.[28] Eventually, local states, the actual owners of local land, become the beneficiaries of this huge value creation process. By constantly mobilizing agricultural land into cultivated land through a monopolistic land market, local governments stand to reap the best fiscal benefit from this great movement.

The new incentive structure put heavy pressure on local officials to concentrate on physical infrastructure, construction projects, and real estate development in the pursuit of positive reviews and promotion. The skylines of China's bigger cities demonstrate the speed with which local governments rush to build skyscrapers. Back in the early 1990s, China scarcely had a dozen skyscrapers, and even the famous Pudong skylines in Shanghai were dotted with only a few high-rises, with mostly low buildings and even peasant houses. By 2017, China had fifty-nine structures towering above 300 meters and 586 structures above 200 meters, accounting for more than half of all such buildings in the world.[29] Behind all these skyscrapers and their related facilities, there is a range of booming economic activities, from land development and relocation to electricity generation and manufacturing of steel, cement, heavy vehicles, and various electronic and electrical devices.

[27] *China Daily*, "Local Debt Surges to 3 Trillion," December 30, 2013.
[28] Canfei He, Zhiji Huang, and Rui Wang, "Land Use Change and Economic Growth in Urban China: A Structural-Equation Analysis," *Urban Studies* 50 (2013), p. 15.
[29] www.skyscrapercenter.com/countries [accessed on May 3, 2018].

The monetization of land and the rise of real estate represents a redistribution of wealth and power in the Chinese society. In a sense, this relatively recent movement has no parallel in human history in terms of its scope and pace. In general, it redistributes revenue from migrants to local residents, from young people of marriageable age to propertied elder generations, and from the real to the financial sector. The young middle-class families who incur heavy mortgages in China's metropolitan areas are bound to shoulder a heavy financial burden, while working-class families are barred from the market due to the prohibitive housing prices. For example, in Beijing, where the average college graduate earns about RMB5,000–7,000 and a migrant worker about RMB3,000–4,000, the average housing price was about RMB30,000 per square meter. Since the great leap in housing prices, housing has become a major source of social grievance for urban residents.[30]

The new fiscal system also means that the local government will not have adequate resources to finance social infrastructure such as public health, public education, a universal pension scheme, and a comprehensive system of public housing. This does not mean an absence of social policy, but certainly there is a disequilibrium between local economic development and social policy, especially for the rural and migrant population. In the Maoist era, urban and rural residents had at least some basic health care coverage, nearly free public education, and subsidized housing. Under the 1994 system, all the welfare schemes were considered fiscal burdens and thus marketized to make room for economic development. During the Hu Jintao era (2002–2012), the central government had sought to rebuild these new systems, under the new ideology of "harmonious society" and *minsheng* (people's livelihood), but the results were rather limited, especially in comparison with China's East Asian neighbors.[31] Since the local states have been heavily corporatized, welfare provision is considered as a cost and financial burden rather than an investment for economic growth.

---

[30] According to the *2013 Evaluation Report on Chinese Urban Governments' Public Service Capacity*, high housing prices and public hospitals are ranked as the top grievances among urban residents in China's thirty-four major cities. See He Yanling et al., eds., *Zhongguo chengshi zhengfu gonggong fuwu pinggu baogao 2013* (The 2013 Evaluation Report on Chinese Urban Governments' Public Service Capacity) (Beijing: Social Sciences Academic Press, 2014), p. 24.

[31] Chack Kie Wong, "The Evolving East Asian Welfare Regimes: The Case of China," in Zhao Litao, ed., *China's Social Development and Policy* (London and New York, NY: Routledge, 2013), pp. 224–225.

At the local government level, welfare provision makes up only a very small percentage of the local government revenue.

The lack of incentive for welfare provision is aggravated by the fact that public sector employees, especially local officials, could enjoy substantial exceptions to China's poorly provisioned welfare schemes, such as health care, basic pensions, and public housing, since they enjoy various privileges such as higher pensions for public servants and cheap housing units built by public units for their own employees.[32] As a result, in sharp contrast to economic and financial reforms, there is a perpetual lack of incentive for social reforms at the local levels. Whenever there is such an incentive for both economic development and public welfare provisions, as we shall discuss below, it is often the result of top-down political and ideological considerations of the local leadership, rather than on behalf of residents.

POST-1994 LOCAL FINANCE AND THE CASH NEXUS

Local States between Politics and Money

The evolution of the fiscal–financial system in contemporary China reflects a process of central–local dynamics. Though the center has the supreme command, most innovative initiatives seem to have emanated from local practice. When mobilizing resources via centrally managed vehicles, local cadres often face a dilemma: The excessive activism necessary for high growth often runs into constraints and risks punishment, whereas passivity and low growth correlates with low chances of promotion. Under the unitary state system, the central state is always able to play the politics of subordination to centralize fiscal and financial resources. While local states are constantly pressed for money, they also have the opportunity to be innovative under China's *de facto* federal institutional arrangement.[33] In the age of reform, local states have played an important role in terms of development and institutional innovations.

There are two ways in which local governments can act with a high degree of autonomy: when there is a powerful local leader, often the party boss at the provincial level who is well connected to the central

---

[32] Zheng Yongnian and Huang Yanjie, "Political Dynamics of China's Social Policy Reform," in Zhao Litao, ed., *China's Social Development and Policy* (London and New York, NY: Routledge, 2013), pp. 183–184.

[33] On the basic dynamics of China's *de facto* federalism, see Yongnian Zheng, *De Facto Federalism in China: Reforms and Dynamics of Central–Local Relations* (Singapore and London: World Scientific, 2007), pp. 31–71.

government, or when the central state takes a particularly keen interest in local development and makes an exception, such as in the cases of the Special Economic Zones in the 1980s and the Pudong District of Shanghai in the 1990s. Under these circumstances, the local governments can mobilize economic resources nationally for rapid local economic development, without compromising local societal interests, but often infringing on local private businesses. When the local leaders do not have such strong political connections, but still have a penchant for growth and revenue maximization, contemporary local development models are often based on an alliance between government and local business interests, and, most frequently, real estate developers. When the logic of politics predominates, local states' actions are more self-restrained and more in line with the central government's policies. When the logic of money predominates, the local states act like pure corporate entities, privileging profits over other concerns. But until recently, there has been a convergence of both logics, as both central and local governments place GDP growth as a national priority.

Before discussing different modes of local fiscal and financial strategies, there is a need to clarify the concept of the local state in the Chinese setting. In China, local government, broadly speaking, includes four layers of substate government systems: provincial level, city level (district level for metropolitans), county, and township. While the CCP cell reaches into the village, the village government is nominally an elected, self-governed committee. Parallel to the hierarchy are vice-provincial-level cities, including some capital cities of key provinces and economically strategic cities. As fiscal and economic units, these key cities are directly administered by the central government and enjoy a high degree of autonomy from the province.[34] Under such a complex system of local government, it will be hard to follow all these different layers of actors at the same time. It suffices to say that subnational-level interactions are like national-level interactions: higher levels of local government gather the best fiscal resources and national assets, whereas the lower levels must settle for an inferior share of state-owned resources. And the fiscal conditions often deteriorate the lower one looks in the hierarchy. The fiscal condition of grassroots government in the less developed inland regions is severely undermined in

---

[34] Currently, there are sixteen vice-provincial cities: Shenyang, Dalian, Ha'erbin, Changchun, Nanjing, Hangzhou, Qingdao, Jinan, Ningbo, Xiamen, Wuhan, Chengdu, Xi'an, Guangzhou and Shenzhen. Of these, Dalian, Qingdao, Ningbo, Xiamen, and Shenzhen are economically strategic coastal cities. The rest are provincial capitals.

its basic functions and completely dependent on higher governments.[35] In other words, the logics of politics are more likely to operate at higher levels in the local system; lower to the grassroots, economic or money motives often predominate.

A few cases can illustrate the fiscal strategies and innovations of local governments. The best example of political logics is the Chongqing model under the ousted political star Bo Xilai, former Party Secretary of Chongqing and a full member of the CCP Political Bureau, China's top decision-making body. There are numerous examples of economic logics in local finance, all centered on a land-based economic development model. We shall survey some of these examples to examine their respective mechanisms of finance. In both cases, we can observe the interactions between the local governments and central players, from the powerful central party organs, through the State Council, through centrally managed SOEs, to the famous superbank of local development financing, the National Development Bank of China. Although it is in the spirit of the 1994 system to pursue thorough centralization and stringent regulatory oversight, it is worth noting that this principle of centralization and regulation has been undermined by central actors, who embrace other principles of development.

High Politics of Money: The Chongqing Miracle

The political dynamics of local development were at their zenith when there was congruence between strong local leadership and national political economy strategies. The crucial condition here is a local party leader of high caliber, who can act as an autonomous power vis-à-vis the bureaucracy. This condition has been relatively rare since the fiscal–financial centralization of 1994, as this reform generally tilted power toward the center. However, there are exceptions, from times at which the local leaders happened to have both power ambitions and a power basis at an opportune moment. The former Party Secretary of Chongqing, Bo Xilai, is perhaps the best example in this category of strong local leaders.

Bo Xilai was unique in that he was a political superstar among the revolutionary "princelings." After making his political debut in the

---

[35] Victor Shih and Zhang Qi, "Who Receive the Subsidies? A Look at County Levels in Two Time Periods," in Vivienne Shue and Christine Wong, *Paying for Progress in China: Public Finance, Human Welfare and Changing Patterns of Inequality* (London: Routledge, 2007), pp. 160–161.

vice-provincial city of Dalian, Bo successively served as governor of Liaoning and Minister of Commerce. He had a reputation as an innovative and
decisive leader at both local and central levels. At the Seventeenth Party
Congress, Bo was promoted to Party Secretary of Chongqing and the
Political Bureau. Bo's political future was critically conditioned on his
performance at his next position. Thus, when Bo was transferred from
Minister of Commerce to Party Secretary of Chongqing as a full member
of the Political Bureau, he brought along a new concept of development
for Chongqing.

Bo's strategy in Chongqing was to mobilize maximum political
legitimacy and economic sources within the constraints of a local leader.
On the political front, he promoted the Maoist notion of equality and
social justice. He engineered large-scale cultural movements such as mass
singing sessions to affirm CCP ideological orthodoxies and carried out
massive anticriminal campaigns to crush the so-called organized criminal
gangs, many of which were no more than large private businesses. Another
central message in Bo's development strategy was *minsheng* (people's
livelihood), one of Sun Yat-sen's *Three Peoples* enshrined as the top
priority for the party-state in recent years. Seeing that the national *minsheng* project was at times no more than rhetorical in many localities, Bo
sought to put it in concrete policy terms, such as lowering inequality and
huge investment in public housing projects. This movement was widely
regarded as an overtly aggressive ideological stance, especially given the
apparent absence of a strong official ideology from Beijing.[36]

Bo's aggressive political strategy was reflected in the building of public
infrastructure financed by state capital from a host of state-owned banks,
from light railways, highways, urban renovation, greening projects, and
environment protection facilities to huge public housing projects. In June
2010, the Chongqing government issued a resolution to invest RMB340
billion in ten major *minsheng* projects over the course of two and half
years.[37] But even more eye-opening was Chongqing's massive infrastructure construction projects, seeking to remake Chongqing as a southwest
metropolitan city. During the height of the construction campaign of
2010–2011, the Chongqing government spent about RMB1.45 trillion on

---

[36] For a brief review of Bo's political motivations, see Willy Lam, "China Leader Revive
Marxist Orthodox," in *Jamestown China Brief*, 10:9 (April 29, 2010), available at
www.jamestown.org/uploads/media/cb_010_36.pdf [Accessed on January 10, 2014].

[37] http://news.xinhuanet.com/local/2010–06/29/c_12274308.htm [Accessed on December
30, 2013].

its infrastructural development projects – 650 billion more than the 800 billion it brought in through local government revenue and central fiscal transfers. One estimate puts the total outstanding debts of the Chongqing government at one trillion by mid-2012.[38]

How did Chongqing under Bo manage to secure such hefty financial resources, given the systemic constraints set by the centralized fiscal system? At the center of Bo's huge construction projects were the so-called LGFVs, companies set up by local government to raise funds for infrastructural and real estate development. As discussed earlier, the gist of the fiscal–financial reforms of the mid- and late 1990s was the removal of local control over local branches of state banks and centralizing of revenue from the most lucrative state assets to the central coffers. When the land-based local fiscal–financial nexus was developed, LGFVs were created as the corporate entities responsible for mobilizing such revenues for infrastructural projects. Called variously investment or development corporations, the LGFVs were in fact platforms for local government to acquire financial sources from banks and investors based on the current and future land supplies. In a sense, the existence of LGFVs, by repeatedly converting locally controlled state-owned land into cash and credit, found a way to circumvent the centralized system. Though not a Chongqing innovation, these fiscal instruments quickly became famous for their outstanding ability to amass financial resources for the Chongqing government to finance economic projects under Bo's powerful leadership.

The fiscal–financial model had taken shape long before Bo came to Chongqing. The model was initially built by Mayor Huang Qifan, an innovative local financier and later Bo's right-hand man in economic affairs, who had served as deputy director of the Pudong Development Office in Shanghai in the late 1990s. Since Huang had come to Chongqing as vice mayor in charge of economic development in 2001, the Chongqing government had created a set of eight so-called investment corporations, covering areas such as urban construction, highway development, high-tech industrial development, real estate development, urban construction, development investment, and water management, among others. The city government regularly injected state assets, including fiscal resources, public shares, and land reserves, to the eight companies, which in turn converted these assets into bank loans and investments. Within six years, Chongqing's state assets increased from RMB170 billion in 2002 to 700

---

[38] http://cn.reuters.com/article/CNAnalysesNews/idCNCNE84106R20120502 [Accessed on December 30, 2013].

billion in 2008.[39] In the same period, these investment corporations financed the lion's share of Chongqing's public infrastructural projects.

The major source of financing for the Chongqing Miracle was the National Development Bank of China (CDB), China's leading policy bank for national and international development financing, headed at the time by another princeling, Chen Yuan. In the search for the quickest way to boost Chongqing's economic growth, Bo found his political ambition in the vision of a developmental coalition between the national bank and national economic agencies, such as the CDB and some leading centrally managed SOEs. Chongqing's LGFV model was strongly backed by Chen Yuan, a longtime champion of such a path of development. In 1998, the CDB had helped the local government of Wuhu, a city in the inland province of Anhui, to establish one of the first LGFVs in China – the Wuhu Construction Investment Corporation, which for the first time utilized the local government's land reserves as collateral for massive loans from the CDB.[40] In 2004, the CDB lent its help to the Chongqing government in creating the Chongqing Yufu Asset Management Group, a state-asset management company modeled after Singapore's Temasek. With support from the CDB, the Yufu Asset Management Group succeeded in buying out local SOEs' bad loans and underutilized industrial land owned by these state firms, thus saving Chongqing's key state-owned sectors, which later turned out to be profitable.[41] The cooperation between Chongqing and the CDB intensified in the later part of the decade. Among the largest sources for Chongqing's eight LGFVs were CDB soft loans. For instance, Chongqing Expressway Development Corporation, by far the largest and most important of the eight LGFVs, received 64 percent of the Chongqing loans from the CDB.[42]

The centrally managed SOEs also represented a central player in Chongqing. Like the CDB, the central SOEs were favored by the Chongqing government under Bo to play a key role in industrial and construction development. The political agenda of Chongqing's "red development" model targeted many private entrepreneurs, who were often accused of involvement in "mafia societies" and causing income inequality.[43] But the crackdown on private entrepreneurship risked a decline of growth dynamics.

---

[39] Henry Sanderson and Michael Forsythe, *China's Superbank: Debt, Oil and Influence – How China Development Bank Is Rewriting Rules of Finance* (Singapore: John Wiley & Sons, 2012), p. 12.

[40] *Ibid.*, pp. 8–9.   [41] *Ibid.*, p. 10.   [42] *Ibid.*, p. 11.

[43] Simon Denyer, "Chinese Entrepreneurs, Unsettled, Speak for Reform," *Washington Post*, August 2, 2013.

To fill the gap, the Chongqing government made an all-out effort to enlist the financially powerful central SOEs to its cause of rapid industrialization. From 2011 to 2012, Sinopec and China Petrol alone invested RMB10 billion in Chongqing, mostly in the refinery and petrol-based heavy chemical industries.[44]

After Bo's downfall in March 2012, the centrally managed SOEs headed to Chongqing on an unprecedented scale. In May 16, a team of SOE bosses headed by the top leadership of the State-Owned Assets Supervision and Administration Commission of the State Council (SASAC) came to Chongqing to sign investment contracts with a net worth of RMB30 billion with the Chongqing government.[45] It was likely that the investment was again as political as it was economic, as the central government feared that the Chongqing miracle would suffer a sudden economic dip and political disturbance in the absence of Bo.[46] Ironically, Bo had created a political economy model which survived his political life, due to a heavy path-dependent effect.

While Bo's political clout was indeed the exception rather than the rule, Chongqing's LGFVs were by no means unique in the country. In many other provinces, as well as in metropolitan cities and vice-provincial ranking cities, LGFVs have evolved in different but equally significant ways. A comparable miracle is the Caofeidian project in Tangshan, in Hebei province. A leading development zone, the Caofeidian project was initiated in 2003. But it was only during the global financial crisis, when state banks made easy credit available, that Caofeidian began to highlight ever bigger ambitions, with average annual investments of RMB100 billion from 2009 to 2011. It promised to deliver a large petrochemical industrial complex, a large steel plant, a mega-sized power station, a world-class port, and even an ecocity. Most of these projects were new production bases for centrally managed SOEs. Even when the warning signs of excess capacity and industrial upgrading were imminent, the investment still poured in, in tens if not hundreds of billions. However, since 2012, the financing of the

---

[44] News available from Sinopec's website: www.Sinopec.com.

[45] *The Economic Observer News*, "30jia yangqi yu chongqing qianding hezuoxieyi" (30 Central SOEs Sign Cooperation Agreements with Chongqing), May 19, 2012.

[46] The centrally managed SOEs are trusted economic and political agents of the central government. Well aware that political stability and economic growth are closely related, the central government usually orders central SOEs to pour massive investment into regions that are considered politically unstable. The most common destination is Xinjiang, a resource-rich but economic backward region inhabited by both Chinese and Muslim Uyghurs.

zone has been in deep trouble, as the planned projects failed either to materialize or deliver projected returns. The interest on existing loans, which has reached RMB10 million a day, is difficult to replay out of local finance.[47] As in Chongqing, it seems that there are only two possible solutions: Either the central government must come in to solve the problem, or the project must be curtailed.

The Local Cash Nexus: The Curse of Natural Sources and Real Estate Bubbles

A perpetual structural problem of the 1994 system is the lack of stable fiscal sources for local governments. For most local governments, even with new income from land sales, perpetual fiscal restraint means it is challenging to meet their ends while achieving reasonable growth rates. However, there is a major exception to this rule. Deep inside China's landlocked regions, some local governments have in fact improved their balance sheets within a very short period of time. This occurs when a region suddenly experiences an economic and fiscal windfall, most commonly in the discovery of natural resources. When this abrupt shift in external conditions suddenly offers an extra source of income, the logics of money often interact with the logics of local politics of growth to produce an instantaneous "miracle" like that of Chongqing under Bo. But unlike the Chongqing miracle, without strong political backing from Beijing, these miracles often disappear rapidly.

Ordos is a prefecture-level city situated at the Ordos Loop of the Yellow River, in central Inner Mongolia. For decades, it has been the poorest prefecture in Inner Mongolia and one of the poorest cities in China. But from 2000 to 2012, the local GDP of Ordos increased from RMB150 million to 3.0 billion, with an annual growth rate of above 20 percent. Meanwhile, the local government has been growing at a rate of 40 percent.[48]

The secret of Ordos's success lies in its natural resources. It has a rich store of coal, raw earth, and natural gas. For decades, demand for these

---

[47] He Jun, *Caofeidian, zhengfu tuidong dakaifaqude zuihou wange* (Caofeidian, the Elegy for Government-Sponsored Mega Development Zones), *Anbound Daily Economic Research*, May 26, 2013, available at www.hibor.com.cn/docdetail_1026114.html

[48] "Zuoyue dechangjiu, shenke debianqian, shushuo er'erduosi gaige kaifang 35 nian" (Outstanding Achievement and Profound Changes: 35 Years of Reform and Opening in Ordos), available at www.ordostj.gov.cn/TJFX/201312/t20131218_1029970.html [Accessed on June 13, 2015].

resources was relatively low and they remained largely unexploited. In the first decade of the 2000s, as the Chinese economy entered a period of rapid heavy industrialization, market prices for natural resources surged to unprecedented levels. To accommodate this change, the Chinese government introduced more market mechanisms in energy pricing from 2000. Between 2000 and 2007, the standard price for coal from major state mines increased dramatically, from RMB123 to 300 per ton, resulting in a surge in the profit rate from 3 percent to 44 percent.[49]

Since underground coal deposits are everywhere beneath Ordos's vast grassland and farmland, the Ordos government's strategy is to clear land for mining use as quickly as possible in order to achieve maximal coal production. This strategy has been popular and extremely well-received by local inhabitants, since it yields an almost instantaneous fortune for the grazers and farmers in the form of huge compensation. Moreover, opportunities for even greater fortunes are opened through the acquisition of open mining rights. This in turn leads to a huge wave of investment in mining.

Although Ordos, like many of China's economic miracles, relies heavily on investment in natural resources, it has become a little more famous due to a spectacular real estate boom between 2004 and 2012. This real estate boom was first initiated by a real demand for housing, as resettled grazers and farmers from the coal area came to the city seeking housing. But soon it developed into the most prosperous sector, with property prices topping Inner Mongolia. Moreover, the speculative real estate market encouraged the participation of all local residents. In 2010, it was estimated that property sales had reached 15 square meters per capita.[50]

Whereas many local governments have difficulty with real estate development due to a lack of cash, Ordos has other incentives for real estate development. In 2008, the party's leading national theoretical monthly endorsed Ordos as the model for Western development and "harmonious

[49] Wang Hongying and Horii Nobihiro, *Zhongguo de nengyuan shichang yu jiage zhidu gaige* (China's Energy Market Price Reform), *Joint Research Program Series* No. 146, Institute of Developing Economics, Japan External Trade Organization, 2008.

[50] Liu Yiding, "Guicheng e'erduosi huo fuzha siqianyi, cengchuan fangjia diezhi sanqian" (The Ghost City Ordos May Owe 400 Billion, Unit Housing Price Once Rumored to Have Fallen to RMB3000), *New Beijing Daily*, August 31, 2013. The figure of fifteen square meters is more staggering when compared with China's average urban housing area per capita, which is only about eighteen square meters.

development outlook," a policy goal under the Hu Jintao leadership of the time.[51] As the premier example of economic success in less developed regions, the government of Ordos has no option but to pursue a single-minded drive for growth. This objective seems to be best served by real estate development supported by both government and local private funds, as nothing else yields such an immediate return in an investment-driven growth model. In the years of super-high growth, there emerged a rare grand alliance of growth between the central state, the local government, and residents. Moreover, a decade of rapid economic growth has further fueled the confidence of the local leadership. The stakes are high in the Ordos leadership's attempts to continue such a growth pattern.

In 2004, awash with tax revenues from coal mines, the local government decided to invest in a new district on the outskirts of the old town. But this new plan soon ballooned into a full-fledged new city that could cater to more than one million people. The combined effects are an oversupply of housing and a real estate bubble. In 2010, Ordos received worldwide attention, as *The New York Times* reported on the ghost city of Kangbashi new district.[52] Eventually, market forces exerted their final blow against the rickety real estate sector. In late 2011, the housing market began to stagnate; in early 2013 average housing prices plummeted 70 percent, from RMB10,000 to 3,000.[53]

An example that is comparable with Ordos is Shenmu County in Shanxi. Although the scale is much smaller, the nature of the miracle is the same. Located in the northwest corner of the landlocked province of Shaanxi, Shenmu is a likely candidate for an economic miracle. Like Ordos, Shenmu has been a poor county. Until the late 1990s, its socioeconomic development was far behind national and provincial standards. All these have changed since the energy price reform of the early 2000s, when Shenmu's coal reserves of fifty billion tons suddenly became the county economy's largest asset by far. This radical change of endowment has since led to a dramatic shift in the economic fortunes of local residents and the fiscal fortunes of the local government. In 2011, at the zenith of its wealth, the small provincial backwater's economy and government revenue all grew at

---

[51] "Xibu Fazhan moshi de Chenggong tansuo: guanyu e'erduosi moshi de sikao" (Successful Experiment with Developmental Models in the Western Region: Some Reflections on the Ordos Model of Development), available at http://theory.people.com.cn/GB/49154/ 49155/7248949.html [accessed on August 15, 2013].

[52] David Barboza, "Chinese Cities Have Many Buildings but Few People," *New York Times*, October 19, 2010.

[53] *New Beijing Daily*, August 31, 2013.

17 percent, while there were approximately 2,000 persons in the county with a net worth of more than RMB100 million.[54] Similar to the Ordos case, local government used its newly found wealth to fund a variety of economic and social projects, including countywide free healthcare, free schooling, and full state provision for the elderly and the disabled. Likewise, the Shenmu experience became emblematic of scientific development and *minsheng* projects in state media, especially in the central party's ideological system.[55]

However, what happened later in Shenmu bore a surprising resemblance to events in Ordos. After a rapid initial accumulation of wealth, there was a countywide rush toward underground high-interest loans and real estate investment. The cash flow from coal mines became the engine for a massive real estate investment fever, driving housing prices in this provincial backwater to unprecedented heights. Meanwhile, the cash-laden local government was unable to devise a development plan for the regional economy outside the trio of coal mines, high-interest loans, and real estate bubbles. In 2012, when coal prices suffered a major downturn after a decade of continual growth, the housing bubble burst instantaneously and the local economy fell into deep trouble.[56]

While the Chongqing miracle depended on political networks of top elites, local miracles such as Shenmu were based on private networks with well-connected but sometimes obscure figures at their center. A telling example is the tale of a certain Shenmu woman called Gong Aiai, nicknamed *fangjie* (property sister) by cynical netizens after her story was exposed. Coming from a peasant family, Gong began her career as an accountant in a rural branch of a state-owned local credit association upon graduation from high school. Working as a low-rank credit officer, Gong developed a unique acumen for investment, and intimate knowledge of the coal sector. In 2004, private coal mining in Shenmu entered a period of explosive expansion and began to seek large amounts of bank credit. But local branches of large state-owned banks were not ready to help due to a

[54] The Gohigh Fund, *Zhongguo minjian ziben touzi diaoyan baogao: Shanbeipian* (China Private Capital Investment Investigative Report: North Shaanxi), p. 4.

[55] For example, the *Ban Yuetan* (Half-Monthly Talk), a leading ideological monthly from the CCP Central Propaganda Department, hailed the Shenmu experiments with free welfare provision as a breakthrough in China's local welfare reforms. See "Jiedu minsheng gaige: Shenmu xianxiang gei women shenmen qishi?" (Interpreting Minshen Reforms: What Can Learn from the Shenmu Phenomenon?), *Ban yue tan* 22 (2009).

[56] Kang Zheng, *Shenmu zenmeban?* (Whither Shenmu?), *Oriental Outlook*, 18 (2013), pp. 2–3.

combination of state regulations and cumbersome bureaucratic processes. Instead, Gong actively courted local coal tycoons and quickly established a financial network with the coal mines.[57]

Even at the height of her wealth and power, Gong was merely the vice-director of Shenmu Rural Commercial Bank, a local joint-stock bank founded – among many other banks – during the best days of underground finance in Shenmu. But she was easily the richest woman in town, given her 11 percent share in the bank (and possibly other credit firms engaged in illegal high-interest loans). In addition to the credit business, Gong had control over several key mines in Yulin, Shaanxi, and received large shares of the profits.[58] Through coal mining and the private credit business, Gong was able to receive yearly dividends amounting to millions and accumulate a huge fortune in a short period. With her newly acquired cash, Gong bought more than 300 properties across China, including forty-one luxurious flats in Beijing with a total area of 10,000 square meters, based on forged identity certificates.[59] When her ownership of these Beijing flats was exposed, her story of wealth brought a national outcry, especially among young, middle-class netizens who could barely afford even one shabby flat on the outskirts of the capital. But even given media exposure, she managed to fend off legal investigations thanks to some degree of local protection. Such protection proved limited, however, as the media exposure reached the national level. In September 2013, Gong was charged with forging identity certificates and sentenced to three years in jail. This verdict led to public speculation regarding Gong's real identity and power, as the courts recognized her as only a "contract worker" rather than a formal state employee.[60] Later, an *Oriental Weekly* report added another dramatic twist to the story. It turned out that Gong was also a victim of the Shenmu Miracle: She attempted suicide when a private fund manager, Zhang Xiaochang, fled with RMB120 million in loans obtained through Gong. When angry

---

[57] He Baoli, "Fangjie yinxing shangye diguo fuxian" (Hidden Commercial Empire of the Property Sister Surfaces) *Fazhi Ribao* (Legal Daily), January 30, 2013.

[58] Gao Long, "Meilaoban Gong Aiai de heijindiguo" (The Black Gold Empire of the Coal Boss Gong Aiai), *Southern Metropolitan Daily*, March 6, 2013.

[59] http://finance.sina.com.cn/china/20130131/154714465742.shtml [Accessed on August 30, 2013].

[60] Wang Chuanbao, "Fangjiean bushe fang, yinggai zhiyi gengduo huiying" (The Property Sister Case Does Not Involve Property, but There Should No Room for Public Doubts), *The Global Times*, September 30, 2013.

depositors were unable to sue Gong, they exposed her ownership of Beijing flats and forged identity cards to the mass media.[61]

Gong's story is instructive in the way that it clearly outlines the mechanisms through which the local economy works in a corporatized and networked model. The issue revolves around the cash nexus that she has managed to weave with local banks, coal mines, local society, and local state bureaucracy, despite not being a high-ranked local official. Unlike the logics of politics, the logics of economy enjoin local government to comply and cooperate with various local economic forces, which can be more aggressively speculative and opportunistic than state actors. Although Gong is not a state agent in the cash game, her identity and credit are still embedded in the local state financial system. In Shenmu, Ordos, and many other rich localities, there are perhaps thousands of such figures, who have the necessary connections and abilities to situate themselves at the node of the local financial nexus.

Rich in natural resources, both Ordos and Shenmu managed to gain some degree of economic autonomy from the central state. Both cities were for a time highly regarded by the Central Propaganda Department as paragons of economic development. And indeed, these cities had taken a great leap not just in terms of economic growth but also in providing public services, in line with the "harmonious society project," as evidenced in the opinion pages of top party magazines such as *Half Monthly Talk* and *Seeking Truth*. But again, in both cases, the short-lived economic miracle ended with a disastrous real estate bubble.

After all, Ordos and Shenmu, just like the Chongqing and Caofeidian projects, are part of the same story of the local growth games of fiscal–financial mobilization. The only difference is that Chongqing and Caofeidian could mobilize on a national scale with real political might; fortunate places such as Ordos and Shenmu lacked such resources, but could nevertheless mobilize natural resources under the same banner of social and economic development. For most Chinese local governments, however, such options are not available. And the only option left is to carefully capitalize any existing abundant resources – mostly urban and suburban land, but also cultural heritage, cheap environment, cheap labor, tourist resorts, and even the human body.[62] In short, GDPism comes in different

---

[61] Zheng, "Shenmu zenmeban?" pp. 5–6.

[62] The so-called *xuejiang* (blood plasma) economy, based on receipts from poor peasants' "voluntary" blood donations, was one example in this category. These donations were widely practiced in Henan in the late 1990s and caused thousands of HIV cases due to

guises and at different levels. Although market mechanisms and especially financial institutions are involved, they are mobilization mechanisms rather than mechanisms for resource optimization.

Locally Backed Underground Banks and Financing Platforms

The rationale behind China's financial reforms of the 1990s is centralization and consolidation, as the central state's control over banking, stock, and foreign exchange demonstrates. This leaves few formal channels for the local and grassroots. But the formal financial system has never been able to meet the social demand for high-yield channels of investment. Since the global financial crisis, numerous private financial institutions have sprung up to meet such demand by gathering funds from private investors and channeling them into high-yield, high-risk, short-term investments. Collectively known as underground banks, they have often had a complex relationship with local government and the formal financial system. We shall only discuss one of the most prevalent of these underground banks here – the Internet-based P2P (Peer-to-Peer) lending platforms – as they are representative of the new trend of underground banks.

Underground banks developed in China in response to a structural need for high-yield investments for private investors and inadequately financed small and medium private entrepreneurs (SMEs). In 2007, the traditional lending institutions began to build frameworks on the Internet. This development picked up pace in 2010–2013, as more and more offline lenders, including some fraudulent and unqualified agencies, began to establish online frameworks, leading to an explosion of risk and investors' losses in 2013.[63] In 2014, the government started to regulate the P2P sector. In 2015, when the central government began to crack down on such dangerous financial schemes, the judicial system identified 3,000 cases which involved 150 billion RMB of private investments. Among these

---

contamination through shared use of syringe needles. According to one estimation, 140,000 to 470,000 Henanese donors contracted HIV in this way; the same report highlighted that at the end of its study period, in 2004, most victims had little access to medical care. See Zhang Ke, "Henan Aizibing wunian baogao" (A Report on AIDS in Henan, 1999–2004), electronic version available at http://paper.usc.cuhk.edu.hk/Details .aspx?id=4955 [Accessed on August 17, 2017].

[63] Naiwen Zhang and Yangjie She, "The Evolution of Peer to Peer Lending in China," *Crowdfund Insider*, September 12, 2014, available at www.crowdfundinsider.com/2014/09/48954-evolution-p2p-lending-china/ [Accessed on August 20, 2017].

cases, Ezubao, Zhuoda, and Fanya could be rightfully called "seismic" due to their huge impact on the financial market.[64] They are devastating because of the involvement of local governments or state banks, or because their sheer size and influence changed the nature and significance of these vehicles. In other words, these cases crossed the borderline of self-regulated underground banks and moved into the dangerous middle ground of state–society relations.

The Fanya case is indicative of such an entanglement with political economy. Established in Kunming, the capital city of Yunnan, in 2011, Fanya was an Internet-based metal exchange platform which specialized in rare metals such as indium, cobalt, and tungsten. The first of its kind in China's economically backward southwest, the exchange opened to fanfare and official support, with the Yunnan and Kunming governments regarding it as a major business start-up and potential tax base. The Kunming municipal government even established a commission consisting of heads of local fiscal and other authorities to supervise Fanya Metal Exchange.[65] In 2013, Fanya, together with Internet giants such as Taobao and Baidu, became one of the eleven signing parties to the National Bureau of Statistics' National Big Data Cooperative Frame Agreement, with a recognized leading edge in metal trading data.[66] Emboldened by government support and endorsement, the Fanya management claimed to control 95 percent of the world's stock of indium, a small but indispensable ingredient for filming liquid-crystal display (LCD). Based on the reserves said to be available, it issued a financial product, *rijinbao* (daily gold jewel), with a promised annualized return of 13.68 percent. The selling point of Fanya, unlike other similar projects, was the murky notion of "state" and apparent local government support, which seemed to provide a degree of confidence in the otherwise risky P2P investments for certain groups of urban residents, who leveraged their life savings in the hope of a high, stable yield. By early 2015, the Fanya platform had collected about RMB40 billion (6.4 billion USD) from more than 220,000 investors from twenty provinces.[67]

---

[64] Wu Hong, Liu Ran, and Han Yi, "Jizi pianju dabaofa" (A Massive Explosion of Ponzi Games), *Caixin Weekly* 49 (2015), p. 3.

[65] http://finance.sina.com.cn/zl/bank/2016-02-07/zl-ifxpfhzk9066908.shtml [Accessed on August 20, 2017].

[66] "Fanya shuju nairu guojia dashujuku jianshe" (Fanya Data incorporated into the Construction of National Big Database), *Yunnan Daily*, November 22, 2013.

[67] Cao Jiaru, "Duanya rensheng: Fanya touzizhe quanxiang" (Lives Broken: A Group Sketch of the Fanya investors), *Phoenix Weekly* 5 (2016), pp. 1–2.

Fanya's claim of a monopoly over indium supply turned out to be unfounded. But it had indeed created a clever business model. It buys indium at a price 25–30 percent higher than the open market, pays 80 percent as loans to the seller, and retains 20 percent as a security deposit. Meanwhile, it gathers funds from millions of small investors and pays an annualized interest rate of 13.68 percent. Fanya made a profit from the difference between the 13.5 percent annualized interest rates and the 20 percent security deposit. The indium suppliers earned the difference between Fanya's purchasing price and the market price. Rather than acting as a rare metal exchange, Fanya merely hoarded indium as an illiquid asset, never selling it back to the market since it was perpetually overpriced. Fanya's survival depended on the projection that the market price of indium would increase annually at a rate of at least 20 percent.[68] The Fanya model thus amounted to a Ponzi scheme in which investors paid cash in exchange for illiquid metal stock with the assumption that the price would rise in perpetuity. But the indium price collapsed in 2015, plummeting from USD700–800 to 300–400 per kilogram in both the Chinese and the world markets.[69] The foundations of the Fanya platform collapsed.

A key factor in the scheme was the regulatory failure of the local governments. When investors learned about the potential loss of their savings, they mobilized against the Fanya management and the Kunming local police. But the Kunming Public Security Bureau initially refused to investigate, citing instructions from the "top" that any investigation would lead to Fanya's bankruptcy. It appeared that the Kunming government had known about the nature of the scheme long before its collapse. While there was a proposed patchwork of regulation in place in 2011, the Kunming financial regulators had ceased to supervise and regulate Fanya Metal Exchange as early as 2012, despite two central policy circulars that demanded urgent inspection of all potential fraud. The Yunnan Settlement Office made an attempt to regulate and examine the case from November 2013 but the investigation yielded little evidence against Fanya, although it clearly violated all the "bottom lines" stated in the policy circulars.[70] After their reports and appeals fell on deaf ears, hundreds of investors from across the country began to organize themselves into rights-activist groups and petitioned relevant government agencies in Beijing. Over the course of

---

[68] Tan Na, "Zhongguoban pangshi pianju fenxi – Fanya moshi fenxi wojian" (Analysis of the Chinese version of Ponzi Game: My View of the Fanya Model), available at www.750208.com/14245.html [Accessed on August 20, 2017].

[69] www.theatlas.com/charts/4kY_GyTR [Accessed on August 20, 2017].

[70] Guo Fang, He Fangzhu, "Fanya moshi: youyige pangshi pianju" (The Fanya Model: Another Ponzi Scheme?), *China Economic Weekly* 37 (2015), pp. 21–25.

a year, they visited the Letters and Visits Office, the Supreme People's Procuratorate, and China Securities Regulatory Commission.[71] Finally, a special team headed by a new governor stepped in and arrested the management of Fanya Metal Exchange. After a major reshuffle of party and government leadership in Yunnan and Kunming, a new team of provincial leadership under the new party secretary, Chen Hao, began attempts to cope with the aftermath of the crisis in 2016.[72]

Fanya is an exceptional case among the general efflorescence of Internet-based wealth management products (WMPs) in China since 2008. It is exceptional because most WMPs are affiliated with local governments and built on nonfinancial exchange platforms. Moreover, they are usually more experienced financial actors that provide meaningful financial mediation between the financially depressed private sector and eager retail investors. There are many Ponzi schemes exposed each year, but these are decidedly not the majority. The WMPs are also not heirs to the private grassroots banking sector in traditional China. Rather, they are typically affiliated with China's large state banks, state security companies, and the two state-run stock exchanges, drawing funds from both the super-rich and the ordinary middle-class households. Unlike Fanya, WMPs typically yielded interest only 2–3 percent higher than the benchmark deposit rates between 2010 and 2014. Most WMPs are not long-term products and the over-whelming majority mature after nine months.[73] As such, although the WMPs or the larger part of the shadow banking system still operate outside the traditional orbit of state banking, they are not necessarily a major threat to financial stability if properly regulated.

Unlike land and real estate, the shadow banking sector is usually not directly involved with state power, but it can become extremely dangerous if entangled with the local state. This can happen when clever financiers leverage political capital but lack the power to control the financial market. China's shadow banking sector, despite its staggering growth in recent years, is still small compared with developed economies, which are more financialized.[74] Nevertheless, the proliferation of these WMPs is indicative of the hypermonetization and financialization of Chinese society, as the whole society is drawn into the process.

---

[71] Guo Changhai, *Zhongguo qianju* (China's Money Traps) (Taipei: Caida Chubanshe, 2016), pp. 74–75.
[72] *Ibid.*, pp. 75–76.
[73] Emily Perry and Florian Weltewitz, "Wealth Management Products in China," *Bulletin of the Reserve Bank of Australia*, June 2015, pp. 64–65.
[74] Douglas Elliot, Arthur Kroeber, and Yu Qiao, "Shadow Banking in China: A Primer," *Brookings Papers*, March 2015, pp. 16–17.

EPILOGUE: MONEY AS THE MEDIUM IN THE MIS SYSTEM AND CHINESE SOCIETY

Monetization is one of the most important engines of China's spectacular growth and structural change, as the country sees a transformation from a highly demonetized and definancialized planning economy to a highly monetized and financialized economy. It is just as significant as urbanization and industrialization in China's transformation from an overwhelmingly rural economy into the world's leading industrial power. Money has replaced ideology, power, and organizations in today's China as the most effective medium between the central and local governments, and between the state and society. Under the new system, the central state dominates local states not only legally and administratively but also through centralized fiscal and financial control via a major share of value-added taxes under the tax-sharing scheme. In the government echelons, cadres are evaluated on performance indicators such as GDP growth or investment and money-making ability, along with less comparable criteria such as qualifications, reliability, and experience, among others. Between the state and local society, a variety of matters are settled through money rather than through law courts, from compensation for land and houses to payment for the relocation of families of victims of state violence.

But the most remarkable feature in the monetization process is perhaps China's local development models based on land and natural resources, and their remarkable potential for mobilization. When politics and money are intimately intertwined, it becomes natural to expect a magical process of economic development, as millions, if not trillions, in investment transforms the local landscape within a short timeframe. This alliance of local politics and national money rests on *de facto* local ownership of urban land and credit monopolies working in tandem under the banner of developmentalism. But when the local state is seeking to maximize its receipts, it sometimes has no choice but to usurp this right, thus coming into conflict with local communities. The famous Wukan Incident, where villagers from a coastal Guangdong village ousted the village's party secretary and elected their own interim committee by vote, was initiated by the sale of collective land and bribery by the lowest ranking party-state agents, namely, the party secretary and his associates.[75]

---

[75] Minnie Chan, "Probes Confirm Villagers' Complaints," *South China Morning Post*, January 10, 2012.

The monetization of Chinese society in the aftermath of the fiscal–financial reform of 1994 has spawned a large pool of middle-ground actors between the central state and local markets. Local governments, in their various corporatized forms, constitute a group of mighty and autonomous actors, on a par with the leading centrally managed SOEs. Since a large percentage of their variable income is from land, they have a vested interest in high property prices. Closely allied with the local governments are real estate developers and a string of downstream sectors associated with property construction and sales. Since they have deep-seated shared interests, real estate developers and government officials often develop long-lasting implicit partnerships. Besides land receipts paid by and various taxes levied on the developers, real estate development also generates a large space for corruption and rent-seeking by government officials, as money becomes the most effective lubricant between the corporatized local government bureaucracy and the real estate sector. As real estate development involves a range of bureaucratic agents, from land suppliers and city planners to the municipal government, corruption occurs at almost all levels of the local bureaucracy.[76] Structurally speaking, part of the lower realm of the government has been transformed into a self-profiting network, at the cost of the interests of the state and the common people.

From the central state to its local agents, from real estate developers to residents, from underground bankers to state-owned super-bankers, the functioning system of money in contemporary China is a multilayered, complex structure containing many players. There appears to have been a major break with the Maoist past in the sense that the state no longer exercises full control over money supply. Compared with the Maoist system, nowadays the Chinese fiscal and monetary system has the appearance of a typical economy in transition, with some remaining oddities. China's accumulation of a huge current account surplus and dollar reserves further lends some credence to this apparent normality. But its continuities with the older commodity standards are also revealing: Instead of control over both factors and commodities, the state has merely retreated from control over commodities, having retained and

---

[76] Jiannan Zhu, "The Shadow of Skyscrapers: Real Estate Corruption in China," *Journal of Contemporary China* 21 (2012), pp. 251–259.

even tightened its grip on key factors of production such as land, infrastructure, natural resources, and credit.[77]

Whereas in the past a single, gigantic planning system controlled all factors of production as well as commodities, today the central state has entrusted control over factors of production to three key agents: urban land to local government; strategic infrastructure and natural resources to central SOEs; and most credit to state-owned major banks. The central government prioritizes the control of credit expansion and inflation, but it has been much harder to do so under this new agency structure, since all three commanding agencies are motivated to expand credit and money supply through powerful interventions in the market. But as the cases of Chongqing and Shenmu demonstrated, among others, the real drivers behind spectacular credit mobilization and wealth creation were often powerful actors with political and economic stakes in such a process. Finally, the tripartite structure allows credit creation by local and central state agents. China experienced an investment fever spearheaded by banks, central SOEs, and local government, and subsequently a period of high inflation following the four trillion RMB investment boom in 2009 in the aftermath of the global financial crisis. The scale of the expansionary policies far exceeded the fiscal stimulus as Chinese banks loosened the floodgates to provide easy credit, with a significant portion going into the LGFVs, fueling local debt to a sky-high level. From 2009 to 2014, the debt-to-revenue ratio for local government rose from 200 percent to more than 300 percent; only central government fiscal transfers and centrally managed funds that significantly boosted the local budget kept the actual debt-to-revenue ratio below 150 percent.[78]

China's local finance and economic development is critically dependent on the financial mobilization of land and natural resources. As such, the

---

[77] The 1982 amendment is a good example of this type. In fact, throughout the 1980s, the state did not establish particularly tight control over urban land use, as there were no authorities in areas such as urban planning, national land and natural resources, and building and construction. There were also minimal boundaries between urban state-owned and rural collectively owned lands. It was still common, for example, for locals to appropriate land on the urban outskirts for private construction projects. From the 1990s onwards, and especially in recent years, however, state control over land and other factors of production became ever tighter and more regularized through new bureaucratic agencies.

[78] Xun Wu, "An Introduction to China's Local Government Debt," *MIT Golub Center for Finance and Policy Working Papers*, October 2015, pp. 6–7, available at http://gcfp.mit.edu/wp-content/uploads/2013/08/Policy-Report-of-Chinese-Local-Government-Debt-final.pdf [Accessed on August 17, 2017].

contemporary local cash nexus is an extension of the mobilization of the Maoist era, with all its mighty promises of rapid industrialization and destructive potential for the society. As one researcher has pointed out, this local development model centered on land and natural resources has led to underinvestment in socially productive goods, such as technological innovation, public education, and health care, and an overreliance on cheap labor, low environmental standards, and high energy consumption.[79] In other words, the local development model is a mobilization model, which can only sustain itself through ever increasing resource mobilization. In a way, the current system is like the old system of mobilization in the Great Leap Forward years under Mao, except that the ideology and organization of the Party have been replaced by money and financial organizations. Chongqing, Ordos, and Shenmu are all classic cases of such mass mobilization. It remains to be seen whether such a model will continue.[80] If the same model were to continue indefinitely, the Chinese economy would be at risk of a major crisis when land and natural resources become depleted.

---

[79] Wang Lianli, *Zhongguo fangdichan zhi'e* (The Conundrum of China's Property Business) (Hong Kong: Tianxingjian Publisher, 2012), p. 16.

[80] Indeed, the new leadership's policy of cracking down harshly on corruption had a strong influence on the local cash nexus. As a result, some local officials were loath to become involved in credit creation through infrastructure, land sales, and industrial projects, for fear of a heightened political risk. According to the online database of the National Bureau of Statistics, growth in fixed capital formation (investment) declined from 20.1 percent in the period 2003–2012 to 14.5 percent in 2013–2016, contributing significantly to lower GDP growth. But as economic growth has slowed sharply, it remains to be seen whether central government will again loosen the reins.

8

State Capitalism

The Centrally Managed State-Owned Enterprises and Economic Domination

In contemporary China, enterprises above a certain scale are officially classified as state-owned enterprises (SOEs) and nonstate enterprises (NSEs) in terms of ownership. In the 1980s, collective enterprises, especially township and village enterprises (TVEs), constituted the majority of the NSEs. Later, foreign-invested enterprises (FIEs) and Hong Kong, Taiwan, and Macau-funded enterprises became the other major NSEs. Many FIEs are joint ventures with SOEs and so retain a significant element of state ownership. Within the SOE sector, enterprises can further be divided into those managed by the central government and those managed by different levels of local government in the provinces and cities. This chapter deals with centrally managed SOEs.

This purpose of this chapter is not to describe the process of China's SOE reform. It is a very large and complex project beyond the scope of this study. The detailed process of China's SOE reform has been closely monitored in China studies and there is a growing body of the literature on this subject.[1] In earlier chapters, we also sketch out the basics of the process as part of China's market reform since 1978. The task of this chapter is to answer the questions: Why are China's SOEs still an essential

---

[1] For a classic description of the reform in the 1990s from the Chinese perspective, see Justin Lin Yi-fu et al., eds., *State-Owned Enterprise Reform in China* (Hong Kong: Chinese University of Hong Kong Press, 1999). For a more polemical and case study-based study of the reform, see Edward S. Steinfeld, *Forging Reform in China: The Fate of the State-Owned Enterprises* (New York, NY: Cambridge University Press, 1998). For a sociological perspective, see You Ji, *China's Enterprise Reform: Changing State/Society Relations after Mao* (New York, NY: Routledge, 1998). For a recent collection of papers on the reform, see Juan Antonio Fernandez, and Leila Fernandez-Stembridge, eds., *China's State-Owned Enterprise Reforms: An Industrial and CEO Approach* (New York, NY: Routledge, 2007). For an examination of the politics of the reform, see Jin Zeng, *State-Led Privatization in China: The Politics of Economic Reform* (London: Routledge, 2013).

part of the postreform political economy? Why are they organized in the way they are? In other words, we want to find out the rationales behind the SOE reform and evaluate the products of the reform, especially the centrally managed SOEs. Building on these discussions, we shall make some observations on SOEs' role in the overall state domination of the economy.

As discussed in Chapter 2, in Chinese political philosophy, the economy and the state are not only regarded as inseparable; more importantly, the economy, understood as "management of the world," is a tool for the state to achieve its economic as well as noneconomic goals. In traditional China, the state was expected to achieve these goals through state monopoly over key industrial sectors such as iron and salt. It is important to note that state monopoly does not deny the role of the market. State monopoly might not be as efficient as private ownership, but the state sector and the market can coexist. Indeed, as discussed in Chapter 2, state enterprises were often operated either through a state–private partnership or privately. In the contemporary era, while the state has continued that old practice, it has also introduced drastic changes in the state sector, particularly centrally managed SOEs. The state sector might not be totally new, but the centrally managed SOE sector is drastically different from either the traditional state salt and other monopolies or the state-run enterprises in the Maoist era. While traditionally most state enterprises were operated privately, centrally managed SOEs today are operated by state officials. Needless to say, the large scale of the contemporary state sector cannot be matched by the traditional state sector. The contemporary state sector also differs from that of the Maoist era. First of all, most state enterprises are now no longer the Maoist three-in-one economic, political, and social entities. State enterprises no longer directly deal with all the various social services that the state sector in the Maoist era bore the weight of. Instead, the government bears these responsibilities through various state and market providers of service, such as schools and hospitals. Contemporary state enterprises have partially differentiated themselves from the state, behaving more like business corporations than typical government agencies. Second, unlike in the Maoist era, where there was no space for a national market, some of the contemporary state enterprises, especially the centrally managed SOEs, not only employ market mechanisms but also act as monopolies, oligopolies, or the largest of the competitors in the natural markets, depending on the sector and industrial policy. The national market might not be perfect; it does, however, exist.

However, SOEs also inherit from their historical forms the status and function of the economic arm of the state. While the purpose of the market-oriented reform in the contemporary era was to fundamentally transform the Maoist mobilization economy, it does not mean in any sense that China's SOEs will operate in the same way that private enterprises operate in the market system in the West. As in traditional China, the state sector continues to be the most important economic arm of the state in order to mobilize resources and dominate the economy. The introduction of the market system into the state sector only increases the efficiency of this sector's pursuit of economic wealth. For the state, the question now is not whether the market should exist or not, but how to efficiently make use of the market while continuously maintaining its domination over the state sector via other means.

In this chapter, we focus on two related processes in the larger transformation of China's enterprise systems. On the one hand, we shall discuss how state enterprises have been differentiated from the state. On the other, we shall examine how the state has established various mechanisms through which it continues to exercise its domination over the state sector. In other words, we want to explore how the contradiction between market development and political domination has been managed. Exploring the state's management or mismanagement of these inherent contradictions, we will be able to see how the contemporary political economy system functions and how dynamism for changes has been created. Another important process in the transformation from Maoist command economy to a largely market-oriented economy was the privatization of small and medium SOEs. This move has created a condition for the development of private enterprises. Some of these private enterprises have risen to political prominence and become increasingly coopted by the state, as we discussed in Chapters 5 and 6.

This chapter proceeds as follows. First, we conceptualize the "family plot" economic practice and make an analogy between the family plot – an economic institution under Mao – and the state sector to explore the rationale of the state sector's existence. Second, we briefly examine the process of differentiation between state enterprises and the state, namely, the process of the corporatization of centrally managed SOEs. Third, we discuss how the state has created various mechanisms to continuously dominate the state sector. Finally, we discuss the contradictions between economic liberalization and political dominance, and dynamics for change.

THE "FAMILY PLOT" THEORY AND THE STATE SECTOR

We discussed the philosophical reasons for the existence of China's state sector in Chapter 2. In this chapter, we want to further discuss the practical political and economic rationales behind the Chinese government's efforts to build a strong and centrally managed state sector, and how the state sector can prosper in an increasingly market-oriented environment. In doing so, we first conceptualize China's "family plot" economic practice and make an analogy between the family plot system and the state sector.

The Family Plot System

The family plot system (FPS) refers to a land system in which a rural collective unit, usually a production brigade or production team, allocated a plot of land to each household under its jurisdiction on a long term basis without much intervention from the production brigade or production team. It was a unique rural land system during Maoist China, but elements of it had been seen in Chinese history.[2]

After the establishment of the People's Republic in 1949, the Communist regime embarked on a large-scale nationwide land reform movement (1950–1952) to distribute land owned by landlords to rural individual households.[3] A few years after the land reform, the regime further initiated

---

[2] A family plot is created out of a private plot under the collective ownership scheme. In the Well-Field System of the Zhou dynasty, a piece of land was divided into nine identically sized plots. The plot in the middle was the public plot whereas the other eight of the nine were private plots. By definition, the public plot provided tax revenue whereas the revenues of the other eight were private. While the system was honored as the most just land system created by Confucians since Mencius, it was not an effective system, as farmers tended to focus on the private plot and neglect the public ones. Except for a failed experiment under Wang Mang, the Well-Field System was not exercised for more than two thousand years. But the Maoist system of collectivization reversed the Well-Field System: now the overwhelming majority of the land would be public and only a tiny portion remained as, effectively, a family plot. For a discussion of Mencius' view of the well-field ideal, see Kung-chuan Hsiao, *History of Chinese Political Thought*, vol. 1 (Princeton, NJ: Princeton University Press, 2015), pp. 172–174, and Mark Edward Lewis, *The Construction of Space in Early China* (New York, NY: SUNY Press, 2005), pp. 248–249.

[3] China's land reform started in the rural north and northeast China under the Communists in October 1947. As the Communists took control of most of China in 1949, land reform spread to all over the country. In June 1950, the Communist Party unveiled the Land Reform Law, making it mandatory for, and a priority task of, the local governments to implement land reforms. By early 1953, land reforms in China proper were completed. Throughout the 1950s, similar reforms would be implemented in Tibet, Xinjiang, and

the agricultural collectivization movement to collectivize land owned by each household under the ownership of a production brigade or production team. The movement eventually led to the establishment of the People's Commune system.

This process of Maoist collectivization was characterized by the unification and equalization of all individual human needs, which were no longer defined by individuals themselves (endogenous) but rather by forces and actors (exogenous). The problem with this system lies in the fact that human beings by their nature cannot be permanently unified and equalized by external forces, be they material or ideational. If a system is forced upon the people, over time social dissatisfaction and crisis become inevitable. Despite efforts by the leadership to eliminate private plots, both at the local and central levels, individual households demonstrated their strong resistance against the collectivization movement. In many places, peasants retreated from their collectives and returned to the previous collectivization system. The resistance was often violent. Under these circumstances, the FPS was invented in some localities as a compromise, and eventually was recognized by the Communist regime. In November 1955, the government issued a policy titled "The Draft of the Demonstration Regulations on the Agricultural Production Cooperatives" and legalized the FPS. The draft stated that everyone in a production brigade was allowed to own no more than 5 percent of the total per capita agricultural land of that production brigade. The government would not collect tax revenues over products of the FPS. The family plot was defined as a family sideline production business, a complementary system to agricultural collectivization, which was designed to absorb "surplus labor" and "surplus labor time" to produce products which met each household's agricultural demands. In other words, the purpose of the FPS was to meet the needs of different households which could not be met by rural collectives. For each household, by its nature, the FPS was a minimum institutional guarantee of the rural subsistence economy. The rural collective system did not provide an incentive mechanism for its members and the level of productivity was low. Rural collectives could hardly produce sufficient product for their members to survive. Without the FPS, the rural collectives might not even be able to exist.

Southwest China. For a classic overview, see John Wong, *Land Reform in the People's Republic of China: Institutional Transformation in Agriculture* (New York, NY: Praeger Publishers, 1973).

During the People's Commune movement, the FPS system was regarded as a residual aspect of capitalism and thus abolished through radical policies in many localities. However, such policies immediately became a threat to the commune system itself, to such a degree that it had to be restored after 1960. In the 1960s and 1970s, while state regulations set the upper limit of FPS at 5–7 percent of communally owned collective land, there was regional variation in local and grassroots practices, with some regions allocating as much as 20 percent of collective land as FPS to the peasants due to the system's overwhelming appeal.[4] In March 1981, a few years after the beginning of the post-Mao agricultural reform, the Communist regime issued another policy circular titled "A Report of Actively Promoting Multiple Agricultural Production Activities," and expanded the FPS. Under the new policy, a rural resident in an agricultural unit was allowed to own no more than 15 percent of the total per capita agricultural land of that agricultural unit. Since ownership of the family plot belonged to rural collectives, individual households only owned the use rights of the plot and did not have the rights to transfer. After the post-Mao leadership's establishment of the household responsibility system (HRS), the economic significance of the FPS faded. The FPS was largely incorporated into the HRS.

The FPS as an Economic Institution

Treating the birth and development of the FPS as an institution helps our understanding of the rationale of China's state sector. Rural peasants' invention of the FPS to overcome the difficulties produced by the rural collective system is not the subject of this research. We are interested in understanding the political economic logic of the FPS by looking at China's political economy system via the FPS. By exploring the FPS, we will be able to identify key political economic factors and institutions to explain China's political economy system, its economic growth, and its problems, both historically and in contemporary times. While the FPS was a very simple institution, with each rural household owning a plot of land, it reflected the principles of China's state sector economy. In making the analogy between the family plot and the state sector, we intend to examine the following key aspects of the FPS, among others.

[4] Gao Yuling, *Zhongguo nongmin fanxingwei yanjiu 1950–1980* (Counteractions of Chinese Peasants, 1950–1980) (Hong Kong: Chinese University of Hong Kong Press, 2013), pp. 155–161.

The first aspect is the household as a self-interested rational actor. It always aims to maximize its interests within the FPS but is also constrained by the system. Two perspectives can be adopted for the analysis. From the agency perspective, we can look at how rural households invented the FPS to suit their own interests – namely, to seek the survival of family members at difficult times and to improve their welfare in normal times – and how the Communist regime accepted the system for its own interests, for example, to reduce its burden in providing welfare when the subsistence economy failed. From the structural perspective, we can look at how the FPS provides incentives while constraining rural households' behavior.

The second aspect is the FPS as a property rights institution. The term "family plot" was sometimes interpreted as "private plot." This translation is certainly incorrect. Individual families only had *de facto* property rights over the family plot, not *de jure* rights. In legal terms, this plot of land was owned by the collective, and the household only had the user rights. As history shows, the collective or the local state could reclaim its user rights from the household when needed. Since the household only had user rights, the land could not be transferred and transacted. The *de facto* property rights thus served as an institutional constraint on the household in the family plot economy.

The third aspect is the FPS as an incentive mechanism. The FPS was a supplementary institution to the rural collectives. It was operated by the private household within a large collective system. Individual households would divide their labor and time into two parts, one for the FPS and the other for the collective. In such a circumstance, it is easy to observe how the household worked. Understandably, the household allocated the most resources to the FPS. For example, family members devoted their most valuable time (e.g., the early morning, when they were still energetic) to working in the family plot, where they used the best fertilizer, etc. Compared to the collective sector, the *de facto* property rights led to a higher level of productivity in the FPS.

The fourth aspect is the FPS as a unique pattern of transaction. These products were largely for household consumption. Only the surplus would go to the market, and indeed, from time to time it was not even allowed to be sold on the market. Without a market, transactions did not occur in the FPS. In this sense, the FPS was also self-sufficient, with no "trade" taking place between and among households. Of course, no "transaction" took place between the household and the local state either, since the household made all decisions regarding the family plot and the state did not place any levy on the family plot. "No transaction" implies that no institutions exist between the FPS and other systems (e.g., the market, the state, etc). Only transactions (e.g., buying and selling) will lead to institutional creation.

The fifth aspect is the FPS as a form of welfare improvement. The FPS was an important part of the rural subsistence economy, and could also become a "welfare" improvement above the level of the subsistence economy when the collectives were able to meet subsistence requirements. Through the FPS, rural residents could produce cash crops and raise farm animals (e.g., pigs) for the market.

China's State Sector: The FPS Writ Large

The FPS can be regarded as a mini political economy system. By expanding the collectively owned commune land to entire national economy and comparing the Communist Party to the farmer who runs the family plot, we may assume that the party-state also has its own "family plot" as its own domain in the economy, be it traditional imperial factories under the Imperial Household Department or contemporary centrally or locally managed SOEs under the State Assets Supervision and Administration Commission (SASAC).

The political rationale for this FPS writ large is evident enough. At the structural level of China's political economy, an analogy can also be made between the utilities of the traditional imperial economy and the state sector in the contemporary era. The FPS writ large is an integral part of political power, aiming at achieving the self-sustainability of the regime. In the West, the economy is conceptualized as a separate and autonomous field of the society, independent from the polity. As discussed in Chapter 2, the economy, as "management of practical affairs under Heaven" in traditional China, was regarded as an integral part of the emperorship, and the former was subject to the latter.[5] While the imperial economy was transformed into a modern economy, domination of the economy continues to sustain the regime. The economy is the bloodline of the regime. While the economy also serves the political purpose of the regime in other political economy systems, the Chinese economy was a structured part of the regime. The state sector is the minimum institutional guarantee of regime sustainability. The existence of the state sector means the survival

---

[5] In the ancient model, we may assume that emperorship also had other domains outside the "economy," such as a large domain of "sacrifice," which managed the relationship between the realm and Heaven, and the domain of the "military," which managed the physical boundary of the realm and thus the economy.

of the state is not dependent on its interaction with other parts of the economy and with society in general.

At the next level, the state needs a state sector within the economy to bear its overall governance responsibilities. In this context, the state sector not only guarantees the sustainability of the regime but also serves the regime's interest in governing society. As discussed in Chapter 2, China's mainstream classical political philosophy held that it was part of the ruler's responsibilities to provide economic welfare to the ruled. In this sense, the state sector has to not only generate revenue for the regime (the household writ large), but also play an important role in maintaining the health of the whole economy, such as balancing other economic sectors, building important economic infrastructure which the private sector is not capable of addressing, and coping with economic crises.

An analogy can also be made between the family plot and the state sector in terms of operation and management of the state sector economy. The state does not manage an economy; its agencies do. There is a principal–agent issue. The imperial economy in traditional China was managed by imperial family members and other private agents, and the contemporary state sector is managed by CCP cadres and government officials. The principal–agent issue matters since it often distorts the purpose of the imperial economy, namely, its sustainability. Frequently, the agents of the state economy who have their own vested interests seek to satisfy their own interests rather than the interests of the state. Their access to both economic resources and power becomes an effective tool to maximize their self-interest. This deviation thus inevitably undermines state interests. This is also true in the contemporary state sector. In pursuing its own interests, the state sector can easily deviate from the interests of the state. As we will discuss later, this holds particularly true when the state sector is differentiated from the state due to the reform's corporatization of the state sector. For the imperial or party-state, the major issue is how to exercise its dominance over the state sector, which attempts to avoid state domination in order to maximize its corporate interests in the market system.

FPS and "Market in State"

More significantly, the family plot theory reveals the nature of the relationship between the state and the market in both traditional and contemporary China. In Chapter 2, we discussed how the emperorship dominated the economy. Despite its modern transformation, such dominance continues. In modern times, most countries in the West have developed a strong public sector. The state delivers public services through this sector. The state sector in China is similar to the public sector in the West in that it also delivers some public services. But in China, delivery of public services is not the primary function of the public sector. The state sector differs from the public sector in various important ways. First of all, the Chinese state itself behaves as a firm, since it owns a large number of enterprises. This aspect differentiates China drastically from other countries with a market economy. Second, the state sector in China is primarily for the state, or, more precisely, for the agents of the state, particularly the central government. Through the state sector, the state not only regulates the market, but is also capable of subjecting the market to state power. The Chinese political economy system is thus characterized by what this book has called "market in state" (MIS). While the existence of the FPS writ large does not deny the existence of the market, the purpose of the market is to serve the state, at least in theory. While the state makes use of the market to serve its purpose, it will also make sure that the market is under its political control. Third, as already discussed, the state sector enables the state to dominate over other sectors of the economy. In the West, states have developed financial and monetary means to regulate the economy. In China, the primary means for the state to dominate the economy is the state sector. The development of financial and monetary means to regulate the economy has come about only recently in China.

As discussed, the MIS rationale is to serve the fiscal and political interests of the state through state-dominated market mechanisms. In accordance with this logic of MIS, the FPS also dictates that the state, as a self-interested economic actor, allocates the maximum and best resources to itself. Through the state sector, the state gains the essential part of social resources for production and reproduction. Monopoly over key industries and commerce is only a part of this large picture. The state sector also contributes some of its fiscal revenue directly to the central government coffers. The Chinese fiscal regime thus differs from Western systems in that it has its own fiscal resources, independent from society, which is dominated by households and the private sector. The state thus allows the private (nonstate) sector to exist not to serve the fiscal needs of the state but to support the basic employment and material needs of the society. As we shall discuss in this chapter, the nonstate sector is populated by smaller and strategically insignificant actors with little control of the market. FPS writ large thus guarantees the state the capacity to mobilize all kinds of resources to boost the economy within a short period of time, even if there is a recession in the private sector. This is unimaginable in a state-in-market situation, unless under the special condition of war.

The most notable aspect of the FPS writ large is the lack of endogenous dynamics for institutional building or innovation. Due to its unique pattern of transaction, the FPS writ large does not have a strong incentive to develop institutions as market actors. This is different from a state-in-market case in the contemporary West. In such economies, the state needs to foster institutions such as property rights, rule of law, a regulatory framework, and a financial system so that it can collect sufficient revenue to provide various public services. By contrast, in the FPS writ large, the state derives income from the profits and tax earned through its investment financed by its own banks. The transactions are largely carried out within the expanded state sector and guided by its various agents. Limited transactions between the state and the market in this sector mean there is little incentive for institutional innovations.

However, the FPS's unique transaction pattern and the lack of institutional innovation often lead to low levels of productivity and technology development. The system favors extensive economic expansion rather than intensive economic growth. Therefore, sustainable development often becomes problematic. A level will be reached at which there is a bottleneck in economic growth.

For contemporary Chinese political economy, the most important part of the state sector is constituted by more than one hundred centrally managed SOEs. They are not only the mainstay of the state sector but also clearly take on FPS characteristics. Thus, this chapter focuses on these large enterprise groups. While the discussion below is not on the history of reform, we shall begin with some background on the formation and current situation of these giant players in both politics and the economy.

THE SOE REFORM

As discussed in earlier chapters, China's SOE reform was initiated in the late 1970s. At that time, most SOEs were mired in a situation of inefficiency and low profitability, and burdened with the provision of basic social welfare and employment. From managers to individual workers, there was little incentive to make a full effort and perform well. Starting in 1978, the first round of the SOE reforms was mostly characterized by the so-called *fangquan rangli* (decentralizing powers and sharing profits), where central ministries gradually transferred some decision-making powers to the SOEs. Similar to the HRS, the SOEs' managers were granted powers to make key decisions regarding production, investment, and personnel appointments, and responsibility for the performance of their firms. The reforms were generally unsuccessful. Instead of improvements in productivity and profitability, the incentive scheme did not work properly to encourage productivity and the retained profits were often channeled into the wages and welfare support of their employees.[6]

In 1984, with the onset of full-fledged urban economic reforms, the focus of SOE reforms shifted to fiscal and financial aspects. Reformers in this period aimed to transform the SOEs into more autonomous, self-disciplined, but still strictly state-run economic entities. These efforts included the so-called *li gai shui* (turning profits into tax revenues) reforms, which restructured the fiscal relations between SOEs and governments. In addition, SOEs were urged to wean themselves off budgetary support and depend instead on bank loans. In 1987, another milestone in SOE reform was reached with the introduction of a new contract system. Under the new system, SOE managers were given free rein to manage their enterprises on the condition that they turned over a contracted amount of taxes to the government. But these reforms were generally unsuccessful as well. Although the central ministries had weakened their control over SOEs, the powerful local governments had every reason to support the local state enterprises under their jurisdictions by forcing banks to back them. The financial situation deteriorated during the bank loan booms in 1993 and 1996. The result was ill-enforced financial discipline, continued losses, and the accumulation of huge bank loans.[7]

Beginning in 1993, the second phase of reforms was carried out under Premier Zhu Rongji, after the Communist Party's Fourteenth National Congress in 1992 formally renamed state-run enterprises (*guoying qiye*) as state-owned enterprises (*guoyou qiye*, or SOEs). In November 1993, at the Third Plenary Session of the Fourteenth Congress, the objective of SOE reform was redefined formally as building a modern enterprise system. In 1995, the central government put forth a new grand strategy of *zhuada fangxiao* (grasping the large and letting go of the small) to streamline the entire SOE sector through consolidation of the large

---

[6] Holz A. Carlson, *China's Industrial State-Owned Enterprises: Between Profitability and Bankruptcy* (Singapore: World Scientific, 2006), pp. 63–64. Also see Andrew Walder, *Communist Neo-Traditionalism: Work and Authority in Chinese Industry* (Berkeley, CA: University of California Press, 1988), pp. 228–229.

[7] Barry Naughton, *Growing Out of the Plan: Chinese Economic Reform 1978–1993* (Cambridge: University of Cambridge Press, 1996), p. 64.

Table 8.1 *List of main sectors in the strategic market*

Coal mining and dressing (CMD)
Petroleum and natural gas extraction (PNGE)
Ferrous metals mining and dressing (FMMD)
Nonferrous metals mining and dressing (NFMMD)
Tobacco processing (TP)
Petroleum processing and coking (PPC)
Medical and pharmaceutical products (MPP)
Smelting and pressing of ferrous metals (SPFM)
Smelting and pressing of nonferrous metals (SPNFM)
Electric power, steam, and hot water (EPSHW)
Gas production and supply (DPS)
Tap water production and supply (RWPS)

Source: Compiled by the authors

state-owned enterprises and selective privatization of small and medium-sized state-owned enterprises.

The first part of the grand strategy, the *zhuada* strategy, concerned large enterprise groups in strategic and heavy industry sectors. Newly created enterprises were typically formed from former industrial ministries, their major departments, subsidiaries, and affiliated research institutes. These enterprises were regrouped according to their core businesses and recapitalized in a variety of ways, in particular by shareholding reforms that transformed them into stockholding companies. A new system was established whereby the parent companies held controlling shares over their provincial, regional and functional subsidiaries. Table 8.1 lists the main state sectors identified in the strategic market. The petroleum, nuclear, and telecommunication industries provide the best examples. The reform resulted in a few hundred large state-owned enterprise groups in the capital-intensive sectors and the manufacturing industries that had significant administrative and economic barriers to entry.

The second part of the grand strategy, the *fangxiao* strategy, aimed to pull the state out of competitive sectors, especially businesses where private entrepreneurs enjoy a clear comparative advantage. The best example here is the tens of thousands of loss-making small and medium-sized enterprises under the local branches of the Ministry of Light Industry and Ministry of Textile Industry. Private entrepreneurs, most significantly former managers of these enterprises, were given the opportunity to acquire the enterprises through selling and buying state assets at a very low price. This strategy spawned a leap forward in the number of private

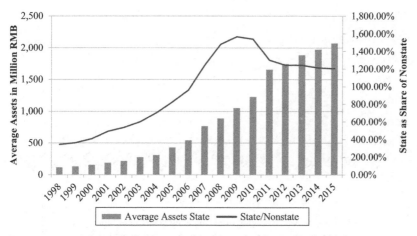

Figure 8.1 Capitalization of state-owned and state-holding manufacturing enterprises, 1998–2015
Source: National Bureau of Statistics. Compiled by the authors

and joint-stock companies. At the same time, much of the task of restructuring was decentralized to local governments, which, for their own fiscal motives, usually kept the more efficient and profitable firms and sold the inefficient and loss-making ones, in the spirit of the *zhuada fangxiao* policy of the center in Beijing. The resultant industrial ownership structure was a highly capital-intensive state sector and a much less capital-intensive private sector. In 2009, the average assets of state sector enterprises were sixteen times the average assets of nonstate enterprises, up from about three times in 1998. While the percentage later declined, it still remained at 1,200 percent in 2013 (see Figure 8.1). In other words, within only a decade, the assets of the state sector expanded more than fivefold relative to the nonstate sector.

Since the mid-1990s, the reforms have achieved considerable success in some of their key objectives. Above all, they have successfully reduced the amount of employment in the SOEs without marginalizing the state sector in overall output. As Figure 8.2 shows, the state sector's share in urban employment declined from 40 percent to less than 16 percent from 1999 to 2014, while its share of total output still made up more than a quarter of the economy in 2011.

Meanwhile, there have also been significant structural changes in the overall macromanagement system of the manufacturing industry. By the late 1990s, almost all of the industrial ministries (except the Ministry of

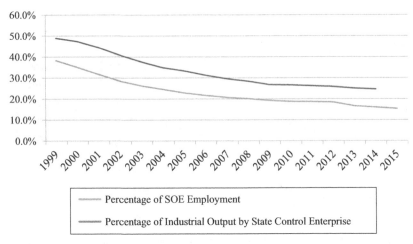

Figure 8.2 Share of the state sector in overall economy
Source: National Bureau of Statistics. Compiled by the authors

Railways, which existed until 2013) had been abolished or corporatized into ministerial-ranking SOEs.[8] Both centrally and locally managed SOEs became autonomous corporate actors, at least on paper. Their relations with the state are no longer mediated by industrial hierarchies but rather by a new overarching agency representing the state as ultimate owner and regulator – the State Asset Supervision and Administration Commission (SASAC), under the State Council. In 2013, all these remaining SOEs were placed under the supervision of either central or local (provincial, municipal, and county) branches of the SASAC. The centrally managed SOEs were defined as enterprises under the direct supervision of the central SASAC in Beijing. They have both political–administrative and economic dimensions. In political–administrative terms, they are owned by all the people in the full sense, and politically managed by the party. At least equivalent to a ministry in administrative ranking, some of these enterprises were corporatized from industrial ministries. In an economic sense, they are the largest and most dominant enterprises in the economy, with

---

[8] The same reform was introduced with regard to the Ministry of Railways (MOR) in 2013. With this reform, the MOR was abolished. The government formed a new State Railway Administration (SRA) to oversee the railway administration function, under the Ministry of Transport (MOT). Meanwhile, a new China Railway Corporation (CRC) was established to take over the commercial function previously performed by the MOR.

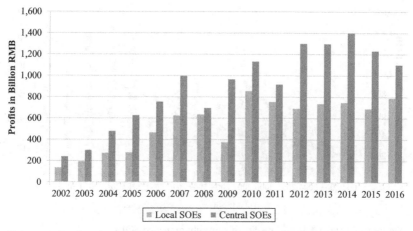

Figure 8.3 Profits of centrally managed and locally managed SOEs, 2002–2016
Source: SASAC. Compiled by the authors

huge resources and monopoly positions in their respective sectors. As shown in Figure 8.3, total profits of centrally managed SOEs have been consistently higher than those of local SOEs in recent years.

The rise of centrally managed SOEs was in a way a response to the weak state regulatory framework centered on the SASAC. Compared with the large enterprises under its nominal jurisdiction, the SASAC system is a much weaker bureaucratic system of supervision and administration. Although it has a very large nominal jurisdiction, it lacked the political authority and administrative resources to exert significant influence over rich and powerful large SOEs. The SASAC is often characterized as a weak regulator, but on the other hand it is a successful promoter when its interest in ensuring steady growth of state assets neatly coincides with the centrally managed SOEs' drive for investment and expansion. Not only are the centrally managed SOEs the greatest profit-makers, they are also consistently the largest enterprises in terms of sales revenue, total assets, value added, and almost all other quantitative indicators.[9] Measured in net wealth, China's most powerful SOEs consolidated their positions on the Fortune 500 list of the largest global corporations in 2017, pushing the

[9] The number of centrally managed SOEs has decreased over time. There were more than 190 such SOEs in 2003, when the SASAC was set up; as of August 2017, however, there were only 98 central SOEs. See www.sasac.gov.cn/n2588035/n2641579/n2641645/index.html [Accessed on August 30, 2017].

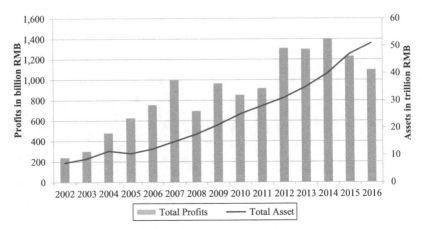

Figure 8.4 Total assets and profits of centrally managed SOEs
Source: SASAC. Compiled by the authors

number of mainland Chinese firms on the list to an unprecedented eighty-nine.[10] Most of these giant SOEs, not surprisingly, are centrally managed corporate groups and state banks in the most profitable and strategic state-dominated sectors, such as banking, energy, electricity, and insurance. Sinopec, China National Petrol Corporation, and State Grid, the three largest centrally managed SOEs, have been ranked among the ten largest enterprises in the world in recent years.[11]

THE EXPANSION OF CENTRALLY MANAGED SOES

The rapid expansion of centrally managed SOEs was already evident long before the global financial crisis in 2008. Since 2003, both the profits and the gross assets of centrally managed SOEs have increased tenfold (Figure 8.4). This was during a period in which GDP rose by 200 percent and total assets for all manufacturing enterprises increased by 400 percent. China's leading state-owned manufacturing enterprises, which formed the bulk of the centrally managed SOEs, routinely generated more than a

---

[10] Of the eighty-nine mainland Chinese firms on the list, forty-seven were centrally managed SOEs and another twelve were state-owned banks or financial enterprises. The detailed list is available online at http://en.wikipedia.org/wiki/Fortune_Global_500.

[11] In 2016, State Grid, Sinopec, and China Petrol were ranked as the second, third, and fourth largest firms globally by revenue: see http://fortune.com/global500/list/ [Accessed on August 27, 2017].

quarter of the profits made by the country's 400,000–450,000 above-scale manufacturing enterprises (revenues from main business above the scale of 20 million RMB).

While most enterprises around the world regarded the global financial crisis as a cause of woe, China's centrally managed SOEs must have seen it as a great opportunity for expansion. Although their profits did experience a temporary sharp dip in 2008, investment and asset accumulation continued unabated. Under China's new economic system, centrally managed SOEs, as part of the economic arm of state power, have an inbuilt obligation to implement the key macroeconomic objectives of the central government, in particular economic growth and structural adjustment.

Although 2009 was a significant year for large investment projects following the RMB4 trillion rescue package, the centrally managed SOEs were in fact not the leading actors in this investment spree. In 2009, gross investment made only by the central SOEs increased by 15 percent, far below the 30 percent increase at the national level. Furthermore, 61 percent of these investments were funded by their own profits rather than bank loans.[12] Instead, the centrally managed SOEs expanded structurally. The crisis helped the centrally managed SOEs in two ways. First, the centrally managed SOEs strengthened their relative positions vis-à-vis other players facing an immediate worsening of financial and economic conditions in the immediate aftermath of the crisis. Second, the financial position of the centrally managed SOEs was further strengthened since the government was forced to pursue a painful policy of credit squeezing to quench inflation as a result of its loose credit policy in the preceding years. In both cases, small and medium-sized enterprises were the major casualty, followed by smaller state firms and even the financial positions of local governments. The centrally managed SOEs had managed to take full advantage of their strong financial position, ensured by a monopoly over key sectors. The scale of the expansion can be demonstrated by the doubling of the centrally managed SOEs' assets between 2008 and 2013.

While almost all large centrally managed SOEs have tightened their grip on their respective markets and explored new territories outside their main businesses, the most telling example is perhaps the State Grid. According to an investigative article in *Business Watch Magazine*, the general manager of the State Grid, Liu Zhenya – who had a vision of building a Chinese Siemens – had sped up the corporation's forceful expansion into control

[12] *SASAC Annual Report 2010*, p. 7; available at www.sasac.gov.cn [Accessed on June 15, 2011].

manufacturing of power transmission and distribution machinery, small hydropower stations, and even wind power.[13] In particular, despite protests from the China Machinery Industry Federation, the State Grid was able to push forward with the takeovers of Xuji Group and Gaoping Group, two leading electrical manufacturers, after they suffered large losses at the outset of the crisis in 2008.[14] En route to achieving a grand monopoly, the State Grid adopted a range of aggressive practices to ensure control and profits, including barring external wind generators access to its grid, procrastinating on further reforms to separate transmission and distribution, and conducting aggressive price bargaining with the major five power plants to achieve handsome profits. This practice inadvertently caused severe power shortages for several months in 2011.[15]

Meanwhile, the State Grid has been a leading force in the technological transformation of the sector. The core system of the electrical grid is fast transforming into an Ultra-High Voltage (UHV) transmission system, in preparation for a planned nationally integrated smart power grid – a visionary strategy for the next-generation power grid championed by State Grid management since 2007. In every aspect, the State Grid, regularly ranked among the largest firms in Fortune Global 500, is rapidly reshaping the national power sector. The State Grid has also been at the forefront of change at the global level. For example, at the United Nations Sustainable Development Summit in New York on September 26, 2015, it proposed a global network for global power demand for green and renewable energy. As Xu Yi-chong suggests in his study of the State Grid, rather than acting as an agent of the central state, the State Grid takes its own global business initiatives, while the state takes advantage of such initiatives.[16] The usual logics of dependency are thus reversed in such a case.

If the State Grid directed its expansionary strategy at a system centering on its own sectoral turf, some other, larger centrally managed SOEs have explicitly crossed over to naked profit maximization. The best example is the central SOE expansion in the real estate sector after the 2008 global financial crisis, which saw the most rapid revenue and profit increases of all

---

[13] Wang Qiang, "Guowang diguo" (The Empire of the State Grid), *Shangwu Zhoukan* (Business Weekly) 11:3 (2011), pp. 31–37.

[14] Fan Ting, "Guojia dianwang longduan kuozhang" (The Expansion of State Grid Monopoly), *Economy & State Weekly* 2 (2011), p. 21.

[15] "Dianhuang zhebizhang zenmesuan?" (How to Account for Power Shortage), *Guangming Daily*, May 20, 2011.

[16] Yi-chong Xu, *Sinews of Power: Politics of the State Grid Corporation of China* (Corby: Oxford University Press, 2017), p. 301.

major sectors. It is reported, for instance, that seven of the ten most expensive land lease deeds were made between the centrally managed SOEs and local government. This news came at a time when the central government and the media were seriously concerned about increasing land and property bubbles, which had caused severe economic and social concern among urban dwellers.[17]

The coal mining sector was another field in which the centrally managed SOEs crushed their private rivals in a series of high-profile mergers and integrations.[18] In the steel sector, the state consolidated its control over the larger manufacturers and recovered some formerly privately owned steel mills. In the coal sector, the state revoked the permits previously issued to private individuals and firms operating hundreds of small coal mines in an effort to "rationalize" the sector through renationalization. Spearheading this *de facto* nationalization were China's largest central and provincial SOEs in the coal sector, such as the Shenhua Group. Similarly, in Inner Mongolia, coal sector restructuring did not involve private investors; the mines were redistributed among about twenty large SOEs, led by Shenhua and Huadian International.[19]

It is clear that China has seen the rise of a new SOE paradigm which is decidedly different from the old SOEs during the Maoist planning period, as well as the early reform years under Deng Xiaoping. As a new type of economic organization, the new SOE paradigm carries much less social responsibility, but no less political and economic weight. More importantly, the new SOEs are distinguished from the old SOEs by a very high degree of autonomy from both the economic forces of the market and the fiscal and administrative control of the central government. In this sense, they no longer represent even a vague sense of national interest, but rather their own corporate interests. This arises partly from a relationship of autonomy and interdependence which the new SOEs have developed with the other significant economic interests within the state.

The rise of the new SOEs presents a significant challenge to the leadership in China. Since 2009, centrally managed SOEs have been the subject of

---

[17] "Fangjia yijing paiqi putongren, yangqi diwang shegai huanghuang" (Housing Price Is Above All Affordability. Centrally Managed SOEs Land Acquisition Raises Concerns), *Southern Daily*, April 12, 2010.

[18] For a review of the debate on the expansion of the state sector, see "Guojin mintui: yangqi kuozhang yin reyi" (Advance of State Capital and the Retreat of Private Capital: Debating Boundless Expansion of Centrally Managed SOEs), *Southern Weekly*, August 20, 2009.

[19] Wang Xiaolu, *Grey Income and Income Inequality in China* (Beijing: National Economic Research Institute of China Reform Foundation, 2010), pp. 75–76.

severe media criticism. They are described by some liberal economists and observers as *de facto* nonstate-owned in the sense of being controlled by a bureaucratic capitalist class.[20] In consequence, a number of SOE-related policy directives have been released as a symbolic gesture to rein in the centrally managed SOEs, but no concrete reform has so far been enforced. As will be discussed later, a more systemic approach, through tightened regulatory or legal frameworks, may also have major shortcomings. More specifically, there seems to be a lack of policy enforcement power on the part of regulatory and legal authorities vis-à-vis the politically vocal large SOEs.

CENTRALLY-MANAGED SOES AS FISCAL REGIME

The rise of new SOEs is part and parcel of the most profound structural change in China's political economy – that of a state which is resurgent in the economic life of the country. In many ways, this is a consequence of Zhu Rongji's mid-1990s reforms, albeit an unintended one. Indeed, what makes the new state economy different from the Communist economic system in place since the mid-1950s is the fact that, despite the reformers' grand design to create an efficient, growth-promoting and centrally coordinated system that complements and supports the market – as in the case of the East Asian NIEs – the outcome is a fiscal system that strengthens state dominance in the market . As Figure 8.5 illustrates, while the SOEs' (including state-owned shareholding firms) share of government revenues declined significantly from 2005 to 2016, the state sector in general, and centrally managed SOEs in particular, still remains the pillar of government revenue, contributing between one-fifth and one-quarter of current government revenue. Thus, even as the state allows the nonstate sector to expand rapidly and share this expansion through VAT and other taxes such as business and corporate income taxes, the state could still achieve stability in the fiscal base by taxing the principal business of a smaller

---

[20] There is a growing body of the literature on this topic. See for example Wu Jinglian, "Tiaozhan quangui zibenzhuyi: zhongguo gaige jinru shenhuichu" (China's Reform into Deep Waters: Challenging Crony Capitalism), *Green Leaves* 21 (2010), pp. 90–95; Zheng Yongnian and Huang Yanjie, "Zhongguo guojiazhuyi jingji moshi hechuqu" (Whither China's Model of Economic Statism), *China Entrepreneurs* 11 (2010), pp. 16–19; and Xu Xiaonian, "Zhongguo zhengzai zouxiang quangui zibenzhuyi" (Making Big Strides towards Crony Capitalism), *Nanfangchuang* 16 (2010), www.nfcmag.com/article/2249.html [Accessed on August 15, 2014].

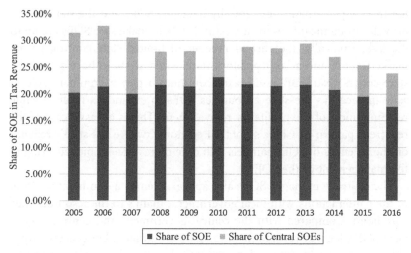

Figure 8.5 SOEs' contribution to fiscal revenue
Source: National Bureau of Statistics. Compiled by the authors

number of central SOEs, whose monopolistic or oligopolistic nature would ensure a more stable stream of income from their principal business.

The expansion of the centrally managed SOEs is both the outcome of and an important driver in the decade-long expansion of the state. Since the SOEs started to make a profit around 1998, the one-way dependency of the 1990s, where the loss-making SOEs depended on government bailouts, has been reversed. Since the early 2000s, it has been the government counting on the centrally managed SOEs as the most stable and secure source of tax revenue. In 2010, for example, all SOEs together accounted for 31 percent of the total tax revenue and 122 centrally managed SOEs alone contributed 19 percent. The continuously rising tax revenues from the centrally managed SOEs add new force to the fiscal bonds binding the centrally managed SOEs and the central government. Under the existing tax-sharing system, the central government claims all corporate taxes and about 75 percent of value-added taxes of the centrally managed SOEs, and tax revenues from the centrally managed SOEs routinely account for more than 30 percent of central government revenue.[21] The fiscal links between

---

[21] According to the SASAC's five-year review, total tax collected from central SOEs reached 1.4 trillion RMB. This amounted to about 19 percent of the total government tax revenues. Of this 1.4 trillion, more than 1.1 trillion were central taxes, contributing about

the market performance of centrally managed SOEs and the state coffers provide strong incentives for the central state to make sure SOEs are up to the task. Ironically, the current practice of limited state control, partial marketization, and a lax regulatory framework seems to have served the state coffers best: SOE-based taxes continue to play a dominant role in state finances, as the state encourages SOEs to expand its revenue while retaining most of the profits for reinvestment. This is a classic case of the recurrent pattern in China's political economy, where the state's reliance on the revenues of SOEs compels it to cede more space of maneuvering to the management of the SOEs.

The centrally managed SOEs also appear to enjoy a dominant position in their interactions with local government, thanks to the resources they command. Compared with the central government and centrally managed SOEs, local governments have relatively strained budgets and arguably the highest incentives for economic growth. Under this prevailing incentive structure, the centrally managed SOEs have played the game to their advantage by making use of their political autonomy and economic monopoly. In the aftermath of the global financial crisis, the number of cooperative projects involving centrally managed SOEs and local governments (*yangdi hezuo*) increased rapidly. In the past, local government had courted Hong Kong and Taiwan companies, in the 1990s, and foreign enterprises, in the post-WTO era. In the immediate post-2008 years, the financially empowered centrally managed SOEs became the most favored partner for entrepreneurial local officials. Cooperation contracts in this category often involve local government offers of cheap land, infrastructure, and sometimes loosening of environmental standards. The centrally managed SOEs have been more successful than foreign enterprises in securing local markets with low entrance costs and almost zero political risk.

The most successful recipients of investment from centrally managed SOEs were initially governments in the central and western regions, especially provinces in the middle range in terms of economic development, including Anhui, Henan, Hunan, Jiangxi, Liaoning, Hubei, and Chongqing. But since late 2008, developed economies such as Guangdong, Zhejiang, Shandong, and Jiangsu have also joined the competition. Anhui, for example, concluded 585 investment agreements with

---

35 percent of central government tax revenues. SASAC, *The SASAC Annual Report for 2010*, available online at www.sasac.gov.cn [Accessed on July 6, 2015].

the centrally managed SOEs, with a total value of RMB1.6 trillion, by May 2011.[22] At least twenty of these projected 585 investment packages exceeded RMB60 billion. The record set by Anhui was soon broken by Guangdong, which signed RMB2.5 trillion worth of contracts with seventy-one centrally managed SOEs during the annual session of the National People's Congress in 2011, when local, central, industrial, and other elites of the party got together in Beijing.[23] Perhaps only a fraction of these investments would eventually materialize, but their size and the trend of expansion were still staggering. As the monopoly profits and potential financial might of the centrally managed SOEs and the growth fever of local government join hands, these emergent relationships of structural interdependence will likely emerge as a new pattern in China's state economy.

The rise of the centrally managed SOEs as powerful players in the economy with strong bonds with local government has produced many unexpected outcomes. The centrally managed SOEs have gained so much autonomy that they are beginning to change the functional division on which the system is based, as some of the most powerful SOEs expand their subsidiaries in the real estate sector. From late 2009 to early 2010, when the real estate fever reached a head, 78 of the 122 centrally managed SOEs took part in the fervent expansion.[24] Although they were not the main force in the real estate sector, they nevertheless flexed their muscles by producing seven of the ten most expensive land sales. In 2009, it was reported that some cash-rich centrally managed SOEs created their own internal banks in addition to complex financial departments – a move signifying further financial autonomy of the centrally managed SOEs, as self-sufficient corporate groups akin to the industrial–financial conglomerates in other East Asian countries (*zaibatsu* in Japan and the *chaebol* in South Korea).

CENTRALLY-MANAGED SOES AS POLITICAL ACTORS

Since the reform, China's largest SOEs have undergone many important changes that have made them more like the East Asian conglomerates. But there remains an important difference between the industrial–financial

---

[22] The full report is available at http://gb.takungpao.com/place/anhui/2011-05-12/802179 .html [Accessed on August 30, 2011].

[23] Li Peng, "Yangqi ruyue chaoyong" (Centrally Managed SOEs Ride Wave to Enter Guangdong), *The Economy & Nation Weekly* 7 (2011).

[24] "Yangqi tuishu fangdichan zhimi" (The Myth of Centrally Managed SOEs Exit from Real Estate), *Xinhua News Agency*, March 25, 2010.

conglomerates and the centrally managed SOEs, namely, the institutional links between the centrally managed SOEs and the central party-state. While SASAC may lack the authority to exercise regular administrative control over the centrally managed SOEs, there are always the central organs of the Chinese Communist Party, which appoints and manages the top managers of the centrally managed SOEs. The corporatization of the SOEs has not weakened their links to the party, as has been the case in relation to the state. Instead, in terms of elite representation and circulation, the centrally managed SOEs seem to have acquired a new importance, as the party tends to reward economic performance and recognize actors with autonomous sources of power.

Indeed, due to the vital importance of SOE cadres, the CCP has held steadfast to the "party controls cadres" principle in the SOE sector.[25] There have been many changes to the Chinese Communist Party as a result of the marketization of the economy, but this principle remains the holy grail of CCP rule. In a genuine market economy, top business executives, including CEOs, CFOs, COOs, chairs, and board members, are human resources allocated by the market. In China, however, SOE executives are considered cadres of the party-state. Most of them are party members and some are even CCP Central Committee members or alternative members. For instance, in 2009, seventeen alternative members and two full members of the Central Committee came from the centrally managed SOEs.[26] All the appointments to important Chinese business groups were made through the central nomenclature of the Chinese Communist Party (see Appendix).

Since the elite management class are also high-ranking party cadres, the CCP's Central Organization Department (COD) has legitimate jurisdiction over their offices and exercises considerable discretionary power over job appointments.[27] This organizational commanding height is enforced by the fact that the CCP also controls the ministerial-level SASAC, the party group embedded within it. The COD, in conjunction with SASAC, which formally exercises the power of ownership, manage the top-tier personnel of all centrally managed SOEs. Likewise, the provincial- and municipal-level Organizational Department and SASAC exercise the same command

---

[25] Since the late 1990s, this "principle" has been expanded to include "the party-controlling talents" regardless of party membership.

[26] Kjeld Erik Brødsgaard, "Politics and Business Group Formation in China: The Party in Control?" *China Quarterly* 211 (September 2012), pp. 624–648.

[27] The organization departments of provincial party committees manage city-level SOE cadres.

over the personnel of the provincial and municipal-level SOEs. In general, the COD thus has a higher vintage and larger purview than SASAC, since it appoints all the cadres of all important organizations in the party, the government, the people's congress, the people's political consultative conference, the trade union, and institutions of higher education. In addition to personnel matters in each sector, the COD is also put in charge of cadre rotation between these vertical systems of nomenclature.

In line with the spirit of the "CCP Central Committee's Decision on Strengthening the Party's Ruling Capability,"[28] the COD routinely rotates cadres among different positions and locations so that they gain broad experience and exposure to various aspects of the Chinese political establishment's operation. On August 6, 2006, the COD promulgated "Regulations for the Rotation of the Leading Cadres of the Party and Government," which formalized a system of cadre rotation to be carried out between localities, between departments, between localities and departments, and between party-state bureaucracies and SOEs and various auxiliary organizations of the party-state such as the Youth League, the Women's Association, the official Trade Union, and various nonprofit organizations. Article 16 of the regulation states: "carry out cadre rotation between party-state organs and state-owned enterprises and non-profit organizations, selecting the leadership talent from the latter to serve in the former and recommending party-state cadres to positions in state-owned enterprises and non-profit organizations." Cadre swapping between SOEs and local government has sped up since this time.

As cadre promotion through the circulation of elites between the center (ministries and departments), local government (provinces and municipalities), and the industrial sector (centrally managed SOEs) gradually became the norm in the *nomenklature*, many top managers in the centrally managed SOEs have become regional or national leaders. For instance, at the end of 2011, 43 of China's 263 current provincial party secretaries, governors, and vice governors had an SOE background, mostly with centrally managed SOE affiliations.[29] Outstanding performance in the centrally managed SOEs could well offer an ideal starting point for a career in provincial leadership.

---

[28] Passed by the Fourth Plenum of the Sixteenth Party Congress on September 19, 2004.

[29] Lance Gore Liang-Ping, "China Recruits Top SOE Executives to the Government," *EAI Background Brief No. 661*, East Asian Institute, National University of Singapore, September 30, 2011.

In addition to being rotated, top SOE executives are also included in a comprehensive cadre-training system, which consists of six institutions: the Central Party School; the National School of Administration; the three "China Executive Leadership Academies" at Pudong, Jinggangshan, and Yanan; and the China Business Executives Academy, Dalian. They constitute the top-tier cadre-training facilities in the nation and all except the Central Party School are run by the COD. Of the six schools, China Business Executives Academy, Dalian specializes in training SOE executives or business cadres for the party. The trainees are business executives, but first and foremost they are cadres of the party. They are not simply human resources to be allocated by the market, but part of China's ruling elite.

The SOE group is a force to be reckoned with on the Chinese political stage. The "Petroleum Faction," which was formed during the Mao era and suffered greatly in the anticorruption campaign beginning in 2013, was a primary example. Besides this faction, many of today's top leaders have experience running businesses. Table 8.2 highlights the business experience of the current members of the Political Bureau and Political Bureau Standing Committee – the apex of political power in China. For instance, in 2012, prior to the eighteenth National Congress of the Chinese Communist Party, nine of the twenty-eight political Bureau members (32 percent) and three out of the nine members (44 percent) of the Political Bureau Standing Committee had at least some experience managing a business. Recent anticorruption campaigns have often targeted CEOs-turned-local and central leaders, especially those associated with Zhou Yongkang, but such extraordinary measures do not necessarily mean a fundamental change in the model of elite circulation. On the list of the representatives to the Nineteenth Party Congress in 2017, fifty-three came from centrally managed SOEs, one more than was the case at the Eighteenth Party Congress in 2012.[30]

The institutional links between the centrally managed SOEs and the party-state have significant consequences. In theory, since the party-state makes all personnel appointments to the centrally managed SOEs, the relationship between the two is a principal–agent one. The principal–agent problem does arise where the two parties have different interests and asymmetric information (with the agent having more information),

---

[30] http://news.takungpao.com.hk/mainland/focus/2017–07/3472025.html [Accessed on August 27, 2017].

Table 8.2 *Political Bureau members with business administration background (2012)*

Name	Current position	Business administration experience
Wu Bangguo	Political Bureau Standing Committee member Chairman, National People's Congress	General Manager, Shanghai No.3 Electric Tube Factory; Deputy Manager, Shanghai Electron Tube Industrial Co.
Jia Qinglin	Political Bureau Standing Committee member Chairman, CPPCC	CEO, China Machinery and Equipment Import and Export Corporation; President, Taiyuan Heavy Machinery Co.
Zhou Yongkang	Political Bureau Standing Committee Member Chairman of Central Politics and Law Committee	President, CNPC (PetrolChina)
Li Changchun	Political Bureau Standing Committee Member	General manager, Shengyang Electrical Control Equipment Industrial Company
Wang Zaoguo	Political Bureau Member; Vice Chairman of NPC; Chairman of All China Confederation of Trade Unions	Party secretary, China No. 2 Automobile Plant
Wang Qishan	Political Bureau Member; Vice Premier	President, China Construction Bank; General manager, China Rural Investment Trust Co.
Liu Qi	Political Bureau Member; Beijing Party Secretary	CEO, Wuhan Iron and Steel Co.
Liu Yandong	Political Bureau member; State Councilor	Deputy party secretary, Beijing Experimental Chemical Plant
Zhang Gaoli	Political Bureau Member; Party Secretary of Tianjin	General Manager, Maoming Petrol Industrial Co (a subsidiary of Sinopec)
Yu Zhengsheng	Political Bureau Member; Mayor of Shanghai	Acting General Manager, Kanghua Trading Co.

Source: Compiled by the authors

such that the principal cannot directly ensure that the agent is always acting in the principal's best interests, particularly when actions that are useful to the principal are costly to the agent and where elements of what the agent does are costly for the principal to observe. However, the interaction between the two is often reciprocal and forms a relationship of "reciprocal accountability," a term that Susan Shirk used to describe the relationship between central leaders and provincial government officials.[31] In this situation, the leaders choose the officials and the officials also choose the leaders. The political influence that the centrally managed SOEs can exercise over the central leadership means that the latter must allow the former greater operational and decision-making leeway than the principal could give to the agent. More importantly, the central SOE sector is actually the "family plot" of the central government, and it makes a vital revenue contribution to the latter. Thus, more often than not, in their daily operations, the centrally managed SOEs are frequently able to "hijack" the central government. As we will show, the centrally managed SOEs can often behave against the interests of society in the domestic market and against China's national interest in the international market. They also make it impossible for the central government to establish a regulatory regime over the SOE sector.

CENTRALLY-MANAGED SOES AS ECONOMIC ACTORS

Despite their huge revenues and profits, China's SOEs, particularly the centrally managed ones, are often criticized as major sources of resource misallocation, hotbeds of poor corporate governance, and chief culprits for the widening income gap.[32] While all these criticisms could stand further examination to a certain degree, the solutions are not straightforward, since the SOEs' fundamental problems are inextricably linked to more profound structural problems in the Chinese political economy.

Governance Problems

While the economic performance of both central and local SOEs has improved significantly since 1998, they still lag on all other indicators of competitiveness, such as unit job creation, investment efficiency, productivity, value added, and technological innovation, considering the amount of the financial resources they control. Despite the rapid rise in the amount

---

[31] Susan L. Shirk, *The Political Logic of Economic Reform in China* (Berkeley, CA: University of California Press, 1993), pp. 82–84.

[32] The Unirule Institute of Economics, *The Nature, Performance and Reform of the State-Owned Enterprises*, Beijing, March 2011.

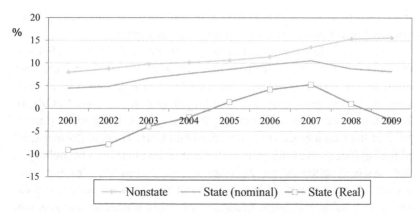

Figure 8.6 Return on capital for state and nonstate enterprises
Source: Adapted from Sheng Hong and Zhao Nong, *State-Owned Enterprises in China: Nature, Performance and Reform* (Singapore: World Scientific, 2012), p. 81

of profits and assets available, the profit-to-asset ratio of the centrally managed SOEs has been dismal at best, achieving either negative or only slightly positive growth for recent years.[33] While some of these inefficiencies might be justified as costs for the provision of public goods, a lack of competition and poor corporate governance are more likely to have caused poor performance.

According to a study by the Unirule Institute of Economics, China's leading private economic research institute, the state sector lags far behind the nonstate sector in its overall economic performance as measured in terms of average rate of return on equity (Figure 8.6). From 2011 onward, nominally, the gap between SOEs and non-SOEs seems quite narrow, but if the full scale of subsidy, including subsidized capital, land, and energy, is accounted for, the gap increases to a staggering 10–15 percent. The worst year was 2009, when the efficiency gap went back to the pre-2005 level of more than 15 percent. In particular, sectors in which the centrally managed SOEs dominate were the least efficient and contributed the most toward this efficiency gap.[34] Even though this measuring method might understate the efficiency of the more capital-intensive

---

[33] "Special Report on Central SOEs" (*Guanzhu yangqi*), *Jingji Ribao* (Economic News Daily), December 29, 2010.
[34] The Unirule Institute of Economics, *The Nature, Performance and Reform of the State-Owned Enterprises*, pp. 49–51.

state sectors vis-à-vis the nonstate sector, there is no doubt a huge efficiency gap between the two sectors' uses of capital.

Besides inefficiency, poor corporate governance and a high incidence of corruption in the state sector have also long attracted attention from both domestic and overseas analysts. High-profile corruption cases were often seen in the top management of the largest centrally managed SOEs. In 2009 alone, two ministerial-ranking SOE magnates, Kang Rixin (former CEO of the China Nuclear Corporation) and Chen Tonghai (former CEO of the Sinopec), were both arrested for embezzling hundreds of millions of state assets. Another recent investigation into Wuliangye, a leading state-owned wine manufacturer, was carried out by China's Securities Regulatory Commission (SRC) due to serious financial misconduct and resultant heavy losses of state assets.[35] In the light of numerous cases of SOE financial fraud in the past few years, this is hardly an isolated case.

Income Distribution

The effect of the state sector, and especially centrally managed SOEs, on income distribution has raised concern on two levels: executive incomes and overall societal income distribution. The first level is relatively simple. Since the partial corporatization of the state sector and especially the listing of larger SOEs, the CEOs have enjoyed exorbitant salaries and bonuses pegged to their performance. This problem aroused grievances both in wider society and inside the SOEs themselves. In August 2014, China's new leadership adopted measures to cap these salaries, as well as other perks and benefits.[36]

The distributional consequences for the SOEs were far more intractable, as they involved millions if not tens of millions in the urban workforce. Official surveys were available but rarely focused on SOEs' effects on income distribution. Based on a 2008 income survey, the average wage rate in the state sector is 63 percent higher than in the private sector and 17 percent higher than the national average wage rate, including government organizations and public service-providing institutions (e.g., the

---

[35] The first news about the scandal was covered by a Shanghai-based newspaper: "Wuliangye under the Investigation of SRC," *Diyi Caijing Ribao* (The First Financial News), September 24, 2009. The next report came twenty months later in the same paper, on May 27, 2011. The indictments and punishments appeared to be much lower than public expectation.

[36] http://politics.people.com.cn/n/2014/0830/c1024-25569328.html [Accessed on June 12, 2015].

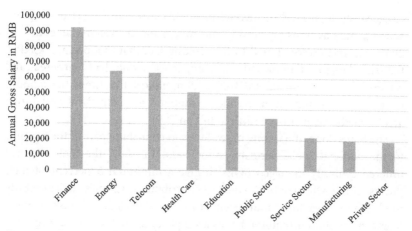

Figure 8.7 Intersectoral wage differentials in Zhejiang, 2008
Source: Zhejiang Statistical Bureau, 2009. Compiled by the authors

public education and health care sectors).[37] A provincewide survey by the Zhejiang Statistical Bureau in 2009 found that workers in a sector controlled by state banks – finance – and two sectors dominated by the centrally managed SOEs – energy and telecommunication – enjoyed the highest salaries across the economy, while the manufacturing and non-manufacturing private sectors paid the least (Figure 8.7). The actual income gaps between SOE employees in the monopoly sectors and those in other enterprises and sectors are likely to endure, since real income levels and welfare provisions for SOE employees far exceed published salaries.[38]

An even more worrying development is the fast widening gap in hidden income, better known as "gray income," which seldom registers in official statistical surveys on income. As in the case of the official income difference, the gaps in gray income are also a function of market control and rent-seeking. Two studies by a team of researchers led by Wang Xiaolu, a leading scholar in the study of China's income distribution, listed SOE monopoly as one of the top five factors contributing to China's

---

[37] The Unirule Institute of Economics, *The Nature, Performance and Reform of the State-Owned Enterprises*, pp. 56–57.

[38] Ren Zhong and Zhou Yunbo, "Dui longduan dui hangye nei shouruchaju de guiji" (An Assessment of the Monopolistic Contribution to Intra-sector Inequality), *Jingji Lilun yu Guanli* (Journal of Economic Theory and Management) 29:4, pp. 52–53.

dangerously high level of income inequality through a myriad of "gray" sources, such as housing subsidy and miscellaneous welfare benefits.[39] In 2007, observers were alerted to the striking fact that Sinopec and CNPC, the two largest state-owned oil companies, alone had garnered and retained a total profit of RMB100 billion, almost five times the amount China spent in minimum livelihood supports for both rural and urban areas, which was just over RMB20 billion.[40]

The State Council has long urged SOEs to contribute part of their profits to the national social security endowment. In 2007, the State Council ordered centrally managed SOEs to give a minimum 5 percent of their profits to the Ministry of Finance to contribute to China's social security fund. But in three out of four recent years, the SOEs failed to meet even the 5 percent minimum requirement as a simple token of their social responsibility. Except in 2009, the profits given to the state accounted for an average of just 2 percent of the total profits of the centrally managed SOEs. Since even the minimum standard was rarely met, there was doubt that the SOEs would turn over 10–15 percent of their profits to meet the State Council's requirement for 2012 onwards.

The distributional consequences for the SOEs have a critical political dimension. As economists from the Unirule Institute of Economics have rightly argued, since SOEs are nominally state-owned entities, they should contribute to the welfare of all the country's citizens, instead of redistributing after-tax profits internally in the form of high salary and welfare payments to its employees – not to mention the outright corruption and embezzlement seen to have occurred on the part of its management.[41] Unless the government finds mechanisms to redistribute SOEs' after-tax profits to society, SOEs are bound to experience greater criticism on social and political grounds.

Price Distortions

The centrally managed SOEs' monopoly-pricing behavior has been a particular concern. Some centrally managed SOEs, as sole suppliers of energy and transportation services, were frequently reported as exploiting

---

[39] Wang Xiaolu, *Grey Income and Income Inequality in China* (Beijing: National Economic Research Institute of China Reform Foundation, 2010), pp. 75–76.

[40] Fu Ziheng, "Ruhe shi yangqi zhenzheng guoyou" (How to Make Centrally Managed SOEs Truly State-Owned), *Southern Daily*, January 2, 2011.

[41] The Unirule Institute of Economics, *The Nature, Performance and Reform of the State-Owned Enterprises*, p. 97.

their monopolistic position by marking up the prices of key products. In addition, Sinopec and CNPC's monopoly of petrol supply networks, to the exclusion of local private retail suppliers, has prevented the market from reacting promptly to price signals when there is a shortage of supply, particularly in the more export-oriented southern region. These factors led to a severe oil shortage in 2010.[42] As discussed earlier, this practice of artificial supply shortage is even more prevalent in the power sector, where the State Grid controls the major part of the country's electricity network. The State Grid's control over access to its nationwide transmission system and thus the price structure of electricity has already led to persistent power shortages, while it makes huge profits at both consumers' and generators' cost.

Similarly, monopolistic pricing behaviors are also widely observed across the state-owned telecommunication sector, such as when China Netcom and China Telecom priced Internet broadband at over 300 percent of its operation costs.[43] According to the initial results of a joint study on mobile communication and Chinese society, the average Chinese person spends 5.4 percent of their income on mobile telecommunication; for those who earn less than 10,000 RMB, the share is as high as 5–10 percent of personal income, whereas the similar estimated share in developed countries is about 1–2 percent.[44] The underlying implication is that the price of necessities provided by the centrally managed SOEs acts like a regressive indirect tax.

---

[42] Wang Kangpeng, *"Youhuang miju yiwai yu biran"* (The Puzzle of Oil Shortage: The Unexpected and the Inevitable Factors), *Economy & Nation Weekly* 10 (2010), pp. 41–45.

[43] Interestingly, this criticism first came from the top state media, in the form of a letter from a reader. See "How to Reform the State Telecom Sector?" in *People's Daily*, September 21, 2010. But in a more interesting episode, on November 9, 2011, China Central Television (CCTV) used a popular social investigative program to launch an attack on two state telecom companies' monopoly pricing of broadband Internet service. This time, the state telecom companies fought back through the state-run, ministerial-level China Telecommunication News. Later, *People's Daily* and *Xinhua News Agency* joined CCTV's side. It is widely speculated that the criticism came from the major state media and the growing dissatisfaction of its party boss, the Department of Propaganda, with the Internet monopoly of China Telecom and China Unicom, as well as the obstacles to its own ambitions. The latter had the possible backing of the Ministry of Trade and Information and the SASAC. The state media seemed to enjoy the upper hand in the political struggle, since China's highest economic regulator, the National Development and Reform Commission (NDRC), had filed a monopoly pricing case against the two state telecom operators. But according to First Finance News, the three sides seemed to reach an agreement, as the two centrally owned enterprises admitted their wrongdoings and agreed to lower the Internet access price.

[44] http://tech.sina.com.cn/t/2011-01-07/11225070502.shtml [Accessed on September 1, 2011].

Although there are usually public hearings regarding price hikes for monopoly enterprises, most of these hearings are simply formalities.

A hidden source of price distortion came from the external costs of the monopoly, such as environmental pollution and public health. China's oil companies have been identified as a major source of air pollution for cities such as Beijing due to their refineries' low environmental standards.[45] Ironically, the regulations are written and supervised by a Committee of Petrol Chemical Standards consisting mainly of representatives from the state-owned petrol system (Sinopec and CNPC being the principal members).[46] The Committee has naturally found it in their interest to stick to the old environmentally unfriendly standards. This is also the case for tobacco. Responsibility for public health consequences and antitobacco supervision is placed on the shoulders of the state tobacco system. As a result, the price of ordinary tobacco is extremely low in China. This arrangement has largely distributed the hidden costs of health hazards solely among customers, and indeed the whole Chinese population.

The Overseas Market

The paradoxical nature of the SOEs is exposed when they become global actors in overseas markets. As in the domestic market, they play both the market card and the state card to their advantage. When seeking profit, they play the market card even against national interests. When faced with losses and failures, the state card becomes desirable as the central state will bear the costs.

The brawl between Sinopec and CNPC in Sudan is a classic example in this category. The two oil giants are oligopolies created from the corporatizing of China's Ministry of Petroleum and its regional subsidiaries. As the company with a greater specialism in upstream oil extraction, especially for overseas oilfields, CNPC has long been recognized as the principal agent of the Chinese central government in securing stable Sudanese oil.[47] But in 2000, Sinopec decided to participate in critical

---

[45] Tom Orlik, "Cost of Clean Air Fogs Outlook for Sinopec," *The Wall Street Journal*, February 4, 2013.

[46] Ye Tan, "Tanlan zaojiu dibiaozhun chengpinyou" (Avarice Makes Low-Standard Refined Oil Possible), *The Beijing News*, February 4, 2013.

[47] Liou Chin-shian, "Bureaucratic Politics and Overseas Investment by Chinese State-Owned Oil Companies: Illusory Champions," *Asian Survey* 49:4 (2009), pp. 682–683.

bidding for two projects in conjunction with a Malaysian oil company, when CNPC had almost secured its anticipated majority share. As a result, China's national team secured fewer oil imports than had been expected. Even when Sinopec came under pressure from the Ministry of Commerce to cooperate with CNPC in the national oil team, its leadership held firm and the negotiation with CNPC never progressed beyond discussion stage.[48]

Compared with the energy sector, the infrastructure sector is even more competitive for China's SOEs seeking overseas projects. In many cases, the large state-owned construction companies seemed to be more concerned with gaining contracts and expanding the overseas market rather than seeking profits. This led many firms to behave in an excessively aggressive way in cut-throat bidding for contracts. The severe losses incurred by China Railway Group in Poland and Saudi Arabia are classic cases. In both cases, the overseas subsidiaries of China Railway Group deliberately underbid to secure the contracts while overlooking their details. Eventually, unable to cover the costs, the Chinese side had to break the contract and abandon the projects. Finally, the fully state-owned China Railway Group had to bail out its loss-making subsidiaries.

Examined more clearly, the SOEs might have been victims of their unique style in overseas investments. In the case of the Polish highway project, China Overseas Engineering Company (COVEC) deliberately underbid because it was confident that it could somehow control and raise overall costs while pursuing the projects, just as would usually be possible in the domestic market. It was reported that their overconfidence meant they did not even study or specify the terms and conditions in detail.[49] In fact, not only was COVEC unable to renegotiate the costs under the European institutional framework, but unexpected costs associated with such understudied issues like environmental concerns and particular geological conditions greatly increased the actual final costs.[50] In the end, COVEC had no choice but to give up work on the projects. Total losses reportedly reached RMB470 million.[51]

---

[48] *Ibid.*

[49] "Zenyang gaoza haiwai xiangmu" (How Does the Overseas Project Go Sour: A Special Report), *Caixin New Century*, July 25, 2011. Full text available at: http://finance.sina.com.cn/chanjing/sdbd/20110725/121810202007.shtml [Accessed on May 20, 2015].

[50] *Ibid* [51] *Ibid.*

THE REGULATORY DILEMMA OF CENTRALLY MANAGED SOES

The government's response to the many criticisms leveled at the SOEs, in particular the centrally managed ones, is lukewarm at best. On the one hand, the government clearly realizes the critical nature of the problems and has repeatedly reaffirmed its commitment to future reform. A policy directive by the State Council during the Wen Jiabao administration called for more policy support for the large number of privately owned small and medium-sized enterprises (SMEs). The new policies included, among others, more equal access to bank loans and opening more sectors previously dominated by SOEs to domestic private capital.[52] But there has been little sign of systematic reform, which would entail an overhaul of the whole system. Observers and critics have put forward three approaches, namely, the regulatory approach, economic approach, and legislative approach.

The regulatory approach aims to strengthen the current regulatory and supervisory systems. This will require the current supervisory body, SASAC, to exercise tight control and carry out necessary SOE reform. But under the current institutional design, SASAC appears more likely to be an obstacle than a vehicle for further SOE reforms. It is noticeable that while the NDRC and other ministries are increasingly concerned with the problems associated with SOEs, the governing body itself seems reluctant to lay more blame on its supervisees. The five-year review of SASAC in 2009 consistently stressed its achievement in increasing the assets it administered from RMB7.3 to RMB21 trillion, while barely addressing critical issues such as income inequality and excessive SOE involvement in the real estate markets.[53]

In fostering the growth of state assets, SASAC has established a symbiotic relationship with all the SOEs and tapped much political benefit from its swelling size and apparent prosperity. Although SOEs' aggressive expansion has attracted much criticism in the past decade, SASAC tends to strongly defend their internal governance practices instead of chastising them for malpractice and mismanagement. For instance, in response to the criticism of super-high bonus for SOE management based on their

---

[52] Policy Directives on Further Promoting the Development of the Small and Medium-Sized Enterprises. Available at www.gov.cn/zwgk/2009-09/22/content_1423510.htm [Accessed on October 12, 2012].

[53] SASAC, *The SASAC Five-Year Review*, December 2009, p. 26.

monopolistic profits, Li Rongrong, then the head of SASAC, claimed that he would feel sorry about not awarding top management of centrally managed SOEs appropriate bonuses, given such spectacular surges in the companies' profits.[54]

With the erosion of regulatory controls, the centrally managed SOEs have largely left the orbit of the government's macroeconomic and social management. The central government's feeble control of the centrally managed SOEs is vividly demonstrated by the failure to restrict the involvement of these expansionary SOEs in the real estate sector. In view of an increasing real estate bubble, SASAC ordered seventy-eight centrally managed SOEs whose principal business was not real estate to withdraw their real estate investment by March 2010.[55] But as late as early December 2010, it was reported that only seven out of the seventy-eight centrally managed SOEs had actually divested their subsidiary real estate business. In view of the ineffectiveness of their orders, the government then ordered state banking facilities to refuse lending to the real estate businesses of these SOEs. But this policy was not able to constrain the SOEs either, since most could simply fund the real estate investment out of their own profits.[56]

While a general regulator such as SASAC is unlikely to be successful, under the prevailing institutional arrangement a specialized and independent regulator is no better option. Up to now the only experiment with a national-level regulator has been the State Electricity Regulatory Commission (SERC) for the power market. It is a vice-ministerial-level agency formed from the corporatization of the Ministry of Power, responsible for regulating the market behaviors of the State Grid, the Southern Grid, five state-owned major generators, and other lesser actors in the power market. Despite being an independent agency directly under the State Council, its strength is entirely unable to compare with the political clout of the mighty State Grid in terms of administrative ranking, informal support, and formal legal backing.[57] Despite the SERC's concern over the State Grid's

---

[54] Li Rongrong, "Guoqi duiyu guojia jingji de juese" (On the Role of SOEs in National Economy), *Guangdong Daily*, August 4, 2009.

[55] "Yangqi chehui de zuihou qixian" (Timetable for Centrally Managed SOEs Withdrawal), *Daily Economic News*, March 20, 2010.

[56] "Yangqi tuichu fangdichan meiyou zuihouqixian" (No Deadline for Centrally Managed SOEs' Real Estate Business), *Xinhua News Agency*, December 6, 2010.

[57] Tsai Chung-min, "The Reform Paradox and Regulatory Dilemma in China's Electricity Industry," *Asian Survey* 51:3 (2011), pp. 535–536; see also Lin Kun-Chin and Mika M. Purra, *Transforming China's Industrial Sectors: Institutional Change and Regulation*

new Ultra-High Voltage project, the State Grid's ambitions have smoothly been subsumed into national policy.[58] Indeed, with further reform in the NDRC, the centrally managed SOEs will only become more powerful actors in negotiating terms with the central government.

While the regulatory approach toward the SOEs may not be very effective, since the central managing authority might easily turn from regulator to protector of vested interests, the legislative approach toward monopoly and corporate governance is not much better. Even before China enacted a very inclusive Anti-Trust Law in June 2007, scholars had cast serious doubt on the proposed antitrust laws' applicability to China's large SOEs.[59] Since this time, there have been so few successful cases that few legal scholars have judged it an enforceable legal tool to tame the large centrally managed SOEs.[60]

Although the legal system was supposed to regulate monopolistic practices for both domestic and foreign firms, it has rarely been applied to state monopolies. The first high-profile case came in May 2009, when the Ministry of Commerce (MOC) warned China Unicom and China Netcom about breaching the Anti-Trust Law through their planned merger.[61] However, a closer look at the issue would suggest that this was the exception rather than the rule. And even in this specific case, where the MOC dared to stand up, SASAC promptly stepped in to exonerate the two telecom giants under its aegis, arguing that the merging and restructuring of state assets were not under the jurisdiction of the Anti-Trust Bureau of the MOC.[62] Therefore, there is very little space left for a legal approach to SOE regulation, especially for the largest centrally managed SOEs, as their CEOs are often also high-ranking party officials who are not directly subject to the rule of law.

Another, more radical approach, as proposed by some liberal scholars, is to make SOEs accountable to the National People's Congress – China's nominal legislative body – and its local versions, just as they are to the

---

of the Power Sector in the Reform Era, Lee Kuan Yew School of Public Policy, Working Paper No. 10–12, pp. 25–29.

[58] Tsai, *ibid.*, p. 537.

[59] Bruce M. Owen, "Anti-Trust in China: The Problem of Incentive Incompatibility," *SIER Paper No. 340*, Stanford Institute of Economic Research, 2009, pp. 37–38.

[60] Lin Shi, "Research on the Efficiency of China's Anti-Trust Laws," *Asian Social Sciences* 5 (2009), pp. 97–100.

[61] See a Ministry of Commerce official's comment on the case of the Unicom-Netcom Merger, in *Jingji Guancha Bao* (Economic Observer), May 1, 2009.

[62] Available at http://ccnews.people.com.cn/GB/87320/7611027.html [Accessed on August 26, 2011].

government and the judicial establishment. For example, the Unirule Institute proposed establishing a "State Asset Governance Committee" under the NPC to supervise and administer the SOEs. It is hoped that by transferring the authority of state assets from governments to the NPC, SOEs' management will be more accountable to the people.[63] In many ways, this legislative approach is even more far-fetched and impractical than the legal one, as it requires fundamental changes in the political system to revamp the current legislative system.

Any political moves against the vested interests of SOEs certainly run into strong political resistance. Ultimately, the central SOEs are the cream of the economic system that embodies "public ownership" and represents "advanced productive powers" in the "Three Represents," proposed by the then party secretary Jiang Zemin in 2001 and consequently written into both the state and party constitutions. As in many previous cases, recent policy directives suggest that any moves against the SOEs have largely remained on paper. This has to do with the remarkable political power and influence of SOEs' management, as discussed earlier. According to a research report, 31 percent of ministers and vice-ministers in the State Council have working experience in SOEs.[64] Furthermore, the CEOs of top SOEs usually hold important political office in the CCP Central Committee as high-ranking party officials. The political capital of large SOEs is a formidable hurdle for any SOE reform.

As an important institutional phenomenon in China's state-led development, the phenomenal yet problematic rise of SOEs underlines a serious conundrum faced by the Chinese development model in general. The state, which enlisted the SOEs as its top economic agents, has become reliant on the SOEs while exercising little effective control over them, in particular concerning the state's share in monopoly profits. This is an interesting development, since it was the loss-making large SOEs who turned to the state for protection only slightly more than a decade ago at the time of writing.

While an aggressive state sector's impact on economic growth still remains debatable at this point in time, the quality of that growth is certainly worrying. Much political determination as well as institutional innovation will be required to resolve the issue in a systematic way. In this respect, even the most comprehensive policy directive aimed at

---

[63] The Unirule Institute of Economics, *The Nature, Performance and Reform of the State-Owned Enterprises*, p. 187.

[64] *Ibid.*, pp. 112–113.

increasing private capital in sectors previously dominated by the state requires new political dynamics to be realized. Unfortunately, the global financial crisis of 2008, which could have provided an opportunity for the generation of such dynamics, proves to have produced exactly the opposite effect.

EPILOGUE: SOES AND THE DYNAMICS
OF STATE DOMINATION

In the pre-reform era, China's SOEs were the workshop and economic department of the all-encompassing party-state. Since the creation of the market in the reform era, however, the SOEs' roles have undergone a period of highly uncertain shifts and changes. When put under market discipline, most SOEs suffered losses and had to be rescued by the party-state, leading to a fiscal–financial crisis in the mid and late 1990s. It was once argued by some economists that all but a few SOEs should be privatized, and their fate left to the market. Since then, the SOEs' fate has improved decisively; they have become powerful and profitable enterprises in China and even the world. Due to their size and industrial positioning, the SOE sector, and especially centrally managed SOEs, naturally form the upper bound in the large institutional space between the central state and the local market.

Upon careful examination, the statist view of the centrally managed SOEs as the most important source of China's economic power is problematic. The functions of SOEs, especially the centrally managed SOEs, are not primarily economic. Being hand-picked and groomed by the central state, they are designed to make the best use of the market and monopolize resources in the service of the state. The SOEs are not really susceptible to the full range of market discipline, such as free market access for nonstate firms and competition from global actors (the multinational companies, or MNCs) in the domestic market. At the same time, they retain access to state-owned land, natural resources, and public funds, and most importantly, seats on key decision-making bodies in the central party-state. In other words, they are provided with a portfolio of market and state mechanisms. In practice, markets are used strategically and selectively (and symbolically) by these SOEs to buttress their positions against the state, such as fending off the state's claims on their profits and control over their corporate management, just as the mechanisms available from the state and its entire central and local bureaucratic machinery are similarly enlisted strategically and selectively (and symbolically, also) to secure interest from the market. For the most powerful of the centrally managed SOEs, the regulators are effectively on their side; local government mostly only acts as a humble business partner; even the State Council and the Central Committee of the Chinese Communist Party are under their influence. It is only from a purely short- or medium-term fiscal perspective that SOEs directly serve the state interests.

But market fundamentalists are also inaccurate in their indictment of SOEs as simply inefficient and uncompetitive market actors. For one thing, the contemporary Chinese market is not an autonomous, self-equilibrating and self-regulating system. Operating through and interlacing with a multivalent state system, the Chinese market can only be understood as a set of mechanisms subject to the fiscal and political interests of the state. Therefore, the operation of the market in China already assumes the built-in structures of the state and the SOEs as preconditions. It is true that privately owned small and medium enterprises are more efficient than SOEs. But efficient functioning of the downstream market, where most private firms operate, is actually vouchsafed by the smooth functioning of the centrally managed SOEs in the upper stream. The SOEs and private enterprises are mutually independent but not mutually replaceable parts of the same system. A world of market-obeying small and medium-sized firms without politically influential SOEs lying in between the central state and substantive local market is not a realistic picture in the political system. Private actors could, however, play an effective role in the state-managed market system if the central state allowed them to take a share in the central SOEs, such as in the ongoing mixed-ownership reform experiment under the Li Keqiang administration, namely, the private–public partnership (PPP).

This political economy of China's centrally managed SOEs thus presents a unique pattern of institutional evolution in both the economic and political domains. For the SOEs and many other middle-ground actors, institutionalization of political control and marketization often proceed in tandem. The current leadership's approach seems to consist of tighter political and disciplinary control and some experiments with mixed ownership. The latest developments in SOE reform again testify to this pattern. In July 2017, the debate on mixed-ownership reform finally settled as the China Unicom Group, a major centrally managed SOE, obtained SASAC's permission to introduce fourteen strategic investors – including some of China's biggest Internet giants, such as Alibaba, Tencent, and Baidu – as shareholders in its key subsidiary enterprise, China Unicom, one of the largest state-owned telecommunication operators. These private investors will hold 35 percent of the shares,[65] but such a move should not be regarded as the state losing control. Instead, it may have been conditioned on further institutionalization of political control of the SOEs. In mid-August, it was reported that China's SOEs listed on the Hong Kong Stock Exchange had added a line on party leadership into their company laws.[66] If the party intends to allow marketization of central SOEs in the form of increasing private shares and possibly an effective voice in the management, it can only do so *after* consolidating its control over the management of the central SOEs, and even the largest private enterprises.

The privatization of state firms in post-Soviet Russia provides a sharp contrast to China's SOE reform and hints at China's road not taken. There was no presence of SOEs or strong state power in the economy, but the rosy picture of millions of small and medium enterprises competing freely and fairly did not emerge in Yeltsin's Russia. Instead, there quickly emerged a hierarchy of economic organizations, on top of which were a dozen oligarchies – private enterprises run by well-connected former cadres and parvenus – dominating the most important sectors of the economy. Most of these big businesses relied on age-old nonmarket informal practices, including barter chains and informal exchanges with government.[67] In the Yeltsin era, the oligarchs not only developed monopolistic controls but also attained political clout strong enough to affect policies and even manipulate political processes such as elections.[68] Like China's centrally managed SOEs, these oligopolies were mainly domestic players with few intentions of international competition. But unlike China's SOE system, these oligarchs were not market-constructing and law-abiding in the post-Soviet political economy, nor did they provide stable tax income for central government. The sweeping crackdown on the oligarchs and subsequent consolidation under Vladimir Putin since the early 2000s can be seen as a political response to the destruction and social costs of such chaotic marketization. But the upshot of this campaign was not the disappearance of the oligarchs in most sectors, but a highly

---

[65] Bien Perez, "China's Unicom Parent Firms Get Go-Ahead for Mixed-Ownership Reform," *South China Morning Post*, July 15, 2017.

[66] Jennifer Hughes, "Chinese Communist Party Writes Itself into Company Law," *Financial Times*, August 14, 2017.

[67] For a discussion of these institutions, see Alena V. Ledeneva, *How Russia Really Works: The Informal Practices that Shaped Post-Soviet Politics and Business* (Ithaca, NY: Cornell University, 2006), chapter 5.

[68] For an account of the rise and impact of the oligarchs, see David E. Hoffman, *The Oligarchs: Wealth and Power in the New Russia* (New York, NY: Public Affairs, 2011). For a case study, see Andrew Barnes, *Owning Russia: The Struggle over Factories, Farms, and Power* (Ithaca, NY: Cornell University Press, 2006), pp. 209–227.

personalized form of control focused on Putin as the final arbiter in charge of carrots and sticks.[69] This differs fundamentally from the Chinese experience, where a degree of institutional control exists between the state and its economic agents. After all, China's centrally managed SOEs are still part of the institutional framework that keeps a more stable balance of central state and market economy possible.

Straddling the state and market, the centrally managed SOEs sometimes choose the game they are playing and set its rules themselves. In this sense, their behaviors are similar to those of other actors, such as local government, large private enterprises, state-owned financial institutions, and other state corporate actors. In this regard, they differ from the powerful large private enterprises in the West, whose access to political power and public resources are based on their market performance. But the centrally managed SOEs are perhaps the classic example in this group because they have access to a full range of state and market mechanisms, ranging from membership of the Central Committee of the Chinese Communist Party, administrative ranking, and exclusive rights to a limited-access market to full claim to their receipts. Thus, they also enjoy the highest degree of autonomy from both the central state and any local market. Not only are the centrally managed SOEs out of the reach of any regulatory agents, but they sometimes directly undermine the central state in many of its key areas of interest, such as social equality and pollution control. The increasingly uncontrollable asymmetrical pattern of income distribution is to a large extent a product of this misalignment. However, there is no simple and quick solution to all these problems. The SOEs have become such a formative element in the system that it is simply impossible to reformulate them into private enterprises without changing the nature of the entire political system. As a consequence, it could be argued that the centrally managed SOEs present the most fundamental challenge to the market-in-state political economy system in China.[70]

---

[69] David Szakonyi, "Why Russian Oligarchs Remain Loyal to Putin," *Moscow Times*, December 1, 2017.

[70] The Xi Jinping leadership is keenly aware of the issue of political importance. Xi purged the entire leadership of the powerful petroleum industrial complex in the last round of the anticorruption campaign, including the former CEO of Petrol China and the head of SASAC, Jiang Jiemin, whose older connections to Zhou Yongkang made them suspects. But this kind of measure will not change the situation entirely as long as the SOEs continue to serve as the economic arm of the party state. See Te-Ping Chen and Aredy James, "Jiang Jiemin Trial Links Key Officials in China's Corruption Crackdown," *The Wall Street Journal*, April 13, 2015.

APPENDIX: Chinese Business Groups in the Central Nomenklature circa 2013 (excluding the financial sector)

	Corporation	Industry
1	China National Nuclear Corporation (Zhongguo hegongye gongsi)	Nuclear power
2	China Nuclear Engineering & Construction (Group) Corporation (Zhongguo gegongye jianshe gongsi)	Nuclear Power
3	China Aerospace Science and Technology Corporation (Zhongguo hangtian keji jituan gongsi)	Aerospace
4	China Aerospace Science and Industry Corporation (Zhongguo hangtian kegong jituan gongsi)	Aerospace
5	China Aviation Industry Corporation (Zhongguo hangkong gongye jituan gongsi)	Aviation
6	China State Shipbuilding Corporation (Zhongguo chuanbo gongye jituan gongsi)	Shipbuilding
7	China Shipbuilding Industry Corporation (Zhongguo chuanbo zhonggong jituan gongsi)	Shipbuilding
8	China North Industries Group Corporation (Zhongguo bingqi gongye jituan gongsi)	Weaponry
9	China South (Zhongguo nanfang gongye jituan gongsi)	Automobiles
10	China Electronic Technology Corporation (Zhongguo dianzi keji jituan gongsi)	Electronics
11	China National Petroleum and Gas Corporation (Zhongguo shiyou tianranqi jituan gongsi)	Oil and Gas
12	China National Petrochemical Corporation (Zhongguo shiyou huagong jituan gongsi)	Oil and Gas
13	China National Offshore Oil Corporation (Zhongguo haiyang shiyou zong gongsi)	Oil and Gas
14	State Grid Corporation of China (Guojia dianwang gongsi)	Electrical power supply
15	China Southern Power Grid (Zhongguo nanfang dianwang youxian zeren gongsi)	Electrical power supply
16	China Huaneng Group (Zhongguo Huaneng jituan gongsi)	Power generation

	Corporation	Industry
17	China Datang Group (Zhongguo Datang jituan gongsi)	Power generation
18	China Huadian Corporation (Zhongguo Huadian jituan gongsi)	Electricity
19	China Guodian Corporation (Zhongguo guodian jituan gongsi)	Power
20	China Power Investment Corporation (Zhongguo dianli touzi jituan gongsi)	Power investment
21	Three Gorges Project Corporation (Zhongguo changjiang sanxie gongcheng kaifa zong gongsi)	Power
22	China Shenhua Group Corporation (Shenhua jituan youxian zeren gongsi)	Chemicals
23	China Telocom Corporation (Zhongguo dianxin jituan gongsi)	Telecommunications
24	China Unicom Corporation (Zhongguo lianhe wangluo tongxin jituan youxian gongsi)	Telecom
25	China Mobile Corporation (Zhongguo yidong tongxin jituan gongsi)	Telecom
26	China Electronics Corporation (Zhongguo dianzi xinxi chanye jituan gongsi)	Electronics
27	China First Auto-Works Corporation (Zhongguo diyi qiche jituan)	Automobiles
28	Dongfeng Automobile Corporation (Dongfeng qiche gongsi)	Automobiles
29	China First Heavy Machinery Corporation (Zhongguo diyi zhongxing jixie jituan gongsi)	Machinery
30	China National Erzhong Group Corporation (Zhongguo erzhong jituan gongsi)	Machinery
31	Harbin Power Equipment Corporation (Haerbin dianqi jituan gongsi)	Electrical power equipment
32	China Dongfang Electrical Corporation (Zhongguo Dongfang dianqi jituan youxian gongsi)	Electrical power equipment
33	Anshan Steel Corporation (Anshan gangtie jituan gongsi)	Steel
34	Shanghai Baosteel Corporation (Baogang jituan youxian gongsi)	Steel
35	Wuhan Steel Corporation (Wuhan gangtie [jituan] gongsi)	Steel
36	Aluminum Corporation of China (Zhongguo lue gongsi)	Aluminum
37	China Ocean Shipping (Group) Company (Zhongguo yuanyang yunshu [jituan] zong gongsi)	Shipping
38	China Shipping Group (Zhongguo haiyun [jituan] zong gongsi)	Shipping
39	Air China (Zhongguo hangkong jituan gongsi)	Aviation

(continued)

(*continued*)

	Corporation	Industry
40	China Eastern Airlines Corporation (Zhongguo dongfang hangikong jituan gongsi)	Aviation
41	China Southern Airlines Corporation (Zhongguo Nanfang kongkong jituan gongsi)	Aviation
42	Sinochem Corporation (Zhongguo zhonghua jituan gongsi)	Chemicals
43	China National Cereals, Oils, and Foodstuff Corporation (Zhong Liang jituan youxian gongsi)	Foodstuff
44	China Minmetals Corporation (Zhongguo wukuang jituan gongsi)	Metals
45	China General Technology (Group) Holding Limited (Zhongguo tongyong jishu [jituan] konggu youxian zeren gongsi)	Equipment and technology
46	China State Constuction Engineering Corporation (Zhongguo jianzhu bongcheng zong gongsi)	Construction
47	China Grain Reserves Corporation (Zhongguo chubeiliang guanli zong gongsi)	Food
48	State Development and Investment Corporation (Guojia kaifa touzi gongsi)	Investment and construction
49	China Merchants Group (Zhaoshangju jituan youxian gongsi)	Transportation and Logistics
50	China Resources (Huarun [jituan] youxian gongsi)	Retail, food
51	China National Travel Service (Holdings) Hong Kong Limited (Xianggang zhonglu [jituan] youxian gongsi)	Travel and tourism
52	State Nuclear Power Technology Corporation (Guojia hedian jishu youxian gongsi)	Nuclear
53	China Commercial Aircraft Corporation (Zhongguo shangfei jituan gongsi)	Aviation

Source: Compiled by the authors. The authors would like to thank Kjeld Erik Brødsgaard for sharing the information.

Conclusion

In this study we have discussed the basic structure of the Chinese political economy from conceptual, historical, and contemporary perspectives. Chapters 1 and 2 laid out a comparative framework of analysis by contrasting China's economic system with several predominant Western models. In Chapters 3 and 4, we focused on the historical evolution in relations between the market and the state from imperial China to the immediate prereform period. The main part of the study, in Chapters 5–8, offered an overall analysis of the contemporary Chinese political economy, including grassroots markets, private capital, the fiscal and financial systems, and the centrally managed SOEs. Throughout our analyses, we foregrounded the market-in-state or MIS system as an overarching conceptual framework to explain the basic logics of the Chinese political economy.

As discussed throughout the book, we argue that the MIS model is a type of historically evolved system of political economy. The system has a long pedigree, from its archaic forms in the Legalist–Confucian debate in the early Han Empire to its more mature late imperial synthesis. In the past two centuries, it has survived the process of modern state-building through war and revolutions and developed into its contemporary postreform configuration. By and large, MIS is a model of political economy where the fundamental logic of the market is made structurally subordinate to the political imperatives of the state. It is conceptually distinctive from the "state in market" model dominant in modern Europe and the United States and the developmental model of East Asian newly industrial economies (NIEs).

The "state in market" model which has been prevalent in the mainstream economic discourse and policy practices in the West dictates that the state operates in strict accordance with market principles of social contract, property rights, and the rule of law. In political life, the principles are realized through multiparty democracy with free elections, majority rule, and parliamentary deliberation. The parliamentary system converts the political choices of voters into state action through a combination of the popular vote and interest groups. Fiscally, state revenues are mostly based on direct taxes from the rich and large corporations. In a sense, this system often allows capital to be an effective means to control or circumvent the sovereignty of the state, especially under the currently prevalent neoliberal ideology. In this case, state autonomy could be severely compromised by organized interests of political and business elites who can tactically dominate the policy process, such as in the contemporary United States.[1]

Compared with the state in the "state in market" model in the West, the developmental state in East Asian NIEs assumes a closer alignment or shared interests between the state and national economic actors. Such a vision could also accommodate the rule of law and property rights, but not necessarily a full spectrum of free choice and competitive competition. Where the free market is allowed to dominate the domestic economy, a state–private alliance is the guiding principle for global market competition. These logics work best with a stable political core that has a clear ideological vision and strong organizational power, such as a single dominant party in a multiparty system or a powerful authoritarian regime. Equally important to the developmental state are institutional arrangements that enmesh the state and the market actors according to the principal interest alignment so that the market actors have full state backing in the global arena. As discussed in Chapter 2, this model has served postwar Japan well, as the political elite, bureaucracy, and business have worked in tandem through institutional alliances such as the Keidaren and central agencies such as MITI (the Ministry of International Trade and Industry) to promote economic growth.[2] East Asian NIEs, particularly the so-called "four little dragons" – South Korea, Singapore, Taiwan, and Hong Kong – have also followed this model.

Unlike the "state in market" model and the developmental state, the MIS system gives the state absolute sovereignty over domestic market actors. As discussed throughout the preceding chapters, this principle is institutionally supported by state control over industry, finance, and land through its economic arms such as state-owned enterprises (SOEs), state banks, and

---

[1] Martin Gilens and Benjamin I. Page, "Testing Theories of American Politics: Elites, Interest Groups, and Average Citizens," *Perspectives on Politics* 12:4 (2014), pp. 575–576.

[2] For example, see Chalmers Johnson, *MITI and the Japanese Miracle: The Growth of Industrial Policy, 1925–1975* (Stanford, CA: Stanford University Press, 1982).

local government, as well as its comprehensive cooptation of powerful private actors. Under such arrangements, the state is equipped with the necessary resources and mechanisms to make the market a tool rather than a source of ideological authority and political principle. As discussed in this book, while the MIS model does allow a market system to function, it is difficult for such a model to adopt important and fundamental institutions of capitalism which are prevalent in the West such as the rule of law, private ownership, and property rights. As such, while the MIS model is well disposed to tap the market's potential in mobilizing resources, it has been less successful in its efforts to build an innovation-based model of economic development. Moreover, marketization under MIS conditions does not necessarily lead to the decline of the state. In fact, it can even create favorable conditions for the expansion of state powers, as discussed in this book.

In the contemporary world, no modern state is as empowered to preside over such a vast network of markets as the Chinese state, centered on the leadership of the Chinese Communist party. The contemporary rise of the MIS model has many key economic consequences. As discussed in this book, this model has evolved from the late 1970s onward, as the post-Maoist state fully embraced the wave of globalization led by the United States and transformed the nature of its mobilization structure from military–political to economic. China's economic transformation is one of the most significant developments in contemporary world history. Within barely four decades, China has transformed from a predominantly planned economy with a predominant rural sector to a vibrant market economy dominated by modern manufacturing and service sectors. The breathtaking growth rate of almost 10 percent between 1979 and 2009, known as the Chinese economic miracle, bears remarkable testimony to the powerful dynamics unleashed and structured by the economic reform.

This hypergrowth is a process of rapid industrialization, underlined by the growth of modern industries and the relative decline of the traditional agriculture. Since the reform and opening policy, the manufacturing and service sectors have grown at a much faster pace than the primary sectors. The manufacturing and construction sector has become the one with the greatest economic weight. The strengthening of the manufacturing industry since the mid-1990s accords with the fundamental changes in the principal growth dynamics from consumption to investment. The sweeping changes in industrial structure are equaled by those in employment structure. From 1978 to 2008, and especially since the mid-1990s, there was a consistent and significant shift from primary to modern sectors, in particular the tertiary sector. The share of modern sector employment has more than doubled as the Chinese economy modernizes and industrializes. Changes in employment structure also took place in terms of the ownership of modern enterprises. Employment in SOEs contracted most rapidly in the late 1990s, when small and medium enterprises were privatized under the Zhu Rongji reform. The rise of the private sector since the mid-1990s to become the major employer of the urban labor force was the defining feature of the Chinese economy as a mixed economy.

Also important is the fact that the Chinese economy has retained the logics of political control of the market and has weathered three major crises in the past three decades, namely, the post-Tiananmen political and economic crisis of 1989–1992, the Asian financial crisis of 1997–1998, and the global financial crisis after 2008. Each time, the system strengthened itself in the direction of selective marketization, targeted state control, and adaptive globalization. Needless to say, the economic rise of China is largely the product of this model.

However, the rise of the MIS in contemporary China also has many social and political consequences. Indeed, the social and political consequences are equally, if not more, far-reaching and destructive. For one thing, while the modern Chinese state has transformed the parts of Chinese society under its direct influence beyond recognition, the model has also covertly marked a return to the old imperial model of economy, society, and state. In the main body of this study, we have barely discussed the social and political consequences of the MIS model. These are obviously important topics given the rise of China on the global stage, but such discussion would have taken more space than would be warranted by the scope and goals of the study. In this concluding chapter, we take up this issue and draw some social and political implications of the MIS model from theoretical and policy perspectives.

SOCIAL CONSEQUENCES OF THE MIS SYSTEM

Society is a concept that we have not discussed in terms of the MIS system. How does society fit, or not fit, into the model? This is clearly an important theoretical question. First, it is meaningful to consider the meaning of society in the modern Chinese political configuration. In general, the Chinese concept of society (*shehui*) is not conceptually equivalent to "society" in Western usage. In classical Chinese, the word *shehui* is associated with an annual gathering for agricultural festivities in the rural society. In late imperial and Republican China, *shehui* came to refer to social organizations such as secret sects and underground societies (*mimi shehui*). The concept of the society as a nonstate unit only emerged in the early twentieth century, under the influence of Western social concepts.[3]

The contemporary Chinese concept of society has two important implications, especially when it is evoked vis-à-vis the state (*guojia*). In official discourse, society is equivalent to nonstate actors (*minjian*), namely, various social organizations not under direct state control, including, importantly, private entrepreneurs.[4] But in colloquial usage, society (*shehui*) often refers to unorganized and thus potentially dangerous elements of society. It is similar to the popular concept of *jianghu* (literally, river and lake), which means "the world of floating population" or "the land of the outlaws." Whereas the state often carries a positive and formal connotation, the concept of society conveys a sense of disorder and lawlessness. This is the opposite of the Western liberal concept of civil society but is akin to the Hobbesian state of nature. As such, the most authentic Chinese notion of society as acknowledged in official and popular discourse is an anarchical marginal society beyond the reach of state power. In other words, it is the area where state power is weak or even nonexistent.

The modern discourse of society conceals the truth of the relationship between the state and society in China. In fact, it is the norm for the Chinese state to directly organize and control society. In premodern China, as briefly discussed in the main body of this book, the imperial state controlled society through its grassroots organization and fiscal apparatus, including the household registry and monopolies over key industries. In modern China, the party state controls society through a vast array of infrastructural powers, from grassroots party organs, to the household registration system, to family planning. In addition, the state organizes society through government-controlled social organizations such as the Chinese Communist Youth League, the All-China Federation of Commerce and Industry (ACFCI), and the All-China Women's Federation. Recently, the party even started setting up its own grassroots organizations

---

[3] Jin Guantao and Liu Qingfeng, *Guannianshi yanjiu: zhongguo xiandai zhongyao zhengzhi shuyu de xingcheng* (Study in the History of Ideas: The Formation of Important Terms in Modern Chinese Politics) (Beijing: Falu Chubanshe, 2009), pp. 187–192.

[4] In classical and even modern Chinese political vocabulary, a much more common synonym for society is *min*, as defined vis-à-vis the agent of the state (*guan*). Such a conceptualization of society is a vivid testimony to the centrality of the imperial state or party state in the definition of the social.

within nongovernmental organizations (NGOs).[5] Society as a nonstate actor only implies indirect rather than direct control. And even in this aspect of uncontrolled order, society often has a derogatory rather than positive connotation. But even this extensive system of social control is only a remnant of the socialist system of even more extensive and intensive social control, which reached way beyond grassroots organizations to every single household unit.

From this perspective, one can see a critical similarity between the Chinese vision of the market and the concept of society. Whereas the autonomous market only exists at the grassroots level, beyond the reach of SOEs and fiscal apparatus, the autonomous "society" only survives at the margins of a society-wide system of state organization and control. As the organizations of market and society move to higher and more complex levels, they invariably involve and enmesh with state power as the dominant organizational force. At the highest levels of the Chinese society, the notions of market and society are inextricably linked with the ideology and organizations of the party state, whether it is the state capitalist idea of the market or the socialist notion of society. But as we have discussed in this study, between the state and market there is a large gray area of middle ground where the identities of state and market actors are often mixed and indistinguishable. There are similar areas between the state and society; these are areas where the state powers provide direct protection for society in the form of a state-controlled social service sector and state-sponsored social welfare. The most typical of the latter is the state-sponsored mini-welfare state under the Maoist order.

Market reform since the 1990s marked an end to this social order in two important ways. First, as discussed in the previous chapters, it replaced a more stringent state control with a more elaborate system of control. Over the past two decades, the communist state has gradually given up its formerly dominant mode of direct social control and reduced its ideological and organizational control systems, including the hallmark system of mobility control imposed by the household registration system. Second, it has also restructured earlier forms of social protection and provision of social welfare. The Maoist mini-welfare state was dissolved during the

[5] In the recently published CCP Party Group Working Guideline, the Party Committee is defined as the leading committee in social and other organizations. The social organizations here necessarily cover nongovernmental organizations (NGOs) and even include foreign NGOs. In July 2015, the first NGO Party Committee was established in Haishu District, Xiamen City. This model of party building is expected to expand.

reform period, except for some remnants within a much smaller state sector – which means members of the political elite, such as some civil servants and SOE management, are still covered by a downsized welfare system.[6] Now, the state employs the market to codominate the provision of social welfare. In other words, in the current configuration, while the market is secondary to the state, society is subject to both the market and the state. It is important to highlight some social consequences of this shifting balance between the state, market, and society.

Before the marketization reform, both society and market were completely state-dominated. While Mao Zedong had a favorable view of the society and tried to unleash the political potential of autonomous social forces, for example, during the Cultural Revolution, he was much less sanguine about political mobilization through the market. However, this is exactly what happened in the reform era, when the market became the favorable instrument of mobilization and allowed the marketization of society. Unlike the rise of liberalism in the West in the late nineteenth century, this marketization only serves state domination and the reconstruction of the MIS system. What happens in this setting is in a way more destructive, but also more malleable, than what happened in Europe and North America roughly a century ago.

One of the most significant consequences of this MIS system since the mid-1990s has been the rapidly widening income gap among different sectors, professions, and social groups. Measured in numerical terms, most economists have estimated China's Gini index in the range of 0.45–0.50, well above the international red line of 0.40.[7] This level of income inequality sets China apart from its East Asian neighbors and places it in the ranks of least equal countries, well above most developed countries, such as Japan and South Korea, and developing countries, such as India and Russia.

The other side of the skewed distribution is the disproportionate sacrifice made by the rural population, which bears the brunt of China's

---

[6] Zheng Yongnian and Huang Yanjie, "Political Dynamics of Social Policy Reform in China," in Zhao Litao, ed., *China's Development and Social Policy: Into the Next Stage* (London: Routledge, 2013), pp. 171–172.

[7] Estimations of China's Gini Index are a contentious area of research, since the official income data provided by the National Bureau of Statistics and other official agencies are also reported to have underreported income differentials. For example, estimates of the Gini Index can vary between 0.43 and 0.55 based on different sources and methodologies of calculation. However, there is consensus among economists that China's income disparity is among the highest in Asia, and on a par with that of the United States.

development costs. While this is practically the Iron Law of all forms of capitalism, the problem in China has been aggravated by the rapid retreat of the state in fields of social welfare such as health care, education, and environment, especially in rural areas, where the process of marketization has proved most lethal. This is evident in high school dropout rates among the rural young. Although Chinese law requires nine years of compulsory schooling and rural household incomes have been on the rise, recent surveys suggest that 63 percent of students in the rural areas never finished their junior high school education, either due to rational calculations regarding higher earnings in the labor market or short-term financial difficulties.[8]

In this context, it is useful to revisit the Polanyian logic of capitalist development. In *The Great Transformation*, Polanyi explores the social and political upheavals that took place in England during the rise of the market economy. He contends that the modern market economy and the modern state should be understood not as discrete elements, but as a single human invention that he calls the market society. He reasons that a powerful modern state was needed to push changes in the social structure that allowed for a competitive capitalist economy, and that a capitalist economy required a strong state to mitigate its harsher effects. Left to its own devices, the market society is unsustainable because it is fatally destructive to the human and natural contexts it inhabits.

In assessing the state's role in unleashing market forces, Polanyi highlights the historical novelty of the nineteenth-century market economy and its concomitant ideological distortions. He argues that laissez-faire was planned and that the movement toward a market society was a conscious and planned phenomenon in which state action was the driving force. There was no natural evolution toward this occurrence. The road to the free market was paved with state actions to clear the way for the market. On the other hand, as opposed to the careful and deliberate construction of a market society, the countermovement, or social protectionism, was spontaneous, unplanned, and came from all sectors of society in response to the devastating impact of the market. Polanyi argued that the construction of a "self-regulating" market necessitates the separation of society into an economic and a political sphere. While the self-regulating market has

---

[8] Yaojiang Shi, Linxiu Zhang, Yue Ma, Hongmei Yi, Chengfang Liu, Natalie Johnson, James Chu, Prashant Loyalka, and Scott Rozelle, "Dropping Out of Rural China's Secondary Schools: A Mixed-Methods Analysis," *The China Quarterly* 224 (December 2015), pp. 1065–1066.

brought unheard-of material wealth, this separation has also resulted in massive social dislocation and spontaneous moves by society to protect itself. Free market capitalism, once it takes land, labor and money as "fictitious commodities," subordinates the substance of society itself to the tyrannical laws of the self-regulating market. When the free market attempts to break away from the fabric of society, social protectionism is society's natural response – a response Polanyi calls the "counter-movement."[9]

According to Polanyi, this countermovement of protectionism is a movement of general interest toward the goal of general welfare; it especially includes workers, yet also incorporates capitalists, as all sought some form of protection from the vagaries and perils of the self-regulating market. The protection gained by the countermovement impeded the efficiency of the self-regulating market, which in turn created more severe economic conditions and another round of demands for protection. The market system was unstable and its instability generated fear and action. Polanyi demonstrates, historically and comparatively, that market encroachment and political repression immediately inspire resistance and rebellion. Therefore, for Polanyi, social demands against economic uncertainty and market malaise placed heavy pressure on the state to intervene politically. The ensuing state action would have to, at least nominally, provide some relief and protection. The market society must be replaced by a society with democratic control of both political and economic institutions. These institutions could no longer control society, but should instead be controlled by society. Thus state protection of society, or what Polanyi understands as socialism, was inherent in the market-based industrial society.[10]

Avowedly a socialist state, China has relentlessly promoted a market-driven form of economic growth, but has been relatively slow in building a set of social policies to cope with the social consequences of market development. This has led to increasing social instability and even unrest in some marginal sectors of the society. From 1990 to 2006, the only period in which official data was made available, the number of incidences of collective unrest increased from 3,200 to 87,000.[11] While currently official

---

[9] Ibid., p. xxviii.

[10] Karl Polanyi, The Great Transformation: The Political and Economic Origins of Our Time (Boston: Beacon Press, 2001 reprint), pp. 242–243.

[11] Carl Minzner, Social Instability in China: Causes, Consequences, and Implications. Center for Strategic and International Studies, available at http://csis.org/files/media/csis/events/061205_mizner_abstract.pdf [Accessed on July 22, 2015]. For a summary of the rise of

data is not available, the number is expected to have grown significantly since that time. Also, since the March 14 Incident in Lhasa in 2008 and the July 5 Incident in Urumqi in 2009, ethnic violence has become the principal source of terrorism in China. This is partly due to a sense of relative deprivation among ethnic minorities whose native cultures are not as adaptive to the forceful and top-down socioeconomic changes introduced by the MIS system.[12] These protests and the violence that comes with them are symptomatic of a social crisis caused by China's economic rise.

This recent wave of social protest and unrest is much more political than economic. Rather than a dispossessed economic and social class, the most dangerous source of protests and unrest is infringed local communities and marginalized ethnic groups. Three types of social protest and unrest are particularly salient: protests against local authorities' forceful requisition of state-owned urban land and collectively owned rural land for infrastructural and real estate development; protests against industrial projects or factories with a high potential for environmental degradation; and violent protests and even terrorist attacks by some marginalized ethnic groups, such as the Uyghurs and the Tibetans. All these protests and unrest are directly related to the relentless drive to mobilize resources and the lack of adequate social protection.[13]

It is no exaggeration to say that if Chinese society cannot be protected, political disorder will follow.[14] Modern history has a rich store of failed state-building attempts in spite of former economic prosperity. In most of these cases, the most important sources of domestic social and, eventually, political crisis are economic inequality and social injustice. Indeed, Chinese history also supplies such lessons in the form of dynastic cycles: When the political power sustains the economic prosperity that in turn succumbs to revolution, all economic prosperity is but wind and shadow. Whether

social protests, see Yongnian Zheng, *Contemporary China: A History Since 1978* (Oxford: Wiley-Blackwell, 2014), pp. 101–119.

[12] Yang Hongwei and Zhang Jinping, *Zangqu 314 shijian shehuijingji chengying diaocha* (Economic and Social Causes of the March 14 Incidents in the Tibetan Area) (For Internal Circulation), September 2010, pp. 13–14.

[13] For an updated analysis of social protests, see Yanqi Tong and Shaohua Lei, *Social Protest in Contemporary China, 2003–2010: Transitional Pains and Regime Legitimacy* (London and New York, NY: Routledge, 2014).

[14] Yongnian Zheng, "Society Must Be Defended: Reform, Openness and Social Policy in China," *Journal of Contemporary China* 19:67 (2010), pp. 799–818, and "Jingji zhuyi de juxianxing" (The Limits of Economism), in *Baowei Shehui* (Society Must Be Defended) (Hangzhou: Zhejiang Publishing Group, 2011), pp. 1–3.

economic and, eventually, social and political transformation in China can be sustained and materialized critically depends on the response of the MIS system to the social crisis of its own making.

To echo the Polanyian message, society, especially the weakest elements of society, must be defended from the destructive power of the market. The protection of society is not only an economic task but, more importantly, a political one. That leads us to an even more important research agenda on China's political transformation.

THE MIS SYSTEM AND THE CHINESE POLITICAL REGIME

The relations between China's economy and polity have been unendingly debated. The fact that China experienced no major breakthrough in the historical development of its economic system leads to another equally important question: Why was China not able to develop a type of political system or modern state such as we have seen in the West? There were frequent dynastic changes, but the pattern of change was almost identical: Each dynastic change was triggered by peasant rebels, and a new dynastic regime was established without any structural change. One can certainly link this question to the debate on "oriental despotism" in the previous century. Karl Marx focused on the socioeconomic base and attributed a highly centralized state to what he called the "Asiatic mode of production."[15] By contrast, Max Weber tended to highlight the political factors leading to such a system, and called China (and also India) a "hydraulic-bureaucratic official-state."[16] Karl Wittfogel came up with an analysis of the role of irrigation works in Asia, the bureaucratic structures needed to maintain them, and the impact that these had on society. In his view, Asian societies like China relied heavily on the building of large-scale irrigation works; to do this successfully, the state had to organize forced labor from the population at large. This required a large and complex bureaucracy staffed by competent and literate officials. This structure was uniquely placed to crush civil society and any other force capable of

---

[15] Marx's theory of the Asiastic mode of production forms an important basis for Wittfogel's thought. For Marx's theory and its influence, see Maurice Meisner, "Despotism of Concepts: Wittfogel and Marx on China," *The China Quarterly* 16 (1963), 99–111.

[16] For Max Weber's thinking, refer to Richard Swedberg, *Max Weber and the Idea of Economic Sociology* (Princeton, NJ: Princeton University Press, 1989), pp. 70–72.

mobilizing against the state. Such a state would inevitably be despotic, powerful, stable, and wealthy.[17]

Within China, why and how this highly centralized system ("hydraulic society") was established and evolved remains the subject of debate to this day.[18] There is no satisfactory answer as yet. Indeed, many questions can be raised regarding the "hydraulic society" thesis. If we focus on what the state actually did, we can question whether large-scale infrastructure building (such as irrigation works) was the main reason for China's highly centralized system, or if this centralized system was only the consequence of the state's reaction to China's geographical environment. But if we shift to ideational factors, we can explore whether this centralized system was subjectively built based on Chinese economic philosophy – a philosophy which normatively justified the relationship between the state and market, and the state and society. Of course, we can also ask whether this highly centralized system was the consequence of the interplay between China's physical and geographical environment and its rulers' philosophies. We believe that history is always open to future exploration.

The "hydraulic society" thesis can be extended to the contemporary era. If, according to Marx, the economy is base and politics is superstructure, then changes in the economy will definitely lead to changes in politics. This does not appear to be the case in contemporary China. Many scholars are still struggling to answer the question why rapid socioeconomic transformation since modern times has not led to political transformation in China. Indeed, an old and important question has been raised again by scholars in the field of contemporary China: Will China's ancient thesis of the "hydraulic society" repeat itself today, or is China able to avoid this Iron Law of history?

When China initiated its reform and open-door policy in the late 1970s, many, both inside and outside China, believed that this new policy would lead the country to economic liberalization and political democratization – a great convergence with the West. It was also believed that, together with a market economy and a democratic polity, there would be a better society, a society which is rich and equal. However, after three decades of the reform and open-door policy, China did not become the sort of country many had

---

[17] Karl August Wittfogel, *Oriental Despotism: A Comparative Study of Total Power* (New Haven, CT: Yale University Press, 1957).

[18] For a summary of different waves of the debates, see Qin Hui, "zhishui shehui lun pipan" (A Critique on "Hydraulic Society"), www.chinaelections.org/NewsInfo.asp?NewsID=104095 [Accessed on September 5, 2009].

expected; instead, it has evolved into an unusual animal unknown to the world. As discussed in this book, many types of associations between the economy and politics which took place in the West did not happen in China. On the contrary, China's experiences have differed drastically from those of the West. The economic miracle has been associated with so many "unexpected" consequences. In the realm of the economy, a growing market economy does not weaken the power of the state over the market; instead, the state has empowered itself by transforming the economy. Politically, despite the development of a market economy, China's system remains a highly authoritarian one. Indeed, in China's official discourse, it is still a communist state. At the societal level, capitalism did lead to a pluralistic and unequal China, but the degree of social division and inequality was unexpectedly high. China is now among the countries with the largest income inequality in the world. The answers to all of these issues can be partially found in the connectedness between Chinese capitalism and its political regime.

It is certainly true that "capitalism with Chinese characteristics" did not lead to expected consequences such as the rule of law and democracy, which had emerged in the modernization process in the postwar West and Japan. In the history of the West, the rule of law and democracy were both closely associated with the rise of capitalism. According to liberal economists such as Milton Friedman and Friedrich Hayek, economic freedom is a necessary condition for the creation and sustainability of civil and political freedoms. Liberal economists believed that economic freedom can only be achieved in a market-oriented economy, specifically a free market economy. Furthermore, they also believed that sufficient economic freedom can be achieved in economies with functioning markets through price mechanisms and private property rights. For these thinkers, the more economic freedom there is available, the more civil and political freedoms a society will enjoy. According to Friedman, "economic freedom is simply a requisite for political freedom. By enabling people to cooperate with one another without coercion or central direction it reduces the area over which political power is exercised."[19]

Therefore, it is not difficult to make sense of why capitalism with Chinese characteristics alone did not and will not bring democracy to China. Many political scientists have made great attempts to explore why the development of a market economy did not lead to political democracy.

---

[19] Milton and Rose Friedman, *Free to Choose: A Personal Statement* (New York, NY: Harcourt Brace Jovanovich, 1980), pp. 2–3.

Mary Gallagher finds that there is no perceived relationship between economic liberalization and democratization in China. While China's market reforms and increased integration with global capitalism have brought about unprecedented economic growth and social change, the country has managed to proactively engage in economic liberalization without democratization.[20] While private ownership and private entrepreneurs played an important role in political liberalization and democratization in the rest of the world, the same did not happen in China. In her study of China's private sector, Kellee Tsai disproves the assumed perception that privatization leads to democratization, and stated her belief that Chinese entrepreneurs are not agitating for democracy.[21] Indeed, many other scholars have shown how the Chinese regime has successfully coopted capitalists, be they red or private. In his extensive research on the CCP, Bruce Dickson challenged the conventional notion that economic development is leading to political change in China, or that China's private entrepreneurs are helping to promote democratization. Instead, Dickson argued that they have become partners with the ruling CCP to promote economic growth while maintaining the political status quo. Rather than being potential agents of change, China's entrepreneurs may prove to be a key source of support for the party's agenda. Dickson illuminated the CCP's strategy for incorporating China's capitalists into the political system and how the shared interests, personal ties, and common views of the party and the private sector are creating a form of "crony communism."[22]

This term apparently stems from "crony capitalism." Crony capitalism has been used to describe an economy in which business success depends on close relationships between businesspeople and government officials. It can be exhibited by favoritism in the distribution of legal permits, government grants, special tax breaks, or other forms of state intervention-ism. "Crony capitalism" has been widely applied to explain the political

---

[20] Mary Elizabeth Gallagher, *Contagious Capitalism: Globalization and the Politics of Labor in China* (Princeton, NJ: Princeton University Press, 2005).

[21] Kellee S. Tsai, *Capitalism without Democracy: The Private Sector in Contemporary China* (Ithaca, NY and London: Cornell University Press, 2007).

[22] Bruce Dickson, *Wealth into Power: The Communist Party's Embrace of China's Private Sector* (Cambridge and New York, NY: Cambridge University Press, 2008) and *Red Capitalists in China: The Party, Private Entrepreneurs, and Prospects for Political Change* (Cambridge and New York, NY: Cambridge University Press, 2003). Also see Jie Chen amd Bruce Dickson, *Allies of the State: China's Private Entrepreneurs and Democratic Change* (Cambridge, MA: Harvard University Press, 2010).

economy systems in East Asian NIEs.[23] Economists within China such as Wu Jinglian have also apply this concept to explore many negative consequences of the economic reform.[24] However, the concepts of "crony capitalism" or "crony communism" cannot explain political developments in China if they mean close connections between the government and business. In East Asia, many economies which have been described as featuring "crony capitalism," such as Japan, South Korea, and Taiwan, are also democracies, and a close relationship between the government and business did not prevent democratization from taking place. A form of "crony capitalism" has existed in China, but one needs to explain why it has performed differently from other East Asian economies.

Our findings in this study certainly support this growing body of literature on the market economy and political regime. We have demonstrated how the Chinese state has been capable to making use of capitalism to promote economic growth while "digesting" its political consequences. However, we have added value to this body of literature by pointing to the hierarchal structure of the market system in China, namely, three layers of the market. We believe that this market hierarchy has empowered the Chinese state to accommodate the market while retaining its control over the market.

However, the fundamental contradictions between the state, market, and society remain in the MIS system. On September 23, 2008, Wen Jiabao, then China's premier, was interviewed by CNN's Fareed Zakaria. In answering Zakaria's question on the market and socialism, Wen stated:

The complete formulation of our economic policy is to give full play to the basic role of market forces in allocating resources under the macroeconomic guidance and regulation of the government. We have one important piece of experience of the past 30 years: that is to ensure that both the visible hand and the invisible hand are given full play in regulating the market forces. If you are familiar with the classical works of Adam Smith, you will know that there are two famous works of his. One is *The Wealth of Nations*, the other is the book on morality and ethics. *The Wealth of Nations* deals more with the invisible hand that are the market forces; the other book deals with social equity and justice. If most of the wealth is concentrated in the hands of the few in a country, then this country can hardly witness harmony and stability.

---

[23] For example, David C. Kang, *Crony Capitalism: Corruption and Development in South Korea and the Philippines* (New York, NY and Cambridge: Cambridge University Press, 2002).

[24] For example, Jinglian Wu, *Understanding and Interpreting Chinese Economic Reform* (Mason, OH: Thomson, 2005).

Wen Jiabao here touched on two actors, namely, market and government, or money and power. Society does not feature in this equation of money and power. However, in the same interview, Wen also mentioned that he was very much impressed by stoic philosopher Marcus Aurelius's *Meditations*, and asked: "Where are those people that were great for a time? They are all gone, leaving only a story, or some even half a story. Only people are in the position to create history and write history."[25]

Regulate or die: This is the lesson one can draw from the 2008 global financial crisis in the United States. The issue is who regulates whom. While the government can regulate the market, the two sides can also share mutual benefits. If this is the case, then there will be no morality or social justice. No one can regulate money, and no one can regulate power. If one refers to Wen's discussion of the *Meditations*, one may reach the conclusion that only society can regulate both money and power, and only by bringing society into the equation can social justice be served. But the issue is how society can be empowered to control both money and power. It is certainly a political question.

This is the political question that China will have to answer in the coming decades. Currently, the societal side of the triangle is too weak to build a stable order. The marketization reform has enabled state and market domination of society. This arrangement has maximized the capacity of the modern state and market to mobilize social resources while putting the autonomous order of the Chinese society in jeopardy. The ongoing social crisis in China wrought by income inequality, social protest, and environmental degradation is the best indicator of the relative weakening of society. This weakening is further exacerbated by the hemorrhaging of middle-class professionals and entrepreneurs from China in the recent wave of global migration, as they come to find China a less appealing option to live in despite its growth potential and job opportunities.[26] By further weakening the middle class, this can only delay social policy reforms to counter the ills of skewed marketization.

---

[25] CNN, "Transcript of interview with Chinese Premier Wen Jiabao," available at www.cnn .com/2008/WORLD/asiapcf/09/29/chinese.premier.transcript/index.html [Accessed on October 1, 2008].

[26] "China's Brain Drain May Be the World's Worst," *China Daily*, July 29, 2013.

MIS IN A GLOBAL SETTING

Lastly, the contemporary Chinese MIS system should be understood against the global setting in terms of its social, economic, and political dimensions. The significance of this issue certainly warrants a systematic treatment, but such extensive analysis would have exceeded the limited scope of our study. Still, this global dimension, as a key factor, cannot simply be ignored. We have offered some preliminary discussion of the issue of the modern transformation of the Chinese political economy; here, we shall outline a simple global framework as the basic external conditions for the contemporary Chinese MIS system, and in turn discuss China's transformation in this global context.

The emerging global political economy alignment consists of a dozen large economies and hundreds of smaller economies. But the key political players are only few: the United States, Europe, China, and the East Asian NIEs. The working of the system is primarily determined by their inter-actions, at both economic and political levels. As the only MIS system in the global system of multiple players, the Chinese market and state are also unique in their interactions with the external world. Moreover, in between these national players are the powerful multinational companies (MNCs), transnational networks of trade and finance, and, to a much greater degree, the flow of migrant labor. Since there is no effective world government that can take overall control of these flows, the global capitalist system operates without a "political shell," producing huge wealth but also creating gaping inequalities and environmental disaster.[27]

Under the MIS system, market forces initiated during the transform-ation of Chinese society pervade the global economy and national econ-omies of advanced countries, even as Chinese market actors, including those private entrepreneurs and migrant laborers who play increasingly important roles in the global economy, are subject to stricter state control. When the Chinese state power seeks to enforce market discipline and exert political control over its domestic market actors (and increas-ingly global actors as well). Meanwhile, it is able to keep the country somewhat insulated from the institutional rules of the global market

---

[27] We borrow the phraseology of Guoguang Wu, who aptly characterizes the system that increasingly encompasses the whole world economy as "global capitalism without a political shell." See Guoguang Wu, *Globalization Against Democracy: A Political Economy of Capitalism after Its Global Triumph* (New York, NY: Cambridge University Press, 2017), pp. 235–230.

except in the case of special arrangements that serve political purposes. When the Chinese state seeks to harness the global market for its own industrialization and modernization projects, it can be more forceful in its efforts to court global companies and promote the growth of an export-oriented economy, while supplying hundreds of millions of disciplined laborers for the global production process. Despite the huge differences between the Maoist economy and the current MIS system, the defining role of the state has remained unchanged. In both cases, the political logics assume supreme importance.

An interesting pattern of "varieties of capitalism" thus emerges when this type of political economy becomes enmeshed with the global market. Unlike the East Asian developmental state and the "state in market" system in the United States and Europe, the Chinese MIS system tends to integrate with the global market in a bottom-up rather than top-down fashion. In other words, the grassroots, downstream, or market layer of the MIS system integrates much more closely with the global market than the most powerful economic forces in China, such as the SOEs and even some large private businesses. This creates a somewhat misleading surge of Chinese enterprises in the Fortune 500. While China ranks top in the league table of exporting economies and second in terms of the number of large firms, most of the top-ranking Chinese firms have only very limited global clout, since the mainly domestic central SOEs always dominate the table.

Rather than China's large domestic SOEs it was foreign capital that invigorated the Chinese economy and rallied its standing in the global market. Since the late 1980s, there has been a huge influx of global economic actors, and the concurrent investment and technology, into China as the Chinese market becomes accessible to the global market. This pattern long predates China's entry into the WTO and the explosive growth of exports. Even in the 1990s, China numbered among the open economies of Asia that were most reliant on foreign direct investment (FDI).[28] One of the most important implications of FDI in China has been the rapid building of export capacity. From the early 1980s to the late 2000s, foreign-invested firms' contributions to China's exports grew steadily until they reached an unprecedented 55.2 percent.[29] From 2008 to 2013, while FIEs still dominated China's exports, contributing 46 percent, the

---

[28] Yasheng Huang, *Selling China: Foreign Direct Investment in the Reform Era* (New York, NY: Cambridge University Press, 2005), p. 10.

[29] Chunlai Chen, *FDI in China Local Determination, Investor Difference and Economic Impact* (Westchester, OH: Edward Elgar Publishing, 2011), p. 15.

share of private enterprises grew significantly to about 35 percent in 2013; SOEs contributed about 17 percent.[30] But since China's private businesses on average have fewer assets and employ more labor-intensive technology than SOEs, the private sector may play a role similar to that of FIEs, as they produce with borrowed technology and supply finished products to developed markets.

From 1980 to 2013, China's exports have grown at a staggering rate of 15.6 percent, most of which consists of merchandise exports, from heavy machinery to consumer durables. Meanwhile, China's manufacturing value-added grew at a similar rate of 15.1 percent.[31] In a matter of three decades, China has developed from a closed, semi-industrialized and semiagricultural economy into the world's factory, relying on marketization but also, and most importantly, access to newly opened global markets. This pattern of growth has been sustained by strenuous efforts on the part of the central and local states to promote the growth of manufacturing, including, among other matters, efforts to keep key factors at competitive prices, from low costs of land and labor to tax exemptions and export subsidies, as well as lax enforcement of environmental and intellectual property protection. As discussed in Chapters 6 and 7, such work is mainly carried out by the local state, which shares most of the benefits from short-term growth in GDP, industrial output, employment, and fiscal income. But the same pattern also benefits global entrepreneurs who can tap into cheap factor prices in China and foreign consumers who enjoy cheap Chinese exports.

But such an interest alignment also has an important impact on the distribution of income. The all-out effort to create industrial capacities is not sustained by corresponding growth in consumption and average household income. In fact, while the Chinese economy entered its most rapid phase of growth in the period 1992–2008, the share of household income in GDP declined from 67 percent to 58 percent and consumption in GDP fell from 48 percent to 35 percent.[32] This relative level of consumption compared unfavorably not only with the 70–80 percent level found in developed economies, but also with the 50–60 percent level seen in developing countries such as India and Russia. In other words, many of the fruits of growth were not distributed to average households. We have

[30] China National Bureau of Statistics online database, www.stat.gov.cn
[31] Calculated based on the World Bank Databank.
[32] Nicolas Lardy, *Sustaining China's Economic Crisis after the Global Financial Crisis* (Washington, DC: Peterson Institute of International Economics, 2012), pp. 60–61.

analyzed how the MIS system has created income inequality in the Chinese society. With the combined effects of income inequality and suppressed consumption, Chinese lower and middle classes have benefited relatively less than might have been expected given the economic growth experienced. Even as per capita GDP in China rose to around USD7,000 in 2013, the average annual household income was only USD4,700 even in Shanghai, and much lower elsewhere.[33]

Sluggish growth of household income and consumption vis-à-vis GDP and trade since the mid-1990s has had a negative long-run structural effect on the Chinese economy. For one thing, it created a vicious cycle, as lower income and consumption fed into lower domestic demand and the further need for a world market in order to create sufficient growth and employment. The same pattern of growth would only lead to repetition of the same structure of income distribution. This was the growth pattern from 1994 to 2008, when the global financial crisis broke out. After this, China found itself in a more serious conundrum. In response to a plunge in long-term demand for Chinese exports in the aftermath of the crisis, Beijing decided to launch a stimulus package of four trillion RMB, primarily focused on infrastructure investment. While this timely intervention salvaged economic growth for a few years, the Chinese economy is now burdened by an inflated money supply and heavy debt levels, and has seen a sharp fall in growth rates in recent years.

The global financial crisis signaled a bigger crisis in the contemporary model of global political economy. In previous decades this model worked well, as a rapidly industrializing China sought to embrace the global market and the United States reciprocated with an engagement strategy to draw China into its own system. This system was created in the aftermath of World War II, consolidated in the early Cold War, and then revamped in the 1970s. As discussed in Chapter 4, this was also a period in which China transformed its own modern state and adapted it from a form of political to a form of economic mobilization. Since the late 1970s, and increasingly in the early 2000s, the America-centered order incorporated a rising China in the name of neoliberalism.

But in recent years, the "state in market" model centered on the United States has no longer been able to fully accommodate the industrial capacity of the MIS as the growth of trade stagnates. There are two reasons for this structural imbalance. First, the old system of global imbalance became

---

[33] Edward Wang, "Survey in China Reveals a Wide Gap in Income," *New York Times*, July 19, 2013.

unsustainable. More than a decade after the onset of the global financial crisis, advanced economies in Europe and North America are still struggling to recover their old patterns of consumption. The irregular growth seen in recent years was to a large extent based on quantitative easing and low interest rates, which are soon to be phased out. As global demand slows, China will no longer be able to count on this external engine of growth. Also, as China approaches resource constraints such as decreasing labor supply and depletion of land, sharply rising factor prices will also put an end to export-led growth.[34]

Second, and equally important, as discussed earlier, China's phenomenal economic growth has led to the expansion of the Chinese state, including in terms of its fiscal and geopolitical clout, instead of fostering the growth of a vibrant civil society. The mobilization approach to economic development inherent in the MIS system has worked well with the logics of global capitalism, enabling it to cater to its profit motives without the countervailing societal and political forces. In the end, the Chinese model will continue to evolve its own modernized political and perhaps even geopolitical institutions with influence far and wide. For the United States, this means the loss of not only economic advantage, but also geopolitical interests and ideological dominance.

Most recently, the global financial crisis of 2008 expanded from a subprime crisis in the United States to encompass economic and trade issues and reshaped the global geopolitical and political economy. Since Obama's second term, the United States has been seeking to revise the rules of the game for global trade. Between 2012 and 2016, this was evident in a new proposed framework of trade and investment under the rubric of the Trans-Pacific Partnership (TPP) which effectively excluded China from the new rules. After the election of Donald Trump, the United States abandoned the institutional approach of the TPP and began to ponder more confrontational measures, including a trade war on China.[35] In response, China sought to strengthen and expand a China-centered trade order. In 2014, China launched its own Belt and Road Initiative, which includes, among other things, the construction of mammoth elements of infrastructure and the strengthening of trade relations across Southeast

---

[34] Jae Wan Chung, *Global Economic Disparity: Dynamic Forces in Geo-economic Competition of Superpowers* (Lanham, MD and New York, NY: Lexington Books, 2015), pp. 25–26.

[35] Shawn Donnan, "Trump Trade War with China May Not Be Imminent but It's Coming," *Financial Times*, August 7, 2017.

Asia, the Eurasian Continent, and the Eastern Pacific and Indian Ocean. In an effort to fund these infrastructure projects, China has also developed alternative financial institutions, such as the China-dominated Asia Infrastructure Investment Bank (AIIB), which has so far attracted all major economies apart from Japan and the United States.[36]

The Chinese economy, and that of the world, is at a crucial turning point. Against the background of the approaching crisis, the domestic rebalancing among society, market, and state in the MIS system in China thus assumes global significance. A stronger and better protected society will be able to strengthen domestic demand and foster a stronger civil society. If the balance between society and state and between society and market can swing toward society, the MIS system will only become more stable and sustainable. The MIS system would lose some of its capacities, but will no longer witness the aggressive growth of a mobilization state and ruthless marketization. As society rises relative to the market and state, the Chinese system will also approach global standards in civil and human rights. This will be the best antidote to the unfolding crisis in China and any global conflict between China and the United States.

---

[36] Gabriel Wildau and Charles Clover, "AIIB Launch Signals China's New Ambitions," *Financial Times*, June 29, 2015.

Bibliography

Aglietta, Michel, and Bai, Gao. *China's Development: Capitalism and Empire*, London: Routledge, 2012.

Arrighi, Giovanni. *Adam Smith in Beijing*, New York, NY: Verso, 2009.

Atweh, William. "Ming and the Emerging World Economy," in Denis Twitchett and Frederick W. Mote, eds., *The Cambridge History of China*, Vol. 8, Cambridge: Cambridge University Press, 1988, pp. 376–416.

Ba, Shusong. "Report on Small and Micro Business: Chinese Experience and Asia Paths," *Boao Review*, April 25, 2014.

Bai, Gang, ed. *General History of China's Political Institutions*, Vol. 5, Beijing: Renmin Publishing House, 1996.

Bakker, Karen. "Neoliberalizing Nature? Market Environmentalism in Water Supply in England and Wales," *Annals of the Association of American Geographers*, 95:3 (2005), pp. 542–565.

Barboza, David. "China Boss's Fall Puts Focus on a Business Ally," *New York Times*, August 21, 2013.

Barnes, Andrew. *Owning Russia: The Struggle over Factories, Farms, and Power*, Ithaca, NY: Cornell University Press, 2006.

Bayly, C. A. *The Birth of the Modern World, 1780–1914*, Oxford: Blackwell Publishing, 2004.

Beattie, Hilary J. *Land and Lineage in China: A Study of T'ung-Ch'eng County, Anhui, in the Ming and Ch'ing Dynasties*, Cambridge: Cambridge University Press, 1977.

Bergère, Marie-Claire. "The Chinese Bourgeoisie, 1911–1937," in John K. Fairbank, ed., *The The Cambridge History of China*, Vol. 13, Cambridge: Cambridge University Press, 1979, pp. 721–825.

Bian, Morris L. *The Making of the State Enterprise System in Modern China: The Dynamics of Institutional Change*, Cambridge, MA: Harvard University Press, 2005.

Bianco, Lucien. "Peasant Movements," in John K. Fairbank, ed., *The Cambridge History of China*, Vol. 13, Cambridge: Cambridge University Press, 1979, pp. 270–328.

Bodde, Derk. "The State and Empire of Chin," in Denis Twichett and Michael Loewe, eds., *The The Cambridge History of China*, Vol. 1, Cambridge: Cambridge University Press, 1986, pp. 20–103.

Bonnin, Michel. *The Lost Generation: The Rustication of Chinese Youth (1968–1980)*, Krystyna Horko (trans.), New York, NY: Columbia University Press, 2013.

Botho, Harold. "The Han," in John Whitney Hall, ed., *Cambridge History of Japan*, Vol. 4, Cambridge: Cambridge University Press, 1991, pp. 193–234.

Bourdieu, Pierre. *Acts of Resistance: Against the Tyranny of the Market*, New York, NY: The New Press, 1999.

Branstetter, Lee, and Lardy, Nicolas. "China's Embrace of Globalization," in Loren Brandt, Thomas Rawski, and John Sutton, eds., *China's Great Economic Transformation*, New York, NY: Cambridge University Press, 2008, pp. 633–681.

Braudel, Fernand. *Civilization and Capitalism, 15th–18th Century*, in 3 volumes, Sian Reynold (trans.), New York, NY: HarperCollins, 1981–1985.

Brødsgaard, Kjeld Erik. "Politics and Business Group Formation in China: The Party in Control?" *China Quarterly*, 211 (September 2012), pp. 624–648.

Brook, Timothy. *The Troubled Empire: China in the Yuan and Ming Dynasties*, Cambridge, MA: Harvard University Press, 2008.

Bureau of Township and Village Enterprise, the Ministry of Agriculture. *Zhongguo xiangzhan qiye tongji ziliao* (Statistical Materials on China's TVEs). Beijing: Zhongguo nongye chubanshe, 2003.

Byrd, William A., and Qingsong, Lin, eds. *China's Rural Industry: Structure, Development, and Reform*, Oxford: Oxford University Press, 1990.

Cai, Lingyue. "Wenzhou minjian ziben de fazhan yu yingdao yanjiu" ("Study on the Development and Guidance of Wenzhou's Private Capitals"), *Zhejiang Jinrong* (Zhejiang Finance), No. 1, 2005, pp. 26–28.

Cai, Yongshun. *The State and Laid-Off Workers in Reform China: The Silence and Collective Action of the Retrenched*, London: Routledge, 2006.

Callon, M. "Introduction: The Embeddedness of Economic Markets in Economics," in Michel Callon, ed., *The Laws of the Markets*, Hoboken, NJ: Basic Blackwell, 1998, pp. 1–57.

Cao, Nanlai. *Constructing China's Jerusalem: Christians, Power, and Place in Contemporary Wenzhou*, Palo Alto, CA: Stanford University Press, 2010.

Cao, Shuji. *Zhongguo yiminshi*, (History of Chinese Migrations, Vol. 5, Ming Dynasty), Fuzhou: Fujian Renmin Chubanshe, 1997.

Carsten, Holz A. *China's Industrial State-Owned Enterprises: Between Profitability and Bankruptcy*, Singapore: World Scientific, 2006.

Chai, Joseph C. H. *An Economic History of Modern China*. London: Edward Elgar, 2011.

Chan, Wellington K. K., "Government, Merchant and Industry to 1911," in John K. Fairbank, ed., *The Cambridge History of China*, Vol. 11, Cambridge: Cambridge University Press, 1978, pp. 416–462.

Chang, Chung-li. *The Chinese Gentry: Studies on Their Role in Nineteenth-Century Chinese Society*, Seattle, WA: University of Washington Press, 1955.

Chang, Kia-ngau. *The Inflation Spiral: The Experience in China*, Cambridge, MA: MIT Press, 1958.

Chao, Kang. *Man and Land in Chinese History: An Economic Analysis*, Stanford, CA: Stanford University Press, 1986.

Zhongguo chengshi fazhanshi lunji (Collected Discussions on the History of Development of Chinese Cities), Beijing: New Star Publisher, 2006.

Chen, Baorong. *Zhonggug jingji* (China's Private Household Economy), Shanghai: Shanghai Social Science Academy Press, 1990.

Chen, Chunlai. *FDI in China Local Determination, Investor Difference and Economic Impact*, Westchester, NY: Edward Elgar Publishing, 2011.

Chen, Edward. *Hyper-Growth in Asian Economies: A Comparative Study of Hong Kong, Japan, Korea, Singapore and Taiwan*, London: Macmillan, 1979.

Chen, Jiaxi. *Gaige shidai de Zhongguo minying qiyejia de zhengzhi yingxiang* (Political Influence of Private Entrepreneurs in the Reform Era), Chongqing: Chongqing Chubanshe, 2007.

Chen, Jian. *Mao's China and the Cold War*, Chapel Hill, NC: University of North Carolina Press, 2001.

Chen, Jie, and Dickson, Bruce. *Allies of the State: China's Private Entrepreneurs and Democratic Change*, Cambridge, MA: Harvard University Press, 2010.

Chen, Teping, and Aredy, James. "Jiang Jiemin Trial Links Key Officials in China's Corruption Crackdown," *The Wall Street Journal*, April 13, 2015.

Chen, Yinghong. *Creating the New Man: From Enlightenment Ideals to Socialist Realities*, Honolulu, HI: Hawaii University Press, 2004.

Chen, Yun. *Chen Yun Wenji* (Collected Works of Chen Yun), Vol. 2, Beijing: Zhongyang wenxian chubanshe, 2005.

Transition and Development in China: Towards a Shared Growth. London: Ashgate, 2008.

Chen, Zhen, ed. *Zhongguo jindai gongyeshi ziliao* (Materials on the Industry of Modern China), Vol. 4, Shanghai: Shanghai Sanlian Books, 1962.

Cheung, Linsun. *Banking in Modern China: Entrepreneurs, Professional Managers and the Development of Chinese Banks, 1897–1937*, Cambridge: Cambridge University Press, 2007.

Chinese Academy of Social Sciences. *China Trade Report 2012*, p. 17, available at www.iwep.org.cn/upload/2013/03/d20130307160336894.pdf

China Economic Reform Foundation. *Zhongguo gaige yu fazhan baogao* (A Report on China's Reform and Development), Beijing: Zhongguo jingji chubanshe, 2002.

Chu, Samuel, and Liu, Kwang-ching. *Li Hung-Chang and China's Early Modernization* Armonk, New York, NY: M. E. Sharp, 2000.

Chu, Tung-Tzu. *Local Government in China under Qing*, Cambridge, MA: Harvard University Press, 1962.

Chung, Jae Ho. "The Evolving Hierarchy of China's Local Administration: Tradition and Change," in Jae Ho Chung and Tao-chiu Lam, eds., *China's Local Administration: Tradition and Change*, London and New York, NY: Routledge, 2010, pp. 1–13.

Chung, Jae Wan. *Global Economic Disparity: Dynamic Forces in Geo-Economic Competition of Superpowers*, Lanham, MD and New York, NY: Lexington Books, 2015.

Clark, Donald, Durrell, Peter, and Whiting, Susan. "The Role of Law in China's Economic Development," in Loren Brandt and Thomas Rawski, eds., *China's Great Economic Transformation*, New York, NY: Cambridge University Press, 2008, pp. 375–427.

Clark, Hugh R. "The Southern Kingdoms between Tang and Song," in Denis Twitchett and Paul Jakov Smith, eds., *The Cambridge History of China*, Vol. 5, Cambridge and New York, NY: Cambridge University Press, 2009, pp. 907–979.

Coase, Ronald. "The Nature of the Firm," *Economica*, 4:16 (1937), pp. 386–405.

"The Problem of Social Cost," *Journal of Law and Economics*, 3 (1960), pp. 1–44.

Coble, Parks M. Jr. *The Shanghai Capitalists and the Nationalist Government, 1927–1937*, Cambridge, MA: Harvard University Press, 1980.

Cook, Simon J. *Foundations of Alfred Marshall's Science of Economics: A Rounded Globe of Knowledge*, New York, NY: Cambridge University Press, 2009.

Dardess, John. "Shunti and End of Yuan Rule in China," in Herbert Frank and Denis C. Twitchett, ed., *The Cambridge History of China*, Vol. 6 (Cambridge and New York, NY: Cambridge University Press, 1994, pp. 561–586.

Deng, Kent. *China's Economy in Modern Times: Changes and Economic Consequences, 1800– 2000*, London: Routledge, 2011.

Deng, Xiaoping. *Deng Xiaoping wenxuan III* (Collected Works of Deng Xiaoping), Beijing: Zhongyang Wenxian Chubanshe, 1993.

Denyer, Simon. "Chinese Entrepreneurs, Unsettled, Speak for Reform," *Washington Post*, August 26, 2013.

Dickson, Bruce J. *Red Capitalists in China: The Party, Private Entrepreneurs, and Prospects for Political Change*, Cambridge and New York, NY: Cambridge University Press, 2003.

Wealth into Power: The Communist Party's Embrace of China's Private Sector, Cambridge and New York, NY: Cambridge University Press, 2008.

Dittmer, Lowell. *Liu Shaoqi and the Chinese Cultural Revolution, revised edition*, New York, NY: M. E. Sharpe, 1998.

Dikötter, Frank. *Mao's Great Famine: The History of China's Most Devastating Catastrophe, 1958–62*, New York, NY: Walker Co., 2010.

Dong, Zhikai. *Jiefang zhanzheng shiqi de tudigaige* (Land Reform in the War of Liberation), Beijing: Beijing University Press, 1987.

Donnan, Shawn. "Trump Trade War with China May Not Be Imminent but It's Coming," *Financial Times*, August 7, 2017.

Duara, Prasenjit. *Culture, Power, and the State: Rural North China, 1900–1942*, Palo Alto, CA: Stanford University Press, 1988.

Eastman, Lloyd. *Seeds of Destruction: Nationalist China in War and Revolution, 1937–1949*, Stanford, CA: Stanford University Press, 1984.

Eisenstadt, S. N. *The Political Systems of Empire: The Rise and Fall of the Historical Bureaucratic Societies*, New York, NY: The Free Press of Glencoe, 1963.

Elliott, Douglas, Arthur Kroeber, and Yu Qiao. "Shadow Bank in China: A Primer," *Brookings Papers*, March 2015.

Elliot, Mark C. *The Eight Banners and Ethnic Identity in Late Imperial China*, Stanford, CA: Stanford University Press, 2001.

Elliot, John E. "Introduction," in Joseph A. Schumpeter, *The Theory of Economic Development*, New Brunswick and London: Transaction Books, 1983, pp. vii–lx.

Elman, Benjamin. *A Cultural History of China's Civil Examinations in Late Imperial China*, Berkeley, CA: University of California Press, 2000.

Etienne-Will, Pierre, and Wong, Roy Bin. *Nourish the People: The State Civilian Granary System in China, 1650–1850*, Ann Arbor, MI: University of Michigan Press, 1991.

Evans, John. *Tea in China: The History of China's National Drink*, Westport, CT: Greenwood Press, 1992.

Fairbank, J. K, Eckstein, A., and Yang, L. S. "Economic Change in Early Modern China: An Analytic Framework," *Economic Development and Cultural Change* 9 (1960), pp. 1–26.

Fairbank, John, and Reischauer, Edwin, eds. *China: Tradition and Transformation*, Sydney: George Allen & Unwin, 1979.

Fallows, James. *More Like Us: Making America Great Again*, New York, NY: Houghton Mifflin, 1989.

Fan, Ting. "Guojia dianwang longduan kuozhang" (The Expansion of State Grid Monopoly), *Economy & State Weekly* 2, 2011, pp. 11–15.

Fardoust, Shahrok, Yifu Lin, Justin, and Luo, Xubei. "Demystifying China's Stimulus Package," *Policy Research Working Paper No. 6221* (Washington, DC: World Bank, October 2012).

Faure, David. *China and Capitalism: A History of Business Enterprise in Modern China*, Hong Kong: Hong Kong University Press, 2006.

Ferguson, Adam. *An Essay on the History of Civil Society*, Cambridge: Cambridge University Press, 1995.

Fernandez, Juan Antonio, and Fernandez-Stembridge, Leila, eds., *China's State-Owned Enterprise Reforms: An Industrial and CEO Approach*, New York, NY: Routledge, 2007.

Feuerwerker, Albert. "Economic Trends, 1912–49," in John K. Fairbank, ed., *The Cambridge History of China*, Vol. 13, Cambridge: Cambridge University Press, 1979, pp. 28–127.

Chinese Social and Economic History: From the Song to 1900: Report of the American Delegation to a Sino-American Symposium on Chinese Social and Economic History, Ann Arbor, MI: The Center for Chinese Studies, University of Michigan, 1982.

Fewsmith, Joseph. *Dilemmas of Reform in China: Political Conflict and Economic Debate*, London and New York, NY: Routledge, 1994.

Fitzgerald, John. *Awakening China: Politics, Culture, and Class in the Nationalist Revolution*, Stanford, CA: Stanford University Press, 1996.

Forsythe, Michael. "Alibaba I.P.O could be Bonanaza for the Scions of Chinese Leaders," *New York Times*, July 20, 2014.

"Wang Jianlin, a Billionaire at the Intersection of Business and Power in China," *New York Times*, April 28, 2015.

Frank, Andre Gunter. *Reorient: The Global Economy in the Asia Age*, Berkeley and Los Angeles, CA: University of California Press, 1998.

Frieden, Jeffry R. *Global Capitalism: Its Fall and Rise in the Twentieth Century*, New York, NY: W. W. Norton, 2006.

Friedman, Milton, and Friedman, Rose. *Free to Choose: A Personal Statement*, New York, NY: Harcourt Brace Jovanovich, 1980.

Fukuyama, Francis. *The Origin of Political Order: From Prehuman Times to the French Revolution*, New York, NY: Farrar, Straus and Giroux, 2012.

Gallagher, Mary Elizabeth. *Contagious Capitalism: Globalization and the Politics of Labor in China*, Princeton, NJ: Princeton University Press, 2005.

Gao, Yuling. *Zhongguo nongmin fanxingwei yanjiu 1950–1980* (Counteractions of Chinese Peasants, 1950–1980), Hong Kong: The Chinese University of Hong Kong Press, 2013.

Gibson-Graham, J. K. *Postcapitalist Politics*, Minneapolis, MN: University of Minnesota Press, 2006.

Gilens, Martin, and Page, Benjamin I., "Testing Theories of American Politics: Elites, Interest Groups, and Average Citizens," *Perspectives on Politics* 12:4 (2014), pp. 564–581.

Gilley, Bruce. *Model Rebels: The Rise and Fall of China's Richest Village*, Berkeley and Los Angeles, CA: University of California Press, 2001.

Gilpin, Robert. *Global Political Economy: Understanding the International Economic Order*, Princeton, NJ: Princeton University Press, 2001.

Gohigh Fund. *Zhongguo minjian ziben touzi diaoyan baogao: Shanbeipian* (China Private Capital Investment Investigative Report: North Shaanxi).

Gao Long. "Meilaoban Gong Aiai de heijindiguo" (The Black Gold Empire of the Coal Boss Gong Aiai), *Southern Metropolitan Daily*, March 6, 2013.

Glossner, Christian L., and Gregosz, David. *The Formation and Implementation of the Social Market Economy: Incipiency and Actuality*, Berlin: Konrad Adenauer Stiftung, 2011.

Gore, Lance Liang-Ping. "China Recruits Top SOE Executives to the Government," *EAI Background Brief No. 661*, East Asian Institute, National University of Singapore, September 30, 2011.

Guthrie, Doug. *China in the Global Economy: The Social, Economic, and Political Transformation of the Chinese Society*, London: Routledge, 2006.

Guo, Changhai. *Zhongguo qianju (China's Money Traps)*, Taipei: Caida Chubanshe.

Guo, Xuezhi. *China's Security State: Politics, Philosophy and Evolutions*, Cambridge: Cambridge University Press, 2012.

Haddad, Mona. "Trade Integration in East Asia: The Role of China and Production Networks," *World Bank Policy Research Paper*, no. 4160, March 2007.

Hall, Peter A., and Soskice, David W. *Varieties of Capitalism: The Institutional Foundations of Comparative Advantage*, New York, NY: Oxford University Press, 2001.

Hamashita, Takeshi. *Intra-East Asian Trade in Ming Times*, Ithaca, NY: Cornell University Press, 1997.

Harding, Harry. *China's Second Revolution: Reform after Mao*, Washington, DC: The Brookings Institute, 1987.

Hartford, Kathleen, and Goldstein, Steven M. *Single Sparks: China's Rural Revolutions*, New York, NY: M. E. Sharpe, 1989.

Hao, Yen-ping, and Wang, Ern-Min. "Changing Chinese Views of the Western Relations, 1840–1895," in Fairbank, John K. ed., *The Cambridge History of China*, Vol. 10, Cambridge: Cambridge University Press, 1978, pp. 142–201.

Harvey, David. *A Short History of Neoliberalism*, Oxford: Oxford University Press, 2005.

Hasan, Parvez. *Korea, Problems and Issues in a Rapidly Growing Economy*, Baltimore, MD: Johns Hopkins University Press, 1976.

Hayek, Frederick. *The Collected Works of F. A. Hayek*, Chicago, IL: University of Chicago Press, 1989.

He, Baoli. "Fangjie yinxing shangye diguo fuxian" (Hidden Commercial Empire of the Property Sister Surfaces) *Fazhi Ribao* (The Legal Daily), January 30, 2013.

He, Canfei, Huang, Huang Zhiji, and Rui, Wang. "Land Use Change and Economic Growth in Urban China: A Structural-Equation Analysis," *Urban Studies* 50 (2013), pp. 2880–2898.

He, Kai. *Institutional Balancing in the Asia-Pacific: Economic Interdependence and China's Rise*, Abingdon and New York, NY: Routledge, 2009.

He, Wenkai. *Paths towards the Modern Fiscal State: Britain, Japan, and China*, Cambridge, MA: Harvard University Press, 2013.

He, Yanling, et al., eds. *Zhongguo chengshi zhengfu gonggong fuwu pinggu baogao 2013* (The 2013 Evaluation Report on Chinese Urban Governments' Public Service Capacity), Beijing: Social Sciences Academic Press, 2014.

He, Zengke. "Zhongguo zhuanxingqi fubai he fanfubai wenti yanjiu" (A Study of the Problems of Corruption and Anti-Corruption during China's transition), *Jingji Shehui Tizhi Bijiao* (Comparative Studies of Social and Economic Systems) 1 (2003), pp. 19–29.

Heilbroner, Robert L. *The Nature and Logic of Capitalism*, New York, NY: W. W. Norton & Company, 1985.

21st Century Capitalism, New York, NY: W. W. Norton & Company, 1993.

Heng, Kuan, and Gale, Esson M. (trans.) *Discourses on Salt and Iron: A Debate on State Control of Commerce and Industry in Ancient China*, Taipei: Ch'eng-Wen Publishing Company, 1967.

Hipsher, Scott A. *The Private Sector's Role in Poverty Reduction in Asia*, Oxford: Chandos Publishing, 2010.

Ho, Ping-ti. *Studies on the Population of China, 1368–1953*, Cambridge, MA: Harvard University Press, 1959.

The Ladder of Success in Imperial China: Aspects of Social Mobility, 1368–1911, New York, NY: University of Columbia Press, 1962.

Hoffman, David E. *The Oligarchs: Wealth and Power in the New Russia*, New York, NY: Public Affairs, 2011.

Hou, Jiaju. *Zhongguo Caijin Zhidu Yanjiu* (Study on the Fiscal History of China), Taipei: Lianjing Publishing House, 1989.

Hou, Xudong, *Beichao cunmin de shenghuo shijie* (Life World of Villagers in the Northern Dynasties), Beijing: The Commercial Press, 2010.

Hsiao, Kung-Chuan. *Rural China: Imperial Control in the Nineteenth Century*, Seattle, WA: University of Washington Press, 1960.

History of Chinese Political Thought, Vol. 1, Princeton, NJ: Princeton University Press, 2015 (reprint).

Hsu, Choyun, *Han Agriculture: The Formation of China's Agrarian Economy*, Seattle, WA: University of Washington Press, 1980.

Hsu, Immanuel, C. K. *The Rise of Modern China*, New York, NY: Oxford University Press, 1999.

Hu, Angang, and Wang, Shaoguang, *The Chinese Economy in Crisis: State Capacity and Tax Reform*, New York, NY: M. E. Sharpe, 2001.

Hu, Qirui, "Jindai Guangzhou Shangren yu Zhengzhi, 1905–1926" ("Merchants and Politics, Modern Canton"), MA thesis (Taipei: National Chengchi University, 2003).

Hu, Tieqiu. *Ming-Qing xiejia yanjiu* (A Study of Innkeepers in Ming and Qing Dynasties), Shanghai: Shanghai Guji Chubanshe, 2015.

Huang, Jianhui. *Shanxi piaohao shi* (A History of the Shanxi Banks), Taiyuan: Shanxi jingji chubanshe, 1992.

Huang, Jiuli, and Kunwang, Li. "Chukou Kaifang, defang jingjiguimo he jingji zengzhang" ("Export Openness, Regional Market Size and Economic Growth"), *Jingji yanjiu* (Economic Studies) 6 (2006), p. 37.

Huang, Jiuli. "Foreign Trade, Interregional Trade, and Regional Specialization," in Ming Lu, Zhao Chen, Zhu Xiwen, and Xu Xianxiang, eds., *China's Regional Development: Review and Prospect*, London and New York, NY: Routledge, 2015, pp. 169–210.

Huang, Mengfu. *Zhongguo minying jingji fazhan xingshi baogao 2005* (China Private Economy Development Trend Report 2005) (Beijing: China Social Sciences Press, 2006).

Huang, Qichen, and Xinping, Peng. *Mingqing Guangdong shangren* (Merchants in Ming and Qing Canton), Guangzhou: Guangdong People's Publishing House, 2003.

Huang, Ray. *Taxation and Government Finance in Sixteenth Century China*, New York, NY: Cambridge University Press, 1974.

China: A Micro-history, Armonk, NY: M. E. Sharp, 2000.

Zibenzhuyi yu ershiyi shiji (Capitalism and the Twenty-First Century), Beijing: Sanlian Books, 2001.

Huang, Yanjie. "China's Young Generation Comes of Age: Generation Shift and How It Augurs for China's Future," in Zheng, Yongnian and Gore Liangping Lance, eds., *China Entering the Xi Jinping Era*, London: Routledge, 2014, pp. 235–254.

Huang, Yanjie, and Yongnian, Zheng. "China's Centrally-Managed State-Owned Enterprises," in Eric Kjelk Brødsgaard, ed., *Globalization and Public Sector Reform in China* (London: Routledge, 2014), pp. 125–127.

Huang, Yasheng. *Inflation and Investment Control in China: The Political Economy of Central–Local Relations in the Reform Era*, New York, NY: Cambridge University Press, 1996.

Selling China: Foreign Direct Investment in the Reform Era, New York, NY: Cambridge University Press, 2005.

Capitalism with Chinese Characteristics: Entrepreneurship and the State, Cambridge and New York, NY: Cambridge University Press, 2008.

Huang, Zongxi, and De Barry, Wm Theodore (trans.) *Waiting for the Dawn, a Plan for the Prince: Huang Tsung-his's Ming-i-tai-fang-lu*, New York, NY: Columbia University Press, 1993.

Hughes, Jennifer. "Chinese Communist Party Writes Itself into Company Law," *Financial Times*, August 14, 2017.

Itoh, Mokoto. "The Theoretical Possibilities of a Socialist Market Economy," in Nobuharu Yokokawa, Jayati Ghosh, and Bob Rowthorn, eds., *Industrialization of China and India: Their Impact on the World Economy* (London: Routledge, 2013), pp. 151–169.

Izutani, Yoko. *Chūgoku kenkoku shoki no seiji to Keizai: taishu undō to shakai shugi taisei* (Politics and Economy in Early PRC: Mass Movement and the Socialist System), Tokyo: Ochanomizu Books, 2007.

Jiang, Yonglin. *The Mandate of Heaven and the Great Ming Code*, Seattle and London: University of Washington Press, 2012.

Jin, Guantao, and Qingfeng, Liu. *Shengshi yu weiji: lun zhongguo fengjian shehui de chaowending jiegou* (Prosperity and Crisis: On the Ultra-Stable Structure of Chinese Society) (Hong Kong: The Chinese University of Hong Kong Press, 1992).

Guannianshi yanjiu: zhongguo xiandai zhongyao zhengzhi shuyu de xingcheng (Study in the History of Ideas: The Formation of Important Terms in Modern Chinese Politics) (Beijing: Falu Chubanshe, 2009).

Johnson, Chalmers. "MITI and Japanese International Economy Policy," in Robert Scalopino, ed., *The Foreign Policy of Modern Japan*, Berkeley, CA: University of California Press, 1977, pp. 227–281.

MITI and the Japanese Miracle: The Growth of Industrial Policy, 1925–1975, Stanford, CA: Stanford University Press, 1982.

"Political Institutions and Economic Performance: A Comparative Analysis of the Government-Business Relationship in Japan, South Korea, and Taiwan," in F. Deyo, ed., *The Political Economy of the New Asian Industrialism* (Ithaca, NY: Cornell University Press, 1987), pp. 136–164.

"The Developmental State: Odyssey of a Concept," in Meredith Woo-Cumings, ed., *The Developmental State* (Ithaca, NY: Cornell University Press, 1999), pp. 32–60.

Jones, Eric. *The European Miracle: Environments, Economies and Geopolitics in the History of Europe and Asia*, 3rd edn., Cambridge: Cambridge University Press, 2003.

Kashiwai, Kisao. *Kindai Shina Zaiseishi* (Fiscal History of Modern China), Tokyo: Tokyo Kyoiku Tosho, 1942.

King, David C. *Crony Capitalism: Corruption and Development in South Korea and the Philippines*, New York, NY and Cambridge: Cambridge University Press, 2002.

Kirby, William. "Continuity and Change in Modern China: Economic Planning in Taiwan and China, 1943–1958," *The Australian Journal of Chinese Affairs* 24, pp. 121–141.

"China's Internationalization in the Early People's Republic: The Dream of a Socialist World Economy," *The China Quarterly* 188 (2006), pp. 870–890.

Koh, Gui Qing. "Is China's Debt Nightmare a Province called Jiangsu?" *Reuters*, July 24, 2013.

Kroll, J. L. "Toward a Study of the Economic Views of Sang Hung-Yang," *Early China* 4 (1978–1979), pp. 11–18.

Kuhn, Dieter. *The Age of Confucian Rule: The Song Transformation of China*, Cambridge, MA: Harvard University Press, 2009.

Kuhn, Phillip. *Soul Stealers: The Chinese Sorcery Scare in 1768*, Cambridge, MA: Harvard University Press, 1990.

Kuo, Ting-Yee and Kwang, Ching Liu. "Self-Strengthening: The Pursuit of Western Technology," in John K. Fairbank and Liu Kwang Ching, eds., *The Cambridge History of China*, Vol. 11, New York, NY: Cambridge: Cambridge University Press, 1978.

Lardy, Nicholas R. *China's Unfinished Economic Revolution*, Washington, DC: The Brookings Institute, 1998.

Sustaining China's Economic Crisis after the Global Financial Crisis, Washington, DC: Peterson Institute of International Economics, 2012.

Lam, Willy. "Chinese Leaders Revive Marxist Orthodoxy," *Jamestown China Brief* 10:9, April 29, 2010, available at www.jamestown.org/uploads/media/cb_010_36.pdf [Accessed on January 10, 2014].

Lau, Lawrence, Qian, Yingyi, and Rolland, Gerard. "Reform without Losers: An Inter-
    pretation of China's Dual Track to Transition," *Journal of Political Economy* 108:1
    (2000), pp. 120–143.
Layton, Robert. *Order and Anarchy: Civil Society, Social Disorder and War*, Cambridge:
    Cambridge University Press, 2006.
Ledeneva, Alena V. *How Russia Really Works: The Informal Practices That Shaped Post-
    Soviet Politics and Business*, Ithaca, NY: Cornell University, 2006.
Levine, Martin. *Worker Rights and Labor Standards in Asia's Four New Tigers:
    A Comparative Perspective*, New York, NY: Plenum Press, 1997.
Lewis, Mark Edward. *The Construction of Space in Early China*, New York, NY: SUNY
    Press, 2005.
Li, Guangtao. *Mingji liukou shimo* (A Historical Inquiry into the Rebellions of Late
    Ming), Taipei: The Academy Sinica Press, 1962.
Li, Hongbin and Zhou Li-an Zhou. "Political Turnover and Economic Performance:
    The Incentive Role of Personnel Control in China," *Journal of Public Economics*
    86:9–10 (September 2005), pp. 1743–1762.
Li, Huarui. *Wang Anshi bianfa yanjiushi* (The History of the Studies on the Wang
    Anshi Reform), Beijing: Renmin Chubanshe, 2004.
Li, Mo. "Jinri Daqiuzhuang" (Today's Daqiu Village), *Xiaokang* 9 (2007), pp. 52–59.
Li, Peng. "Yangqi ruyue chaoyong" (Centrally-Managed SOEs Ride Wave to Enter
    Guangdong), *The Economy & Nation Weekly* 7 (2011), pp. 15–17.
Li, Weiguang. *Zhongguo caizhengshi lungao* (Essays on China's Fiscal History), Beijing:
    Zhongguo Caizheng Jingji Chubanshe, 2000.
Li, Xi and Xu, Dianqing. *From Trade Surplus to Dispute over the Exchange Rates*,
    Singapore: World Scientific, 2016.
Liang, Fangzhong and Wang, Yu-chuan (trans.) *The Single Whip Law of Taxation in
    China*, Cambridge, MA: Harvard University Press, 1956.
Lin, Chaochao. Sulian jingji hesuanzhi yu zhongguo jihua jingji (Soviet Economic
    Accounting and Chinese Planned Economy), *Shilin (Historical Review)* 1 (2016),
    162–174.
Lin, Kun-Chin and Mika M. Purra. *Transforming China's Industrial Sectors: Insti-
    tutional Change and Regulation of the Power Sector in the Reform Era*, Lee Kuan
    Yew School of Public Policy Working Paper No. 8, 2012.
Lin Yifu, Justin. *New Structural Economics: A Framework for Rethinking Development
    Policy*, Washington, DC: The World Bank, 2010.
Lin, Yifu Justin, Cai, Fang, and Zhou, Li. *The China Miracle: Development Strategy and
    Economic Reform*, Hong Kong: The Chinese University Press, 1996.
    State-Owned Enterprise Reform in China, Hong Kong: The Chinese University Press,
    2001.
Lin, Yunhui. *Xiang shehui zhuyi guodu: zhongguo shehui he jingji de zhuanxing*
    (Transition to Socialism: The Transformation of Chinese Society and Economy).
    History of Contemporary China Series, Vol. 2, Hong Kong: The Chinese Univer-
    sity of Hong Kong Press, 2009.
Lin, Yi-min. "The Institutional Context of Rent-Seeking in Economic Transition," in
    Tak-Wing Ngo and Wu Yongping, eds., *Rent Seeking in China*, London: Rout-
    ledge, 2000, pp. 59–78.

Wutuobang yundong: cong dayuejin dao dajihuang (The Utopian Movement: From the Great Leap Forward to the Great Famine). History of Contemporary China Series, Vol. 4, Hong Kong: The Chinese University of Hong Kong Press, 2008.

Ling, Zhijun. *The Lenovo Affair: The Growth of China's Computer Giant and Its Takeover of the IBM-PC* (trans. Martha Avery), Singapore: John Wiley, 2005.

Liou, Chin-shian. "Bureaucratic Politics and Overseas Investment by Chinese State-owned Oil Companies: Illusory Champions," *Asian Survey* 49:4 (2009), pp. 670–690.

List, Frederick. *The National System of Political Economy* [1885], New York, NY: Augustus Kelley, 1966.

Liu Guanglin, William. *The Chinese Market Economy, 1000–1500*, New York, NY: SUNY Press, 2015.

Liu, Qiao. *Corporate China 2.0: The Great Shake Up*, New York, NY: Palgrave Macmillan, 2016.

Liu, Wei and Zhizhou, Cai. *Zouxiashentan de GDP zhuyi: cong jingji zengzhang dao kechixu fazhan* (Demystifying GDPism: From Economic Growth to Sustainable Development), Beijing: China CITIC Press, 2006.

Liu, Xin. *The Otherness of Self: A Genealogy of the Self in Contemporary China*, Ann Arbor, MI: The University of Michigan Press. 2002.

Liu, Zehua, Wang, Maohe, and Wang, Lanzhou, *Zhuanzhi quanli yu zhongguo shehui* (Absolutist Power and Chinese Society), Changchun: Jining Wenshi Chubanshe, 1988.

Liu, Zhiying. Wangwei zhengfu liangzheng shuping (Outline and Comments on the Grain Policy of Wang Jingwei Puppet Government), *Kangri zhanzheng Yanjiu* (Study on Sino-Japanese War) 1 (1999), pp. 135–153.

Loewe, Michael. "The Former Han Dynasty," in John K. Fairbank and Denis Twitchett, eds., *The Cambridge History of China Vol. 1: The Chin and Han Empires, 221 BC–AD. 220*, Cambridge and New York, NY: Cambridge University Press, 1986, pp. 103–122.

Low, Linda, Heng, Toh Mun, Wong, Soon Teck, Yam, Tan Kong and Hughes, Helen. *Challenge and Response: Thirty Years of the Economic Development Board*, Singapore: Times Academic Press, 1993.

Locke, John. *Two Treaties of Government*, Cambridge: Cambridge University Press, 1960.

Lou, Jiwei. "The Reform of Intergovernmental Fiscal Relations in China: Lesson Learnt," in The World Bank, *Public Finance in China: Reform and Growth for a Harmonious Society*, Washington, DC: The World Bank, 2009.

Lou, Jiwei, and Wang, Shulin. *Public Finance in China: Reform and Growth for a Harmonious Society*, Washington, DC: The World Bank, 2008.

Lü, Xiaobo. "Minor Public Economy," in Lu Xiaobo and Elizabeth Perry, eds., *Danwei: The Changing Chinese Workplace in Historical and Comparative Perspective*, New York, NY: M. E. Sharpe, 1999, pp. 21–40.

Lufrano, Richard John. *Honorable Merchants: Commerce and Confucian Self-Cultivation in Late Imperial China*, Honolulu, HI: University of Hawai'i Press, 1997.

Ma, Ming and Zhu, Ying, *Zhongguo jingji tongshi* (General Economic History of China), Vol. 9, Changsha: Hunan Publishing House, 2000.

Macfarquar, Roderick, *The Origins of the Cultural Revolution*, Vol. 3 (1961–1966), New York, NY: Columbia University Press, 1999.

MacPherson, C. B. *The Political Theory of Possessive Individualism: From Hobbes to Locke*, Oxford: Clarendon Press, 1962.

Maddison, Angus. *The World Economy: A Millennial Perspective*, Paris: OECD, 2001.

Marcus, Alfred. *Innovation in Sustainability*, Cambridge: Cambridge University Press, 2015.

Marx, Karl. "The Communist Manifesto," in Robert C. Tucker, ed., *The Marx-Engels Reader*, New York, NY: W. W. Norton, 1972, pp. 469–500.

Mason, Edward S., Kim, Mahn Je, Perkins, Dwight H., Kim, Kwang Suk and Cole, David, *The Economic and Social Modernization of the Republic of Korea*, Cambridge, MA: Harvard University Press, 1980.

Mckeown, Adam, *China Migration Networks and Cultural Change: Peru, Chicago, and Hawaii, 1900–1936*, Chicago, IL: University of Chicago Press, 2001.

Meisner, Maurice. "Despotism of Concepts: Wittfogel and Marx on China," *The China Quarterly* 16 (1963), pp. 99–111.

Miller, H. Lynman, "The Late Imperial Chinese State," in David Shambaugh, ed., *The Modern Chinese State*, New York, NY: Cambridge University Press, 2001, pp. 15–41.

Ministry of Commerce, *2013 nian quanguo shichang zhuti fazhan baogao* (Report of National Survey on Development of Market Entities), Beijing, 2014.

Ministry of Land and Natural Resources. *China National Land and Natural Resource Report 2011*, Beijing, January 2012.

Minzner, Carl. *Social Instability in China: Causes, Consequences, and Implications*, Washington, DC, Center for Strategic and International Studies, 2016.

Mitchell, Timothy. *Rule of Experts*, Berkeley, CA: University of California Press, 2002.

Moore, Malcolm. "The Rise of Wang Jianlin, China's Richest Man," *Daily Telegraph*, September 21, 2013.

Morris, Ian. *Why the West Rules – For Now: The Patterns of History, and What They Reveal about the Future*, London: Profile Books, 2011.

Mote, Frederic W. *Imperial China, 900–1800*, Cambridge, MA: Harvard University Press, 1999.

Mulvenon, James C. *Soldiers of Fortune: The Rise and Fall of the Chinese Military-Business Complex, 1978–1998*, Armonk, NY: M. E. Sharpe, 2001.

Nagakane, Katsuji, "Manchukou and Economic Development," in Peter Duus, Ramon H. Meyers, and Mark R. Peattle, eds., *The Japanese Informal Empire in China* (Princeton, NJ: Princeton University Press, 1989), pp. 133–164.

Nagle, D. Brendan. *The Household as the Foundation of Aristotle's Polis*, New York, NY: Cambridge University Press, 2006.

Naito, Torajiro and Xia Yingyuan (trans.), *Zhongguo lishi tonglun* (General Discussions on Chinese History), Beijing: Sheke Wenxian Chubanshe, 2006.

National Bureau of Statistics. *China Statistical Yearbook 2002*, Beijing: Zhongguo tongji chubanshe, 2002.

    China Statistical Yearbook 2012, Beijing: China Statistical Publishing House, 2012.

    China Statistical Yearbook 2013, Beijing: Zhongguo tongji chubanshe, 2013.

Naughton, Barry. *Growing Out of the Plan: Chinese Economic Reform, 1978–1993*, New York, NY: Cambridge University Press, 1995.

"Cities in the Chinese Economic System: Changing Roles and Conditions for Autonomy," in Deborah Davis et al. eds., *Urban Space in Contemporary China: The Potential for Autonomy and Community*, Washington, DC: Woodrow Wilson Center Press and Cambridge University Press, 1995, pp. 61–89.

The Chinese Economy: Transition and Growth, Cambridge, MA: MIT Press, 2007.

Nee, Victor and Opper, Sonja. *Capitalism from Below: Markets and Institutional Change in China*. Cambridge, MA: Harvard University Press, 2012.

Nishijima, Sadao, *Chugoku Keizaiji Kankyu* (Study on Economic History of China), Tokyo: Tokyo University Press, 1982.

"The Economic and Social History of Former Han," in Denis Twichett and Michael Loewe, eds., *The Cambridge History of China*, Vol. 1, Cambridge and New York, NY: Cambridge University Press, 1986.

Oi, Jean C. *Rural China Takes Off*, Berkeley, CA: University of California Press, 1999.

"Fiscal Reform and the Economic Foundations of Local Corporatism in China," *World Politics* 45:1 (1992), pp. 99–126.

O'Sullivan, Arthur, and Sheffrin, Steven M. *Economics: Principles in Action*, Upper Saddle River, NJ: Pearson Prentice Hall, 2003.

Ou, Yangsong. *Gaige kaifang koushushi* (Oral History of the Reform and Opening Up), Beijing: Renmin University Press, 2014.

Owen, Bruce M. "Anti-Trust in China: The Problem of Incentive Incompatibility," *SIER Paper No. 340*, Stanford Institute of Economic Research, 2009.

Patrick, Hugh. "The Future of the Japanese Economy: Output and Labor Productivity," *Journal of Japanese Studies* 3:2 (Summer 1977), pp. 419–439.

Peck, J. "Economic Geographies in Space," *Economic Geography* 81:2 (2005), pp. 129–175.

Pei, Minxin. *China's Trapped Transition: The Limits of Developmental Autocracy*, Cambridge, MA: Harvard University Press, 2009.

Peng, Xinwei. *Zhongguo huobi shi* (A Monetary History of China), Shanghai: Shanghai People's Publishing House, 2009.

Peng, Zeyi. *Zhongguo jindai shougongye shiliao* (Historical Materials on Handicraft in Modern China) Vol. 4, Beijing: Zhonghua Shuju, 1962.

Pepper, Suzanne. *Civil War in China: The Political Struggle, 1945–1949*, Berkeley, CA: University of California Press, 1978.

Pereira, Alexius A. *State Collaboration and Development Strategies: The Case of the China Singapore Suzhou Industrial Park, 1992–2002*, London: Routledge, 2003.

Perkins, Dwight H. *Market Controls and Planning in Communist China*, Cambridge, MA: Harvard University Press, 1966.

East Asian Development: Foundations and Strategies, Cambridge, MA: Harvard University Press, 2013.

Perry, Emily, and Florian Weltewitz. "Wealth Management Products in China," *Bulletin of the Reserve Bank of Australia*, June 2015, pp. 64–65.

Piketty, Thomas, and Goldhamer, Arthur (trans.). *Capitalism in the Twenty-First Century*, Cambridge, MA: Harvard University Press, 2014.

Pilling, David. "Round Two in America's Battle for Asian influence," *The Financial Times*, April 1, 2015.

Pines, Yuri. *Everlasting Empire: The Political Culture of Ancient China and its Imperial Legacy*, Princeton, NJ and Oxford: Princeton University Press, 2012.

Polanyi, Karl. *The Great Transformation: The Political and Economic Origins of Our Time*, Boston, MA: Beacon Press, 1944.

Pomeranz, Kenneth. *The Great Divergence: China, Europe, and the Making of the Modern World Economy*, Princeton, NJ: Princeton University Press, 2000.

Pomfret, John. "Beijing Tries to Push beyond Made in China to Find Name-Brand Innovation," Washington Post, May 25, 2010.

Qi, Xia. *Wang Anshi bianfa* (The Wang Anshi Reform), Shanghai: Shanghai Renmin Publishing House, 1957.

Qian, Changzhao. "Liangnianban chuangban zhonggongye zhi jingguo ji ganxiang" (Experience and Thoughts of Building Heavy Industry in the Last Two and Half Years), *New Economy Biweekly* 2 (1939), pp. 29–31.

Qian, Yingyi. "How Reform Worked in China," *William Davidson Institute Working Paper No. 473*, June 2002.

Qiu, Jian. "Nian Guangjiu yu shazi guangzi de liangci fuchen" (Two Rises and Falls of Nian Guangjiu and The Fool Melon Seed), *Yanhuang Chunqiu* (China through the Ages) 4 (2000), p. 43.

"Nian Guangjiu yu shazi guangzi de liangci fuchen," *Yanhuang Chuanqiu*, pp. 44–46.

Ren, Fang. *Mingqing changjiang zhongyou shizhengjingji yanjiu* (Study of Market Towns in Ming and Qing Dynasties), Wuhan: Wuhan University Press, 2003.

Ren, Xuefei. *Urban China*, London: Wiley & Sons, 2013.

Ren, Zhong, and Zhou, Yunbo. *Longduan dui woguo hangye nei shouruchaju de yingxiang daodi you duoda* (An Assessment of the Monopolistic Contribution to Intra-Sector Inequality), *Jingji Lilun yu Guanli* (Journal of Economic Theory and Management) 29:4, pp. 25–30.

Rogers, Mike, and Ruppersberger, Dutch. *Investigative Report on National Security Issues Posed by Chinese Telecommunication Companies Huawei and ZTE*, a report by Chairman Mike Rogers and Ranking Member C. A. Dutch Ruppersberger of the Permanent Select Committee on Intelligence, Washington, DC, October 2012.

Rickett, Allyn. *Guanzi: Political, Economic and Philosophical Essays from Early China*, Princeton, NJ: Princeton University Press, 1985.

Rowe, William T. *China's Last Empire: The Great Qing*, Cambridge, MA: Harvard University Press, 2007.

Saich, Tony. *The Origin of the First United Front in China*, Leiden: Brill Academic Press. 1997.

Sanderson, Henry and Forsythe, Michael, *China's Superbank: Debt, Oil and Influence – How China Development Bank Is Rewriting Rules of Finance*, Singapore: John Wiley & Sons, 2012.

Sasagawa, Yuji and Okumura, Satoshi. *Tougo no Chugoku Shakai, Chunichi senso shita no sodoin to nozo* (Chinese Society Led by the Guns: Total Mobilization and Countryside during the Sino-Japanese War), Tokyo: Iwanami Books, 2007.

Saw, Swee Hock and Ge Yun. "Enhancing Education Collaborations between China and Singapore," in Saw Swee Hock and John Wong, eds., *Advancing Sino-Singapore Relations*, Singapore: Institute of Southeast Asian Studies, 2014.

Schram, Stuart R., ed. *The Scope of State Power in China*, Hong Kong: The Chinese University of Hong Kong Press, 1985.

Schran, Peter. *Guerrilla Economy: The Development of Shangxi-Gansu-Ningxia Region*, New York, NY: SUNY Press, 1976.

Schumpeter, Joseph. *History of Economic Analysis*, London: George Allen & Unwin Ltd., 1954.

Smith, Adam, and Edwin Cannan (eds.). *An Inquiry into the Nature and Causes of the Wealth of Nations*, Chicago, IL: Chicago University Press, 2009.

Shanxi Provincial Academy of Social Sciences, ed. *Shanxi piaohao shiliao* (Historical Materials on the Shanxi Banks), Taiyuan: Shanxi jingji chubanshe, 1992.

Shao, Qin. *Culturing Modernity: The Nantong Model, 1890–1930*, Palo Alto, CA: Stanford University Press, 2003.

Shanghai Gone: Domicile and Defiance in a Chinese Megacity, Lanham, MD: Rowman & Littlefield, 2014.

Shapiro, Judith. *Mao's War Against Nature: Politics and Environment in Revolutionary China*, Cambridge and New York, NY: Cambridge University Press, 2001.

Shen, Daming. *Daqing luli he qingdaide shehuikongzhi* (The Qing Legal Cases and Social Control in Qing Empire), Shanghai: Shanghai Renmin chubanshe, 2007.

Sheng, Shihao and Zheng, Yanwei. *Zhejiang xianxiang: Chanye jiqun yu quyu jingji fazhan* (The Zhejiang Phenomenon: Industrial Clustering and Regional Economic Development), Beijing: Tsinghai University Press, 2004.

Shi, Jingchuan and Jing, Xiangrong. *Zhidu bianqian yu jingji fazhan: Wenzhou moshi yanjiu* (Institutional Change and Economic Development: A Study of Wenzhou Model), Hangzhou: Zhejiang University Press, 2004.

Shi, Lin. "Research on the Efficiency of China's Anti-Trust Laws," *Asian Social Sciences*, 5 (2009), pp. 97–100.

Shi, Yaojiang, Zhang Linxiu, Ma Yue, Yi Hongmei, Liu Chengfang, Natalie Johnson, James Chu, Prashant Loyalka, and Scott Rozelle. "Dropping Out of Rural China's Secondary Schools: A Mixed-Methods Analysis," *The China Quarterly* 224 (December 2015), pp. 1048–1069.

Shi, Yun, and Li Danhui. *Nanyi jixu de jixu geming: cong pi Lin dao pi Deng* (The Hard-to-Continue Continued Revolution: From Anti-Lin Biao to Anti-Deng Xiaoping Campaigns), History of Contemporary China Series, Vol. 2, Hong Kong: The Chinese University of Hong Kong Press, 2008.

Shih, Victor and Zhang, Qi. "Who Receives Subsidies? A Look at the County Level in Two Time Periods," in Vivienne Shue and Christine Wong, *Paying for Progress in China: Public Finance, Human Welfare and Changing Patterns of Inequality*, London: Routledge, 2007, pp. 145–165.

Shirk, Susan. *The Political Logic of Economic Reform in China*, Berkeley, CA: University of California Press, 1993.

Shiroyama, Tomoko. *China During the Great Depression: Market, State and World Economy*, Cambridge, MA: Harvard University Press, 2008.

Skinner, William G. "Marketing and Social Structure in Rural China," *Journal of Asian Studies* 24 (1964), pp. 1–64.

Marketing in Rural China, Ann Arbor, MI: Association for Asian Studies, 1964.

Skinner, William G. ed., *The City in Late Imperial China: Studies in Chinese Society*, Stanford, CA: Stanford University Press, 1977.

Skinner, William G. *Marketing and Social Structure in Rural China*, Ann Arbor, MI: Association for Asian Studies, 2001.

Smith, Paul Jakov. "Shen Tsung's Reign and the New Policies of Wang An-Shih," in Denis Twitchett and Paul Jakov Smith, eds., *The Cambridge History of*

China, Vol. 5, Cambridge and New York, NY: Cambridge University Press, 2009, pp. 347–483.

Song, Zheng, Kjetil Storesletten, and Fabrizio Zilibotti. "Growing like China," *American Economic Review* 101:1 (2011), pp. 196–233.

So, Sherman, and J. Christopher Westland, *Red Wired: China's Internet Revolution*, London and Singapore: Marshall Cavendish, 2010.

Spiegel, Henry William, ed., *The Growth of Economic Thoughts*, Durham, NC: Duke University Press, 1991.

Steinfeld, Edward S. *Forging Reform in China: The Fate of the State-Owned Enterprises*, New York, NY: Cambridge University Press, 1998.

Sun Lijian and Zhang Shengxing. "An Externally Dependent Economy and Real Estate Bubbles," in Ross Garnaut and Ligang Song, eds., *China: Linking Markets for Growth*, Canberra: Asia Pacific Press, 2007, pp. 344–368.

Sun, Yat-sen. *Sun Zhongshan quanji* (The Complete Works of Sun Yat-sen), Vol. 2, Beijing: Zhonghua shuju, 1986.

Sun, Zen E-zu. "Sericulture and Silk Textile Production in Ch'ing China," in William E. Willmott, ed., *Economic Organization in Chinese Society*, Stanford, CA: Stanford University Press, 1972, pp. 84–85.

Swedberg, Richard. *Max Weber and the Idea of Economic Sociology*, Princeton, NJ: Princeton Unversity Press, 1989.

    "Markets as Social Structures," in Neil Smelser and Richard Swedberg, eds., *The Handbook of Economic Sociology*, Princeton, NJ: Princeton University Press, 1994, pp. 235–254.

Tackett, Nicolas. *The Destruction of Medieval Chinese Aristocracy*, Cambridge, MA: Harvard University Asian Center, 2016 (reprint).

Tang, Lixing. *Shangren yu jinshi Zhongguo shehui* (Merchants and Early Modern Chinese Society), Taipei: The Commercial Press, 1997.

Tang, Taomo. "Kangri zhanzheng shiqi Shang-Gan-Ning bianqu de caizheng" (Finance and Economy at the Shan-Gan-Ning Border Region during the Sino-Japanese War), in Institute of Financial Science in the Ministry of Finance, *Geming genjudi de caizheng jingji* (Finance and Economy in the Revolutionary Base Areas), Beijing: China Caizheng Jingji Chubanshe, 1985.

Ter Haar, B. J. *The White Lotus Teaching in Chinese Religious History*, Leiden: Brill, 1991.

Tilly, Charles. *Coercion, Capital and European State: AD 990–1992*, Cambridge, MA: Blackwell, 1990.

Tong, Yanqi and Lei, Shaohua. *Social Protest in Contemporary China, 2003–2010: Transitional Pains and Regime Legitimacy*, London and New York, NY: Routledge, 2014.

Torbert, Preston. *The Ching's Imperial Household Department: A Study of Its Organization and Principal Functions, 1662–1792*, Cambridge, MA: Harvard University Press, 1977.

Toby, Hoff. *The Rise of Early Modern Science: Islam, China and the West*, Cambridge and New York, NY: Cambridge University Press, 2003.

Trescott, Paul B. *Jingjixue: The History of Introduction of Economic Ideas to Modern China*, Hong Kong: The Chinese University Press, 2007.

Tsai, Chung-min. "The Reform Paradox and Regulatory Dilemma in China's Electricity Industry," *Asian Survey* 51:3 (2011), pp. 520–539.

Tsai, Kelle. *Capitalism without Democracy: The Private Sector in Contemporary China*, Ithaca, NY: Cornell University Press, 2007.

The Unirule Institute of Economics. *The Nature, Performance and Reform of the State-Owned Enterprises*, Beijing, March 2011.

Van Cleve, George William. "The Anti-Federalist's Toughest Challenge: Paper Money, National Debt, and the Ratification of the Constitution," *Journal of the Early Republic* 34:4 (2014), pp. 529–560.

Van Slyke, Lyman. "The Chinese Communist Movement During the Sino-Japanese War 1937–1945," in John K. Fairbank, ed., *The The Cambridge History of China*, Vol. 12, Cambridge: Cambridge University Press, 1983, pp. 609–722.

Vogel, Ezra F. *The Four Little Dragons: The Spread of Industrialization in East Asia*, Cambridge, MA: Harvard University Press, 1991.

  Deng Xiaoping and the Transformation of Modern China, Cambridge, MA: Harvard University Press, 2013.

Von Glahn, Richard. *Fountains of Fortune: Money and Monetary Thoughts in China, 1000–1500*, Berkeley and Los Angeles, CA: University of California Press, 1998.

Vu, Minh Khuong. The Dynamics of Economic Growth: Policy Insights from Comparative Analyses in Asia. Cheltenham: Edward Elgar, 2013.

Wade, Robert. *Governing the Market: Economic Theory and the Role of Government in East Asian Industrialization*, 2nd edn., Princeton, NJ: Princeton University Press, 2004.

Walder, Andrew. *Communist Neo-Traditionalism: Work and Authority in Chinese Industry*, Berkeley, CA: University of California Press, 1988.

Waldron, Arthur. *From War to Nationalism: China's Turning Point, 1924–1925*, 2nd edn., Cambridge: Cambridge University Press, 2002.

Wallerstein, Immanuel, *The Modern World-System I: Capitalist Agriculture and the Origins of the European World-Economy in the Sixteenth Century*, New York, NY: Academic Press, 1974.

  The Modern World System II: Mercantilism and the Consolidation of the European World-Economy, 1600–1750, New York, NY: Academic Press, 1980.

  The Modern World-System III, San Diego, CA: Academic Press, 1989.

Wang, Fei-ling. *Organizing through Division and Exclusion: China's Hukou System*, Stanford, CA: Stanford University Press, 2005.

Wang, Gungwu. *Renewal: The Chinese State and the New Global History*, Hong Kong: The Chinese University of Hong Kong Press, 2013.

Wang, He. *Youzou zai hongxian shang de wuxi chengtou* (The Wuxi City Investment Co. on the Verge of Bankruptcy), *China Securities Weekly*, June 16, 2012.

Wang, Hongying and Horii Nobihiro. Zhongguo de nengyuan shichang yu jiage zhidu gaige (China's Energy Market Price Reform), Joint Research Program Series No. 146, Institute of Developing Economics, Japan External Trade Organization, 2008.

Wang, Jiafan. *Zhongguo lishi tonglun* (A General Study of Chinese History), Taipei: Wunan Book Co., 2002.

Wang, Lianli. *Zhongguo fangdichan zhie* (The Adversity of China's Property Business), Hong Kong: Tianxingjian, 2011.

Wang, Mengkui. *China in the Wake of Asia's Financial Crisis*, London and New York, NY: Routledge, 2009.

Wang, Qiang. "Guowang diguo" (The Empire of the State Grid), *Shangwu Zhoukan* (Business Weekly) 11:3 (2011), pp. 31–37.

Wang, Xiaolu. *Grey Income and Income Inequality in China*, Beijing: National Economic Research Institute of China Reform Foundation, 2010.

Wang, Yanling. "Cheap Labor and China's Export Capacity," in Kelvin Zhang Honglin, ed., *China as a World Factory* (London: Routledge, 2006), pp. 69–81.

Wang, Yi. *Zhongguo huangquan zhidu yanjiu* (A Study of the Institutions of Emperorship in China), Beijing: Peking University Press, 2007.

Wang, Guotai. *Youmin wenhua yu Zhongguo shehui* (Vagrant Culture and Chinese Society), Beijing: Tongxin, 2007.

Wang Kui. *Qingmo shangbu yanjiu* (Study on Late Qing Ministry of Commerce), Beijing: People's Publishing House, 2008.

Warner, Malcolm. "On Keynes and China: Keynesianism 'with Chinese Characteristics'," Cambridge Judge Business School Working Paper No.2/2014, University of Cambridge, 2014.

Weber, Max, Gerth, H. H. and Mills, C. Wright (trans. and ed.). *From Max Weber: Essays in Sociology*, New York, NY: Oxford University Press, 1958.

Wedeman, Andrew H. *From Mao to Market: Rent Seeking, Local Protectionism, and Marketization in China*, New York, NY: Cambridge University Press, 2003.

White, Gordon, "Developmental States and Socialist Industrialization in the Third World," *Journal of Development Studies* 21:1 (1984), pp. 97–120.

White, Gordon, and Wade, Robert. "Developmental States and Markets in East Asia," in Gordon White, ed., *Developmental States in East Asia*, London: The Macmillan Press, 1988, pp. 1–29.

Whyte, Martin, ed. *One Country, Two Societies: Rural–Urban Inequality in Contemporary China*, Cambridge, MA: Harvard University Press, 2010.

Wildau, Gabriel and Clover, Charles. "AIIB Launch Signals China's New Ambitions," *Financial Times*, June 29, 2015.

Willmott, W. E, ed. *Economic Organization in Chinese Society*, Stanford, CA: Stanford University Press, 1972, pp. 9–46.

Wittfogel, Karl August. *Oriental Despotism: A Comparative Study of Total Power*, New Haven, CT: Yale University Press, 1957.

Woetzel, Jonathan R. "Reassessing China's State-Owned Enterprises," *The McKinsey Quarterly*, July 2008.

Wong, Bin Roy. *China Transformed: Historical Change and the Limits of European Experience*, Ithaca, NY: Cornell University Press, 1997.

Wong, Christine and Bird, Richard. "China's Fiscal System: A Work in Progress," in Loren Brandt, Thomas Rawski, and John Sutton, eds., *China's Great Economic Transformation*, New York, NY: Cambridge University Press, 2008, pp. 429–466.

Wong, John. *Land Reform in the People's Republic of China: Institutional Transformation in Agriculture*, New York, NY: Praeger Publishers, 1973.

The Political Economy of Deng's Nanxun: Breakthrough in China's Reform and Development, Singapore and London: World Scientific, 2014.

Wong, John, Rong, Ma, and Mu, Yang, eds. *China's Rural Entrepreneurs: Ten Case Studies*, Singapore: Times Academic Press, 1995.

Wong, Chack Kie. "The Evolving East Asian Welfare Regimes: The Case of China," in Zhao Litao, ed., *China's Social Development and Policy*, London and New York, NY: Routledge, 2013, pp. 207–229.

Woo, Wing Thye. "Improving the Performance of Enterprises in Transition Economies," in Wing Thye Woo, Stephen Parker, and Jeffrey Sachs, eds., *Economies in Transition: Comparing Asia and Eastern Europe*, Cambridge, MA: The MIT Press, 1997, pp. 299–324.

World Bank. *World Development Report 1981*, Oxford: Oxford University Press, 1981.

Wright, Teresa. *Accepting Authoritarianism: State–Society Relations in Reform Era China*, Stanford, CA: Stanford University Press, 2010.

Wu, Guoguang. *Globalization Against Democracy: A Political Economy of Capitalism after Its Global Triumph*, New York, NY: Cambridge University Press, 2017.

Wu, Jinglian. *Understanding and Interpreting Chinese Economic Reform*, Mason, OH: Thomson, 2005.

Wu, Xun. "An Introduction to China's Local Government Debt," *MIT Golub Center for Finance and Policy Working Papers*, October 2015.

Wu, Yiqing. *The Cultural Revolution at the Margins: Chinese Socialism in Crisis*, Cambridge, MA: Harvard University Press, 2014.

Xi, Wang. *Wenzhou moshi de lishimingyun* (The Historical Destiny of Wenzhou Model), Beijing: Economic Science Press, 2005.

Xu, Yi-chong. *Sinews of Power: Politics of the State Grid Corporation of China*, Corby: Oxford University Press, 2017.

Xu, Dixin and Wu Chengming, eds., Li Zhengde, Liang Miaoru, and Li Siping (trans.), and Curwen, C. A. (annotator). *Chinese Capitalism, 1522–1840*, London: Macmillan Press Ltd, 2000.

Xu, Fuguan. *Zhouguan chengli shijian jiqi sixiang xingge* (Zhouguan Jing: Its Time of Compilation and the Characters of Its Thoughts), Taipei: Taiwan Xuesheng Shuju, 1980.

Yang, Dali. *Remaking the Chinese Leviathan: Market Transition and the Politics of Governance in China*, Stanford, CA: Stanford University Press, 2004.

Yang, Hongwei and Zhang, Jinping. *Zangqu 314 shijian shehuijingji chengying diaocha* (Economic and Social Causes of the March 14 Incidents in the Tibetan Area) (For Internal Circulation), September 2010.

Yang, Jufeng. "Woguo chengshi tudi suoyouzhi de yanjin he laiyuan" ("Origin and Evolution of China's State-Ownership of Urban Land"), *Southern Weekly*, June 13, 2007.

Yang, Lijun. *Bungaku daigakumei to chugoku no chakai kozo: komeigen no bunpai to kyodanteki boryoku koi* (Social Structure and the Cultural Revolution in China: The Distribution of Citizenship and Collective Violence), Tokyo: Ochanomizu Shobo, 2003.

Yang, Lien-sheng. "Economic Justification for Spending—An Uncommon Idea in Traditional China," *Harvard Journal of Asiatic Studies* 20 (1957), pp. 36–52.

Money and Credit in Ancient China, Cambridge, MA: Harvard University Press, 1962.

Yang, Yongzhi and Yang, Zhigang. *Zhongguo caizheng zhidu gaige 30 nian* (Thirty Years of China's Fiscal Reform), Shanghai: Shanghai People's Publishing House, 2007, pp. 78–81.

Ye, Min. *Diasporas and Foreign Direct Investment in China and India*, New York, NY: Cambridge University Press, 2014.

Young, Arthur. *China's Wartime Finance and Inflation, 1937–1945*, Cambridge, MA: Harvard University Press, 1965.

You, Ji. *China's Enterprise Reform: Changing State/Society Relations after Mao*, New York, NY: Routledge, 1998.

Yu, Lei. *Zhuixun shangye Zhongguo* (A History of Commerce in Contemporary China), Beijing: CITIC Press, 2009.

Yu, Xinyan. *Zhongguo shangye shi* (A Commercial History of China), Beijing: Zhongguo shangye chubanshe, 1987.

Zanasi, Margherita. *Saving the Nation, Economic Modernity in Republican China*, Chicago, IL: University of Chicago Press, 2010.

Zarrow, Peter. *China in War and Revolution: 1895–1949*, London: Routledge, 2006.

Zelin, Madeleine, *The Magistrate's Tael: Rationalizing Fiscal Reform in Qing China*, Berkeley, CA: University of California Press, 1992.

"A Critique of Property Rights in Prewar China," in Madeleine Zelin, Jonathan K. Ocko, and Robert Gardella, eds., *Contract and Property in Early Modern China*, Stanford, CA: Stanford University Press, 2004, pp. 1–33.

The Merchant of Zigong: Industrial Entrepreneurship in Early Modern China, New York, NY: Columbia University Press, 2006.

Zeng, Jin. *State-Led Privatization in China: The Politics of Economic Reform*, London: Routledge, 2013.

Zhang, Haipeng and Wang Tingyuan. *Huishang yanjiu* (A Study of the Anhui Merchant Groups), Hefei: Anhui renmin chubanshe, 1995.

Zhang, Jia. *Xintianxiazhihua: Mingchu lisu gaige yanjiu* (Renewing the Transformation of the World: A Study of Reforms of Rituals and Customs in Early Ming), Shanghai: Fudan University, 2015.

Zhang, Jun. *Shuangguizhi jingjixue: Zhongguo de jingjigaige, 1978–1992* (The Economics of Dual Track System: China's Economic Reform: 1978–1992), Shanghai: Sanlian Books, 1997.

Zhang, Wenxian, and Ilan, Alon, *Biographical Dictionary of New Chinese Entrepreneurs and Business Leaders*, Cheltenham: Edward Elgar Publishing, 2009.

Zhang Xiaoling. *Transformation in Political Communication in China*, London: Routledge, 2010.

Zhang, Ying. "Zeng Chengjie: Shengqian sihou" (Zeng Chengjie: Before and After a Death). *Observer Weekly*, July 22, 2013.

Zhang, Zhengming, Sun Liping, and Bai Lei, eds. *Zhongguo jinshang yanjiu* (A Study of Shanxi Merchants in China), Beijing: Renmin chubanshe, 2006.

Zhao, Dingxin. *The Power of Tiananmen*, Chicago, IL: The University of Chicago Press, 2001.

Confucian-Legalist State: A New Theory of Chinese History, New York, NY: Oxford University Press, 2015.

Zhao, Jing. "Fu Guo Xue and the 'Economics' of Ancient China," in Cheng Li, Terry Peach, and Wang Fang, eds., *The History of Ancient Chinese Economic Thought*, London and New York, NY: Routledge, 2014.

Zhao, Shiyu. "Weisuo junhu zhidu yu mingdai shehui: shehuixue shijiao" (The Garrison System and Ming Chinese Society: A Social History Perspective), *Journal of Tsinghua University (Philosophy and Social Sciences)* 30:3 (2015), pp. 114–127.

Zhao Ziyang. *Gaige Licheng* (Roads to Reform), Hong Kong: The New Century Press, 2010.

Zheng, Jin. *State-Led Privatization in China: The Politics of Economic Reform*, London: Routledge, 2013.

Zheng, Yongnian. *Discovering Chinese Nationalism in China: Modernization, Identity, and International Relations* (Cambridge and New York, NY: Cambridge University Press, 1999.

Zhu Rongji xinzheng: Zhongguo gaige de xin moshi (The New Deal of Zhu Rongji: A New Model of China's Reform), Singapore: The Global Publishing Co, Inc., 1999.

"Ideological Decline, the Rise of an Interest-Based Social Order, and the Demise of Communism in China," in John Wong and Zheng Yongnian, eds., *The Nanxun Legacy and Chian's Development in the Post-Deng Era* (London and Singapore: World Scientific and Singapore University Press, 2001), pp. 173–195.

Globalization and State Transformation in China, New York, NY: Cambridge University Press, 2004.

Will China Become Democratic? Elite, Class and Regime Transition, Singapore: Eastern Universities Press, 2004.

De Facto Federalism in China: Reforms and Dynamics of Central–Local Relations, Singapore and London: World Scientific, 2007.

Technological Empowerment: The Internet, State, and Society in China, Stanford, CA: Stanford University Press, 2008.

"Society Must Be Defended: Reform, Openness and Social Policy in China," *Journal of Contemporary China* 19:67 (2010), pp. 799–818.

The Chinese Communist Party as Organizational Emperor: Culture, Reproduction and Transformation, London and New York, NY: Routledge, 2010.

Zhongguo moshi: Jingyan yu tiaozhan (The China Model: Experiences and Challenges), Beijing: Zhongxin Publishing House, 2015.

Zheng, Yongnian and Huang, Yanjie. "Political Dynamics of China's Social Policy Reform," in Zhao Litao, ed., *China's Social Development and Policy*, London and New York, NY: Routledge, 2013, pp. 161–185.

Zheng, Zhenman and Michael Szonyi, trans. *Family Lineage Organizations in Ming and Qing Fujian*, Honolulu, HI: University of Hawai'i Press, 2001.

Zhou, Boli. *Zhongguo caizheng shi* (Fiscal History of China), Shanghai: Shanghai Renmin Publishing House, 1981.

Zhou, Wei. "The Changing Face of Rural Enterprises," *China Perspectives* 50 (2006), pp. 1–18.

Zhou, Xueguang, *State and Life Chance in China: Redistribution and Stratification, 1949–1994*, Cambridge and New York, NY: Cambridge University Press, 1999.

Zhou, Yumin. *Wanqing caizheng yu shehui bianqian* (Late Qing Government Finance and Social Changes), Shanghai: Shanghai Renmin Publishing House, 1997.

Zhou, Zhichu. *Wanqing caizheng jingji yanjiu* (Studies in Late Qing Economy and Government Finance), Jinan: Qilu Book Publisher, 1999.

Zhu, Jianhua. *Dongbei jiefangqu caizhengjingji shigao* (Fiscal and Economic History of North East Liberated Regions), Harbin: Heilongjiang People's Press, 1987.

Zhu, Jiannan. "The Shadow of Skyscrapers: Real Estate Corruption in China," *Journal of Contemporary China* 21 (2012), pp. 243–261.

Zhu, Ying. "On Late Qing Economic Laws and Regulations," in Douglas R. Reynolds, ed., *China, 1895–1912 State Sponsored Reforms and China's Late-Qing Revolution: Selected Essays from Zhongguo Jindai Shi (Modern Chinese History, 1840–1919)*, New York, NY: M. E. Sharpe, 1995, pp. 87–126.

Index

Adam Smith, 35–38, 43, 48–49, 55, 114, 175, 191, 439, 447
Alibaba, 317–319, 333–334, 336, 419, 451
All Under Heaven, 82, 84, 86, 111
All-China Federation of Commerce and Industry, 429
All-China Federation of Industry and Commerce, 295, 329
Anhui, 120, 122, 184, 207, 252, 258–259, 261, 301, 362, 400, 447, 466
Anti-Trust Law, 416
Asia Infrastructure Investment Bank, 446
Asian financial crisis, 23, 65
asymmetrical equilibrium, 19, 24, 111
Australia, 4, 214, 325, 373, 451, 455, 459
autarchy, 236–237

Baidu, 316–318, 371, 419
Bank of China, 125, 210, 223, 287, 293, 339, 345
Bastid, Marienne, 82
Beijing, 6, 11, 13, 122, 134, 140, 147, 156, 160, 173, 176, 191, 197–199, 201–202, 204–207, 210–211, 215, 219, 221, 224–225, 230–231, 240, 245, 253, 257–258, 260–262, 266, 271, 273, 278, 284, 292, 302, 306–307, 310, 312, 320, 331, 341–342, 356, 360, 364–366, 368, 372, 391–392, 397, 401, 405–406, 410, 412, 429, 444, 447–450, 453–466
Beijing-Tianjin region, 198
Belt and Road Initiative, 445
Bo Xilai, 321, 323, 335, 359
Board of Revenue, 87, 173
Board of Rite, 112
Book of Songs, 136

Book of Zhou Rituals, 154
Bramall, Chris, 11
Braudel, Fernand, 45, 48
Britain, 10, 203, 453
British Empire, 194, 196
brokerage, 177, 212
business ventures, 244
Business Watch Magazine, 395
BYD, 314–315, 318, 327

California School, 10, 134
centralization, 81, 86, 153, 166–169, 173, 210, 237–238, 340, 345–346, 353, 359, 370
central–local relations, 166, 168, 273, 311, 350
centrally managed SOEs, 254, 296, 336, 352, 378–379, 383, 386, 392–394, 397, 400–404, 406–407, 409–410, 414–416, 418–421
central-provincial tax contract, 345
Chao Kang, 175–176
Chaofangtuan, 310
Chen Liangyu, 321
Chen Yun, 224, 231, 235, 255, 449
chengxiang jiaoliu, 225
Chiang Kai-shek, 209, 211
China Merchants Steamship Company, 197
China Overseas Engineering Company, 413
China Petrol, 363, 394
China Railway Group, 413
Chinalco, 4
Chinese Communist Party, xi, 7, 17, 80, 193, 301, 307, 332, 402, 404, 419–421, 427, 454, 467
Chinese Medieval Age, 156
Chinese People's Political Consultative Conference, 256, 329

Chinese-ness, 119
Chongqing, 217, 273, 335, 359–364, 367, 369, 376–377, 400, 449
Church, 33, 81
Civil Service Examination, 109, 147–148, 163, 182, 203
civil society, 37, 57, 82, 114, 429, 435, 445–446
Civil War, 157, 204, 219–223, 228, 244, 342, 459
class struggles, 54, 213
CNPC, 405, 410–412
coal, 10, 145, 165, 285, 288, 310, 333, 362, 364–369, 397
Coase, Ronald, 59
Cold War, 114, 191–192, 214, 227, 232, 243, 245, 303, 342, 444, 449
collective incidents, 433
collectivization, 233, 283, 381–382
command economy, 67, 140, 215, 223, 243, 380
commanding heights, 21, 290
commercial capitalism, 85, 310
commercial revolution, 9, 162
commercial rivalry (*shangzhan*), 201
commercialization, 8–9, 73, 152, 154, 158, 163, 169, 269, 288
commodification, 73
Common Good, 33
commune and brigade enterprises, 236, 251, 300–301
communism, 8, 12, 65, 115, 231, 270, 438
Communist Revolution, 282
Communist Youth League, 429
comprador, 170
Confucian, 2, 19, 33–34, 65, 82, 84, 88–91, 93–94, 96–105, 107, 109–112, 115, 120, 142–144, 150, 154–157, 159–160, 162–163, 165, 175, 183, 197, 199, 201, 203, 231, 236, 300, 381, 425, 455, 457, 466
Confucian school, 91, 93, 96–97, 101, 108
Confucius, 84–85, 93, 96, 158
Conghang, 172
cooptation, 121, 148, 274, 296, 300, 323, 329–331, 333–334, 337–338
copper coins, 152
corporate lineage, 163
corruption, 20, 68, 149, 159, 167, 170, 220, 268–269, 304, 321, 332–333, 339, 375, 404, 408, 410, 421
CPPCC, 256, 329–330, 336, 405

crony capitalism, 31, 65, 221, 438
Cultural Revolution, 193, 228–229, 234–236, 238, 240, 244, 258, 263, 300, 339, 431, 450, 458, 465
currency, 4, 48, 92, 101, 103, 124–125, 154, 178–179, 203–208, 210–211, 213, 218, 220, 223, 225, 243, 245, 292–293, 341, 347

Da Xue, 93
dahu, 145
Dalian, 358
danwei, 230
Daqiu Village, 258, 263, 265, 456
decentralization, 20, 57, 65, 81, 232–233, 237, 253, 268, 282, 301, 340, 344–346
defense industry, 198, 214
deflation, 57, 210
demobilization, 231, 244, 249
democracy, 15, 68, 207, 290, 337, 426, 437–438
demographic revolution, 195
Deng Xiaoping, 7, 20, 228, 231, 234–235, 237–239, 241, 244, 251, 259, 261, 271, 291, 303, 397, 450, 461, 463
Dengist, 240, 245, 252
development zones, 291, 364
developmental state, 62, 65, 68–70, 299, 312, 314, 324, 332, 398, 426, 442
Dickinson, Bruce, 438, 449
Discourses on Salt and Iron, 153
Discourses on Salt and Iron, 88, 93, 95–97, 99, 103, 116, 453
distortions, 42, 63, 127, 166, 432
domination, 19, 24–26, 31, 39, 71, 80, 86, 102, 111, 116–120, 126–127, 133, 135, 139, 143–145, 148, 150–151, 157, 164, 168, 186, 190, 206, 222, 272, 292, 297, 300, 312, 318, 328, 333–334, 337, 343, 379–380, 385, 387, 431, 440
Dual-Track System, 267–268, 466
Dutch East Indian Companies, 172
dynastic cycle, 83, 133, 151, 165, 434

East Asia, xi, 13, 24, 29, 31, 62, 64–65, 67–71, 75, 78, 81, 172, 219, 255, 281, 290, 292, 342, 356, 398, 401, 403, 425–426, 431, 439, 441–442, 452, 459, 463, 465
economic freedom, 49, 437
economic growth, 4–5, 7, 16, 20, 55, 57, 60, 67, 69, 134, 234, 241–242, 254, 270, 273–274, 279, 292, 297–298, 314, 325, 331–332,

343, 352, 354, 356, 362–363, 369, 383, 388, 395, 400, 417, 426, 433, 438–439, 444–445
economic rectification, 241
economic statism, 19, 111, 113, 120, 134, 150, 152–153, 192, 206, 212
economics, 88–89
  neoclassical economics, 33, 111, 227
economics, 85
education, 21, 30, 33, 62, 104, 109, 168, 183, 201, 235, 239, 275–276, 279, 281, 356, 377, 403, 409, 432
efficiency, 5, 21, 39, 42, 59, 85, 111, 141, 159–160, 170, 198, 230, 254, 256, 285–286, 288, 294, 301, 304, 346, 352, 380, 388, 406, 408, 433
emperorship, 19, 25, 133, 142, 145, 187, 385–386
Empire Wu of Han, 89
Empress Dowager Cixi, 199–201
environmental degradation, 434, 440
equality, xii, 20–21, 93–94, 96, 105, 109, 151, 157, 160, 229, 238, 268, 276, 359–360, 397, 410, 421, 434, 437, 444, 460–461, 464
equalize distribution, 95
Eurasian continent, 86, 446
Europe, 1, 5, 7–9, 12, 21, 29, 34, 37, 47–48, 50, 52, 54, 57, 73, 81–82, 85–86, 119, 122, 131, 134, 148, 164, 172, 176, 187–188, 191–192, 194, 207, 243, 270, 292, 302, 315, 325, 339, 413, 425, 431, 441–442, 445, 455, 460, 462–465
export-oriented, 289, 294, 411, 442

fabi, 211, 213, 218, 220, 341
Fairbank, John, 9, 83, 84
family planning, 429
family plot, 380–384, 386, 406
fangquan rangli, 388
Fanya, 371–372
fascism, 30
fiat money, 192, 342
financialization, 26, 340, 352
fiscal agents, 10, 112, 137–139, 141, 143–146, 149, 151, 159, 162, 166, 170, 172, 175
fiscal state, 34, 133, 188, 255, 340
Foochow Shipbuilding Enterprise, 197
Fool's Melon Seeds, 261
Foreign direct investment, 291, 442, 454, 466
foreign reserve, 294, 339, 347, 351
foreign trade, 125, 172, 179, 199, 251, 347
Fortune 500, xiv, 393, 442
Four classes, 94

Four Modernizations, 239
Foxconn, 280
France, 34, 48, 245
Friedman, Milton, 64, 437

Gaoping Group, 396
Gallagher, Mary, 438
GDP, 15, 232, 239, 242, 244, 269, 273, 295, 311–312, 335, 352–355, 358, 364, 369, 374, 394, 443–444, 457
GDPism, 273
geming, 83, 207, 231, 237, 461
General Theory of Employment, Interest, and Money, 55
Geopolitics, 12, 25, 110, 190–192, 194, 243, 455
Germany, 55, 75, 208
Gernet, Jacque, 81, 83
Ghost City, 365
Gini index, 431
global capitalism, 73, 132, 192, 196, 210, 227, 289, 438, 441, 445
Global Financial Crisis, xii, 5, 23, 57, 255, 296, 325–327, 363, 370, 376, 394–396, 400, 418, 428, 440, 443–444, 455
globalization, 54, 69–70, 249, 272, 291–293, 295, 314, 427–428
Gong Aiai, 367–368, 452
granary system, 138, 141, 179
grassroots fiscal organizations, 166
grassroots markets, 112, 155, 176, 250–251, 295, 425
Great Depression, 55, 57, 63, 210, 212, 461
Great Leap Forward, 222, 228, 232, 243, 300, 341, 343, 377, 457
gray income, 409
guanban, 198–199, 202
guandu shangban, 170, 197, 199–200, 202
Guangdong, 70, 120, 173, 192, 207–208, 213, 290, 292, 374, 400–401, 415, 454, 456
guangdu shangban, 198–199
Guangzhou, xiv, 173, 208–209, 284, 358, 453
guanshang, 170
Guanzi, 92, 143, 169, 460
guild, 49, 125, 177
guojia, 285, 352, 371, 398, 415, 429

Half Monthly Talk, 369
Han dynasty, 88, 91, 103, 107, 178
Hangzhou, 309–310, 358, 434, 461
harmonious society, 356, 369
harmony, 84, 93, 439

Hayek, Friedrich, 57, 437
Heilongjiang, 228, 468
Henan, 369, 400
hereditary households, 148
hierarchy, 25, 48, 80, 112, 123, 133, 166,
    229–230, 267, 271, 280–281, 288, 297,
    311, 333, 351, 358, 420, 439
homo economicus, 36
Hong Kong, xiv, 1, 8, 13, 31, 63–64, 69, 75, 81,
    83, 131, 133, 184, 208, 228, 231–232, 284,
    289–290, 292, 303–304, 311, 313, 317,
    320, 377–378, 383, 400, 420, 424, 426, 449,
    451, 455–457, 460–463, 467
household economy, 133, 151, 163, 187, 225,
    300
household enterprises, 240, 259, 266, 302
household entrepreneur, 261–262
household registration system, 180, 234, 245,
    276–277, 301, 429
household responsibility system, 234, 263, 267,
    284, 301, 383
Hu Angang, 254, 352
Hu Jintao, 320, 356, 366
Hua Guofeng, 252, 327
Huaihai Campaign, 220–221
Huan Kuan, 88–89
Huang Yasheng, 15, 18, 269
Huang, Ray, 152, 160–161, 167
Huawei, 268, 313, 316, 318, 460
Huishang, 120, 122, 466
human rights, 446
hydraulic empire, 114

imperial agents, 25, 133, 146, 148, 162, 168
imperial Chinese state, 10–11, 131, 133, 135,
    186
imperial factories, 118, 138, 164, 174, 198, 385
imperial household, 134, 137, 140, 145, 148,
    173
Imperial Household Department, 138, 164,
    170, 174, 385, 462
imperialism, 190
income inequality, xii, 270, 362, 410, 414, 431,
    437, 440, 444
India, xii, 3, 15, 64, 114, 196, 278, 291, 431, 435,
    443, 446, 454, 466
Indonesia, 64
industrial revolution, 9
industrialization, 9–10, 20, 49, 61, 63, 69, 131,
    157, 163, 190, 196, 214, 216, 226, 241, 243,

256, 275, 290, 292, 342, 345, 354, 363, 365,
    374, 377, 427, 442
inflation, xii, 56, 155, 160, 178, 216, 218–223,
    269–270, 346, 376, 395, 448, 454, 466
infrastructure, xii, 5, 21, 39, 41, 47, 57, 62, 73,
    99, 108, 114, 116, 137, 141, 149, 153, 165,
    186, 203, 214, 216, 227, 238, 240, 256, 282,
    285–286, 304, 311, 314, 316, 318, 341, 345,
    354–356, 360, 377, 386, 400, 413, 436, 444,
    446
Institutional Economics, 58
interest groups, 151, 426
intermediary, 122, 172, 224, 251, 283, 325, 346
IPO, 317, 319, 334
Italy, 55

Japan, 6, 29, 31, 64–65, 67, 69, 75–76, 87, 119,
    134, 164, 168–169, 171, 187–188, 190,
    192–196, 199–201, 203, 211–213,
    215–219, 223, 229, 233, 239, 243, 290, 292,
    311, 339, 342, 365, 401, 426, 431, 437, 439,
    446, 448–449, 453, 455, 457–460,
    462–463, 467
Jiang Zemin, 271, 274, 417
jianghu, 260, 429
Jiangnan region, 162
Jiangxi, 161, 201, 400
Jin Empire, 156
jingji, 2, 13–14, 85, 87, 122, 136–137, 177, 198,
    202, 211, 222, 224–225, 228, 240, 243, 257,
    268–269, 273, 292, 302, 306–307, 309,
    342, 398, 415, 434, 449, 454, 456–457,
    460–461, 464–466, 468
jingshi jimin, 85
joint-stock company, 307
Johnson, Chalmers, 65, 426
junshu, 95

Keynes, John, 55
Keynesianism, 30, 53, 55, 57–58, 62, 464
KMT, 192–193, 205, 207–213, 215–223, 231,
    233, 341
Kong Xiangxi, 210
Korean War, 223–225
Kunming, 371–372

labor market, 230, 278–279, 281–282, 289, 295,
    432
laissez-faire, 34–35, 42, 90, 100, 133, 135, 151,
    153, 432

land reform, 156, 213, 221–222, 283, 381
land tax, 97, 138, 152, 158, 164
land transfer, 284, 319, 353
late imperial state, 132, 159, 162, 168, 171–172, 179–182, 187–188, 199
lay-off, 306
Least Developed Countries, 69
Legalism, 110
Legalist school, 88, 91–97, 99–101, 104, 108, 111
Legalists, 34, 84, 88–89, 91–95, 97–98, 100–106, 109–110, 112, 143
legitimacy, 204, 236, 252, 273, 303, 360
Lenovo, 268, 313, 316, 318–319, 457
LGFV, 353, 362–363, 376
Li Changchun, 405
Li Hongzhang, 197, 199
Li Ruihuan, 264
Liang Qichao, 93, 159
Liao Zhongkai, 208
liberalism, 30, 36, 40–41, 52, 58, 61–62, 73, 77, 79, 452
lijin, 197, 202
Limited Liability Company, 307
Lin Biao, 231, 235–236, 461
lineage, 144, 163, 179
literati-bureaucrats, 138, 141, 149, 157–158, 160, 168, 183
little dragons, 31, 67, 426
Liu Chuanzhi, 268, 313
Liu Kunyi, 201
Liu Shaoqi, 231, 234–235, 450
local corporatism, 345

Macao, 172, 192
Machiavellian idea of power, 83
Machinery Bureau, 197
macro-region, 123, 176
Malaysia, 64, 413
Manchu Heavy Industrial Company, 212
Manchukou, 212, 458
Manchuria, 195, 206, 212, 214–215, 221
Mandate of Heaven, 82–84, 131, 144, 161, 165, 204, 454
Mao Zedong, 20, 114, 120, 188, 229–230, 289, 431, 457
Maoism, 227, 309
Maoist, 25–26, 61, 72, 126, 161, 225, 229–231, 233–237, 239, 241–242, 244–245, 250, 253, 256–258, 263, 275, 277, 280,

282–283, 285, 296–297, 300, 311, 337, 339, 341, 356, 360, 375, 377, 379–382, 397, 427, 430, 442
Mao–Khrushchev conflict, 231
market economy, 2–4, 6–7, 14–16, 20–22, 26, 30, 37, 39–40, 42, 45–46, 50, 61, 134, 158–159, 175, 193, 227, 245, 250, 253–254, 270, 272–273, 275, 278–279, 297–298, 300, 304, 309, 328, 336, 338, 352, 387, 402, 421, 427, 432, 436–437, 439, 454
Market Economy Status, 3–6
market fundamentalists, 419
market in state, xi–xii, xiv, 19, 23–24, 31–32, 126–127, 131, 188–189, 194, 250, 334–335, 345, 351, 387, 421, 425
Market Networks, 122
marketization, 7, 25, 227, 244–245, 250–251, 253–258, 261–262, 265–267, 269, 271–272, 275–277, 279–284, 286–288, 290–292, 294, 297–298, 301, 307, 334, 347, 400, 402, 419–420, 427–428, 431–432, 440, 443, 446
Marx, Karl, 8, 37, 39, 73, 114, 435
Marxism, 11, 30, 39–40
material interest, 109
material standard, 218, 223, 225, 342–343
McKinsey, 4
Mencius, 94, 97, 100, 116, 381
mercantilist, 34, 51, 81, 172
Metzger, Thomas, 117
Michel Callon, 42, 76, 448
middle class, 368, 440, 444
middle ground, 26, 116, 250, 256, 274, 294, 297–298, 305, 332, 336–338, 340, 352, 371, 375, 419, 430
migrant labors, 272, 277, 441
Ming, 10, 114, 118, 134, 138, 142–143, 149, 151–152, 155, 160–162, 165–168, 170–173, 176–178, 181, 183–184, 186, 195, 198, 287, 290, 323, 341, 447–448, 452–454, 456–457, 460, 466–467
Ming dynasty, 10, 114, 137, 142, 167, 171, 174, 181
Ming Empire, 160
Ming Taizu, 160, 168, 178, 181
mining, 67, 90, 94, 102, 113, 120, 174, 191, 198, 230, 333, 365, 367, 390, 397, 421
Ministry of Agriculture, Industry and Commerce, 201

Ministry of Commerce, 201–202, 260, 262, 342, 351, 413, 464

Ministry of Finance, 86, 201–202, 205, 287, 296, 339, 343, 345, 349, 354, 410

Ministry of Petroleum, 412

Minsheng, 207, 356, 360

MIS framework, 126, 132

MIS system, 25–26, 190, 245, 250, 338, 425–426, 428, 431, 434–435, 439, 441–442, 444–446

MITI, 66, 426, 455

mixed economy, xiii, 56, 58, 80, 298, 428

mobility, 143–144, 161, 181, 430

mobilization, 20, 90, 95, 145, 155, 192, 194, 204, 210, 212, 216–217, 219, 221–223, 226–233, 236, 239–241, 243–245, 249, 252, 280, 282, 288, 324, 327, 334, 337, 341, 343, 345, 369, 374, 376, 380, 427, 431, 444, 446

mobilization state, 20, 241, 245–246

modernization, 9, 159, 198, 203, 207, 209, 226–227, 232, 239, 251, 437, 442

Moist School, 92

Monetization, 341, 356, 374

Mongolia, 195, 364–365, 397

moral economy, 161, 223

multinational companies, 418, 441

Nanjing, 204–206, 211, 220, 243, 310, 358

national defense, 19, 113

National Development Bank of China, 359, 362

national economy, 4, 11, 46, 113, 126, 187, 210–211, 215, 219, 223, 241, 253, 266, 274, 282, 290, 385

National People's Congress, 256, 330, 401, 405

National Planning Commission, 228

national salt market, 112

nationalism, 201, 207

nationalization, 286

natural disaster, 141, 165, 177, 182

NDRC, 411, 414, 416

Needham, Joseph, 9

neo-classical economics, 62, 64–65, 73

neoliberalism, 444

netizens, 322, 334, 367–368

New Deal, 57

New Structural Economics, 69–70, 456

New York Stock Exchange, 317

New York Times, 319, 321, 323, 331, 366, 444, 447, 451

nexus of power, 151

NGOs, 430

Nixon, Richard, 238

Nian Guangjiu, 252, 258, 260, 263, 279, 294, 460

Ningbo, 121, 124–125, 257, 358

Nolan, Peter, xiii, 11

nomenclature, 402–403

North Dynasty, 134

North, Douglass, 39

NPC, 276, 330

nuclear war, 232

NYSE, 325, 333

Oikonomia, 85, 219, 342

Old-Text School, 154

oligarch, 420

One Whip Law, 178

Opium War, 192, 196

opportunism, 59, 288

Ordos, 364–367, 369, 377

organizational dependency, 139, 144, 147, 150, 158–159, 161, 170, 179, 186–187

organized dependency, 146–147, 164

Oriental Despotism, 8, 114, 436, 464

Oriental Weekly, 368

Otto Bismarck, 55

overseas Chinese, 291

P2P (Peer-to-Peer), 370

Pacific War, 218, 289

Pakistan, 242

paper money system, 160, 341

party chief, 264

Party Congress, 233, 252, 261, 303, 328, 330, 336, 360, 389, 404

party-state, xi, 256, 421

Pax Americana, 249

PBOC, 339–340, 345–347, 350

Pearl River, 191, 198, 277

peg, 223, 347

People's Daily, 233, 239, 252, 312, 318, 325, 411

People's Liberation Army, 225, 313

People's Republic of China, 193, 226, 289, 341, 343, 382, 464

physiocrat, 34

Piaohao, 120–122, 124–125, 180

Piketty, Thomas, 23

Pingyao, 121

pingzhu, 96

planned economy, 3, 14, 20–22, 26, 30, 134, 162, 214, 227, 231, 235, 243, 249, 252, 259, 267, 269, 271, 281, 340, 343, 427
Poland, 232, 413
Polanyi, Karl, 36, 37, 45, 432
poll tax, 137–138
Pomeranz, Kenneth, 7, 10, 122, 134, 191
Ponzi scheme, 322, 373
Portuguese, 172
powerful households, 144
price reform, 366
Prince of Gong, 199
princeling, 319, 359, 362
private entrepreneurs, xiii, 16, 199, 209, 223, 254, 256, 262, 273, 277, 280, 283, 285, 298–300, 305, 308, 314, 328, 330–335, 337–338, 362, 370, 390, 429, 438
private property, 8, 60, 66, 437
private–public partnership, 192, 308, 419
privatization, 5, 15, 57, 73, 205, 271, 285, 304, 307, 323, 380, 390, 420, 438
proletariat revolution, 209
property rights, 4, 59–61, 68, 73, 175, 285, 323, 384, 388, 427
proto-Daoist Huang-Lao School, 92
proto-industrial production, 163
public debts, 192
public housing, 21, 356–357, 360
public works, 38–39, 165, 169
put-out system, 163

Qianlong, 159, 166, 195–196
Qianzhuang, 124, 180
Qin Empire, 79
Qin Shihuang, 166
Qing, 10, 25, 86–87, 117–118, 133, 137–138, 141, 147, 150–151, 159, 162, 164, 166–167, 170, 172, 174, 176–178, 180, 182, 187–188, 190–196, 198–207, 212, 236, 243, 245, 256, 262, 266, 268, 300, 311, 358, 405, 429, 448–449, 453, 455, 460–461, 464, 466–467
Qing dynasty, 117, 147, 174
Qing Empire, 148

real estate, xii, 269, 281, 284, 293, 305, 310, 319–321, 323, 335–336, 353, 356, 358, 361, 365, 367, 369, 373, 375, 396, 401, 414–415, 434

Receiving Bureau, 99
Reciprocity, 47
reconstruction, 57, 73, 231, 243–245, 257, 271, 431
redistribution, 22, 46, 136, 139, 163, 167, 235, 344, 356, 397
reform and opening, 193, 364, 427
Ren Zhengfei, 268, 313
Renminbi, 223, 341
Revolutionary Base Area, 219, 462
Ricardo, David, 35, 56
Rishengchang Piaohao, 121
Robert Heilbroner, 48
Roman Empire, 48–49, 191
Rome, 72
rule by virtue, 83
rule of law, 299, 323, 416, 425
Russia, 3, 6, 194, 207, 244, 420–421, 431, 443, 447, 453, 456
rustication, 176

salt gabelle, 202, 207
salt monopoly, 113, 117, 138, 152, 160, 171, 187
Sang Hongyang, 98
Sansi, 173
Sany Heavy Industry, 328
SASAC, 325, 363, 385, 392–395, 399, 402, 411, 414–416, 419
Saudi Arabia, 413
Schumpeter, Joseph, 33, 44, 132
Science and Civilization in China, 9
Seeking Truth, 366, 369
self-regulating market, 34, 37, 45, 50, 52, 432–433
self-reliance, 218, 230, 235, 301
service tax, 140, 158, 165
Shang Dynasty, 82
Shang Yang, 104, 169
Shan-Gan-Ning border region, 219
Shanghai, 4, 124–125, 138, 141, 159, 161–162, 167, 195, 198, 203–205, 210, 217, 220–221, 224, 226, 243, 259, 261, 268, 284, 302, 310, 315, 320, 334, 343–344, 355, 358, 361, 405, 408, 423, 444, 449–450, 453, 459–461, 465–467
Shanxi merchant, 170, 180
Shanxi, 121, 366
Shaofu, 173
share-holding, 86, 282, 305, 398

shehui, 13, 133, 136, 141, 147, 161, 167, 204, 228, 275, 428–429, 434, 436, 454, 456–457, 461–462, 464–467
Shenmu, 343, 366, 368–369, 376
Shenyang, 358
Shenzhen, 261, 280, 314–315, 327, 358
Shenzhen Special Region, 314
Sichuan, 112, 123, 176, 222
Sierra Leone, 242
silver standard, 152, 205, 210, 341
silver yuan, 205–206, 210–211, 213
Sina Weibo, 318
Singapore, xi, xiii, 31, 63–64, 69, 75, 219, 228, 266, 271, 274, 291, 303, 311–313, 317, 328, 342, 346–347, 357, 362, 389, 403, 407, 426, 448–449, 452, 456–457, 459–460, 462, 464, 467
Sino–Japanese War, 211, 214–215
Sinopec, 319, 363, 394, 405, 408, 410–412
Sino–Soviet alliance, 231
SIP model, 312
Skinner, William, 112, 123, 164
small and medium enterprises, 290
social Darwinism, 188
socialism, 18, 20, 22, 72, 126, 143, 207, 223, 230, 242, 260, 264, 283, 433, 439
socialist market economy, 250, 252–253, 303, 342
Society of Perfect Liberty, 43, 49
SOE, xii, 4–5, 7, 21, 26, 30, 71, 217, 254–255, 267, 271–274, 277–283, 285–286, 288, 294, 296–297, 299, 304–307, 313, 316, 318, 323–324, 328, 335, 340, 343–344, 348, 350, 352, 359, 362–363, 375–376, 378–380, 385, 388–389, 392–404, 406, 408–421, 425, 428, 430–431, 442–443, 452, 456
Son of Heaven, 136
Song dynasty, 114, 173, 176, 179
Song Ziwen, 209, 211
South Korea, 29, 31, 63, 66–67, 70, 290, 292, 303, 401, 426, 431, 439, 455
Southeast Asia, xiii, 68, 290, 292, 312, 446, 460
Southern Grid, 315, 415
Southern Tour, 260–261, 271, 303
Soviet Union, 193, 207–208, 211, 214–215, 228, 236, 238, 242–243, 270, 303, 341
Sovietization, 235
Spain, 55
stability, 55, 62, 66, 100, 125, 137, 149, 154, 166, 178, 185, 188, 217, 220, 222, 256, 265, 278, 287, 295, 306, 322–323, 327, 337, 341, 363, 373, 398, 433, 439, 458

Stalin, 231, 234, 243, 289
Standing Committee of the Political Bureau, 264
State Administration of Industry and Commerce, 333
State Assets, 351, 385, 408
State Assets Supervision and Administration Commission. See SASAC
state assets, 306
state capacity, 117, 139, 255, 352
state capitalism, 2, 4, 15, 26, 30, 42, 143, 159, 193, 254, 430
state control, 20, 34, 88–89, 97, 104, 107, 119, 134–135, 139, 143, 151, 154, 157, 166, 170, 209, 211, 213, 224, 228, 234, 241, 245, 250, 257, 259, 286, 293, 305, 341–342, 376, 400, 426, 428–430
State Grid, 319, 394–396, 411, 415, 422, 451, 464–465
state ideology, 109
state monopoly, 224
state ownership, 7, 21, 117–118, 192, 207, 245, 283, 318, 378
state sector, xi–xii, 5, 15, 26, 41, 115–116, 119, 138, 241, 250, 253, 262, 267, 270–272, 277–279, 281, 295–296, 299, 301–302, 306, 316, 366, 375, 379–380, 383, 385–388, 390–391, 397–398, 401, 407–408, 417, 431
state-building, 11, 25, 34, 61, 90, 147, 153, 159, 169, 188, 190–193, 196, 199–200, 211–212, 227, 243, 245, 249, 256, 280, 425, 434
statecraft, 33, 81, 90, 92, 109, 194
state-in-market, 388
stock market, 72, 125, 203, 287–288, 351
Sun Yat-sen, 188, 207, 360, 462
Suntech Power, 324–326
superpower, 214, 235
surtax, 141
Suzhou, 118, 298–299, 310–311, 324, 459
Suzhou Industrial Park, 311, 459
Suzhou model, 299, 311–312, 324

Taiping Rebellion, 197
Taiwan, 31, 63–64, 66–67, 70, 75, 154, 195, 214, 291–292, 303, 309, 378, 400, 426, 439, 449, 455, 465
Tang dynasty, 169, 178, 191
Tang–Song transition, 157
Tanzania, 242
tariff, 52, 272, 347
tax base, 133–134, 139, 157, 165, 171, 204, 217, 273, 343–344, 346, 348, 350, 371

tax grain, 156, 162
tax-sharing reform, 273, 319, 353
Tencent, 419
The Communist Manifesto, 73, 458
The Great Divergence, 7, 10, 122, 134, 191, 460
The Great Transformation, 37, 46, 50, 52, 432–433, 460
The Plan for National Agricultural Development, 233
The Wealth of Nations, 38, 175, 439
The World Development Report, 242
theory of *Qing-Zhong*, 169
Three Frontiers Movement, 235
Three Peoples, 360
Three Represents, 274, 417
Tiananmen Square, 243, 270
Tianjin, 197–198, 205, 263–264, 284, 343, 405
Tibetans, 434
To Get Rich is Glorious, 241
Tokugawa, 168
total war, 90, 188, 193, 213, 226–227, 245
trade surplus, 172, 292, 294
trade war, 445
Tsai, Kellee, 438
TVE, 236, 254, 264–266, 290, 302, 306–307, 311, 345, 378, 448

Ultra-High Voltage (UHV) transmission system, 396
unemployment, 53, 55–57, 99, 296
United States, 3–6, 29, 75, 103, 193–194, 210, 215, 219, 238–239, 242–244, 289, 292, 313, 355, 425–427, 440–442, 444, 446
urbanization, 20, 157, 176, 194, 215, 235, 241, 265, 275–276, 284, 299, 320, 354, 374
Uyghurs, 363, 434

value-added tax, 273–274, 296, 348, 374, 399
varieties of capitalism, 24, 29, 75, 442
viceroy, 199–201
Vietnam, 3, 6, 238–239

wan yuanhu, 262
Wanda Group, 268, 321
Wang Anshi, 113, 120, 140, 151–152, 156–159, 161, 173, 179, 188, 206, 456, 460
Wang Jianlin, 268, 321–323, 451, 458
Wang Jingwei, 209, 211, 216, 457
Wang Mang, 113, 120, 137, 140, 151–155, 157, 159, 178, 188, 381

Wang Qishan, 405
Wang Shaoguang, 254, 352
war economy, 214, 228, 235
Warring States, 91–92, 115, 175
water management, 233, 361
wealth management products, 373
Weber, Max, 8, 37, 39, 73, 114, 435
welfare state, 21, 52, 430
Wen Jiabao, 320, 350, 414, 439–440
Wenzhou, 287, 290, 299, 308–310, 312, 333, 448, 461, 465
Wenzhou model, 299, 308–309, 312
Will, Pierre Etienne, 115
Wittfogel, Karl, 8, 114, 435
Wong, Bin, 450
Words of Warning in Times of Prosperity, 200
WTO, 3, 6, 291, 307, 347, 400, 442
Wu Bangguo, 405
Wu Jinglian, 439
Wuhan, 177, 358, 405, 423, 460
Wuhu, 258–261, 362
Wuxi Suntech, 324, 326–327

Xi Jinping, 279, 421, 454
Xi'an, 201, 315, 358
Xia Dynasty, 82
xiahai, 279
Xiamen, 358
Xiejia, 162
Xinjiang, 195, 363, 381
Xiongnu, 89–90, 153, 169, 190
xitong, 230
Xiyuecheng Dye Company, 121
Xue Muqiao, 218
Xuji Group, 396

Yan Fu, 93, 188
Yang Lien-sheng, 92
yanglian, 167
Yangtze Delta, 163, 215–216
Yangtze River Delta, 277
Yangzhou, 179
Yellow River, 364
Yeltsin, 420
Yongzheng, 151, 166
Yu Zuomin, 263–264, 279, 294
Yuan dynasty, 171, 181
Yuan Shikai, 204, 206–207
Yunnan, 371–372

Zeng Chengjie, 322, 338, 466
Zeng Guofan, 197
zero-sum, 80, 115, 143, 148

Zelin, Madeleine, 61, 167, 206
Zhang Gaoli, 405
Zhang Juzheng, 151, 166
Zhang Zhidong, 201
Zhang Zuolin, 206
Zhao Ziyang, 289, 467
Zhejiang, 70, 205, 287, 290, 302, 309–310, 331, 333, 400, 409, 434, 448, 461
Zheng Guanyin, 200
Zheng He, 171

Zhou dynasty, 136
Zhou Enlai, 231, 235
Zhou Yongkang, 404, 421
Zhou Zhengyi, 320, 323, 338
Zhu Rongji, 188, 237, 253, 271, 304, 346, 348–349, 389, 398, 428, 467
Zhu Yuanzhang, 114, 120, 137, 152, 160–161, 188
zhuada fangxiao, 304, 328, 389, 391
ZTE, 268, 313, 316, 318–319, 460